JOHN LELAND ITINERARY

John Leland

ITINERARY

A Version in Modern English

edited by

John Chandler

THE HOBNOB PRESS

First published as *John Leland's Itinerary: Travels in Tudor England* in 1993 by Alan Sutton Publishing Ltd.

This revised and enlarged edition with additional material published in 2022 by The Hobnob Press,
8 Lock Warehouse, Severn Road,
Gloucester GL1 2GA
www.hobnobpress.co.uk

© John Chandler, 1993, 2022

The Author hereby asserts his moral rights to be identified as the Author of the Work.

All rights reserved. No part of this publication may be reproduced, stored in a retrieval system, or transmitted in any form or by any means, electronic, mechanical, photocopying, recording or otherwise, without the prior permission of the publisher and copyright holder.

British Library Cataloguing in Publication Data
A catalogue record for this book is available from the British Library

ISBN 978-1-914407-29-1

Typeset in Chaparral Pro 11/14pt, with headings in Caslon Antique
Typesetting and origination by John Chandler

CONTENTS

Foreword	vii
Introduction	ix
The Tudor Scholar	ix
The Topographer	xix
The Afterlife	xxxi
This Edition	xxxiv
Editorial Note	xxxix
Note ~ Dating the Itinerary	xli
The New Year's Gift to King Henry VIII, given January 1544	xlix
Bedfordshire	1
Berkshire	8
Buckinghamshire	19
Cambridgeshire	24
Cheshire	26
Cornwall	34
Cumberland	66
Derbyshire	70
Devon	72
Dorset	94
Durham	110
Essex	120
Gloucestershire	121
Hampshire	151
Herefordshire	163
Hertfordshire	179
Huntingdonshire	182
Kent	184
Lancashire	201
Leicestershire	211

Lincolnshire	221
London and Middlesex	239
Monmouthshire	242
Norfolk	250
Northamptonshire	253
Northumberland	267
Nottinghamshire	277
Oxfordshire	286
Rutland	302
Shropshire	304
Somerset	320
Staffordshire	350
Suffolk	359
Surrey	361
Sussex	363
Warwickshire	367
Westmorland	383
Wiltshire	387
Worcestershire	405
Yorkshire	417
Appendix ~ The Welsh Itinerary	467
Index of Names	481
Index of Subjects	494
Index of Places	497

FOREWORD

I SPENT SEVERAL YEARS, three decades ago, working intermittently on this book, because I thought then, and still do, that Leland's achievement as a topographer, flawed and unfinished as it is, deserves to be seen and appreciated as a whole, and not just in the bite-size quotations which pepper virtually every local history. His questing observations on what he saw in towns and villages, how things had come about and what they meant, have been valued by historians ever since that cruel day, 21 February 1547 (exactly 475 years ago as I write) when his mind collapsed and his work came to an abrupt end. The notes that he made of his journeys, now mostly in the Bodleian Library at Oxford, were published in the 18th century, and again in a highly respected edition (by Lucy Toulmin Smith) in five volumes between 1906 and 1910, and it is to her work that scholars have turned ever since, and will continue to do so. It is a handy and reliable source of reference, where through its index one can quickly find and extract what Leland said or thought about a particular place. But unless one is well versed in Tudor English and can cope with the frequent lapses into Latin, his writing does not make for easy reading. Words change their meaning, places change their names.

And so I decided to do to what he had intended, had his sanity endured, to rearrange it all by county and to try to make it more intelligible. For Leland, with the scholarly readership he envisaged, that would have involved turning it all into Latin, as his successor William Camden did with his research; for my readership this meant reworking it into modern English. I wanted his work to be accessible and affordable, so that anyone like me with a fascination for English landscapes and townscapes could travel around with him, experiencing the places we know and visit, as they appeared to the most acute of eye-witnesses almost half a millennium ago.

My book appeared in 1993 and has been out of print for many years; its publisher no longer exists. A publisher myself since 2001 in a small way, I had put Leland to one side until recently, but renewed interest in his work in recent years by archaeologists, local historians and topographers suggested that it was time to give him another airing. In the interim more has been discovered and published about his life and work, by James Carley and others, so that some of what I wrote about him in 1993, notably the chronology of his journeys, needed revision. I have now also included much of his descriptive material about Wales, which I omitted before, and I have made small corrections and changes to the text. All of this is explained in more detail in the introduction, which is substantially different from its predecessor.

Although I have distributed Leland's text to the counties to which it relates, some readers may still want to follow him on his journeys around the country. At the end of most itinerary extracts, therefore, is a note of the page on which the narrative continues. And at the end of every extract, in square brackets, is the year that it was written, if known with reasonable certainty, followed by a cross reference to the Toulmin Smith edition, in the form volume no./pages nos. When quoting him in publications one should always refer to Toulmin Smith.

The first edition of this book was dedicated to my parents, Marion and Stanley Chandler, who both died many years ago. If I were to include a dedication in this edition (which I am not, as its recipients would heartily disapprove, I am sure) it would be to the distinguished scholars of the present, notably James Carley, Caroline Brett and Dana Sutton, and long before them Lucy Toulmin Smith and Thomas Hearne, who have brought academic rigour and wisdom to the study of John Leland. My role and aim, by contrast, is far more modest – merely to allow Leland, that quintessential sightseer, to communicate with his fellow-travellers of today.

I should be grateful to be made aware (via Hobnob Press, the publisher) of errors of interpretation or identification of places and people.

John Chandler
Gloucester
February 2022

INTRODUCTION

Abbreviations used in the introduction:
DVI James P Carley (ed.) 2010, *John Leland De Viris Illustribus: On Famous Men* (P.I.M.S. Studies and Texts 172).
HBC F M Powicke and E B Fryde (ed.) 1961, *Handbook of British Chronology* 2nd edn. (R.H.S. Guides and Handbooks, 2)
HP *History of Parliament 1509-1558* (online edn.)
L&P *Letters and Papers of Henry VIII.*
LTS Lucy Toulmin Smith (ed.) 1906-10 (and reprinted 1964), *The Itinerary of John Leland*, 5 vols.
ODNB *Oxford Dictionary of National Biography* (online edn.)
TNA The National Archives
VCH Victoria History of the Counties of England

THE TUDOR SCHOLAR

AN ORPHAN who rose to become one of the most formidable scholars of his generation, John Leland's active life coincided precisely with the reign of his idol, Henry VIII. The date of his birth is uncertain; it can hardly be later than 1505, and was probably around 1503.[1] His birthday was 13 September, and he was born in London. Of his family we know only that he had an older brother, apparently also named John. There can be little doubt that he was related in some way to Sir William Leyland of Morleys Hall near Leigh. Not only do we find Leland receiving hospitality from him during his travels through Lancashire, but Sir William was also the recipient of one of Leland's short poems, or *encomia*. He may also have been related to an earlier John Leland, an Oxford grammarian from Lancashire, who died in 1428, and whose life he described.[2]

---

1 The best introduction to Leland's life is by James Carley in ODNB, written in 2004, and supplemented by his introduction to his edition of DVI, especially pp. xxi-xxvi. I cite other modern authorities only when adding to, or diverging from, Carley's accounts. I am most grateful to James Carley for his help and encouragement throughout.
2 DVI, pp. 742-5 (no. 537).

Convention, incidentally, dictates that our subject's surname is written 'Leland', but during his lifetime the name, and indeed the Lancashire town from which it was ultimately derived, was spelled in various ways, with and without the letter 'y'. In fact it has been claimed that the inscription on his long-destroyed gravestone began, 'Here lieth interred the body of John Leland or Leyland ...'.[1] It seems reasonable, therefore, that his name should now be pronounced in the same way as the town, and the motor vehicles which have been its most conspicuous product.

Under the patronage of a certain Thomas Myles the orphan was enabled to receive an education which could not have been more stimulating, nor more useful to his later career.[2] He attended St Paul's School in London, then newly refounded along humanist lines, and studied under England's foremost humanist scholar, William Lily. This opened his eyes to the rediscovered world of classical literature and ideas, and enabled him to begin friendships which would later help and affect his career. One of his fellow pupils, for example, Thomas Wriothesley, became Henry VIII's chancellor, and was created earl of Southampton; in 1542 Leland visited and commented on his house at Titchfield in Hampshire.

From St Paul's Leland moved to Cambridge, as a student at Christ's College, and after graduation in 1522, was appointed tutor to the duke of Norfolk's son Thomas Howard, an appointment which ended when the duke died in 1524. From the Norfolk household at Lambeth Leland went to Oxford and stayed about two years, but was dissatisfied with what he viewed as the reactionary teaching still being offered there. The first great turning-point in the young intellectual's career came in 1526, when under the patronage of Cardinal Wolsey he was given a royal exhibition or scholarship to enable him to study abroad. He went to Paris, perhaps with the intention also of visiting Italy. In Paris he immersed himself in the dynamic world of Renaissance scholarship, and moved in the same circles

---

1 W Huddesford (ed.), 1772, *The Lives of those Eminent Antiquaries John Leland, Thomas Hearne and Anthony à Wood*, vol. 1, 35.
2 Myles is known from a poem (LXVII) dedicated to him, and was probably a mercer: J P Carley, forthcoming, 'After the Dissolution: John Leland and his Neighbours in Charterhouse Square'. Another (XX), expressing gratitude for his patronage, is dedicated to William Gonson, a senior naval official (d. 1544): see http://www.philological.bham.ac.uk/lelandpoems/.

as its most influential professors. He perhaps knew the great classical scholar Guillaume Budé, and he may even have come to the attention of Erasmus himself.[1] The intellectual excitement of Paris nurtured Leland's ambitions as a Latin poet, as well as a nascent antiquarianism and a fascination with manuscripts. Other facets of this truly Renaissance education – medicine, art, and Greek literature – are also reflected in his poems written during this period.[2]

With Wolsey's fall in 1529 the heady Paris days came to an end, and Leland returned to England, where he had to make new arrangements to support his academic pursuits. With influential friends at court, such as Anthony Denny and Brian Tuke (both recipients of poems),[3] it was perhaps not difficult for him to obtain sinecure ecclesiastical posts. He was given an absentee living in the Calais Marches in 1530, permitted to hold up to four benefices in 1533, appointed to two Wiltshire prebends in 1534, and was by then also a royal chaplain. Before 1533 he may also have become involved in developing the royal libraries, although the notion that he held some fomal position, as librarian or 'antiquary' has been discredited.

Whatever scholarly pursuits he was following during the first few years after returning to England, in 1533 we find him once more in the limelight. These were momentous years, both in terms of international politics, and probably in Leland's own intellectual development. Henry broke with Rome, declared himself head of the English Church, and married Anne Boleyn; the writing was on the wall for monasticism, and for the tradition of learning which the monastic libraries enshrined. To celebrate Anne's coronation in 1533 Leland was engaged to write poems for a pageant, a sign not only that he was keeping up his literary composition, but also, since they were actually recited at the coronation, that he was consolidating his position at court. In the same year, at the age of about thirty, he procured a document which was to change the direction of the rest of his career.

---

1 J P Carley, 1986, John Leland in Paris: the evidence of his poetry, *Studies in Philology*, 83, 1-50; J P Carley, 1981-2, Four poems in praise of Erasmus by John Leland, *Erasmus in English*, 11, 26-7.
2 L Bradner, 1956, Some unpublished poems by John Leland, *Publications of the Modern Language Association of America*, 71, 827-36.
3 Bradner, 1956.

Arguments about the legitimacy of Henry's divorce and remarriage appealed to precedent as chronicled in manuscript books, and many unique and potentially significant works were scattered in monastic libraries, sometimes in deleterious conditions. In 1533 Leland received a commission from the king (in the words of Anthony Wood), 'to make a search after England's Antiquities, and peruse the Libraries of all Cathedrals, Abbies, Priories, Colleges, etc. as also all places wherein Records, Writings and secrets of Antiquity were reposed'. There was perhaps a precedent for this kind of search, as a surviving list of the contents of Lincolnshire libraries may predate Leland's work, and have served as his model.[1] The precise nature of his commission has never been discovered. He referred to it as a 'diploma', a Greek word used in the Roman empire to mean an official pass; clearly it was a powerful weapon when Leland needed to bludgeon a recalcitrant janitor into granting him access to inspect a library. At the Oxford Grey Friars, 'But I pressed them and, armed with the king's letter ('diploma'), more or less forced them to open up their shrines'.[2] Henry's attitude to the monastic libraries, and to libraries in general, as well as the attempts by the intelligentsia to prevent their wholesale destruction, are large questions which need not concern us directly. What is more important, so far as Leland's later career is concerned, is that it took him out of the study (or the royal library) and on to the road.

In 1533, therefore, Leland became peripatetic, and for the next three years or so much of his energy was devoted to examining the contents of monastic libraries. Detailed booklists survive among his notes, arranged sequentially by monastic house, and from these it has been possible to reconstruct six principal journeys that he made between 1533 and 1535, which took him as far as Devon and Northumberland.[3] They are important precursors to the surviving itineraries of later years, not only because they shaped Leland's research interests for the rest of his working life, but also because many of the surviving notes on people and places, which are jumbled and cannot be assigned to a later journey, almost certainly derive from these monastic library tours, either as eye-witness reportage, or as preparatory research and subsequent enquiries. These notes have

---

[1] J P Carley, 1989, John Leland and the contents of English pre-dissolution libraries: Lincolnshire, *Trans. Of the Cambridge Bibliographical Soc.*, 9, 330-57.
[2] DVI, pp. 480-1 (in no. 269).
[3] DVI, lxi-xcv.

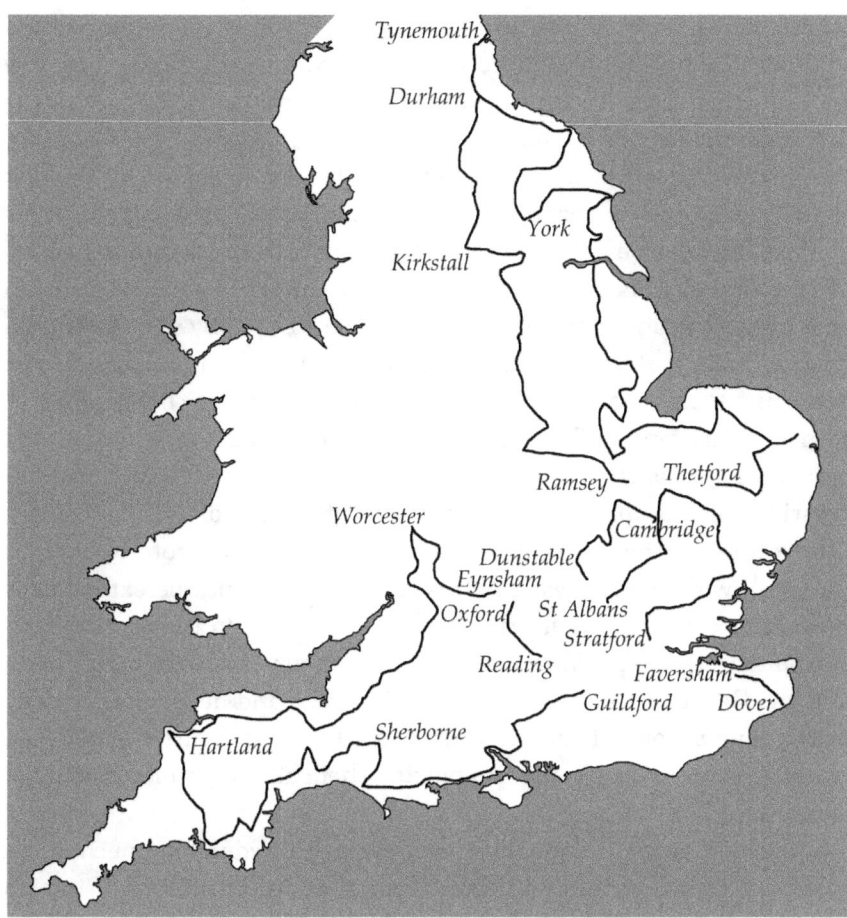

Monastic library journeys, 1533-5 (Sources: DVI, lxiii-xcv; Leland, *Collectanea*, vol. 4):
- **1533:** Guildford–Waverley–Winchester–Southwick–Southampton–Netley–Beaulieu–Christchurch–[Salisbury]–Abbotsbury–[Cerne]–Sherborne–Montacute–Newenham–Dunkeswell–Exeter–Totnes–Buckfast–Plympton–Buckland–Tavistock–Hartland–Barnstaple–Cleeve–Taunton–Glastonbury–Wells–Bath–[Keynsham–Bristol]–Malmesbury–Cirencester–Gloucester–Tewkesbury–Worcester–[Warwick]–Pershore–Evesham–Winchcombe–Eynsham.
- **1533-4:** Stratford Langthorne–[Merton]–Waltham–Coggeshall–Colchester–Bury St Edmunds–Ely–Saffron Walden– St Albans
- **1534:** Faversham–Canterbury–Dover–[Battle]
- **1534:** Dunstable–Woburn–Newnham–Warden–St Neots–Godmanchester–Huntingdon–Barnwell–Cambridge
- **1534:** Thetford–[Ipswich]–Eye–Wymondham–Norwich–Holme St Benets–Walsingham–Castle Acre–Kings Lynn–Crowland–Thorney–Peterborough–Bourne–Sempringham–Spalding– Swineshead–Boston–Revesby–Kirkstead–Tupholme–Bardney–Thornton on Humber–Beverley–Meaux–Watton–Bridlington–Malton–Kirkham–York–Newburgh–Rievaulx–Whitby–Guisborough–Durham–Newcastle–Tynemouth–Jarrow–Easby–Jervaulx–Fountains–Kirkstall–Selby–Pontefract–Worksop–Welbeck–Newstead–Melton Mowbray–Leicester–Launde–Sawtry–Ramsey
- **1534-5:** London and Westminster
- **1535:** Reading–Abingdon–Oxford

traditionally been bundled with the itineraries proper, and in this edition all those of topographical interest are included for each county after any relevant itineraries. A summary of these journeys is given above in the caption to the map on p. xiii.

James Carley has shown that in 1535 Leland embarked on the first of the great projects that he proposed (and failed) to complete in his lifetime. This was *De Viris Illustribus* ('On Famous Men'), a comprehensive biographical dictionary of writers and other eminent figures. He worked on it until 1537 and then laid it aside until late 1543.[1] By 1538 he was on the road again. But before establishing the chronology of his journeys and describing their routes, it will be worthwhile to set this change of focus both in the national and in Leland's personal context.

In 1536, as the dissolution of the monasteries began, and their libraries were despoiled and dispersed (often to foreign collectors), Leland foresaw the need for a salvage operation. He wrote to Thomas Cromwell with the request that his terms of reference be extended to allow him to collect manuscripts and deposit them in the royal library. 'It would be a great profit to students and honour to this realm; whereas, now the Germans perceiving our desidiousness and negligence do send daily young scholars hither, that spoileth them, and cutteth them out of libraries, returning home and putting them abroad as monuments of their own.'[2]

Leland's anger, it should be noted, was directed not so much at the wanton destruction going on all around, as at the effrontery of foreign scholars who purloined monuments of English history, and claimed them as their own. The liberal humanist of cosmopolitan student days in Paris was developing a streak of chauvinism. If not the original cause of Leland's fervent nationalism, certainly an important contributor was the Italian scholar working in England, Polydore Vergil, who in 1534 published a history of England, *Anglica Historia*. Polydore's treatment of the legendary account of early British history, known as the *Brut*, has been described as, 'a reasonable and sympathetic criticism'.[3] But in it he cast doubt on the existence of Arthur – an unthinkable suggestion, particularly from a foreigner. The question of the veracity of Arthur and the other early

---

1 DVI, xxvii and *passim*.
2 quoted by Huddesford, 1772, 17.
3 T D Kendrick, 1964, Foreword to LTS, 1964 reprint, vol. 1.

British kings was no mere academic debating-point to Tudor historians; the Tudor kings claimed direct descent from Arthur, and therefore upon his existence depended the legitimacy of the claims of Henry VII and his son Henry VIII to the English throne. An attack on Arthur was an attack on Henry, and this had to be rebutted. In 1536 he produced *Codrus*, a vitriolic pamphlet attacking Polydore, and defending his monarch against this preposterous slur.

This was the first of several short works which cast him as propagandist for the king's affairs. In 1537 he wrote a poem, *Genethliacon*, to celebrate the birth of Henry's son, the later Edward VI, and two years later responded to an attack by a Dutch theologian, Albert Pighius, on Henry's break with Rome by writing a lengthy work (probably commissioned by Cromwell) couched in the form of a dialogue attacking the pope, and entitled *Antiphilarchia*.[1] From about this date we detect a shift, too, in Leland's antiquarian interests. Not only was he turning into the king's collector, as well as cataloguer, of monastic manuscripts; he was also becoming, as he wrote to the king, 'totally enflammid with a love to see thoroughly al those partes of this your opulente and ample reaulme .. .' (*New Year's Gift*, see below, pp. xlix-liv). Despite his urgent request to Cromwell for greater powers to salvage books, his enthusiasm seems to have turned from libraries and their contents to recording and understanding the towns and villages that he visited in order to see them. He was becoming a topographer.

Between 1538 and 1544 he embarked on a series of journeys, undertaken most likely between spring and autumn each year, which are known as the itineraries. The descriptions that he recorded of these journeys form the bulk of this edition, and they are dated and discussed in greater detail later in this introduction. Outside the somewhat rarefied scholarly worlds of medieval bibliography and Renaissance Latin poetry, it is for these descriptions that Leland is chiefly remembered, and his work has been quarried relentlessly by historians of places for more than four centuries.

During these years, when not on the road, it is assumed that he was living mostly in London. He was assessed for a tax as resident in Cornhill ward in 1541, and by 1543 and still in 1546 he held a tenement in an affluent

---

1   I owe this observation to James Carley, pers. comm..

neighbourhood within the site of the former London Charterhouse.[1] A letter written by him to a contact in Louvain, and dated 12th November (but no year) is addressed from London.[2] It is probable, however, that he spent some time also in Oxford and nearby at Haseley in Oxfordshire, whence he set out on one of his journeys. This is because, so as to support himself at this period he secured further ecclesiastical preferments – in 1542 he was presented to the living of Haseley, and in 1543 to a canonry of King Henry VIII College, Oxford. His rectory at Great Haseley, now 'The Old Rectory' and within earshot of the M40 motorway, has retained some of its late-medieval fabric. The Oxford post came to an end in 1545 when the college was dissolved. But he retained the Wiltshire prebends of North Newnton and West Knoyle, and visited one and probably both during his 1544 itinerary.

By this time he had become a scholar of international reputation, with a wide circle of friends and acquaintances (and not a few enemies), but he had published virtually nothing. This deficiency began to be set right in 1542, with the appearance in print of an elegy on the death of Thomas Wyatt, and thereafter six other works were published up to 1546. These included other occasional poems – a celebration of the capture of Boulogne in 1544, an encomium on the peace of 1546, and another elegy – as well as two long poems with a topographical bias. These were a reworking and expansion of the *Genethliacon*, the poem which he had written to celebrate the birth of Edward in 1537, and which he now enriched with the topography of Cornwall, Wales and Cheshire, the three domains to which the young prince's titles referred. It was published in 1543, the year after Leland's journey to Cornwall. In 1545 appeared a poem of almost 700 lines, entitled *Cygnea Cantio*, 'The Song of the Swan'. It describes, in ample topographical detail, a swan's journey down the Thames from Oxford to Greenwich, and ends with a long panegyric on Henry's reign. The other product of these years was a prose work of 1544, a sturdy defence of the authenticity of the Arthurian tradition, entitled *Assertio inclytissimi Arturii;* its editor has commented that, 'his disquisition upon Arthur is more notable for heat than light'.[3]

---

1 Carley, 'After the Dissolution . . .'
2 LTS, vol. 2, 146.
3 W E Mead (ed.), 1925, *The famous historie of Chinon of England . . .* (Early English Text Soc., orig. ser. 165), viii.

One other work written during this period, but not published until a few years' later, is generally referred to as the *New Year's Gift*, and has already been cited. It is a kind of report to Henry VIII on his work so far achieved, and his plans for the future. His labours in monastic libraries on the king's behalf had come to an end several years earlier, and for the previous six years he had been travelling. He had by now completed these explorations in England and Wales, and with a mass of notes and memoranda was ready to write up a series of ambitious works derived from them. As well as the biographical dictionary of British writers in four volumes, there would be a history of England and Wales in as many volumes as there were shires, six books about offshore islands, three books about the British nobility, and a written description of England suitable for turning into a map – this to be ready within a year.

When this ambitious prospectus was published, in 1549, its editor, John Bale, dated it to New Year, January 1546, and until very recently that date has generally been assumed to be correct (including in the earlier edition of this work). Leland's claim to have spent the previous six years travelling would therefore refer to the period 1539 or 1540 to 1544 or 1545. But in his detailed analysis of the composition of *De Viris Illustribus* James Carley has now convincingly shown that Bale, who was in exile on the continent for most of the 1540s, misdated the work, and that the likely composition date was actually between July and December 1543 for presentation to the king in January 1544.[1] This has obvious implications for the chronology of Leland's activities during these years, so that a redating of the itineraries is now necessary, and is attempted below.

By the end of 1543, therefore, the six years of travelling (which must therefore have begun in 1538) had been completed – although it will be seen that Leland did set out on one more journey, during 1544 – and work could resume on the *De Viris Illustribus*. This was a productive period, which has given us also the lengthy *Cygnea Cantio*, and other prose and poetry. In 1546 there was even an excursion to France, to collect apple and pear seedlings and grafts for Henry from Rouen. But all the great works were left unfinished, and some not even begun. On 28 January 1547 Henry VIII died, and three weeks later, 21 February, Leland suffered a severe mental

---

1   DVI, xxvi-xxix.

breakdown which rendered him incapable of further work.¹ A grant of March 1551, entrusting his care to his brother, described the illness in the following terms: '[John Leland] is mad, insane, lunatic, furious, frantic, enjoying drowsy or lucid intervals, so that he cannot manage his affairs'.² A year after the official grant of custody, on 18 April 1552, Leland died at the home of his publisher, Reginald Wolfe,³ and was buried in the church of St Michael le Querne in London. The church was destroyed little more than a century later, in the great fire of 1666.

There have been many theories about the cause of Leland's mental illness. Fuller, in the seventeenth century, was 'uncertain whether his brain was broken with weight of work, or want of wages: the latter more likely; because, after the death of King Henry, his endeavours met not with proportional encouragement'.⁴ John Bale, who perhaps knew him as well as anyone, gave the following diagnosis, which he put into the mouth of an unnamed mutual friend: 'I muche do feare it that he was vaynegloryouse, and that he had a poetycall wytt, whyche I lament, for I iudge it one of the chefest thynges that caused hym to fall besydes hys ryghte dyscernyhges'.⁵ A recent professional diagnosis, cited by Carley, suggested that he suffered from 'manic-depressive illness which may well have been aggravated by Henry's death, as well as from a "magpie complex", that is an obsession with collecting, from which insanity provided the only escape'.⁶

A disillusioned, highly-strung poet, or an arrogant scholar who overreached himself; a fanatical devotee adhering to a dead monarch, or the schizophrenia of a humanist besotted by the middle ages? We cannot tell. Indeed, despite his voluminous notes, his poetry, his well-documented life, there is a great deal that we do not know about him. We can deduce little of his personal circumstances, family, private life. We assume that he was never married. As we travel around England with him we are at once impressed by his dogged and insatiable curiosity, his thoroughness and persistence, but we never come to know him as a person. There are almost

---

1   DVI, p. xxiv.
2   *Calendar of Patent Rolls, 1550-3*, 181.
3   A L Clarke, 1911, John Leland and King Henry VIII, *Library*, 3rd ser., 2, 132-49
4   quoted by E H Bates, 1887, Leland in Somersetshire, 1540-1542, *Somerset A&NHS Proc.* 33, 60-136 (on pp. 60-1).
5   Bale's preface to *New Year's Gift,* reproduced in Huddesford, 1772.
6   ODNB.

no sparks of humour,[1] no personal details, no grumbles. But we must respect his privacy, and turn instead to the cornucopia which he offers.

THE TOPOGRAPHER

ONE OF THE most striking discoveries that anyone beginning to research Leland will quickly make is that today he is studied and his work valued by three distinct bodies of scholars. A select band of academics is interested in him as an exponent of Renaissance Latin poetry, a competent if not outstanding practitioner of a recondite art. A second group pores over his lists of manuscripts and notes on medieval authors, many of whose books are now lost and would be entirely unknown were it not for his meticulous work as a bibliographer. The third, and by far the largest, group is acquainted with him as topographer and antiquarian, usually because he is an eyewitness source of evidence about particular places and buildings in the sixteenth century. But whereas the students of Renaissance literature and medieval bibliography are aware of his value to historians, it is probably true that the majority of historians who casually cite the *Itinerary* have no idea of its author's importance in other fields.

It has been said that Leland himself thought that it would be his poetry that would generate his greatest fame,[2] and that he saw his strength in the field of antiquarian research as an authority on the general subject of British antiquities:

> He would not perhaps have understood why we now count him so great an antiquary; for we should have to tell him that his supreme antiquarian merit resulted from his resolution to go to look at places of interest instead of merely reading about them. There is no evidence that he had any idea of the important contribution to antiquarian practice that his long journeys had made; he just said that he had been exceedingly anxious to see these places, and had been rewarded by the acquisition of a mass of valuable notes.[3]

---

1 There may be deadpan humour in his note about a man who 'fayned hymselfe Christ, whiche was brought to Oxford, and ther crucified' (LTS, vol. 5, 93).
2 Carley, 1986, 1.
3 T D Kendrick, 1950, *British Antiquity*, 52.

This mass of notes, which is now referred to as Leland's *Itinerary*, owes its origin, as we have seen, to the travelling which he undertook, from 1533 onwards, initially in connection with his visits to monastic libraries. Much of the material included in the 'notes' portion of each county in this present edition probably dates from the mid 1530s, when his bibliographical work was still the main concern. Examples may be found of references in the present tense to monasteries which were dissolved in 1536, so we must assume that he had begun to take notes before this date. Indeed there survives an extended description of parts of Cornwall which contains several indicators that it was compiled before 1536.

By the later 1530s his notetaking was becoming more systematic. Information on a number of midland and northern counties in England and most Welsh counties survives which has been arranged under a series of standard headings. Staffordshire, for example, has notes on: market towns; castles; rivers; abbeys and priories; forests, parks and chases; position and mineral resources. Very often a heading followed by a blank occurs in the manuscript, signifying presumably that Leland was unable to gather any information on a particular subject. Much of the surviving corpus of notes on Wales defies arrangement into any coherent sequence and seems not to follow the course of a journey; it is omitted from this edition. The exceptions are his account of Monmouthshire and the first part of the 1538 itinerary (see below), which is included as an appendix (pp. 467-79).

In the *New Year's Gift*, which as we have seen was probably written towards the end of 1543, Leland claimed that, 'by the space of these vi. yeres paste', he had been travelling throughout Henry's domain, 'al my other occupations intermittid'. This would take us back to 1538. And it was very probably in 1538 that the first of the five recognizable itineraries was undertaken. (For a detailed explanation of the evidence for dating the itineraries see the note which follows this introduction.) The writing, though still in the form of notes and *aides-memoire*, includes eye-witness accounts, speculations and reports of conversations, linked by passages in the form: 'then I travelled six miles to ...', and similar.

The first page of the 1538 itinerary is lost, so Leland's starting-point is unknown. He arrived at Hailes in Gloucestershire and made his way to Montgomery in mid-Wales, then through south and west Wales to Pembrokeshire and Strata Florida above Aberystwyth before returning to England. He entered Shropshire and travelled north through Cheshire

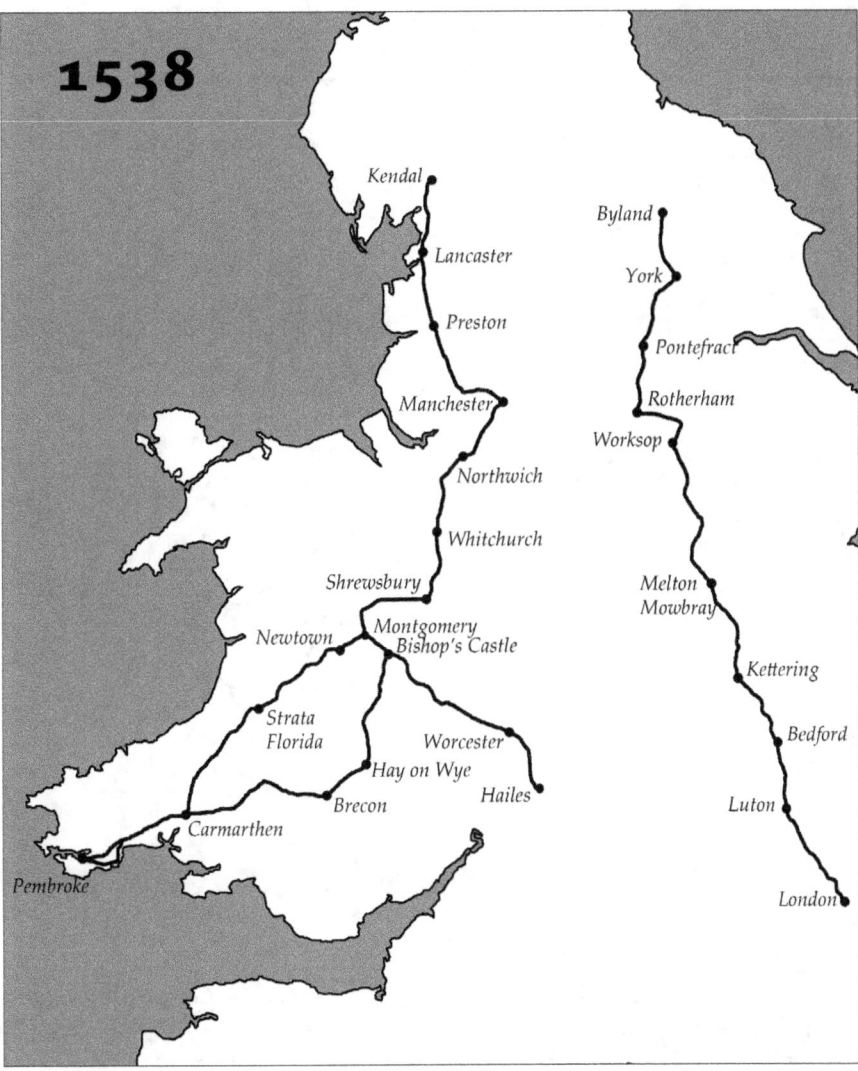

to Manchester, and then to Sir William Leyland's house near Leigh. From there we can trace his movements north as far as Kendal, at which point the narrative breaks off. The story is taken up again at Byland Abbey in Yorkshire, and we can follow Leland's journey back southwards, through Yorkshire and the east Midlands, to Worksop and Bedford, and ending at London. We can possibly reconstruct the missing leg of the journey from a series of notes, in Leland's 1530s style, relating to Cumberland, Hadrian's Wall and Northumberland.

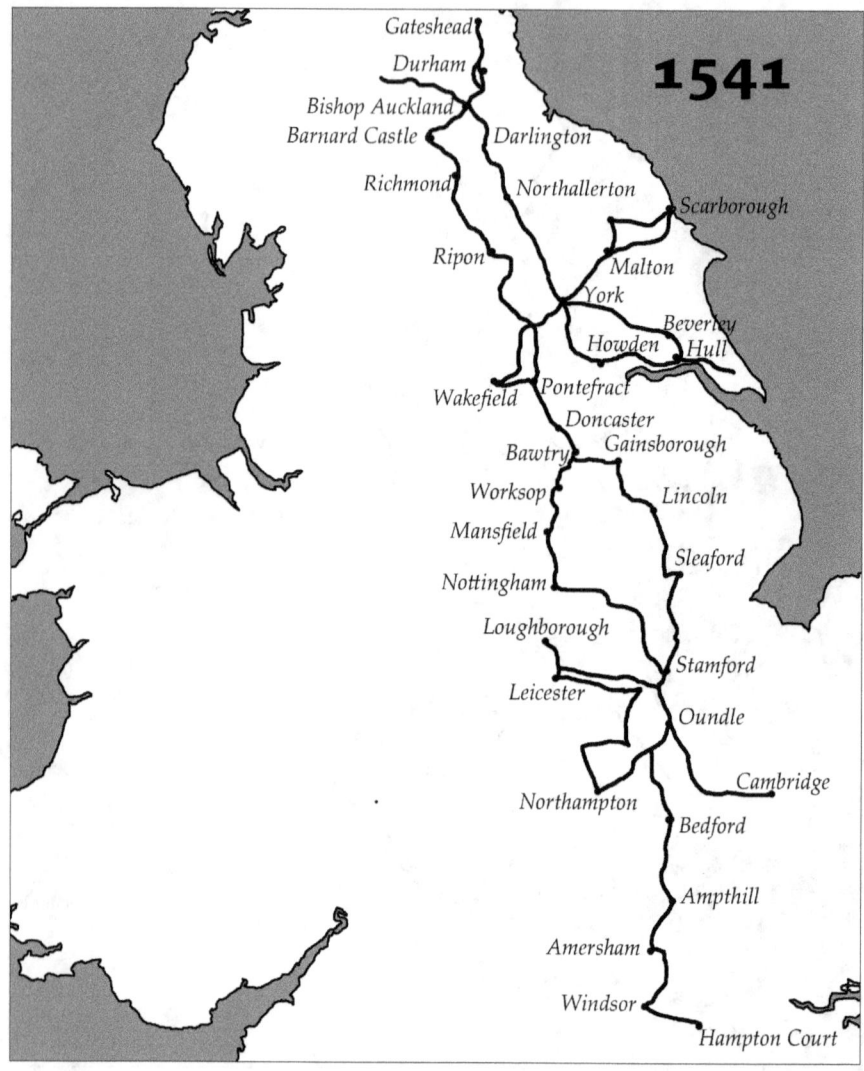

The narrative portions of this 1538 itinerary are much briefer than those of the later journeys (the leg from Bedford to London is described in four sentences), but they nevertheless record Leland's opinions on some of the architecture and scenery along the way. They also give us three glimpses of the practicalities of travel. At Hay on Wye his mistaking the true fording place 'did sore troble my horse'. In south Lancashire he mentions that he was given information by his guide – apparently the sole reference to any kind of travelling companion. And when he had to cross the River Trent at Hoveringham he tells us that he went in the ferry-boat, but his horse had to wade across at the ford.

None of the surviving itineraries, apart from a foray through Monmouthshire into Glamorgan, appears to date from the years 1539 or 1540; if therefore the evidence of the *New Year's Gift* is to be trusted we must assume that the manuscripts of journeys taken during these years have been lost. Since East Anglia is not the subject of any of the surviving narratives (apart, perhaps, from some fragments relating to Hertfordshire, which mention as recent an Act of Parliament passed in 1540) it is probably safe to assume that he went there during this period – an extant letter of 1539 (or perhaps 1540) announcing his intention to look for books at Bury St Edmunds adds strength to this assumption. Another journey may have explored Sussex and parts of the south coast; his descriptions of Petworth and Winchelsea in Sussex seem to be surviving fragments of a missing journey, and he makes an interesting comment when travelling through east Dorset in 1542, 'I have the description of Wareham in an other Itinerarie of myne'. Since no account of Wareham has survived this reference seems to prove, not only that itineraries (now lost) took place before 1542, but also that by this time he was using the word 'itinerary' to describe the notes resulting from his travels.

In 1541 Leland set out from Cambridge and travelled through the East Midlands and Lincolnshire to York, and then around Yorkshire and Durham and finally back south, ending at Hampton Court. He was in fact following in the train of Henry's royal progress to the north of that year, which he refers to several times, and at York he appears to have joined the king's entourage. On the way he indulged in a number of excursions, apparently using the homes of friends, such as Thomas Brudenell of Deene in Northamptonshire, as his bases. From York he made long detours, to Beverley, Hull and the Humber estuary; to Scarborough and the Vale of Pickering; and to Durham and Gateshead, the furthest north he ventured on this occasion.

The 1542 itinerary began from London on 5 May (the date heads the manuscript). Leland travelled first to Haseley in Oxfordshire, the living to which a few weeks earlier he had been presented, and then made his way west as far as Cirencester, before striking south to Somerset and the Arthurian sites of Glastonbury and South Cadbury (the supposed Camelot). The journey continued across north Devon and north Cornwall as far as the Godolphin family seat near Helston, and then he set off back along the south

coast. On the way he appears to have picked up a commission to compose a few lines to be inscribed on St Mawes Castle, which was then being built (the inscription is still there). From Cornwall he travelled through south Devon and Dorset to Salisbury and Winchester, where, after an excursion to Southampton and Portsmouth, the narrative ends.

The following year, 1543, was devoted to exploring the west Midlands. A meandering route took him from Haseley to Warwick, down the Avon to Gloucester, and then up the Marches to Hereford, Ludlow and

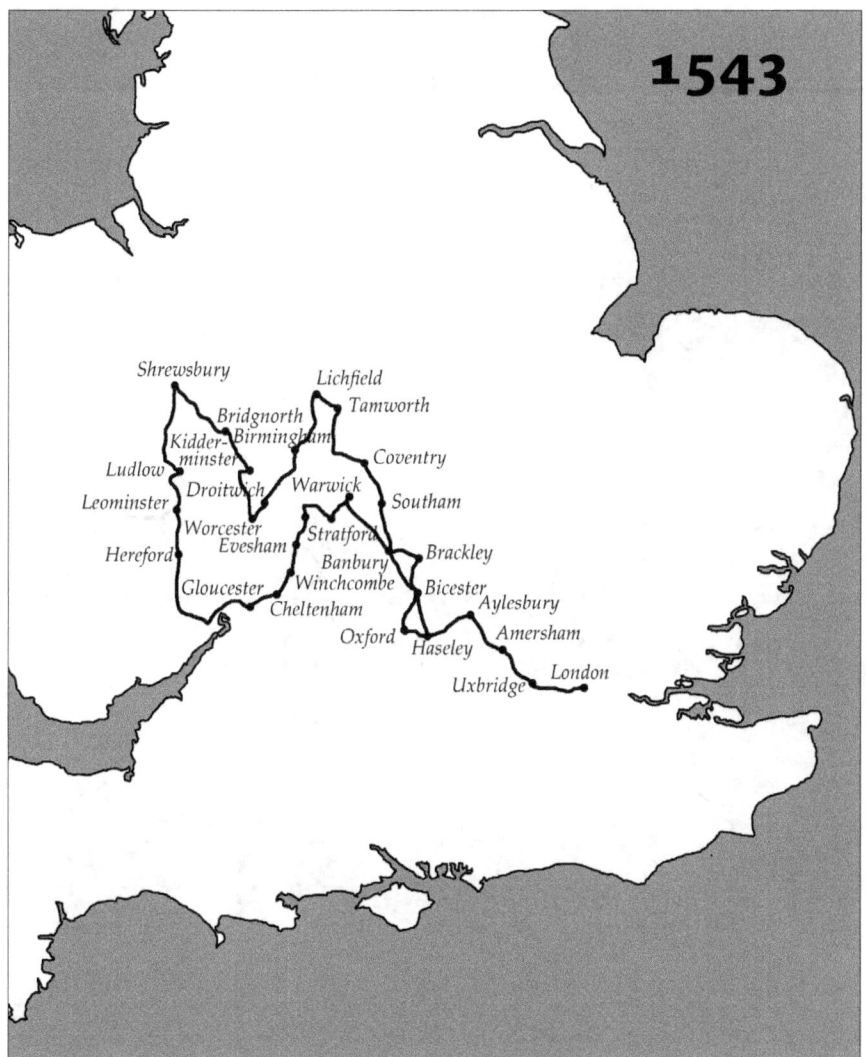

Shrewsbury. This was his furthest point, and he returned down the Severn valley to Worcester, before heading north-west through Birmingham to Lichfield and Coventry, and back via Haseley to London.

Back in London, we must assume, he penned his new year's gift to Henry and began to turn his attention to the projects he had begun or was proposing for the years ahead. But there was one more summer of travelling, a reappraisal of an area which he had already explored. Starting from Oxford he returned to Bath, but by a different route

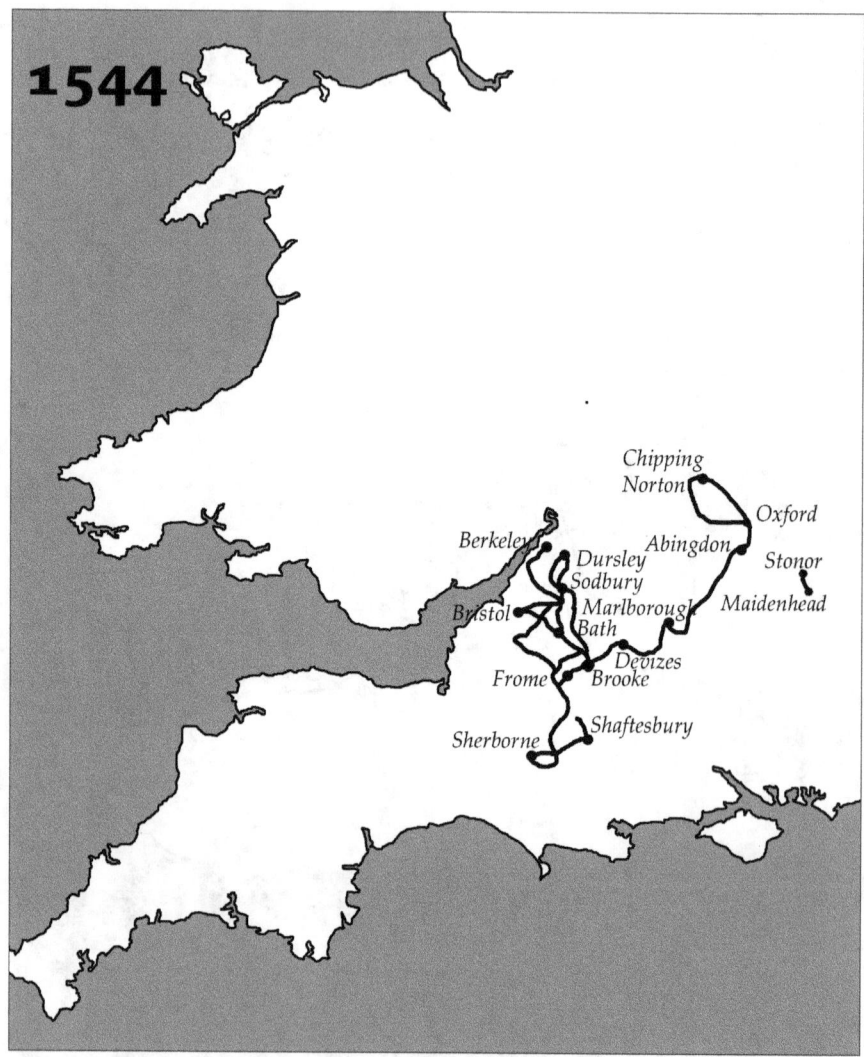

through Wiltshire, and then visited the Bristol area and Somerset. The narrative of this journey ends abruptly in Gillingham Forest, near the point where Dorset, Somerset and Wiltshire meet, and some two miles away from Leland's living at West Knoyle, which was perhaps his destination.

These, then, are the itineraries with which most of this book is concerned. Sir Thomas Kendrick has summarized Leland's method as urban historian thus:

When he came to a town, he recorded its distance from other places, and he made notes about its wall and gates, its castle, its parish church, its streets and markets, and its finest houses; he observed, if there was one, the course of the river through it, and recorded the bridges; he also mentioned the suburbs, if any, and he inquired about the staple industry; then he asked about any archaeological discoveries that had been made, and occasionally he recorded some bit of local folklore or speculated about the meaning of the town's name.[1]

Cathedral cities and regional capitals received this treatment, but also a host of smaller places – Brackley, Malmesbury, Ludlow and Richmond (Yorkshire) are among the best of several hundred towns in the following pages which were subjected to Leland's unique mixture of observation and enquiry.

Between towns our traveller was no less astute. His careful, if not always consistent, reference to distances and directions was of course necessary in order to execute his proposed map. The same purpose led him to describe the courses of rivers, and the relationship of tributaries within a river system. Leland's mile was considerably longer than our mile,[2] and so to the modern reader his distances appear to be underestimates. He also used a variety of other linear measurements, including 'long miles', furlongs and bow-shot lengths. On the road he would describe the terrain and scenery, buildings or parkland glimpsed at a distance, the types of agriculture and land use, and the presence or absence of woodland as a source of fuel. Sometimes when noting a treeless landscape he would explain that local people burnt turf, bracken or some other fuel.

Villages often received a few sentences of description, using adjectives such as 'meane' (modest) or 'praty' (pleasant), and including a short notice of the church or manor house, often with some information about the landowning family. Some villages were 'thoroughfares', or settlements which depended for their livelihood partly on the traffic which passed through them. Others lay at important river crossings, and then the number of arches and type of construction of the bridge were usually noted.

---

1 Kendrick, 1950, 53.
2 R D Connor, 1987, *The Weights and Measures of* England, 69-74.

We tend to think of Leland as an antiquary, and it is certainly true that he was fascinated by archaeological sites such as hillforts (which he called 'camps of men of war') and standing stones. He was also very good at recognizing and interpreting earthworks of village desertion and shrinkage. But a great deal of what he described was not from his perspective ancient. Time and again he referred to structures built within living memory, including many examples of late medieval church architecture. He was interested too in recent adaptations of former monasteries and castles to become the mansions of Tudor gentry, and regularly described new buildings of brick.

There is no need, in this introduction, to attempt to paint a portrait of Tudor England from the 'hole worlde of thinges very memorable' which Leland described. Nor should we be concerned here, as some recent commentators have been, to assess his qualities and shortcomings as a propagandist and trailblazer for English nationhood.[1] But it may be helpful to consider Leland's achievement as a fieldworker and topographer – indeed, as some have suggested, the founder of topography.[2] As an example we may cite a passage from his 1538 return journey through Leicestershire as perhaps being the first ever (albeit brief) report of archaeological fieldwork: 'At first I assumed that it [Burrough Hill] was a hillfort, but then I saw clearly that a stone wall had been built around it. To make sure I pulled out some stones at its entrance, where there had been a large gate, and there I found lime between the stones' (my version, below p. 212). Even though this be disallowed as a proper excavation report, his note on Silchester (Hants.) demonstrates that he was able to recognize cropmarks, if not explain their significance; and his descriptions of other Roman sites, such as Kenchester, Knollbury and Ancaster, qualify him for the title of pioneer field archaeologist, as well as pioneer antiquary.

---

1 e.g. Cathy Shrank, 2004, *Writing the Nation in Reformation England, 1530-1580*, 65-103; Andrew McRae, 2009, *Literature and Domestic Travel in Early Modern England*, 3-7; John Cramsie, 2015, *British Travellers and the Encounter with Britain, 1450-1700*, 139-78.

2 W G Hoskins, 1963, *Provincial England: essays in social and economic history*, 209; J M Levine, 1987, *Humanism and History: origins of modern English historiography*, 79; S A E Mendyk, 1989, *'Speculum Britanniae': regional study, antiquarianism and science in Britain to 1700*, 44.

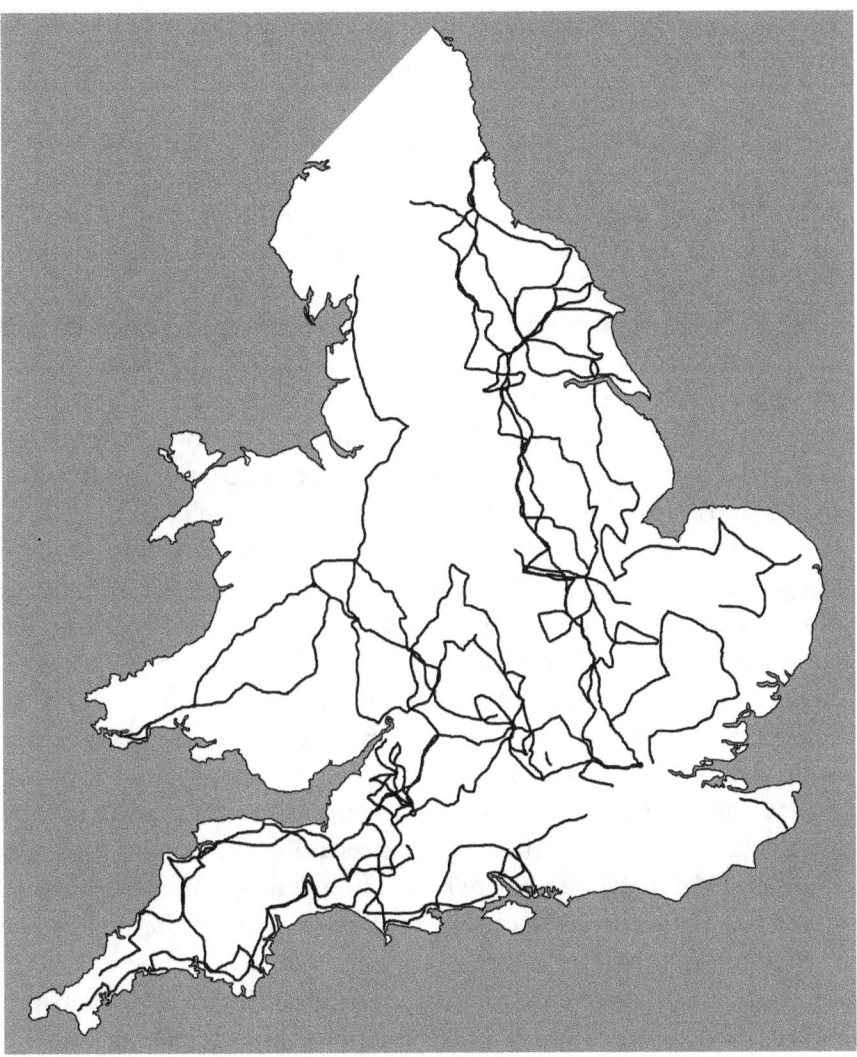

This map combines the five extant itineraries, 1538-44, with the earlier monastic library tours, 1533-5, to give an idea of Leland's known travelling to record the information included in this edition. (The imprecise 1539 journey into south Wales is omitted.)

Without denying an element of truth in such claims, we must beware of hyperbole. In fact a geographical description of England, and other countries, had already been written more than two centuries earlier, by Ranulf Higden, a monk at Chester Abbey. His work, the *Polychronicon*, held great sway in the intellectual life of the late middle ages; it had been translated into English before 1400, and part was printed by Caxton under the title *The discrypcion of Britayne* in 1480.

Higden's work was the product of the study, rather than the field, but another historian and antiquary, William Worcestre, had actually produced a volume of *Itineraries,* describing in Latin his travels through parts of England during the period 1478-80.[1] He also wrote a meticulous description of his native city, Bristol, in far more detail than anything Leland ever produced.[2] Then there was John Rous, the fifteenth-century Warwickshire antiquary whose work on the Earls of Warwick and on his native town anticipated Leland's genealogical and local history endeavours; Leland visited his tomb in the parish church at Warwick. In fact it has been claimed that, 'almost all the forms of topographical-historical-antiquarian literature existed by 1500: descriptions of an entire country and of individual regions, cities, and various ruins'.[3]

Leland, if the *New Year's Gift* is to be believed, was driven to travel by a genuine enthusiasm to see and discover. In this respect his motives were similar to those of the contemporary explorers who discovered the new world and proved, by circumnavigating it, that the earth was a sphere. The rediscovery of England by the Tudor antiquaries complemented the pioneering voyages of Tudor sea-captains to exotic shores.[4] And because the needs of sailors included accurate charts, so the consequent development of cartographic skills enabled the English regions to be mapped in faithful detail. It seems to have been the idea of presenting Henry VIII with a map of the kingdom that gave point to Leland's notetaking. His intention was, 'such a description to make of your reaulme yn writing, that it shaul be no mastery after for the graver or painter to make a like by a perfecte exemple'. Hence, as we have seen, we find him listing mileages between a town and its neighbours, describing in detail the twists and turns of stretches of coastline, and taking pains to discover the source, direction and tributaries of each river he encountered. He even sketched the relationship of rivers flowing into the Humber estuary and Lincolnshire, and produced a rough outline of the east coast.

---

1   J H Harvey, 1969, *William Worcestre Itineraries.*
2   Frances Neale (ed.), 2000, *William Worcestre: the topography of Medieval Bristol* (Bristol Record Society, 51).
3   Mendyk, 1989, 43.
4   Hoskins, 1963, 209-11.

But as it turned out his map was never drawn (and because of irreconcilable discrepancies in his data could never have been drawn); as it happened, too, his efforts were anticipated by another, and almost certainly hostile, intellectual camp. In 1546, two years after Leland presented his *New Year's Gift* to his king, the first of the long series of sixteenth- and seventeenth-century maps of the British Isles was published. It appeared anonymously in Italy, and its authorship is generally attributed to George Lily, the son of Leland's old schoolmaster, William Lily.[1] George Lily was a Catholic, a friend of Leland's arch-enemy Polydore Vergil, and a member of the household of the exiled Cardinal Pole.

What, therefore, was Leland's contribution to knowledge by collecting the material that we call his Itinerary? He was not a particularly original thinker; he could be grossly uncritical when dealing with arguments in conflict with the Arthurian tradition and the Tudor monarchy; and he failed, through illness, to achieve any of his stated aims. But perhaps his supreme value to historians, topographers and archaeologists is that he found himself in the right place at the right time. Here was a man educated to the pinnacle of humanist achievement, abreast of all the latest intellectual quests of his day, and equipped with a brilliant memory, linguistic talent, and a thirst for discovery; but who nevertheless understood and was fascinated by the medieval world which his own world was displacing, and was able to spend its last crucial decade describing its death-throes in meticulous detail. On virtually every page we feel a sense of the old giving way to the new, the clock striking midnight.

THE AFTERLIFE

MORE THAN 150 years separated the onset of Leland's madness from the first publication of the *Itinerary* in 1710-12. During this long period the history of the manuscript volumes, both of the *Itinerary* and of the so-called *Collectanea* (which contain many of Leland's topographical and other notes), falls into two distinct halves. Up until 1632, when most of what survived was presented to the Bodleian Library in Oxford, they passed through the hands of various antiquaries, and were consulted

---

1   E Lynam, 1934, *The Map of the British Isles of* 1546, 1-2; reproduced in P D A Harvey, 1993, *Maps in Tudor England*, 10 (fig. 2).

by all the great names of Tudor topographical writing. During this time they were vulnerable to damage and loss, but were several times copied. After 1632 further copies were made, and one more manuscript volume was presented to the Bodleian, but continued heavy use seems to have hastened the illegibility of some portions.

The editing and first publication of the *Itinerary* in 1710-12 were the work of Thomas Hearne, second keeper of the Bodleian, using the surviving manuscript volumes and various copies then available. This edition, in nine volumes, was followed in 1715 by Hearne's edition of the *Collectanea,* in six volumes. New, improved editions of both works appeared later in the eighteenth century, and a thorough re-examination of Leland's originals, all the surviving manuscript copies, and the printed editions, was undertaken by Lucy Toulmin Smith over several years leading up to 1907. Daughter of Joshua Toulmin Smith, an authority on guilds who had emigrated to the United States (where Lucy was born in 1838) and then returned to England in 1842, she was particularly well equipped for the task of editing Leland. She had helped her father in his work and had edited volumes for the Camden Society and the Early English Text Society. In 1894 she was elected librarian of Manchester College, Oxford, the first woman in England to hold such a post. She died in 1911.[1] Her meticulous edition was published between 1906 and 1910 in five volumes, and reprinted in 1964; and it is from this that the present work has been compiled.

The complicated history of the manuscript originals and copies need not concern us, except to note the remark of William Burton in the seventeenth century that three books of the original were 'imbesiled and gone'; and that of Hearne that 'a vast deal, and I am afraid much the better part, is now quite lost'.[2] Among these losses, as suggested above, may have been an itinerary of East Anglia, and perhaps also one of parts of the south coast; other missing portions must have included accounts of Wareham and of some Warwickshire towns, referred to by Leland himself (see pp. 103, 381-2). The reason for these losses, of course, was the usefulness of Leland's notes to his successors, not all of whom were scrupulous in preserving them. This doubtless explains also why individual folios are

---

1 ODNB.
2 LTS, vol. 1, xx-xxxii

missing, sometimes depriving us of the starting-point or final destination of a journey.

At the time of his insanity and death Leland's mantle was picked up by two of his contemporaries, John Bale and Laurence Nowell. Bale, a colourful character whose career had included spells in a Carmelite friary, a gaol, on the road with strolling players, and eventually as virulently anti-papist bishop of a conveniently distant Irish diocese, was the first to champion Leland and use (with due acknowledgement) his unpublished notes. He published the *New Year's Gift* in 1549 (below, pp. xlix-liv), and an enlarged version of his own biographical dictionary of British writers, incorporating much of Leland's work in this field, in 1557.[1] Another area of Leland's work, his ambition to collect information about places and antiquities so that a map could be drawn, was continued by Laurence Nowell. Nowell was younger than Leland, but probably knew him. He was appointed master of Sutton Coldfield grammar school in 1546, some three years after Leland noted it during his visit to the town, and became Dean of Lichfield in 1559. An avid transcriber of documents, and an Anglo-Saxon enthusiast, he plotted Old English place-names on a detailed series of manuscript maps which are now in the British Library.[2]

The works of Bale and Nowell, and to a lesser extent those of Sir John Prise (a collector of monastic manuscripts) and Robert Talbot (an expert on Roman Britain), stand as a bridge between Leland and the next generation of antiquaries.[3] Five men were in the later Elizabethan period to set the agenda for the next two centuries of topographical and antiquarian study, and all were to a great extent influenced by Leland's work, of which they made extensive use. William Lambarde, whose *Perambulation of Kent,* published in 1576, was the pioneer county historian. William Harrison, who contributed a description of Britain to Holinshed's *Chronicles* (1577).[4] Christopher Saxton was the great

---

1 M McKisack, 1971, *Medieval History in the Tudor Age*, 11-16; Leslie Fairfield, 2006, *John Bale: Mythmaker for the English Reformation.*
2 R Flower, 1935, Laurence Nowell and the discovery of England in Tudor times, *Proceedings of the British Academy*, 21, 46-73; ODNB.
3 McKisack, 1971, 23-4; Brett, 1990, John Leland, Wales, and early British history, *Welsh History Review*, 15, 169-82.
4 J Carley, 2012, 'Leland and other Precursors' *Oxford Handbook of Holinshed's Chronicles* (ed. P Kewes, et al.), ch. 11.

originator of the long series of published county maps (his own maps were first engraved between 1574 and 1579). John Stow may have drawn on Leland's material to compile his *Survey of London* (published in 1598). Greatest of all, the *Britannia* of William Camden (published in 1586), was the realization of Leland's dream, a description of the kingdom, detailing the history, geography and antiquities of each county. These men, perhaps, rather than Leland, should be described as the fathers of their respective disciplines, but if so, then Leland may best be regarded as the grandfather of them all.

THIS EDITION

ANYONE CHANCING on Leland's note about St Just in Cornwall: '... divers sparkeled howses at the west poynt of the shore ...', might conclude that they were in the presence of a poet. They would be right, of course, but for the wrong reason. However felicitous and appropriate may seem the choice of adjective now to describe settlement in west Cornwall, to Leland 'sparkeled' was merely an alternative for 'scattered', with no literary or poetic pretensions. In the present edition the passage is rendered, 'a scattering of houses ...'.

One of the more remarkable features about the itineraries, in fact, is that they are not a poet's notebook. John Leland *poeticus* and John Leland *antiquarius* do not here find common ground. This is not because he did not write landscape poetry – more than 300 lines of the *Cygnea Cantio* describe the Thames landscape from Oxford to Greenwich. It is rather that the itineraries were written (largely) in English, to furnish the raw materials for his antiquarian and historical studies, whereas the language of his poetry was Latin. Proof of this distinction comes in the only passage in the *Itinerary* (translated on p. 372) where Leland the Latin poet shows through, at Guy's Cliffe near Warwick: 'It is a place of pleasure, an howse mete for the muses; there is silence, a praty wood, *antra in vivo saxo*, the river rollynge with a praty noyse over the stones, *nemusculum ibidem opacum, fontes liquidi et jemnei, prata florida, antra muscosa, rivi levis et per saxa discursus, necnon solitudo et quies musis amicissima.*' The English topographer lapses into the Latin poet.

But if Leland's English is not poetry, it is nevertheless (to our ears) quaint. And this, one suspects, is part of the reason why he is so frequently quoted in local histories. A snatch of robust Tudor English brightens up a dull narrative, even when the meaning is unclear or ambiguous. Such treatment has certainly kept his memory alive – he must be one of the most frequently quoted authors in local history publishing – but it does not do justice to his achievement. Worse, quotation of a sentence out of context can give a quite misleading impression of what Leland meant. To come back to our starting point, his work has been 'disparkeled' (by which he meant 'dispersed').

In some instances it must be clear to anyone reading Leland that the meaning has changed. Leland tells us that Hugh Despenser was beheaded and quartered at Hereford, 'and one of the quarters of hym was buried by the lavatory of the high altare in Twekesbyry' . Likewise Edward Langley, during the battle of Agincourt, 'be [by] much hete and thronggid, being a fatte man, he was smoulderid to death, and afterward brought to Foderingey'. He suffocated. But often, in reading Leland, words and expressions are encountered which have disappeared from modern parlance, and sense can only be made of them by recourse to a large dictionary; often, too, Latin words, phrases and abbreviations pepper the text. These annoyances, a deterrent to all but the most persistent 'general reader', may alone be sufficient justification for the present, modern English, version. But there are other considerations too.

More treacherous to our comprehension than the obscure and obsolete words of Tudor vocabulary are the instances of common words, then and now, which have subtly changed their meaning. When Leland described a place, as he frequently did, as 'a praty uplandisch toun' , it is really a little irresponsible for anyone to quote him without a word of caution. 'Praty', a word sprinkled across almost every page of Leland, did not really mean 'pretty' in the modern sense, but was the word normally used when we might say 'pleasant', 'nice', or 'attractive'. 'Uplandisch' did not usually refer to the elevation of a site, but rather to its inland position or its remoteness. And 'town' (variously spelled) is a very slippery customer. For Leland (and for his medieval predecessors) the basic meaning seems to have been 'settlement', or more vaguely 'place', without necessarily an urban connotation. Facets of a settlement which might render it a town, in our sense, were often expressed by a qualifying word such as 'market' or 'privileged'. There may sometimes be an implication of size in Leland's use of 'town', as he also used a word 'townlet', but he was perfectly happy to use 'town' and 'village' indiscriminately of the same place, even in the same sentence. 'Appleby [Westmorland] is the Shire towne, but now yt is but a poore village.' 'The town of Whitington [Salop] is a gret mile north est from Hene Dinas. It is a village in a valley ... '. Leland should never be cited as evidence of urban status on the basis of his use of the word 'town' alone.

'Praty' and 'town' are not the only stumbling-blocks. 'Road' always means 'anchorage'; 'place' often means 'house', in the sense of a manor house or gentry residence; 'bottom' is a valley; 'fair' is a vague word with the general meaning of 'fine' or 'good'; 'meately' means 'quite' or 'reasonably'; 'mean' is best rendered as 'modest'. Sometimes too a word which now carries a fairly wide meaning seems to have been used by Leland in a specific sense; the best example of this is 'defaced', which although in some instances is the equivalent of modern 'damaged' or even 'destroyed', also had the more precise connotation, in the context of walls and buildings, of 'robbed of its facing stone'. Likewise a building said to have been 'discovered' had literally had its roof removed.

Leland's accounts of his journeys across England, and his supporting notes, were envisaged as a means to an end, not as an end in themselves. As they stand they were never intended for publication – and probably not for anyone else but himself to read – and should not be criticized as if they were.[1] They are the research notes of an accomplished literary author, but they are not accomplished literature themselves. Paradoxically, had Leland lived to accomplish his literary intentions, and presented the world with a precursor of William Camden's *Britannia*, the manuscript itineraries would probably have been discarded, and all the freshness and directness of a real traveller visiting real places would have been lost. All this puts the 'translator' of Leland in a somewhat difficult position.

First, should Leland's English be tampered with at all? Indeed, is there any justification for rendering into English something that is already in English? If the itineraries existed in a form in which Leland would have sanctioned their publication the answer would probably be no. All that would be permissible and appropriate would be guidance to the reader about the idiosyncrasies of Tudor language, and Leland could be allowed to speak for himself. But, of course, this is not the case. Since the work is of little stylistic or literary interest, it is the meaning that is paramount.

---

1 For a recent example, see the assessment in McRae, 2009, 3-7.

And we have said enough above to demonstrate that in the form in which the work survives (despite the sterling efforts of its editors) its meaning can be elusive and obscure for all but the specialist reader.

Second, if Leland is not to be left on the academic shelf, but brought within everyone's grasp, how should this be achieved? The solution adopted here has been to rearrange the work by English county, as Leland intended, and then to try as far as possible to render the author's meaning in a serviceable modern English, omitting those passages which seem likely only to be of interest to specialist researchers (see the note on editorial method below). In no sense is this volume intended to replace the Toulmin Smith edition of Leland's work, which must be consulted and considered by anyone intending to make serious use of him as a historical source. The present version is merely intended to give him a platform (and one of which I hope he would approve), on which his unique view of a long-vanished world may be exhibited to the appreciation and enjoyment of a new audience, almost five centuries after it was written. He himself was attempting something similar when he scoured the monastic libraries. His intention, as he explained in the *New Year's Gift,* was that, 'the monumentes of aunciont writers . . . might be brought owte of deadely darkenes to lyvely lighte, and to receyve like thankes of the posterite, as they hoped for at such tyme as they emploied their long and greate studies to the publique wealthe'.

The previous edition of this work was published in 1993, almost three decades ago as I write, and I had worked on it for several years before that. The book was quite widely reviewed and fairly well received. The criticisms, as I had anticipated, were threefold. They either focused on specific errors of interpretation; or they felt that the whole project was pointless since Leland's prose was perfectly intelligible (this mainly from academics); or they regretted that I was somehow depriving historians of the 'robust Tudor English to brighten up a dull narrative', as I described it earlier. For this edition I have corrected numerous small errors that I have discovered or that have been pointed out to me. My response to the second criticism is that this was never intended as an academic work to replace the standard Toulmin Smith edition – which I, and all my academic colleagues, cite and quote where appropriate. To the third complaint, well I had already addressed that in the paragraphs recited above.

In deciding to bring Leland back into print after so long I have been influenced by the growing interest from medieval and early modern historians in travel and communications, including the road network, bridges and early mapping, for which Leland is an important source. In addition, James Carley's careful analysis for his edition of *De Viris Illustribus*, published in 2010, of Leland's activities, year by year, and his consequent revised dating of the New Year's Gift, has rendered some of my previous conclusions about the dates of the journeys incorrect. I believe that a more robust chronology can now be established, so that each of the five major journeys can be assigned to a specific year. My reasoning is set out in the note that follows this introduction, and throughout the text I have appended the presumed year to each itinerary extract.

One other failing of the previous edition that I wished to remedy was my omission of all the material relating to Wales. There remain difficulties of interpretation which only a specialist Welsh historian could resolve, and so I have not attempted to include everything that Toulmin Smith printed in the third volume of her edition, devoted to Wales. Within the jumble of that material, however, there is quite clearly defined a journey made to Pembrokeshire and Strata Florida which then continues through Shropshire and Cheshire to the north (the 1538 itinerary), and so for completeness this has been included as an appendix. Leland's exploration of Monmouthshire also takes the itinerary form and, since topographers after him regarded it as an English rather than a Welsh county (though he placed it in Wales), I have given it a chapter to itself.[1]

I see this book as a companion, not a replacement, of the standard edition by Toulmin Smith – now readily available online. For the casual armchair traveller of the Tudor landscape I hope that it will provide interest and entertainment – and give Leland the voice that his madness deprived him of during his lifetime. But for anyone wishing to quote him in the course of their historical research, I suggest that they use this edition as a handy key to lead them to his actual words, as transcibed by Toulmin Smith. My Foreword explains how I cross-reference to that edition.

One further consideration. The text presented here, despite its length, is only a fraction of his surviving writing. Much of the rest is of

---

[1] I am grateful to Rose Hewlett for encouraging me to take an interest in Monmouthshire, and for constructive comments on the work as a whole, which she saw in proof. She is not to blame for the mistakes that remain.

little topographical interest, with two major exceptions. To both his long poems, the *Genethliacon* and the *Cygnea Cantio*, Leland appended long Latin commentaries explaining and describing the places mentioned in the verse, and these may include information missing or in a different form from anything found in the Itinerary. It should not be assumed that, if a place is not mentioned in the present edition, Leland wrote nothing about it.

EDITORIAL NOTE

THE AIM of this book is to present in a modern English rendering everything about England contained in the corpus of material known as Leland's Itinerary which I adjudge may be of interest to the local historian, traveller, and general reader. (Wales is covered in more cursory fashion, and I have also omitted the brief description of the Channel Islands.) I have worked entirely from the five-volume Toulmin Smith edition, and so, in addition to the *Itinerary,* I have included some material which she selected from the *Collectanea,* vol. 3, as being appropriate to stand alongside it. At the end of each extract, as explained in my Foreword, I print in italics the page references to her edition, in the form: *volume number/page numbers*, preceded (for itinerary passages) by the year that the journey was undertaken.

Miss Toulmin Smith's edition is very highly regarded as being a careful and reliable work of scholarship, and rightly so. Her identification of place-names, however, is not faultless, and I have tried to check and correct, where necessary, all places from modern Ordnance Survey mapping. In a very few instances I have been suspicious of her reading of the manuscript, and have consulted Leland's original, or Stow's copy when the original is lost. A list of these suspect readings was included in my first edition.[1]

I have excluded a great deal of material which I felt would be tedious to all but the specialist (who should in every case consult the Toulmin Smith edition). Excluded are most passages which Leland copied from other writers, most genealogical and biographical lists, most epigraphic material, and much of what may best be described as family history. It has proved difficult, however, to apply criteria for inclusion and exclusion

---

1 J Chandler (ed.), 1993, *John Leland's Itinerary: Travels in Tudor England*, xxxiii-xxxiv.

consistently, and much biographical information related as part of Leland's descriptions of places has been retained.

In my introduction above (pp. xxxiv-xxxvii) I have tried to justify my idea of rendering Leland into modern English. The method which I have adopted has been to attempt to grasp the meaning of Leland's words, and then to express that meaning in straightforward modern English. Leland's original was intended, we assume, solely for his own use; it is abbreviated and repetitious, rough and sometimes confused. In reworking it I have done what I assume Leland would have done with it, had he been transported to the present day and asked to edit it for publication – I have tampered with the structure of sentences and the order of words, tried to avoid repetition and tried to make it flow, while remaining faithful to the author's meaning. There will doubtless be found passages which I have misconstrued, but I hope that a few lapses in a text of over 200,000 words will be forgiven.

Now to some details. Distances have been retained as in the original, although, as mentioned above (p. xxvii), Leland's mile was longer than the modern mile. Points of the compass have also been left, but where they are obviously wrong I have added a correction. Monetary values expressed in round numbers of marks (13s. 4d.) I have rendered as the approximate equivalent in pounds. Place-names and personal names I have converted to their normal modern spelling. I have used the Ordnance Survey as my authority for place-names, and for personal names I have adopted a spelling used by the *Victoria County History,* the *Oxford Dictionary of National Biography,* or the *Handbook of British Chronology,* wherever possible. However, when Leland spelled a name in an interesting or, to us, unusual way, I have retained that spelling when it first occurs (followed by the modern spelling in italics), and thereafter used the modern form. Leland frequently left gaps in his notes to be filled later. If the sentence is meaningless with the gap (such as: 'nearby lives Mr ... ') I have omitted it entirely, but if it conveys some meaning (such as: 'there is a park ... miles east of the town') I have reordered the sentence or inserted a phrase like 'several miles' or 'some distance'. Whenever I am uncertain of an identification, or the meaning of a passage, I follow it with a bracketed question mark, and sometimes an explanation. The rule is that everything printed in roman (upright text) is my rendering of Leland's words, everything in italics is my interpolation or explanation.

I have rearranged Leland's material (as he intended) by historic (pre-1974) English county. I have regarded Lincolnshire and Yorkshire as single, rather than tripartite, counties, and I have placed London and Middlesex together. Within each county section the arrangement is the same. First there is a brief introduction, printed in italics, with a map. Second come the narrative portions of itinerary, printed in what I believe to be chronological order. Third, in smaller type, are Leland's miscellaneous notes. For some counties only notes survive.

NOTE
DATING THE ITINERARY

THE CHRONOLOGY and sequence of Leland's journeys have puzzled his readers since the seventeenth century, and most historians who quote passages of his work have been content to ascribe them to the 1530s or 1540s. Greater precision should be possible – in my first edition I made an attempt to date the journeys (wrongly, as it turned out, in some particulars). Now, following James Carley's detailed analysis of Leland's movements in connection with his monastic visits and bibliographical research for *De Viris Illustribus*, a year can be assigned with reasonable confidence to each of the five surviving journeys which form the major part of what is generally referred to in the singular as Leland's Itinerary. In the following discussion these five will be referred to as: Wales and the North; Durham and Yorkshire; West Country; West Midlands; and the Bristol area.

Clues and Assumptions
It has generally been assumed that, like most early travellers, Leland's journeys took place during the summer months and, in view of the distances he covered, that each was therefore undertaken in a different year. For the years 1541 and 1542 this can be demonstrated, as will be argued below, and it seems reasonable for the other years too.

Before embarking on his Itinerary travels Leland undertook a series of at least six tours visiting monastic libraries, which on the basis of the lists that he compiled have been dated between 1533 and 1535.[1] It can be suggested that some of the additional notes that have found their way

---
1   DVI, lxii.

into the printed editions of the Itinerary were made during these visits.

In the *Laboriouse Journey*, his new year's gift to the king, Leland grandiloquently claimed that: 'all my other occupacyons intermytted, I have so traveled in your domynions both by the see coastes and the myddle partes, sparynge neyther labour nor costes by the space of these vi. yeares past...'. John Bale, who edited and provided a commentary to the *Laboriouse Journey*, ascribed the work to 1546, and thus led (or rather misled) posterity, including myself, to juggle the journeys into the years 1539 or 1540 to 1545. Carley has shown that the dating to 1546 was speculation on the part of Bale, who was absent in exile from 1540 to 1548, and that the true date of the gift was almost certainly new year's day 1544.[1]

Assuming that this date is correct, and that Leland's six years can be taken at face value, he would have been undertaking his journeys each year between 1538 and 1543. We cannot assume, however, that by the end of 1543 he had completed his travelling, and there are good grounds, as argued below, for believing that one of the five extant journeys took place in 1544. Nor, when he implies that his travelling had taken him everywhere in the king's domain, can we dismiss the possibility of hyperbole, or – more charitably – that his claim included his good intentions for the future.

Against this background there are manifold clues from Leland's accounts of his journeys themselves. Foremost are the known dates of the dissolution of the various monastic houses which he saw and commented on – very often he described them as suppressed, or conversely implies that they were still functioning. This provides crucial dating evidence for the years 1538 to 1540. One journey is actually dated, in Leland's hand, to 1542, and another, which closely follows the king's northern progress in 1541, can be dated with confidence to that year. Events such as deaths or transfers of property that can be dated from other sources then provide *termini post quem* and *ante quem*.

Finally, there are known events in Leland's own biography. In 1534 he was appointed to a prebend in Wilton abbey, from which he derived an income from two Wiltshire livings, North Newnton and West Knoyle. In 1542 he was presented to the living of Great Haseley near Thame, and in 1543 to a canonry of King Henry VIII College, Oxford. Leland embarked on his West Midlands journey from Haseley, which suggests a date of 1543 or later.

---

1   DVI, xliii-xlv, xcviii.

INTRODUCTION *xliii*

The Dates of the Five Extant Journeys
In this section is rehearsed in greater detail dating evidence for the five journeys, ascribing them to the years 1538, 1541, 1542, 1543 and 1544.

a. Wales and the North. Although scholars have despaired of extracting a coherent itinerary from Leland's muddled notes that survive about Wales, a route can in fact be discerned with some confidence, which took him from Hailes (near Winchcombe in Gloucestershire) to Hay, then Brecon, and through mid-Wales to Carmarthen, Pembroke and Strata Florida (near Tregaron), then via Welshpool into Shropshire (see Appendix pp. 467-79), whence he travelled north through Lancashire before returning to London. If this be accepted as a single, continuous journey, then his frequent references to the monastic houses he encountered on the way, suppressed or still functioning, when compared with the known dates of their dissolution, make it possible to narrow this itinerary to the year 1538. Several, which he describes as suppressed, desolate, in ruins, or simply in the past tense, were dissolved under the 1536 Act, in either 1536 or early 1537.[1] These include Chirbury, Brecon, Talley, Rufford, Kirby Bellars and (probably) Monkton near Pembroke.[2] Many others, which were not dissolved until 1539, are described as if still functioning, although often Leland's remarks are ambiguous (as referring to surviving buildings rather than an active community) or non-committal. But the range of possible years, 1537-9, may be narrowed to 1538.

At Whitland, which was dissolved in February 1539, Leland had a conversation with the abbot, who told him 'a meri tale'.[3] Strata Florida (also dissolved in February 1539) was clearly still functioning when he visited, although it was in decline. Leland described land (in the present tense) belonging to the abbot.[4] These references appear to rule out 1539 for the

---

1 Listed by S M Jack, 1970, Dissolution dates for the monasteries dissolved under the act of 1536, *Bulletin of the IHR*, 43, 169-81; see also D M Smith, 2008, *Heads of Religious Houses*, III, 1377-1540.
2 Although Monkton may not have been surrendered (with its mother house, St Albans) until 1539, its last recorded prior had resigned by November 1535: see Smith, 2008, 200.
3 LTS, vol. 3, 123.
4 LTS, vol. 3, 121.

Welsh portion of the journey. In fact the last possible date for his visits to places on his return to London can probably be set to October 1538, since he refers to Pipewell near Kettering as if still functioning (p. 212); it was dissolved on 5 November 1538.[1] He also left a detailed description of the Bedford Greyfriars (p. 6), probably made on this visit, which was dissolved on 3 October 1538.[2] At Brecon, near the start of this journey, he refers to Llanthony (Prima, in Monmouthshire) in the past tense, 'this priori was fair, and stoode betwixte ii great hilles', with a marginal note, 'Suppresid'.[3] This was dissolved in March 1538.[4] And later on the journey he came to Thurgarton in Nottinghamshire, 'lately suppressid' (p. 280), which was in June 1538.[5] All this evidence is consistent with a journey made during the spring, summer and autumn of 1538.[6]

b. Durham and Yorkshire. Carley has noted that, in his life of Richard of England, Leland explains that: 'A few years ago, when Henry VIII was visiting York, I happened to turn aside to Ripon . . .'.[7] This remark, linking Leland's journey with Henry's royal progress to the North, fixes it to the summer of 1541. The king left London on 30 June for York and returned shortly before 26 October.[8] Leland, who began his journey from Cambridge, seems to have trailed behind the royal entourage, as he noted in the past tense events that occurred in the course of the king's progress: hunting at Pipewell (p. 261), which took place shortly before 26 July;[9] an unidentified village (in Huntingdonshire) 'wher the king dynid in a meane house' (p. 262), on 19 October;[10] and Berkhamsted Castle, 'and there the king lodgid'

---

1   Smith, 2008, 320.
2   This assumes that the folio on which the description is written forms part of this journey.
3   LTS, vol. 3, 106.
4   Smith, 2008, 469.
5   Smith, 2008, 537.
6   DVI, xcvii-xcviii and notes, concurs with this dating, and includes as evidence some other monasteries, whose status or inclusion on this journey is less certain.
7   DVI, xcvii and note 413; 328-9 (ch. 165). I have abbreviated the translation from Latin (by Carley).
8   L&P, XVI, 941, 1291.
9   L&P, XVI, 1042.
10 This and other dates are taken from R W Hoyle and J B Ramsdale, 2004, The

(p. 180), probably 23 October.¹ Much of Leland's journey to and from the north (from Northampton to Pontefract, and through Lincolnshire back to Hampton Court) shadowed quite closely Henry's progress, and his remark quoted above implies that he was at York while the king was there (18-27 September). But in Yorkshire he must have 'turned aside' (*diverterem*) very considerably during late August and September to explore places Henry and his court did not reach, including the North Riding, Durham and the Tyne.

c. West Country. Leland's account of this journey is headed in his handwriting 'Quinta die Maii Anno D. 1542' (5 May 1542),² and there is no reason to doubt that he set off then or shortly afterwards. During the autumn of 1542 he wrote *Naeniae*, an elegiac poem on the death of his friend and fellow poet Sir Thomas Wyatt, who had died at Sherborne on 6 October.³ It was published in London before the end of the year, so the assumption must be that Leland had returned there after leaving Winchester, where his account ends (p. 161), by October or November at the latest.

Even without Leland's date, internal evidence confirms the year 1542. In Oxfordshire he gives a detailed account of Great Haseley, the living to which he was presented on 31 March 1542,⁴ and with which he had no known former connection. At Wells he notes the lavish cross in the market place then being erected by William Knight, the bishop. Knight was consecrated bishop on 29 May 1541,⁵ and the completed cross had the date 1542 inscribed on it.⁶ Torrington manor, Leland tells us, had recently been given to Fitzwilliam, Earl of Southampton (p. 76); Sir William Fitzwilliam died on 15 October 1542 without issue.⁷

---

  royal progress of 1541, the north of England, and Anglo-Scottish relations, 1534-42, *Northern History*, 41, 239-65, table on 263-5.
1 The table (previous note) shows the king at Ampthill (22 October), St Albans (23) and Hampton Court (24).
2 LTS, vol. 1, 107.
3 Leland *Naeniae* (ed. Dana Sutton), online edn.; ODNB.
4 L&P, XVII, 283, g. 16.
5 HBC, 206.
6 J Collinson, 1791, *History and Antiquities of Somerset*, vol. 3, 376.
7 HBC, 483.

d. West Midlands. That this journey did not take place before 1542 may be inferred from two references within Leland's text. At Gloucester he notes that a merchant named Bell has endowed land to maintain bridges and causeways (p. 128), and Thomas Bell is known to have made this gift in 1542.[1] The manor of Southam (Warwicks.), he tells us, had been acquired through exchange by one Knightley (p. 381); this took place in April 1542.[2] Leland set off on this journey from his living of Great Haseley, to which as we have noted he was presented in March 1542. Since we know that the West Country journey was made in 1542, the following year, 1543, seems to be the earliest that he could have explored the West Midlands. Nor could this have taken place later than 1544, because Fulk Greville's possession of the former Alcester Priory (pp. 375-6) came to an end when it was granted away in November 1544.[3] Leland tells us that Elmley Castle (Worcs.) belonged to the king (p. 415), who in fact sold it to Sir William Herbert in October 1544.[4] And at Eyton near Leominster Leland refers to 'Hakcluit now lyvynge' as the third in descent from William Hakluyt who fought at Agincourt (p. 173). This was Thomas Hakluyt, who died before 15 May 1544, when probate of his will was granted.[5]

So far as can be known, Leland visited Worcester only twice during his Itinerary years, in 1538 before exploring Wales, and on his West Midlands journey. Among his notes is a list of bishops of Worcester (omitted from this edition) which ends with John Bell, 1539. Assuming that Leland compiled the list at Worcester it must therefore have been during his later visit. John Bell was bishop from 1539 until November 1543, and his successor was nominated the following month.[6] Had Leland compiled the list in 1544 he would be expected to have brought it up to Bell's successor, Nicholas Heath. And so it seems very likely that the West Midlands journey was undertaken during 1543.

---

1 VCH Glos, IV, 242-3.
2 L&P, XVII, 285, g. 6; VCH Warwicks, VI, 222.
3 L&P, XIX (2), 690, g. 58.
4 L&P, XIX (2), 527, g. 41.
5 D James, 2017, The Herefordshire Hakluyt houses, *Jnl. Hakluyt Soc*, Jan. 2017, 3-4; TNA, PROB 11/30/104.
6 HBC, 262.

e. Bristol Area. This appears to post-date the 1542 West Country journey. In 1542 at Abingdon Leland made himself a note to ask about a Latin book on the works of the abbots of Abingdon (p. 14); in this account he adds more information about Abingdon (pp. 14-16), which seems to be derived from this book.[1] At Lambourn 'Master Estesex' is described as lord of the town (p. 17), which he only became in 1543.[2] The former priory of St Margaret's, Marlborough, is described by Leland, 'where now dwellythe one Mastar Daniell' (p. 400). Geoffrey Daniell purchased the former priory from the crown in July 1544.[3] Leland tells us of Alderley (Glos.), 'where Mastar John Points dwellith, beying lord of it' (p. 138). Sir John Poyntz died on 29 Nov. 1544, leaving as heir his son Henry, a minor.[4]

On internal evidence, therefore, this journey appears to have taken place during the summer of 1544, arriving at Marlborough no earlier than July, and at Alderley before November. Even without the reference to Poyntz, the alternative, 1545, seems to be ruled out by two, possibly three, references to Leland's other activities in that year. He signed a document on 20 May 1545.[5] He completed his *Cygnea Cantio* and dated its preface from London *tertio calendarum Jul.* (i.e. 29 June) – it was published later in the same year. It was probably also in 1545 that he visited Ampthill (Beds.) where he discussed Latin with Prince Edward and Princess Elizabeth.[6] Edward's only recorded visit to Ampthill occurred before he attained his eighth year (on 12 October 1545).[7] By 1545, in any case, Leland appears to have been busily engaged in writing his *De Viris Illustribus*.[8] Thus we can assign with reasonable confidence the Bristol area journey to the summer and autumn of 1544.

The years 1539 and 1540, and the missing or fragmentary journeys
As we have seen, the corpus of Leland's notes that have come down to us as his commentaries or itinerary is incomplete and disordered. If two of

---

1 LTS, vol. 5, 75 note.
2 VCH Berks, IV, 253.
3 VCH Wilts, XII, 171; L&P, XIX (2), 1035, g. 83.
4 HP.
5 L&P, XX (1), 776 (388), cited by Carley, DVI, xxiii-xxiv, n. 18.
6 Leland *Epigrammata* CLXV (ed. Dana Sutton), online edn.
7 *Ibid*, notes.
8 DVI, civ, where this period is described as 'frenzied activity'.

the claims that he made to the king in the New Year's Gift, were truthful, that he had visited everywhere in the kingdom, and that he had spent the previous six years travelling, he was presumably on the road during 1539 and 1540, engaged on journeys to places for which no description survives, or exists only in a fragmentary state. Can any of this accumulation be dated to these two years?

There is a mass of material, mostly excluded from this edition, relating to Wales, largely in the form of lists of monastic houses, castles, gentry, rivers, bridges, market towns and the like, which cannot be rearranged into any coherent itinerary. While it is possible that some of this was compiled during fieldwork prior to 1538,[1] he appears not to have visited Wales during the library tours of 1533-5.[2] It is perhaps more likely that these notes include material tabulated from reading in the study before setting off,[3] and from information collected during the 1538 itinerary about nearby places that he did not actually see.[4] There is, however, one sequence, beginning with a crossing of the Severn from Aust in Gloucestershire, through Monmouthshire and then into Glamorgan, which appears to be describing a journey (pp. 242-7). It includes the phrases 'as I lernid', 'house, where I lay,' and 'I marked not'.[5] Moreover, based on Leland's descriptions of monasteries it can be dated to 1539. Thus Newport's Austin friary and Cardiff's Greyfriars, both dissolved in September 1538, are described in the past tense, as is Neath, dissolved in February 1539; whereas Ewenny, described in the present tense, was not dissolved until January 1540.[6]

The regions about which Leland's surviving notes are least informative are the Home Counties around London, London itself, and East Anglia. Since, so far as we know, he was usually resident in London, where he had a house

---

1   As suggested by Carley, in DVI, xcviii, n. 417.
2   DVI, appendix 1, pp. 817-21, lists the places he visited.
3   LTS, vol. 3, 58 notes that some folios were written in two inks – heads were put in first and details written later.
4   e.g. his notes on Carmarthenshire and Pembrokeshire, LTS vol. 3, 57-65, which refer to houses dissolved in February 1537 in the past tense (Carmarthen and Haverfordwest), but Whitland and Kidwelly, dissolved in February or March 1539 in the present tense.
5   LTS, vol. 3, 43-5.
6   Dates from https://www.monasticwales.org/.

in 1541 and 1546,[1] short topographical forays would have been possible during 1539 and 1540, and in other years during the winter months when he was not away on his longer expeditions. He is known to have been at Bury St Edmunds on 9 November 1539.[2] Of this fieldwork only fragments have survived, including a description of Kingston on Thames (pp. 361-2), and archaeological remains at Silchester in Hampshire (pp. 161-2).

But two fragments can be closely dated, probably to 1540. One relates to Royston. The town stood astride county (Hertfordshire and Cambridgeshire) and diocesan boundaries, an inconvenience rectified by an Act of Parliament in 1540,[3] which reorganised its parish structure. Leland alluded to this, and described the situation before 'the late parlament', which sat between 12 April and 24 July 1540.[4] The second is a reference to Halnaker during a leg of a journey from Petworth to Arundel and Littlehampton in West Sussex (pp. 363-4). Halnaker is described as 'a late the Lord Delawar house.' The king negotiated in November 1539 to acquire Halnaker from Lord de la Warr in exchange for Wherwell in Hampshire, and the transaction was completed in March 1540.[5] One or more longer journey may also have been undertaken in 1540; there is an intriguing reference when Leland passed through Dorset in 1542: 'I have the description of Wareham in an other Itinerarie of myne'.[6] This description and this 'itinerary' have not survived.

THE NEW YEAR'S GIFT TO KING HENRY VIII, GIVEN JANUARY 1544[7]

This is the text of Leland's prospectus to the king outlining the research he had undertaken and the books he planned to derive from it. Not only does

---

1 DVI, xxiii, n. 15; Carley in ODNB, 'John Leland'.
2 LTS, vol. 2, 148; date discussed by Carley, in DVI, xcix.
3 Act 32Hen.VIII, c. 44.
4 L&P, XV, 498 (51).
5 L&P, XIV (2), 544, 547; XV, 436 (72).
6 LTS, vol. 1, 254.
7 For the date, see above, p.xvii. The text is that edited by Toulmin Smith (LTS, vol. 1, xxxvii-xliii) from Leland's autograph, not the version printed with John Bale's commentary in 1549.

it help to explain the form and purpose of the itinerary. It also illustrates Leland's English prose style when polished for publication.

WHERE AS IT PLEASID yowr Highnes apon very juste considerations to encorage me, by the autorite of yowr moste gratius commission yn the xxv. yere of yowr prosperus regne, to peruse and diligently to serche al the libraries of monasteries and collegies of this yowre noble reaulme, to the intente that the monumentes of auncient writers as welle of other nations, as of this yowr owne province mighte be brought owte of deadely darkenes to lyvely lighte, and to receyve like thankes of the posterite, as they hoped for at such tyme as they emploied their long and greate studies to the publique wealthe; yea and farthermore that the holy Scripture of God might bothe be sincerely taughte and lernid, al maner of superstition and craftely coloured doctrine of a rowte of the Romaine bishopes totally expellid oute of this your moste catholique reaulme: I think it now no lesse then my very dewty brevely to declare to your Majeste what frute hath spronge of my laborius yourney and costely enterprise, booth rootid apon yowr infinite goodnes and liberalite, qualites righte highly to be estemid yn al princes, and most especially yn yow as naturally yowr owne welle knowen proprietes.

Firste I have conservid many good autors, the which other wise had beene like to have perischid to no smaul incommodite of good letters, of the whiche parte remayne yn the moste magnificent libraries of yowr royal Palacis. Parte also remayne yn my custodye. Wherby I truste right shortely so to describe your moste noble reaulme, and to publische the Majeste and the excellent actes of yowr progenitors (hitherto sore obscurid booth for lak of enprinting of such workes as lay secretely yn corners, and also bycause men of eloquence hath not enterprisid to set them forthe yn a florisching style, yn sum tymes paste not communely usid in England of wryters, otherwise welle lernid, and now yn such estimation that except truethe be delicately clothid yn purpure her written verites can scant finde a reader;) that al the worlde shaul evidently perceyve that no particular region may justely be more extollid then yours for trewe nobilite and vertues at al pointes renoumed. Farthermore parte of the examplaries curiousely sought by me, and fortunately founde yn sundry places of this yowr dominion, hath beene enprintcd yn Germany, and now be yn the pressis chiefly of Frobenius that not al only the Germanes, but also the Italians them self, that counte, as the Grekes did ful arrogantely, al other nations to be barbarus and onletterid saving their owne, shaul have a directe occasion openly of force to say that *Britannia prima fuit parens, altrix,* (addo hoc etiam & jure quodam optimo) *conservatrix* cum virorum magnorum, tum maxime ingeniorum.

And that profite hath rysen by the aforesaide journey in bringging ful many thinges to lighte as concerning the usurpid autorite of the Bishop of Rome and his complices, to the manifeste and violente derogation of kingely dignite, I referre my self moste humbly to your moste prudente, lernid and highe jugement to disceme my diligence in the longe volume wheryn I have made answer for the defence of youre supreme dignite, alonly lening to the stronge pilor of holy Scripture agayne the hole College of the Romanistes, cloking theire crafty assertions and argumentes under the name of one poore Pighius of Ultrajecte in Germayne, and standing to them as to theire only ancre-holde agayne tempestes that they know wylle rise if treuth may be by licens lette yn to have a voice in the general concile.

Yet here yn onely I have not pitchid the supreme marke of my labor whereonto yowr Grace moste like a princely patrone of al good lerning did animate me: but also considering and expendinge with my self how greate a numbre of excellente goodly wyttes and writers, lernid with the beste, as the tymes servid, hath beene yn this your region, not only at suche tymes as the Romayne Emperours had recourse to it, but also yn those dayes that the Saxons prevailid of the Britannes, and the Normannes of the Saxons, could not but with a fervente zele and an honeste corage commend them to memory, els alas like to have beene perpetually obscurid, or to have bene lightely remembrid as oncerteine shadowes. Wherfore I, knowing by infinite variete of bookes and assiduus reading of them who hathe beene lernid, and who hath writen from tyme to tyme in this reaulme, have digestid in to foure bookes the names of them with theire lyves and monumentes of lerning, and to them addid this title, "De viris illustribus," following the profitable exemple of Hieronyme, Gennadie, Cassiodore, Severiane, and Trittemie a late writer: but alway so handeling the matier that I have more exspatiatid yn this campe then they did, as yn a thing that desired to be sumwhat at large, and to have ornature. The firste booke begynning at the Druides is deductid on to the tyme of the cumming of S. Augustine yn to Engelande. The secunde is from the tyme of Augustine on to the advente of the Normans. The thirde from the Normans to the ende of the most honorable reigne of the mightty, famose, and prudent Prince Henry the VII. your Father. The fourth beginnith with the name of your Majeste, whos glorie in lerning is to the worlde so clerely knowen, that though emonge the lyves of other lernid menne I have accuratly celebratid the names of Bladudus, Molmutius, Costantinus Magnus, Sigebertus, Alfridus, Alfridus Magnus, Æthelstanus and Henry the firste, Kinges and your progenitors; and also Ethelwarde, secunde sunne to Alfride the Greate, Hunfride Duke of Glocestre, and Tipetote Erle of Worcester; yet conferrid withe yowr Grace they seme as smaule lighttes (if I may frely say my jugemente, yowr highe modeste not offendid,) yn respecte of the day-starre.

Now farther to insinuate to yowr Grace of what matiers the writers, whose lyves I have congestid ynto foure bokes, hath treatid of, I may right boldely say, that beside the cognition of the thre tunges, yn the which parte of them hath excellid, that there is no kinde of liberale science, or any feate concerning lerning, yn the which they have not shewen certeine argumentes of greate felicite of wytte; yea and concerning the interpretation of holy Scripture, booth after the aunciente forme, and sins yn the scholastical trade, they have reignid as in a certeine excellency.

And as touchinge historical knowlege there hath beene to the numbre of a fulle hunderith, or mo, that from tyme to tyme hath with greate diligence, and no lesse faith, wold to God with like eloquens, perscribid the actes of yowr most noble prædecessors, and the fortunes of this your realme, so incredibly greate, that he that hath not seene and thoroughly redde theyr workes can little pronunce yn this parte.

Wherfore after that I had perpendid the honest and profitable studies of these historiographes, I was totally enflammid with a love to see thoroughly al those partes of this your opulente and ample reaulme, that I had redde of yn the aforesaid writers: yn so muche that al my other occupations intermittid I have so travelid yn yowr dominions booth by the se costes and the midle partes, sparing nother labor nor costes, by the space of these vi. yeres paste, that there is almoste nother cape, nor bay, haven, creke or peere, river or confluence of rivers, breches, waschis, lakes, meres, fenny waters, montaynes, valleis, mores, hethes, forestes, wooddes, cities, burges, castelles, principale manor placis, monasteries, and colleges, but I have seene them; and notid yn so doing a hole worlde of thinges very memorable.

Thus instructed I truste shortely to see the tyme that like as Carolus Magnus had emonge his treasours thre large and notable tables of sylver richely enamelid, one of the site and description of Constantinople, another of the site and figure of the magnificente cite of Rome, and the thirde of the description of the worlde; so shaul yowr Majestie have this yowr worlde and impery of Englande so sette forthe yn a quadrate table of silver, if God sende me life to accomplische my beginninges, that yowr grace shaul have ready knowlege at the firste sighte of many right delectable, fruteful, and necessary pleasures, by the contemplation thereof, as often as occasion shaul move yow to the sight of it.

And be cause that it may be more permanente, and farther knowen than to have it engravid in silver or brasse, I entende (by the leave of God) withyn the space of xii. monethes following, such a description to make of your reaulme yn writing, that it shaul be no mastery after for the graver or painter to make a like by a perfecte exemple.

Yea and to wade farther yn this matier, wheras now almoste no man can welle gesse at the shadow of the aunciente names of havens, ryvers, promontories, hilles, woddes, cities, tounes, castelles, and variete of kindredes of people, that Cæsar, Livie, Strabo, Diodorus, Fabius Pictor, Pomponius Mela, Plinius, Cornelius Tacitus, Ptolemæus, Sextus Rufus, Ammianus Marcellinus, Solinus, Antoninus, and diver others make mention of, I truste so to open this wyndow that the lighte shall be seene so longe, that is to say, by the space of a hole thousand yeres, stoppid up, and the olde glory of your renowmid Britaine to reflorisch thorough the worlde.

This doone I have matier at plenty al ready preparid to this purpose, that is to say, to write an history, to the which I entende to adscribe this title, De Antiquitate Britannica, or els Civilis Historia. And this worke I entende to divide yn to so many bookes as there be shires yn England, and sheres and greate dominions yn Wales. So that I esteme that this volume wille enclude a fiftie bookes, wherof eche one severally shaul conteyne the beginninges, encreaces, and memorable actes of the chief tounes and castelles of the province allottid to hit.

Then I entende to distribute yn to vj. bokes such matier as I have al ready collectid concerninge the isles adjacent to your noble reaulme and under your subjection. Wherof thre shaul be of these isles, Vecta, Mona and Menauia, sumtyme kyngedoms.

And to superadde a worke as an ornament and a right comely garlande to the enterprises afore saide, I have selectid stuffe to be distributid into thre bookes, the whiche I purpose thus to entitle, De Nobilitate Britannica. Wherof the first shaul declare the names of kinges, quenes, with theyr childerne, dukes, erles, lordes, capitaines and rulers yn this reaulme to the coming of the Saxons and their conqueste. The secunde shaul be of the Saxons and Danes to the victorie of Kinge William the Greate. The thirde from the Normans to the reigne of yowr moste noble grace, descendinge lineally of the Britanne, Saxon and Norman kinges. So that al noble mene shaul clerely perceyve theyr lineal parentele.

Now if it shaul be the pleasure of Almightty God that I may live to performe these thinges that be al ready begune and in a greate forwardnes, I truste that this yowr reaulme shaul so welle be knowen, ons payntid with his natives coloures, that the renoume ther of shaul gyve place to the glory of no other region; and my great labors and costes, proceding from the moste abundant fonteine of yowr infinite goodnes towarde me, yowr poore scholar and moste humble servante, shaul be evidently seene to have not al only pleasid but also profited the studius, gentil, and equale readers.

This is the briefe declaration of my laborius yorneye, taken by motion of yowr highenes, so much studiyng at al houres the fruteful præferremente of good letters and aunciente vertues.

Christe continue your most royale estate, and the prosperite with succession in kingely dignite of your deere and worthily belovid sunne Prince Eduarde, graunting yow a numbre of princely sunnes by the moste gratius, benigne, and modeste lady your Quene.

Joannes Lelandius Antiquarius scripsit.

BEDFORDSHIRE

RETURNING TO LONDON *from both his northern itineraries, in 1538 and 1541, Leland travelled south through Bedfordshire. His account of the later journey, which took him to Bletsoe, Bedford, Ampthill and Dunstable, is the more informative. After Bedford we find him making a detour to examine castle sites along the Ouse, and perhaps to visit Sir John Gostwick of Willington. He had previously explored another corner of the county, around Melchbourne, soon after he had set out from Cambridge on the 1541 journey, and he had also begun to compile lists of various places and topics of interest.*

FROM HIGHAM FERRERS to Bedford is ten miles beside pasture and arable land. About four miles from Higham Ferrers the road crosses the boundary between Northamptonshire and Bedfordshire. A mile downstream from Bedford is Newnham, a house of canons. There are many small islands, or holmes, in the river between Bedford and Newnham. Newnham Abbey was transferred from St Paul's, Bedford, which had been a house of prebendaries before the conquest. One Simon de Beauchamp refounded it as a house of regular canons, and during the time of the second prior the community was transferred to Newnham.

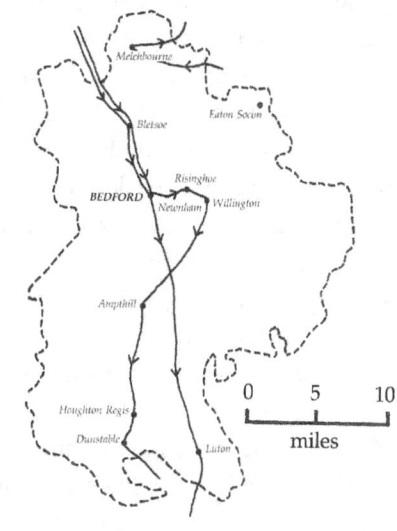

There are seven parish churches in Bedford, three still in use in the south part, four in the north, as well as a house of Grey Friars. Distances from Bedford: Buckingham, 20 miles; Huntingdon, 10 miles.

I travelled the twelve miles from Bedford to Luton, a market town in Bedfordshire, mostly beside arable ground, which is somewhat hilly and the soil chalky. Close to the highway on each side I saw three long trenches, apparently made for a military purpose. From Luton to St Albans is eight miles by wooded and enclosed ground, and the country is similar to Barnet (ten miles) and London (another ten miles). One corner of Enfield Chase extends close to Barnet. [**1538:** 4/33-4]

From Great Staughton to Melchbourne village is four miles, largely by pasture but also some arable land. Here is a very fine house built of squared stone, much of it vaulted on stone pillars, with good gardens, orchards and ponds, and beside a park. Although the house itself is old, the hall was newly built by Lord Weston of the College of St John in London (the third before the last of that name). In the chapel, on the north side, a knight of the Order of St John is buried.

Melchbourne is in Bedfordshire, but almost on the boundary. In this region, although not immediately next to Melchbourne itself, two brooks issue from different springs. One flows from Higham Park. They flow into the same valley and become a single stream, which passes the village of How End, hence the name by which they are known – How Water. There used to be a fine manor house at How End, which once belonged to the Stricklands of Huntingdonshire, and later to the Byfields; it was recently divided between three daughters. How Water flows on to Great Staughton, and into the River Ouse a mile below St Neots.

Distances from Melchbourne: Higham Ferrers market, 3 miles; Wellington [*Wellingborough*] market near the River Avon [*Nene*], 6 miles. The area is quite well wooded, and Melchbourne House is considered to be one of the finest in Bedfordshire. *cont. p. 254* [**1541:** 1/1-2]

I rode across six miles of open country from Higham Ferrers to [*Bletsoe*], where Mr St John lives in a very handsome moated manor house. In the quire wall of the parish church there I saw an old tomb with an effigy, which some think belonged to one of the de Broy family, former owners of the manor. From Bletsoe to Bedford is eight miles, mostly open country, but some good woodland near Bedford.

The principal church in Bedford is St Paul's. This was a pre-conquest college of prebendaries which continued until Newnham Priory was founded, on a site beside the River Ouse scarcely a mile below Bedford. The dwellings of the prebendaries surrounded St Paul's Church; two named prebends remain, with houses belonging to them, but the prebendal stalls are in Lincoln. It was Roais, the wife of Payn de Beauchamp, who translated the secular college to Newnham, a college of regular canons. But it was the son of Roais and Payn, Simon de Beauchamp, who confirmed and completed his mother's action. He is buried in front of the high altar in St Paul's church, Bedford, with the following Latin epitaph engraved in brass and set on a flat marble stone: 'Under this slab lies Simon de Beauchamp, the founder of Newnham'.

Payn de Beauchamp was given the barony of Bedford after King William's conquest. His wife Roais established Chicksands Priory, and was buried in the chapter house there. Caldwell Priory also, which is a little downstream [upstream] from Bedford on the right bank of the River Ouse, was founded by one of the Beauchamps. The barony of Bedford, and Bedford Castle as its residence, remained in the Beauchamp family until Fulk de Breauté took charge of the castle in the time of John and Henry III. I remember reading somewhere that he acquired it by marriage. But after he and his brothers rebelled against Henry III the king seized Bedford Castle and demolished it, giving the site to one of the Beauchamps who had a hereditary claim over it. Subsequently the male line of the Beauchamps failed, and their lands were divided between three Beauchamp daughters. The eldest married Lord de Moulbray; the second, according to some people, was unmarried, and her lands were bought by Lord Latimer. The third married a man called Lestrange, but his share, because he had no male heir, passed to two daughters, who married Pigot and Patishull. A portion of Patishull's share has since come to the best of the St John family in Bedfordshire.

Both the hospitals in Bedford were founded by the townspeople of Bedford. But recently, in order to reduce their annual liability for taxation from £40 to £20, the townspeople have given the title and patronage of one of the hospitals to Sir Reginald Bray. By this means it has lately become the exclusive property of Lord Bray.

From Bedford to Castle Mills is two miles, partly through pasture and corn. A little to the west of the mill, upstream, are indications of the site of the large castle of Risinghoe. No part of the buildings is visible, but it is easy to see the position of the castle baily. The great round hill where the keep or dungeon stood is intact. At present many rough bushes are growing on it, and there is a flourishing burrow in it for badgers and foxes.

A mile further north, according to the miller, in a large open field there is a ditch and a hill, which was probably a tower or fortress; but the prior of Newnham told me that this lay on the road from Bedford to St Neots. So far as I can discover, the castle near Castle Mills belonged to Lord Beauchamp, Baron of Bedford, but I have not been able to find out when it became utterly ruined. However, I would conjecture that it belonged instead to the Espec family, and their heirs, the de Ros family. The Especs founded Warden Abbey in Bedfordshire, and this was a portion of the abbey's lands. Both Castle Mills and the castle baily belonged to Warden Abbey at the time of its recent suppression, and were sold by the king to Mr Gostwick, their present owner. Next to the castle the River Ouse divides into two streams, which meet again just below the mill, and so form an island. The smaller stream serves the mill. I crossed over this by a wooden bridge, and in due course I crossed the main channel by a timber bridge. I was told by the miller here that there was only one other timber bridge across the Ouse between the mill and St Neots.

Having crossed these two bridges I came to rather low-lying ground, with very good meadows and pastures, and so to the village of Willington, about a half-mile from Castle Mills. The village lies in a convenient position on a good gravelly site, with fine woods in some places around it. It belonged to the Beauchamps, barons of Bedford, and when their lands were partitioned it passed to Lord Mowbray of Axholme. Mr Gostwick, a native of Willington, bought the lordship from the present Duke of Norfolk, and has erected in the village a sumptuous new building of brick and timber from the foundations up, with a water supply flowing in lead pipes. Near Mr Gostwick's new building was an old manor house where some of the Mowbrays used to stay for short periods. It has been completely demolished, but the site is clearly visible. Apart from Willington Mr Gostwick has purchased five or six other manors.

From Willington to Ampthill Castle is twelve miles, almost entirely across open ground, partly arable, partly pasture, with some barren heathland and sandy ground. There is fine woodland around the castle itself and the town. Ampthill Castle and town, and several good manors in this area belonged to Lord Fanhope, a man of great renown during the reigns of Henry V and Henry VI. It was he who built the castle in its present noble state, on a hill, with four or five stone towers in the inner ward, as well as a lower courtyard. He built it, so it is said, from spoils which he won in France. But, according to the east window of the castle chapel, it appears that he married into noble blood – his wife, as I recall, was the Duchess of Exeter – so it may be that this marriage was largely responsible for the sumptuous building. I have learnt that this Lord Fanhope is buried at Blackfriars in London, with his wife on his right hand, and a child.

I have been told the following as a true account of how Lord Grey of Ruthin came to own this castle and its surrounding lands. During the civil war between Henry VI and Edward IV a battle was fought close to the southern suburbs of Northampton. Lord Fanhope was wholly on King Henry's side, and so, apparently, was Lord Grey of Ruthin. But shortly before the battle Grey negotiated with King Edward, and either claimed that he was entitled to Fanhope's lands in and around Ampthill, or defamed him with false accusations. As a result Grey and his strong Welsh army went over to King Edward's side, on condition that if Edward won the battle Grey should have Ampthill with Fanhope's lands there. Edward was victorious and so Gray obtained the Ampthill estate. His standing with the king increased further, and eventually Edward made him Earl of Kent. But whether or not Lord Fanhope was killed at this battle I am not sure.

Ampthill is a pleasant, well-built market town, a quarter-mile distant from the castle. One part stands on a hill, but the larger and better part lies in a valley. A small brook, as I recall, runs past the east side of the town.

From Ampthill to Dunstable is ten miles or more. At first I passed wooded and enclosed lands, but most of my journey was over open ground, and about two miles east of Dunstable I passed through a pleasant country town called [?*Houghton Regis*]. A further six miles across open ground, mostly fertile arable land, brought me to Markyate. *cont. p. 179* [**1541**: *1/99-104*]

Notable things in Bedfordshire: Adinggreves [*Renhold*] Castle is on the same side of the river as Castle Mills (also called Risinghoe), about a mile downstream towards St Neots. Here, no more than two stones' throw from the river bank, on a hill, is a ditch and other signs of buildings. Castle Mills is a mile-and-a-half below Bedford. At Barford, about a mile-and-a-half below Adinggreves, is a large stone bridge of eight arches, and on the further bank is a good country town [*Great Barford*].

From Great Barford it is about three miles to Eaton Socon, a good village on the further bank. Here, between the church and the river, almost next to the riverbank, may be seen the remains of a castle belonging to Lord Vaux. There is a small, poor, accommodation bridge across the river at Eaton.

In the southern suburb of Bedford, on this side of the River Ouse, there were two hospitals; the houses and chapels of both survive. As you approach Bedford from the south you come first to St John's on the right hand side; and then also on the right, but a little to one side, is St Leonard's.

Notable things in the Grey Friars, Bedford: The first foundress of the Grey Friars at Bedford was Lady Mabel Pattishall of Bletsoe (where Sir John St John now lives) and, according to some, also of Stoke [*Stoke Rochford*], Lincolnshire, four miles this side of Grantham (which is now also St John property). This Mabel is buried under a flat stone at the south side of the high altar under an arch. Her Latin epitaph runs: 'Here lies Lady Mabel Pattishall, mistress of Bletsoe, first foundress of this place'. One of the Lords Mowbray is also buried on the north side of the high altar, under a plain stone. Right in front of the high altar lies Queen Eleanor, under a flat marble stone with a plain brass plate portraying a crowned figure. Richard Hastings, Esquire, Edward III's chamberlain, is buried in a low tomb on the north side of the quire. In the middle of the nave (which, it is said, he built) is buried Sir Richard Irencester. Recently Blake St John was buried off the quire close to Hastings. The friary lies in the northern part of the town. [4/22-3]

Walter Espec founded the monastery at Warden in 1136. [1/91]

The original town of Dunstable, and the main road, lay a mile from the new town, where the village called Dunestaple Houghtoun [*Houghton Regis*] is now situated. Dunstable has one parish church, but there was also a priory of Augustinian canons, which was founded by Henry I. In the priory were buried the relics of a Saxon nobleman, St Fremund. A popular legend recounts that these relics were being taken to Canterbury to be deposited there, but by some miracle they could be carried no further than Dunstable. Also buried there were two noblemen, called Fitzneele and Nigel Loring, who were both great benefactors to the priory. Loring, a Bedfordshire noble, established three chantries in the parish church at Toddington in Bedfordshire, two miles from Dunstable, and I heard it said that some of his family are buried there. Dunstable also had a house of black friars, which recently claimed an esquire from Devonshire as its founder. [4/127]

Market towns in Bedfordshire: Bedford; Biggleswade, two miles from Warden Abbey, a good market and two fairs; Shefford, three miles from Bedford, and a mile from Chicksands Priory; Luton, a very good market town for barley; Ampthill; Olney; Potton; Woburn; Dunstable.

Castles in Bedfordshire: Bedford Castle close to the town is now completely demolished. Beside the castle there is a place called Falxherbar [*Faux 'Erber*]. Between Kings Cross halfway to Newnham and the castle were found many bones from human burials. Ampthill Castle was built by Lord Fanhope, a very rich man who made his name fighting overseas. Odell Castle, the property of Lord Bray, is now nothing except odd ruins. The settlement at Odell is next to the castle, about eight miles from Bedford, and about a mile from Harrold nunnery. This Odell was a barony. A mile from Lavendon Abbey (which is less than a mile from Olney) is Castle Park, which belonged to the Zouches, but has recently been sold to Lord Mordaunt. Perhaps this was Lavendon Castle. Risinghoe is close to Castle Mills on the River Ouse. It used to belong to Warden Abbey, but is now Mr Gostwick's. A mile or two from Risinghoe, beside the River Ouse at Adinggreves [?*Renhold*], are traces of the ditches of a former fortress.

Rivers in Bedfordshire: Isis, otherwise Ouse; Olney Water; Undal [?*Ouzel*] Water. [5/7-8]

BERKSHIRE

T HE WEST COUNTRY ITINERARY, which Leland began in May 1542, took him up the Thames valley to the Cotswolds, and on his way he was able to record in detail most of the Berkshire towns, notably Maidenhead, Reading, Wallingford and Faringdon. He also described Abingdon, but realised that there was much more to be found out about its history. A second itinerary, to visit the Bristol region, took him back to Abingdon in 1544 and enabled him to write a fuller account, before continuing via Wantage and Faringdon into Wiltshire. Apart from the Kennet valley, therefore, with its towns of Newbury and Hungerford, Leland explored and described most of Berkshire; his rough notes add little to the more vivid narratives of his itineraries.

T WO OR THREE MILES after crossing the River Burne I came to the timber bridge over the Thames at Maidenhead. A little above the bridge on this bank of the Thames I saw a cliff overhanging the river with some bushes growing on it. I conjectured that this had been the site of some ancient building. There is a large wharf for timber and firewood at the west end of the bridge. This wood comes from Berkshire, from the great woods in Windsor Forest, and from the great Frith [*woodland between*

Maidenhead and Henley]. It should be noted that all the land from the arm of the River Colne which flows through Colnbrook up to Maidenhead Bridge is in Buckinghamshire; beyond is Berkshire.

The town of Maidenhead stands at a good distance from the riverside, and is moderately well built. The south side of the town is in the parish of Bray, and the north side is in Cookham parish. From here it is two miles by a narrow, wooded road to the Frith, then more than three miles through the Frith, and a further two miles to Twyford, which is a pleasant little town. At the west end of Twyford flows the Lodden, a nice river but here so divided into different channels that I passed over four bridges.

Sonning is a mile-and-a-half further on. It is a remote place, but set in fine, fruitful country. The Thames runs below it in a pleasant valley. I did not notice anything of great antiquity in the church, the living of which belongs to the dean of Salisbury. In the sanctuary is buried one Fyton, an esquire; and in the south aisle are the tombs of two or three vowesses, kinswomen of a bishop of Salisbury. At the east end of the church there is an old chapel of St Sarik [?*Cyricus*], and here until recently many people came as pilgrims to be cured of madness. Before the conquest the bishop of Salisbury, who owned Sonning, had an ancient manor house here. A good, old, stonebuilt house still survives right next to the bank of the Thames, with a fine park beside it, and this belongs to the bishop of Salisbury. Sonning is in Berkshire three miles above Henley. It is two miles from here to Reading, and as you approach Reading there is a park which belonged to the former monastery.

There is no evidence that Reading was ever a walled town; but it is a very ancient place, and at present is the best town in the whole of Berkshire. In Saxon times there was a castle here, and even now the name Castle Street is used of the street which runs from east to west and leads towards Newbury. I could not see nor find out for certain where the castle had stood, but in all probability it was at the west end of Castle Street, near where executions take place, in the opinion of some. It is very likely that part of the abbey was built from its ruins, so perhaps it stood where the abbey was.

I have read that St Edward the Martyr's stepmother built a monastery for nuns at Reading as an act of penance. It is widely believed that St Mary's parish church in Reading is on the site of this nunnery. When Henry I founded an abbey at Reading for black monks he suppressed the nunnery, so I have heard, and used its lands to endow his abbey. To ascertain this I must find out whether the old nunnery did not in fact occupy the site on which Reading Abbey was built, and whether St Mary's is not a newer foundation. Until recently there was a good house of grey friars on the north side of Castle Street.

In the town there are three parish churches, St Giles's on this side of the River Kennet, St Mary's and St Laurence's on the other side. In terms of age St Mary's is the principal parish church in Reading, and stands in the centre of the town. St Laurence's lies to the west, close to the main entrance into the abbey. An almshouse for poor sisters lay WNW of St Laurence's church; it was probably established by one of the abbots of Reading, and it continued until the time of Henry VII, when Abbot Thorne suppressed it and give its lands for the use of the abbey almoner. But when Henry VII came to Reading he asked what this old building was, and when the abbot told him, the king ordered him to turn the house and its lands back to some pious use. Whereupon the abbot desired that it be made into a grammar school, and so it was. William Dene, a rich man who worked for Reading Abbey, gave the sum of £130 to promote this school, according to the epitaph on his grave in Reading Abbey church.

The River Kennet passes through the centre of Reading, but divides into two main streams, the larger of which flows under a great wooden bridge on the south side of the town. The other channel is generally known in the town as the Hallowed Brook. It leaves the main stream of the Kennet upstream from Reading to the WSW, near the Bere, where the Abbot of Reading had a fine brick manor house. Then it flows down through meadows towards Reading, running through part of the abbey and washing away its filth. A little below this it rejoins the main stream, and the reunited River Kennet flows into the Thames a little further down. The River Thames itself comes within half a mile of Reading on the ENE side. In the lower part of the town, where the two Kennet streams run close together, I noticed a number of little channels branching out of them and creating small islands, which are approached over various wooden bridges. These channels are very suitable for dying and many dyers are settled there, since Reading's mainstay is its cloth industry.

From Reading to Caversham, which is shortened to Causham, is about half a mile. Here there is a large, strong bridge of timber over the Thames, and I noticed that its foundations were mostly of timber, but in some places of stone. Towards the northern end of this bridge, on the right hand side, there is a good, old stone chapel, which is protected against the river's surge by piles driven into the foundations. There is no bridge over the Thames further upstream for about ten miles, at Wallingford. And downstream from Caversham Henley Bridge is five miles, with the wooden bridge at Sonning halfway between, and then Great Marlow Bridge. Three miles above Maidenhead on the Berkshire bank of the Thames is Bisham Priory, and a further mile upstream is Hurley, a cell of Westminster Abbey. On the Buckinghamshire side there was a priory of nuns at Little Marlow, two miles above Maidenhead, and then one mile further is Great Marlow, where there is the timber bridge over the Thames. One mile up the river above Bisham, on the Buckinghamshire side, is Medmenham, a cell of Woburn Abbey in Bedfordshire. *cont. p. 286* [**1542**: *1/108-11*]

From the Thames ferry to Wallingford is a mile, through really fine and fertile open arable countryside. Wallingford has been a very considerable town, with a good wall. The town ditch and the bank on which the walls stood are still very clearly visible, and run for more than a mile from the castle around to Wallingford Bridge, which is a large stone construction across the Thames.

Among the street names which survive are Thames Street, Fish Street, Bread Street, Wood Street, Goldsmith's Row. From the evidence of documents and grants by Edmund, Earl of Cornwall and lord of the honour of Wallingford it appears that there were fourteen parish churches in the town. Indeed there are men still alive who can point out all the sites and graveyards in which they stood. But now there are only three meagre parish churches in the town. Just inside the west gate of Wallingford there was a priory of black monks, a cell of St Albans, which was suppressed by Cardinal Thomas Wolsey.

The town and castle were badly damaged during the Danish wars; but they flourished again to a certain extent in the time of Richard, Earl of Cornwall, who was Henry III's brother, and king of the Romans. He spent a large sum on the castle. The castle adjoins the north gate of the town, and has three ditches, large, deep and well-watered. Around the first and second ditch, on the banks made by the spoil from excavating them, runs a battlemented wall, now in very bad repair, and much of its facing robbed. All the substantial buildings, with the towers and dungeon, are within the third ditch. Among them is a collegiate chapel, which was founded and endowed by Edmund, Earl of Cornwall, who was Richard's son. I was told that Edward the Black Prince enlarged this college. It has a dean, four priests, six clerks and four choristers. The predecessor of Dr London, the present dean, built a fine stone tower at the west end of the college chapel, and it is said that in so doing he damaged, without permission, a part of the king's lodging, which adjoins the east end of the chapel. The dean has a handsome timber lodging inside the castle, with a house for the ministers of the chapel attached to it.

Mackney in Berkshire is a good mile from Wallingford. Here Mr Moleyns has a pleasant manor house of brick, which was built in recent times by his uncle, a man named Court. Moleyns owns not only this manor, but also one in Oxfordshire, near Dorchester, called Mongewell, with an annual income of £50, and fine woodland. Before Court's death Moleyns lived in Hampshire, in a good manor house at a place called Sandhill [near Fordingbridge], about eight miles from Salisbury.

From Wallingford to Sinodun is about a mile-and-a-half. This place is surrounded by a remarkable ditch, approximately half a mile in length, and stands on a hill overlooking the Thames on the Berkshire side. There used to be a settlement inside it, popularly believed to have been a castle in the time of the Britons, and probably destroyed by the Danes. At present it produces good crops of barley and wheat, and Roman coins are turned up there during ploughing. The fertile Vale of White Horse begins about Sinodun and stretches away south-west to the Faringdon area. The vale has not much woodland. From Sinodun it is six miles to Abingdon.

A short distance on this side of Abingdon Bridge two streams, which branch out of the River Isis near the east end of Abingdon Abbey, and so form two little islands, come together. At the very point where they meet they flow under a very fine bridge of seven arches, and then together in one channel they rejoin the Isis almost immediately. The great bridge of Abingdon over the Isis has fourteen arches.

Before the abbey was built there Abingdon was called Seukesham. Work on the first abbey began at Bagley Wood, two miles above the site of Abingdon on the Berkshire side of the Isis. But the foundations and building works there were not successful, and so the abbey was moved to Seukesham and completed there, mostly at the expense of King Cissa, who was later buried in it. The exact positions of his grave and tombstone were never known after the Danes had destroyed Abingdon. I have heard that a holy man, a relation of King Cissa, was living as a hermit in the woods and wasteland about Seukesham, and that it was through him and for his sake that the abbey was built there.

Ethelwold, who was abbot of Abingdon, and later bishop of Winchester, in King Edgar's reign, completely rebuilt and enlarged the abbey. He dug a channel to draw a flow of water out of the Isis under pressure so as to serve and cleanse the domestic quarters of the abbey. Later on, in the early Norman period, his church and buildings were taken down and rebuilt by the Norman abbots. The eastern portions of this work may still be seen. The crossing tower, all the nave of the church and the western towers were built by the four abbots immediately preceding the last four abbots of Abingdon. The names of the last two of these four, responsible for the western part of the church, were Ashendon and Sante. Sante was a doctor of divinity, and served as ambassador to Rome for both Edward IV and Henry VII. At the west end of the abbey church precinct stands a charnel chapel, which was endowed with the income from a chapel at Bayworth near Bagley Wood. On the south side of the precinct are all the dwellings of the abbot and the community.

In the past many of the villages around Abingdon were served only by chapels-of-ease, with Abingdon Abbey as their mother church, and place of burial. Outside a gate at the west end of the abbey is a church dedicated to St Nicholas, which was built by an Abbot Nicholas for the benefit of the town when its population increased. On the opposite side outside the abbey gate is a church dedicated to St John, and this has a hospital for six almshouse men. This hospital is reckoned to be a royal foundation. There is a parish church of St Helen at the southern end of the town, beside the Isis and downstream from the abbey. There was formerly a nunnery on this site, and during the time of Ethelwold (who rebuilt Abingdon Abbey) strange things and burials were found when digging took place. I understand that there is now a hospital for six men and six women at St Helen's, which is maintained by a fraternity there.

Not far below St Helen's the River Ock, which flows through the Vale of White Horse, joins the Isis. Almost at the confluence is Ock Mill, and there is another mill further upstream. In Abingdon market place there is an excellent stone cross with handsome steps and statues. There is also a good house for market people, with open pillars covered by a lead roof. Abingdon is a clothing town, and has a busy market.

I must remember to ask Mr Bachelar in Abingdon, and the prior of Abingdon, who lives one mile from the town, about the Latin book, 'The works of the abbots of Abingdon'. *cont. p. 291* [**1542:** *1/118-22*]

From Oxford I went through the south gate and across the bridge of several arches over the Isis, and then along the causeway on the Berkshire side for at least a quarter of a mile or more, and so up Hincksey Hill, which is about one mile from Oxford. From Hincksey for about one mile the hill is partly wooded, but the next ten miles to Faringdon is all across open country, some arable but mostly pasture.

Faringdon is built on a hillside in stony country. It is sometimes called Chipping-Faringdon [*i.e. Faringdon Market*], but its market, if indeed it is still held, is now very small. There is only one parish church, with transepts, in this little town; but in the churchyard is a very fine chapel to the Trinity, built by one of the Cheneys, who is buried there in a high marble tomb, and endowed with a chantry. Lord Cheney, Warden of the Cinque Ports, pays for it at present. The living of Faringdon, which is worth £40 annually, belongs to a prebend of Salisbury, which is now occupied by that young Florentine, Calvacante.

I asked about the castle which was built here by the supporters of the Empress Matilda, and later pulled down by King Stephen, but no-one could tell me anything about it. However I did learn for certain that one mile from Faringdon to the right of the Highworth road can be seen a large ditch marking the site of a fortress or military camp, which some said had been thrown up as a Danish stronghold. Highworth itself, five miles from Faringdon, has a good Wednesday market serving Berkshire.

From Faringdon to St John's Bridge (a three-arched stone bridge with a causeway) is three and a half miles across low-lying ground prone to flooding from the Isis. As I rode over the river I discovered that the further bank was in Gloucestershire and the nearer in Berkshire, with Oxfordshire not far away. *cont. p. 121* [**1542:** *1/125-6*]

Abingdon is four miles from Oxford, and stands on the right bank of the Isis in Berkshire. A very long time ago the town was called Seusham, but was then renamed Abingdon. There is a foolish tradition that the name is derived from a certain monk and hermit called Aben, who began a monastery in this area. But the truth is that a Saxon nobleman by the name of Eanus was granted permission by his master, the Saxon king Cissa, to begin building a small monastery at a place called Chilswell, two miles NNE of Abingdon along the footpath to Oxford. Later this site was thought to be unsuitable, and the monastery was transferred to Seusham. The new monastic buildings were given the name Abingdon – 'the abbot's town'.

Not long after this Abingdon nunnery was built on the left bank of the River Ock (or Coche), close to its confluence with the main stream of the Isis. This house of nuns was dedicated to St Helen, and her name has been retained. The Danes destroyed both abbey and nunnery. I do not know whether the nunnery was rebuilt, but the abbey rose again, although it remained impoverished until King Edgar enlarged and enriched it, on the advice of Ethelwold, bishop of Winchester.

A little while after the conquest a foreign physician named Faricius was made abbot of Abingdon. He removed the old church, which had stood further north where the orchard is now, and he built a new east end and transept, which he decorated simply with a number of small marble pillars. Later another abbot, who saw that the community had an insufficient water supply, contrived to alter the course of the Isis, and managed to bring it right alongside, and partly through, the abbey. Previously the main stream ran between Andersey Island and what is now the southern end of Culham.

The other channel, which branches out of the Isis about a quarter-mile above Culham to flow past the village and under Culham Bridge, is now the lesser stream of the river. During great floods or after the banks have been breached Culham Water partly reverts to the old course of the Isis, and so then there are three streams. In former times a fortress or castle-like stronghold stood on Andersey south-west of Abingdon, almost in the centre between the old and new channels of the river. The site is a meadow, a quarter-mile across, lying opposite St Helen's. Part of this fortress was still standing after the conquest, when it housed the royal hawks and hounds. But one of the abbots realised how much trouble this had caused and was likely to cause the community, and so he acquired it in exchange for the manor of King's Sutton [*Sutton Courtenay*], a mile-and-a-half downstream, on the Berkshire bank of the Isis. There is now an old barn on the site of this little castle or fortress, and because the river flows close by it is still commonly known as the Castle of the Rhae ['ree' is an obsolete word for river].

The west part of Abingdon abbey church was rebuilt by Abbot William Ashendon. Most of St Edward the Martyr's relics were kept at Abingdon, where, according to some authorities, he spent his childhood. Members of the Blessells family are buried there. Nearly all the land between Eynsham and Dorchester belonged to Abingdon, which received almost £2,000 annually in rents. During their campaign for self-government the inhabitants of Abingdon, Newbury and Oxford ransacked Abingdon Abbey, and in consequence were heavily punished. There was a park belonging to Abingdon at Radley, but it was disparked because it became popular with Oxford scholars as a hunting ground.

Long ago the principal parish church in Abingdon used to be St Nicholas's by the abbey. The abbot built the Hospital of St John the Baptist next to it, and the two were joined together. There are twelve men in the hospital. St Helen's is now a parish church, and is used by the majority of the townspeople. When the course of the Isis was diverted several curious things were found, including an inscribed cross. The present hospital at St Helen's is on the exact site of the nunnery.

Formerly there was no bridge over the Isis at Abingdon, but only a ferry. The road from Gloucester to London did not then pass through Abingdon and Dorchester, as it does now, but through the important town of Wallingford. Various mishaps occurred at the ferry crossing before the bridge was built, and a number of people were drowned. The inhabitants of Abingdon made a successful petition at court for a bridge to relieve the danger, and in 1416, the fourth year of Henry V's reign, the king gave his approval for bridges to be built at Bordford and Culhamford near Abingdon. The work was begun on St Alban's day, and employed three hundred men through the summer. Geoffrey Barbour of Abingdon was the main benefactor, giving money towards the building costs and to procure land to pay for maintenance. (These details are taken from a hanging notice-board.) Some people at Abingdon say that Geoffrey Barbour was also the principal founder of St Helen's Hospital. Another tradition is that at about the same time a certain John of St Helen's had two daughters who produced no heir, and so he decided that his land should be put towards the maintenance of the hospital and the bridges. There is a stone bridge over the River Ock by St Helen's Hospital, and in the market place is a fine cross.

Near Abingdon may still be seen the remains of two military camps. One is at Serpenhil, a quarter-mile ENE of the town along a footpath. A popular tradition explains that a battle was fought here between Danes and Saxons. Part of the ditches of the earthwork are still visible. The other, of which ditches also survive, is called Barow, and is just to the west of Abingdon in the Faringdon direction. There is a tradition that the abbot of Abingdon sent a band of men to one of these camps, with the result that the Danes were defeated, and lands were given to the abbey in consequence of the victory.

It is eight miles from Oxford to East Hanney. For the first five miles the terrain is hilly with much woodland and fertile cornland, but the last three miles are across flat, low-lying ground which is marshy in places. A mile before I reached East Hanney I crossed a brook running from the north-west towards the south. This is either the River Ock, which rises in the Vale of White Horse and flows to Abingdon, or else one of its tributaries. Two miles beyond East Hanney, through low-lying wooded country, I came to Wantage.

Wantage stands on the right bank of a pleasant stream which flows to Abingdon, six or seven miles away. There are two churches in this market town in a single churchyard, although one is only a chapel. Lord Fitz Warin is one of the principal landowners in Wantage, and his name and family are commemorated by two monuments in the parish church.

Cheping Lanburne [*Lambourn*], which is six miles from Wantage, has a poor Friday market. The road passes hilly arable ground and some woodland, and when I was more than halfway along I saw a large rabbit warren. This belongs to Mr Essex, who inherited the lordship of the town, and lands worth more than £200 annually, through his mother, the only daughter and heiress of Mr Rogers. Lambourn lies on the right bank of the River Lambourn, which rises above the town a little to the north; it flows on ten miles to Donnington, and then a little further on it enters the River Kennet. *cont. p. 399* [**1544**: 5/75-9]

The reason for Wallingford's great desolation was a severe epidemic in the reign of Edward III. In consequence the town made a successful petition to King Richard to have its assessment for tax reduced from £40 to £17, Mr Pollard told me that there is documentary evidence for twelve parish churches in Wallingford in Richard II's time. When John de St Helen built Abingdon's great stone bridge people from Gloucestershire began to travel via Abingdon instead of Wallingford, to Wallingford's great detriment.

My approach into Abingdon took me over a stone bridge across the River Ock. Immediately after this bridge the Ock, which flows down from Wantage in Berkshire, enters the River Isis next to the hospital to the west of St Helen's church. At Abingdon they regard Henry V as the principal founder of this hospital. [1/306]

The town of New Windsor has been built since King Edward III rebuilt the castle there. [2/28]

The first of the Berkshire Achards was favoured with seven manors in the county by the gift of Henry I. The two main ones were called Sparsholt and Aldermaston. At Sparsholt one of the Achards was buried with honours in a chantry chapel adjoining the side of the parish church. Two wives of his lie on either side of him, and there is a popular tradition that one was a duchess, and the other a countess; but there is little evidence that the legend is true. [4/99]

John de St Helen's, so-called because he lived in St Helen's parish in Abingdon, initiated and built the great stone bridge over the Isis at Abingdon. Before his time there was a ferry. The construction of the bridge was a serious setback to the town of Wallingford, because its trade had been with travellers from Gloucestershire, but now they passed through Abingdon instead. This John de St Helen's lived about the beginning of Henry VI's reign, and was also responsible for building the fine hospital next to St Helen's in Abingdon. He gave land worth £50 annually to maintain the hospital and the bridge. The stone-arched bridge at Dorchester is relatively new, replacing a ferry which plied across the Thames when the water was high. [5/1-2]

BUCKINGHAMSHIRE

THREE ITINERARIES *passed through Buckinghamshire, but Leland's treatment of the county is on the whole disappointing. Buckingham itself and the whole of northern Buckinghamshire are ignored, and only Aylesbury and its immediate surroundings are described in detail, as he made his way back to London in 1543 after his West Midlands tour. Leland had already collected notes about Aylesbury during the 1530s (the friary was dissolved in 1538), and these he revised in the light of his visit. The southern tip of the county he visited on his way to the West Country, as well as on his return from the North-East.*

UNDER THE TIMBER BRIDGE at Colnbrook flows the second (and in my estimation the smaller) of the two principal arms of the River Colne. It leaves the main stream two miles above Colnbrook in a marshy area about a mile below Uxbridge. It then continues by itself for about a mile-and-a-half beyond Colnbrook until it joins the Thames just above Ankerwyke, where there was a priory of nuns. Colnbrook is three miles from Uxbridge and two miles from Staines. Although the town of Colnbrook lies on both banks of the River Colne, by far the larger part is on the west side; here there is a brick chapel, recently built. The parish church is a mile away. From Colnbrook it is four or

five miles to the place where I crossed the River Burn. The source of this river is a marshy area on the left hand side as I rode from Stoke Poges, where the Earl of Huntingdon is buried. I imagine that it continues past Burnham and around Eton College on its way to the Thames. *cont. p. 8* [**1542**: 1/108]

BEFORE I APPROACHED Chenies I crossed a small brook, and another in the valley nearby. Both flow into the Moore Water [*River Colne*] near Rickmansworth. The old house of the Cheyne family has been transformed to such an extent by Lord Russell (to whom it belongs by right of his wife) that little or nothing remains unrestored. A great deal of the house is entirely new, and built of brick and timber. Fine apartments have recently been constructed in the garden. Inside the house in various places are sumptuous old paintings in black and white. The manor house lies at the west end of the parish church and is surrounded, as I recall, by two parks. On the north side of the church, as if in a chapel, are two tombs to members of the Cheyne family, who were lords of the manor and of the small village which bears their name.

After Chenies I passed much good pasture and arable land for five miles until I came to [?*Chalfont*], a pleasant, remote place in a valley. The next five miles took me across largely waste ground, similar to Hounslow Heath (to which, in all probability, it may extend), and then three miles of enclosed land and woods as far as Windsor. After Windsor I travelled through three more miles of woodland and enclosed pasture. Chertsey lay a mile away on my left hand, where the fine timber bridge over the Thames has recently been repaired. Rather more than two miles further on, in fine open and flat meadowland, I could see Ankerwyke Priory across the Thames, a former nunnery, and about half a mile downstream I crossed the Thames by Staines Bridge. Another six miles, largely over open, arable ground, brought me to Hampton Court. Hampton village lies a further half-mile this side of the court and next to the Thames. [**1541**: 1/105-6]

A SHORT DISTANCE NNW from Thame church I crossed the River Thame by Crendon Bridge, which has four stone arches, and journeyed the ten miles to Quarrendon in the Vale of Aylesbury. My way was hilly in places and then through large pasture grounds and fertile bean-fields. Quarrendon once belonged to the Spencers, but Mr Anthony Lee lives there now. There is a stone bridge between his two houses there, under which flows a tributary stream of the River Thame.

Two miles further, across an expanse of open land which is good for beans and pasture, lies Burston in the Vale of Aylesbury, where Mr Lee has a fine house with good orchards and a park. Burston is three miles from the fine market town of Aylesbury, and sits almost in the middle of the Vale of Aylesbury, which is the name given to the open country all around the town. This vale extends in one direction as far as the forest beyond Thame. In other directions it reaches to Buckingham, Stony Stratford and Newport Pagnell, and along the foot of the Chiltern Hills from Aylesbury almost to Dunstable.

On my way to Aylesbury I rode over a small stone bridge called Woman's Bridge, and along a stone causeway from the bridge to the town. The stream which passes under this bridge, and which flows on the right hand side of the causeway, is the River Thame, so far as I can ascertain. By comparison with the surrounding land, the town of Aylesbury stands on a hill, three miles due north of the Chiltern Hills. It is quite well built of timber, and has a noted market. It stands on the main roads from Banbury to London, and from Buckingham to London. The town hall, which stands in the middle of the market place, has lately been rebuilt by John Baldwin, chief justice of the common pleas, using timber supplied by the king. The communal gaol or prison for Buckinghamshire is at Aylesbury.

Although Aylesbury boasts only one parish church – which lies in the WNW part of the town – it is clear from the life of St Osyth that it is one of the oldest foundations in the region. Its parish included Quarrendon, a mile-and-a-half north of Aylesbury, as well as Bierton, Ellesborough on the Chilterns three miles south, and several other hamlets. It is said that a bishop of Lincoln was asked by the pope to grant the benefice of Aylesbury to a relation of his, a foreigner, but the bishop found a way of turning it into a prebend of Lincoln Cathedral. At the same time the benefice of Thame also was impropriated and made a prebend of Lincoln. So the care of both churches devolved upon vicars, who receive extremely meagre stipends.

St Osyth, Frithwald's daughter, was born at Quarrendon in Aylesbury parish, and brought up by an aunt at Ellesborough in the Chiltern Hills, three miles south of Aylesbury. The Earls of Salisbury were formerly lords of Ellesborough, but now it is in the king's hands by attainder. For a time the body of St Osyth was translated to Aylesbury from Chich (St Osyth Priory) for fear of the Danes.

There is a tradition that the present parsonage house is on the site of a nunnery, or other religious house, and documentary evidence suggests that it was in fact a house of Maturin (or Trinitarian) friars, similar to those at Tickhill, and at Hounslow, ten miles from London. On the south side of the town was a house of grey friars, founded about the time of Richard II. Lord Ormonde was, within living memory, reckoned to be the chief landowner in Aylesbury, but since his property was divided this distinction has passed to Boleyn.

Almost at the southern limit of Aylesbury town a pleasant stream runs under a wooden bridge. It flows from east to west, and joins the Thame about a mile below Aylesbury, rather lower than Stone Bridge over the Thame. I assume that its source is near the roadside place called Wendover, three miles due south. The River Thame itself, as I discovered there, drains the eastern part of all the Chiltern Hills towards Dunstable, and its source is approximately seven miles above Stone Bridge, which crosses it between Quarrendon and Aylesbury.

Distances from Aylesbury: Dunstable, about 8 miles; Thame, 8 miles; Buckingham, 10 miles; Banbury, 19 or 20 miles.

Three miles from Aylesbury is Wendover, a pleasant place on the main road, with two streets of good timber buildings. A causeway runs almost the whole way between the two towns, as otherwise the low-lying heavy clay would make the going very tedious and difficult in wet weather. The little town of Wendover is situated partly on a spur of the Chiltern escarpment. The remainder, the north-east part of the town, lies at the foot of the hills. Just as most of the Vale of Aylesbury has an open, entirely treeless appearance, so it is noticeable that the Chilterns by contrast are well-wooded and full of enclosed fields.

From Wendover it is three miles to Great Missenden in the Chilterns. This is a nice roadside place, but not a market town. There is a pleasant brick chapel on the south side, and a little beyond, outside the town, was Missenden Priory, for black canons. It is situated right at the foot of a hill, surrounded by ample grounds, and with several pleasant wooded hills to the south and east. Its founder's name was Doyley. A further mile-and-a-half towards London is Little Missenden, built along a single street; and two-and-a-half miles beyond is Amersham, also in Buckinghamshire and on the Chilterns.

Amersham (also known as Hagmondesham) is a very pleasant town, with a Friday market, and a single street of good timber buildings. Its principal owner was the duke of Buckingham, but then it passed to the king, who granted it to Lord Russell, the occupant of Chenies, three miles to the east. The parish church stands near the centre of the town, on the north-east side, and has a north chapel in which are buried members of the Brudenell family: Edmund, father of Sir Robert Brudenell, the former chief justice of the common pleas; Drew, Sir Robert's elder brother; and Helen his wife, the daughter of a man named Broughton, who lived on one of his manors, with an annual value of £40. A stream rises almost by Missenden, and flows close beside Amersham (which lies south of it on its right bank), before continuing down the valleys of the Chiltern Hills towards the River Colne. *cont. p. 240* [**1543**: 2/110-13]

Next to the church at Newport Pagnell certain ditches are visible, as if it was the site of a castle. [4/118]

Aylesbury, which is five miles from Notley, is a good market town with one parish church and a house of grey friars. It stands on a little brook, and is a mile from the River Thame. From Henley in Oxfordshire to High Wycombe in Buckinghamshire is eight miles, and from High Wycombe to Dunstable in Bedfordshire is eighteen miles. This route runs right along the Chiltern Hills, the chalky clay soil of which provides a good store of woodland, and some arable.

Rivers in Buckinghamshire: The Use or Ise. Another Use or Ise [*River Wye*], whose main headwater rises in the Chiltern Hills near West Wycombe and flows past the market town of High Wycombe. At the west end of High Wycombe it is joined by the Hughenden Brook, which also rises in the Chiltern Hills a mile above the town. The united streams flow in a valley to Hedon, then to Woburn, where the bishop of Lincoln has a fine house, and so another mile or more to fall into the Thames. [5/7]

The Vale of Aylesbury covers a large area, extending in one direction from the edge of the forest alongside the Thame, and running along the foot of the Chiltern Hills almost as far as Dunstable. Its boundaries in other directions are Newport Pagnell, Stony Stratford and Buckingham. The centre of the vale is reckoned to be Burston Park and manor, which occupy fairly high ground. Quarrendon, a dependent hamlet of Aylesbury, which once belonged to the Spensers, stands a good mile from the town, and between them lies St Osyth's Well. There is a house of grey friars at Aylesbury. Ellesborough, sometimes pronounced Hilborough, is three miles south of Aylesbury. It stands on one of the Chiltern Hills, and formerly belonged to the Montacute estate. Bierton is a mile from Aylesbury. Sir Anthony [?*Ormonde*] has recovered his property here, after his father was attainted for fighting on King Richard's side at Bosworth Field. [5/233]

CAMBRIDGESHIRE

T*HE JOURNEY to the North-East in 1541 began at Cambridge, but all that Leland gave us is a brief description of Eltisley. More detail is supplied by a note. A fragment of an otherwise lost itinerary has survived in the British Library, and this takes us rapidly from Cambridge to Royston. Leland also noted some family history associated with Grantchester, and elsewhere copied out a list of Cambridge Colleges (here omitted) which had been compiled by the Warwick antiquary, John Rous.*

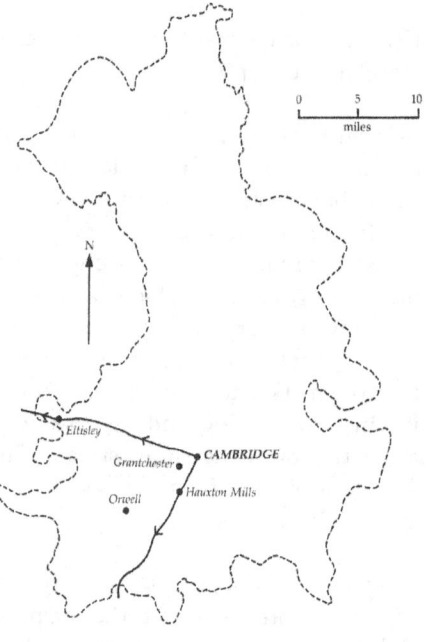

I T IS EIGHT MILES across open country from Cambridge to Eltisley village. At one time there was a nunnery at Eltisley, where the Scottish virgin Pandonia was buried. A well by the south side of the quire bears her name. I was told that when Eltisley nunnery was destroyed a new one was built at Hichingbrook near Huntingdon. The boundary of Cambridgeshire is one mile from Eltisley in the St Neots direction. *cont. p. 182* [**1541:** 1/1]

O RWELL IN CAMBRIDGESHIRE is part of the Richmond estate, and in one of its townships there are some traces of an ancient house. This estate is very important in many parts of Cambridgeshire; it has many vassals and tenants.

From Cambridge it is three miles to Hauxton Mills and a further seven to Royston. Four miles before Royston the road passes over a small

CAMBRIDGESHIRE 25

stream and beside a mill. It is open country with neither enclosure nor wood the whole ten miles. [**?1540:** *1/327-8*]

Besides his many other manors Henry Lacy, earl of Lincoln, owned Grantchester near Grantebridg [*Cambridge*], and here he established one of his relatives, along with an endowment of estates there and elsewhere. I assume that this relative was a bastard child of his. Henry decreed that every son and heir of this Grantchester branch of the Lacy family should be given the name Henry, a requirement which has been religiously adhered to up to the present day. I was told all this about the establishment of the Lacy family of Grantchester in Cambridgeshire by the present heir to the estate. The sixth Henry to inherit from Henry Lacy, earl of Lincoln, gave the manor of Grantchester as part of his endowment to the college which he founded in Cambridge. [*2/1*]

According to the Legend of St Pandonia it seems that she was the daughter of a king of Scotland, who fled from those intent on deflowering her, and came to one of her relatives, the prioress of the nunnery at Eltisley in Cambridgeshire, four miles from St Neots. After her death she was buried at Eltisley next to a well which is called St Pandonia's Well. In 1344 her body was translated into Eltisley church, according to an account of the translation made by the parish priest there, a certain Sir Richard. Some people maintain that the old priory was next to the vicarage. Croxton is a half-mile from Eltisley, and is still in Cambridgeshire, but Elnig [*?Yelling*], a further half-mile, is in Huntingdonshire. In recent years Eltisley has been appropriated by Denney Abbey. The owner of Eltisley village is Sir Manok [*George Mannock*] of Suffolk. [*5/218*]

CHESHIRE

LELAND'S ONLY SURVIVING JOURNEY through Cheshire formed part of an itinerary which took him from Wales to Carlisle and the Scottish border in 1538. Although there is an interesting description of the Northwich salt industry, his route, from Whitchurch to Manchester, avoided most of the Cheshire towns, and he has left us no account of them. The lack of any description of Chester is particularly regrettable. By way of compensation, however, his notes on Cheshire are fuller than for most counties; they include a long directory of the leading families, as well as a detailed description of the Wirral coastline, which was probably compiled around the same time.

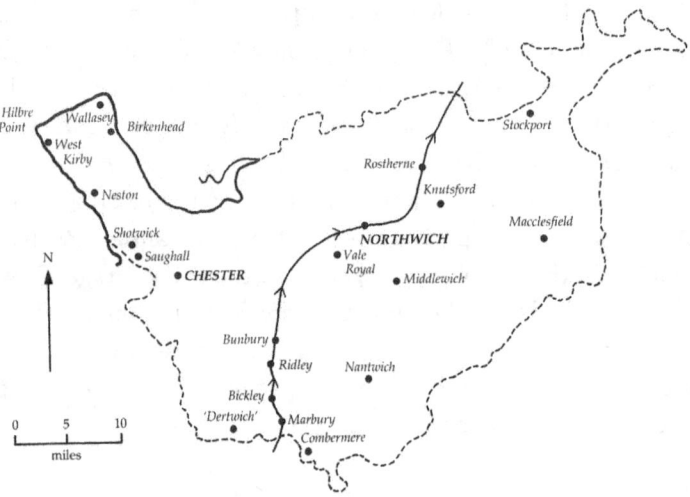

LESS THAN HALF a mile after Black Mere Park I passed the parish of Marbury; the church here stands in a valley between two good meres or lakes. From Black Mere to Bickley is three miles in a sandy hollow, close to Cholmondeley Moss. Here for the first time I saw the huge number of fir tree roots, which are often dug up by the inhabitants for firewood, although I did not see any fir trees growing. Very often when digging in this moss or marsh for peat or turves they find instead whole trees, some short but others very long, neither twisted nor bowed, and anything from less than a foot to three or four feet below the ground. How or when these trees came down, other than by cutting or windblow, no-one there is able to say. When burnt the wood gives off a resinous odour.

As I passed by this moss for nearly two miles I saw on my right hand a large wood belonging to Mr Cholmondeley, and at the far end of the moss was a wooden chapel. In the valley nearby was Mr Cholmondeley's house, a fine timber building with a moat watered by a pool. From here to Ridley Park is about a half-mile. A very fine stone and timber house, built by Sir William of Standeley (who championed the cause of Henry VII at Bosworth Field), stands next to the park. Later Henry VII gave the house to one of the Egertons. The mere at Ridley Park contains pike, bream, tench and perch. It is a half-mile wide, one-and-a-half miles long, and is reckoned to be the finest mere in Cheshire.

From there I went on to Spurstow, a stone and timber house belonging to Mr Spurstow, with a large pool which abuts the house on one side. The arable and pasture fields around the house are surprisingly good. Less than a quarter-mile from the house is a large reedy pool, to which countless starlings resort at night. A half-mile further is Bunbury, with a very fine collegiate church, which was once endowed by a knight called Sir Hugh Calveley. Pecforton is less than a mile-and-a-half from Bunbury; it is a fine manor, with a large stone house.

From Bunbury I rode ten miles across sandy ground all the way to Northwich. After three miles, as I entered Delamere Forest, I left Sir John Downe's house a half-mile away to my left. In one direction the forest, which has red and fallow deer, is twelve miles long, or more, but my way crossed it in no more than six or seven miles. Two miles into it I crossed a small brook called Sandiford, and from there to Northwich I noticed several forest pools. As I reached the end of the forest I could see Vale Royal on my right hand. There are several good and large pools near the house, and one within a mile of it is called Petty Pool, although in fact it is very big. In Delamere Forest there is a place called 'The Seven Loos' which the local people are eager to point out. Seven manmade ditches are visible, which I take to have had a military function. I saw little arable in the forest on account of the deer. I noticed as I rode through it that to my right was flat, dark heathland, whereas to my left it was somewhat hilly and wooded.

Apart from the smell Northwich is a pleasant market town. Beside the houses of the saltmakers are large stacks of wood chopped up small, which are used in boiling the brine to make white salt. The brine-pit is close to the bank of the River Dane, less than a bow-shot above its confluence with the Weaver. From the bank which lies between the River Dane and the pit of the saline spring I could see Congleton, a market town ten miles away, and Maxwel [*Macclesfield*] Forest which lies close to it.

There are two salt springs at Middlewich, which, if I remember correctly, stands on the River Dane, but the one which produces the most salt water is at Nantwich, and in consequence 300 saltmakers work there. Within living memory part of a tree-covered hill one mile from Combermere Abbey slipped and a spring of salt water filled the resulting pit. The abbot there began to make salt, but the men of the salt wiches came to an agreement with the abbey which forbad it from making salt. There is still brine in the pit, but a great deal of filth has polluted it.

A system of channels enables the salt water to be drawn from the pits easily to each man's house, and at Nantwich many such channels cross over the River Weaver in order to supply the saltmakers' troughs with the water. They boil it in lead furnaces and scoop the salt into wicker cases, through which the water drains leaving the salt behind. There are also two or three very small saline springs in a low valley at Dertwiche [*Higher Wych and/or Wychough, near Wigland*], where salt is sometimes made. Dertwiche is a mile-and-a-half from Malpas village, the home of Sir Randol of Brereton.

My ride from Northwich to Manchester took me over a small river in the town of Northwich, and then along a five mile causeway, which crosses the Waterless Brook and River Peover (presumably tributaries of the Weaver). By this route I passed on my left hand Tabley, the house and park of Mr Leyrcestre. There is a fir wood near here in a moss. Four miles beyond Tabley I passed on my left hand the house and park called Dunham Massey, the seat of Mr Bouth. Good husbandry has turned the neighbourhood here, which used to be fern-infested common land, into excellent corn ground. And there is a lake, called Rostherne Mere, nearby, which is two or three miles long, and very well stocked with fish. It is by Rostherne church, to the right of the road. Three miles before I reached the great wooden bridge over the Mersey at Crossford I passed over a pleasant river, the Bollin. This, I discovered, rises in Macclesfield Forest, and falls into the Mersey quite a distance below Crossford Bridge. *cont. p. 201* [**1538**: 4/2-5]

Wirral begins less than a quarter-mile from the city of Chester itself, not two bow-shots from the suburb outside the north gate. Here a small stream called Flokars Brook flows into the River Dee, and there is a basin known as Porte Poole sufficient to hold a ship at spring tide. A half-mile downstream is Blacon Head, a kind of peninsula, where there is a former residence of Sir William Norris, an old manor house which belongs to the Earl of Oxford.

Continuing a mile down the Dee there is a small village close to the bank called Saughall, and less than a mile lower is Crabwall. Then a further mile, right on the shore, is the royal castle of Shotwick, with a park adjoining; Shotwick village is three-quarters of a mile beyond. Two miles lower there is an anchorage in the estuary called Salthouse Roads, which corresponds to a salterne cottage on the shore. At Burton Head, almost a mile further, is a village, and two miles lower is Denhall Roads, offshore from a farmhouse called Denhall Hall (which belongs to Mr Smith) and Denhall village, which lies further inland. Rather more than two miles beyond Denhall is Neston Roads, with Neston village a mile inland, and then three miles further is the Red Bank, corresponding to the village of Thurstaston, a half-mile inland. West Kirby village, however, more than a mile beyond, is right on the shore, and is only a half-mile from Hilbre, the extreme point of Wirral.

At high tide Hilbre is like an island, entirely surrounded by the sea, and is separated from the mainland by a stretch of water a quarter-mile wide and four fathoms deep, but at low tide it can be reached across the sand. It is about a mile in circumference, and rabbits live on its sandy soil. The monks of Chester had a cell here, and Our Lady of Hilbre was a place of pilgrimage. Chester Bar, as the spit of sand brought down by the River Dee is called, lies eight or ten miles WSW from Hilbre.

Hilbre Point is approximately sixteen miles in a straight line from the Lancashire coast at its nearest point. Liverpool lies ten miles inland from the mouth of the River Mersey, and not far short of twenty miles from the true Mersey Bar, out in the open sea. It is ten miles from Hilbre Point overland to Liverpool. Continuing round the coast from Hilbre to the Mersey side of Wirral it is seven or eight miles to the village of Wallasey, right on the shore, where there is a great trade in salting the herring caught in the sea at the mouth of the Mersey. Then two miles further along the Wirral shore is the ferry house, from which is the shortest crossing (three miles) to Liverpool. A few hundred yards along the shore is the former Birkenhead Priory, a cell of Chester with sixteen monks, but there is no village beside it. There are high embankments along both the Dee coast of Wirral and on the Mersey coast as far as Birkenhead, but it is not very hilly country. The passage over the Dee in a diagonal line from Hilbre to a point between Flint and Basingwerk is seven miles at high tide. [3/91-2]

The principal, and probably the original, cause of the numerous pools and lakes in Cheshire has been the digging of marl pits to enrich the poor soil there so as to produce good crops. Water from the rivers and springs in the area has flowed into them, and in addition, because the ground there is so deeply fissured, many springs rise naturally in them.

There is evidence in Cheshire of several salt pits in addition to those generally now in use. For example there was one in a wood near Combermere; another at Dertwiche where a new pit has recently been made beside the derelict one; while at Aldersey, a poor village of six houses, which is four miles from Malpas somewhat to the west of the Chester road, there has been a salt pit, now derelict, for almost as long as anyone can remember.

Fallen fir trees submerged in bogs and marshes, such as occur in Cheshire, Lancashire and Shropshire, are also found in some parts of the Isle of Axholme. [5/6]

Market Towns in Cheshire: Chester on the Dee. Nantwich on the Weaver, 14 miles west [*east*] of Chester. Combermere Abbey is the impropriator of the parish church which, according to some people, is a daughter church of Acton. Nantwich has no market. Northwich on the Weaver, 12 miles from Chester. The parish church, a living of Norton Priory, is at Budworth, one mile away, and Northwich has only a chapel. Maxwelle [*Macclesfield*], which lies 24 miles north-west [*east*] of Chester towards Derbyshire, stands below Macclesfield Forest, right on the edge but just outside. Congleton on the Dane is 20 miles from Chester, due directly east, and 6 miles from Northwich. Knutsford, a market town is 18 miles north-east [*of Chester*]. It has only a chapel, the parish church being a mile away at Aspebyri [*Leland is the only source for this lost place-name, which refers to the site of St John's church*]. Stoppord [*Stockport*], on the Mersey, 6 miles from Manchester. The parish church is in the town. Mr Warren is called Baron of Stockport locally. This is because in about the time of Henry IV one of the Cheshire Warrens married the daughter and heir of a certain Stockport, Baron of Stockport. The earlier seat of the Warrens was at Poynton, and this is where Mr Warren now lives, as Stockport manor house is derelict. Poynton, which has a park, is halfway between Stockport and Macclesfield, four miles from each. It is one of several houses of old gentry families which lie in the parish of Prestbury.

Castles in Cheshire: Chester. Beeston Castle was built or rebuilt by Ranulf, Earl of Chester. Halton Castle was built by Randol, Earl of Chester. It stands alongside the Mersey, less than a mile from the bank, and less than a mile from what is now a small, poor town by a salt creek, called Runcorn. Shotwick is in the Wirral. There used to be a house, which is now demolished, called Newhall Tower, between Combermere and Nantwich. It belonged to the Lord Audeleys. Moats and a fine stretch of water survive there.

Rivers in Cheshire: Dee (I have its course). Weaver (I have its course). Above Frodsham, the Weaver flows on its own to the sea. The River Dane, or Daven, rises

CHESHIRE

in Macclesfield Hundred, in the forest region. Its source is right on the border of Macclesfield Forest with Derbyshire, where, it is said, the three counties of Cheshire, Staffordshire and Derbyshire meet. There is a place three miles below the source where, after heavy rainfall, the river rushes violently over rocks, but by the time it has flowed through Congleton its course is across somewhat marshy ground.

Abbeys and Priories in Cheshire: At Norton, which is two miles from the Mersey, and right next to Liverpool [*perhaps Lancashire is intended*] there was a priory of canons, which has now been suppressed.

Forests, Chases and Parks in Cheshire: I cannot recall any to compare with Delamere, a fine, large forest, with an abundance of red and fallow deer. Macclesfield Forest, apart from a tiny portion, lies entirely in Cheshire.

Notable Houses of Gentry in Cheshire: South of Delamere Forest: Sir John Downe (or Dane) lives at Utkinton. This is less than three miles from Gunbyri [*i.e. Bunbury*], one mile from Tarporley (a long, paved, roadside village), and four miles from Vale Royal. The principal seat of the Egertons is at Egerton in Malpas parish. He also owns the manor of Oulton, where the oldest branch of the family now lives, and he is carrying out building work there at present. The Starkeys' second house is at Darley; this is about five miles from Northwich, three miles from Vale Royal, and barely a mile from Oulton.

Bunbury is a gentleman next to, but not within, the Wirral. Iriene Breton married William Hanford, who inherited Handforth. But she already had a son by Sir John Standely, the illegitimate son of Standely, bishop of Ely. Sir Richard Brereton, younger son of Sir Randol of Brereton, married Wylken Standeley's only daughter, who inherited from Sir Geoffrey Massey the manor and park of Tatton. Mere of the Mere, two miles from Knutsford, has land worth £70 annually.

Lee of High Leigh, one mile from Knutsford, is the oldest branch of the family in this district. Lee of Booth, a half-mile from Knutsford, has a park. Lee of Adlington, one mile from Prestbury, has land worth £200 annually.

Leicester is from Tabley between Northwich and Knutsford, three miles from each. His younger brother has his manor house at Tofte Hall, and owns land with an annual value of £70. Daniel is also of Tabley, a mile from Leicester's house.

Booth of Dunham lives at Dunham, three miles from Knutsford. The estate has a fine park, and is a mile from the poor mayoral town of Altrincham. The oldest branch of the family is Booth of Barton in Lancashire. Booth, the bishop of Hereford, was the younger brother of Booth of Barton.

Davenport of Bramhall lives at Bramhall, two miles west [*south*] of Stockport. He has land worth [£130] annually. There is another Davenport at Woodford, two miles from Bramhall. But the best and first house of the Davenports is at Davenport. This is a large, old house roofed with lead, on the banks of the River Dane, three miles above [*below*] Congleton. Davenport of Henbury springs from this branch, and his house, Henbury Hall, is two miles due north [*west*] of Macclesfield. It has a large lake. This Davenport owns a portion of Becheton's lands, and Fitton of Gawsworth has another portion. He is now living at Gawsworth, but not on the part which was Becheton's.

The principal seat of Sir Piers Dutton is at Dutton, eight miles from Chester, but he also owns Hatton, a fine house four short miles from Chester.

The daughter and heir of Bostock of Bostock (a very ancient family in Cheshire, and in Davenham parish) married Sir John Salvage during the time of Henry VII. Bulkley and Lestwick were other families from the parish of Davenham. The last Bulkley of Eaton was a nephew, whose wife, the daughter of Venables, is still alive. Bulkley of Whatcroft, two miles from Northwich, now lives in Wales. William Bulkley, chief justice of Chester, established Eaton Hall, but owned some land before he became justice. Whether the Eaton or Whatcroft branch is the older is a matter of dispute. A lawyer made the family name prominent, but Bulkley of Wales owns far more land than his namesake. Bulkley of Eaton's estate passed to a daughter, who married Lestwich; but Sir William Breton bought Eaton.

Egerton, a younger brother of Egerton of Egerton, lives at Ridley, not a halfmile from Bulkeley Hill, where the River Weaver rises. Nearby is a lake more than a mile long, and from this a stream flows a little distance into the Weaver, greatly augmenting it. Sir William Stanley, supporter of Henry VII, transformed Ridley Hall from an old and poor house into the finest gentleman's mansion in the whole of Cheshire; but he was attainted, and Ridley was given to Ralph Egerton. It has a very large [*park*]. Ridley belonged to Daniel, Sir [*?William*] Stanley's servant, but few people know what happened to him.

Spurstow has a house one mile away, and a lake beside it called Newpool. Bunbury College, which is a half-mile away, was founded by Sir Hugh Calveley about the time of Henry V. Sir Hugh Calveley and Sir Robert Knolles were companions and great military men.

Beeston lives at Beeston, a half-mile from Beeston Castle. One of the Davenports, who has fewer lands than the others, lives three and a half miles east of Beeston at a place called Calveley. His house is surrounded by some very tall trees, which may be seen from a great distance. A mile from Calveley is Wardle, the home of Prestland, in Bunbury parish. A further one and a half miles away is Barbridge and the Bar stream, which later flows into the Weaver.

Sir Randol Manoring lives at Baddiley, three miles south-west of Nantwich; he has a park, and a mere called Baddiley Mere. The oldest branch of the Starkey family lives at Wrenbury, one and a half miles from Cumbermere. The park there is stocked with surprisingly fine wood, but there are no deer. There is an abundance of woodland around these two houses.

One Needham, a knight, lives at Shenton, four miles east of Combermere, and in Shropshire; he has built a fine, moated house there. The Needham name was brought to prominence by Sir John Needham, chief justice of Chester. The manor and house of Cranage (in Cheshire, three miles from Middlewich) belong to Needham of Shenton. Three other manors – Baddington, Broomhall and

Austerson – have been inherited by the present Sir Robert Needham from his mother, one of the three heiresses of Sir John Bromley. The second daughter married Gerald of Brin (Lancashire), and he inherited Bromley, the principal seat, and Winnington, which are both in Staffordshire, as well as various other manors. Harper of Rushall married the third, and she brought him the manor of Cholmondeston, two miles from Nantwich. The principal seat of the Bromley family, at [*Gerrard's*] Bromley in Staffordshire, lies in the very large parish of Eccleshall, where the bishop of Chester has his castle.

Sir John Oldford of Oldford, one mile from Northwich. One Fowleciste [*Fouleshurst*], a knight, has a fine house and lands four miles south-east of Nantwich. John Ashley of Ashley, two miles from Knutsford. Sir Henry Delves lives three miles east of Nantwich, and has a fine house. Richard Leftwich of Leftwich. Calveley lives at a manor house called Leigh, five miles south-west of Beeston.

The second house of the Breretons, where Sir Randol used to live, is at Malpas, a small town of three paved streets with a Sunday market. Sir Randol built a grammar school and a hospital there; his fine house is at the far end of South Street. Cholmondeley lives at Cholmondeley Hall. This is a good house, with a little mere beside it, a fine wood, and a moss of firwood. It is halfway along the road from Malpas to Bunbury, three miles from each. The oldest house of the Breretons is Brereton Hall, near Middlewich, which now belongs to Sir William Brereton.

Minshull lives at Minshull, five miles west of Middlewich. Venables, Baron of Kinderton, an ancient gentry family, lives at Kinderton near Middlewich.

In the Wirral: Stanley, a knight; Pole, a knight; Massey at Puddington. [5/23-30]

CORNWALL

CORNWALL AND SOMERSET, the two counties with the strongest Arthurian connections, receive greater attention from Leland than anywhere else. He visited both at least twice, and his descriptions, as well as providing a wealth of vivid depictions of Tudor life, are also helpful in piecing together his working methods. The earliest portion of his Cornish text is here printed as the first and longest of the notes. It includes lists and general information, such as have survived for many counties, but it seems also to have served as a prototype for the whole series of itineraries. There are detailed descriptions of many towns and villages, strung together as a journey; and a journey which, unlike his later visit, extended to the very tip of west Cornwall. It is clear from several references that this account dates from before the main phase of the dissolution of the monasteries; the neighbouring houses of Tywardreath and St Carrok (St Cyricus and Juliette) were both suppressed in 1536, and Leland's descriptions of them in the present tense show that he must have been writing earlier than this, probably when visiting monastic libraries during 1533.

Leland returned to Cornwall on his itinerary of the West Country in 1542, and his account of the journey is printed after this introduction. He revisited many places, and reworked his earlier material, a task which included turning all the monasteries into the past tense. However, it is doubtful whether on this occasion he ventured further west than the houses of two Cornish gentlemen, Mr Arundel of Gwarnick (near Truro), and Mr Godolphin of Breage near Helston. Evidently he received hospitality from them, and they furnished him with the extensive family and topographical notes which now interrupt the account of his journey half way through.

A third host and informant must have been Thomas Treffry of Fowey, and it is likely that this encounter resulted in Leland being commissioned to compose Latin inscriptions in praise of Henry VIII for the new St Mawes Castle. The result is given in a note, and the originals may still be seen inscribed on the castle walls. During his visit Leland must have been shown a chart, similar to that now in the British Library which depicts the fortifications along the English channel coast; he mentions it in connection with a creek near St Mawes.

In addition to Leland's main narrative of his journey, briefer and perhaps earlier drafts of two portions have survived, and are printed here as notes. They cover the legs from Launceston to Wadebridge, and from Wadebridge to Gwarnick.

A MILE BEFORE I reached Launceston I crossed a stone bridge of three arches and one small arch, called New Bridge. The River Tamar, which divides Devonshire and Cornwall for almost its entire length from source to mouth, flows under this bridge. New Bridge was built and maintained by the abbots of Tavistock – for the abbey had substantial possessions in this area.

The River Tamar rises three miles north-east [*south*] of Hartland and then flows to [*North*] Tamerton, a village on the east bank in Devonshire, where there is a stone bridge over the river (this bridge is twenty miles from Padstow). Yealmbridge (of stone) is two miles lower, and then New Bridge, Polson Bridge and Greystone Bridge are at two-mile intervals further downstream. Greystone Bridge is about four miles from Tavistock and three from Launceston, on the road between them. Then Horse Bridge, another New Bridge, and Calstock Bridge, which is next to the seat begun by Sir Piers Edgecumbe. Lydford Bridge is not on the Tamar.

Shortly after entering the suburb of Launceston I crossed a brook called the Ottery [*confused here with the Kensey*] flowing in the valley below the steep hill on which the town stands. I discovered that the Ottery rises ten miles WNW towards Bodmin, and after passing by Launceston it flows east into the Tamar, so I gathered, just above Polson Bridge. Having crossed this brook I climbed the hill through the extensive suburb until I came to the town wall and gate, and then into the town, still climbing the hill, until I reached the very top. Here are the market place and St Stephen's parish church, which has lately been rebuilt.

Launceston Castle is large and ancient, and occupies the summit of the hill just south of the parish church. Much of the castle remains standing. The motte is large and of fearsome height, and its keep, surrounded by three separate wards, is the strongest, if not the biggest, of any ancient monument that I have seen in England. The upper part of Launceston receives its water supply from a small rivulet.

Launceston Priory stands at the foot of the hill, in the WSW quarter of the town's suburb. There is a fine wooded slope beside it, through which a rivulet issues from a nearby hill, and this provides water and sanitation for the whole priory. In its church I noticed two remarkable tombs, to Prior Horton and Prior Stephen, and I was told that a certain Countess Mabilia was also buried there, in the chapter house. The priory was built by William Warelwast, bishop of Exeter, who was later buried at another of his foundations, Plympton Priory. Warelwast had previously suppressed a collegiate church of St Stephen, along with its staff of prebendaries, and had given the best part of its lands to Launceston Priory, but had kept the remainder for himself. There is still a church of St Stephen about a half-mile from Launceston; it stands on the hill formerly occupied by the collegiate church. A chapel dedicated to St Catherine lies a short distance from Launceston, due WNW, but it has been desecrated. Gawen Carow has charge of the priory.

My journey from Launceston to Botreaux Castle, commonly called Boscastle, took me for the first two miles past enclosed ground with some woodland and good corn. Then came eight miles of hill and wasteland, with scarcely any wood, so that in consequence gorse and heather are the fuel throughout these parts. The last two miles to Boscastle were also by enclosed arable ground, moderately fertile but virtually treeless. The exposed north-facing coast is inhospitable for trees.

Boscastle sits on the brow of a rocky hill, at the south-east end, and extends northwards down towards the sea, though not all the way. It is a very filthy, uncared-for town. Its church, as I recall, is dedicated to St Symphorian. Boscastle belonged to Lord Botreaux, a member of an old Cornish family. His manor house here was not very highly thought of, so far as I could gather, and in its present state can certainly not be described as a castle. Local people call it the Court. A small brook flows from high ground south-east of the town, and runs west past it to the Severn Sea [*Bristol Channel*] between two hills. But it is a poor harbour, affording uncertain protection.

One of the Hungerfords married an heiress of Botreaux, and so Boscastle passed to Hungerford. Then through a Hungerford heiress it came to Lord Hastings. One of the Botreaux manors was held jointly by Hastings, Earl of Huntingdon, and the late Lord Hungerford. This is six miles south of Boscastle at Park, where there is a manor house or small castle.

Moving north-east along the Severn Sea coastline from Boscastle to Hartland Point there is no noteworthy place or building except Stratton, twelve miles from Boscastle and about a mile inland, where there is a pleasant market. Ebbingford, commonly called Efford, is near here; John Arundale of Trerice was born here, and the fine manor house belongs to him, although its present occupant is Sir John Chaumon, who married John Arundale's mother. She is still alive. Old Treviliane, who is descended from a younger brother of the principal branch of that family, has a pleasant estate and lives in the Stratton area. Hartland Point is ten miles further up the Severn Sea from Stratton.

From Boscastle it is about a mile to Trethevey village on the shore, to which flows down a brook which rises in the great rocky hills nearby. A further mile along the shore brings us to Bossiney. This has been an important fishing settlement, with great privileges granted to it. A large number of ruined houses are still visible there. As at Trethevey, so here there is a brook flowing through the place, and the two make their course to the sea together between two hills. The hill to the east stands out like an arm, or cape, which gives it the appearance of a small harbour or jetty, so that sometimes boats take shelter by it. Not long ago a friar attempted to build a harbour here, but he was unable to make much of an impression. Due WNW by the point or side of this creek there lie two little islands of black rock, separated from each other by a narrow channel of water. It is very likely that gulls breed on these islets.

A mile along the shore from Bossiney is Tintagel. The castle has been an incredibly strong and remarkable fortress, made almost invincible by virtue of its position – the dungeon especially so, which sits on a huge and fearfully high crag surrounded by the sea, but it connected to the rest of the castle by a drawbridge. A chapel of St Ulette or Uliane still stands within the dungeon, but the dungeon itself is now grazed by sheep. The remainder of the once extensive castle buildings are now badly weather-beaten and in ruins. The castle lies within the parish of Trevena, whose church is dedicated to St Symphorian – but Simiferian is the local pronunciation.

I had travelled a mile from St Symphorian's church over heather-covered hills when I crossed a brook flowing north from the south-east into the Severn Sea. About a half-mile down the coast from the mouth of this brook a great black rock lies just offshore like a small island. And three miles from the mouth, westward along the coast, is the fishing village of Port Isaac. A brook flows to Port Isaac, and there is a pier and some shelter for fishing boats. Similarly at another fishing village, called Portquin, two miles downshore, is a pier and the mouth of a brook. Three miles further is the mouth of Padstow harbour.

St Teath, which is four miles from Tintagel, has quite good land immediately around it. Two miles further is Trelill, and then [*St Kew*], where Mr Carniovies or Carnsey has a pleasant house and fine estate, surrounded by good woodlands. A further three miles, past good arable ground but no woods, brings us to Wadebridge.

Eighty years ago there was only a ferry where Wadebridge is now, and it was often very dangerous to cross the river on horseback. But then the vicar of Wadebridge, one Lovebone, began the bridge out of his concern, and accomplished it after a great deal of trouble and thought, and with assistance from well-wishers. The completed bridge has seventeen fine, large arches, which are stone-built and identical. I was told that originally the foundations of some of the arches were laid on such shifting, sandy ground that Lovebone almost despaired of completing his bridge, but that he solved the problem by laying down packs of wool as foundations.

The River Alaune [*Camel*] flows through Wadebridge, and is clearly seen further down. The first important bridge on the Camel is called

Hellandbridge, which is downstream from Camelford (although the river is almost a mile from Camelford town), There is a three-arched bridge two miles lower at Dunmere, and here the Camel flows within a mile of Bodmin. Wadebridge is three miles lower over land, or four miles by water. This is the lowest bridge on the Camel. A brook flows from St Teath, five miles from Wadebridge, and joins the Camel on the east side of the harbour a little above Wadebridge. Its source is two miles ENE of St Teath. Another brook flows from Mr Carnsey's house and enters the Camel estuary by a tidal creek on its east side three miles below Wadebridge. Between Dunmere and Bodmin the road is carried by a bridge of one stone arch over a pleasant little stream. This is close to Dunmere, and shortly afterwards the stream, which runs past the east end of Bodmin town and powers the mills there, flows to the west bank of the Camel beneath Dunmere Bridge. Another stream flows into the Camel from the west side about two miles below Dunmere Bridge. It rises to the south-east, and I crossed it by a bridge on the road to Mitchell at St Lawrence, barely a mile after I had left Bodmin.

Four miles from Wadebridge is Padstow, a good fishing town, which is busy but dirty. It is an ancient town, called Lodenek in Cornish, but its real English name, according to old documents, is Adelstow, the place of Athelstan. Indeed it regards King Athelstan as the main bestower of its privileges. The parish church is dedicated to St [*Petrock*]. Many small ships from Brittany come to Padstow to trade in goods from their own country and to buy fish. The town is full of Irishmen. It lies on the west side of the estuary, [*?two*] miles from its real mouth.

After riding a mile from Wadebridge I crossed a brook, which rises two miles ENE beyond St Teath, flows past St Teath, then five miles to this bridge, and so to the River Camel above Wadebridge. Another brook flows from Carnsey's house into the Camel on the east bank a mile above Padstow. This brook is called the Laine [*?Allen*]. Two miles from the bridge is another, of three arches, called Dunmere Bridge over the Camel. And just beyond it is a single-arched bridge, carrying the road over a brook which rises at Bodmin and flows into the Camel just below Dunmere Bridge. Another brook flows from the south-west into the Camel on the same side two miles lower, but above Wadebridge. A mile from Dunmere Bridge is Bodmin, which is aligned roughly east-west.

At the west end of the town is a chapel, and at the east end is the parish church, with a chantry chapel in the churchyard. The priory stood in the ESE part of the parish churchyard. In front of the high altar in a high tomb of very dark grey marble lies buried Thomas Vivian, prior of Bodmin and suffragan bishop of Megara, who died not long ago. The house of grey friars lay on the south side of Bodmin market place. It was founded by a merchant, John of London, and later Edmund, earl of Cornwall, was a great benefactor. Two other benefactors, Sir Hugh Peverelle and Sir Thomas Peverelle, are buried there.

From Bodmin to St Columb Major is eight miles. From Bodmin to St Laurence is about a mile. There is a poor hospital or lazar house here, which was given a small annuity by one of the Peverelles. There is also a bridge over a pleasant brook which flows from the hills to the south-east into the Camel two miles above Padstow on the west bank. Its creek is tidal. After St Laurence I travelled across treeless moorland for six miles, and then passed St Columb Major about two miles to my right. Castle an Dinas is at least a mile away to the right near here. All I could see was a hill of that name, with no building on it. Two or three miles further across this treeless moor brought me to Mitchell, a small roadside place, and then it was another five miles to a small village and parish church called St Allen, surrounded by very good cornland. Gwarnick, Mr Arundel's house, is a mile from here.

This family is not related, heraldically speaking, to the great Arundel family of Lanherne near St Columb Major. Mr Arundel told me that he thought his descent was from the lords of Culy Castle in Lower Normandy, which has now passed by marriage to a certain Frenchman, M de la Fontaine. To distinguish them from the Lanherne family he is called Arundel of Trerice, which is one of his manors three or four miles from St Allen. His first wife was one of the two heiress daughters of Boville (or a Beville). Granville married the other, and the estate which they shared between them was worth about £250 per annum. John Arundel of Trerice lives in the house that belonged to Boville, and it is from him that he derives the red ox on his coat of arms. One of the Boville family is still alive, and owns land worth £100 which was purchased by his grandfather. Two men called Humphrey Arundel, both with large estates, are brother and nephew of old Arundel of Lanherne, but his heir was his son, Sir John Arundel. The Arundel family living beside Falmouth harbour is related to the Lanherne family. Caerhays, where Trevanion now lives, used to belong to the Arundels.

Arms in Cairdine [*Godolgan*] Castle: 1. Sir William Godolphin and his wife, the daughter of Strode of Parnham in Dorset. 2. Sir William Godolphin and Margaret Glynne, his first wife. She was one of the three heiresses of Glyn of Morval, which is beside Looe Water near St Germans. Vivian of Trelowarren married another, and Richard Kendale of Worngy the third. Vivian's grandfather had a modest estate, and his father was a gallant courtier, Somerset Lord Herbert's protegé. The present Vivian heir, in spite of owning more land than his father, has an annual income of little more than £70. His uncle, a lawyer, has a modest estate. The heir of the senior house of the Vivian family is now the Lord of Treryn Castle at the south-west point of Cornwall, where a brass pot full of Roman money was found within living memory while digging out a fox. 3. William Godolphin the younger, and his wife Blanch Langdon. The Langdon family live at Keveral near St Germans, and are descended from a Breton family, the St Albines, who have another branch at St Albine's in Somerset. 4. Graineville. 5. Milatun, who lives at Pengersick. 6. Devon families: Fortescue of Filleigh; Fortescue of Preston; Fortescue of Spriddlestone; Fortescue of Wymestun [*?Whelmstone, near Copplestone*]; Robert Fortescue of Wood; Fulford, a knight from Fulford. 7. Campernulphus (or Chambernoun), formerly of Tywardreath and founder of a priory of monks, which later acquired the lordship of this manor. Campernulphus is now the lord of Modbury in Devon, and was the lord of Bere near Exeter.

Miscellaneous notes: Carew of Mohuns Ottery, Carew of Haccombe by Torbay, Carew of Antony in Cornwall, near Saltash – all men with fine estates. Three families all from Meneage – Vivian, Roskymer and Erisey (from Erisey in Meneage). Cowlin at Treveglos. Cavel married Sir William Godolphin's sister. Petite was the owner of very fine estates in Cornwall; they included the isle of Pryven [?], which has now passed to Kiligrew. Bewpray is from the Latin for 'beautiful meadow'. Archdeacon. Tresinny of Penryn has land worth £27 annually, mostly in the Padstow area.

Pencaire is a hill in the parish of Penbro, which is commonly called St Banka [*Breage*]. Riviere, Theodoric's castle, which stood on the east side of the mouth of the River Hayle, has now, it is thought, been engulfed in the sand. It was on the north coast. Before the parish church was established at Penbro it lay at Trenewith, a short distance away. Talmeneth is a mansion in Penbro, and Cairdine, an old mansion of the Cowlins, is now the home of William Godolphin. But the main seat of the Godolphins, with a ditch and a tower, used to be at Carne Godolphin on top of a hill. The ditch is still to be seen there, and much masonry has recently been taken from the site. It is three miles ENE of St Michael's Mount. Cair Kenin (or Gonyn or Conin) stood on Pencaire hill, and two ditches are still visible. According to some, Conan had a son called Tristrame.

The church of St Germoe is three miles ESE of St Michael's Mount, and a mile from the sea. St Germoe is buried there and his tomb may still be seen. His chair is in the churchyard, and just outside is his well. Gersick or Pengersick is close to the shore three miles east of St Michael's Mount. It used to belong to one Henry Force, but recently it was given as a dowry by the wife of one of the Worth family to a member of the Devon family of Millaton. Millaton owns Millaton in Devon, as well as part of the Devon lands of Mewis, through a blood-heir. Urth, daughter and heir of the Godolphins, married Henry Force. The daughter of Sir [?William] Godolphin is married to young Millaton.

Marazion, an important and extensive town, was burnt by the French in about 1512. It has a pier opposite St Michael's Mount, and both Marazion and the Mount are in the parish of St Hilary, whose church is a mile away. A monastic cell was formed on the Mount by the Count of Mortain and Cornwall. It was once given to a Cambridge college, and more recently to Syon Abbey. There is a good spring on the Mount.

One mile west of Marazion is Ludgvan, and here is supposed to have been a castle belonging to Lord Brooke. Then going west along the coast Penzance is two miles, Newlyn a further mile and Mousehole a mile beyond. Each place has a pier. Newlyn is a hamlet of Mousehole, and the bay between them is called Gwavas Lake. Mousehole in Cornish is Portenis, the port of the island, and the island, which has a chapel dedicated to St Clement, is just beyond it. Much land, including woodland and buildings, has been swallowed up by the sea between Penzance and Mousehole. A few years ago in tin workings near the Mount in St Hilary's parish were found spearheads, warriors' axes and copper swords, wrapped in linen in a good state of preservation. An old legend of St Michael's speaks of a small town in this area which was demolished and submerged beneath the water.

The college at St Buryan was founded by King Athelstan, who granted it privileges and sanctified it, so it is said, as a votive offering for a safe journey from there to the Scilly Isles and back. The college is on the site of an oratory made by St Buriana, a holy woman from Ireland, who at one time lived there. Treryn Castle lies in ruins at the south-west point of Penwith; its remains are still clearly visible. I heard it said that its lord was one Myendu, which means black mouth or chimney.

Some people believe that Riviere Castle, which belonged to Theodore and lay almost by the mouth of the River Hayle on the east bank near the coast, was submerged beneath the sand. But of the site of Coombe Castle there are still indications, and Basset has an excellent manor in this coombe called Tehidy. A good brook flows down past Coombe. Pencombe is a small headland on the north coast a mile further up from Connor, and Cayl Castle, in Phillack parish, is a mile east of Riviere. Connor, which is two miles from Riviere, was formerly a large place, but now has gone. Two parish churches, quite separate from one another, stood in the town, and substantial remains of them may still be seen, although little or nothing of the town itself survives. Its site, which is where a small brook flows into the sea, is now usually considered to be part of Gwithian parish. The Basset family had a small fortress or tower on Carn Brea hill a mile west of Redruth town. It used to have a park, but that is now broken.

The Isles of Scilly: There are reckoned to be 140 islands on which grass grows, and they provide exceptional pasture for cattle. St Mary's is five miles or more in circumference; there is a poor settlement on this island, and a castle of moderate strength. But the roofs of the castle buildings are badly weathered and defaced. The soil of the island grows extremely good corn – so good in fact that all that is needed is to sow seed where the pigs have rooted and it will come up. Iniscaw, called by some people Tresco, is the largest of the islands, six miles or more in circumference. It belonged to Tavistock Abbey, and there was a poor cell of Tavistock monks on the island. St Martin's Island. St Agnes Island is named after the chapel on it. Within living memory this island was depopulated as a result of an accident. Almost everyone from the five households which inhabited it attended a marriage or feast on St Mary's, and on their way home all were drowned. Rat Island. St Lide's Island – her tomb there used to be a place of great superstition. There is evidence of habitations, now completely demolished, on several islands. Some are well-stocked with rabbits, wild garlic grows on some, whilst on some gulls and puffins can be taken. But despite all this abundance, few people are happy to live on these islands, as French and Spanish robbers come over the sea and take their cattle by force. The owners of the Scillies are Danvers, a Wiltshire gentleman whose principal seat is at Dauntsey, and Whittington, a gentleman of Gloucestershire. But their annual revenue from rents and goods is less than £30. Scilly is a 'kenning' [*the maximum range of vision*] from the westernmost point of Cornwall, that is to say, about twenty miles.

[*Notes on Cornish landholdings:*] The principal seat of the Petite family was at Ardeveraman [*Ardevora*] in Falmouth Harbour by the Ardaverameur peninsula. But their estates have now descended to Arundel of Trerice, Granville (the knight) and Kiligrew. Thomas Levelis around St Buryan. Kiwartun at Newlyn near Mousehole, and John Godolphin at Mousehole. In St Kew parish Cavelle at Trearch [*Treharrock*] and Carnsew at Bokelly. Trecarrel at Trecarrel near Launceston.

Mr Godolphin owns all the land between his house and Penbro, where the parish church is. The living belongs to Hailes Abbey in Gloucestershire. Penbro is about a mile from the south coast. From Mr Godolphin's house to Lelant is four miles, and in all Cornwall there are no greater tin workings than on Sir William Godolphin's land. Hayle Harbour is choked with sand from the tin workings. Four main streams make up the River Hayle; they flow from the south, south-west, south-east and north-east. At low tide it is possible to cross a wide beach, and then the river itself. Mr Mohun has a fine manor near St Erth, and a gentleman called Trewinard lives at a place of the same name in St Erth parish. St Erth is more than a mile above Lelant; it has a three-arch bridge just below the parish church, which stands on the east side of the harbour. The bridge is two hundred years old, and replaced a ferry. There was a time before the harbour was blocked up and choked by the tin workings, when good tall ships used to come to this place. And not far from the bridge there was a castle, so it seems, or manor house now completely demolished, which was called Carnhangibes. Some say that Dinham was lord of this place, and many knights and gentlemen owed suit to his court. Lelant is a pleasant place; its church is dedicated to St Uny.

St J[um]es *Ives*] is two miles or more from Lelant. The main part of the town, on which part of it is built, is a true peninsula, almost a mile around, which juts out into the Severn Sea like a cape. The majority of houses on this peninsula are badly afflicted and smothered by sand which is thrown up during high winds and storms; it has been a problem for more than twenty years. Consequently the best part of the town stands at the south side of the peninsula towards another hill which protects it from the sand. A blockhouse stands on the east side of the peninsula, and a good pier, although it is badly choked with sand. The church is dedicated to St Ia, an Irish nobleman's daughter who was a follower of St Barricus. She and Elwine were two of many who arrived in Cornwall by landing at Pendinas, which is the name of the peninsula and craggy rock on which St Ives is built. At Ia's request one Dinan, a great Cornish nobleman, built a church at Pendinas, or so it is written in the legend of St Ia. But now there is a chapel dedicated to St Nicholas at the very tip of Pendinas, and a lighthouse for ships which sail in this region at night. St Ives receives fresh water from streams which rise in the nearby hills. The town belonged to the late Lord Brook, but now Blunt, Lord Monjoy, and young Poulet own it. Perranzabuloe is 18 miles from St Ives going up the coast, and Crantock two miles further. All this shoreline, from St Ives to Crantock, is badly affected by the sand, and there is hardly anything of note the whole way. A gentleman of St Ives called Glynne owns land with an annual value of £35.

It is about four miles from Mr Godolphin's house to Trewennack, where Sir William's younger son Thomas is building a nice house, and has made an exceptionally good blockhouse and mill in the rocky valley nearby. All the brooks which issue from the hills in the area join in this valley and flow two miles down to the Loe. The Loe is two miles long, and there is only a sand bar between it and the open sea. Once every three or four years the build-up of fresh water and the force of the sea combine to break the bar, and when the fresh and salt water meet there is an amazing noise. But it does not take long for the sand bar to form again. Normally the excess water in the Loe drains through the bar into the sea. If the bar could be kept open all the time it would make a good harbour for Helston. Trout and eels are the fish usually found in the Loe.

Helston (or Hellas) stands on a hill. It is a good market town, with a mayor and privileges, and twice each year blocks of tin are stamped here. There was a castle, and the parish church is situated at the north-west end of the town. At the WSW end a hospital, established by a certain Kylligrin and dedicated to St John, is still standing. The fresh water which enters the Loe flows fairly close to the town on its west side, and the stream from Gweek mill comes within about a half-mile of its east side.

From Helston it is about two-and-a-half miles to Mawgan bridge. A small brook which rises further up to the west flows under this bridge at low tide; the river is tidal for about a mile further upstream. I saw the main arm of the Helford estuary on my left hand near this bridge. It is called Gweek, which is also the name of two small freshwater streams which flow into it. It extends some three miles inland northwards to Gweek mill. A bow-shot beyond Mawgan Bridge I reached a stone causeway, with a one-arch bridge in the centre. It is tidal above this bridge, but at low tide a brook flows under it from the south-west. Both brooks flow together into the Gweek water a little further down. The bridges are rather more than four miles from the mouth of the Helford estuary.

On the east [*north*] bank some two miles below this confluence there is a salt-water creek called Poulpere. Polwheveral is about a half-mile lower, with a brook flowing into it, and this, together with the creek and the sea water of the estuary, hems in part of Mr Reskymer's park at Merthen so that it is strengthened on three sides. Cheilow (or Calamansack) is the name of another creek on the same side, a half-mile lower. On the south bank of the estuary there are four creeks, which are each fed by a stream. The lowest is called Pen Kestel [*?Helford*]; it is four miles below the bridges, and a mile from the estuary's mouth. It is frequently used by ships as an anchorage, and there is a ferry across the estuary at this point. The next is Caullons, a half-mile upstream. Then Mawgan Creek two miles higher, with St Mawgan's church next to it, and the bridge with the broken stone. Gear is a creek branching out of Mawgan Creek, and here is the causeway and one-arch bridge.

Mawnan church stands at the very tip of the Helford estuary on the Falmouth side, and is a landmark from the sea. Opposite, but just outside the estuary, lies Gillan Harbour; the head of its creek divides into two. On the headland between the Helford River and Gillan Harbour stands St Anthony's church or chapel; the living belonged to Tywardreath. St Keverne is two miles from Gillan Harbour and less than a mile inland. It belonged to Beaulieu Abbey in Hampshire, and the church of St Keverne (or Piran) had the privilege of sanctuary. One of the Reskymer family gave land at St Keverne for the support of certain poor people.

Mr Reskymer, whose arms include a wolf, owns a manor bearing his name a mile from Merthen. There was a fine house on this manor which has become ruined during living memory; his present house at Tremayne, a mile or more from Gear Bridge, is small. It was inherited within living memory from the Tremayne family (one of whom still has a good estate in Devonshire) by a certain Trederth, who also owns land and a pleasant manor house elsewhere. John Reskymer's mother was Trederth's daughter. Across the Helford River from Tremayne is Merthen, where Mr Reskymer has a manor house in ruins and a good, well-wooded park, which is hemmed in on three sides by the river and a creek called Poole Penreth. Merthen is in the parish of Constantine.

From Merthen I rode to Budock. After rather more than a half-mile I crossed a freshwater stream that rises in the nearby hills and flows straight into Poole Penreth creek. Then about a half-mile further I crossed the brook that flows down to Polwheveral creek, and not long after that the greater arm of this same brook, with the salt-water creek lying below in the valley nearby. Then four miles over rocky moorland brought me to within a half-mile of St Budock's church. Budock was an Irishman who came to Cornwall and lived at this place. Not far from the church there is a short creek which lies between two hills close to the shore, and looks like a small harbour, but it has a bar across it.

A further quarter-mile and I arrived at Arwennak, Mr Kiligrew's house, which stands right on the edge of Falmouth Harbour, and has always belonged to the senior branch of the family. But there used to be a second Kiligrew family, related to them, who lived in the town of Penryn. Now the two branches are reunited. At the very tip of the harbour mouth there is a hill which belongs to Mr Kiligrew, and on this the king has built a castle called Pendennis. The hill is a mile in circumference and is surrounded by the sea on almost every side. Where it is not the ground is so low-lying that only a short channel would be necessary to make it an island. Almost opposite Mr Kiligrew's house, about a mile-and-a-half away, there is a small cape or headland in the harbour, which is called Penfusis, and a large arm of the harbour runs up between this cape and Arwennak to Penryn town. Penryn is at least three miles from the true harbour entrance and two miles from Penfusis. At Penfusis is a man called Trefusis, of an old gentry family.

By sea it is four miles from Mawnan to Pendennis, where the king has built his castle on one of the points of Falmouth Harbour, which is virtually an island. Between Budock and Pendennis is Levine Prisklo, or Levine Pool [*Swan Pool*], which would make a good harbour were it not for the sand bar. The first creek on the north-west side of Falmouth Harbour leads to Penryn, where it divides into two. The smaller leads to Glassiney

College, a kind of green nest or quagmire at Penryn, and the other to the parish church of Penryn, St Gluvias. One arm breaks out of Penryn Creek on each side before it reaches the town. Just below the place where the creek divides into two there are stakes and stone foundations set in the water, with a chain across a gap in the middle. There is good woodland on the south and west sides of Penryn. In a marshy area called Glassiney a certain bishop of Exeter, Walter Good [*Bronescombe*], founded a collegiate church with a provost, twelve prebendaries and other clergy. This college, which lies in the valley of the bishop's park at Penryn, has fortifications and strong walls, with three strong towers and guns at the end of the creek.

Between Trefusis Point and the point of Restronguet Wood is the mile-long Mylor Creek, where there is a church dedicated to St Mylor. Beyond the church there is a good anchorage for shipping, and there is good woodland in Restronguet. The next creek after the headland in Restronguet Wood is called Restronguet, and this runs two miles inland before branching into two arms. Between these arms stands St Piran's church, and Carr Bridge, of stone, carries the Truro road over one branch of the creek. Between Restronguet Creek and Truro Creek are two other creeks, one called Feock, and the other St Scaf [*?Saveock*] or Kea. Truro Creek is next, and extends two miles from the main river. Within a half-mile of Truro it branches to the west by Newham Wood.

Just before it reaches the town Truro Creek divides into two. Each arm is fed by a brook, and each has a bridge. The town of Truro lies between them. The western arm separates the town from Kenwyn Street, where there was a house of white friars, and Clement Street is separated from the town by the eastern arm. Truro itself has one parish church, but both Kenwyn and Clement Streets have separate churches, after whose saints they are named. Truro has the privileges of a borough, and tin is stamped here at midsummer and Michaelmas. A quarter-mile west of Truro there is the Earl of Cornwall's castle. It has been completely demolished, and its site is now used for archery and recreation. One mile east of Truro another creek branches off the eastern bank, and runs a mile-and-a-half to a stone bridge at Tresilian. The parish church there is dedicated to St Michael. Where this creek joins the Truro Creek there is an anchorage called Malpas Roads, and recently a fight took place here between eighteen Spanish merchant ships and four warships from Dieppe. The Spaniards had pursued the Frenchmen here.

Lamorran Creek, named after its church dedicated to St Moran, is a mile-and-a-half up the River Fal beyond Truro Creek, and it runs inland a quarter-mile. The Fal is tidal a further two miles beyond Lamorran, within a quarter-mile of a place called Tregony (commonly shortened to Tregny). There is a stone bridge of several arches across the river here. The Fal rises a mile or more from Roche Hill, and flows to the borough of Grampound, where there is a stone bridge over it. Grampound is four miles from Roche and two short miles from Tregony. Mr Tregyon is building a sumptuous manor house, which he has not yet finished, at Wulvedon, (or Goldoun) on the Fal between Grampound and Tregony.

Two miles down the Fal from Tregony we come to the entrance to Lanihorne Creek or Pool on the south-east side. This runs a half-mile inland from the main estuary, and at its head stands Lanihorne Castle, once the principal house of the Archdeacon family. It had seven towers, but now it is roofless and falling into decay. The estate passed by inheritance to the main branch of the Shropshire Corbetes, and to Vaulx of Northamptonshire, although the latter's share has since been purchased by Tregyon of Cornwall. A mile below the pool of Lanihorne Creek there is a peninsula of about forty acres called Ardevora Veor. It is formed by two creeks; the smaller on the SSE side is quite insignificant, and only runs inland about a half-mile, but that on the WSW side is larger. From here it is four miles or more to St Just Creek, where the parish church of St Mawes, dedicated to St Just, is situated. A further mile-and-a-half from St Just Pool or Creek brings us to St Manditus [*Mawes*] Creek.

There is a point of land between St Just Pool and St Mawes, at the entry into St Mawes Creek, which is sometimes called Pendinas, and here the king has recently begun to erect a castle or fortress. St Mawes Creek is tidal for the first two miles inland to the ENE [*north*], and at the limit of the tidal creek there is a mill powered by a freshwater stream which flows into it. Barely a quarter-mile from the castle up the creek on the same side there is a pleasant fishing village with a pier. This is St Mawes, and there is a chapel dedicated to him here, as well as his stone chair just outside, and his well. Locally they call him St Mandite; he was a British bishop, who is depicted as a schoolmaster. A half-mile down towards the estuary from the head of this creek there is another creek, which is shaped like a pool (on the chart it is depicted by a round mark), and on this there is a mill worked by the tide. A mile below this on the south side a half-mile long creek enters the estuary, but it has a small sandbank barring it from the open sea. Another mile lower, almost opposite St Mawes, a creek or pool runs a mile inland, and at its head is a cell dedicated to St Antony. It belongs to Plympton Priory, and until recently two canons from Plympton lived here. All the creeks of the River Fal are well-wooded.

It is three-and-a-half miles from St Anthony Head at the open sea to Nare Head, and barely a half-mile further east lies Gref Islet [*Gull Rock*], where gulls and other seabirds breed. Gull Rock lies due north of the Forne [*?le Four*], a headland in Brittany, and the sleeve of the ocean enters between them. The distance between these two points is five kennings [*100 miles*], and this is reckoned to be the shortest passage from Cornwall to the Breton mainland. About a mile west of Nare Head near the coast and in the parish of Gerrans there is a single-ditched fort. No more than a bow-shot to its north can be seen a hole which was made by ploughing. The plough had broken the roof of a tunnel which led from the castle to the sea. There is another fort on the hillside a mile-and-a-half away. Also due north of the castle are four or five barrows or mounds.

Dodman Point is about five miles from Gull Rock, and although there is some woodland inland there is none along the coast itself the whole way from St Anthony Head to Dodman Point. Chapel Point lies within Bodrugan Park, which also contained the house of Sir Henry Bodrugan, of an ancient family. He took Richard III's side against Henry VII, fled to Ireland and was attainted. Bodrugan and other pieces of his estate were acquired by the father of Sir Piers Edgecumbe, Sir Richard. Other portions of the Bodrugan estate, including Restronguet and Newham in the Fal estuary, went to Trevanion.

Pentewan, two miles from Chapel Point, is a sandy bay to which fishing boats resort for shelter. A pleasant river, which flows from St Austell two-and-a-half miles away, has its mouth here, and there is a stone bridge named after the place. St Austell is a poor town, with nothing worthy of note except the parish church, and this river passes to the west of it, beneath the hill on which it stands. Between Pentewan and Black Head (which is about a mile away) there is a fine quarry of white freestone on the rocky shore. Some of it was used in the interior of St Mawes Castle. The rest is granite and slate, as at Pendennis, which is all granite except the filling. Between Black Head and Tywardreath Bay there is a cave in the cliffs where the rock formation looks like pictures of gold. The same cliffs have veins of copper and other metals. A mile from the opening of Tywardreath Bay, at the bay's inland limit, there is a parish church dedicated to St Blazey, and a new stone bridge named after this saint has been built across the brook which flows into the bay at this point.

Tywardreath, a pleasant place but not a market town, lies a quarter-mile from the east side of the bay, and two miles from Fowey. It has a parish church, and there used to be an Augustinian priory, which was an offshoot of a house in Normandy. Its founder is variously given as Campernulphus, or Cardinham, or recently Arundel of Lanherne has been put forward. A tomb which I saw in the west part of the priory church was inscribed in Latin, 'This is the tomb of Robert, son of William'. This Robert Fitz William owned a large estate during the reign of Edward III. The headland on the east side of Tywardreath Bay is called Penarth Point [*Gribbin Head*], and two miles beyond it is the mouth of the Fowey estuary.

At the western point of Fowey harbour mouth there is a blockhouse designed by Thomas Treffry, the cost of which he shared with the town of Fowey, On the hillside above this point is a chapel dedicated to St Catherine, and there is a little bay or creek with the same name at the foot of the hill just inside the harbour mouth. Approximately a quarter-mile along on this west side there is a square stone tower built in about the time of Edward IV to defend Fowey harbour, and just beyond the tower on the same side is Fowey itself. The town is built by the shore on the side of a great hill of slaty rock. In the centre there is a house built foursquare out from the shore into the harbour, which conceals ships beyond it from three-quarters of the harbour mouth, and protects them from storms. The Cornish name for Fowey is Couwhath [*see the correction at the end of Leland's notes on Cornwall*]. It is built on the north side of the harbour, perched on a strong rocky hill, and extends for about a quarter-mile. Its owner, a highly regarded man called Cardinham, gave it to Tywardreath Priory, and this is why Cardinham is sometimes credited as the priory's founder, although others say that it was Campernulph of Bere. When he made this gift Fowey was merely a small fishing community. Its parish church is dedicated to St Fimbarrus, and the living belonged to Tywardreath.

Fowey rose to prominence during the hundred years' war, partly through feats of war, and partly through piracy. When it grew rich it became devoted entirely to trade; it was frequented by ships from various nations, and its own ships sailed to every country. When their ships sailed past Rye and Winchelsea in about Edward III's time the men of Fowey would not raise their hats, as was required of them, and so the men of Rye and Winchelsea engaged them in a fight. But the Fowey men won, and thereafter they included the arms of Rye and Winchelsea on their own. Consequently they became known as the Gallants of Fowey. On various occasions the French have attacked this town. The most recent notable occasion was in about Henry VI's time, when the wife of Thomas Treffry the younger with her retinue managed to repel the French from her house during her husband's absence. As a result Thomas Treffry built a very fine and strong fortified tower on to the house, and embattled all the walls after the fashion of a castle. Even now it is the showpiece among Fowey's town buildings.

In Edward IV's time two strong towers were made just below the town, one on each side of the harbour, and a chain was stretched across between them. During the same reign when hostilities ceased between England and France the men of Fowey, who were accustomed to plundering, continued to attack the Frenchmen at sea with their ships, against the king's orders. And so the Fowey ships' captains were arrested and sent to London, and men from Dartmouth were ordered to confiscate their ships. It was at this time that the men of Dartmouth came to Fowey and took away not only the ships, but also the great chain that had been made to extend between the towers across the harbour. And so Thomas Treffry, who is still alive, and the townspeople, made the blockhouse at the foot of St Catherine's Hill.

Going north up the Fowey estuary we come first to Chagha Mill Pool, which is close to the northern end of the town, and on the same side. More than a mile upstream on this west side is Bodmin Pool or Creek, where goods are unloaded for carriage to Bodmin. A quarter-mile further on the same side is Golant, a small fishing community. Lantyan Pool or Creek, which does not extend far, is about a half-mile upstream from Golant. Barret, a man of modest estate, lives between Golant and Lantyan; the manor of Lantyan belonged to the earl of Salisbury. Nearly a mile above Lantyan Pool is an insignificant creek called Bloughan Pool or Creek, and between here and Penknek (near Lostwithiel) is the home of Carteis, a gentleman with land worth almost £70 annually. Lostwithiel is barely a mile above Bloughan on the main stream of the River Fowey. The river used to be tidal above Lostwithiel, but the tide does not now flow as far as the town.

The shire hall of Cornwall is at Lostwithiel, and there is also the Coinage Hall for tin. The town has borough privileges, and there is a weekly market held on Thursdays. Richard, King of the Romans and Earl of Cornwall, granted the town its privileges. The parish church is dedicated to St Bartholomew. A stream flows from the west alongside the town and into the River Fowey, It divides Lostwithiel from Penknek, which is in the parish of Lanlivery. Immediately to the north of the town is Restormel Park, which contains good woodland and tin workings. The earls of Cornwall used to occupy the castle in this park. Although the base court is badly dilapidated the fine large keep is still standing, and there is a chapel built on to it, of later work, and now without a roof. Another chapel, dedicated to the Trinity, is in the park not far from the castle. Cardinham Castle is more than four miles north of Lostwithiel, and many knight's services were attached to it. Arundel of Lanherne, Lord Zouch, and Compton are among those who have divided up the Cardinham lands.

The course of the River Fowey is as follows: it rises on Fowey Moor, about two miles south of Camelford in a real quagmire on the side of a hill. Then to Draynes Bridge which is built of flat granite slabs. Then two miles or more to Clobham Bridge which is submerged in the sand. Then one mile to Largin Bridge of two or three arches. Then two miles to Newbridge of stone arches. Then two miles to Resprin or Laprin Bridge, also of stone arches. Shortly before it reaches the stone bridge at Lostwithiel the river divides into two channels. At the present day the lesser stream flows under the stone bridge and the greater stream under a wooden bridge which is only a little distance away. They join again in one valley a considerable distance lower. It is deliberate policy to divert most of the flow of the river away from the stone bridge, in order to prevent the sand from choking the bridge, and to remove it away from the lower part of the town. Men still alive can remember when the arches could be seen to be very deep, but now the sand has come up to within four or five feet of their tops. The main cause of this is the sand washed down from tin workings, and in the course of time this will badly affect the whole Fowey estuary. At present barges still bring their goods to within a half-mile of Lostwithiel.

St Winnow, with its abbey church, lies more than a mile below Lostwithiel on the River Fowey. A gentleman by the name of John of St Winnow used to live beside the church; then it belonged to Lord Hastings, who sold it to William Lower, the great-grandfather of its present owner.

The wife of this Lower is one of Thomas Treffry's two daughters. Beside the church is a wharf for building ships; there is plenty of good timber to be obtained from St Winnow's Wood (the point of which is a half-mile downstream), and from woodland on the opposite bank of the estuary. Next to St Winnow's Wood on the east bank a salt creek extends a half-mile to Lerryn Bridge, and this creek is also called Lerryn. Almost at the head of this creek on the north bank is Ethy, Laurence Courtney's house. It used to belong to the Stonnard family, and then to Cayle, and now to a branch of the Devonshire family of Courtney. The next creek, about a half-mile lower on the east side, is called St Carac's Pool or Creek [*Penpoll Creek*]; it is about a mile-and-a-half long, and there was a small cell of Ss Cyret and Julette [*Cyricus and Juliette*] belonging to Montacute Priory half-way along on the north bank. A mile further downstream is Poul-Morlande [*Mirrow Pill*], which is hardly a quarter-mile long and divides into two arms at its head. From here it is only a half-mile to Bodinnick village, where the ferry crosses to Fowey. Mr Mohun has a manor house called the Hall on the hill above the village.

At Pelene Point, a quarter-mile below Bodinnick, a pool or creek half a mile long enters the estuary. At its head there is a chapel dedicated to St Willow, and next to it a house called Lamelin which until recently belonged to Lamelin, but has now been inherited by Trelawny; his seat is at Menheniot. On the south side of this creek is the parish church for both Bodinnick and Polruan, which is known as Lanteglos-by-Fowey. From this creek's mouth it is only a quarter-mile to Polruan, a good fishing settlement. On its hill is a chapel dedicated to St Saviour, and in Polruan itself is a fortified tower, which corresponds with the tower on the Fowey side. They say that a chain used to be extended between the towers across the harbour. At its mouth Fowey Harbour is two bow-shots wide. On this east side the land at the very tip of the harbour mouth is called Pontus Cross, or commonly Paunch Cross.

From Lostwithiel to Castle Dore is at least three miles over fertile corn and grassland. Castle Dore belonged to the Earl of Salisbury, but is now completely demolished. There is a broken cross a mile from here with the Latin inscription: 'Conomor and his son with the Lady Clusilla'. It is about six miles from Pontus Cross to Polperro, where there is a small fishing community and a pier, with a tiny creek and a brook. From Polperro to the creek at Looe, which is dry at half tide, is two miles, and there is another small creek on the way. By the mouth of Looe Creek there is a town on each bank, East Looe and West Looe. East Looe is a pleasant market town. A great bridge of twelve arches crosses Looe Creek to connect the two towns. Salmon are taken in the creek, and good woodland surrounds it. A manor house called Trelawne is nearby; it belongs to the Marquis of Dorset, but was once owned by the Bonvilles. Two gentry families, Kendal and Code, live in Morval parish on the east side of this creek. Two miles from Looe Creek is Seaton Bridge, a two-arch stone bridge over the River Seaton, which is three miles long. It is about nine miles further from Seaton to Rame Head.

My journey from Fowey to Liskeard took me first across the harbour to the fishing settlement of Bodinnick, near which Mr Mohun has a manor house; then through five miles of most agreeable countryside, with pleasant woodland and abundant corn and grass. This was followed by three miles of heather-clad moorland, and two miles of hills and woods, which brought me to Liskeard. But in the wood about a half-mile before I reached the town I passed a chapel of Our Lady known as Our Lady in the Park, which used to be much frequented by pilgrims. It is one of three or four chapels dependent on Liskeard.

Liskeard stands on rocky hills, and at the present day is the second best market town in Cornwall, after Bodmin. Its market is kept on Mondays. The parish church, which is dedicated to St Martin, stands on a hill, and is a fine large building. There was a castle across the town from St Martin's, to the north. It is now all in ruins, and only broken pieces of walls are still standing. It occupied a magnificent site overlooking the whole town. It belonged to the earls of Cornwall, but now it is used from time to time as a cattle pound. The town recognizes Richard, King of the Romans and Earl of Cornwall, as the granter of its freedom and privileges. A fine conduit in the town centre provides it with an abundant water supply. Distances from Liskeard (in miles): Fowey, 10; Launceston, 12; Lostwithiel, 10; Bodmin, 10; East Looe, 7; St Germans, 6; Plymouth, 12.

About a half-mile after I left Liskeard I passed on the right hand the old manor house of Cartuther. It is a fine manor, with an annual value of £100, although it has now been divided up between heirs. Mr Trelawny told me that the lordship of Cartuther, along with that of Tregelly (the old name for Menheniot), used to belong to one Heling or Eling. Menheniot is two miles from Liskeard, and here there is a fine, large, old church.

The manor used to be called Tregelly, and some ruins as well as the name survive. The present Trelawney is the fourth of that name to have been lord of Menheniot. The first was the son of Sir John Trelawney (of an old gentry family), but probably not the eldest son, as the present Trelawney owns none of Sir John's lands; these have descended by the female line. From Menheniot it is two miles to Bodulcan's ruined house. A half-mile from here is a large brook which flows for four miles before joining the River Lynher. St German's Creek runs one side of the town, and another stream a quarter-mile further on flows to the other side [?]. From here it is four miles to Notter Bridge, of two or three arches, which crosses the River Lynher. This river, as far as I could ascertain, rises in the north-east towards the Launceston area. The soil is very good between Menheniot and Notter Bridge. The land is enclosed, and reasonably well-wooded. It is two miles from Notter Bridge to St Germans, which is on the near bank of the river as I approached the bridge. St Germans is now only a poor fishing town; it owed its renown to the priory there. It lies about three miles up the Lynher Creek away from the Tamar estuary.

Saltash is about four miles from the bridge over the Lynher, across rather similar countryside. It is a pleasant and busy market town which extends from the top of a rocky hill at its western end and right to the foot of the hill by the Tamar estuary to the east. The inhabitants rely on both trade and fishing. The town has a chapel-of-ease, but the parish church, which is called St Stephen's, is about a half-mile to the south, and the living belongs to Windsor College. Near the church and in its parish is the grand and ancient castle of Trematon on a rocky hill. Large portions of it still stand, and in particular the keep, the ruins of which are used as a prison. The castle enjoys great liberties. The Valetortes, who were large landowners, possessed the castle and, so far as I can discover, were its builders. They were also owners and lords of the town of Saltash.

The course of the Tamar: It passes more than two miles from Tavistock; Greystone Bridge is three miles below Launceston on the Tamar, and six miles from Tavistock. The Tamar passes close to the abbot of Tavistock's house at Morwell, which is about a mile from Morwellham. Calstock Bridge or New Bridge is two miles from the first creek, which is Millbrook Lake. St John's Lake is the second, the third is the River Lynher, and the fourth is just above Saltash. The fifth is undoubtedly the main stream of the Tamar. From Reddon there is a six-mile stretch of land lying

south-west of the river on St Nicholas' Isle as far as Cargreen, and here the river, after running north, turns towards the west for a mile. On the west bank I noticed the following creeks: First I judged by eye that the main branch of the Tamar estuary [*left the other branches*] about two miles or more above Saltash; it is tidal almost to Calstock Bridge, some ten miles further inland. Ships come up to a place called Morwellham, which is less than a mile from this bridge, and only three miles from Tavistock. The shortest route from Saltash to Tavistock is reckoned to be only ten miles. Along the two-mile stretch of estuary from Saltash to the main Tamar river I could see three creeks running inland from the shore. The first ran north-west, the second WNW, and the third west, although this was scarcely a half-mile long. Nearly a mile downstream (on the other side of Saltash town, which stands between them) is Lynher Creek running up to St Germans. Then there is a small creek called St John's or Antony, and at the mouth, near St Nicholas, is a creek which runs two miles inland from the estuary to Millbrook, a prosperous fishing community. Penlee Point is a headland three miles below this creek, and Rame Head is a mile further.
cont. p. 77 [**1542**: *1/173-9, 183-212*]

Plymouth is the easternmost port along the south coast, between [*Cornwall and*] Devonshire, for this is where the Tamar flows into the sea.
    The Middle Part of Cornwall: Along the River Tamar from its source in the NNE to its estuary in the south the terrain is hilly, the soil fertile for corn and grass, and some tin is won by streaming. Hingston, which is a high hill near the Tamar in east Cornwall, would be barren waste were it not for its rich workings of tin, which is both mined and streamed. From the middle of Cornwall eastwards is high, rocky, mountainous country, barren except for some tin working. High mountainous waste extends the length of Cornwall, closer to the north than to the south. Between Launceston and Bodmin the land is fertile, with some tin working, and in a dry summer it is good cattle pasture. Note Dozmary Pool, also called Dounevet, near St Anne's Hill. The high, barren, mountainous ground, which offers rough pasture and tin, continues west of Bodmin as far as the village of Redruth, which is nearer the north than the south coast. From Redruth to Carne Gotholghan the terrain is hilly, bereft of grass, but with plenty of tin. From Lelant to St Just (or Justinian), the westernmost point of Cornwall, the northern part is mountainous waste abundant in tin. The extreme west point has the Cornish name Penwolase, which means 'the furthest headland'.
    The North Part of Cornwall: From Stratton, which is close to the source of the Tamar, the country along the north coast as far as Padstow is hilly rather

than mountainous, and produces very abundant grass and corn. The cliffs along this stretch of coast produce thin blue slates of good quality, which are suitable for roofing houses; there are also strata of lead and various other metals not yet known. And in the Camelford area there are some ancient mine workings, but it is not known what metal was extracted. Less than a mile south of that poor village flows the river which enters the Severn Sea at Padstow. It is the largest of the rivers along the north Cornwall coast, and is called in the vernacular Dunmere; but in the royal grant of privileges to the canons and burgesses of Bodmin it is called Alan, which may be a reference to the Alaune. In some histories it is called Cablan. It was beside this river that Arthur fought his last battle, and evidence of this, in the form of bones and harness, is uncovered when the site is ploughed.

Less than four miles from Camelford on the northern cliffs is Tintagel. It seems likely that the castle once had three wards, but that two have been washed away by the sea's inroads, to such an extent that the castle is a virtual island, and the only access to it now is across tall elm trees which have been laid as a bridge. The only remains off the island are a gatehouse, a wall, and a parapet with ditch and wall. On the island old walls remain, and on the more easterly part, where the ground is lower, there is a battlemented wall, which still had its iron postern door within living memory. There is a nice chapel on the island with a tomb on the left side; and there is a well, with a pit nearby which has been hewn out of the stony ground to the length and breadth of a man. Also on the island is a square plot surrounded by a wall as if it were a garden, and the ruins of a vault can be seen next to the wall. Now the island nurtures sheep and rabbits.

Padstow is a town of fishermen, with one parish church, and a harbour which ships may only enter at high tide. On the east side of Padstow Bay are two rocky headlands. The more easterly is called Pentire, and gives its name also to the land nearby. Down the coast from Padstow to St Anne's Hill [*St Agnes Head*] (which has no building on it), the terrain is quite hilly; there is little tin, but abundant corn and grass. Eight miles from Padstow is a small house of secular canons called Crantock. From St Agnes Head to Lelant village the coastline is fairly hilly, sandy and barren, but in various places along it there are good deposits of tin. There is a river called Dour Conor which flows past Conarton [?*Connor Downs*], and enters the sea near the Lanant river mouth [*Hayle estuary*]. Seabirds breed on Godrevy Rock, which lies in the estuary of the river flowing past Lelant. From Lelant it is a barren coastline, but with good tin workings in various places, all the way to St Just (or Justinian). Here there is only a parish church and a scattering of houses at the westernmost point of the shore.

All along the north Cornish coast there are various creeks, in which small fishing boats can be beached, and in good weather the inhabitants go fishing in them. But in Padstow Bay, and at Lelant and St Ives, there are quays or piers to shelter the ships and sloops in all weathers. Dozmary Pool, which lies a little way inland to the south at the eastern end of this coast, is reckoned to be two bow-shots long by one bow-shot wide. It is situated on a hill, and at its east end it is thought to be 14 or 15 fathoms deep. A river flows from it; it is called Deep Hatch, and a mile-and-a-half from the pool it is two fathoms deep. I must find out where it flows to the sea. There are red deer on this hilly moorland, and when hunted they take refuge in the pool.

The Scilly Isles include 147 islands which grow vegetation (not counting barren rocks), and they are reckoned to be thirty miles west of the Cornish mainland. The largest of the Scillies, which is called St Nicholas Isle, has a small tower or fortress, and a parish church which a monk from Tavistock Abbey has been left in peace to serve. There are about sixty households in his parish. One of the Scillies is called Rat Isle, because there are so many rats on it that if a horse or any other live animal is taken there they devour it. Another is called Bovy Isle, and there is one called Innisschawe, 'the isle of elder', because stinking elder grows on it. Wild boars or pigs inhabit it.

The land from St Just eastwards to Newlyn is quite hilly and good for grass, and tin is both streamed and mined; but there are no harbours or creeks, only winches in various places with which boats are drawn up on to dry land. These winches look like the capstans used on board ship for weighing anchor. The boats only go fishing in good weather. At the south-westerly point between St Just and Newlyn there is a promontory also entirely surrounded by the sea. To all appearances it is just a hill enclustered with rocks; but there used to be a castle here, and proof of this can be seen on the landward side where there are the remains of two wards which have completely fallen down. Their fine squared masonry is still there. Nowadays the ruined castle on the point is an impregnable refuge for foxes. Four miles from this south-westerly point, between it and Newlyn, and a mile or more inland, is a place of sanctuary called St Buryan. There is a church and no more than eight dwelling-houses nearby. It has a dean and a few prebendaries, but they are very seldom resident there.

Newlyn is a poor fishing community. All it has is a small quay for ships and boats, and a little freshwater shelter. A small, low, grass-covered island with a chapel on it lies opposite the quay or pier, less than a bow-shot away. Mousehole is a pleasant fishing place next to the shore on the western side of Mount's Bay, with no protection for ships except an artificial pier. In the bay to the east of Mousehole there is a good anchorage for ships called Gwavas Lake. About a mile from Mousehole, and close to the shore of Mount's Bay, is Penzance, the most westerly market town in the whole of Cornwall. There is no shelter for boats or ships except a manmade pier or quay. As at Newlyn, there is only a chapel within the town; their parish churches are more than a mile away.

Marazion, or Market Jew, is a fishing town with a market, and it is built right against the shore of Mount's Bay north of St Michael's Mount, the foot of which lies directly opposite. On the western side of the town a lake or small river flows down from within a mile of Lelant, which lies due north. Marazion is a poor town with a poor chapel in its centre, and another small chapel in the sand nearby, between the town and the mount. Less than a mile separates the small river, at its nearest point, from the River Hayle, which flows into the sea at Lelant. And the distance between high water mark at Marazion and the tidal limit of the Hayle estuary is less than two miles.

St Michael's Mount is less than a half-mile around its foot. The SSE part is pasture land where rabbits breed, but the rest is a high crag. There is a garden with some fishermen's houses and workshops in the NNE quarter, and in the NNW quarter is a jetty for boats and ships. There is a path on the north side, accessible at half-tide and lower, which begins at the foot of the mount, and climbs by flights of steps first westwards and then turning eastwards until it reaches the outer ward of the church. In this ward there is a courtyard with a strong wall, and it contains two chapels – St Michael's on the south side, Our Lady's on the east. Lodgings for the chaplain and the priests are also on the south side, and to the west of St Michael's chapel. Between half-tide and full-tide the Mount is surrounded by the sea, but at other times it is accessible on foot.

Between the Mount and Penzance can be found at various places in the bay near low water mark the roots of trees, as evidence of the erosion of the shoreline. The Mount's Bay coast runs for some twenty miles from Newlyn to the Lizard Point, and less than three miles from the Lizard there is a small island in the bay of about two acres called Inispriuen [?*Mullion Island*], where birds and rabbits live. Although the land along this coastline from Newlyn as far as The Loe is not very fertile, it has good tin workings. Further along the south coast, from the Lizard to the Helford River, the soil produces good corn and grass, but less than three miles inland, and so between Helford and Mount's Bay, there is a wild moor called Goonhilly, which means 'hilly heathland'. Cattle are bred here. Also due west of the headland at the mouth of the Helford estuary, in the area called Meneage, there is a parish church dedicated to St Keverne, or Piran. It is a place of sanctuary, with ten or twelve dwellings, and there used to be a cell of monks nearby; but they have gone back to their mother-house, and their monastery survives only as ruins.

Less than two miles from the tidal limit of the River Hayle is Helston. This is a market town, and twice each year a court is held there for the stamping of tin. It has both a chapel and a parish church, and traces if its castle are still to be seen in the west part of the town. A river runs beneath these remains and flows south towards the coast. But the south-easterly winds pile up sand to form a bar, which turns it into a pool called The Loe. It is a bow-shot wide, and in summer two miles around. But in winter, because the pool floods back up to Helston and prevents the mills near the town from working, it is necessary for men to cut through the sand bar between The Loe and the sea, so that the water can be released, and the mills grind again. The cut thus made enables the sea to flow in and out of the pool with the tide, and allows sea-fish to enter. But as soon as there is a south-easterly wind the channel becomes filled with sand and blocked again. Then the sea-fish are trapped, and can be caught in the pool along with trout and eels.

The land from Newlyn to Helston is moderately fertile for corn and grass, and there is abundant tin near the south coast.

From the Helford estuary to Falmouth is four miles by sea. Falmouth is a most noteworthy and celebrated harbour, and in one sense is the most important in the whole of Britain. For the channel in its mouth, usually known as Carrick Roads, extends two miles upstream to a depth of 14 fathoms, and so offers a safe refuge for even the largest of ocean-going ships. At the harbour entrance, nearer the west than the east side, there is a blind rock which at high tide is underwater. It is called Caregroyne, which means island (or rather rock) of seals. Seals come to land in order to give birth, and they place their young on a dry ledge which they can visit; they make their young stay there for a while before introducing them to the sea.

On the east side of Falmouth Harbour there is a creek which runs two miles inland, and is fed by fresh water at its head. On the south bank of this creek there is a place called St Antony's, which is a cell belonging to Plympton Priory, but there are only two canons there. On the north bank near the harbour mouth is a poor fishing village called St Mawes, or La Vousa, and nearby, on the harbour side of the village, a small fortress has recently been built by the government to defend the harbour. On the west side of the harbour a creek runs inland from the harbour mouth for more than three miles. Penryn, a very pleasant trading town with a victuals market, stands at the head of this creek. In the town St Thomas's College, which is well defended by a wall and ditch, has secular canons and a provost. There is also a chapel in the town, but the parish church is a quarter-mile outside. More than eight miles due ENE of the harbour mouth is the market town of Truro, which has a mayor, a parish church, a house of black friars, and the right to stamp tin. Also on the south-east [north-east] side, more than twelve miles inland, at the former tidal limit of the River Fal, is another market town, called Tregony. This place has an old castle, with the parish church of St James standing close to it on wasteland. Another parish church stands at the east end, and in the town centre is a [?chapel].

Six miles east of Tregony is St Austell, a poor village with a parish church. Tywardreath stands at the head of its bay on the east side. It is a poor village with a parish church and a priory of Cluniac monks. All the way along this south coast from Falmouth to Tywardreath the soil is reasonably fertile for growing corn and grass, and there are no tin workings between Falmouth and Dodman Point. Halfway between these two places there is a grass-covered rock of two acres in area, called Grefe [Gull Rock], with a peak rising vertically in the centre. Seabirds breed on this island. From Dodman Point to Tywardreath there is rather less arable and grassland, but tin workings make up for this, and there are seams of copper in the sea-cliffs. – Also a reasonable amount of pasture, corn and woodland.

Tywardreath is two miles from Fowey, and along the coast between them there is abundant corn and grass, but no tin workings. Fowey is a market town defended on the seaward side by a wall, and it also has gates. There is only one church in the town; its houses are well-built but badly lived-in. On the west side of the harbour entrance there is a blockhouse next to a chapel dedicated to St Catherine. Also on this side is a tower equipped with weapons to defend the harbour.

Two miles up the estuary on the west bank is a fishing community called Golant, and about a quarter-mile above the tidal limit is the market town of Lostwithiel. This is the shire-town of Cornwall, for it is here that the sheriff holds the monthly shire-court. Tin is stamped in this town twice each year. Next to the shire hall can be seen the ruins of ancient buildings, once a house belonging to the Duke of Cornwall. There is no doubt that the River Fowey was once tidal right up to Lostwithiel, and that the flow is blocked now on account of sand discharged by the tin workings. In the king's park near Lostwithiel stands the small round castle of Restormel.

On the east side of Fowey harbour mouth there stands a tower to defend it, and a little above it is a chapel dedicated to St Saviour. Nearby is the fishing village of Polruan. A mile upstream on the east bank stands a poor fishing village called Bodinnick, which is where the ferry crosses to Fowey. Two miles inland from Bodinnick due north, up a creek on the north [*east*] bank, there is a cell of black monks from Montacute, which is dedicated to Ss Syricus and Juliette.

Four miles due east of the Fowey estuary is a small creek called Polperro, with a poor and simple fishing village on its eastern side, and a pier or quay to protect the fishing boats. Two miles further east is another creek called Looe, which is a tidal creek. At low water in summer time it is possible to wade or ride across it beneath the bridge. On each side of this creek there is a small fishing village right next to the shore, called East Looe and West Looe. East Looe has a market, and both have chapels. In the mouth of this creek, closer to its south-west bank and less than a quarter-mile from the sea shore, is a low island of six or eight acres in area called St Nicholas' Isle. Sheep and rabbits graze on it, and it is a breeding ground for seabirds. A little above the two villages is a stone bridge of ten or twelve arches, and this is used when the tide comes in.

From Fowey Harbour to Looe Creek the land beside the shore yields very good corn and grass, and there are no tin workings. From Looe Creek eastwards towards Plymouth it is twelve miles to the Tamar, and on the west bank of this estuary, less than three miles from its mouth, there is a simple fishing settlement called Millbrook. Up another creek further along the west bank is a place called St Germans, where there is now an Augustinian priory incorporating a parish church. Next to the high altar on the right hand side there is a tomb set into the wall with a statue of a bishop, and above it are painted eleven bishops with names and verses. This is a reminder of the number of bishops that are buried there, or of the number of bishops of Cornwall that had this as their cathedral. Even now the bishop of Exeter owns a house here. It is called Cudden-Beck, and adjoins the south-east side of the town.

Six miles north-east of St Germans there is a market town on the Tamar called Saltash, and from here a ferry makes the quarter-mile passage across the river. Less than two miles west of Saltash there is a round castle belonging to the king and called Trematon – that is to say, 'the second Tamar fortress'. Two miles inland from Saltash going north is the small village of Cargreen; Bere house and park in Devonshire lie to its east, and are separated from it only by the width of the Tamar. Along the south coast from Looe to the Tamar the soil is fertile for corn and grass, but there is no tin working.

Cornwall is divided into hundreds as follows: on the south side from east to west the hundreds are – East [*Wivelshire*], West [*Wivelshire*], Powder and Kerrier; on the north side from east to west – Stratton, Lesnewth, Trigg, Pydar and Penwith.

Launceston, otherwise called Lostephan and once Dunevet, stands two miles west of Polson Bridge on the Tamar. The town wall, nearly a mile in circumference, is now in ruins. A castle with three round wards stands on a high hill on the northern side of the town, and the north-west portion forms part of the town wall. The town has three gates and a postern, and another gate leads from the castle into the old park. Some of the Cornish gentry hold their estates by castle-guard, that is to say, they must keep the town and castle in repair. The castle contains a chapel, a hall for holding quarter sessions and assizes, and the common gaol for the whole of Cornwall. The town has a market, a mayor and burgesses, and a chapel-of-ease dedicated to St Mary Magdalene. At the foot of the town hill, in a valley about a bowshot north of the castle, is a priory of canons regular dedicated to St Stephen. And almost a half-mile north-east of the priory is a small village set on a hill, which contains the parish church of St Stephen. It is believed that at first the canons lived on this hill, but then came down to the better and warmer site. There is another parish church standing in the priory churchyard. The wall of Dunevet is high, large and strong, and a good defence. A small river runs past the north side of the priory. There are two conduits of channelled water in Dunevet. [1/315-26]

Bridges on the Tamar: A stone bridge at North Tamerton, a village on the east bank; Yealmbridge, 2 miles lower; New Bridge, 2 miles lower, with three large high arches and one low arch; Polson Bridge 2 miles lower (Tavistock Abbey built this bridge and has good landholdings in the area); Greystone Bridge, about 2 miles lower; another New Bridge; Lydford Bridge.

Launceston: A long suburb. The town wall is about a mile in circumference on a craggy hilltop. The castle keep has three wards. There is one parish church. A small brook or stream of water flows from a hill nearby and passes through a portion of the town within the wall. Another stream, called the Ottery, flows through the suburb in the valley; it rises twelve miles WNW towards Bodmin. Bodmin is twenty miles from both Launceston and Tamerton, which are four miles apart. The priory of black canons is next to the suburb of Launceston. A small stream derives from a nearby hill and after passing through an attractive wood near the priory, flows through its domestic buildings, and so to the Ottery.

An old college of priests at St Stephen's on the hill a mile outside the town. A countess called Mabilia was buried in the chapter house. Prior Horton had a fine tomb in the south aisle, and Prior Stephen a rich monument. Gawen Carow is the leaseholder of the priory. St Catherine's chapel on a hill outside the town has now been robbed of stone.

The first two miles of my ride to Boscastle were through reasonably good enclosed ground, partly wooded. The next eight miles were over wild moorland, with no crops or trees visible, and for the last two miles to Boscastle there was some arable land but absolutely no wood. For the most part the inhabitants there burn gorse and heather. Six miles south of Boscastle Lord Huntingdon has a house called Parkwalls, where Lord Botreaux had a fine manor house or castle. The late Lord Hungerford owned half this manor.

There is an attractive market town called Stratton, a mile inland, twelve miles up the Severn shore [*Bristol Channel coast*] from Boscastle. Hartland Point is six or eight miles further up, and Hartland is eighteen miles from Boscastle. Trevethy and a brook, with two rocks as little islands. Bossiney is a privileged town, and the stream of Trevethy Water flows out to the sea here. There is a little headland at Bossiney, and if the pier were made up it would provide a small harbour. Trevena. St Symphorian's church. St Julian's chapel in Tintagel Castle.

A mile from where I rode a brook flowed into the sea, and a rock stood as an island in the sea just to the west of the mouth. From there it was three miles to Port Isaac, an attractive fishing village; a brook flows here and forms a small creek. Two miles further was another fishing village, Portquin, with another brook flowing into a small creek. From here the mouth of Padstow harbour was about three miles. St Teath is about four miles from Tintagel, and in this area the soil is more fertile for everything. Mr Carnsey has a house about a mile beyond Trelill (which is two miles from St Teath), and here there is a little woodland. From St Teath to Wadebridge, however, there is virtually no woodland, but there is good arable.

The vicar of Wadebridge, whose name was Lovebone, started to build the fine bridge of seventeen arches there eighty years or more ago, and completed it with the help of his fellow countrymen. There are no bridges worth mentioning between Camelford and Wadebridge, nor indeed at Camelford on this river, apart from Hellandbridge, and Dunmere Bridge, which is two miles lower. This has three arches, and from Wadebridge it is three miles upstream over land, and four miles by water. Padstow is four miles down from Wadebridge, but there is no bridge either on this stretch or from Padstow to the sea. [1/301-3]

From Wadebridge to Dunmere is three miles, and Bodmin is a mile further. Bodmin's Saturday market draws people to the town like a fair. The centre-piece and show-piece of the place is its main street running east-west. At the west end of the town is a chapel of St [*Leonard*], and at the other end stands the fine, large parish church, with chantry chapel at its east end. The former Augustinian priory, whose patron and sometime resident was St Petrock, lay in the churchyard of Bodmin parish church, at the east end. There have been monks, then nuns, then secular priests, then monks again, and finally regular canons in St Petrock's church, Bodmin. The latest priory foundation was the work of William Warelwast, bishop of Exeter, but he kept for himself some of the former lands of Bodmin Abbey. The only tomb of note which I saw in the priory was that of a former prior, Thomas Vivian, who had the title of suffragan bishop of Megara. St Petrock's shrine and tomb are still standing in the east part of the church.

There was a good house of grey friars on the south side of the town, which had been founded by a merchant, John of London, and augmented by Edward, earl of Cornwall. Two of the house's benefactors, Sir Hugh Peverelle and Sir Thomas Peverelle, knights, are buried in the grey friars. Bodmin has also a second chapel-of-ease, in addition to the one at the west end, and an almshouse, which however has no endowment of lands. King Athelstan is regarded as Bodmin's chief founder and granter of privileges to it. St Columb Major is eight miles from Bodmin.

My journey from Bodmin to Gwarnick: It is about a mile to St Laurence, where there is a poor hospital or lazar house. Then five miles of hills and waste until Castle an Dinas, a hill which lies barely a mile off the road on the right hand side. Then four more miles of hilly, treeless moorland, to Mitchell, a poor roadside place. Then six miles to St Allen parish church, which is surrounded by fertile arable and grassland. Another mile to Gwarnick.

Gwarnick used to be one of the manor houses of the Boville or Beville family, whose name came from Lower Normandy. The lineage continued at Gwarnick for a long time until recently, when it descended to two daughters. One married the present Arundel of Trerice, the other a Graneville; and so nearly £200 worth of lands were divided between them. [1/180-1]

Latin inscriptions made at St Mawes Castle [by John Leland] at Mr Treffry's request: 'Henry VIII, King of England, France and Ireland, the most invincible, placed me here as protection for the state and deterrent to its enemies. Submit your sails, O ships, to the authority of Henry. Your glory and fame, Henry, will endure for ever. Edward reflects his father by his deeds and reputation. Let fortunate Cornwall now rejoice at Edward its duke.' [1/248]

The main source of the River Fowey is in Fowey Moor, at a place popularly known as Codde Fowey. It is sixteen miles overland from the town of Fowey, less than two miles from Camelford, and only four miles from the Severn Sea. It rises to the north, and flows into the sea to the south. [4/128]

My reference in the manuscript I wrote about Cornwall to 'Cowwath' as the old Cornish name for Fowey should be corrected to 'Fawathe'. [5/6]

CUMBERLAND

ALTHOUGH LELAND'S ACCOUNT of Cumberland is not written as if it were part of an itinerary, it was probably compiled during his ride through north-west England in 1538. The narrative of that journey breaks off at Kendal and is picked up again at Byland Abbey in Yorkshire, so this passage, and the account of Northumberland which follows it in the manuscript, provide us with a substitute for the missing portion of itinerary.

[*Distances around the coast:*] From Carlisle to Burgh by Sands, 6 miles; from Burgh to Workington, 12 miles; Workington to St Bees, 14 miles; St Bees to Furness along the sea coast, 14 miles; Furness to Lancaster, 12 miles; Lancaster to Preston, 20 miles.

The River Esk marks the border between England and Scotland. It has a tributary, the Liddel Water, which joins it at Liddel Moat. There used to be a moated house here which belonged to a gentleman called Sir Walter Selby. But he was killed here, and his house destroyed, when the Scots went to Durham during Edward III's reign. This was the occasion when the Scottish king was captured by Copeland on a hill next to Durham, where many Scots were buried.

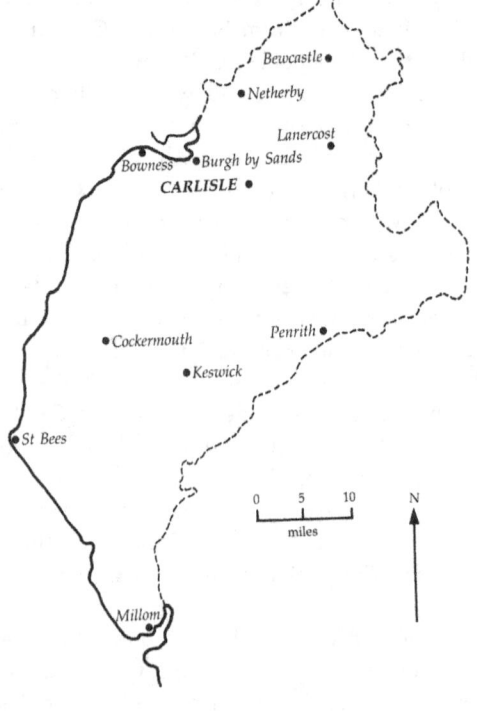

Bowness is a low-lying tract at the mouth of the River Eden. It is on the nearer side of the Eden about eight miles from Carlisle. There is a small, poor tower here for defence against assault, and part of Hadrian's Wall clearly survives in this area. One may speculate that Bowness is so-called because it is the 'eye' or point, or end, of the wall.

Burgh by Sands lies about one mile inland from the nearer shore of the Eden. Next to the village survive the ruins of a great house, now completely deserted, in which Edward I died. Burgh is three miles from Bowness, and four or five miles from Carlisle. Burgh once belonged to the Morville family, and it was here that about fifteen years ago Lord Maxwell was badly wounded, and many were killed or drowned in the Eden.

About half-way between Bowness and Burgh, at Drumburgh, the father of Lord Dakers built a good fortress to defend the surrounding country. It was erected on old ruins, and part of Hadrian's Wall, which is very close by, was pulled down to provide building stone for it.

Netherby is seven miles north of Carlisle, and the River Esk flows past its north side. The surviving ruined walls prove that there were remarkable buildings here, and within living memory there were rings and staples in the walls, which appear to have been moorings for ships. To one side of it is disputed territory, so it is in effect the boundary between England and Scotland. The remains are now at least three miles from the tidal reaches of the Solway Firth, and the ruined walls are overgrown with grass. Rockcliffe is a good fortress or castle belonging to Lord Dakers. It is on the further bank of the Eden, about four miles from Carlisle.

Cockermouth stands on the River Cocker, which flows right through the town; it joins the Derwent right by the tip of Cockermouth Castle. The River Derwent, where its course narrows, throws off a branch, and the abundant water forms a pool or lake, called Use. This then narrows, and eventually flows back into the Derwent, thus making an island.

Forests: The great forest of Inglewood; the Duke of Lancaster's Nichol forest; Ennerdale Forest.

Thirty years ago, not far from Moor chapel, which is in the parish of Cumwhitton in Gilsland, six miles east of Carlisle, there was found a grave containing bones of extraordinary size. And twenty years ago, within a quarter-mile of Carlisle the pipes of a conduit were dug up, which probably brought water from a place called Tipping Castle.

Carlisle city is scarcely a mile in circumference, and has a very fine strong wall made of squared blocks of a reddish stone. There are three gates in this wall: Butcher Gate (south), Caldew Gate (west) and Richard Gate (north). In a sense the castle, which lies within the town, closes off the town wall. The Irish word for a town is 'bal', so it may be that this was the Old Scottish word too – in which case 'Lugubalia' could mean 'Luele [*Lisle*] town'.

There are two parish churches in Carlisle. One is dedicated to St Cuthbert, but the other is in the nave of the cathedral. This is the only English cathedral which has regular canons. There is also a chapel in the town dedicated to St Alban, and two friaries, black and grey, which are both within the walls.

In the past, and recently, when excavation took place in the town for new buildings there were frequently uncovered various foundations of the old city, such as paved street surfaces, old door arches, cornerstones and stone blocks, painted pottery, and money hidden in pots which was so old and decayed that, when handled at all roughly, it virtually disintegrated. This occurred, for example, well to the south of the town during digging in connection with squaring off the garden and orchard of a house. In fact the whole layout of the town has completely changed, for where there used to be streets and large buildings, now are empty plots and gardens. The cathedral nave belongs to an older building than the quire. It was colonised from St Oswald's [Nostell] Priory, close to Pontefract. Carlisle stands within Inglewood Forest. Ploughing in the fields around the city has turned up various cornelians and other stones with intaglio carvings as for seals; and elsewhere in Cumberland ploughing has uncovered ancient stamped bricks.

In length Cumberland extends along the coastline from the Duddon Channel, which separates Furness and Cumberland, up to a small stream or pond called Polt Rosse, which divides the county of Northumberland on the east side from Cumberland. In breadth Cumberland extends from the River Eamont to the River Esk. The Eamont defines the county's southern boundary with Westmorland as far as its confluence with the River Eden, two miles east of Penrith, and then the boundary follows the east bank of the Eden as far as a brook; this also divides Cumberland from Westmorland. The Esk is the northern boundary, and separates Cumberland from the disputed territory until it reaches an arm of the sea which divides England from Scotland.

Market towns in the county: Carlisle. Penrith is a market town sixteen miles south of Carlisle and five miles south-west of Kirkoswald. It has a strong royal castle, and is only one mile from the earl of Cumberland's place or castle at Brougham. It is notable that Penrith lies half a mile away from the River Eamont, and is served by an artificial channel cut by Bishop Strickland of Carlisle. This leaves the River Petteril at Ingmer Meadow, flows through Penrith, and joins the Eamont at Carleton, half a mile from the town. Penrith has one parish church and a Franciscan friary.

Cockermouth is a market town built on the west bank of the River Derwent four or five miles from the coast and twenty miles from Carlisle. Also on the Derwent's west bank is a good creek for ships, and a pleasant little fishing community called Workington, where Sir Thomas Culwyn has his principal house. Next to the source of the Derwent, on the east side of the island, is a small, impoverished, market town called Keswick; it is one mile from St Herbert's Island, which has a chapel and is mentioned by Bede. Several springs flow down from Borrowdale to form a great lake which we call a pool. There are three islands in it. On one are the principal houses of Mr Radclyf, another is St Herbert's Isle, and the third is Vicar Isle, which is covered in trees like a wilderness.

Abbeys or priories in Cumberland: The canons of Carlisle. Wetheral, which was a cell of St Mary's Abbey [in York], lies three miles up the River Eden south-east of Carlisle and on the same bank. Lanercost is an abbey of Augustinian canons eight miles from Carlisle, on the north bank of the River Irthing. Holmcultram

Abbey, of Cistercian monks. St Bees in Coupland, next to the western sea, was a cell of St Mary's Abbey, York, and lies about 26 miles or more directly west of Carlisle. Calder Abbey, a Cistercian monastery, is in Coupland, close to Egremont Castle and not very far from St Bees.

[*Castles in Cumberland:*] Egremont, south of Cockermouth, belonged to Lord Fitzwalter. It stands next to the market town of Egremont. The Earl of Northumberland's castle at Cockermouth adjoins the town, which has a good market. Bewcastle, or Belcastle, is a royal castle ten miles east of Carlisle. In the vicinity are discovered old foundations containing British bricks, with inscriptions and portraits. Four miles south of Bewcastle and eight miles from Carlisle is Naworth, a fine castle belonging to Lord Dacers. Millom Castle stands beside the Duddon Channel or Duddon Sands. It belonged to Sir John Hudelstan. In a creek close to the sea shore a fish was found forty years ago of infinite greatness. High Head Castle stands on the River Ive six or seven miles south of Carlisle. Kirkoswald Castle stands close to the River Eden, twelve miles SSE of Carlisle, and south of Naworth. Penrith has a royal castle close to the town. It is sixteen miles south of Carlisle and five miles south-west of Kirkoswald. Greystoke Castle, which belongs to Lord Dacors, is fourteen miles south of Carlisle and three miles west of Penrith. Rose Castle belongs to the bishops of Carlisle. It lies six miles south-west of Carlisle, and was greatly rebuilt by Bishop Kite.

Ruins of deserted castles and towns: Six miles from Carlisle in Inglewood Forest may be seen the ruins of a castle called Castel Luen. I must remember to find out from the [*Antonine*] Itinerary the positions of the old towns. [5/50-6]

DERBYSHIRE

BOTH THE SURVIVING ITINERARIES *to northern England took Leland through Nottinghamshire rather than its neighbour, Derbyshire. Consequently we have no proper description of a county about which, to judge from the brevity and inaccuracy of the sketchy notes which follow, our traveller knew very little.*

Bolsover is a fine manor belonging to the king, in Scardale, four miles from Chesterfield. Substantial remnants of an ancient castle survive, and there is an attractive little town (also called Bolsover) next to it. [2/28]

Market towns in Derbyshire: Derby; Oresworth [*?Wirksworth*]; Bakewell; Ashbourne in the Peak; Chesterfield in the Peak; Mansfield [*actually in Nottinghamshire*].

Castles in Derbyshire: Duffield had a castle; Horeston [*Horsley*]; Codnor, five miles east of Horsley. It once belonged to Lord Grey, but is now all in ruins. High Peak [*Peveril*] Castle belongs to the king.

Rivers in Derbyshire: Trent. Manifold. The Derwent rises directly west and just above the market town of Blakwel [*Bleaklow – here confused with Bakewell*]. It flows through Darley in the Peak to Wensley village, Matlock village, Cromford village and under Cromford Bridge. Then to Whatstandwell Bridge, Darley, Derby, and Sawley Ferry, five miles overland from Derby, where it flows into the Trent. The Amber rises east [*west*] of Chesterfield, which it leaves on its left hand (as it flows towards us), then eight miles to Wingfield village, two miles to Amberbridge, then to Crich

Chase, a wood close to where it flows into the Derwent. The River Wye, a good trout stream, rises in Derbyshire close to St Anne's Well at Buxton, then to the market town of Bakewell, then to Haddon, which is near its confluence with the Derwent. The source of the River Ecclesbourne is a rock in the parish of Wirksworth. It then flows three miles to Idridgehay, and a further three miles to Duffield church. It flows into the Derwent a little beyond the church at a place called Ecclesbourne Mouth. [5/30-1]

DEVON

LIKE MANY TRAVELLERS *exploring the south-western peninsula, Leland made his way to Cornwall across north Devon, and returned through south Devon. The long description which he has left us is part of his 1542 itinerary, and is easily followed, from Exmoor, through the north Devon towns to Launceston, and returning via Plymouth, Totnes and Exeter (where he makes a detour to visit Crediton), then to Mohun's Ottery near Honiton, where Sir George Carew gave him hospitality, and so to the Dorset coast. With a view to the map which he was intending to draw, Leland tried to collect information about the course of rivers, and their bridges, as well as giving distances between points along the coast. These passages, as well as genealogies and extracts from chronicles (which have here been omitted), interrupt and sometimes confuse the narrative; in the following text some paragraphs have been transposed to give a more logical order.*

Apart from the account of his itinerary Leland has left us few notes on Devon. An earlier draft of the north Devon leg of the journey has been preserved near the end of the manuscript, but nearly all of it he incorporated into his fuller account. Only a few items of additional information are given, and they are printed here among the notes at the end, along with a mention of Hemyock Castle and a correction to a passage in the itinerary about Stoke Fleming.

FROM SIMONSBATH BRIDGE I rode up a high hill on to moorland, which continued for about two miles. But then the soil became more fertile, and the hills were full of enclosures. After three miles of this I reached Brayford, a poor village beside a stream, which presumably flows into Simonsbath Water and the River Exe. Brayford is eight miles from Barnstaple, over hilly ground, with many enclosures for both pasture and corn.

Barnstaple used to be surrounded by a wall of some half-mile in circumference. Nearly all of it has fallen down entirely, although clear traces survive of the four gates, and their names – East, West, North and South – have been kept. I think that the former name of the town, in the British language, was 'Abertaw', because it lay near the mouth of the River

Taw. 'Berdenes' then, I suppose, was a corruption of 'Abernesse'. The suffix 'staple' refers to a market.

Barnstaple's present suburbs are larger than the town itself. The houses are stonebuilt, as indeed are all the houses in good towns in this area. Of the great castle, which stood on the north-west side of the town a little downstream from the town bridge, there are substantial ruins, and part of the keep is still standing. The earliest reference which I can find to an occupant of this castle is to a certain Judhael of Totnes, son of Alfred, and he, as lord of both the town and the castle, also founded an Augustinian monastery at the north end of Barnstaple. However, one of his successors, by the name of Tracy, has been credited with its foundation.

Although Barnstaple has only one parish church, there have been four chapels in the town, and three of these survive; they include All Hallows by the north gate, and, as I recall, St Nicholas's by the west gate. There is also a fine chantry chapel in the parish churchyard, which was established by a vicar of Barnstaple named Holman. But a chapel dedicated to St Thomas Becket, which stood at the east end of the bridge, is no longer consecrated.

Barnstaple Fair is held on the feast of the nativity of Our Lady. According to some people it was a member of the Tracy family who built the very large and costly stone bridge of sixteen high arches at Barnstaple. It is endowed with lands for its maintenance.

A later lord of Barnstaple was a certain Philip de Columbariis [*of the Dovecote*]; he died in about 1344 or 1347 and is buried with his wife in Barnstaple Priory. Also in the priory are buried some of the barons of Slane in Ireland. Subsequent lords of Barnstaple have been Sir William Mertun, the Duke of Exeter, the Countess of Richmond (Henry VIII's grandmother), and Henry, the late Duke of Richmond and Somerset. Barnstaple has a mayor, and the burgesses trace the borough's privileges back to King Athelstan.

Pilton is separated from the north suburb and the priory only by a great stone causeway, with an arched bridge at each end. A London merchant named Stawford was responsible for making this bridge long ago, under the following circumstances. Once when he happened to be in Barnstaple buying cloth he watched a woman riding from Pilton across the low-lying salt marsh towards Barnstaple. But the influx of the tide was so great through a channel which connected the estuary to the marsh that she could not make it across. She cried out for help, but no-one would risk going out to her, and so she was drowned. In consequence Stawford gave the prior of Barnstaple a certain amount of money in order to begin a causeway, embanked on each side, and the bridges. Later he paid the balance.

A pleasant stream flows from the hills to the east of Barnstaple. It runs past the priory wall, and under the bridge at the town end of the causeway; immediately after this it turns a mill, and then flows into the estuary. River-barges and other small craft use a channel which leads up from the estuary to the other bridge on the causeway at the Pilton end. Pilton extends along one good street, and depends for its livelihood on clothmaking. Barnstaple Priory owned most of the place on the WNW side, and Cleeve Abbey most on the east side. King Athelstan gave a good estate in and around Pilton to Malmesbury Abbey, which also appropriated the living.

The bishop of Exeter has an old manor house called Tawton on the east bank of the estuary a mile above Barnstaple Bridge. Recently Bishop Vesey has reduced the size of the house but improved its appearance. At

Tawstock, on the west bank a mile above the bridge, the earl of Bath has an excellent estate and manor house; and another large manor, called Fremington, has recently been given by the king to the Earl of Hampton. It occupies the west bank of the estuary from Barnstaple Bridge as far as the point.

The River Taw, which rises on Exmoor, ESE of Barnstaple, does not seem to flow strongly along its tidal reach past the town. Even at the mouth of its estuary, five miles below Barnstaple, it is not particularly large. A little beyond the mouth is a bar. Along the west bank of the estuary is a beach, and three miles below Barnstaple at the ness or point is the confluence of the Rivers Taw and Torridge. They form a wide expanse of water, which flows into the Severn Sea [*Bristol Channel*].

Bideford Bridge crosses the Torridge four miles upstream from this ness. It is a remarkable structure, with 24 stone arches, and good masonry on each side. The arches, however, are not so high as those of Barnstaple Bridge. A poor priest, inspired, so it is said, by a vision, began this bridge. Then the whole neighbourhood set themselves to complete the task, and subsequently land has been given to provide for its upkeep. A fine chapel dedicated to our Lady stands right next to the far end of the bridge, and in the town there is a guild dedicated to preserving it; someone is always on duty to keep the bridge free from all dirt.

On the nearer [*east*] side of the bridge is a pleasant, busy street of smiths and ship-builders; but most of the town lies over the bridge, where there is a fine parish church. Bideford has no regular market on a fixed day of the week.

Two miles below Bideford on the further bank there is a good village called Appledore; from there it is about a mile to the mouth of the estuary. Mr Cophin lives three miles north-west of Bideford. From Bideford it is ten miles to Hartland, mostly over moorland which is nonetheless a very good breeding-ground for cattle. Hartland Point lies NNE three miles closer to the mouth of the Taw than Hartland. It is seven or eight miles from Barnstaple to Bideford Bridge.

From Barnstaple to the poor village of Newton Tracy is three miles over stony and hilly terrain with some enclosures. Three miles further in similar country brought me to Alscote [*Alverdiscott*], where Mr Bedlaw lives. I passed his house nearby on the left hand side, and continued to Torrington, two miles beyond.

Torrington is a large and important town, with three fine streets, and stands on the brow of a hill. It has a good weekly market, and its annual fair on St Michael's day is the best in the whole region. There is only one parish church, and Dr Chaumbre is the incumbent. Most of the inhabitants earn their living by clothmaking. The town has a mayor, and the privileges of a liberty.

The River Torridge flows at the foot of the hill on which Torrington stands, and here it is crossed by two stone bridges. The South Bridge has three stone arches, and a half-mile lower is the West Bridge, which is the larger. The road to Hartland, twelve miles away, crosses the West Bridge. A little upstream from the south bridge a fine castle stood on the brow of the hill overlooking the Torridge valley. Nothing now remains standing except a neglected chapel, but I discovered there that the castle and town once belonged to a certain Sir William of Torrington; they still pray for him and his son in the parish church. The king has recently granted the manor of Torrington to Fitzwilliam, earl of Southampton.

Little Torrington, the seat of a gentleman, a Mr Monk, lies on a hill beyond the River Torridge one mile SSW. Less than one mile east of Torrington there is a hamlet called St Giles in the Wood, which is dependent on the town. George Rolls has built here a very fine house of brick. Frithelstock Priory is also about one mile from Torrington.

The River Torridge rises on moorland three miles north-east of Hartland close to the principal source of the Tamar. At first it flows SSE for a few miles. The first important bridge over it is Kismeldon Bridge, and a half-mile lower is Putford Bridge. From there it is two miles to Woodford Bridge and a further two miles to Dipperford Bridge, which has three arches. Between this and the next bridge, which is Torrington South Bridge, the river changes direction from south to north-west. The West Bridge at Torrington is followed by Bideford Bridge four miles lower; two miles beyond this the Torridge and Taw meet, and flow through the mouth of the estuary into the Severn Sea.

My journey from Torrington took me over the South Bridge and through hilly and largely enclosed country with some woodland to Dipperford Bridge, a distance of eight miles. A further twelve miles across hills and treeless moorland brought me to Launceston. *cont. p. 35* [**1542:** 1/169-73]

THE CREEKS ALONG the east side of the Plym and Tamar estuary from its mouth are as follows: The Mill Bay. The Stone House Creek. Kaine Place Creek, which is two miles long and has a mill at its head. Mr Wise has a manor house beside this creek. Four miles upstream there is a creek which reaches up to the estate and manor house of Mr Budock, and to St Budeaux church. Also living beside this creek is Copston of Warley, whose estate is said to be worth more than £1,300 annually. The highest creek is that formed by the River Tavy flowing into the Tamar. On its east side, two miles from its mouth, is Buckland; and one mile from its mouth on the west side is Bere Ferrers, where Lord Broke had his house and park. Plymouth town is about three miles from the Saltash crossing, which is itself a half-mile wide. Between the crossing and Plymouth there is good arable ground, but little woodland.

Plymouth is a very large town, and is at present divided into four wards – Old Town Ward, Venarward, Low Ward, and Vintry Ward, which lies alongside the bay. Each ward has a captain, with three constables answerable to him. Until about the time of Henry II Plymouth was a meagre fishing community, but then it gradually increased. The oldest part of the town, which is now badly dilapidated and the least important of the four wards, lies away to the north and west.

Plymouth's right to its name and to mayoral privileges was granted by act of Parliament in the 16th year of Henry VI [1437/8]. Until then government was exercised by the prior of Plympton's courts in the town. The old name for Plymouth was Sutton, and it was divided into Valletort (which occupied the northern, and now least important, part, and which belonged to someone called Valletorte), Sutton Prior (the centre and heart of the town), and Sutton Ralf, which lay to the east, and contained both Carmelite and Franciscan friaries.

Plymouth has only one parish church, which is dedicated to St Uthu. It stands in Sutton Prior, and the living was appropriated by Plympton Priory. A rich merchant named Painter, who has recently died, built a fine house towards the estuary, and it was here that Dowager Princess Catharine stayed when she came from Spain. Another Plymouth merchant, Thomas Yogge, also built a fine house, of granite, on the estuary side of the town, and another good granite house on the north side of the parish churchyard. He also built a fine chapel on the north side of the church, and recently paid for the building of the church tower, although the town paid for the materials. There is also a hospital house on the north side of the church.

The church and much of the land on which has been built Sutton, now called Plymouth, belonged to one of the prebends of Plympton, called the prebend of St Peter and St Paul. Before the conquest Plympton had been a collegiate church, or royal free chapel. Everyone who, since the time of Henry II, has built houses at Sutton Prior, now the largest part of Plymouth, has done so by licence of Plympton Priory as overlord.

There is an excellent walk on a hill outside the town to the south, called the Hoe, where there is also a fine chapel of St Catherine. The entrance to the bay which harbours the ships of Plymouth has walls on each side, and a chain is suspended across when occasion demands. On the south-west side of the entrance is a blockhouse, and next to it on a rocky hill is a strong square castle with a large round tower at each corner. It does not appear to be very old. Vesey, the present bishop of Exeter, started to build part of a high, strong wall next to the castle wall. Piers Edgecumbe had an estate near Rame Head, and a fine house at the mouth of the Tamar estuary on the Cornish side.

Between Plymouth and the point where I crossed the Plym at ebb-tide is about three miles, through hilly but good enclosed land. The Plym rises six miles NNE of this point, and I reckoned that for about one mile above my crossing-place the river is tidal. The two noteworthy bridges over the Plym are Bickleigh Bridge and Plym Bridge. I noticed that the Plym estuary has only two creeks of note, one running inland from the western bank about a mile from the estuary mouth, and a larger one, called Schilleston, on the eastern bank about two miles from the mouth. Between this creek and the estuary mouth is a fine anchorage for large ships.

At ebb-tide it is possible to see the confluence of the Torey Brook and the Plym near my crossing-place. Having crossed, I left the Plym on my left hand side, and rode along beside the Torey Brook for about a half-mile. This brook is always stained red, from the sand which it flows over and which it carries with it from the tin workings. Then I came to Plympton St Mary, which is so-called because its church is dedicated to Our Lady.

Plympton was renowned for the priory of Augustinian canons which was established there and which attracted rich endowments of lands. Its origins were as follows: A bishop of Exeter, named William Warelwast, became displeased with the canons or prebendaries of a free chapel which had been founded by the Saxon kings, because they would not leave their concubines. He found a way of dissolving their college, which consisted of a dean or provost and four prebendaries with other ministers. One of these prebends was of Plympton itself, and another was called the prebend of St Peter and St Paul at Sutton (which is now Plymouth). To make up for the loss of revenue from the prebendaries at Plympton he built a college of similar size at Bosham in Sussex, and attached its income to the bishopric of Exeter for his successors. Then he established at Plympton a priory of regular canons, and was subsequently buried in the chapter house there. Some members of the Courtenay and other gentry families were also buried in Plympton Priory.

Several noblemen endowed the priory with land, including Walter de Valletorte. He owned Trematon in Cornwall, and some say (although it remains uncertain) that he also had Totnes. I do know that he owned good estates around Plymouth, and that he gave to Plympton Priory the island of St Nicholas, with its rabbit warren of some two acres or more, which lies at the mouths of the Rivers Tamar and Plym. I heard it said that, because one of the Valletortes committed a murder, their lands were confiscated by the king, who has retained the majority of them.

Plympton St Mary stands not on the River Plym, which is almost a half-mile away, but on the east bank of the Torey Brook. Consequently the lower-lying and earliest of the buildings in the priory precinct have become almost completely choked with sand, which is brought down by the brook from the tin workings. The priory church, which stood until recently, was substantially the work of Prior Martin, the third or fourth prior. A midsummer fair is kept at Plympton St Mary on St John's day.

Plympton St Thomas is a quarter-mile from Plympton St Mary. It is named after Thomas Becket, although the church there is now dedicated to St Maurice, knight and martyr. To one side of this place is a fine, large castle with a keep which is still standing, although its domestic quarters are in disrepair. Many of the gentry hold their lands through service to this castle. Baldwin Redvers, earl of Devonshire, owned the town and castle; a later owner was Isabella de Fortibus (the last of that line), and she gave the town privileges, including the pleasant market which is still held. More recently the Courtenay family, earls of Devonshire, have owned Plympton.

After Plympton St Thomas I came to Lee Mill Bridge. This is a three-arched stone bridge across the River Yealm, which flows from the NNE. Two miles downstream there is another bridge, Yealmbridge, which crosses the river one mile before it flows into the sea. This, I estimate, must be four miles south-east along the coast from the principal mouth of the Plym.

From Lee Mill Bridge it is three miles to Ivybridge. The river here is the Erme, which rises in the north-east, and flows noisily over great rocks. There are dangerous rocks too in the river mouth, where there is no shelter, and some say that Philip of Castile's navy was driven towards this estuary. There is another bridge, two miles below Ivybridge, at Ermington, and the distance from Ivybridge to Modbury is also two miles. The land between Plympton and Modbury is fertile for both corn and pasture, and there are some good woods.

The small town of Modbury has privileges, and various dependent hamlets. Opinions differ as to whether the Ruans or the Oxtons were its owners. The current owner, Campernulph, told me that Oxton was lord immediately before his family, but he contended that before the Oxtons it had been Campernulphs. The grandfather of the present Campernulph of Modbury married the only daughter and heir of Childerleigh, a Devonshire family from near Exeter, and through her received land with an annual value of £80. But there was an older branch of the family, Campernulph of Bere. The last of this line left as his heiress a daughter named Blanch, who first married Copestan of Devonshire, but later divorced him and married Lord Brooke. He was Henry VII's steward, and by this marriage he acquired land worth nearly £500 annually.

In Modbury there lives a man named Prideaux, who is a member of an ancient family which had fine estates. There is a Prideaux aisle in Modbury church. But one of his parents happened to kill a man, and a member of the Courtenay family, earls of Devonshire, acquired Columb St John and other Prideaux lands. Also in the parish is a gentry family named Hill, which came to prominence through a lawyer and judge who left to his heirs land worth £200 annually. Half of this was sold by the present Hill's grandfather. At Modbury too lives one of the Fortescues, and his father married the mother of Sir Philip Chaumburne, who is still alive.

There was an alien house of monks of the French order at Modbury, and the site of their premises may still be seen on the north side of the church. Little is known about the founder, whom I take to have been Ruan or Oxton. In the time of Edward IV this priory, and the living of Modbury appropriated to it, were given to Eton College.

From Modbury it is four or five miles to the ford by which I crossed the River Avon. This river flows past Estbrenton [South Brent], which is on the main road from Plymouth to Exeter, and a little downstream from it is a bridge. The ford which I used is six miles below South Brent, and two miles upstream from Gara Bridge. This river, the Avon, enters the sea at the mouth of the Erme.

A little beyond the ford I passed Mr Stour's house on a hillside, and after two miles I came to Rolster Bridge. This crosses a brook which is generally called Harbourne Water, but I discovered that it is written as 'Hurbertoun'. It derives from a spring two miles north-east above Rolster Bridge, and flows another two miles lower to Bow Bridge in the valley between Ashprington and Cornworthy. Just below Bow Bridge it forms one of two arms which flow into a salt-water creek, and this joins the main stream of the Dart estuary; the other arm turns towards Cornworthy. From Rolster Bridge it is two miles to Totnes. All the country from Modbury to Totnes has an abundance of good grass, corn and woodland.

The town of Totnes extends from the top of a high, rocky hill on its western side, eastwards to its foot. It was a walled town, and although the walls are entirely gone the site of their foundations is still visible. There are still three gates – West, East and [one other]. Totnes Castle stands on the hill north-west of the town. The castle wall and the strong keep are maintained, but the domestic buildings are utterly ruined. Many gentry estates are held by guard and service of this castle. For a long time the Lords Zouche owned town and castle, but since the attainder of Zouch they have been given to Edgecumbe.

The first to grant Totnes mayoral privileges was King John, and its liberties were augmented by Edward I. It has only one parish church, and this is in the centre of the town. It has a large tower, and the largest bells in the whole area. There was a Benedictine priory by the north-east side of this church, which had appropriated the living. There was also a hospital by the churchyard, and a lazar house in the southern part of the town which was endowed with some lands. Totnes is served with water by conduits, and there are three conduit houses in the town.

Totnes Bridge crosses the Dart by seven arches. A bowshot further downstream is Little Totnes, and here its owner, Lord Delabont, built a cell of Trinitarian friars. Bishop Oldham of Exeter suppressed this house and gave its lands to the vicars choral of Exeter Cathedral. Berry Pomeroy church lies almost one mile from the bridge, and its castle about a half-mile from the church, but the settlement itself is situated right by the east end of the bridge. A half-mile upstream, on the Totnes bank, is Dartington Park. There is a large manor house in the park which belonged to the duke of Exeter, and when St Leger married the duchess of Exeter he set up home here. Just below the park, on the same bank, a stream called Gulle [*Bidwell Brook*] flows into the Dart from the west.

Because of tin workings the River Dart brings down a great deal of sand to Totnes Bridge, which chokes the river all the way downstream, and is very harmful to the Dart estuary. The river flows from Dartmoor, and its source is reckoned to be fifteen miles above Totnes. Dartmoor covers a very large area, and its wild moors and forests are comparable with Exmoor.

From Totnes I went across hilly but fertile ground for two miles to Ashprington, and another mile of similar country to Cornworthy, where a priory of nuns has recently been suppressed. Harbourne Water flows in the valley between Ashprington and Cornworthy. The terrain is similar between Cornworthy and Dartmouth, four miles beyond. About a half-mile above Dartmouth there is a creek branching from the main stream of the estuary called Old Mill Creek.

Before I entered Dartmouth town I came to a small place called Hardnesse, which is inhabited mostly by fishermen and some merchants, and which has a chapel dedicated to St Clare . Here also are the substantial ruins of Hawley's Hall – he was an exceptionally rich merchant and a noble soldier. All that divides Hardnesse from Dartmouth is a tidal salt-water bay, which drives two tide-mills. There is a stone causeway with two flat bridges across this bay.

There are clear signs that at some time in the past there were many buildings between the present town of Dartmouth and Stoke Fleming; from which it must follow that, either Old Dartmouth lay in that direction, or else Stoke Fleming was larger than it is now. Dartmouth town extends lengthwise for about a quarter-mile along a very rocky hill beside the estuary, about a half-mile from the harbour entrance. The town boasts good merchants, and to its harbour belong good ships. The town has a conduit water supply, and a fine church; but the parish church, to which it is subordinate, lies at Townstal, a half-mile away on the hilltop. There is a theory that the parsonage house at Townstal is on the site of a house or cell of French monks. Torre Abbey appropriated the living of Townstal.

John Hawley, the rich merchant and noble fighter against the French, died in 1403 and is buried before the high altar in Dartmouth church with his two wives. Copestan, a man who now has extensive property in Devonshire, married the heiress of Hawley, and by this means greatly increased his estates. The Brien family, of whom Guy Brien achieved fame, were owners of Dartmouth.

King John gave Dartmouth mayoral privileges, and Edward III licensed the town to own property. Edward IV remitted £20 of its tax assessment, and Richard III and Henry VII a further £10 each [?]. A good fortification has recently been built in the town. There are two towers at the harbour mouth, with a chain to draw across it between them. One tower stands beside Sir George Carew's castle, known as Stoke Fleming, at the harbour mouth.

Dartmouth seafarers reckon that Plymouth harbour is about one kenning [*twenty miles*] from Dartmouth. Salcombe harbour, which lies about seven miles WSW of Dartmouth, suffers to some extent from a sandbar and a rock at its entrance. Salcombe itself is a fishing community which comes under the jurisdiction of Dartmouth, and lies about a half-mile within the harbour mouth. The eastern point of Salcombe harbour is a great foreland projecting into the sea called Start Point. Ilton Castle, a possession of Courtenay of Powderham, is about one mile above Salcombe on the same side of the harbour. And three miles further, at the head of the estuary, is Kingsbridge, which was once an attractive town.

Almost halfway between Dartmouth and Salcombe harbour, near the coast at Slapton, there is a pleasant college which was founded by Guy Brien. At Slapton is a very large lake two miles in length, which is separated from the sea merely by a sand bar. Fresh water drains through the sand bank into the sea, but sometimes the weight of fresh water and the rage of the sea break through it. There is good fishing in Slapton lake.

The estuary of the Erme lies beyond Salcombe harbour. Its mouth is strewn with rocks and shallows, so that it is only in desperation that ships seek refuge here from storms. Two of Philip of Castile's ships were wrecked in this estuary when a storm forced him to run to England for shelter. The River Erme flows into this estuary, and so, I have been told, does the River Avon. Further along the River Yealm flows into the Yealm estuary, and after that is Plymouth.

I crossed by ferry from Dartmouth to Kingswear opposite. It is a pleasant fishing community belonging to Sir George Carew, and it is built on a small point which juts out into the harbour. On the eastern side of Dartmouth harbour mouth I noticed the following: First there is a large and lofty point called Doune [*Froward Point*], which has a chapel on it. This point projects a half-mile further into the sea than its counterpart on the western side of the harbour. Less than a mile into the harbour from Downesend is a small point called Wereford, and between them a little bay. Another pleasant little bay separates Wereford from Kingswear, also on a small point. Not far above Kingswear a small creek runs inland from the main stream of the harbour. It is called Water Head, and is suitable for shipbuilding. Noss Creek, a half-mile above Water Head, is another, longer, creek running inland, and one mile further is a large creek called Galmpton, with Galmpton village at its head. This place is roughly equidistant between the Dart estuary and the sea around the coast in Torbay.

My way from Kingswear to Galmpton took me three miles over hilly ground, and nearly three miles further to Paignton. A pleasant stream flows down here and into the sea in Torbay beside a sandy shore. A mile beyond Paignton is Torbay village and Torre Abbey. The abbey has three fine gatehouses, and the inlet beside it has a breakwater and a harbour for fishing boats. The first William Brewer built the abbey on his own land, and bought Torre Mohun next to it to give to the abbey. Other donors were Peter son of Matthew, who is buried there, Dawney who gave it Northton, and a rich merchant who was also a great benefactor.

The westernmost point of Torbay is called Berry Head, and less than a mile from it within the bay is a pleasant fishing town called Brixham. It has a breakwater, and comes within Dartmouth's jurisdiction. Dartmouth men say that it is five miles between the mouth of the Dart and Torre, but I reckon that it is further than that even to Berry Head. It is my estimation that the sweep of Torbay is more than ten miles, and that Berry Head and Petit Tor Point are a great league, or four miles, apart.

From time to time fishermen in Torbay have caught in their nets deer antlers, and it is thought therefore that at some time in the past the bay was a forest. Almost halfway around the bay I noted one building set right up against the shore, which had a small pier forming a harbour for fishing boats. The eastern point of Torbay is called Petit Tor, but it does not appear to project so far out into the sea as Berry Head. Next to Petit Tor is a large rock called Isleston, which is like an island surrounded by the sea. There is also a far bigger rocky island called Ore Stone, which lies in the sea one mile south-east of Petit Tor. Another islet, called Black Rock, lies near the shore about one mile south-east of Petit Tor towards Teignmouth. The distance from Petit Tor to Teignmouth is scarcely five miles, and the shoreline curves to form a slight bay.

All the land between Torbay and Exmouth alongside the coast and especially further inland is well enclosed, with fertile arable and grassland, and some woods. This region, the most fertile in the whole of Devonshire, is known as the South Hams [*the South Hams in fact lie between Salcombe and Dartmouth*].

From Torre Abbey and village it is three miles to Haccombe. This manor formerly belonged to one of the Archdeacon family, and there are several fine tombs of this family in the church there. But then it passed with other estates to one of the Carews, and several members of this family also are buried in the church.

The very westernmost point of land at the mouth of the Teign is called the Ness, and is a very high red cliff. The eastern point is called the Poles. This is a low sandy piece of land which has been formed either from sand deposited by the Teign, or through the action of raging winds and waves. It covers a very large area between Teignmouth town, where the ground rises, and the Teign estuary.

There are two towns on this side of the estuary mouth. Both are called Teignmouth, and they abut one another. The more southerly is Teignmouth Regis, which has a market, a church dedicated to St Michael, and part of a wall with battlements facing the shore. This is regarded as the older of the two towns, and on its west side, on a part of the sandy area mentioned above which is called the Dene, there were until recent years a number of houses and a wine cellar. Inhabitants told me how their town was damaged by the Danes, and more recently by the French. The other town is called Teignmouth Episcopi, and has a church dedicated to St James. It lies a little to the north, further along the same bank of the estuary.

The Teign is tidal for five miles, almost up to Newton Bushel. A short distance above the mouth of the estuary on the western bank I noted quite a small creek called Stokeinteignhead, and another, callled Combeinteignhead, which is about a half-mile further on, and which penetrates a little further inland than the first.

Bridges on the Teign: The River Teign rises on Dartmoor at a place called Teign Head, twenty miles from Teignmouth. Chagford Bridge, four or five miles from Teign Head and a half-mile above the town, which has a market and two fairs. Clifford Bridge of stone, four miles lower. Bridford Bridge of stone, more than four miles lower. Chudleigh Bridge of stone, five miles lower. Teign Bridge, which is halfway between the market town of Newton Bushel and Kingsteignton, three miles lower. On my journey Newton Bushel was on the nearer side of the Teign, one mile away, whereas Kingsteignton was close to the Teign, on the further side. The River Lemon flows past Newton Bushel from five miles to the north-west, and joins the Teign one mile downstream. The River Aller rises about three miles south-west and joins the Teign in almost the same place and on the same bank as the Lemon.

From Teignmouth to Exmouth is about four miles, and from Exmouth to Exeter is seven miles.

Noteworthy places on the west bank of the Exe estuary: At the extreme western point of the estuary there is a huge expanse of firm and barren sand. A little above this sand on the western side a creek runs about a mile inland; it is sometimes called Kenton Creek. But Kenton itself is two miles further up the estuary and very close to the main channel. It is a very insignificant roadside settlement, but it has an excellent church, and the living belongs to Salisbury Cathedral. Powderham was Sir William Courtenay's castle. It is strongly-built, and stands beside the estuary a little above Kenton, with a barbican or bulwark as sea defence. Some people say that the castle was built by a widowed lady, and I think that it was Isabella de Fortibus. After Kenton I travelled two miles to a village, where I saw a nice lake on my left hand side, with a stream flowing from it. Then I came to Exminster, which is a pleasant little town. There is a ruined manor house here with a battlemented front, which I believe was owned by the marquis of Exeter.

Noteworthy places on the east bank: Exmouth is a small fishing community just inside the mouth of the estuary. Four miles further up beside the shore is Topsham, a pleasant little place. This is the trading port and anchorage for ships which frequent the estuary, and especially for

Exeter's ships and merchandise. The Exeter men are making great efforts to bring the estuary right up to the city, but at present it is navigable for ships only as far as Topsham.

The town of Exeter is more than a mile in circumference, and has extremely strong walls in good repair. Between the south and west gates are several fine towers in the wall. But when the walls have been renewed, the old towers have fallen into decay. Exeter Castle occupies an imposing, lofty site between the east and north gates. The town has four gates, named east, west, north and south. The east and west gates are built in similar style and are now the best; the south gate used to be the strongest. There are several fine streets in Exeter, but the High Street, which extends from the west to the east gate, is the finest. In it are the castle, the water channel and the guildhall.

There are fifteen parish churches in the town. The cathedral church is dedicated to St Peter and St Paul, and its yard, which has four gates, is surrounded by many fine houses. The college house, in which the chantry priests live, was built recently by John Rese, Dean of St Buryans. There is a vicars' college. The charnel chapel in the cathedral yard was built by a treasurer of Exeter Cathedral by the name of John. There is also a parish church in the cathedral yard. On the north side of the town there was a priory of St Nicholas, which was a cell of Battle Abbey. And beside the east gate there is a hospital of St John, which was built and endowed with lands by Bishop John Grandisson of Exeter. Another poor hospital in the town still cares for sick men.

A Franciscan friary lay between the north and west gates near the town wall, but this is now an empty plot called Friernhay. The friary was removed by Bishop Bytten of Exeter, who built the Franciscans a house just outside the south gate. A house of Dominican friars lay on the north side of the cathedral yard, but outside the close. Lord Russell has turned this into a fine house for himself. Two fragments may be seen of Roman inscriptions which by chance happen to have been reused when the town wall to the rear of the former Dominican friary was being renewed. One is built into a tower on the wall, and the other is in the wall next to the tower.

The suburb which lies outside the east gate of Exeter is the largest of all its suburbs. It is called St Sidwell's, because she is buried there, and a church there is dedicated to her. Outside the north gate the suburb is called St David Down. St Thomas's suburb lies outside the west gate, and boasts a large stone bridge of fourteen arches across the River Exe. The suburb outside the south gate is given the name of St Magdalen.

Bridges on the Exe: Exeter Bridge of fourteen arches. Cowley Bridge more than a mile upstream; it has twelve arches beneath the channel and causeway. Thorverton Bridge, about four miles further upstream, and Tiverton Bridge another five miles. The town of Tiverton is on the east bank of the River Exe.

From the time of its first bishop, Leofric, Exeter Cathedral remained unaltered until the present cathedral was begun by Bishop Peter the first [Quinil, 1280-91]. He levied a subsidy on the clergy of his diocese to pay for its commencement. John Grandisson, bishop of Exeter, extended the west end of the church by making seven arches instead of the five of the previous design. He also made the vault of the cathedral nave.

At Ottery St Mary he made the church collegiate, and granted it lands and tithes there which some people believe had previously belonged to a cell of French monks in Ottery, or to some religious house in France with property there. In Exeter Grandisson renovated St John's hospital, an old foundation, and converted it to a house of Crutched friars. And he turned an old almshouse for twelve poor men and twelve women (who had been given the name 'Calendar Brethren') into lodgings for the vicars choral of Exeter Cathedral. The building work of this college was completed by Bishop Brentingham. Bishop Hugh Oldham obtained and granted to it the revenues of a small cell of Trinitarian friars at Totnes to pay for its provisioning. John Grandisson compiled the lessons which are now read at divine service in the diocese of Exeter.

Bishop Stapleton of Exeter built the presbytery vault of the cathedral, as well as the richly-carved stone pulpitum for the high altar, and the precious silver table at its centre. Some people attribute the silver table to Bishop Lacy, but this is unlikely. I was told that Bishop Neville built the chapter house in its present form, but I have since learnt that it was begun by Edmund Lacy and completed by Neville.

From Exeter to Cowley Bridge is about a mile. A stream leaves the Exe a little above the bridge on the nearer bank (as I approached it); it turns several mills and then rejoins the river above Exeter. From Cowley Bridge it is two-and-a-half miles to Newton St Cyres Bridge, which spans the River Creedy by four arches. The village or small town of Newton itself is a half-mile further, and two miles short of Crediton. The country between Exeter and Crediton produces exceptionally fine corn, grass and woods.

Crediton has a pleasant market. The town depends on the cloth trade, to which most of its inhabitants owe their livelihood. The site of the former cathedral church at Crediton is now occupied by houses next to the new churchyard. The old church was dedicated to St Gregory, but the present church shows no sign of ancient work. In its north transept are buried Sir John Scylley and his wife, who once lived in the parish. The bishop of Exeter has a manor house or palace next to the churchyard, with a park attached to it. There are twelve good prebends in Crediton, as well as certain bursars, ministers and choristers. The parish priest is called the dean, but he does not hold a prebend as a matter of course.

Crediton stands on the west bank of the River Creedy. The river rises some two miles above Crediton to the north-west. Three and a half miles below the town it flows under the four-arched Newton Bridge, and about two-and-a-half miles lower under a stone bridge of two arches. Then it flows directly south for barely half a mile to join the River Exe a little above Cowley Bridge.

From Exeter to Clyst Bridge is three miles. A pleasant stream runs under this stone-arched bridge, and about a half-mile lower it flows past the bishop of Exeter's fine manor house of Clyst. Five miles further on I forded a small river called the Tale. This is a tributary of the River Otter, which it joins a mile-and-a-half lower above Ottery St Mary. Beside the ford is a stone bridge. After the ford I rode about two miles to Fenny Bridges, where the River Otter has been divided deliberately into four courses, in order to serve grist and fulling mills. Over three of these streams I rode on good stone bridges, but the first, which was the smallest, had no bridge so far as I could see. On the north side of the first bridge was a chapel no longer consecrated. Honiton is two miles from Fenny Bridges, and lies on the east bank of the River Otter. It is a fine, long, roadside and market town, which belongs to Courtenay of Powderham. It is on the main road to London just twelve miles east of Exeter. A little beyond Honiton I left the London road on my right hand and rode north-east for three miles to Mohun's Ottery.

The origin and course of the River Otter: The Otter rises five miles due directly north of Mohun's Ottery near a house called Otterford. It flows four miles to a village called Upottery, and another mile to Mohun's

Ottery, which was once called Ottery Fleming. Sir George Carew, who owns a fine park at Mohun's Ottery, told me that this had not been part of the estate of the Mohun who was earl of Somerset, but of a baronial family of the same name. The arms of Mohun, earl of Somerset, were 'or, a cross engrailed sable [*an indented black cross on a gold field*]', whereas the Devonshire Mohuns used a maunch [*a lady's sleeve*] on a powdered field. Much of the estate of the Devonshire Mohuns was inherited by marriage to an heiress of the Flemings, who owned Dartmouth Castle and the manor of Stoke Fleming. Alan Fleming was a famous member of that family. Carew married an heiress of the Devonshire Mohun family. The real name of the family was Montgomery, and in an old deed it is written as Montgomery, Lord of Carew. Sir Nicholas Carew was a member of this family. The original arms of the Carews are three black lions on a gold field. I recall that in Dartmouth Castle there was and is a chapel dedicated to St Patrick, which has the appearance of having been in the past a small cell dependent on some great abbey.

From Mohun's Ottery the River Otter flows three miles to Honiton, two miles further to Fenny Bridges, and from there to Ottery St Mary. Then it is about a mile to Newton Poppleford Bridge, and five more miles to Ottermouth and the sea. Otterton is a pleasant fishing community which stands on the east side of the estuary about a mile from Ottermouth. Almost opposite Otterton, on the west side of the estuary but further from the shore, is East Budleigh. Within the last hundred years ships have used this estuary, but now it is completely blocked by a sand bar. The estuary is sometimes called Budleigh Haven on account of East Budleigh. The mouth of the Otter lies to the south-west. Below Otterton, at the extreme ESE point of Ottermouth, there is a fishing village callled Salterton. This was a considerable place in the past, and the Otter estuary was named after it Saltern Haven, although this name possibly only referred to a creek branching off the main estuary.

From Mohun's Ottery to Colyton is about five miles, across good arable and pasture with some woodland. About a mile before I reached Colyton I could see from a hill the lord marquis of Dorset's excellent manor house on the hillside at Shute, with a fine, large park beside it. Colyton itself is not a very remarkable town. Its vicar, who has a good house there, is the bishop of Exeter's chancellor. The town stands on a hill, at the foot of which flows the River Coly.

This brook rises, so far as I could gather, WNW of Colyton. I noted that it flows past Colcombe Park, which is close to Colyton, and a former property of the marquis of Exeter; it runs on for a mile or more before joining the River Axe between Axe Bridge and Axmouth. It is scarcely two miles from Colyton to Seaton, and before I arrived I crossed the River Coly again, at Colyford.

Seaton used to have a very important estuary, but now a massive ridge and bar of pebbles lies between the two points of the former estuary at its very mouth. And the River Axe is forced to the easternmost point, which is called White Cliff, where it enters the sea by a very small channel, which is right at the foot of the cliff. Small fishing boats put in here for shelter. Seaton itself is now a very inconsiderable place inhabited by fishermen, although it used to be much larger when the estuary was good. The abbot of Sherborne owned the town and the living.

To the west, over a hill beyond Seaton, is Wiscombe, a fine manor house which used to belong to Lord Bonville and now to the marquis of Dorset. Seaton had, and still has, a dependent chapel at Beer, close to the sea, where there is a hamlet of fishermen. A good breakwater for the protection of small ships had been begun at Beer, but three years ago a storm, such as had never in living memory occurred along this coast, dashed this breakwater to pieces. Recently the men of Seaton began to build up a strong wall inside the estuary, with the intention of diverting the course of the Axe into a channel cut through the bar almost in the centre of the old estuary, and so letting out the river and letting in the open sea. But their plans came to nothing. I should have thought that the forces of nature would have broken through the bar close to Seaton itself, and let the sea in at that point.

Beer, the westernmost point of the Axe estuary, is barely a half-mile from Seaton. It is almost a mile from Beer to the eastern point, White Cliff. Sidmouth is six miles further west from Seaton; it is a fishing town, with a river and bay of the same name. I left Seaton at low tide by crossing the salt marshes and the River Axe, and came to Axmouth, an old and large fishing community on the east side of the estuary. Syon Abbey was its patron, although I discovered here that Monteburgh Abbey in Normandy has written evidence that there were cells dependent on it at Axmouth, Sidmouth and Otterton.

The descent and course of the River Axe from its source: The Axe rises one mile east of Beaminster, a market town in Dorset, at a place called Axe

Knoll, which is a marshy area on the side of a hill, and the property of Sir Giles Strangeways. It flows four miles south-west to Forde Abbey, which stands on the further bank, in Devonshire. In this area the river defines the boundary between Devonshire and Somerset.

The Axe then flows three miles to Axminster, a pleasant, lively market town on the nearer bank, and in Devonshire. I discovered that the living of Axminster belongs to York Minster. The church is famous for having the tombs of many Danish noblemen and some Saxon lords who were killed in a battle on Brunsdown [?*Rousdon*] nearby during the time of Athelstan. The Axe then flows under Axminster Bridge, which is of stone and lies about a quarter-mile downstream from the town.

Somewhat below this bridge the Axe is joined by the River Yarty, which at times is a raging torrent. It rises in the north-west but enters the east bank of the Axe. About a half-mile before the confluence the Yarty is crossed by a stone bridge, which is sometimes called Kilmington Bridge, after a nearby village.

About a half-mile below Axminster Bridge, on the nearer (eastern) bank but in Devonshire, is Newenham, formerly a Benedictine abbey, which was founded by Mohun, Earl of Somerset. Axe Bridge, of two stone arches, is a mile and a half downstream; it is impassable at high tide. From here the Axe flows a half-mile to Axmouth, and a quarter-mile further, right at the foot of White Cliff, it enters the open sea, which is here called Axe Bay. *cont. p. 97* [**1542:** 1/212-44]

There is a sand bar across the mouth of the Taw estuary, making entry into it dangerous. From the extreme tip of the estuary mouth in a straight line to Hartland Point is six or seven miles. Hartland Priory is three miles above Hartland Point, and less than a mile from the sea. But between the mouth of the Taw and Hartland Point is a very rounded bay, and almost halfway around it is a house called Clovelly, home of the Carys. From here is the shortest passage to Lundy Island.

Distances in north Devon: Dipperford is seven or eight miles overland from Torrington; Bideford is three or four miles below Torrington; Dipperford is nine miles from Hartland; Bideford is ten miles from Hartland; Torrington is twelve miles from Hartland; Lydford is eighteen miles from Torrington.

[*South*] Molton is a good market town seven miles east of Barnstaple. The earl of Bath has a fine manor house called Bampton, near Tiverton. [1/298-301]

Hemyock Castle lies three miles from Dunkeswell. It belonged to the Brewer family, but has been demolished apart from two or three towers. [4/74]

When I wrote that the castle and village of Stoke Fleming stood at Dartmouth I made two mistakes. First, the castle is called Dartmouth, not Stoke Fleming, Castle in an old document, even though the Flemings built and owned it long before it came into the hands of the Carew family. Second, Stoke Fleming is an attractive and old little town near the coast about a mile-and-a-half west of Dartmouth. Several members of the Fleming family are buried there. In Dartmouth Castle there is a chapel dedicated to St Patrick, and some old documents suggest that it was a monastic cell. I still hear people arguing that it was called Stoke Castle. [5/230]

DORSET

The West Country tour of 1542 saw Leland visiting Sherborne on the outward journey, and crossing Dorset from Lyme Regis to Cranborne on his return. In doing so he has left us interesting descriptions of Sherborne, Portland and Wimborne, and an especially perceptive account of Poole. But Dorchester, the county town, he neglected, and about Wareham he made few comments – he had apparently visited and written about the town previously, but his description has not survived.

He returned to Dorset when visiting the Bristol area in 1544, and two short passages of itinerary describe his wanderings in the Blackmore Vale area, around Stalbridge, Sturminster Newton and Shaftesbury. The narrative of this journey ends suddenly in Gillingham Forest.

Preliminary drafts, or collections of notes, have survived for parts of his 1542 journey, and a few passages omitted from the fuller version are printed here among the notes which follow the Dorset itineraries. A stray passage in which Leland transcribed documents about Blackmore and Gillingham Forests, and made comments on lists of Dorset landowners [4/106-9] has here, for the most part, been omitted. His remark about daggers made at Bridport is a misunderstanding – the town was famed for rope-making, so that to be killed by a Bridport dagger was a euphemism for being hanged.

The town of Sherborne stands partly on the brow of a hill, and partly in a valley. I reckon that it cannot be much less than two miles in circumference. It depends to some extent on clothmaking, but more important are all kinds of crafts. It is my opinion that, apart from Poole, which is only a small place, Sherborne is at present the best town in Dorset, despite being inland [?]. For a long time it was the seat of the bishops of Salisbury, and afterwards a college of monks was established there.

Until a hundred years ago the nave of the abbey church, dedicated to Our Lady, served as the principal parish church of the town. But this arrangement came to an end because of the following circumstance. A dispute arose between the monks and the townspeople because the town presumed to celebrate the sacrament of baptism in All Hallows Chapel.

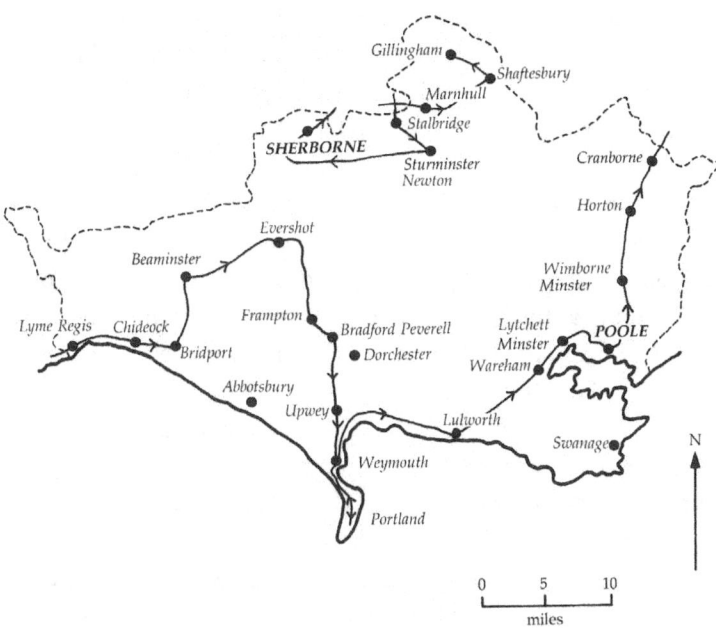

As a result a headstrong butcher who lived in Sherborne, named Walter Gallor, completely destroyed the font-stone. The dispute escalated to a full-scale riot, with the townspeople supported by the retinue of an Earl of Huntingdon, then staying nearby, and the monks supported by the bishop of Salisbury. A priest of All Hallows Chapel shot a burning arrow into the top of the partition which divided the eastern part of St Mary's church (used by the monks) from the townspeople's part. At the time this partition was thatched, and caught fire, with the result that the lead and bells melted, and the whole church was destroyed. Abbot Bradford of Sherborne demanded compensation for this injury, and the townspeople were forced to contribute to the church's rebuilding. But from then on All Hallows, and not St Mary's, was used as the parish church.

All the eastern part of St Mary's was rebuilt during Abbot Bradford's time, apart from the Lady Chapel. This was an old piece of work not affected by the fire, because it was part of an older building. In ancient times two kings, sons of King Ethelwulf of Wessex, were buried in a place behind the high altar of St Mary's, but now there are no tombs, and no legible inscription referring to them. Philip Fitzpayne, a nobleman, was buried with his wife under an arch on the north side of the presbytery, but their tomb has recently been destroyed. All the western part of St Mary's church was built from its foundations by Peter Ramsam, the next abbot but one after Bradford. The porch on the south side of St Mary's nave is an ancient piece of building which was not destroyed in the fire, because it had a much lower roof line than the nave. The abbey cloister, on the north side of the church, was built by a certain Abbot Frithe, who was abbot not long before Bradford's time. The penultimate abbot, whose name was Mere, built the fine castle-like structure over the conduit in the cloister, and its spouts. The water supply is drawn from a place in the town called New Well. The chapter house is ancient, and on its vault are painted the portraits of bishops of the see of Sherborne. A nobleman called St John is buried in the chapter house. Abbot Ramsam built a chapel against the south side of the old Lady Chapel which was dedicated to Our Lady of Bow. At the ESE end of St Mary's church there is the archway of an old gate; this is evidence that the close of the canons or monks once had a wall around it.

There used to be a parish church dedicated to St Emerentiana. It stood on the north side of the town, but has completely fallen down, and its site is marked by an enclosed plot. There was a chapel dedicated to St Michael in the town, and a hermitage of St John by the mill; both are now demolished. A chapel of Thomas Becket survives on Sherborne Green, although it is no longer consecrated, and a hospital supposed to have been founded by the king also remains; it originated as an act of devotion by good people in Sherborne in the fourth year of Henry VI's reign [1425/6]. There is also a chapel in St Mary's churchyard, which was built recently by a canon of Salisbury named Dogget.

The bishop of Salisbury owns the town of Sherborne. It stands on the north side of an adjacent brook. At the east end of the town, on a small rocky hill, stands Sherborne Castle. It has marshy ground on two sides of it – WNW and ESE. It was built by Roger Poore, who was bishop of Salisbury in the time of Henry I. He dug a large ditch around it, and built a false wall outside the ditch. There are four large towers in the castle wall, including the one which is the gatehouse. Each is three storeys high. The main domestic building, which is very strong and fully vaulted, lies in the middle of the castle courtyard. There are few buildings in England as old as this that survive so completely and solidly. Since it was first erected the only addition of note has been at the west end of the hall, where a stone accommodation block was recently built by a certain Bishop Langton.

Outside the castle on the east side there is a chapel in a small precinct; and at the end of the castle is a lake which is now choked with weeds and rushes, but was formerly very much larger. The lake is fed by a stream which rises two miles or more due east on a hillside at a place generally called Horethorne. Its source is five springs called the Seven Sisters, which shortly flow together into one valley and form the stream. After the lake this stream flows in a narrow valley to the mills at Sherborne, and near the lower mill it is joined by another stream of similar stature, which enters it on its south bank. This second stream rises three miles directly east of the confluence at a place called Purse Caundle, and flows west in a valley. Between the two streams is a park. After Sherborne the stream flows three miles or more to Clifton [*Maybank*], Mr Horsey's residence, and a little lower joins the River Ivel. A little further up the Ivel from this confluence, and on the same bank, another stream joins it. This is the West Coker stream, which rises three miles to the west. *cont. p. 332* [**1542:** 1/152-5]

FOUR MILES of fairly good ground but not much woodland separate Axmouth from Lyme. Lyme is a pleasant market town set at the foot of a high rocky hill which descends to the foreshore. It has good ships, and depends on fishing and trade. Merchants from Morlais in Brittany frequent the town. A shallow stream comes from the hills about three miles to the north, flowing rapidly over large stones and under a stone bridge in its valley. Townspeople generally call this stream the Buddel. Within living memory a merchant named Burrow built a fine house at Lyme, with an excellent tower at its entrance. There is only one parish church in the town, and no harbour; but a quarter mile to the WSW is a large [*breakwater – the Cobb*] in the sea to shelter ships. Lyme is five miles from Colyton.

It is a long mile from Colyton [*i.e. Lyme*] to Charmouth, past fairly good land. Approaching Charmouth, which is a good fishing community, I crossed a small stream, and at the far end of the place I crossed the River Char, from which it takes its name. This river rises three miles to the north in a royal park called Marshwood, and flows into the sea a little below Charmouth. Three more miles across moderately good land brought me from Charmouth to Chideock. This fishing village lies a mile inland and belongs to Arundell of Lanherne in Cornwall, who has a manor house and park here. At the far end of Chideock I crossed a brook which flows from there into the sea, and came another two miles to Bridport, past arable, pasture and woodland. A river flows past the west end of this town, and enters the sea a mile downstream. The natural position of this river mouth in a valley between two hills is such that, if money were spent on the project, the sea might be led into it to make a harbour.

Bridport (sometimes written Bruteport) is a fine, large town, and its principal street runs from west to east. A second fine street crosses it in the middle and runs to the south. At its northern end is St Andrew's chapel, which according to some lies on the site of the former parish church. The present parish church stands at the southern end of this street, and in it I saw a tombstone on the north side of the high altar with the following Latin inscription: 'Here lies William, son of Elizabeth de Julers, Countess of Kent, whose sister was Philippa, once queen of England.' Before I crossed the river to enter Bridport I could see a lazar house; and nearby was a chapel of St Magdalene in which a chantry was established. And just across the bridge in the western part of the town is St John's chapel. There is also a chapel in the town dedicated to St Michael. Bridport belongs to the king, and holds the privilege of a market and two bailiffs. It is about five miles from the town along a somewhat curving shoreline to the north-western end of Chesil Bank, which runs to Portland.

The course of the river which flows to Bridport: This river rises little more than a half-mile above Beaminster to the north, and descends while still a small stream to the east end of Beaminster, where it flows under a little stone bridge with two attractive arches. Beaminster is a pleasant Dorset market town, and depends largely on agriculture. It consists of one street running north–south, and another running east–west. It is a prebend of Salisbury Cathedral, and has a chapel-of-ease within the town, although the parish church is at Netherbury. Crewkerne, a Somerset market town, is only four miles north of Beaminster, and Sherborne is six miles to the east. Hooke Park, containing an ancient manor house, is only a mile-and-a-half due ESE. A mile downstream from Beaminster the river flows past Netherbury, which is a remote place set on a hill. It has three prebends belonging to Salisbury Cathedral – the first is usually called Netherbury in the churches (it belongs to Anthony Chalcedon), the second is Netherbury in the lands, and there is also a third. The river leaves Netherbury on its west bank and flows three more miles to Bridport Bridge. A mile further to the south it enters the sea.

From Bridport I rode the three miles to Netherbury, and then another mile to Beaminster. The soil is exceptionally good all the way, and this stretch of country is almost the best in the whole of Dorset for arable, pasture and wood. My ride from Beaminster took me after one mile to the top of a high hill, and I passed on my left hand Axnoller to the north, the source of the River Axe which flows to Axmouth. After a further mile of corn, pasture and wood, I came across three miles of largely waste, which was nevertheless good pasture for breeding cattle, and arrived at Evershot, a very unpretentious and poor market town. Then it was another mile of very good ground to Melbury.

Mr Strangeways has recently carried out much building work at Melbury using stone blocks, and has raised the inner part of the house with a tall, new tower. The church adjacent to the manor house contains the tombs of two members of the Browning family, former owners of Melbury; but although their tombs and epitaphs are in the church, I was told there of a rumour that the body of one was actually buried at Milton Abbey, and the other at Cerne. The Strangeways acquired the manor of Melbury by purchase. Next to the manor house is a fine park with a pond, out of which a small stream flows and after a very few miles joins the River Ivel.

My journey from Melbury took me uphill for about a mile, past fertile and quite well-wooded land, and then six miles along a high ridge across open country. From this ridge I could see little arable and no woodland, but everywhere were large flocks of sheep, which are of great benefit to the soil locally. Before I rode down from the end of the ridge I noticed two streams flowing into the River Fraw or Frome. One, which was no more than two miles long from its source to the confluence, was called the Sidling or Silling, and it joined the Frome on the right hand side near Bradford Peverill. The other was on the left hand side, and flowed into the Frome from Compton Valence. From the ridge I rode a mile down the hill to Frampton, which is a pleasant farming village with a three-arched bridge at one end across the River Frome.

The course of the River Fraw or Frome from its source: It has been alleged that the ultimate source of the Frome is at a place called Kenford about two miles above Hooke Park, but most people are of the opinion that it rises in a large pond in Hooke Park itself. From there it flows in due course to Frampton, which lies on the south-west side of the river, and two miles further to Bradford [*Peverell*], on the same bank. Dorchester is another two miles downstream, and a little below Dorchester is a stone bridge at Fordington; then Woodsford Castle, two miles lower on the left bank and left hand side going down. Wool Bridge is five miles further, and a little below this is Bindon, which is on the right bank and right hand side going downstream. Holme is barely three miles further, and also on the right bank; and about a quarter-mile beyond Holme is Holmebridge, of four arches. The six-arched bridge at Wareham is two miles lower.

I crossed Frampton Bridge and rode four miles entirely over hilly ground with no woodland but exceptionally good for sheep, until I came to Upwey. Here, on my right hand side as I rode, is the true source of the River Wey, sometimes called the Wile. At Upwey I joined the road from Dorchester to Weymouth, which is a good three miles distant, and rode along it across flat, low-lying country. Dorchester and Weymouth are eight miles apart.

There is a small town with mayoral privileges called Melcombe on the nearer side of Weymouth harbour. There are evident signs that this town was formerly much larger than it is now, and this is attributed to the French, who during times of war took advantage of its lack of defences and razed it. All the houses which remain in the town are well and strongly built of stone. Melcombe has a chapel-of-ease; its parish church is a mile away, which is a clear indication that the town is not very old. The eastern part had a good friary, which was established and supported by the principal branch of the Rogers family in Dorset. Just above the town the harbour opens out to form a bay; this and the gulf created by the open sea on the other side make the site of the town a peninsula.

Weymouth is a small town lying directly opposite Melcombe on the other side of the harbour. The width of the channel here is only small, and the crossing is by a ferry boat without oars and a rope fastened across the harbour. Although Weymouth has certain liberties and privileges, there is no mayor, and the parish church is a mile away. It has a chapel-of-ease on a nearby hill, and there is a quay and wharf for ships. The River Wey or Wile rises less than four miles above Weymouth, at Upwey to the north-west on the side of a great hill. It is tidal for about two miles above Weymouth, and there is a small sand bar at the harbour mouth. A great arm of the sea flows up to the right of the harbour, and barely a mile along its shore from the harbour mouth has been built an excellent castle equipped for war, with one open barbican. This arm of the sea continues for another mile like a bay, up to a headland where there is a crossing over to Portland by a long causeway of pebbles and sand. From the narrow part of this crossing the arm of the sea continues to be quite wide, and extends about seven miles to Abbotsbury, where a small stream of fresh water flows into the sea.

The furthermost point of Chesil Beach lies a little beyond Abbotsbury to the north-west. From there it extends in a straight line as a strong but narrow bank seven miles to the south-east, until it abuts Portland, scarcely a quarter-mile beyond the new Portland Castle. The nature of Chesil Beach is such that whenever there is a strong south-easterly wind blowing the sea breaks against the bank, loosening it and soaking through it. If the wind were continually in this direction the bank would soon be broken up, and the sea would invade completely, cutting off Portland and turning it into an island – which I can only assume it must have been in the past. But to the same extent as the south-east wind batters and breaks Chesil Beach, so the north-westerly comes to its rescue by strengthening and building it up again.

At the far end of the Portland crossing as you come from Weymouth there is a point of land like a causeway, which is entirely composed of pebbles and sand thrown up by the sea during storms. Barely a mile along this I came right to the foot of the high ground of Portland, and here an extremely strong and magnificent castle has recently been built. It is only a short distance from this castle to the south-eastern point of Chesil Beach, and a gulf is formed between them by the arm of the sea which runs up to Abbotsbury.

Portland. It is very likely that in ancient times Portland was surrounded by the sea, and even now it is called an island. It has hilly ground protruding along its coastline, and a large flat area in the centre. Its circumference is reckoned to be about seven miles, but if one were to go round it along the shoreline at the foot of the cliffs, the distance would rise to ten miles. The soil is rather stony, and there are many rocks along the coast; it produces good corn and grass, and has abundant sheep. At the present time there are about eighty houses on the island, although ruins suggest that there were once nearly twice as many. There is only one street of houses; the remainder are scattered. Near this street is a small castle or tower built on a high rock a little above the east end of the church and next to the sea cliffs. The only parish church which now exists on the island is long and rather low; it stands by the shore at the foot of a steep hill. The shortest route from this church to the new royal castle is about a mile and a half, but going round by the coast the distance is three miles or more. I could not verify a rumour that there had once been another parish church on the island.

Apart from the elms around the church there are very few trees on the island, or none at all. If trees were planted there more would grow, although it is very exposed. The inhabitants fetch their wood from the Isle of Wight and elsewhere. They also burn cow-dung which they dry by the heat of the sun. The fishing industry has declined somewhat, and most of the inhabitants depend now on agriculture. They are good at slinging stones, which is their method of defending the island. When it comes to selling their produce they are quite shrewd, not to say greedy. The best building on the island is the parsonage house, which stands in the high street. The bishop of Winchester is patron of the living, but the island belongs to the king.

The ESE point of Weymouth harbour is a little foreland called St Aldhelm's Point, and from here I rode beside a small bay, scarcely two miles wide. Seven miles further on I saw on the coast a little fishing community called Lulworth. It used to belong to the Newboroughs but is now Poyninge's property, and it has a channel or creek running inland from the sea, in which small ships take shelter. West Lulworth is on the west side of this creek, but East Lulworth is more than a mile away, and inland. The soil between Weymouth and Lulworth is not very fertile; it is better for cattle than for corn, and there is not much woodland. However around East Lulworth the land is quite good, and there are abundant woods.

The fine manor house of the Newborough family, lords of East Lulworth, is next to the parish church, but their tombs were at Bindon Abbey, which they founded. The last to bear the family name died in Essex or Suffolk and was buried there, although the tomb which was erected for his burial still survives in East Lulworth church. His daughter inherited, and she married Sir Henry Marney. In the glass windows of the parlour at East Lulworth manor house is set out the Newborough genealogy, together with the names of those who inherited by marriage into the family.

The land of Purbeck Forest begins at the further boundary of East

Lulworth. (I must find out whether the name Purbeck is not a corruption of 'Corbek'.) My journey of two miles to Holme, a monastic cell of Montacute, and a little further to Holmebridge, took me for the most part across low-lying black and marshy country, overgrown with heather and moss. The land is much the same as far as Wareham, except that around the town itself it is more fertile. Wareham's orientation now is north to south, and there is a fine six-arched bridge at the south end across the River Fraw or Frome. Wareham's walls have fallen down, and land within them has been converted to gardens for growing garlic. I have described Wareham in another of my itineraries.

Two furlongs north of Wareham is a large six-arched bridge across the River Trent (or Pyddildour [*Piddle*]). Five miles of rather low-lying and marshy terrain, like that in Purbeck Forest, separate Wareham from Lytchett Minster. Before I reached Lytchett I encountered a small channel like those in fenland country; it extends from Poole Harbour to Lytchett. From here I rode around to Poole, a distance of three miles; but there is another route from Lytchett to Poole which uses the ferry opposite the town and is only two miles.

Poole is not an old-established trading town; in fact it used to be a poor fishing village, and a hamlet or dependent chapelry of the parish church. But within living memory much good building has taken place, and trade has greatly increased. Its position in Poole Harbour is almost that of an island, but it is connected to the mainland, which is almost a bowshot away, on its north-east side. At this point there is a fortified stone gate giving access to the town, and a channel through which water often flows out of the harbour. The town is orientated almost directly north–south, and it has a quay for ships, with a fine town hall beside it, on the south-east. At one end of the quay Richard III began to build part of a town wall, and promised the town great things. Poole has a fine church.

The only explanation I can find is that in the past ships sailed up the harbour quite close to Wareham, and disposed of their goods there, but that more recently the water has been too shallow for them to anchor there. Consequently they stayed and berthed closer to Poole, enhancing that town a little, but leaving Wareham to fall completely into ruins. It should be said, however, that Wareham had been badly damaged once before, during the Danish wars.

Opposite Poole quay there is a causeway shaped like a broad sword, with its sharp point facing the town, and its broad part joined to the land. This causeway is used by people coming from Lytchett Minster to the ferry. On both sides of this point or causeway there are bays formed by the water of Poole Harbour. If one were to travel right around the shoreline within the harbour mouth the distance would be the best part of twenty miles. The best known of the three islands in Poole Harbour is Brownsea. Some people maintain that it used to have a parish church, and even now it has a hermit's chapel, which belonged to Cerne Abbey. There are men still alive who remember seeing almost the whole of the town of Poole covered with sedge and rushes.

Distances from Poole: To Christchurch (Twyneham) eight miles; to Weymouth it is reckoned twenty miles. From the harbour mouth three miles south-west along the coast is Sandwiche [*Swanage*], a fishing community set in a bay, with a small stream and a pier. The very furthest point of St Aldhelm's Head is five miles from Swanage, and beyond it to the west is West Lulworth, whose bay offers some shelter for ships. From Poole to Wimborne Minster is four miles, of which three-and-a-half are across waste and heathland. But around Wimborne itself the soil is very good for corn, grass and wood. A half-mile before I reached the town I passed over Allen Bridge, a twelve-arched bridge across the Stour.

Bridges on the Stour below Blandford Bridge: Blandford Bridge is four miles below Sturminster Newton on the Stour. From Blandford Bridge it is three miles to Sturminster [*Marshall*] Bridge. Next is Julian Bridge at one end of Wimborne, and a furlong lower, at the other end, is Allen Bridge, of twelve good arches. Iford Bridge is six miles downstream, and two miles above Christchurch, which is usually reckoned to be eight miles from Wimborne.

Wimborne is still quite a good town with a considerable population. It used to be very large, and achieved pre-eminence in the time of the West Saxon kings. In and around it are various chapels which, as I discovered, used to be parish churches of the town itself. Close to Wimborne the Saxon kings had a castle, now completely demolished, which is now called Badbury. The banks and ditches and site of the castle are still visible, but now rabbits burrow into it. More recently there was a fine manor house called Kingston Hall, but this too has to a large extent been destroyed. In documents it is referred to as Kingston Lacy, and from this I assume that it was built by a Lacy, one of the predecessors of Henry Lacy, earl of

Lincoln. I assume, too, that the Lacys owned Wimborne, and that through Lacy it passed to John of Gaunt, duke of Lancaster. It still belongs to this dukedom, and the courts for Wimborne are still held at Kingston. Kingston lies more or less to the north-west, close to Wimborne, and not far also is the famous Bathan Wood, now usually called Bothom.

The church of Wimborne Minster was originally a nunnery built by St Cuthberga, and it is only in recent years that a dean and prebendaries have been attached to it. The crypt in the eastern part of the church is an old piece of work. St Cuthberga was buried on the north side of the presbytery, and King Ethelred next to her. His tomb has recently been repaired, and a marble slab has been placed on it. A brass plate carries a portrait of a king and the following Latin inscription: 'In this place reposes the body of St Ethelred, king of the West Saxons, martyr, who met his death at the hands of the pagan Danes on the 13th day of April in the year of our Lord 827'. Cuthberga was later translated to the east end of the high altar. Under an arch on the south side of the presbytery lie buried in a fine tomb John, earl of Somerset (or more likely his son John, duke of Somerset), with his wife. And in the south aisle by the quire a certain Barok or Berwike (so I was told) lies buried in a fine, large, marble tomb. The mother of Henry VII, Lady Margaret, founded and endowed a grammar school in Wimborne. The clergy of Wimborne church have a pleasant house or college as their dwelling, and the dean has a fine house.

The course of the Wimborne River: The Wimborne rises approximately three miles above Wimborne St Giles and flows north-east past Mr Ashley's manor house and park there. It descends six miles to a stone, four-arched bridge at the edge of Wimborne town called Walford Bridge, and then a furlong further downstream it divides into two courses. Each runs beneath a three-arched bridge in the very centre of Wimborne; they are called the Isebroke Bridges, and are close to each other. The courses reunite and flow a little further to a mill. Shortly below this the Wimborne joins the Stour on its ESE side, not far above Allen Bridge.

Four miles from Wimborne, largely through woodland, I came to Horton. The monastery here used to be an abbey in its own right, but later it became a cell of Sherborne. The village has recently suffered a fire. In its valley a little stream, which is crossed by two small bridges, flows towards Wimborne St Giles and into the River Wimborne. The three miles between Horton and Cranborne is all open country with neither enclosure nor woodland. Cranborne is a pleasant roadside place, and its single street has quite good buildings. A swift stream flows through it, and is channelled along the right hand side of the street itself. It is my guess that it flows to Horton, but I am not sure. Cranborne too used to have an abbey in its own right, but an earl of Gloucester converted it to a cell of Tewkesbury. Two miles from Cranborne, all across open country, I passed the great royal park of Blagdon on my left hand. Then after another six miles of similar terrain I reached Homington, a good village. *cont. p. 393* [**1542**: *1/244-58*]

A MILE FURTHER I reached Stapleford [*Stalbridge*], which is a pleasant but remote town with a single street of quite good buildings, and a church at its north end. Here a certain Thornhill of Thornhill lies buried on the south side of the quire in a fine chapel which he built himself. The manor and small town of Stalbridge in Blackmore was an ancient possession of Sherborne Abbey. The River Cale flows down from Morelande [*?Marnhull*] and leaves Stalbridge on its right bank. Stalbridge lies approximately seven miles north [*i.e. south*] of Wikehampton [*Wincanton*], the source of the Cale. A mile from Stalbridge, across good enclosed ground, is Thornhill, where dwells Mr Thornhill, of an old gentry family. Two miles further, through enclosed ground and woodland, brought me to Sturminster. Halfway along I crossed a five-arched stone bridge over a stream called the River Lydden, and just above Sturminster I crossed the Stour by a wooden bridge.

The little town of Sturminster stands in a valley. There is not much to it, and the buildings are indifferent, although it has a very good market. It stands on the left bank of the Stour. An excellent stone bridge of six arches has recently been built on the edge of the town chiefly by the vicar of Sturminster and the parson of Shillingstone. Shillingstone lies on the right bank of the Stour on the Blandford road next to Eyford [*Hayward*] Bridge, which is two miles downstream from Sturminster. On the right bank of the Stour by the end of the bridge there is a fine manor house on a hill which has been made artificially more precipitous. Old documents refer to this as Newton Castle, and it was given, with Sturminster, to Glastonbury Abbey by one of the kings. Later the castle was completely demolished, and the abbots of Glastonbury built the fine manor house, in which they used to stay. The living of Sturminster, with an annual revenue amounting to £80, belonged to Glastonbury.

I crossed Sturminster Bridge, and less than a mile further I came to another bridge, of four arches, which crossed the River Divelish, if I remember correctly. Then it was about a mile to Thornhill, and another mile to [*Stourton*] Caundle, which is a pleasant village. Lord Stourton has a fine manor house here which used to belong to the Chideock family. There are several villages called Caundle. After three miles of rather hilly enclosed country with a certain amount of woodland I reached Sherborne. The park at Sherborne, apart from a short length around the lodge, is enclosed by a stone wall. From Sherborne it was barely two miles to Wyke, which lies on the right bank of the Sherborne Water, or River Ivel. This was a manor house of the abbots of Sherborne, but now it belongs to Mr Horsey. Bradford Abbas, a pleasant village, also lies on the right bank of the Ivel, and from there it is scarcely a mile to Mr Horsey's manor house at Clifton. Bradford Bridge is a little above the village, and has two arches.

Clifton stands on the right bank of the Ivel in the parish of Yetminster, which has three prebends in Salisbury Cathedral. It belonged to the Maybank family, and passed by inheritance to the Horsey and Ware families, who partitioned the estate. About the time of Edward IV Ormond, earl of Wiltshire, seized Clifton and held it by force with a bogus title. He started work on massive foundations for stabling and domestic buildings, and it was his intention to build a castle there, but shortly afterwards the property was restored to the Horsey family. The original manor house of the Horseys, from which they derive their name, lay about a mile from Bridgwater at the end of the great hill which extends from Glastonbury almost to Bridgwater. Sir John Horsey still owns this land. Sherborne and Millbrook waters join a quarter-mile or more below Clifton. *cont. p. 347*
[**1544:** 5/107-9]

[F*ROM MILBORNE PORT*] it is a mile to Toomer Park, which is surrounded by a stone wall. Ownership passed from the Toomer [?Tonmers] family through inheritance by marriage to the Carent family, who as a result increased their estate substantially. A mile further is Stalbridge. The abbot of Sherborne procured for this town the privileges of holding a market and fair. The market has declined, but the fair continues. As owner of the town the abbot of Sherborne had a manor house there, which lay on the south side of the church. Also on this side is an excellent spring with a wall around it. The Stour is the nearest river, and this leaves Stalbridge about a mile away on its right bank. Cale Bridge on the River Cale is a mile and a half away. Marnhull, which is about six miles from Shaftesbury, is a good secluded place beside the Stour. It belonged to Glastonbury.

Stalbridge is a mile from the causeway which leads to Shaftesbury. Then it is about two miles to Five Bridges over the River Cale, which does indeed have five main arches, and hence the name. But the bridge is joined to a long stone causeway, and this has a number of small arches. The country around Five Bridges is a flat valley of great extent, surrounded by high hills. A mile further on I rode over a stream which, in all probability, flows into the Stour.

Shaftesbury lies about three miles beyond this. It is a large market town which stands on a hill and has four parish churches. The abbey stood to the [*west*] of the town. As one entered the chapter house there was an inscription on the right hand side which had been placed there by Alfred king of Wessex to the effect that he had rebuilt Shaftesbury after its destruction by the Danes. But the remains of the inscription mentioned by William of Malmesbury stood in the wall of St Mary's Chapel on the edge of the town. This chapel has now been pulled down. The River Stour passes Shaftesbury [*some distance away*] on its left bank.

Going from Shaftesbury towards Mere I travelled through two miles of woodland, and crossed a stream which flowed down to my left towards the Stour. As I went through part of Gillingham Forest I crossed another stream. [**1544**: 5/110-11]

Abbot Ramsam built the New Inn and several houses in the northern part of Sherborne. All Hallows parish church has recently been demolished, and the abbey church of Our Lady has replaced it as the parish church. The chapel of Thomas Becket is near the New Inn. John Mere, abbot of Sherborne, said that he had read in Latin books belonging to his abbey that Sherborne was called 'clarus fons' ['the bright spring']. [1/295-6]

Woodsford Castle, which stands three or four miles downstream from Dorchester on the River Frome, at one time belonged to Guy de Brian, then to Stafford, and now to Strangeways as part of his share. At another Strangeways property, Melbury Sampford, which he acquired by purchase, he has recently begun lavish building work on the communal dwelling house, and has ordered 3,000 loads of freestone to be brought there from Hamdon quarry, nine miles away.

One of the headwatersof the River Ivel rises in the pond in Melbury Park. The Sherborne Water rises in Blackmore, and the River Frome in a valley three or four miles above Frampton. A tributary flows into it from a pond in Hooke Park. [4/73-4]

Gillingham Forest, in its present form, is four miles long and approximately one mile wide. Tarrant nunnery until recently stood near Crawford Bridge, which crosses the River Stour below Blandford. [4/107,109]

Blackmore, until its disafforesting in William the Conqueror's time, was a forest which extended from Yeovil to the Shaftesbury area. It adjoined Gillingham Forest, near Shaftesbury. At that period, and for a long time previously, notable families in the Blackmore area included the Thornhulls of Thornhull ('hul' was the Saxon version of our word 'hall'), the Lewestons of Leweston, and the de la Lynes. Blandford belonged to the earldom of Lancaster, and there was a very rich miser in Blandford called Ryves. The Martins are an old gentry family in Dorset. [4/142-3]

On a map at Merton College Bridport is marked as lying halfway between Weymouth and Lyme. They make good daggers at Bridport. [5/44-5]

DURHAM

COUNTY DURHAM *seems to have been the limit of Leland's 1541 north-eastern itinerary, and it is possible to reconstruct much of his journey. He appears to have been entertained by several Durham gentry, including the Conyers family at Sockburn, the earl of Westmorland at Brancepeth, and Lord Bergavenny at Raby. He traversed the county from south to north, and back again, largely ignoring the coastal region, but making excursions up both Weardale and Teesdale.*

The fairly extensive notes on the county were probably compiled several years earlier, perhaps during a monastic library tour in 1534, and Leland must also have passed through the area as he returned from his 1538 itinerary to the north-west. But of this no record has survived.

SOCKBURN IS THE OLDEST seat of the Conyers family, and the house and estate have been since ancient times their genuine inheritance. In old documents their name was written not as Conyers but Congres (Conyers told me this himself). The house, with a mile of extremely attractive ground surrounding it, is almost made into an island by the meandering of the River Tees around it, and a little below the manor house there is a large weir for fish. The tomb of Sir John Conyers is in Sockburn parish church. He married Elisabeth, the eldest daughter of Bromflete, Lord St John. This Bromflete, as I once saw it written, was created Lord Vescy by Henry VI, since he had acquired much of Lord Vescy's estate through marrying the daughter and heir of a knight named Aton, who in turn had

inherited it through a daughter. Anastasia, the second daughter, married Lord Clifford, and Katharine married Eure.

Neasham on the Tees is three miles from Sockburn, and Darlington is five miles further, entirely over good cornland. Apart from Durham itself Darlington is the best market town in the diocese, and it has a stone bridge of three arches, as I recall. The parish church is collegiate, with a dean and prebendaries belonging to it, and at the high altar there is an exceptionally long and fine altar stone of variegated marble, mottled in black and white. In the town the bishop of Durham has an attractive palace.

Auckland is a good eight miles' journey from Darlington, over reasonably good arable and pasture ground. One mile this side of Auckland Castle I crossed the River Gaunless by a bridge of a single large arch. This attractive river rises six miles to the west and flows past West Auckland, St Helen Auckland, St Andrew Auckland and Bishop Auckland before passing to the south of Auckland Castle and shortly afterwards joining the main stream of the River Wear. Auckland itself is an inconsiderable town but it has a good market for corn. It is situated on a pleasant hill between two rivers, the Wear to the north and the Gaunless to the south. These rivers meet a bowshot or more below the town and flow eastwards. Each has a hill next to it, so that Bishop Castle Auckland stands on a small hill between two large hills.

The bishops of Durham had a manor house at Auckland a very long time ago, but Anthony Bek was the first to fortify it. His work included the great hall and an exceptionally fine great chamber, both of which contain a number of pillars of black marble mottled with white. In addition he built an extremely fine chapel of squared masonry, a college with a dean and prebendaries, and a quadrangle for the college servants on the south-west side of the castle. Bishop Skirlaw of Durham built the fine gatehouse at the entrance to Auckland Castle. Next to the castle is a good park containing fallow deer, wild bulls and cattle.

My journey up Weardale took me seven miles to Wolsingham, and then at two-mile intervals to Frosterley, Stanhope, Eastgate, Westgate and St John's Chapel. All except the last lie on the north side of the Wear. The Westgate is the name given to an attractive square tower on the north bank of the Wear which belongs to the bishop of Durham. It adjoins a park enclosed by a rough stone wall of twelve or fourteen miles in total length. I was told that there are some small leased holdings within the park. This is sixteen miles up Weardale from Auckland Castle; twelve miles from Auckland and beside the river is Stanhope, the chief parish of Weardale, and seven miles above Auckland on the Wear is Wolsingham, which formerly had a small market, but not any more.

The Wear originates, some eight miles or more above Stanhope, from the confluence of two small burns, the Burnhope from the south and the Killhope from the north. A third, Wellhope Burn, flows into Killhope. Although Upper Weardale is not very good for growing corn, the dale itself through which the river flows produces excellent grass. Many red deer stray on to the mountains of Weardale. Lying as it does towards Westmorland on the western border of the diocese Weardale is well wooded, as also is the area around Auckland; indeed its name suggests that it was full of oaks.

No more than half a mile below Auckland Castle, on the south bank of the Wear, stands Binchester. It is now a poor village situated on the brow of a hill, but as I rode past on the south side I could see a small ditch, and indications of old buildings. In the ploughed fields next to the village Roman coins and many other archaeological remains have been, and still are found. There is an extremely fine one-arch bridge over the Wear between Auckland and Binchester; there is another a little above Durham called Sunderland Bridge.

Four miles of mountainous country, like that around Auckland, separate Binchester from Brancepeth. It does not produce good corn, but it is well wooded. Rather more than a mile before Brancepeth I crossed the River Wear by a ford. Brancepeth village and castle stand on an outcrop of rock surrounded by higher hills. A small stream flows down from the nearby hills and rocks to the south-west part of the castle.

Brancepeth Castle is strongly positioned and built. It has high buildings arranged about two courtyards, and a small moat surrounds a large part of the first courtyard. Here are three towers of living quarters, and three small ornamental towers. But the charm of the castle is its second courtyard; I entered it by a large tower, on the front of which I saw escutcheoned a lion rampant. Some claim that Ralph Neville, first earl of Westmorland, built much of this house. The present earl has added a new piece of building to it.

The parish church of St Brandon at Brancepeth contains several tombs of the Neville family, including a high tomb in the quire depicting

DURHAM

one of them with his wife. This Neville had no male heirs, and consequently a great dispute arose between the nearest male relative and a member of the Gascoyne family. In a chapel on the south side of the quire is buried a countess of Westmorland who was the sister of Archbishop Booth of York. The chapel also contains the tomb of Lord Neville, the present earl's father. This Lord Neville predeceased his father, who was then earl, and his death caused the earl such distress that he died at Hornby Castle in Richmondshire, and is buried in the parish church there. The present earl of Westmorland had an elder brother, but he lies in a small marble tomb beside the high altar on the south side, and at his feet are buried four of the present earl's children. I was told at Brancepeth that Ralph, the first earl of Westmorland, was buried at the college he founded at Staindrop near Raby; and that another was buried at the friary in Northallerton.

The distance from Brancepeth to Durham is about three miles, and rather more than half a mile before I approached Durham I crossed over a bridge with one large arch, as well as another, smaller bridge, which spanned a pleasant river called Deerness or Devernesse. This river is joined a little above the bridge by the River Browney, which rises above and flows past Repaire [*Beaurepaire*] Park.

Durham itself stands on a rocky hill. Approached from the south it lies on the north bank of the Wear, but the natural meandering of the river's course in the valley is such that from the great stone bridge of fourteen arches at Elvet the river steals right around the town to be crossed by another bridge, of three arches, at Framwellgate. Between these two bridges, or rather slightly lower, at St Nicholas', the town comes within a bowshot's length of being an island. Indeed some people believe that anciently the Wear flowed from the site of the present Elvet Bridge directly past the hill on which St Nicholas' now stands; and that the other course is an artificial valley into which it has been channelled partly as a matter of policy and partly as a result of the quarrying of building stone for the town and minster. I am not entirely convinced by this suggestion.

The close of the minster is situated on the highest part of the hill; it has good walls and several fine gates. The church itself and the cloister are very strong and fine, and right at the east end of the church is a transept. This is in addition to the central transept of the minster church. The noble castle stands on the north-east side of the minster, with the Wear flowing below it. At the top stands the splendid keep, built in the shape of an octagon and four storeys high. Bishop Fox carried out extensive renovations on this dungeon, and he also built within the castle a new kitchen complex and many attractive dwelling-quarters. Tunstall also spent money on the keep and other parts of the castle, as well as building an excellent new gallery approached by a handsome flight of stairs, and providing an extremely strong iron gate for the castle.

The part of Durham town virtually surrounded by the Wear has three parish churches and a chapel. St Oswald's is reckoned to be ancient. There are three more parish churches in the suburbs. The largest of these suburbs is beside Elvet Bridge; it has a number of small streets. Across Framwellgate Bridge there is another suburb divided into three parts. South Street is on the left hand side, Cross Street (which leads to Auckland) is in the centre, and Framwellgate, the road to Chester-le-Street and Newcastle, is on the right. Durham town is reasonably strongly-built, although the houses are neither lavish nor tall. Some fragments of town walls may be seen adjoining a gate in the palace wall, but compared with the size of the noble close that part of the town within the peninsula is but small; the close by itself may really be described as the walled town of Durham.

On the south side of Durham Minster lies the sanctuary or consecrated churchyard, and here there are very many old tombs. At the head of one of them is a cross seven feet tall, with several rows of an inscription which is now illegible. Some people say that this cross was brought from the consecrated churchyard on the island of Lindisfarne.

Monkwearmouth is about eight miles from Durham, and about six miles from Tynemouth, or rather from Newcastle. There is no notable bridge on the Wear below Durham apart from Chester Bridge. The river comes within a quarter-mile of the town of Chester-le-Street. My journey there from Durham took me across Framwellgate Bridge, and then past a little arable ground, but mostly across upland pasture, with some waste and gorse. Approaching Chester I could see barely a half-mile away from the town Lumley Castle, which is set on a hill surrounded by pleasant woods; there is also some woodland around Chester itself. The town consists largely of very poor buildings ranged along a single street. There are also one or two small streets around the church, but this, although it is collegiate with a dean and prebendaries, is also very poorly built. In the nave is a tomb with an effigy of a bishop, which symbolises that St

Cuthbert was once buried here, or at least his shrine was placed here. Right at the far end of the place I crossed the Cong Burn by a good three-arched bridge of stone. Then I made my way to Gateshead across mountainous country, with pasture, heath, waste and gorse. There is a large coal pit a little this side of Gateshead.

I left Durham by Elvet Bridge and travelled two and a half miles to Sunderland Bridges. Here for a short distance the Wear divides into two channels and creates an island. The first bridge which I came to was of a single arch, but the other had three. A mile or more further on I crossed Valley Burn which flows into the Wear nearby, and on the hill just above it is Burnham Claxton's house. Burnham's estate has an annual value of nearly £70. Then I rode through a large wood growing on a hill, and across hilly waste and heathland to St Andrews Auckland [*South Church*], which is eight miles from Durham. On my right hand side I passed close to the stone wall around one of the parks of Auckland. The dean of Auckland has substantial premises at St Andrews Auckland, consisting especially of barns and other agricultural buildings.

Most of my five-mile journey from St Andrews Auckland to Raby took me across pasture grounds and treeless, hilly moorland, though part was arable. Raby is the largest inhabited castle in northern England; it is strongly built, although sited on neither a hill nor a very strong position. My entrance was by a causeway with a small pond to its right. The first precinct had no buildings except two entrance towers at opposite ends; my way into the second precinct was by a great iron gate with a tower, and there were two or three more towers to its right. But the principal towers lay in the third or central courtyard of the castle. The hall and all the service buildings are large and noble; in the hall I saw the antlers of a stag of unbelievably huge size. The great chamber used to be extremely large, but now it has been given a false ceiling and partitioned into two or three rooms. In a small chamber there I saw the whole pedigree of the Neville family depicted in coloured glass in the windows; but this has been removed and replaced with clear glass. One of the castle towers has a design of two capital Bs, derived from Bertram Bulmer. Another is named after Jane, the illegitimate sister of Henry IV, who married Ralph Neville, first earl of Westmorland.

Two of the three parks attached to Raby are stocked with deer. The middle park contains a lodge. Next to Raby also is Langley Chase, which is three miles long and has fallow deer; and there is a royal forest of red deer on moorland at Middleton in Teesdale, eight miles west of Raby. The parson at Middleton is Dr Noteres.

Staindrop is a small market town about a half-mile from Raby. There is a collegiate church here with a nave and two aisles. I was told that before Ralph of Raby's time it only had one, the present south aisle. I was also told that Ralph's grandparents made a chantry in this aisle, where they are buried. In the wall of this aisle may be seen the tombs and effigies of three ladies (one wearing a coronet), the tomb of a male child, and a flat tomb of mottled marble. Another flat slab has a plain brass figure and inscription marking the tomb of Richard, the son and heir of Edward, Lord Bergavenny. This Edward was de Raby's fifth son, and Joanna Beaufort was his mother. Edward was succeeded by another son, George, whose own son George succeeded him and left Henry the present Lord Bergavenny.

Ralph's son John, by his first marriage, was Lord Neville. Richard, his son by his second wife Joanna, was Earl of Salisbury. Robert became bishop of Durham. George was Lord Latimer. Edward was Lord Bergavenny, and, if I remember correctly, Ralph also fathered William, who became Lord Falconbridge. Ralph himself, the first Neville to be Earl of Westmorland, is buried in a magnificent alabaster tomb in the quire of Staindrop collegiate church. His first wife, Margaret, lies on his left hand side, and on his right hand side is an effigy of his second wife, Joanna, although she is buried at Lincoln next to her mother Catherine Swineford, Duchess of Lancaster. It was this Joanna who erected the actual college building at Staindrop, which lies on the north side of the collegiate church, and is strongly built entirely of stone. Flowing past the north side of the college is a stream called Langley Beck. Its source is five miles to the west in Middleton parish, and it passes through Langley (from which it takes its name) before joining the Tees a mile or more lower below Selaby, the seat of Mr Brackenbury.

Five miles of reasonable corn and pasture land separate Staindrop from Barnard Castle. This is quite a pleasant town, fairly well built and with a good market. The town actually lies in the parish of Gainford, where the mother church is, six miles further down the Tees and in Durham diocese. The castle stands proudly above the Tees. The first precinct contains nothing of great note except a fine chapel, which contains two chantries. In the centre of the chapel nave is a fine marble tomb with an effigy and an inscription around it in French. A similar effigy graces a freestone slab in the nave south wall. They are said by some to have belonged to the Balliols. The inner precinct is very large and partly moated, with well-appointed living quarters in towers. The castle possesses two parks; one is called Marwood, and adjoins a chase of the same name, which borders the river up into Teesdale. Langley and Marwood Chases are separated by nothing more than a hill.

This is the approximate course of the River Tees: It rises on Yade Moor, and then takes its course among rocks, receiving several other small valleys or streams, and flowing over much wild country for eight or ten miles to a bridge with a good arch at Eggleston. Next comes the excellent three-arched bridge at Barnard Castle, and then Piercebridge. This formerly had five arches, but has recently been rebuilt with three. Close to Piercebridge is a nice chapel of Our Lady which was founded by John Balliol, king of Scotland. Five miles on to Croft Bridge, next to Yarm bridge, then three miles to Stockton, where there is a ferry, and from there a further four miles to Teesmouth. *cont. p. 447* [**1541:** 1/69-78]

The Bowes family were gentry in County Durham long before Henry V's time, and their principal house and estate, which they still own, is also called Bowes. One member of this family, Sir William Bowes, served as chamberlain to the Duke of Bedford, Henry V's brother and Henry VI's uncle, who was protector and governor in France. Bowes spent seventeen years with him in France, where he was known as Monsieur de Arches, and was able to grow rich, so that when he returned home he increased his estate and his standing. It was he who built from its foundations the manor house at Streatlam, not far from Barnard Castle in Durham. His great-grandson is Bowes of the king's counsel at York, who is the younger brother and uncle of the present leading members of the Bowes family. [2/9]

Dr Belasyse told me that a duck, with the customary markings of ducks in the bishopric of Durham, was placed in one of the pools between Darlington and the bank of the Tees, which are called Hell Kettles; and that this duck was subsequently found at [Croft] Bridge on the Tees, where Clarivaulx lives. So that local people came to the conclusion that an underground passage connected these two places. [4/84]

Market towns in County Durham: Durham; Auckland; Whickham; the busy market of Darlington which lies between the Rivers Tees and Wear; Stockton on Tees; Wolsingham, which lies on the Wear about halfway between Stanhope and Auckland; Hartlepool.

Castles in County Durham: Durham; Auckland; Prudhoe on the Tyne; Stockton on Tees; Barnard Castle; Lumley Castle not far from Chester-le-Street.

Abbeys and priories in County Durham: Durham on the River Wear; Finchale on the Wear, which is a cell of Durham with thirteen monks; Monkwearmouth; Jarrow. I recall that there was a priory close to the River Tees not far from Darlington.

The boundaries of County Durham: River Tees; River Tyne as far up as the confluence with the River Derwent. [5/48-9]

There is a strong guarded gate at Gateshead.

Bishops' tombs in the chapter house at Durham: Robert of Holy Island, in mottled marble; Bishop Turgot, Aldun and Walker in one tomb; Eadmund and Eadred in one tomb; William of St Carilef; Robert Graystanes, a native, lies buried here; Bishop Nicholas Farnham; Bishop Philip; Richard Marsh; another tomb without an inscription; Bishop Ranulf, Bishop Geoffrey, a second William, Walter. Some people maintain that Ranulph built Norham Castle. Walker, who was killed at Gateshead, was previously buried at Jarrow.

Tombs in the Quire: Skirlaw on the north side under an arch; Hatfield on the south side under a arch; Lewis de Beaumont in front of the high altar under a marble slab. In the eastern transept of the church: Anthony Bek under a stone slab on the north side; Richard of Bury on the south. In the Galilee: Thomas Langley, who was chancellor of England during three reigns, is buried in the Galilee. This Galilee chapel adjoins the main church at the west end. It is five separate bays wide, and each bay is of four arches.

Langley established the choristers' and grammar schools at Durham. Robert Neville, bishop of Durham, lies in the Galilee in a high tomb of plain marble. Some say that he was responsible for making the existing reliquary of St Cuthbert. At Bishop Neville's head lies Richard of Barnard Castle under a flat stone, and at his head is one of the Nevilles. There is also a tomb of the noble monk Bede. Two members of the Lumley family lie in a mottled marble tomb in the churchyard on the north side of the church.

I was given the following information by Mr Hinmar, Chancellor of Durham: There is written evidence that a bishop of Durham gave the manor of Ravensworth-on-Tyne to his nephew. Later it passed to one Humfrevill, then Lumley, and now Gascoyne. Not very long ago the castle belonged to Bointon.

The land now occupied by Greatham Hospital near Hartlepool used to belong to Peter de Montfort, one of the Leicester family, but when he was attainted the king took possession of the land. But the bishop of Durham appealed to the king, claiming that attainted land within the diocese should pass to him. He established the truth of this claim, and so received the land, on which he built and with which he endowed a hospital.

Henry of Pudsey, Hugh of Pudsey's brother, was the founder of Finchale Priory, which lies on the Wear two miles below Durham. He is buried there, as is

St Godric the hermit. There is a place right at the head of Weardale which is called the Bishop's Stones, and this marks the diocesan boundary.

At Norton-on-Tees, about one mile above Stockton, the living comprises eight prebends or portions. Two miles further up is Yarm Bridge, which was built by Walter Skirlaw, bishop of Durham. He also built the gatehouse at Auckland, and Finchale Bridge over the Wear one mile above Durham. This bridge had two arches, or rather a single arch supported by a central column, but it collapsed two or three years ago because repairs were not carried out in time. The same bishop Skirlaw constructed all, or part, of the lanterns in York Minster, which spring from the aisle vaults on either side of the high altar. His arms are incorporated into the work. And at his birthplace, Swine in Holderness, he built a fine chapel, and endowed two chantries in it. It is said that his father made meal-sieves.

Iron and lead ores are found in Weardale, as well as coal. The River Wear is always discoloured, because of the marshy and ore-bearing land through which it flows. Fish cannot thrive in it, and hardly any are caught, except eels in the upper reaches. The market at Wolsingham in Weardale is in complete abeyance. No goods or carved stone are brought there now on the customary market day. In the case of Stanhope informed opinion is that a market has never been held there.

It is the Chancellor of Durham's opinion that the marble employed in various parts of Durham Cathedral was quarried from neither the Tees nor the Wear but from a less important stream near Wolsingham. There is a very good quarry for grey marble at Eggleston.

The Dean of Durham told me that the house of the bishops of Durham at Darlington was built by Hugh of Pudsey. [5/125,127-9]

ESSEX

If Leland's claim to have explored the whole kingdom is correct, we may suppose that an itinerary of East Anglia (or perhaps more than one) has been lost. Essex, in common with Suffolk and Norfolk, is virtually ignored in the surviving manuscripts, and can only be represented here by two brief notes.

A member of the collegiate church at Pleshey told me that he had heard from informed men that the town, and the site where the castle now stands, was originally called Tumblestoun, and that the new name is written in the following form – 'Castel de Placeto'. It was owned by the Mandevilles, but whether or not they obtained it immediately after the conquest I am unable to find out for certain. A man of

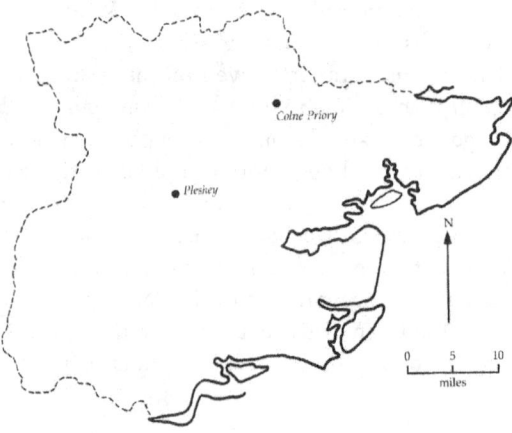

importance called de Placetes married the heiress of the earl of Warwick. Edward III's son, Thomas, earl of Buckingham, owned the castle, and it was he who built the college there. He married Eleanor, who was the daughter and one of the heiresses of Humphrey de Bohun, earl of Hereford. They had a daughter, called Anne. Eleanor is buried in St Edmund's chapel, Westminster. Anne, their heiress, married Stafford, earl of Stafford. More recently a certain Humphrey, duke of Buckingham, with his wife and three sons, was buried at Pleshey. I am told that one of these sons was earl of Wiltshire. [2/20]

Mr Sheffield told me that not far from Colne Priory, where the earls of Oxford were accustomed to be buried, they had a manor house, and that the site and earthworks survive there, at a place called Hall Place. After the destruction of this manor house they built another next to the priory. [1/25]

GLOUCESTERSHIRE

*T*HREE OF THE SURVIVING *itineraries, made in successive years, cross parts of Gloucestershire, and Leland also made extensive notes about the county. His West Country tour in 1542 took him via Lechlade and Cirencester, and he may have stayed with the Tame family at Fairford, about whom he seems well informed. The Winchcombe area and Gloucester were covered in detail during his 1543 journey around the West Midlands, and much of south Gloucestershire he explored in meandering fashion when he toured the Bristol area in 1544. His informant here seems to have been Sir John Newton of Barr's Court. The account of Bristol itself is substantial and important.*

The most extensive of the notes about places not visited on the itineraries concerns Tewkesbury and its surroundings, including Deerhurst. Contained within this are family details of the earls of Gloucester, many of whom were buried in Tewkesbury Abbey. There is also additional material about Winchcombe, Prestbury, Dursley and elsewhere, and some classified information about the county in general. A preliminary draft of the itinerary in the Gloucester area has also survived, but apart from one or two points everything is covered in the fuller description, and so most of the draft has here been omitted.

Taken altogether Leland's treatment of Gloucestershire is among the most satisfactory and complete of any county. The only parts which, on surviving evidence, he seems not to have explored were the north-east corner, around Stow, and the Stroud area.

I WAS TOLD that the Northleach Brook [*River Leach*] flows from north to south past Eastleach to join the Isis a little below St John's Bridge. Northleach, a pleasant but remote place, lies eight miles north of St John's Bridge, and like Eastleach, which is five miles lower, it stands (in terms of my route) on the nearer bank of the river. Right at the end of St John's Bridge on the far bank in a meadow on the right hand side I could see a chapel and large stone-walled enclosures. Here within living memory was a priory of Augustinian canons supported by the Duke of Clarence or York. When this priory was suppressed three chantries were established in Lechlade church; they continued until recently, when Dean Underwood of

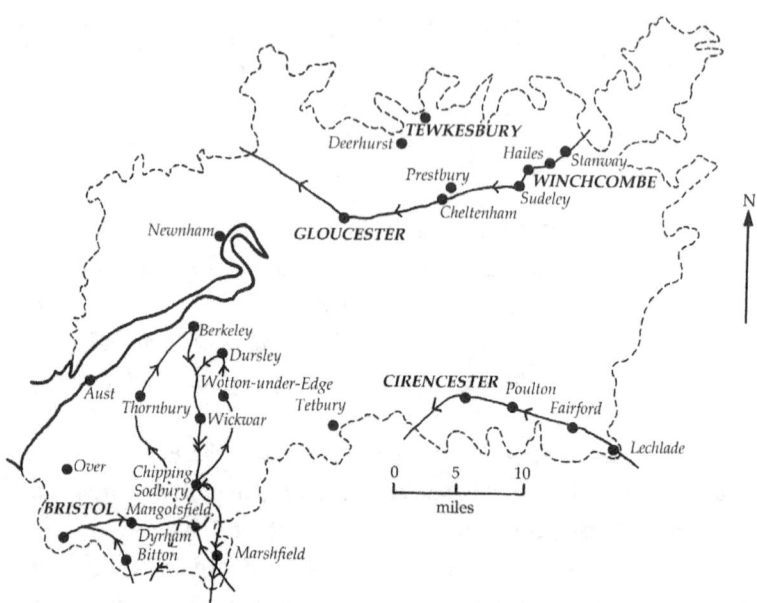

Wallingford found a reason for placing two of them at Wallingford College, and leaving only the third chantry at Lechlade.

It is about a half-mile from St John's Bridge to Lechlade, which is a nice old village, with an attractive stone spire at the west end of the church. Fairford is about four miles from Lechlade, across flat low-lying country very suitable for grass but devoid of trees. Tewkesbury Abbey owns [?owned] much of Fairford, a pleasant but remote place, including the benefice. Close to the churchyard is a fine mansion belonging to the Tame family, and its rear courtyard extends right down to Fairford Bridge. The town never prospered until the Tames arrived. John and Edmund Tame were entirely responsible for the house, and the fine new church of Fairford was begun by John and completed by Edmund. Both are buried in a chapel on the north side of the quire, with these Latin epitaphs:

> Pray for the souls of John Tame Esquire and his wife Alice. John died on the 8th day of May, 1500 in the 16th year of Henry VII's reign, and Alice died on the 20th day of December, 1471.

> Here lies Sir Edmund Tame, and his wives Agnes and Elizabeth. Edmund died on the 1st day of October, 1534, in the 26th year of Henry VIII's reign.

Fairford Water [*River Coln*] rises five miles NNW of Fairford, and then about a mile downstream it flows through the village of Whelford, before joining the Isis another mile or so lower, between Whelford and St John's Bridge. The course of the Isis above St John's Bridge is as follows: St John's Bridge to Lechlade more than half a mile; Lechlade to Castle Eaton two miles; Castle Eaton to Nunne-Eiton [*Water Eaton*] one mile, and two miles to Grekelade or Cricklade. Castle Eaton is in Wiltshire, and substantial remains of a building stand on the further, or Wiltshire, bank of the river. The castle belonged to Lord Zouch; Water Eaton belonged to the nuns of Godstow. Cricklade also lies in Wiltshire, on the further bank. Note that Bradon Water [*River Key*] flows into the Isis here.

As I left Fairford I crossed the Coln by a bridge of four stone arches, and about 2 miles further I came to Poulton. On my way out of Poulton I crossed a small stream, which rises not far above the village; it continues for about a mile before joining the Ampney Brook beside a mill a little above Down Ampney. Just beyond Poulton I could see Poulton Priory, which had a prior and two or three black canons. In the walls of the former presbytery I saw three or four arches which contained the tombs of gentry. I think that some of the Seymours were buried there, including certainly the Seymour who founded the house. I crossed the Ampney Brook on my way to the village of Ampney [*Crucis*], which I left on my right hand side. The source of the Ampney Brook is a rock a little above the village to the north; it flows three miles or more to Down Ampney, where Sir Anthony Hungerford has a good stone house on the far bank, and joins the Isis one mile lower, opposite Water Eaton. Poulton and Cirencester are four miles apart.

Cirencester (called in Latin Coriminum) stands on the River Churn. The town possessed a fine and rich college of prebendaries before the Conquest, but no one can discover who was its Saxon founder. Rumbald, Edward the Confessor's chancellor, was dean of the college, according to the epitaph on his tomb, and is buried in the nave of the church. The college was turned into an abbey of regular canons by Henry I, to which he gave the whole of the prebendaries' estate, and some other property. Richard I gave Cirencester Abbey jurisdiction over, and revenue from, seven hundreds in neighbouring part of Gloucestershire, but otherwise there has been little augmentation of the abbey's estate since Henry I's foundation. The eastern part of the abbey church is clearly of very old construction, but from the transept westwards there is nothing old to speak of. Two noblemen of St Amande lineage are buried inside the presbytery of this church, as well as the heart of Sanchia, who was wife of Richard, Earl of Cornwall and King of the Romans. The first of Cirencester's 29 or 30 abbots was called Serlo, and he made his brother prior of Bradenstoke. Alexander Neckam, the great scholar, was also abbot of Cirencester, and he is buried in the entrance to the cloister from the church of Worcester Cathedral. The last abbot, Mr Blake, spent nearly £500 on building two fulling mills at Cirencester. These are of exceptional importance to the town, because it depends entirely on the cloth industry.

There used to be three parish churches in Cirencester, but St Cecilia's, which was latterly only a chapel, has been completely demolished. St Laurence's still stands, but is not parochial; it supports an almshouse for two women which has an endowment of land. So now there is only one parish church in the whole town, but it is a very fine one, and its nave is entirely new. Bishop Ruthall of Durham, who was born and brought up in Cirencester, promised a large contribution towards this, but his death prevented him from giving anything at all. However his maternal aunt, one Alice Aveling, gave nearly £70 towards building the exceptionally fine porch of the parish church, and his mother was also among those who made a contribution towards its completion. Henry I founded the hospital of St John in the town.

Cirencester is in the Cotswolds, and its market, on Mondays, is the most important in the whole area; but its government is in the hands of a mere bailiff. The road from here to London goes by way of Fairford (6 miles), Faringdon (8 miles), Abingdon, Dorchester (5 miles), and Henley.

Tetbury is a pleasant market town seven miles from Malmesbury. As you ride along the Fosse Way towards Chipping Sodbury Tetbury lies two miles away on your left [*i.e. right*] hand side. The Fosse Way leaves Cirencester, and extends along a large and obvious ridge to Chipping Sodbury, and so to Bristol. The headwater of the Isis rises in the Cotswolds about one mile this side of Tetbury. Coberley, which is six miles north-west of Cirencester, is the source of the Coberley Stream [*River Churn*]. Master Bridges has a good house at Coberley, and Sir Edmund Tame has an excellent house at Rendcomb Park, which is three miles further downstream. *cont. p. 387* [**1542:** *1/126-30*]

GLOUCESTERSHIRE

At Stanway in Gloucestershire there is a fine estate and manor house by the east end of the church. It formerly belonged to and was at one time a residence of the abbot of Tewkesbury, but now it is leased by Mr Tracy. A small stream flows down from the ESE and later joins Toddington Water. Didbrook is one mile from Stanway, and Hailes a quarter-mile further. Another stream flows into Toddington Water from the south side of Hailes Abbey. Winchcombe is a mile-and-a-half from Hailes, over fine, fertile hills.

The town of Winchcombe lies due east of a small valley, and its single main street climbs gently towards the west. There is no doubt that the town was walled; the wall may be seen in several places, especially on the south side towards Sudeley Castle, and it is recorded also in the Life of St Kenelm. There was a fortress or castle right next to the south side of St Peter's. A very long time ago there was a church dedicated to St Nicholas in the eastern part of the town, but it was ruined long since. This parish church, (according to documents at Winchcombe Abbey) was later known as Ivy-castle, and its site is now occupied by a few poor houses and gardens. I suspect that the reason for the name Ivy-castle is that when the old building fell into ruin, ivy grew up its walls. The last prior of Winchcombe told me that he had heard of a fort or castle once existing in the east or north-east part of the town.

Cenwulf, the Mercian king, had a house in Winchcombe, and was the first to build the famous abbey in the town, which was dedicated with a splendid ceremony. On two separate occasions this abbey was destroyed by fire and rebuilt. Richard Kidderminster, the penultimate abbot, spent a large sum on the church, and enclosed the abbey on the town side with a strong wall of squared stone blocks. In the eastern part of the abbey church were buried Cenwulf and his son Cenelm, who were both kings of Mercia. And in the St Nicholas chapel at the east end of the high altar was the tomb of a certain Henry Boteler, who roofed the nave of the abbey church with lead. He was a member of the Boteler family of Sudeley, of whom others were also buried in the abbey church.

In the time of Henry V the nave of the abbey church was in use as the town's parish church, but during the reign of Henry VI William Winchcombe, abbot of Winchcombe, began to build a parish church for the townspeople, with their agreement, at the west end of the abbey, where for a long time up until then had stood a small chapel dedicated to St Pancras. Abbot William built the east end of the church, and the parishioners, having raised £200, started on the nave. But that sum was not sufficient to pay for such a costly task, so Ralph Boteler, Lord Sudeley, helped them to complete it. In the quire south aisle I noted first the effigy of Thomas Boteler, Lord Sudeley. There were also effigies to his sons, John, William, Thomas and Ralph, and another which I assume to have been Elizabeth, the wife of Ralph, Lord Sudeley. In the north quire aisle windows four gentlewomen were depicted in the glass, and one was named as Alice, the daughter of Thomas Boteler, Lord Sudeley. This parish church is dedicated to St Peter.

There was once a hospital in Winchcombe, but now all that remains is the name 'Spittle'. The usual name for the stream which flows beside the south part of the town is the Eseburne [*Isbourne*]. Its source is about three miles above Winchcombe to the west, and it flows east right to the foot of the town before turning somewhat north to Toddington, less than two miles away, and it joins the River [*Avon*] at [*Evesham*]. Sudeley Castle is about a half-mile from Winchcombe.

One Boteler, Lord Sudeley built this castle from its foundations, and at the time of its construction it surpassed all other buildings of its day. The only Boteler whom I could find reference to as Lord Sudeley was called Thomas, and his name can be seen in the glass windows of St Peter's Church, Winchcombe. So I assume that this Thomas was the builder of the castle. But Mr Tracy of Toddington, whose family was set up in land by gifts from the Botelers, told me that it was built by Ralph Boteler, although he could not cite any authority for this. Certainly Thomas did have a son called Ralph, and he is shown as the youngest son in the glass windows of St Peter's Church.

The Lord Sudeley who built the castle was a noted warrior during the reigns of Henry V and Henry VI, and I have been told that he was a naval admiral. And so the assumption has been made and uttered that the castle was partly built on spoils won in France; indeed there is talk of a tower in it called Potmare's Tower, after the man whose ransom money paid for it. Of particular note in this castle is the use of beryl to glaze some of the windows. The site of the former manor house at Sudeley, which existed before the castle was built, can still be seen in Sudeley Park.

Edward IV suspected that Lord Sudeley was at heart loyal to Henry VI and so was not well disposed towards him. Accusations were made against him and he was arrested. On his way to London he looked down on Sudeley from the hill, and said, 'Sudeley Castle, you are the traitor, not I!' After he had cleared his name he sold the castle to King Edward. Henry VII gave it to his uncle, Gasper, duke of Bedford, or at least allowed him to use it. Now it is falling into ruin, more's the pity. An attractive lake extends from Sudeley Park down to the castle, and its water flows into the Isbourne stream on the south side of Winchcombe.

Distances from Winchcombe: Tewkesbury, 7 miles; Worcester, 14 miles; Pershore, 9 miles; Cirencester, 15 miles; Gloucester, 12 miles; Evesham, 7 or 8 miles.

I travelled from Winchcombe the three miles to Southam over good arable, pasture and wooded ground, although rather hilly. At Southam Sir John Huddleston has built an attractive manor house on land which he bought from a certain Goodman. From here another four or five miles brought me to Cheltenham, which is a long town with a market. This place belonged to Tewkesbury Abbey, but is now the king's. There is a stream on the south side of the town.

My ride from Cheltenham to Gloucester was across six miles of low-lying corn, pasture and meadow land. There is a great deal of low ground in this area, extending from Winchcombe to Evesham and Tewkesbury, and all the way from Cheltenham to Gloucester and then on to Tewkesbury, and part of the way beside the Severn down to Newnham. This land is at the mercy of sudden rises in the level of the River Severn, so that after rainfall it is very muddy for travellers. I crossed two or three small streams between Cheltenham and Gloucester, which flow into the Severn.

Gloucester is an old town, well built of timber, and large. Except where fortified by the deep water of the River Severn there are strong walls to defend it. The wall has a gate on each of the four sides, and these are known as the north, south, east and west gates, although the east gate is colloquially known as Aillesgate.

The old castle stands on the south side of the town, beside the left bank of the Severn. Close by is the quay, also on the left bank, which is used by barges and small ships. I discovered there that the former Severn quay stood next to St Oswald's Priory, but that it was moved from this site because of arguments between the town and the monastery. When the quay was by St Oswald's there used to be several nice streets, such as St Bride's Street and Silver Girdle Street, which are now completely ruined. In practice these streets proved to be rather unhealthy and were vulnerable to flooding from the Severn in spate, so that the inhabitants preferred to live in the higher parts of the town. Gloucester's best feature is the two streets which run across the town between opposite gates, and at the cross-roads where they meet is a conduit encased in stone.

Outside Gloucester's east, north and south gates are suburbs, but at the west gate there is only a bridge and its causeway. The bridge over the principal channel of the Severn, which flows next to the town, has seven large stone arches. A little further west is another bridge, with one or two arches which at certain times serve to drain the meadows. Not far away another bridge, of five large arches, stands close to the west gate, and from it a great stone causeway, a quarter-mile long, has been thrown up across the low-lying meadows by the Severn. This causeway has a number of double-arched bridges which drain the meadows when flooded, and at the far end there is an eight-arched bridge which is not yet finished. A Gloucester merchant named Bell, who is still alive, realises the importance of bridges and causeways to the town of Gloucester and to the common good, and has given land with an annual value of £10 towards their maintenance.

Gloucester has eleven parish churches, and there is a church dedicated to St Ewin in one of the suburbs. I am not sure whether this is to be included among the total of eleven. The college of grey friars lay outside the town close to the south gate. It was established by one of the Lords Berkeley, but now it is a brewery. Blackfriars was founded in about 1239 by Henry III and a certain Sir Stephen, lord of Harnhill. It stood inside the town close to the castle, and has been turned into a weaving-house. The college of white friars lay in the suburb outside the north gate. In the same suburb, rather further to the north, there is a hospital for the poor dedicated to St Margaret and endowed with lands. It is controlled by the corporation. To the north of this there is another hospital, also for the poor, and dedicated to St Mary Magdalene. The prior of Llanthony was reckoned to have been the founder, and he was accustomed to support it with a dole of bread. Just inside the west gate there is a hospital of St Bartholomew which has a master and 32 poor men and women (formerly 52 poor men). It is supported by the bishop of Worcester, although some believe that it was a royal foundation. A certain Pancefoot, who died within the memory of old men, is buried in the hospital chapel. A suffragan bishop named

Whitmaster [*Whitney*] is now in charge of the establishment; he has built up the hospital (it used to be very vulnerable to the Severn floods) and has made fine quarters for himself in it.

The following information is gleaned from text on the wall of the north nave aisle in Gloucester church:

Osric, who was the first sub-king and lord of this region, as well as king of Northumbria, was the first founder of this monastery, with the permission of Ethelred, king of Mercia. On the advice of Bosel, the first bishop of Worcester, Osric installed nuns, and made his sister Kineburge the first abbess. During the time that it was a nunnery, 84 years, there were only three abbesses, Kineburge, Edburge and Eva, and they were all noblewomen and queens of Mercia. During the wars between King Egbert and the Mercian kings the nuns were defiled and driven out.

King Beornwulf of Mercia introduced secular canons and priests, and granted them possessions and liberties. But the secular clergy were expelled by King Canute for irregular conduct, who, on the advice of Bishop Wulfstan of Worcester, replaced them with monks. When Bishop Ealdred was translated from Worcester to York he seized most of the Gloucester Abbey estate in order to rebuild York Minster. As penance for killing seven priests a nobleman called Wolphine Lereve was made to support seven monks at Gloucester in perpetuity. Archbishop Thomas of York restored to Gloucester the lands of which Ealdred had wrongfully dispossessed them.

William the Conqueror granted Gloucester Abbey, then in ruins, to his chaplain Serlo, who was a monk of St Michael's in Normandy. William and his sons also gave properties and liberties to Gloucester Abbey. [*The relics of*] St Arilda the Virgin, who was martyred at Kington near Thornbury, were translated to this monastery, and have performed many miracles. Monks of Gloucester have included: Roger Lacy, earl of Hereford; Roger, Lord Berkeley; Hugh de Port; Elias Giffard; and John Maungeant, canon of Hereford. The quire and south aisle of the abbey church were built from the offerings made at the tomb of Edward II.

The following noblemen are buried in Gloucester Abbey: Osric, the abbey's founder, was buried first in St Petronel's chapel; from there he was moved to the Lady Chapel, and recently he has been removed and laid under a fine stone tomb on the north side of the high altar. The Latin legend on a wall at the foot of his tomb runs thus, 'King Osric the first founder of this monastery, 681'. Robert Curthose, son of William Conqueror, lies in the centre of the chancel; there is a painted wooden effigy on his tomb, made long after his death. King Edward II of Caernarvon lies under a fine tomb in an arch at the head of King Osric's tomb. Abbot Serlo of Gloucester is buried under a fine marble tomb on the south side of the sanctuary. When Malvern alias Parker, the former abbot of Gloucester, recently made a chapel for his burial a corpse wrapped in a bull's hide was dug up under a vault at the head of Edward of Caernarvon's tomb. A monk told me that it was the corpse of a countess of Pembroke. Abbot Horton is buried under a flat stone in the north transept, and Abbot Froucester in a chapel in the south-west part of the quire. Gamage, a Welsh knight, is buried with his wife in a chapel in the north-east part of the nave.

There are the following Latin inscriptions on the walls of the chapter house and cloister at Gloucester: Here lies Roger Lacy, earl of Hereford; Here lies Richard Strongbow, son of Gilbert, earl of Pembroke; Here lies Walter de Lacy; Here lies Sir Philip de Foye; Here lies Bernard of Newmarket; Here lies Payn de Cadurcis; Here lies Adam de Cadurcis; Here lies Robert Curtis.

The following information about abbots of Gloucester, which I was given by an old man who was recently made a monk there, is worth recording: Serlo rebuilt Gloucester Abbey; Abbots Hauley and Farley built the chapel of Our Lady at the east end of the church. Abbot Horton built the north transept. The south transept and much of the chancel vault was funded by offerings at the tomb of King Edward II. Abbot Sebroke was responsible for much of the exceptionally fine square crossing tower, which is a landmark from the hills on every side. Abbot Froucester built the cloister, a particularly fine and expensive piece of work. Abbot Morwent renewed the west front of the church, and one arch on either side of the nave; had he lived it was his intention to refurbish the whole nave in similar style. He also built the grand and costly porch on the south side of the nave. A certain Osborne, the abbey's cellarer, recently built the fine new tower or gatehouse at the south-west side of the churchyard.

The following good mansions and manor houses belong to the abbot of Gloucester: Prinknash, which is situated on a hill three miles east of Gloucester and has a fine park; Vineyard, a good house on a mound due west of Gloucester at the end of the causeway; Hartpury, four miles north-west of Gloucester; Bromfield, two miles from Ludlow, where there used to be a small college which was later appropriated by Gloucester Abbey;

GLOUCESTERSHIRE

Frocester, eight miles from Gloucester and a mile beyond the priory at [*Leonard*] Stanley. There used to be a college of prebendaries at Frocester, but it was suppressed and the estate given to Gloucester Abbey; it is now in the king's hands, and has an annual value of nearly £70.

St Oswald's Priory stood beside the Severn NNW of Gloucester Abbey. Its founders were Ethelred, Earl of the Marches, and Ethelfleda his noble wife, who was a daughter of King Edward the Elder. They installed a college of priests in it, and translated to it from Bardney the body of King Oswald of Northumbria, which they placed in a rich tomb. It so happened that soon after the conquest a bishop of Lincoln, who was a favourite of the king, requested either authority or land in Lindsey, which then belonged to York diocese. The king approached the archbishop of York about it (who was then also bishop of Worcester), and he asked that St Oswald's College should be appropriated to the bishopric of York. This duly took place. The archbishop then negotiated with the priests over whether they would become regular canons of a refounded house. Some agreed, but others did not. However, he achieved his design by force, and founded the house of regular canons, granting them benefices and small pieces of land. He kept the worthwhile land for York Minster, to which it still belongs.

Llanthony Priory, for regular canons, stood on the left bank of the Severn, just below Gloucester. It was founded by a certain Milo, Earl of Hereford, and began as a mere cell of Llanthony in Brecknockshire [*actually Monmouthshire*] – a priory with good estates, mostly in Ireland, and many fine manor houses. Llanthony's property included the following: Newark, an attractive stone-built house next to Lanthony; Quedgeley, three miles from Brockworth; Barrington in the Cotswolds; and Alvington beside the Severn three miles from Chepstow.

The River Severn divides into two channels in the meadows a little above Gloucester. The main channel turns to flow right beside the town, and the other passes through a large bridge at the western end of the Gloucester causeway. They meet again just below Llanthony Priory. This island or middle ground between the two channels is all excellent meadowland, as is the area around Llanthony; cheese made there commands a high premium. Below Gloucester there is no bridge across the Severn, nor is there above Gloucester for eleven or twelve miles, until the small town of Upton-on-Severn. At high tides the Severn flows up this far.

There are few remarkable buildings along the Severn between Gloucester and Aust Cliff, which is where the ferry crosses the river to the Forest of Dean. Eight miles below Gloucester on the right bank is a remote little town within the Forest of Dean called Newnham, and here at high tide the Severn is a half-mile wide. But two miles further down the Severn at high tide is two-and-a-half miles wide, and at Aust Cliff it is a good two miles across. Berkeley lies eighteen miles from Gloucester, and is somewhat inland from the Severn shore. Thornbury is 22 miles from Gloucester and four miles above Aust. It is not far from the Severn shore, and there is a creek running up to it across the marshes from the Severn.

Distances from Gloucester: Tewkesbury, 7 miles; Worcester, 20 miles; Cirencester, 18 miles; Monmouth, 26 miles; Newent, 6 miles; Ross on Wye, 12 miles; Bristol, 30 miles; Hereford, 20 miles.

As soon as I crossed the Severn channel at the west end of Gloucester I came into the Forest of Dean. This extends down the Severn as far as the mouth of the River Wye, where it joins the Severn, and from Monmouth along the left bank of the Wye to its mouth, which is the boundary with Wales. On the whole the soil in the forest is better for growing trees and grass rather than corn, although it produces enough good corn for the needs of the inhabitants. The ground is profitable for mining iron, and there are several iron-making forges there. Flaxley Abbey, a Cistercian house, stood in the Forest of Dean some five or six miles from Gloucester. Mr Baynham lives at Westbury in the Forest, six miles from Gloucester. cont. p. 166 [**1543**: 2/53-64]

FROM KELSTON it is two miles to the village of Bitton in Gloucestershire, and a little above Bitton I crossed a three-arched stone bridge over a brook which appeared at this point to be flowing from the north to join the Avon further south. From there it was about two miles to Hanham. There are several villages collectively known as Hanhams, although they are separate. Sir John Newton lives at this Hanham in an attractive old stone manor house called Barr's Court. Three miles further is Bristol, across hilly and stony ground which is overgrown with ferns in several places.

The site of Bristol: The castle and most of the northern part of the town are built on quite high ground between the Rivers Avon and Fraw, or Frome. But from Frome Bridge a considerable hill (by comparison with the site of the town) extends as far as St Augustine's or Trinity Church, which is the cathedral, and there stops.

Gates in the Bristol walls: In some parts of the town there are double walls, which is a sign that the town has been extended. I believe that Newgate, which has a chapel over it, is built in the outer wall, by the castle. It serves as the city's prison. St John's Gate has a church on each side of it. St John's church is right next to it on the north side, and has crypts. St Giles's Gate lies south-west of the Frome quay. St Leonard's Gate has a parish church over it, and at St Nicholas's Gate there is a church with crypts. These are the inner gates to the old town (that is to say, the town standing on the right bank of the Avon, or the side nearer the Severn). In the outer walls are Petty Gate, Frome Gate, Marsh Gate next to the Avon. In the wall on the other side of the Avon and the bridge are two gates, Redcliff Gate and Temple Gate; and there is a large tower called Harry's Tower, which stands right at the end of the wall built along this bank of the Avon from the bridge area as far as the fortification beyond the Frome channel.

Bristol Castle: The River Frome used to run down from the weir next to the castle, where there is now a stone bridge, along its eastern side. Indeed a small branch of the river still takes this course, but virtually all of the flow is now directed past the north side of the castle, and under an arch by Newgate. The castle has two courts, and in the north-west part of the outer court there is a large keep with a dungeon, said to have been built of stone brought by the red earl of Gloucester from Caen in Normandy. In the other court is an attractive church and many domestic quarters, with a great gate on the south side, a stone bridge and three ramparts on the left bank leading to the mouth of the Frome. Many towers still stand in both the courts, but they are all on the point of collapse.

Parish churches inside Bristol city walls: The churches of St Nicholas, St Leonard, St Lawrence, St John the Baptist, Christ Church, or Trinity, St Audoen, St Werburgh, All Hallows, St Mary Port, and St Peter all within the walls this side of the Avon. St Stephen's lies between the inner and outer walls. On the other side of the Avon are the churches of St Thomas the Apostle and the Temple church. This is now dedicated to St Leonard, but it is said that it was once St Sepulchre's, and that there was a nunnery here. The Jews used to live in this area in the same lane, and their temple or synagogue can still be seen, now used as a warehouse.

Parish churches in the suburbs: St Philip's within Ford's Gate on this side of the Avon, but now some distance from it; St Jacob's by Broadmead Street; St Nicholas's on the brow of the hill north of Frome Gate; St Augustine's, a parish church on the green next to the cathedral church; the parish church of St Mark's in the Gaunts. Redcliffe church, beyond the Avon, is the most beautiful of all the churches by far.

Former religious houses in Bristol: St Augustine's, now the Holy Trinity, has a Latin inscription by the entrance: 'King Henry II and Master Robert Fitzharding, son of the king of Denmark, were the first founders of this monastery.' There are three tombs of the Berkeley family in the south quire aisle. The House of St James lies on high ground north of the castle and next to Broad Mead; its ruins abut right on to the east end of the parish church. Robert, count of Gloucestershire was buried in the centre of the quire, in a grey marble tomb set on six low columns. A parchment document was found in his tomb giving details about him and the time of his death. This is now in the possession of a Bristol brewer. This house of St James was a cell of Tewkesbury. Close to the right bank of the River Frome on the north side of the town was the nunnery of St Magdalen, which has recently been suppressed, along with other houses with an annual value in rents of less than £200. Mr Wicks now lives in this house. Sir Henry Gaunt, who once lived not far from Brandon Hill next to Bristol, built a college of priests with a master on the green beside St Augustine's. Soon afterwards he changed the original foundation to a specific religious order, became controller of the house himself, and lies buried under a flat slab in the vestry. This house at the dissolution had an annual value in lands of £200. Henry had a brother, Sir Maurice Gaunt, who established the black friars in Bristol.

Ruined [?] hospitals: The house of St Bartholomew; the house of the Three Kings next to St Bartholomew's outside Frome Gate; another house not far along the right bank of the Frome by the approach to St James's in Lewin's Mead Street; one in Temple Street; another outside Temple Gate; another by St Thomas's Street; St John's by Redcliffe; a hospital of the Holy Trinity just within Lafford's Gate; the Tuckers' [*fullers'*] hospital in the Temple; the Weavers hospital in Temple Street; long ago there was a hospital where more recently has been a nunnery called St Margaret's. The house of grey friars was on the right bank of the River Frome not far from St Bartholomew's hospital. The black friars stood a little higher than the grey friars on the right bank of the Frome. Sir Maurice Gaunt, elder brother of Sir Henry Gaunt (who founded Gaunt's College), was the founder of the black friars. The white friars stood on the right bank of the Frome opposite the quay. The house of Austin friars was built against the north-west side of Temple Gate on the inside.

Chapels in Bristol and neighbourhood, on this side of the Avon: The Back Chapel (so called because it stood by the Back beside the Avon) belonged to St Nicholas; St George's chapel adjoined the council house; a chapel over New Gate; a chapel of Our Lady on Avon Bridge; St Sprite's [?*the Holy Spirit's*] chapel in Redcliffe churchyard was previously a parish church until the great new church of Redcliffe was built; St Brandon's chapel, now demolished, stood on Brandon Hill, a quarter-mile west of Gaunt's; Bedminster, which lies one mile due ESE [*actually south*] outside the town, is now the mother church of Redcliffe, St Thomas's in Bristol, and Leigh outside.

Bridges in Bristol: The great bridge of four stone arches over the Avon; Weir Bridge on the Frome, right next to the north-east part of Bristol Castle. A channel divides from the Frome a bow-shot length above Weir Bridge, flows through a stone bridge of one large arch, and rejoins the other stream of the Frome at New Gate. This stream flows from Weir Bridge, under another stone [*bridge*], and turns the mill just outside New Gate at the confluence.

Bristol harbour: The Avon basin is tidal for about two miles above Bristol Bridge. St Anne's ferry is about a mile-and-a-half upstream from the town, and Keynsham is about five miles from Bristol on the Avon's left bank. There was a time when ships only sailed up to a place on the Avon called the Back, where the water was and is deep enough; but the riverbed is very stony and uneven there, and so the decision was taken in 1247 to cut a channel some distance away to the north-west of this old quay. The consequence of diverting the course of the River Frome into this channel was to create a soft and muddy harbour for the large ships. Hung Road is about three miles further down the river from Bristol, and at this anchorage are some houses on the right bank of the Avon. About a mile lower is King Road, and there are some houses on the right bank here too. Almost opposite Hung Road is a place called Portchester, where Harding and his son Robert had a fine house, as well as another in Bristol town. Some people believe that much of the depth of the passage from St Vincent's to Hung Road was excavated by hand. It is also said that in the very distant past ships used to sail up as far as St Stephen's church in Bristol.

Notes of important events which occurred in Bristol, taken from a small book about the relics of the house of Calendars in Bristol:

Most of the Calendars' relics were accidentally destroyed by fire. The Calendars are also known as the Guild or Fraternity of the Clergy and Commonalty of Bristol. They were originally based in Trinity Church, but later in All Hallows, and their origin has been forgotten.

Before the conquest Bristol belonged to Ailarde Mean and his son Bitrick. Haymon, earl of Gloucester owned the town after the conquest, and his son, Count Robert, was also Earl of Gloucester and lord of Bristol. Count Robert controlled Bristol Castle, and established St James's Priory in the northern suburb of the town; he was also the founder of Tewkesbury Abbey. King Stephen used force to take Bristol from Count Robert.

During Henry II's reign Robert, earl of Gloucester (illegitimate son of Henry I) and Robert Harding removed the Calendars' Fraternity from Trinity Church to All Hallows. They also established schools in Bristol for the conversion of the Jews, and placed them under the control of the Calendars and the mayor. Harding was the founder of St Augustine's Abbey at Bristol, to which belonged the living of All Hallows church. After Henry III's coronation at Gloucester a papal legate called Cardinal Gwalo came to Bristol and held a council here during the time that Henry of Blois was bishop of Worcester. William, earl of Gloucester took from the Calendars the administration and mastership of the school in Bristol, and gave it to Keynsham Abbey, which he had founded.

Watercourses in Bristol: On this side of the river are St John's Conduit, next to St John's Gate; the Quay Pipe, with a very nice conduit house; All Hallows Pipe next to the Calendars, without a conduit house; St Nicholas's Pipe, with a conduit house. Over the bridge are Redcliffe Pipe, which has a conduit house outside the gate close to Redcliffe Church; another pipe outside Redcliffe Gate with no conduit house; and another outside Port Wall. Port Wall is the finest section of the town wall, and a good part of it is said to have been built by certain butchers; it is the highest and strongest section of all the town walls.

In the year 1247 the channel was excavated along the river from the Gibb Taylor to the Quay. The community on the Redcliffe side was involved in this, as well as the Bristol townspeople; and at the same time the inhabitants of Redcliffe and Bristol were united to form a single corporation of Bristol. Also the land on the St Augustine's side of the river was sold to the citizens of Bristol by Sir William Bradstone, who was then abbot of St Augustine's, in return for a sum of money paid to him by the city; this is attested by a deed drawn up between the mayor and corporation on the one hand, and the abbot and his brethren on the other.

In 1221 the first Dominican friars came to England, and in 1225, on St Bartholomew's day, the first Franciscans. In the same year a man from Adderley [?*Alderley*] pretended that he was Christ, so he was taken to Oxford and crucified there. In [1248] the first Austin friars were established in England. The Jews were at Tewkesbury. In 1309 Bristol's statutes were renewed, the stewards were renamed royal bailiffs, additional land was purchased for the town, and King Edward granted the citizens new privileges.

The almshouse outside Temple Gate is named after its founder, Rogers Magdalens of Nunney. The almshouse by St Thomas's Church is called Burton's Almshouse after the mayor of Bristol who founded it and is buried there. There is another hospital close to the Grey Friars, and another in Temple Street. The very tall and lavish tower of St Stephen's was built by a Bristol merchant named Sheppard.

I left Bristol and after three miles or more of wooded country like that of Kingswood Forest I passed Stoke [*Gifford*] away to my left. There is a ruined manor house of the Berkeleys here, and a park wall; it belongs at present to the Berkeley who is at court. After two more miles of heavily forested and in places barren ground I reached the village of Mangotsfield. I saw here an old manor house which used to belong to the Blunt family, and was later bought by Hussey for his son and direct heir. It was then acquired, through purchase or exchange, by the Berkeleys. A mile further on, over very open and fertile arable and grassland with comparatively few trees, I passed by Codrington, a half-mile away to my left. This used to be the residence of a gentleman named Codrington. Another mile-and-a-half brought me to Dyrham, a fine house of ashlar masonry with a park, which is the home of Mr Dennis. I continued to Dodington, two-and-a-half miles away. The manor house and estate used to belong to the Berkeleys, but was purchased by its present owner, Mr Wicks, who lives here and has carried out a good restoration with attractive buildings.

Mr Walch owns and lives at Little Sodbury, where he has a fine house on the slope of Sodbury Hill with a park. Nearby is a good, large hillfort with two ditches, and there is evidence at Malmesbury that a pre-conquest battle took place on Sodbury Hill, for its part in which Malmesbury Abbey was rewarded. There is another, smaller earthwork at Horton, and a third next to the house of Mr Dennis at Dyrham. All three stand on the same steep ridge. A fourth hillfort is sited at Becketbury [?*Brackenbury*] one-and-a-half miles from Alderley.

A mile from Little Sodbury is Old Sodbury, and here may be seen the ruins of an old manor house which belonged, like the rest of the place, to the earl of Warwick, and now to the Crown. The earls of Warwick also owned Chipping Sodbury, a small, attractive market town on the main road to Bristol. There is a royal park next to the town, which used to belong to the Warwicks. Few trees are visible near the southern end of the open country around Sodbury, but there are abundant woods to the south of Sodbury in a large valley. They lie within Kingswood Forest, whose woodland once extended from there right to the Severn. The ridge of hills near Sodbury veers around towards Gloucester.

From Chipping Sodbury I went to Alderley, which is a clothing village owned by Mr John Poynts, who also lives there. In the time of Edward III it belonged to the Chauncy family. Below Alderley, at least a mile away, is Kingswood. The land between them is enclosed, and partly wooded. Kingswood has some clothiers, but otherwise it is a small and mean village. There is a place in the hills ESE of Alderley where stones are found in the shape of cockle-shells, and huge petrified oyster-shells.

The course of the River Acton: Some people call this stream Loden, and colloquially Laden. Its source is above Dodington, the house of Mr Wicks, then it flows four miles to [*Iron*] Acton, Mr Poyntz's house, and on towards Bristol taking the name of Frome. Two streams meet a half-mile below Iron Acton at a mill. The Sodbury stream comes from the hills nearby. The stream near Alderley is referred to in documents as Avon; it flows to Berkeley.

From Kingswood I went on to Wotton under Edge, which is an attractive market town with one fine long street of good buildings. A fair number of its inhabitants are clothiers, and the town clings to the hillside near its foot. Next to the parish church are the ruins of an old manor house; it once belonged to the Berkeleys, and later to the Lords Lisle. More recently Lord Berkeley used force to recover it, by killing Lord Lisle.

From Wotton it was more than two miles over very hilly and wooded country to Dursley, which is a pleasant clothing town built on a site which clings to the hill, and which nine years ago was granted the privilege of holding a market. Within the town there is a good spring, and this functions as the main source of a stream which serves the fulling mills in the neighbourhood of the town. This stream flows through several other villages before reaching the Severn about four miles away. Dursley had a castle which once belonged to the Berkeleys, and later to the Wicks; still later it fell into disrepair and now it has been completely demolished. It had a fairly good ditch around it, and much of the building was constructed of tufa stone, which is full of pores and holes like pumice. There is a quarry of this very long-lasting stone near Dursley.

Next I went to the village of Tortworth, where some good clothiers live. A stream flows through it; I think that it must be the one which comes from Dursley and then goes on to Berkeley three miles lower. Next to Tortworth parish church is a manor house in which Mr Throgmorton lives. Then I rode two miles to an attractive little clothing town called Wickwar; Lord Delaware is the principal landowner. And another four miles, mostly over open country, brought me to Chipping Sodbury, which, like Old Sodbury village and manor house, was the property of the earls of Warwick. Then to Tormarton village (where Sir Edward Wadham lives) and about four miles beyond across flat countryside I came to Marshfield, which was one of Keynsham Abbey's estates. *cont. p. 402* [**1544:** 5/84-96]

IT IS EIGHT MILES from Bath to Tormarton, almost entirely across open country. Tormarton formerly belonged to the De Rivere family, and then descended to the St Loes. Old Wadham has it for his lifetime, by virtue of having married one of the St Loe ladies, who was a daughter of the last De Rivere. In the nave of Tormarton parish church is the tomb of a certain Petrine De Rivere, owner of the manor, with an epitaph in French.

Dyrham village is two miles from Tormarton, and here there is a fine manor house belonging to Mr Dennis. In former times the manor belonged to the Russells, and one John Russell is buried with his wife Elizabeth in the parish church. There was only a poor house at Dyrham then. From the Russells the estate descended in direct line to the Dennis family. Gilbert Dennis was thought to have been the first member to have owned it, and then came Maurice, who built a new range, and Sir William Dennis, who has built another range in recent years. The Dennis family has a fine park at Dyrham, and they also own a good estate with an attractive house at Siston, two miles away, and another house and estate called Alveston, two miles from Thornbury. When the old forest of Kingswood was disafforested Alveston belonged to the Crown.

From Tormarton I travelled on via Sodbury (two miles of open ground) to Iron Acton (a further three miles of enclosed, wooded ground). Acton manor house lies about a quarter-mile from the village and parish church on flat land composed of a red, sandy soil. It is a good house, and there are two parks beside it, one for red deer, the other for fallow. At one time the earls of Hereford owned Acton manor.

It is three miles or more from Acton to Thornbury, over enclosed ground with many trees. Thornbury's position is almost level, and the town plan is like that of a letter Y, with one long street which branches into two. The direction of the street is roughly north to south, with the right fork leading to the west, and the left fork running south. A weekly market is held in the town, which has a mayor and borough privileges. The parish church stands at the north end of the town; it is a fine building, and all of it except the chancel has been built within living memory. There used to be a good cloth trade, but now unemployment is rife in the town.

In the past there was an unremarkable manor house immediately to the north of the parish church. But the late Edward, duke of Buckingham, attracted by the area around Thornbury, and the position of the house, pulled down most of the old building, and rebuilt the south wall with great opulence in good squared masonry. He also completed the western part and built a beautiful gatehouse up to first-floor level. The gatehouse remains in this state, with its roof temporarily strengthened, and there is an inscription on the front which reads: 'This gatehouse was begun in the year of Our Lord God 1511, the second year of the reign of King Henry VIII, by me Edward, duke of Buckingham, earl of Hereford, Stafford and Northampton.' The duke's motto was 'Dorenesavant' ['*Henceforwards*']. The foundations of a very spacious outer courtyard were started, with several gates and towers after the manner of a castle. It stands some four or five yards high, and remains as evidence of the grand scale of the building work which was intended. There used to be a wooden gallery in the rear yard of the house, which was attached to the north side of the parish church.

Edward, duke of Buckingham constructed a fine park next to the castle, and incorporated into it a great deal of very fertile arable farmland, to make good glades for coursing. The inhabitants cursed the duke for enclosing this land. A small tidal creek flows into the park from the Severn, and Duke Edward had intended to make a channel to lead the water up to the castle. Already before Duke Edward's time there were two parks: one next to the manor house is called Marlwood, and still exists; the other lay at Eastwood a mile or more away, and this the duke enlarged twice (not without a great deal of cursing from the poor tenants), so that it totalled six miles in circumference.

The Severn estuary lies more than a mile from Thornbury across the marshes. Thornbury is ten miles from Bristol and eighteen miles (some say twenty) from Gloucester.

Berkeley is a market town, with a mayor and borough privileges, four miles from Thornbury. A mile or more before I reached the town I passed on my left hand the new park which belongs to Berkeley, and which has a good lodge built on the hill within it. And a bow-shot's length before I entered the town itself, which is set on a hillside, I crossed a bridge over the Tortworth River, which flows down on the left hand side to the Severn marshes. Where the town begins there is another bridge, which I crossed, over a stream which issues from springs in several nearby hills. This stream joins the one from Tortworth in the salt meadows just below the town, and within a mile or so they flow past the salt marsh and the little harbour at New Port into the Severn.

Berkeley is not a town of any size, but it has a good position in excellent surroundings. The cloth trade used to be very important here, and still is to some extent. The church stands on an elevated site at the south end of the town, and the castle, which is not large, stands at the south-west end of the church. There are several towers around the edge of the castle, and the guardhouse to the first gate, which is approached by a bridge over a ditch, is fairly strong. The castle has a square keep, but it does not stand on a raised earthen motte. A number of manors in this area belong to Berkeley, with a total annual value of nearly £700; Swinburne [? *Slimbridge*] is one of the best. In addition there are four parks and two chases, including Oakleaze Park next to the castle, Whitcliff, New Park, Hall Park, and Michaelwood Chase.

My route took me seven miles, largely through wooded country, from Berkeley to Iron Acton, then to Chipping Sodbury, and a further mile to Little Sodbury. The double-ditched hillfort here encloses two acres; it was held by Edward IV's army on their way to the Battle of Tewkesbury. Old Sodbury and Chipping Sodbury belonged to the Earls of Gloucester, and then to the Beauchamps, Earls of Warwick. Gilbert de Clare was another owner. The manor house used to stand close to the west end of the church, but has been completely demolished.

I continued another four miles from Little Sodbury to Pucklechurch, where the park and estate belong to the bishop of Bath. For the first mile-and-a-half the ground was enclosed; the rest was open but fertile. Edmund the Elder, King of England, was killed at Pucklechurch and buried at Glastonbury. Savaric, who was bishop of Bath and Abbot of Glastonbury, transferred Pucklechurch from Glastonbury to Bath, but the benefice belongs to Wells Cathedral. *cont. p. 345* [**1544**: 5/98-102]

In the year 1251 the church, dormitory, cloister and refectory of Hailes Abbey were completed; the total building cost was £5,300. Pinnock Well, at the foot of the Cotswolds, is considered by some people to be one of the furthest sources of the Thames. The stream flows to the village of Naunton, and then Bourton-on-the-Water. Some distance below Bourton it joins another stream, which rises at Kensdale [?*Springhill*] on the Cotswolds, and runs to Hinchwick. After flowing underground from near here, it runs through the village of Swell near Stow, then to Slaughter and so into Bourton Water [*River Windrush*]. A stream flows from the Rollright area, down not far from Chipping Norton, and then I imagine to Bruern. About halfway along the road from Chipping Norton to Stow-on-the-Wold you come to Adlestrop and Horse Bridge. Close by is the border between [*Gloucestershire and Oxfordshire*].

Market towns on the Gloucestershire Wolds: Stow-on-the-Wold, 5 miles from Chipping Norton and 7 or 8 miles from Hailes; [Chipping] Campden, 7 miles north-west of Stow; Northleach, 7 miles south-west of Stow almost on the road from Stow to Cirencester; Fairford, where Mr Tame lives, 7 miles from Northleach; Cirencester; Tetbury; Cheltenham, a market town in the vale, 5 miles from Hailes Abbey.

Gloucester stands on a brook which flows into the Severn. Olney or Alney is close to Deerhurst, which remains in Gloucestershire and is a cell of Tewkesbury. Scorgate beside the Severn was repaired by Ethelfleda. [3/38-40]

Market towns in Gloucestershire: Gloucester; Bristol; Cirencester; Tewkesbury.

Castles in Gloucestershire: Gloucester; Sudeley near Winchcombe; Cirencester probably had a castle; Bristol Castle.

Rivers in Gloucestershire: Severn; the Avon touches at Tewkesbury; another Avon at Bristol. The Isis rises three miles from Cirencester, not far from a village called Kemble, and less than a half-mile from the Fosse Way between Cirencester and Bath. From the source it flows four miles to Latinelad [*Latton*], and then Cricklade a mile lower, and soon afterwards it receives the Churn. When there is serious drought in the summer very little water can be seen at the source of the Isis, or none at all, but the stream is fed by many other springs which all flow into the one valley. The Churn is at Cirencester (which should be Churncester) and close to Chesterton (or more correctly Churntown). The main source of the Churn is at Coberley, the chief house of Sir John Bridges. This is seven miles from Gloucester, and five miles or more from Cirencester, which the river flows past. Six miles further downstream, and one mile below Cricklade, the Churn flows into the Isis.

In general there is abundant arable, pasture and woodland throughout Gloucestershire; the Cotswolds, where the huge flocks of sheep are, is an exception, although even here good corn is grown in some places.

Gloucester is walled, except where the Severn provides sufficient defence. The castle is an impressive old building. It has no old British bricks in it, but is mostly built of squared stone masonry. The oldest and strongest part of the whole castle is the high tower in the central courtyard. There is a double ditch around it. There are eleven parish churches in the town, not counting the house of black monks. Until recently there were also black canons outside the town. A bowshot's length from the town in the Hereford direction there is a long stone bridge, and under this flows a large channel of the Severn which, as I recall, is called Owseburne. It flows for about a mile, leaving the main course of the river above the town, and joining it again below. It thereby makes an island of a fine meadow.

Bristol on the Avon is a large city, with a good wall and a fine castle. From memory I believe that it now has eighteen parish churches. St Augustine's, a house of black canons, lies outside the walls; it possesses a chapel in a large courtyard in which St Jordanus lies buried. He was one of the followers of Augustine who brought the gospel to the Angles. I recall that there is a house outside the walls called the Gaunts or Bonhommes. There are four friaries, including a very fine house of white friars. About a quarter-mile below the town in a meadow a great channel or cut leaves the River Avon, and this enables the larger vessels such as ships with main-tops to sail up to the town. The Avon almost surrounds the town, therefore, and ships approach it on both sides. I did not ascertain whether any fresh water feeds into this channel from the land. The Avon flows into the Severn at King Road, which is three miles below Bristol across land, and six miles by water. In the hills around Bristol are found small stones of various colours which imitate precious stones.

Cirencester stands in a valley on the River Churn. The name is a corruption of Churncester, and may be the place called by Ptolemy Coriminum. It seems probable that in the past channels have been made to lead part of the flow of the river through the city, and then return it to its valley. The old wall, of which a few traces survive, was nearly two miles in circumference. Anyone who walks along the river bank can still make out quite clearly the outline of the foundations of towers which were once set into the wall. And close to the place where the abbot recently set up the excellent cloth mill, an old ruined tower was demolished for stone to build the mill walls. In it was found a squared stone which had previously fallen down and broken into several pieces. I was told by a person who saw it, but who was scarcely literate, that it had on it a Roman inscription, of which he made out the words 'Pont. Max.'. Various coins are often found there, and the finest are of Diocletian, but I cannot confirm that the inscription was a dedication to him. A multi-coloured mosaic pavement was discovered in the middle of the old town in a meadow, and close to the town in our own times was discovered the broken shin bone of a horse. One end had been closed off with a peg, and when this was removed by a shepherd he found it filled with silver coins.

There was probably a castle or some other large building on the SSW side of the wall, because the banks and ditches are still there. One explanation is that a siege was laid against the town at this point; not far from here and outside the walls there is a steep circular mound like that of a windmill, which is known as Grismund's or Gusmund's Tower. It is now a rabbit warren, and unusually large human bones have been discovered there, as well as graves made of hewn stone. A round vessel made of lead was found in one of them, which contained ashes and pieces of bone.

More than three-quarters of the old town is now good meadowland. The other quarter is still well inhabited; it has a most lavishly ornamented parish church, and an abbey of black canons which was founded by Henry I. Before that it was an important collegiate church. The nave of the abbey church contains a tomb with a cross of white marble inscribed: 'Here lies Rumbald, a priest, sometime dean of this church, who was chancellor in the time of Edward, King of England.' There is also a small chapel which is an almshouse.

The soil of the stony fields around Cirencester is more suitable for barley than for wheat, and in this area, as on the Cotswolds, there is not a great supply of wood, except in a few places given over to woodland from necessity. About halfway between the point where the woodland runs out and the open country of the Cotswolds begins, between Gloucester and Cirencester, the fine old road made by the Britons can still be seen very clearly, running in a straight line to Cirencester, and from there to Bath. But some people maintain that the road from Cirencester to Bath should be regarded as the Fosse Way, and that the road from Cirencester towards Gloucester is another of the four roads made by the Britons. The Abbot of Cirencester told me that all four roads should meet and cross near Cirencester.

At Little Subbury, or Sodbury, in Gloucestershire twelve miles north-east of Bristol, can be seen on a hill a strong double-ditched military camp. Mr Walsh now has it under arable. [3/99-102]

The senior branch of the Tame family is at Stowell near Northleach. Mr Horne, who lives near Langley in Oxfordshire, is married to the daughter of this family, and she will inherit, bringing him land with an annual value of £80. Sir Edmund Tame of Fairford near Cricklade was related to the Tames of Stowell. The Tame who now lives at Fairford has been married for twelve years, without issue. So it is likely that Sir Humphrey Stafford, who married Tame's sister, and who is the son of old Stafford of Northamptonshire, will inherit the Fairford estate. Thus it seems that the Tame family name is falling into a serious decline. [4/78]

Lord Berkeley and Lord Lisle engaged in a passionate dispute over the ownership of Wotton under Edge, so much so that they arranged to fight, and met in a meadow at a place called Nibley. Lord Lisle raised the visor of his helmet just as Berkeley's archers fired a massive volley, and the arrow of an archer from the Forest of Dean entered his mouth and passed out through his neck. There were several other casualties, and Lisle's men fled. Immediately Berkeley and his men ransacked the manor house at Wotton, and occupied the building. Berkeley had sided with Henry VI, and Lisle had favoured Edward IV. Berkeley had once been a true friend of Richard III, and in order to ingratiate himself with King Edward he promised to make the marquis of Dorset his heir, but in this he was unsuccessful.

Berkeley was parted from his estate in the following way: The circumstances of Lord Lisle's death were at first overlooked and then Berkeley was pardoned. Lisle had no heir, but his brother negotiated and made a deal on behalf of his own son, who had been set to inherit the estate. This enraged Lord Berkeley to such an extent that he named Henry VII as the heir to most of his lands, was created a marquis, and lies buried in the Austin friary in London. [4/105]

Drisilega (alias Dursley) once lay within the forest. Part of Dursley Castle was taken for the new building at Dodington. There is a quarry of tufa stone near Dursley, from which much of the castle was built. The old house at Dodington lies within the moat next to the new. In a grave in the roadway next to Dodington church was found a glass containing bones. And from the soil of Dodington's fields is dug Roman pottery which had been fired and decorated to an exceptionally high standard. Also found in Dodington field was an earthenware pot containing Roman coins.

These are the ancient bounds of Kingswood Forest: The Bristol forks [?crossroads]; Huntingford, near Kingswood Abbey; the River Severn; the ridgeway along the brow of Sodbury Hill from Lansdown in one direction as far as Alderley stream in the other. The witnesses of its disafforesting included Gilbert, earl of Gloucester and Hertford. The whole of the wood in the great valley between Sodbury and Kingswood was called Horwood. Mangotsfield (or Magnusfelde ['*the great field*']) is actually a small manor. There is no doubt that it was once a nunnery – indeed part of the cloister is still standing. It now belongs to Lord Berkeley. Some people maintain that there was also a nunnery at Berkeley.

In recent times Tetbury has been part of the Mowbray estate, but Beverstone Castle, which stands about a mile from Tetbury, is a fortress built by one of the Berkeley family from the spoils he won in France. More than a mile from Little Sodbury is the village of Badminton, and here there is a modest manor house and a park, which within living memory has belonged to three generations of the Butler family, relations of Lord Sudeley. Butler has land worth £180 annually.

There has been a large defensive work on a hill now called Nibley, which is overgrown with trees. It lies about halfway between Wotton under Edge and Dursley, closer to Wotton. In the parish of Nibley Lord Lisle was killed by an arrow, which was fired by a certain James Hiatte of the Forest of Dean.

Cow Berkeley (shortened to Coberley) is the seat of Mr Bridges. Hubley [?Abson] and Wick belong to Lord Cheddar.

Sir William Berkeley, a very old knight, and owner of the well moated castle at Beverstone, has another manor house called Over [*Over Court, Almondsbury*], which is four miles from Bristol. He told me that Thomas, Lord Berkeley, was taken prisoner in France, but later he recovered his losses by taking French prisoners and at the battle of Poitiers. Consequently he was able to build Beverstone Castle entirely, and to make it a very attractive fortress at the time.

Mr Wicks of Dodington maintains with some justification that the Berkeleys of Dursley are as old a family as the Berkeleys of Berkeley, if not older. But the fact that their name is taken from the town and manor of Berkeley suggests to the contrary.

At Boddington, four miles north of Gloucester, there is a fine manor house with a park. It belonged to Lord Beauchamp, but passed to a man named Rede, who was his servant, but married the eldest of his master's three daughters; and it still belongs to the Rede family. The Beauchamps also owned a castle with fine towers, which they had built on a hillside, at Bronsil in the parish of Eastnor, about two miles from Ledbury. It was bought by Sir John Talbot of Grafton near Bromsgrove.

There was a nunnery at Minchinhampton near Tetbury; and at Boxwell, two miles east of Wotton under Edge, there was a house of nuns which, according to some people, was destroyed by the Danes. It now belongs to Gloucester Abbey.

Deerhurst stands beside the River Severn on the left bank (as one goes downstream) a mile below Tewkesbury. The site of the present settlement is like a meadow, so that when the level of the Severn rises substantially the place is almost surrounded by water. It is assumed that in the past it was less prone to flooding, because the river bottom was deeper and less choked with sand, so that less damage was caused during floods.

Deerhurst is now only a poor village, and a portion of its manor belonged in recent years to the abbot of Tewkesbury. The portion which had belonged to Westminster passed to Pershore Abbey until given away by William the Conqueror. The remainder belonged to Deerhurst Abbey until it was alienated from the mother house of which it was a cell, St Denis near Paris. The last alien prior, during the reign of Edward IV, was a certain Hugo Magason, who was a monk of St Denis. About this time it was dissolved, and most of its land was given to Fotheringhay, although it is said that Eton College also had some claim. A dispute followed between these colleges and Tewkesbury Abbey, which after a long interval was settled in Henry VII's reign; Goldcliff Priory with its lands, which had then recently passed to Tewkesbury, were to go to Fotheringhay College, and Deerhurst should go to Tewkesbury.

Bede refers to a notable abbey which existed in his time at Deerhurst. This was destroyed by the Danes, and Werstan, so it is said, fled from there to Malvern. The monastery of the French order was built after the conquest. The old priory stood a bow-shot east of the Severn, and north of the town. Several of the town's street-names survive, including Fisher Street, but their buildings have gone. Two fairs are still kept, on the feasts of the discovery and exaltation of the cross [3rd May, 14th September]. Between Deerhurst and the old site of Holme Castle there is a park, but this belonged to the earl of Gloucester's house at Holme, not to Deerhurst. In this park, Tewkesbury Park, there is a fine manor house of timber and stone; Lord Edward Spencer lived there, and more recently my Lady Mary.

Prestbury is a pleasant little town situated a mile ESE of Cheltenham. Nearby is a quarry of fine stone, from which part of the fine stone masonry at Tewkesbury was constructed. It is alleged by some that long ago it used to be a chartered market town, and its market was revived twenty years ago. The town used to be larger than it is at present, to some extent as a result of accidental damage by fire. It belonged to the earls of Gloucester, and Gilbert de Clare, the second earl of Gloucester, gave it to the bishopric of Hereford to compensate for wrongs he had done to Bishop Cantilupe and his church. A Prestbury freeholder named Simon, who was a servant to the red earl, and who derived £10 income annually from the manor, was required to wait upon the bishop of Hereford if he went to Scotland. Simon's holding now has a fine house built on it, called Overton; it lies a mile-and-a-half outside Prestbury, but still within the parish, and it now belongs to William Bagers. The bishop of Hereford owns Prestbury, and he has a fine house there on the north-west side of the town towards Tewkesbury. It has a good moat, and stands within a quarter-mile of Southam. [4/130-5]

Manor houses which belong to the abbot of Tewkesbury: Stanway was enlarged and virtually rebuilt by Abbot Cheltenham during the reign of Henry VII. Forthampton is a fine house standing on the right bank of the Severn a mile below Tewkesbury, and opposite Tewkesbury Park which lies across the river. The manor house in this park, and the holme where the castle stood, were leased by Henry VII to the abbot of Tewkesbury.

Tewkesbury stands on the left bank of the River Avon at least a bowshot above the confluence of the Avon and the Severn. At the north end of the town there is a large stone bridge, and a short distance above it the Avon breaks into two arms. But the bridge is so large that it spans both arms. The right arm flows into the Severn within a bowshot of the bridge, and at this point there is the town quay for ships which are called picards [*sailing-barges*]. The other arm flows down beside the town and the abbey, which it leaves on its east side, and passing close to Holme Castle enters the Severn.

Bredon is a very notable church and parish, with many dependent villages and hamlets, but it does not now have a market. It stands on the left bank of the Avon two-and-a-half miles above Tewkesbury. From [*Bishop's*] Cleeve a small brook called the River Swilgate flows down and joins the Avon by its left bank at Holme Castle. It is fed by water descending from the surrounding hills, and after a sudden downpour it becomes a raging torrent.

Tewkesbury has three streets, which meet at the market cross. The most important is called High Street. There was no other parish church in the town apart from the west end of the abbey church. King John, who by right of his wife was earl of Gloucester, caused Tewkesbury Bridge to be built of stone. The person entrusted to carry out this order first made a stone bridge across the mainstream of both arms of the river, north and west; but then to save time and money he built a wooden bridge of great length at the northern end across land prone to sudden inundations. The money thus saved was spent on Hanley Castle, five miles from Tewkesbury and a mile from Upton, which formed part of the inheritance of the earldom of Gloucester. The red earl spent much of his time here, and also at Holme, the castle of uncertain date which stood at the south-west end of the abbey. The Clares, earls of Gloucester also lived there. Some portions of the castle remained standing within living memory, but now only ruined footings of some of the walls are visible, and the site is called Holme Hill. The red earl greatly troubled St Thomas [*?Cantilupe*] of Hereford.

To pay for maintaining the bridge King John granted all the tolls of his Wednesday and Saturday markets in the town. This arrangement still continues, but the income is diverted to private gain rather than to repairing the bridge. King Edward's brother George, duke of Gloucester [*i.e. Clarence*], had an idea to divert the Avon around Tewkesbury, and so to enlarge the town.

There was little or no settlement at Tewkesbury at the time when two dukes of Mercia, the brothers Odo and Dodo, built the priory there for Benedictine monks, as a daughter or sister house to Cranborne in Dorset. Odo and Dodo gave Tewkesbury the estate of Stanway, including its dependencies Toddington, Prescott and Didcot [*?Didbrook*]. Tracy now lives at Stanway. Later, towards the end of Danish rule and that of Edward Confessor, the earl of Gloucester was Aylward Meaw [*Snew*], and he was reckoned the founder of Cranborne. Aylward had a son called Brictric, who was earl of Gloucester at about the time of Duke William of Normandy's arrival in England. Matilda, William's wife, asked her husband as a favour to deliver Brictric to her, and she imprisoned him in the castle at Hanley [*?Handley*] near Salisbury, where he died. There is a rumour that before she married Duke William, she wanted Brictric for her husband, but he refused, and so afterwards he received harsh treatment at her hands.

King William gave the preferment of the county of Gloucester to his wife Matilda. Later it passed to Robert Fitzhamon, who was related to William the Conqueror's nephew, Duke Rollo. This Robert Fitzhamon converted Tewkesbury Priory into an abbey, making Cranborne a dependent cell and transferring the principal Cranborne lands to his new foundation. He was buried at Tewkesbury, at first in the chapter house, but later translated to the north side of the quire in a chapel.

Robert Fitzhamon left three daughters. The two elder daughters became nuns, at Shaftesbury and Wilton, but the third was maintained by Henry I, and later married his illegitimate son Robert (the Consul), who was earl of Gloucester. He it was who built Bristol Castle, or at least most of it. Everyone agrees that he was responsible for the great square stone keep, and that the stone for it – like the stone for the tower of Tewkesbury Abbey church – came from Caen in Normandy. Robert was buried at St James's Priory, Bristol, and his son William succeeded to the earldom.

William had two sons, Robert and Roger. Robert died young, but Roger became a priest and a bishop. William arranged that his son Robert should be buried at Keynsham, which was then a small priory; later he repaired and endowed it anew, turning it into an Augustinian abbey. William died at Bristol Castle, and it was his wish that he should be buried next to his father at St James's. But his body was taken secretly by night to Keynsham. William had granted the entire manor of Marshfield, where there was a nunnery, so it is said, to Keynsham, and had appropriated the living of Marshfield to St James's. Consequently this benefice passed to Tewkesbury.

William had three daughters. One married a Breton, Amauri, and he was earl of Gloucester for six years. Another married Richard I's brother, King John, who had no children by her, and lived with her for only a year, before repudiating her and marrying the daughter of the earl of Hereford. Nevertheless through her he became earl of Gloucester, and he retained the town and castle of Bristol within the hundred of Barton, which lies in Gloucestershire between Bristol and Kingswood Forest. This remains crown property up to the present. The wife whom John rejected later married the earl of [Essex].

[Richard] de Clare married another daughter of William, earl of Gloucester, and so succeeded to the earldom. Their son Gilbert became the first of that name to be earl, and he is buried in the quire of Tewkesbury. His son was the second Richard, earl of Gloucester, and he too was buried in Tewkesbury quire, on the right hand of his father, with his effigy in silver. He in turn had a son Gilbert, the second of that name, and he was nicknamed 'the Red', because of his very ruddy and bloodshot complexion. His dealing with the Tewkesbury monks was harsh, and he took away the gifts that his grandfather Gilbert had given them. He was buried on his grandfather's left hand side.

This second Gilbert had a third, who was earl of Gloucester, and who restored to the abbey everything that his father had confiscated. He was killed at the battle of Stirling in Scotland, and was buried to the left of his father. He was only in his 23rd year when he died, and he was greatly mourned because he was a good man. His son John died in infancy and is buried in the Lady Chapel at Tewkesbury. But Gilbert had three sisters, the red earl's daughters. The eldest, Eleanor, married Hugh Despenser, the second son of Hugh, earl of Winchester, and so by her became earl of Gloucester. He was beheaded and quartered at Hereford, and one of his quarters was buried near the piscina by the high altar at Tewkesbury. Another married a member of the Audley family, who thus succeeded to the title. Edward, the third Hugh Despenser's son, had a son Thomas, and he was made earl of Gloucester by Richard II. This Thomas married Constance, the daughter of Edmund of Langley, duke of York. After this the estate was dispersed, and Thomas of Woodstock, the fifth son of Edward III, was made duke of Gloucester. He was followed by Humphrey, Henry IV's son, and by Richard, Edward IV's brother. [4/136-41]

St Arilda the Virgin was martyred at Kington near Thornbury, by a certain tyrant called Muncius, who cut her head off because she refused to lie with him. She was translated to Gloucester Abbey, and has performed great miracles.

Roger, earl of Hereford, founded Flaxley Abbey in the Forest of Dean at the exact place where his brother was killed by an arrow whilst hunting. There was a notice explaining this hung up in the abbey church at Flaxley. One of the bishops of Hereford was of great assistance in building Flaxley. [5/156,160]

Parson Avery of Deene told me that he had read that the murderer of St Cenelm, Askaperius, was married to Quindred [*Cwenthryth*], Cenelm's sister, and that he reigned for two or three years after Cenelm, until one of Cenelm's relatives deposed him. But I must find out more about this. More recently he has told me that this information occurs in the life of St Cenelm, which also says that Winchcombe was a walled town. Parson Avery further said that the town was considerably built up in the direction of Sudeley Castle, and that some evidence of a ditch and the foundation of a wall may be seen there. In another direction there are also settlement remains some distance beyond the High Street and above the church, where Corndean Farm is. So that Winchcombe must have been an extremely large town in the past. The site of the monastery was in the best part of the whole town, and nearby, where the parish church is, was King Cenwulf's palace.

Winchcombe stands at the foot of the Cotswolds. The local name for the river which flows through the centre of the old part of the town is 'Grope cunte', but shortly after Toddington, which it passes, it changes its name, and beyond a small village called Hampton, on this side of Evesham, it flows into the Avon. This little river has its source two miles above Winchcombe in the hills, and it flows within a quarter-mile of Hailes Abbey in the valley below. [5/220-1]

HAMPSHIRE

THE *WEST COUNTRY ITINERARY* of 1542, in its present form, ended at Winchester, and this is the only surviving journey which Leland made into the county. He has left us detailed descriptions of Winchester itself, and of his excursion to Southampton and Portsmouth, but almost nothing about the Isle of Wight, north Hampshire or the New Forest. One distinguished exception is his note on Silchester, which shows that he was able to recognise cropmarks on an archaeological site.

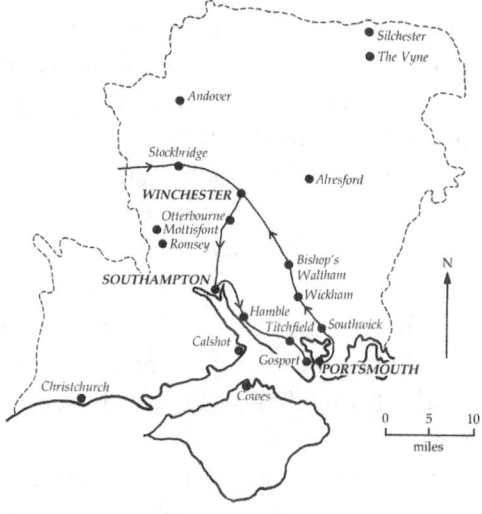

FROM BUCKHOLT WOOD it is eight miles across open unwooded country to Stockbridge. The bridge here across the Andover Water [*River Anton*] has arches of stone, and Stockbridge stands on the left bank (as the river flows) below the Anton's confluence with the Horwel Stream [*?Wherwell Stream, i.e. River Test*]. Andover, which is three miles north of Stockbridge, has a stone bridge over the river, but there is no notable bridge in between, and the Anton rises not far above Andover. Romsey is twelve miles from Stockbridge, and Winchester is eight miles, all across open country without woodland. The soil between Salisbury and Winchester is white clay and chalk.

The circumference of the town wall at Winchester is about a mile-and-a-half, and the distance from east to west is greater than from north to south. The wall has six gates: North, South, East and West; the King's Gate, between South Gate and Wolvesey, the bishop's palace; and Bourne Gate, a small postern between North Gate and East Gate. The castle adjoins West Gate on its south side.

The cathedral church and the close lie on the south side of the town, occupying an area (with the cemetery) nearly half a mile in circumference. From near King's Gate almost to East Gate the limit of the town is marked first by the close wall and then by the wall of Wolvesey castle or palace. The palace is well fortified, and nearly surrounded by water.

An arm of the River Alre provides water for St Mary's Abbey, a little to the east within the town wall, and then flows on to the bishop's palace at Wolvesey. In a courtyard on the north side of St Mary's Abbey church there is a fine chapel approached by steps, with a vaulted charnel-house beneath. It was founded by a gentleman named Inkepen, whose arms were a chequerboard of silver and black. There are three marble tombs of priests who served this chapel.

Entering Winchester by East Gate there was a house of grey friars just inside the gate on the right, and a little further west on the same side is a fine hospital of St John for sick paupers. The chapel there contains an image of St Beornstan, once bishop of Winchester, and I have read that he founded a hospital in Winchester.

The black friars college stood somewhat towards the north within the town. There were also white friars, and an Austin house, which was a little way outside South Gate on the left hand side of the Southampton road. St Swithun's, now called Trinity, stands on the south side of the town. There is a chapel with a charnel-house at the west end of the cathedral church.

The new college lies immediately outside the close wall to the south of the town. The water which flows through Wolvesey and the close passes right by its eastern side and on towards St Cross. Only a narrow causeway separates the new college from St Elizabeth of Hungary's college, immediately to its east, which was founded by Bishop John of Pontoise. The main course of the River Alre divides into two a little above the college, and one arm runs on each side of it. In between them, not far from the college church of St Elizabeth, is a chapel dedicated to St Stephen.

There was a hospital for the poor just outside King's Gate which was maintained by the monks of St Swithun, but it has been suppressed. Several of the parish churches which lay within the town walls were suppressed by Bishop Fox, and he invited the parishioners to maintain those that remained and so provide a reasonable living for their incumbents.

The street which leads from the High Street to North Gate is called the Jury, because Jews lived there and had their synagogue there. The staple houses for wool lay in a back street between the West Gate and North Gate. Ancient writers speak of St Michael's Gate, but the name is not now in use. St Michael's church is beside King's Gate, and so I conjecture that this was once called St Michael's Gate, or else it was South Gate.

At East Gate is the largest of Winchester's suburbs. It is sometimes called the Soken, and has two parish churches. Beyond it to the east beside the London road on top of a hill is a chapel of St Giles, which looks as though it had once been much larger. Waldavus, earl of Northumberland, a noble Saxon or Dane, was beheaded at William the Conqueror's command.

There is also a little suburb outside West Gate, but its church or chapel is now used as a barn. The north suburb, which is called Hyde, still has a parish church. The great abbey of Hyde which stood here was originally called New Minster and lay within the close beside St Swithun's, then known also as the Old Minster. New Minster took the name of Hyde when it moved there. The bones of Alfred, king of the West Saxons, and of King Edward his son were translated from New Minster to Hyde, and were laid in a tomb in front of the high altar. Two small lead tablets inscribed with their names were recently found in this tomb. The bones of St Grimbald and St Judoce also lay here. On the south side of Hyde Abbey towards the wall is Denmark meadow, where Guy, Earl of Warwick, is reputed to have killed the great Colebrande the Dane in single combat.

There is a small suburb outside Dorne (or postern) Gate, and a fine suburb called the King's Street outside King's Gate. Outside South Gate the small suburb had a fine church dedicated to St Faith, but it was suppressed by Bishop Fox, and its parish annexed to St Cross. There was also a very fine chapel to St Catherine on a hill scarcely half a mile south of Winchester, which was endowed with lands. I was told that Cardinal Wolsey had it suppressed.

This is the course of the River Alre: The river rises in a large number of fair silvery springs a good mile above Alresford, which flow into a valley to form a large, wide lake commonly called Alsford Pond. Where the valley narrows the river runs under a stone bridge at the end of Alresford town, which lies on the left bank. Three miles downstream, at Itchen Stoke, there is a small bridge for horsemen and foot passengers, and two miles further, at Easton village, there is a wooden bridge for carts. When it reaches a place called Worthy the river begins to divide into arms, and then into streamlets which flow to Hyde and the lower, eastern end of Winchester, giving a plentiful water supply to the streets, the close, St Mary's Wolvesey and the new college. The main stream flows from Worthy to Winchester east bridge, which is of two arches of stone, and then a furlong downstream it divides into two, to flow on either side of St Elizabeth's College. Next it flows past St Cross, which is a quarter-mile away on the right, and then to Twyford, a mile-and-a-half lower, where all its streams merge into a single course. Six miles further, at Wood Mill, it flows into a salt creek. Mr Philpot lives near Twyford. A little above Wood Mill there is a wooden bridge called Black Bridge, and there is another Black Bridge between St Elizabeth's College and the east bridge at Winchester. At Otterbourne, 3 miles south of Winchester, a brook called the Otter flows into the Alre from the west.

The road from Winchester to London runs as follows: Alresford (7 miles); Alton (7 miles); Farnham (7 miles); Guildford (9 miles); London (25 miles).

From Winchester to Southampton is ten miles; Otterbourne is three miles along the road. In some places between the two towns the soil is fairly good, but there is much dry, ferny ground, more suitable for breeding cattle than for growing corn. Most of the land has been enclosed and is reasonably well wooded. Three miles south of Winchester, roughly to the south, there is a park belonging to the bishop of Winchester called Hursley, and beside it Merdon Castle, of which small ruins or vestiges survive.

Old Southampton was a place noted for its fishermen, and to some extent for merchants; it stood about a quarter-mile north-east of New Southampton and extended down to the water's edge. Good corn and grass now grow on its site, which is called St Mary's Field after the church of St Mary next to it. Men still alive remember seeing several houses actually in the field which is now called St Mary's, up in the area of Old Southampton. And some people believe that the large suburb which lies outside the East Gate of New Southampton adjoining St Mary's church is really part of Old Southampton.

A small and mean chapel dedicated to St Nicholas still stands at the east end of St Mary's church within the large churchyard, and there is a persistent belief that it marks the site of the former parish church of Old Southampton. I was told by one person that the present large church of St Mary was built because the old church was too small, and came about in the following way: Matilda, queen of England, asked why so many people were walking around outside St Nicholas's church, and someone told her that it was because there was not enough room inside. Thereupon she promised with an oath that she would build a new church, and so St Mary's came into being. It had been the intention of either Queen Matilda, or later benefactors, to make St Mary's collegiate, but this plan was not fully implemented. Nonetheless St Mary's, as a mark of the antiquity of Old Southampton, is now regarded as the mother of all the New Southampton churches, and because of this the communal burying-ground of New Southampton is in St Mary's churchyard. In addition there are many fine marble tombs of New Southampton merchants in St Mary's, by virtue of its high status as mother church. On the south side of the churchyard there is a good stone mansion house which belongs to the incumbent of St Mary's.

The old town of Southampton was burnt during wartime, and was plundered and destroyed by French pirates. It was for this reason that its inhabitants removed themselves to a more convenient site, and obtained royal permission and help to build New Southampton, with a good and extremely strong wall around it as protection from enemies. These are the gates in the wall: first the Bargate on the north side. It is large and well-fortified, with the city hall in its upper part and the town prison beneath. There is a large suburb outside this gate, beyond which on either side are a pair of large water-filled dykes. Between here and the east gate are four wall turrets; the third, a corner tower, is of considerable strength. The east gate is strong (although not on the same scale as the Bargate), and it too has a suburb outside it. It is here that St Mary's, the mother church of New Southampton, is situated. Between the east and south gates are six good wall turrets, and it should be noted that the double ditch outside the wall which runs from the castle to the Bargate continues almost as far as the south gate. This south gate is not really on the south side, but on the south-east. A fortress adjoins it with sufficient weaponry to defend that part of the estuary. A little further south is a less important gate called God's House Gate, after the hospital adjoining it; and not far beyond is the Water Gate. This is a fine gate, and leads out to a good square quay for shipping, which has been strengthened by driving piles into the water of the estuary. There are three more turrets between here and the strong west gate, which has outside it a similar large quay for ships as that outside the

Water Gate. In addition there is a postern gate, and another gate next to the castle. The castle has a remarkable dungeon keep, which is large, fine and extremely strong, by virtue of both its site and its construction.

There are five parish churches within the town of Southampton; Holy Rood church stands in the main street. A college of grey friars stood in the ESE part of the town abutting the wall between the east and south-east gates. Towards the south side of the town is a hospital called God's House, which contains a chapel dedicated to St Julian the bishop. The hospital was founded by two merchants who were brothers; they were named (presumably after the saints' days on which they were born) Gervase and Protasius [Roger]. When Old Southampton was burnt by pirates these brothers, so I discovered, were living in the same house as the hospital now occupies; for God's sake they converted their dwelling into a hospital for poor people and endowed it with some land. At Winchester I inspected a register of those abbeys, priories and hospitals in the gift of the bishop of Winchester, and the list included the hospital, or house of God at Southampton. I assume, therefore, that a bishop of Winchester must have refounded the hospital and given it more lands, and thereby acquired the patronage. But more recently, at the request of a queen, it was handed over to Queen's College, Oxford, which maintains the hospital and receives its surplus income.

Southampton has three main streets. The one which leads from the Bargate to the Water Gate is among the finest streets in any English town, and its architecture, despite being timber-built, is good. At the centre of this street has been erected a fine house for making accounts. Fresh water is brought into Southampton by a lead conduit, and there are a number of conduit houses in the town supplied by it. There are many excellent merchant's houses, and the best of all is the one built on the west side of the town by Huttoft, the former customs officer for Southampton. Other fine houses are those of Mr Lyster, chief baron of the Royal Exchequer, Mr Mille the recorder of the city, and the Italians Nicoline [Niccolo de Egra] and Guidotti.

A brief description of Southampton Water: At the mouth or entrance to Southampton Water the distance from shore to shore is roughly two miles. At the western point is a strong castle which has recently been built, called Caldshore or colloquially Cawshot. Opposite it, on the eastern side, is a place called Hamble Hook, consisting of three or four fishermen's houses. On its west side the estuary extends inland for seven miles, until it is opposite Southampton; here the width of the crossing is about a mile. Then it continues another three miles up to Redbridge, and is still tidal a mile beyond that. Both the River Test and the Stockbridge Water [*i.e. River Blackwater*] flow in the same valley into this salt-water arm, which is the furthest and most important head of Southampton Water. On this side of the estuary I noticed little else to comment on. But I did note that at the mouth of the estuary the main flow was on the southern side.

Three miles from Hamble Hook, which lies at the harbour entrance on the eastern shore, a creek usually known as the Hamble Creek or Hamble Harbour flows inland to the north-east, and this offers a very good anchorage for large ships. It is named after a good fishing town called Hamble, which is situated on the left or western side about a mile upstream from the mouth of the creek. This place now belongs to the new college in Winchester, and was previously owned by a priory of religious men, also in Winchester. Three miles above Hamble, right at the head of the creek, is a good village called Budley or Botley. It is my impression that the stream which flows through Bishop's Waltham, a pleasant little town three miles away, issues into this creek.

Barely a mile above the mouth of Hamble Creek, on the shore of Southampton Water itself, stands Letelege [*Netley*], where until recently were the extensive buildings of a Cistercian abbey. Two miles further up the estuary a large creek runs inland to the north. On its left or western side a little way from the shore there stands a chapel to Our Lady of Grace, which used to be frequented by pilgrims. And just opposite it on the eastern side is a small village called Itchen, with a ferry across called Itchen Ferry. Two miles further up this creek on the left or western side is St Denys, where until recently there was a priory of Augustinian canons. On the right or eastern bank almost opposite St Denys is Bitterne. The bishops of Winchester used to have a castle here, and some of its ruins still survive, but now there is a farm belonging to the bishop of Winchester. At the head of this creek, less than a mile further upstream, is Wood Mill, which is a good place for taking salmon. The waters of the Alresford river [*River Itchen*], augmented by several streams which join it, flows into this creek, and Southampton is less than half a mile above its mouth.

The shoreline from Calshot Castle to Christchurch (Twineham): Beyond Calshot to the south-west a creek extends from the coast three or four miles inland. At its head was the Cistercian abbey of Beaulieu, with a small town and a piece of land which had the right of sanctuary. Hurst Castle is reckoned to be fourteen miles along the coast from Calshot, and lies almost directly opposite the furthest point of the Isle of Wight. The crossing here is about two miles, and Hurst Castle serves to defend this narrow point. Six miles beyond Hurst is the town of Christchurch (Twinehambourne). The river here marks the boundary between Hampshire and Dorset.

The new castles on the Isle of Wight: Two new castles have been established and equipped at the mouth of the Newport estuary, which is the only estuary on the island worthy of mention. They have been built on the east and west sides, with a crossing of at least a mile between them, and are called East Cowes and West Cowes respectively; West Cowes is the larger of the two. Cowes is seven miles from the Hampshire mainland and coast.

My journey from Southampton took me about a mile to Itchen village, across the ferry, and then three miles past heathland and bracken with enclosures to the fishing town of Hamble. Here I took a ferry and continued at least two miles to Titchfield. The terrain was similar, although there are some patches of very good land around Titchfield. On my left before I arrived in Titchfield I passed an attractive lake. On the exact site of the former Premonstratensian abbey of Titchfield Mr Wriothesley has built a very grand house, with battlements, a fine gate, and a conduit house in the centre of the courtyard. There is a grammar school close to the river bank, and there is a park, although its soil is rather poor and heathy. Botley is reckoned to be only three miles from Titchfield. Six miles further past a great deal of heath and bracken I reached Gosport, a small fishing village. A chapel, now desecrated, stood here close to the shore of Portsmouth Harbour, and barely a half-mile from its actual mouth.

The course of the Titchfield Water [*River Meon*]: Its source is near East Meon, ten miles north-east of Titchfield. From East Meon it flows five or six miles to a pleasant little town on its right bank called Wickham, where it breaks into two streams for a short distance and runs under two wooden bridges. Three or four miles lower it flows under another wooden bridge near Mr Wriothesley's house, and passes Titchfield on its right bank. Just below Titchfield is a timber bridge called Warebridge, and from this point the river is tidal. Less than a mile downstream it joins Southampton Water.

Places of note on the west side of Portsmouth Harbour: The land at the western point of the harbour is a sandy headland which before long breaks off and gives way to the open sea. On this west point at the mouth of the harbour is a round stone tower containing weaponry. And not far around inside the harbour a large creek, called Ostrepole Lake, extends a mile inland to the west. The village of Gosport is scarcely a quarter-mile above this creek, and about a mile further round is another creek, named Forton after a small village nearby. Bedenham Creek, also named after the village next to it, is a mile-and-a-half further, and lies almost opposite Portchester Castle. The fishing village of Fareham is about another mile up into the harbour, right at its head. The distance from the west point of Portsmouth Harbour to the east point of Southampton Water is about seven miles, and almost halfway between is a fishing village.

Places of note on the east side of Portsmouth Harbour: On this side the land extends south-east from the harbour mouth a great deal further towards the sea than it does on the western side. On this point of the harbour stands the town of Portsmouth, and a large round tower almost twice as great, in both size and strength, as its counterpart on the western side right opposite. A massive iron chain can be drawn across from tower to tower. A quarter-mile in from this tower is a large dock for ships, in which may still be seen part of the rib-timbers of the Henry Grace de Dieu, one of the largest ships to have been made within living memory. Beyond this dock there are two creeks in this part of the harbour, and Portchester Castle stands three miles by water from Portsmouth town.

The fortification of Portsmouth town consists of an earthen wall with timber strengthening, inside a ditch, and topped with large iron and brass cannon. It runs directly SSE for a furlong from the east tower, and it is this portion which is the most important for defending the town on the side which lies open to the harbour. The wall and ditch continue in the same fashion due almost directly east for a certain distance, and then make a circuit of one mile around the town. On the north-eastern side is a timber gate, and next to it has been thrown up an earthen bank inside a ditch. On this there are guns to control entry into the town from the landward side. There is a great deal of open space within the town wall.

Portsmouth has one good street, which runs from the west to the north-east, and only one parish church; but there is also a chapel on open ground on the south-west side of the town near the wall and shore. Peter des Roches, bishop of Winchester, was the founder of a fine hospital in the WSW part of the town; until recently it housed twelve poor men, but now there are six. I was told in the town that the two towers at the harbour mouth were begun by Edward IV, that building work was continued by Richard III, and that Henry VII completed them under the supervision of Bishop Fox of Winchester. When his first French wars began Henry VII built three great breweries in the southern part of the town, which were fully equipped to provide for his ships whenever they went to sea during wartime. He also placed a garrison of officers and a number of soldiers in Portsmouth, but in peacetime the town is empty, with few inhabitants. However, a rich man called Carpenter has recently built himself a town house in the middle of the High Street.

The town stands in one corner of an island also called Portsmouth [*Portsea Island*], which is six miles long and three miles wide, and produces good corn and grass. Part of the island has been enclosed, and in addition to fertile cornfields it has a certain amount of woodland. This area has been formed into an island by two creeks, the one leading off Portsmouth Harbour three miles above the town, through marshy ground to a place called Portsbridge, and the other running up to Portsbridge from the open sea, or Avant Haven [*Langstone Harbour*]. I travelled the two miles from Portsmouth to Portsbridge, which is a bridge of two stone arches and marks the boundary of the island. From here I could see the two salt-water creeks leading from Portsmouth Harbour and the open sea up to the bridge.

Then I continued for four miles, partly over an open area called Portsdown, and partly through woods, until I reached Southwick. This is a good and large roadside place, but does not have an important market. It was renowned for its Augustinian priory, whose image of Our Lady was an object of pilgrimage. To the east of Southwick there is a large area of well-wooded forest known as East Bere, which has a good stock of deer. Another chase or forest called Bere lies three or four miles to the west of Winchester, and this is known as West Bere. Wickham lies three miles from Southwick, across enclosed ground. It is a large and populous roadside town, and next to it, by the left bank of the River Meon, stands Mr Wodale's [*?Uvedale's*] manor house.

From Wickham I travelled three miles through a countryside of enclosures, good pastures, woodland and arable, to Bishop's Waltham.

Here the bishop of Winchester has a very spacious and fine moated manor house close to an attractive stream. Many bishops have contributed to its fabric, including Bishop Langton, who has recently built of brick and timber most of three sides of the lower courtyard. All the remainder of the inner parts of the house are stonebuilt. Several springs within a mile of the town by the Winchester road supply much of the water to the stream, which then flows towards Botley and Hamble Creek. Then I returned to Winchester, seven miles away. For the first three miles the country was enclosed and wooded, but the remaining four were across open ground. [1/269-85]

The original house of the Sandys family, so far as I can discover, is at [East] Cholderton, one-and-a-half miles from Andover. There is still a fine manor house there, largely built of flint.

The Vyne near Basingstoke was also part of the Sandys' ancient estate, but it passed by marriage to one of the Brooks's family; and so it remained until the late Lord Sandys, before he was made a baron, recovered it into his possession. At that time it was not a large and lavish manor house, but consisted of only what lay within the moat. However, Lord Sandys transformed and enlarged it, and built a fine outer court, so that at the present day it is one of the most important houses for good architecture in the whole of Hampshire. The great increase in the estate of Sir William (later Lord) Sandys came about through his wife, the niece of Sir Reginald Bray. When Bray went to the battle of Blackheath he left Sandys as his heir, and on his return from battle he purchased land with an annual value of nearly £700, in addition to what he already had. Later he died, leaving no will apart from the one he had made at the time of Blackheath. Whereupon a great dispute arose between Sandys and Sir Reginald's young nephew, over their rival claims to the estate bequeathed in the will. The argument was eventually settled by the king and his counsel, who made a division of the estate between them.

The Lord Sandys who recently died entered into an exchange with the crown, whereby he ceded Chelsea near Westminster and received Mottisfont Priory in Hampshire. He began to transform the old priory building in order to make a fine manor house, but the work has been left unfinished. The present Lord Sandys is married to the earl of Rutland's sister, and they have four sons and six daughters alive. [2/7-8]

Silchester lies on the very edge of Hampshire (the brook there marks the boundary), and is six miles or more from Reading. In addition to the land around the manor house itself, and the church, it contains three fields, making a total of eighty acres enclosed within the wall. This stone wall is about two miles around, and has four gates. On the wall grow some oak trees weighing ten cart-loads each.

The land inside the wall stands almost level with it, but from outside the wall is six or seven feet high in some places. One farmhouse and the parish church stand inside, but the rest of the settlement is outside. A curious phenomenon observed at Silchester is that in some parts of the land enclosed by the wall the corn appears to the eye to be of wonderful quality, but as it is about to reach maturity it rots. The entire manor, including the area outside the wall, has an annual value of £37. After the conquest this estate passed to one Blewett, but when the male line of the Blewetts failed, the land which was not entailed to the heiress passed by marriage to a knight called Peter de Cusance. Later it came to a certain Edmund Baynard, from an Essex family of that name, which in Essex itself is now lost. [4/110-11]

The New Forest in Hampshire: There are nine walks in it, nine keepers, two rangers, one bow-bearer, and the Lord Warden, a hereditary title belonging to the earl of Arundel. There is a theory that some forest land existed there before the time of William the Conqueror. The place where Tyrrell is believed to have killed King William Rufus is called Truham, and a chapel still stands there. [4/142]

HEREFORDSHIRE

*L*ELAND VISITED HEREFORD *during his exploration of Wales, perhaps in 1539, and has left a short account of the city, as well as a description of Kenchester which shows him at his most observant and thoughtful. He returned to the county on his West Midlands tour in 1543, and was able to write a much fuller account of Hereford, before travelling north via Leominster (which he also described in detail) to Shropshire. His surviving notes on the county and diocese are also quite extensive, and in general do not duplicate the material in the itinerary. Clearly he must have spent some time collecting material about the Golden Valley, and he also made extensive notes (most of which are here omitted) from manuscripts and epitaphs at Hereford Cathedral. For some Herefordshire places along the Welsh border see pp. 469-70.*

M<small>Y JOURNEY</small> from Monmouth to Hereford brought me over a large stone bridge built on four arches. Hereford is a large, old town with strong walls and a mighty castle next to the bank of the River Wye. I estimate that the circumference of this castle is as great as that of Windsor. Its keep is tall and strong, and in the ditch close to the keep is a good spring called St Ethelbert's Well. During digging work at Hereford Castle bones have been found which, whilst not those of giants, are nevertheless remarkably large; bones of similar size turn up in the mud which is found on the riverbank of the Wye next to the castle.

Hereford town wall is surrounded by a ditch which is always full of stagnant water. This drains down and collects in the ditch, where it is retained by some mills which are driven by it before it flows into the valley of the Wye. Were it not for the mills the ditch would often be dry. The town has four parish churches, including one in the cathedral. Some of the churches are excellent, and the cathedral church is very strongly built. It contains a lavish shrine at the tomb of St Thomas Cantilupe, bishop of Hereford. St Ethelbert the martyr was also buried in the cathedral church, but his relics never reappeared after the Welsh destroyed Hereford during the reign of Edward the Confessor. According to one tradition he was martyred at Marden, which is not very far from the ruins of Sutton, the supposed residence of Offa (although my view is that Offa's palace was at Kenchester).

The suburbs of Hereford contain two parish churches, a Benedictine priory dependent on Gloucester Abbey, and two friaries, black and grey. The present name of the town, according to one explanation, is derived from an old ford or river crossing over the Wye close to the castle. Some people maintain that the older name was Fernleigh ('the ferny clearing', according to Mr Taylor), or alternatively Fernhill, and that on the site of the present cathedral church there used to be a chapel dedicated to Our Lady of Fernleigh.

Herefordshire monasteries: There is a Benedictine priory, a cell of Gloucester Abbey, in the suburbs of Hereford. Limebrook is a house of nuns, less than two miles from Wigmore, on the Herefordshire–Shropshire border. Wigmore is a large abbey of white canons less than a mile from Wigmore town and castle, in the border country towards Shropshire. Feverleigh [?] used to be a friary, but at some time it was suppressed and its lands given to Wigmore and Limebrook; all three were founded by the Mortimers, Marcher earls. The nunnery at Aconbury, three miles from Hereford, has now been suppressed. Leominster, on the River Lugg seven miles from Hereford, is a cell of the Benedictine abbey at Reading. Wormsley, a house of Augustinian canons, lies in wooded countryside five miles from Hereford. Monmouth Priory was a French alien house which lay in Hereford diocese, and has been suppressed. Dore Abbey in the Ewyas region was a great Cistercian house, but has been suppressed. It lay in the diocese, but not the county, of Hereford. A stream called the Worm flows nearby.

The River Wye flows right across Herefordshire, past Bredwardine, Sir Richard Vaughan's castle, then eight miles to Hereford, and on to Ross, a market town in the county. There are umber or grayling in the Wye, and I think that they are called in Welsh 'caugin'. The River Lugg rises near Melennith [?Mynachoy], not far from the chapel of Our Lady of Pylale [?Pilleth], and flows nine miles to Presteigne (a market town), seven miles to Leominster (another market town), and seven miles to Mordiford, where it joins the Wye three miles below Hereford. A large brook called the Frome, which is sometimes in spate, flows past Bromyard, as I recall, and into the Lugg. There is very good pasture land in this area.

Leominster is served by three small rivers, the Lugg, the Pinsley, and the Kenbrook. The Lugg receives the other two below the town, and the Pinsley rises only a few miles away. The River Arrow passes quite close to Leominster, but does not flow through the town. It rises between Elvethland and Melenithland [?the Mynachoy area], flows past Old Radnor and Huntington, which was formerly a manor belonging to the duke of Buckingham, and eventually joins the Lugg a half-mile below Leominster. The small river that flows past New Radnor is called Summergil, not Onny. Someone told me that the Onny flowed quite close to Ludlow Castle, but I was doubtful, and I have since discovered that it joins the Teme near Bromfield, which is a priory not far from Ludlow. The local people insist that the Onny does not flow through Radnor. [**?1539:** 3/47-50]

KENCHESTER LIES THREE MILES or more upstream from Hereford on the same side of the river, but it is nearly a mile away from the riverbank. This place is a far more ancient town than Hereford, and was important during the Roman period. There is a great deal of evidence for this, especially the old coins of the emperors which are frequently found there, both within the settlement and in ploughing the fields around it; the local people call them 'dwarf's money'. By my reckoning Kenchester must have covered as large an area as Hereford (if Hereford Castle, which is on a very large scale, is excluded). Portions of the walls and towers are still visible almost at ground level, and more would remain to be seen if people from Hereford and the neighbouring area had not in the past demolished much of it, and removed the best masonry for their building work. Recently a certain Mr Breinton collected a great deal of shaped stone from Kenchester to use in a house he was building at Stretton [*Sugwas*] a mile away. The owner, both of Kenchester and of Sutton, is a Mr Lingham [?Lingen], according to local people.

It is probable that in the past Kenchester was on a route which went on via Hay and Brecon to Carmarthen. The site of the former town is completely overgrown with hazel, brambles and similar bushes. Nevertheless here and there ruined buildings are still visible, and people foolishly call one of these the Fairy King's Chair. In our own time various strange things of the [Romano-] British period have been found, including bricks, pipes, watercourses, tessellated pavements, part of a small golden chain and a golden spur. To put it briefly, Hereford emerged and flourished out of the ruins of Kenchester. Undoubtedly Hereford has the better site, adjacent to the River Wye and so closer to the pastures. But I find no evidence that Hereford began in any substantial form before the time of King Offa, whose palace was probably at Sutton.

Sutton is four miles from Hereford, and here can be seen substantial remains of a large ancient building. Local people are almost certainly correct in believing that it was once the residence of King Offa, when Kenchester was still standing, or at the time that Hereford was just beginning. About a mile from Sutton is Marden, and on a hill next to the village it is said that St Ethelbert was beheaded. The fine church in the village is dedicated to him, but I think that in fact he was killed in King Offa's house at Sutton. The name Marden appears to refer to the Martyr's Hill. [**?1539:** 3/102-4]

HEREFORD CASTLE STANDS on the left bank of the River Wye a little below the bridge. Where the river does not provide a natural defence the castle is strongly ditched, and it has high, strong walls with many large towers. In its time it was one of the finest, largest and strongest castles in England, but now the entire structure is verging on ruin. It has two courts, and both are surrounded by water. A branch of the stream which runs along much of the town ditch was led through an arch in the town wall and into the castle ditch. This flowed around one half of the castle and into the Wye, so that with the main stream also running along the castle ditch, and the River Wye itself, the castle was completely surrounded. This branch of the stream does not flow through the castle any more, but it could easily be made to do so again. The second court, which contains the keep, was also surrounded by water, because a section of the water from the ditch was diverted that way. The castle keep is very tall and strong; it has an outer ward with ten semi-circular towers, and an inner ward

HEREFORDSHIRE

with one large tower. Entry to the castle was on the north-west side by a large bridge with stone arches and a drawbridge in the centre; but this has completely fallen down. The castle has an attractive chapel dedicated to St Cuthbert, with an apsidal east end. There used to be priests attached to it, but one of the Lacy family transferred them to St Peter's, in Hereford town, and later that college was transferred again to the eastern suburb, where a monastery dependent on Gloucester was built. There is a good, abundant spring of water within the castle, and this, together with the stream flowing in the ditch, was enough to drive a mill in the castle complex. There is a belief that the castle was begun by Harold, after he had put down the Welsh rebellion during the reign of Edward the Confessor. But the Lacy and Bohun families, earls of Hereford, are thought to have been its main builders. Since the time of the Bohuns it has steadily fallen into ruin.

The site of Hereford town is rather low-lying on every side. Not far away to the east and south are thickly-wooded hills on the right bank of the River Wye. One Welsh name for Hereford is Henford, which is a reference to an old ford near the castle. This was heavily used before the great Wye Bridge at Hereford was built. Its other Welsh name is Trefarrith, referring to the large number of beech trees which grew in the area. The walls surrounding the town are more than a mile in length, and have six gates: The Wye Gate; Friar Gate on the west side, named after the house of grey friars situated outside it; Inne [*Eign*] Gate on the WNW; Wigmarsh Gate directly north, named after a marshy area just beyond the gate or suburb; Bishop Street Gate on the north-east; and St Andrew's Gate on the east, which is named after St Andrew's parish church in the suburbs outside this gate.

A small stream rises five miles to the west of Hereford, and flows around the ditches outside the town walls (except where the River Wye provides a defence). Then its course continues past the castle, which it leaves on the right hand side after driving two corn mills, and into the Wye a bowshot's length below Wye Bridge and in the shadow of the castle. Hereford Castle stands on the south side of the town below the bridge and close to the Wye.

The walls and gates are maintained in excellent order by the Hereford burgesses. It is the common belief that Hereford had barely any protection in the form of walls when the town was destroyed by Griffin, Prince of

Wales. With the help and connivance of Algar, the son of Leofric, earl of the Marches, Griffin killed Bishop Leofgar and his clergy.

Within the town walls are four parish churches, dedicated to St Peter, St Nicholas, All Hallows and St John. The cathedral church occupies the highest part of the town, on the south side near the castle. Its first founders were the sub-king Milfrid [?*Merewald*] and his wife Quenburg, but a new church was begun on the site by Bishop Robert Lorengo [*Losinga*] of Hereford, and Bishop Kynelm [*Reinhelm*] of Hereford also carried out major building work. A Hereford merchant, one Richard Phillips, has recently been buried in St Mary's graveyard, under the cloister of St Mary's within the precinct of Hereford Cathedral. His grave is covered by a slab which used to be on the altar of Aconbury Priory.

Outside Wye Gate there is a suburb, with a chapel where the road forks dedicated to Our Lady of Alingtre, and another to St Giles. Below the bridge in Wye Gate suburb is St Martin's Church. Wye Bridge has large stone arches. There are few houses outside Friar Gate. The Franciscan friary was established by Sir William Pembrugge, and the friars were given land by the bishop of Hereford. Members of the Chandos and Cornwall families are buried in the friary, as well as Owen Mereduke [*Meredydd*] or Tudor, who lies uncommemorated in a chapel in the nave of the friary church.

The suburb outside Eign Gate has a chapel of St Giles, supported by the burgesses, which was originally founded for lepers, but has now been converted for the use of the poor. The best of Hereford's suburbs lies outside the northern or Wigmarsh Gate. This contained the Dominican friary, which was originally founded by a knight called Deinville [*Daniel*], and completed by Edward III. William, Lord Hastings, earl of Pembroke, was formerly buried there, until his body was removed to the grey friars in London (for which the Hereford Dominicans received £100). Other burials included: William Beauchamp, Lord Bergavenny; Sir Richard Delaber; Sir Roger Chandos and his wife; Sir Nicholas Clare; Sir John Burley; Sir John Ellesforde; Mabilia Rouse; Sir Thomas Rehan; Henry Oldcastle; Alexander Bache, bishop of Castrencis [*i.e. St Asaph*], who was confessor to Edward III. He was buried in the quire, having died at Hereford when Edward III, with the prince and three archbishops, attended the dedication of the black friars' church. In this suburb was also a hospital of St John; it used to be a Templar preceptory, but now it is an almshouse with a chapel. At the north end of this suburb is a brook called Small Purse which flows from Broad Meadow nearby. It passes the black friars, drives mills, and flows under the single stone arch of Eign Bridge and so into the Wye.

Outside Bishopgate Street there is a pleasant suburb which had a priory dedicated to St Guthlac. The priory was a cell of Gloucester, and had formerly been within St Peter's Church in Hereford. Hugh Lacy transferred it to this suburb, and it was built on a new site donated by Bishop Bethune of Hereford. Before this priory was built one of the provosts or masters of St Peter's in Hereford, Bernard Quarre, was killed at the altar, and after the move his tomb was translated to St Guthlac's chapter house.

There is also a suburb outside St Andrew's Gate, with the parish church of St Andrew halfway along the street. St Giles' Hospital, which had previously been a chapel belonging to the Franciscans and the Templars, was presented to the town by King Richard, and was then turned into a hospital.

Distances from Hereford: Leominster is eight miles, and Ludlow (by the road to the right) another seven. About a mile to the north of Leominster there is a hill called Comfort Castle, on which some ruins may still be seen. Hay is twelve miles from Hereford, and almost half-way to Brecon, which is twenty-four miles away. From Hereford to Wormbridge is six miles, then two miles to Ailstone Bridge [?*Pontrilas*], three miles to Lincot Wood [*Lingoed*], and five miles to Abergavenny. Abbey Dore is six miles SSW of Hereford. Distances on the way from Hereford to Bristol are: Monmouth, twelve miles; Chepstow, six; Beachley (on the right bank of the Severn), two; Aust Cliff, across on the ferry, two; Bristol, twelve. From Hereford to Lea is fourteen miles, and to Gloucester a further eight or more. Worcester is twenty miles from Hereford, and Bromyard, a Herefordshire market town on the right bank of the River Frome, is twelve. Wigmore is fourteen miles away; it is eight miles to Leominster, then five to the small town of Wigmore, and a further mile to Wigmore Abbey.

Weobley lies seven miles to the WNW of Hereford. It is a Herefordshire market town with a good, if rather dilapidated castle, which was the principal seat of the Devereux family. They also owned Linshull or Lyonshall Castle, with a park, two miles from Weobley. This they inherited from much more ancient owners, the Marbury family.

From Hereford going upstream there is no bridge on the Wye until Builth, where the bridge has recently been repaired with timber.

Builth stands on the right bank of the Wye upstream from Hay. Going downstream there is a wooden bridge near Ross, but no other bridge until just above the confluence of the Wye and the Monnow. An estate and manor house called Ewyas Castle, seat of Tregoze, lies beside the Wye [*i.e. Monnow*] below Hereford. It was formerly of some importance. There is a wooden bridge giving access from Monmouth to the Forest of Dean, but below Monmouth there is no bridge over the Wye right down to its mouth. There used to be a timber bridge at Chepstow.

The River Lugg joins the Wye a little below Mordiford Bridge. This is a stone bridge over the Lugg three miles from Hereford, and the river itself comes within a mile of Hereford. The following stone bridges cross the Lugg below Leominster: 1. a bridge a quarter-mile below Leominster; 2. Ford Bridge, of three arches, two miles lower; 3. at Hampton, one mile lower (Hampton stands on the left bank – the manor formerly belonged to the Lords Burford, and now to the Coningsby family); 4. at Wisteston village, three miles lower; 5. Lugg Bridge, of stone; 6. Lugwardine Bridge (where, on the left bank, the manor house of the Chandos family was later owned by the Bridges and has now been sold to Warmecombe); 7. Mordiford Bridge, which is larger than any of the others.

From Hereford I travelled to Dinmore Hill across four miles of enclosed ground, not particularly hilly, but with an abundance of good arable and pasture, and reasonable woodland. About a mile before Dinmore I passed a small village called Wellington, and here I crossed a bridge of three stone arches. The usual name for the stream which runs under this bridge is Wormsley Water [*Wellington Brook*]. It rises four or five miles to the west, flows past Wormsley village, from there to Wellington, and a furlong lower it joins the River Lugg on its right bank. Dinmore Hill itself is very steep, high and well-wooded, and it offers a good view over the surrounding countryside. Right on the top of the hill, to the west or left hand as I rode past, stands a commandery and fine house which belonged to the Knights Hospitallers of St John of Jerusalem in London.

A mile beyond Dinmore I saw Hampton Court in passing, an excellent manor house on the left bank of the Lugg, with a stone bridge over the river. This house was built at great expense by a certain Sir [*Rowland*] Leinthall, who achieved a high station through service to Henry IV. He was the king's Yeoman of the Robes, and a handsome fellow; as a result either a daughter or a very close relative of the king fell in love with him, and in due course they were married. He was consequently held in high esteem, and was given estates with an annual value of £1000 to support his wife and himself, and to pass to their heirs. Ludlow formed part of this estate. At the Battle of Agincourt this Leinthall was one of the victors; he took many prisoners, and with their ransoms began to rebuild Hampton manor house. Among the new works he built a small reservoir at the top of the house which was fed by spring water from a hill. He and his wife had a son, who died when a few years old; after this Leinthall left off building at Hampton, and shortly afterwards his wife died. Later he was married again, to the daughter of Lord Grey of Codnor.

The three miles of countryside between Hampton and Leominster include good arable and some enclosures, but not much wood nearby. A half-mile on this side of Leominster I crossed a three-arched stone bridge called Arrow Bridge [*Broadward Bridge*] after the river which flows under it. This River Arrow flows through the town of Pembridge, which has a good market, and a stone bridge over the river. There is another stone bridge two-and-a-half miles lower at the village of Ivington (a former manor of Leominster), then about a half-mile downstream is Arrow Bridge, and about another quarter-mile the Arrow flows into the Lugg, on its right bank. Below Ivington the ground is low-lying, and although there is much good meadowland it is so often inundated that scarcely once in six years can the grass be saved.

The site of Leominster (or Lemster) itself is also rather low-lying, but the land immediately around it is much lower still. At the town's west end are three stone bridges. The first crosses Penfilly [*Pinsley*] Brook which rises five miles away to the WSW. After three miles a small stream which issues not far above Kingsland church joins it, and having flowed under the bridge at Leominster it passes right through the priory building, and a little further joins the Lugg on its right bank. The second bridge crosses the Kenwater. This is an arm of the Lugg, which leaves the main river a quarter-mile above Lugg Bridge, and rejoins it shortly after flowing under Kenwater Bridge. The third bridge, the largest of the three, as I recall, and with the most arches, is called Lugg Bridge. The main stream of the Lugg is controlled by a dam or weir which supplies the king's mills a little downstream from it.

Between Leominster and Presteigne (called Llanandrew in Welsh) there are three important stone bridges. The first, two miles above Leominster, is called Kingsland Bridge after the nearby village. The second, three or four miles above Kingsland, is Limebrook Bridge, and I suppose that it takes its name from some stream which joins the Lugg there, or from a village of that name. Limebrook Priory, a former nunnery, stood not far from this bridge a quarter-mile or more from the left bank of the Lugg. The third stone bridge, two miles further upstream, is at Presteigne. Until about the time of Edward IV Presteigne was merely a Welsh village; but recently Richard Martin, who was bishop of St David's and before that chancellor of the Marches and ambassador to Spain and other foreign countries, obtained for it borough privileges and made it a market town, with what has become a very important corn market.

Leominster is quite a large town with good timber buildings. The best-known evidence for the town's antiquity is its nunnery, which King Merewald of the Marches established there, and which he endowed with all the surrounding country except the manor now called Kingsland. Churchmen believe that the most likely derivation of the name is from the Welsh Llanllieny, 'the place or monastery of the nuns', and not from the lion who is recorded to have appeared in a vision to King Merewald, and which prompted him, so the story goes, to build the nunnery. Merewald's immediate successors as Marcher kings were also benefactors, but one version says that the nunnery was later destroyed during the Danish wars, and a college of priests established instead. What is certain is that Shaftesbury Abbey controlled Leominster and was a major landowner, and that Shaftesbury sent part of the relics of St Edward the Martyr there to be venerated. But Henry I attached Leominster's lands to Reading Abbey, and the abbots of Reading established a cell of monks at Leominster.

Leominster has only one parish church. It is large and rather dark, with ancient fabric; indeed there is a very strong probability that it is the church which existed some time before the conquest. The priory church was attached to the east end of the parish church, but was only small. According to some people, the monks of the priory claimed to possess the skulls of two Marcher kings, Merewald and Ethelmund. However, Mr Hakluyt told me that Merewald's body was discovered in a wall of the old church at Wenlock.

Because of its excellent wool, Leominster carried on an extensive trade in cloth, and this brought it prosperity. But in recent years, following complaints from both Hereford and Worcester that the popularity of Leominster was prejudicial to the markets in the county towns and was harming their own cloth trade, Leominster was deprived of its Saturday market, and a Friday market assigned to it instead. From then onwards Leominster has been in decline.

There is a common belief amongst the townspeople that King Merewald and some of his successors had a castle or palace on a hillside a half-mile east of Leominster. The site is now called Comfort Castle, and there is still some evidence of ditches where buildings used to be. Once a year people from the Leominster area come to this place to sport and play. Another castle stood at Kingsland, two miles WNW of Leominster, and its ditches and part of its keep can still be seen on the west side of Kingsland church. It is always said that King Merewald once lived here. In later times is belonged to the Marcher earls, and now to the king.

From Leominster I travelled to Eyton, one mile WNW. A house was built in this village by one William Hakluyt, who had fought with Henry V at Agincourt, and had taken prisoner a French nobleman called St George. With the house he bought an estate, and the present Hakluyt is the third in descent of the Eyton branch of the family. The principal and senior branch of the Hakluyts has been a gentry family since time immemorial. They derive their name from Clwyd Forest in Radnorshire, and they had a castle and dwellings not far from Radnor. In Edward III's time there were three Hakluyt knights, including one called Edmund. It so happened that one of the Hakluyt knights took the side of Llewellyn, Prince of Wales, against Edward III; as a result his estates were confiscated and passed to the crown, or to Mortimer, Lord Radnor, never to be returned. At the same period one of the Hakluyts fled into the Welsh mountains and lived there in exile. Later he was pardoned and, having no issue, he named as his heir the godson or relative who had served him as his knight; the lands thus inherited remain with the senior branch of the Hakluyts.

I left Eyton on the Ludlow road, and after a mile and a half I could see a mile away on my right hand the manor house [*Berrington Hall*] of a cadet branch of the Cornwall family, barons of Burford. And a mile to my left I could see Croft, seat of the Croft family, which is situated on the brow of a rather craggy hill, with walls and ditches like a castle. Then I rode a further four miles, past good arable land, partly enclosed, and with some nice woods, to Richards Castle.

Richards Castle stands on top of a very craggy, well-wooded hill on the west side of the parish church. Its keep, walls and towers are still standing, but are falling into disrepair. There is a meagre wooden farmhouse in the castle grounds, and the park still has its pale and many trees, but no deer. It is now in the king's hands, having previously belonged to Lord Vaux, and then to Pope. From Richards Castle it is two miles to Ludlow. *cont. p. 305* [**1543:** 2/64-76]

In length Herefordshire extends for about 24 miles, from Clifford (which stands right on the border, but is outside the county) to a village called Lea, three miles from the market town of Ross. Lea is half in Herefordshire and half in Gloucestershire. The first village in Herefordshire on this side of Clifford appears to be Winforton. The breadth of the county is 23 miles or rather less, measured from Ludlow Bridge by Ludlow to the Cistercian monastery at Abbey Dore.

Important rivers in the county are as follows: the Wye; the Kenbrook, which rises in Wales and enters the Lugg at Leominster; the Lugg, which enters the Wye below Hereford at Mordiford, a village three miles east of Hereford; the Pinsley, which rises at Kingsland, two miles from Leominster, where it flows into the Lugg; the Arrow, which joins the Lugg at a village called Wharton nearly a mile below Leominster; and the Frome, which enters the Lugg at Yarkhill, three miles from Hereford.

Visible remains of former castles in the county are as follows (ask Mr Blakston of Peckwater's Inn which castles are still standing): Hereford (inside the city); Bicknor (with a village); Lyonshall (three miles from Weobley, belongs to Lord Ferrers); Weobley (also belongs to Lord Ferrers); Bredwardine; Dorstone; Snodhill; Mapheralt or Ewyasharneis [*Ewyas Harold*] (which is six miles from Abergavenny, and belongs partly to the king, so I have heard, and partly to the Lord Abergavenny); Ewyas Harold; Ewyas Lacy; Wilton; Goodrich; Landamas [?]; Grosmont; Guyn (a large castle); [?*Ganarew*]; Longton (of Ewyas).

Market towns in the county: Leominster, about eight miles north of Hereford, has a Benedictine Abbey (now virtually a cell of Reading Abbey) which is almost attached to the parish church. Pembridge, ten miles NNW of Hereford, has the River Arrow running past the north side of the town. Weobley lies seven miles west of Hereford and four miles south-west of Pembridge; Lord Ferrers has a fine castle here. Ross, three miles from Lea, has the River Wye on its south side, and a small river called the Strood in the direction of Lea market; there used to be a palace of the bishops of Hereford at Ross. Next to Hay Castle (which is outside the county) I am told that a ruined town wall is visible. Many ancient coins are found here, as well as pottery and other interesting items.

Places in the county where brass or silver Roman coins in pots have been found through ploughing, digging, or by other means: At Kenchester, three miles west of Hereford and a mile from the bank of the Wye, was Offa's palace, according to some people. Ruins and some arches survive. Discoveries have been and still are made by ploughing and digging of Roman coins, tesserae, and a small golden cross to wear around the neck. The coins are known as dwarfish halfpence or dwarfs' money. The site used to belong to Sir John Lingain, and now it his heir's. Three miles north of Hereford, on the River Lugg, is King Offa's palace of Sutton, where King Ethelebert was killed. There is nothing but ruins there now, and the place is called Sutton Walls. [4/164-8]

Matilda Walerie [Margery de Lacy] is alleged by some to have founded Aconbury, a priory of nuns in Aconbury Wood, three miles south of Hereford. Fercher and Coryn, the father and mother of St Brendan the abbot, were buried long ago at the exact spot where a new church has now been built for the whole town [of Hereford]. At the west end of the parish church may still be seen evidence of the old tomb. Owen Meredydd, erroneously called Owen Tudor, who was Edmund, earl of Richmond's, father, and King Henry VII's grandfather, is buried on the north side of the nave of the grey friars' church in a chapel. Richard Stradel, doctor of divinity at Oxford and abbot of Dore, wrote homilies on the paternoster, and on the whole text of the gospels. He flourished in the fourteenth century.

In the time of Sir Thomas Cantilupe three preaching friars came to Hereford, and with the approval of William, Bishop Cantilupe's brother, they set up a small oratory at Portfield. But the bishop evicted the friars, and then they were permitted the use of a small plot in the northern suburb by a certain Sir John Daniel. After this the bishop of Hereford gave them a small site next to Daniel's plot, and here they started a building, with Daniel's help, and created a dignified piece of architecture. But then, when the barons' war started between Thomas of Lancaster and Edward II, Daniel was taken by the king and beheaded in Hereford; and his body was buried at the high cross in the minster churchyard there. Work on the black friars' college ceased for a while, but then Edward III gave it his support, and later it was dedicated in the presence of many noblemen. It was on this occasion that Alexander Bache, bishop of Chester [i.e. St Asaph], died at Hereford, and the king attended his funeral there. The bishop was buried in the black friars' quire under a good flat stone slab. [5/160-1]

Kilpeck Castle lies three miles below the source of the River Worm, on the left bank. Apart from Kilpeck there is nothing worth noting on the Worm.

Some say that the valley where the River Dore flows between two hills is called Dyffryn Dore (that is, the golden valley) because of its fertility; but I think that Dore derives from the Latin 'durus', meaning 'harsh'. The low-lying ground where the River Dulas flows is called Dyffryn Dulas. There used to be at Dore a manorial building called Black Berats Hall. The manor of Ewyas Harold itself, at its narrowest point, is one mile wide and nearly two miles long. It produces good corn, grass and wood.

Abbey Dore is six miles from Hereford due directly south, ten miles WNW of Monmouth, and nine miles directly north of Abergavenny. The River Dore runs past the abbey of Dore, breaking into two arms a short distance above it. The larger stream leaves the monastery a bow-shot away on its right bank, but the smaller stream flows through it, and the two rejoin very shortly below the abbey.

The confluence of the Rivers Dore and Monnow occurs eight miles from the town of Monmouth. The River Worm flows into the Dore on the left bank three-quarters of a mile below Abbey Dore. It rises next to Hay Wood, three miles SSE of Hereford, and flows five miles from its source. Half-a-mile lower, on the right bank of the Dore, the River Dulas enters, having risen two miles upstream and flowed through Ewyas Harold. The source of the Dore is a little above Dorstone, which is a small village six miles WNW of Abbey Dore on the right bank. Two miles below Abbey Dore the Dore flows into the left bank of the Monnow.

More than a mile below Dorstone there is a castle on the right bank of the Dore called Snodhill. There is a walled park, which contains the castle built on a hill called South Hill, with a free chapel, and nearby, beneath the castle, is a quarry for marble. The castle, which belonged to the Chandos family, is somewhat ruinous. Several members of the family are buried in the grey and black friars at Hereford.

Abbey Dore was founded during the reign of King Stephen by a certain Robert Ewyas, so called because he owned part of Ewyas. The rumour is that King Harold had an illegitimate son called Harold, after whom part of the estate was called Ewyas Harold. Harold's son was Robert (the founder of Abbey Dore), and his son was also called Robert. His only daughter, Sybil Ewyas, married a Norman called Sir Robert Tregoze, and they had a son John. John Tregoze married Julia, Lord William Cantilupe's daughter, and the sister of Thomas Cantilupe, who was bishop of Hereford and Henry III's chancellor.

The story goes that Mapheralt Castle was built by Harold before he was king, and when he had defeated the Welsh he gave the castle to his illegitimate son. A large part of the castle still stands, together with a chapel of St Nicholas within it. At one time there was a park next to the castle. The castle stands on a modest hill, with the right bank of the River Dulas in the valley close by at its foot. Next to the castle is a village called Ewyas Harold, and here there was a priory or cell of black monks, dependent on Gloucester, which had been transferred here from Dulas a mile further upstream. The village of Dulas belonged to Harold, and his son founded the monastery there. Robert Tregoze translated it from Dulas to Mapheralt, but after John Tregoze and his son-in-law, Grandisson, no-one of high standing lived at Mapheralt. The castle was bought from Grandisson and De La Warre [*the other son-in-law*] by Joanna Beauchamp, Lady Bergavenny. [5/175-7]

Palaces of the bishops of Hereford: [*Stretton*] Sugwas is a bow-shot or more away from the left bank of the River Wye, two-and-a-half miles [*above Hereford*]. It stands at the foot of a hill, and the park next to it is now without deer. Colwall Park, next to Malvern Chase, belonged to the bishop of Hereford, and a portion of Malvern itself from the crest of the hill, demarcated by a ditch, is also the bishop's property. Bosbury, is ten miles north-east of Hereford at the head of the River Leadon, and nearby is a place which belongs to St John's in London, called Upleadon. Whitbourne, seven miles from Worcester, lies right on the edge of Herefordshire on the right bank of the River Teme. There used to be a fine bishop's palace at Ledbury, twelve miles ENE of Hereford, and seven miles or more from Ross, but the building is now all in ruins. The palace at Ross, also now completely ruined, lay just at the west end of the parish churchyard. The bishop of Hereford's prison for convicts used to be at Ross, but is now at Hereford. Bishop's Castle in Shropshire is twenty-three miles NNW of Hereford, and twelve miles from Shrewsbury. John, son of Alan, Lord Arundel, captured Bishop's Castle, where, after pledging good faith, he killed the constable of the castle in the 45th year of Henry III [1260/1]. He held it for almost six years. Prestbury is five miles from Gloucester, and close to [Bishop's] Cleeve. There is a park adjoining it.

It appears from his epitaph that Bishop William de Vere, carried out much important building work. Bishop John Breton was at one time sheriff of Hereford, warden of the manor of Abergavenny and of three castles, and keeper of the royal wardrobe.

Kilpeck Castle is five miles south-west of Hereford, very close to the Worm Brook. Some ruined walls still stand. A quarter-mile from the castle stood a priory of black monks which must have been connected with Gloucester; it was suppressed during the time of Thomas Spofford, bishop of Hereford.

The father of Thomas Cantilupe, bishop of Hereford, was steward of England, and his mother, Millicent, was countess of Evreux in Normandy. His uncle was Walter Cantilupe, bishop of Worcester, and he presented Thomas to benefices. He helped Thomas's brother Hugh in the same way, and Hugh became archdeacon of Gloucester. [5/184-5]

Monastic houses in the diocese of Hereford: Hereford Cathedral; St Guthlac's Priory, Hereford; Wigmore Abbey (canons); Wenlock Priory (Cluniac order); Leominster Priory; Chirbury Priory (canons); Wormsley Priory (canons); Abbey Dore (Cistercian order); Flaxley Abbey, in the Forest of Dean; Aconbury (nunnery); Limebrook (nunnery); Clifford Priory (Cluniac order); Kilpeck Priory; Newent Priory; Bromfield Priory; Alberbury Priory (Grandmontine order). There was also a Grandmontine house (now united with Hereford Cathedral) at Diddlebury in Corvedale. Acle was a manor and dependent cell of the priory at Lire in Normandy; there was also a chapel there. Acle is four miles from Hereford in the Bromyard direction. Excepting in Hereford itself there are no collegiate churches for priests in the diocese of Hereford. Castle Frome is on the River Frome, which flows into the left bank of the Lugg about a mile above Mordiford Bridge.

The bounds of Hereford diocese: The whole of Herefordshire. Also part of Shropshire as far as the River Teme and almost to the town of Shrewsbury. And the Forest of Dean in Gloucestershire.

Richard's Castle is two miles south of Ludlow, and there is a parish church of the same name next to it. The castle stands on a hill, about a mile-and-a-half from the right bank of the Teme. Until recently it was Lord Vaux's, but then Pope bought it, and now it belongs to the king. [5/190-1]

HERTFORDSHIRE

LELAND RETURNED *through Berkhamsted and the western tip of Hertfordshire after his visit to north-eastern England in 1541, but none of the other surviving itineraries describe the county in any detail. The short description of Royston, however, and perhaps the detailed working-out of the multifarious River Lea in the Cheshunt area, sound as if they may have been connected with a now lost itinerary of the eastern counties. But with these exceptions Leland remains almost entirely silent about Hertfordshire.*

THERE WAS A NUNNERY at Markyate until recently, situated in a pleasant wood on a hill close to Watling Street, on its east side. Humphrey Bourchier, who was the illegitimate son of the previous Lord Berners, went to great expense converting the priory into a manor house, but he left the work unfinished. Not far to 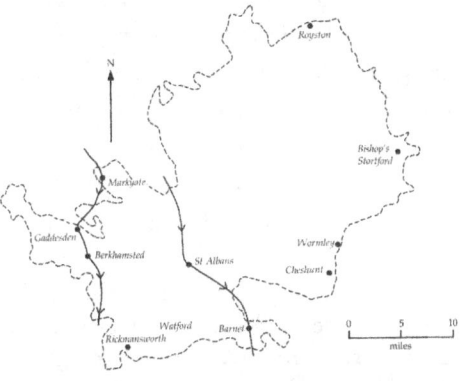 the south of the priory is a straggling roadside settlement along Watling Street, with modest houses reasonably well built. From near the middle of Markyate I climbed up hilly ground on the edge of the Chilterns for half-a-mile, and then saw St Leonards [*Beechwood*], where until recently there was a priory for nuns [*Flamstead Priory*]. It is set in a pleasant wood barely half a mile from the road on the left hand side. Mr Page, the knight, acquired it by exchanging land he owned in the neighbourhood of Hampton Court in Surrey; he has converted the house, and spends much of his time there.

I next travelled four-and-a-half miles through the Chiltern Hills and Woods to Gaddesden, where Lord Derby has an attractive timber manor house. Just before I reached the village I rode across a small brook [*River Gade*] which flows a short distance from the Chiltern Hills to Kings Langley, where the friars were living. A further three miles over the Chiltern Hills, through mainly waste and woodland, with bracken, and chalky soil with flints, which is typical of the Chilterns, brought me to Berkhamsted.

Berkhamsted has a large, old castle, occupying a rather low position at the foot of a hill. It is surrounded by a moat, into which, as I could see, part of the flow of the nearby river is channelled. I noticed several towers and the motte of the keep in the middle ward of the castle, but my impression was that it was largely ruinous. Ashridge, the house of Bonshommes which was founded by Edmund, earl of Cornwall (who owned Berkhamsted Castle), is about a mile away, and it was here that the king stayed. After I had inspected the castle, I crossed the wooden bridge over the river. This river flows past Pendley in the Chilterns, three miles to the north-west, and after passing the east end of Berkhamsted it continues twelve miles southwards to the marshlands in the Rickmansworth area.

Berkhamsted is one of the best market towns in Hertfordshire, with a long street of fairly good buildings running north to south, and a second, rather shorter, street running east to west, where the river flows. The church is in the centre of the town, and in the valley on both sides of the river are very fine meadows.

Then I went past hills, woods and a great deal of wasteland on my way to Chenies, five miles further on. *cont. p. 19* [**1541:** *1/104-5*]

Royston stands in a slight valley between two hills. The town itself, which is only moderately well built, occupies a raised area. The market place lies in Hertfordshire, but the rest of the town is in Cambridgeshire. I was told that Royston is the point where the jurisdiction of three dioceses meet – London, Ely and Lincoln. There is only one parish church, and the eastern part of this served until recently as the priory church for a house of canons. The western part was the chapel for the town. For until the recent [*act of*] Parliament [1540] the town was dependent on two or three outlying parishes; but now the whole town has been allotted to a single parish, which has as its church the eastern end of the priory, and the western end has been pulled down. Royston's Wednesday market is surprisingly busy, especially for corn dealing. [*1/328*]

Rivers of Hertfordshire:] First the St Albans (or Redbourn) water [*River Ver*] flows down; then the River Colne, and they meet three miles above Moor Park by a place (on the further bank) called Munden. They are both small rivers, the Ver the larger of the two. A mile below the confluence at Munden the combined stream flows past an attractive roadside place on the far bank called Watford. Then the [*Hemel*] Hempstead water [*River Gade*] flows down to the Moor stream [*River Colne*] a quarter-mile this side of Rickmansworth, having been joined by the

Berkhamsted Brook [*River Bulbourne*] at Two Waters mill. Hemel Hempstead is nine miles north of the Moor, and the source of the stream is three miles further north at Great Gaddesden. A bow-shot downstream from the confluence with the Gade on the further bank the main river through the Moor is met by the Lowde Water [*River Chess*]. This is before it reaches Rickmansworth, and here the mainstream briefly divides into two arms. Like the Moor, Rickmansworth is in Hertfordshire, but it is not a market town. Next the Amersham Water [*River Misbourne*] joins the river this side of Uxbridge, and is generally taken to be the boundary between the counties of Hertford and Buckingham. Amersham is a market town in Buckinghamshire. [4/98]

The River Lea rises north of Wormley, which is a town three miles upstream from Waltham, and flows almost directly south into the Thames opposite Woolwich. The first arm that divides off to the west from this river is a mile below Wormley at Wormley Lock (in the same parish); it flows past the nunnery at Cheshunt and the parish church, which stand on its west bank. From this arm a sidestream breaks out a little below Cheshunt nunnery. It is called the Shire Lake, because it defines the boundary between Essex and Hertfordshire. Along the length of a meadow called Frithaw this stream runs only during times of serious flooding, but then, half-a-mile below the point where it broke away, it joins a tributary of ditch water at a place called Hook's Ditch. From here another half-mile takes it to North Marsh Point, where it rejoins the arm from which it derived. Next this arm flows to Smawley [*Small Lea*] Bridge, the most westerly bridge on Waltham Causeway, and a half-mile lower, at the corner of Rammey Mead, it returns to the mainstream (or king's stream) of the River Lea.

The second main arm to break away from the west side of the king's stream is at a hamlet called Holyfield, a half-mile lower than Cheshunt nunnery. It flows to the fulling mill, then to the second bridge to the west of the king's stream, and then, a stone's throw lower at a place called Malkins Shelf it rejoins the mainstream. It should be noticed here that the inhabitants of Cheshunt and Hertfordshire say that the king's stream at Waltham divides Hertfordshire from Essex. But the Essex men base their claim on a forest charter that their county extends to Small Lea Bridge.

In Waltham town there are seven or eight bridges, since a number of small tributary streams divide off from the three main courses of the River Lea. Only one significant arm breaks away from the king's stream on the east bank, and this is three-quarters of a mile above Waltham at Holyfield. It flows to the corn mill, and rejoins the king's stream a stone's or quoit's throw below the King's Bridge. [4/112-13]

The ruins of a few sections of the walls of [*Bishop's*] Stortford Castle, as well as the motte, may still be seen right at the far end of the town close to the river. I am told that the bishop's prison is not part of the castle. [4/117]

HUNTINGDONSHIRE

IN COMMON with most other eastern counties Leland's treatment of Huntingdonshire is brief and disappointing. The county town is hardly mentioned, and there is nothing about St Ives or Ramsey. Only one portion of surviving itinerary touches the county, and this is the short description of the St Neots and Kimbolton area which Leland made after he had set out from Cambridge in 1541 on his journey to north-eastern England. Some miscellaneous information received second-hand makes up the note.

ST NEOTS IS FOUR MILES from Eltisley. The older part of the town, where the parish church is, retains the former name of Eynesbury, which is a corruption of 'Enulphesbury'. St Neots stands close to the east bank of a river which here marks the boundary between Huntingdonshire and Bedfordshire, although a short distance downstream both banks are in Huntingdonshire. St Neots bridge is made of timber.

From St Neots I travelled three miles past some enclosures to the Huntingdonshire village of Great Staughton. Close to the church is Oliver Leader's attractive house, with good facilities around it. Then I went to Melchbourne, four miles away and on to Kimbolton. This is a meagre market town on the edge of the county. Its castle has two ditches and is quite strongly built. It belonged to the Mandevilles, earls of Essex, then to the Bohuns, earls of Hereford and Essex, and later to the Stratfords. Sir Richard Wingfield built new living quarters and galleries on the old castle foundations. I discovered that the priory of canons not far from Kimbolton was founded by the Bigrame family. It was a community of only seven canons, and it is unlikely that Bigrame gave them much land, because the annual value of their whole estate was less than £70, of which over £40

HUNTINGDONSHIRE 183

came from the rectory of Kimbolton which they had appropriated. Apart from Bigrames and Conyers there were few named burials in this priory. The manor house of the Bigrames, which has the same name, still survives nearby. Less than a mile west of Kimbolton is the site of a place called Hill Castle; it is now completely deserted, but ditches and traces of former buildings may still be seen there.

Leighton Bromswold is situated on a hill three good miles from Kimbolton, and my ride there took me through level countryside of pastures and arable, but few trees visible except beside the villages. The soil between the two places grows exceptionally good corn. The manor of Leighton village belongs to a prebend in Lincoln Cathedral, and a certain Carnbull, who was the prebendary, built part of an attractive house there within a moat. Smyth, the present incumbent, has turned it into a free school. *cont. p. 2* [1/1-3]

Information from Mr Hall of Huntingdon. Earl Ferrars was lord and landowner around Eynesbury by St Neots. The best and most definite boundary that can be established in the fens of the upper part of Huntingdonshire is the River Nene. Virtually the whole of the Delph lies in Huntingdonshire, mostly in the hundred of [?*Hurstingstone*], with a small part in Norman Cross hundred. If there is any section of the Delph across the Nene in Thorney's territory it is of no consequence.

Spaldwick and Buckden, part of the St Etheldred estate, were given to the bishop of Lincoln by the bishop of Ely in exchange for jurisdiction in Cambridgeshire. Bishop Rotherham of Lincoln built the new brick tower at Buckden, completely transformed the hall, and spent a great deal of money there on other things. The barony of Broughton was at some time acquired by Engayne from the abbot of Ramsey.

It is said that the whole county of Huntingdon used to be within forest jurisdiction, but it is a very long time since its disafforestment. It used to have much more woodland that it has now. The deer used to live in the fens, and at a later period the red deer from this forest occupied Thorney fens.

Lunetot [*Eustace de Lovetot*] transferred the canons from their house on the site of the present St Mary's church in Huntingdon to the building outside the town which stood there until recently. One of the Simons de St Liz founded Sawtry Abbey. At Papworth St Agnes there is the boundary between Huntingdonshire and Cambridgeshire. [2/29-30]

KENT

LELAND'S TREATMENT OF KENT is quite substantial, and full of interesting details. The east Kent coastal towns are fully described, along with the problems caused by the changing shoreline, and there are useful accounts of Canterbury, Sittingbourne and elsewhere. His remark that Judge Fyneux had been advised by his doctor to move to Herne for the sake of his health prefigures the seaside resort movement by several centuries. But, like other counties near London, none of his Kentish material is written in the form of itinerary. Instead we are given rather muddled jottings, with supplementary notes on places already described, and a certain amount of repetition. Doubtless Leland collected material over several years, including during a monastic library tour in 1534, before he had embarked on any of the extended itineraries. He described St Radegund's near Dover as a still functioning monastery (it was dissolved in 1536), and he refers to the recent death of Richard Knight of Hythe (whose will was proved in 1535/6). His disparaging remark about the Canterbury nun's bogus miracles was a topical reference to Elizabeth Barton, the 'holy maid of Kent', who was persuaded to denounce the king's divorce, and suffered the death penalty for it in 1534. A passing reference in his account of Sandwich to Sir Edward Ringeley enables us to date this passage to before 1543, when his will was proved; and another to Sir Thomas Cheney, lord warden of the cinque ports, fixes his remarks as later than 1536, when he took up this appointment.

In the pages which follow I have tried to include all Leland's topographical material about Kent which was written in the form of a coherent narrative. I have however omitted several pages of rather more disconnected notes, which are largely of biographical interest, or extracts from manuscript histories which Leland had consulted. Scattered among these miscellanea are several interesting remarks which suggest that he attached particular importance to Kent: 'Let this be the first chapter of the book... The king himself was born in Kent. Kent is the key of all England.'

Mr Balthasar told me that around the cliffs of Dover hermitage he found snakes turned into stones. And that in the area of Dover Down by the shore there were round stones of considerable size which, when broken, appeared to contain a

KENT

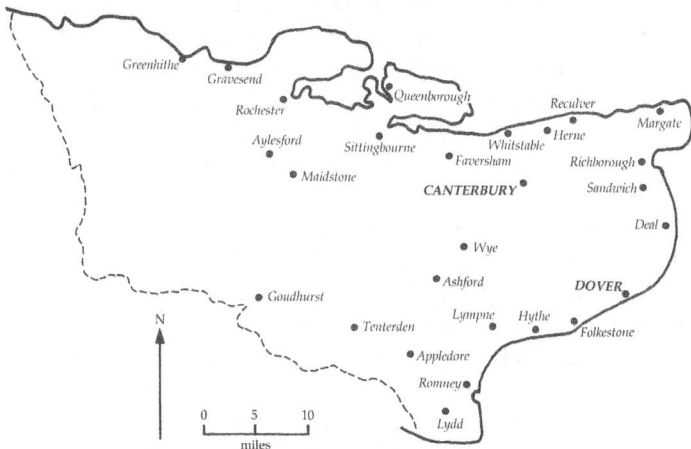

large amount of metal, but when this was broken up and left in a fire it merely turned to ashes. [2/28]

Stone Castle lies in Kent three miles this side of Gravesend and a half-mile from the Thames shore at Greenhithe. Until recently this building belonged to an alderman called Champion.

Sir John Cutte, knight and under-treasurer of England, purchased from a large Yorkshire landowner named Saville, who was then in difficulties, the manor of Goudhurst, including the ruins of a castle which stand about two miles from the bank of the River Medway, and two miles from Maidstone. When he bought it part of the manor was badly overgrown with thorns and bushes, and its annual value was only £14. But now it has been cleared, and its value much enhanced. There remains also a great deal of fine woodland around it. Old Cutte married the daughter and heiress of a certain Roodes from the Yorkshire region, and from her obtained land worth annually £200. He built at Childerley in Cambridgeshire, Salisbury Park near St Albans, and Horham Hall, which is a very lavish building near Thaxted in Essex, with a good pond or lake next to it, and surrounded by fine parks. [2/30-1]

Wingham College lies on the road from Canterbury to Sandwich four-and-a-half miles due precisely east of Canterbury. It has a provost and six prebendaries, as well as other priests attached to the church. It was founded by Archbishop Pecham during the period when the king had retained the temporalities of his bishopric, and he derived his income solely from the spiritualities, and the visitations of the province. When Pecham arrived with his bulls from the pope, by whose grant he was elevated to the see of Canterbury, he entered the monks' chapter, and began his address to them in Latin with the words: 'You have not chosen me, but I have chosen you'.

Wye is a pleasant little market town on the east bank of the River Doure [*Stour*] seven miles upstream from Canterbury. A great fair is held at Wye annually on St Gregory's day. Cardinal Kempe came from Wye, the son of a poor farmer. He was a doctor both of law and of divinity, who became first a deacon, then bishop successively of Rochester, Chichester, London and York, where he remained twenty-five years; finally he was translated to Canterbury, and was made a cardinal. 'Twice primate, thrice bishop, twice performed the cardinal's role.' During the twenty-fourth year of his episcopacy of York he made Wye parish church collegiate under the control of a prebendary and with a staff of priests to take public worship; they are to pray for the souls of those who gave him his education and advanced his career in other ways.

It was intended that Ashford church should be made collegiate. This was the desire of a gentleman named Fogge, who lived in the area and was Edward IV's comptroller [*of the household*]. But Edward died before Fogge had completed the scheme. Consequently Ashford has remained a prebend in name only; lands, priests and choristers are attached to the place, but their position is insecure as they have no common seal.

At Maidstone the college was founded by [*Archbishop*] Courtenay, who carried out much other building work there both at the palace, and in the town of Maidstone itself. The master of the college is a prebendary, and the other staff are priests who conduct public worship.

Noblemen buried beyond the steps at the east end of Canterbury cathedral church: King Henry IV and his wife under a pillar in the north aisle. Edward the Black Prince lies immediately opposite him under a pillar on the south side. He died in the bishop's palace at Canterbury. He gave a large golden chalice to Christ Church [*the cathedral church*], as well as golden vessels and many other precious objects.

Behind the wall of the high altar, between it and the steps at the east end are buried two bishops, Elphege [?*Aelfsige*] on the north side and Dunstan on the south side. Under the south side of the pillars on the south side of the high altar lie three other bishops, as follows: Simon Sudbury, who was beheaded by Jack Straw in London, lies in a high tomb of copper and gilt. He built the stretch of town wall and its towers between the west and north gates. Bishop Stratford lies in a high tomb with a stone effigy. Bishop Kempe lies in a high tomb of marble, but with no effigy. On the north side of the high altar lie Bishop Chichele and Cardinal Thomas Bourgchier, who crowned three kings, Edward IV, Richard III and Henry VII.

In a chapel in the south quire aisle dedicated to Ss Peter and Paul are buried Bishop Anselm behind the altar, and Bishop Mepham in a very fine tomb of black marble. In the south quire transept, right at the far end beside the wall lies Bishop Winchelsey in an excellent marble tomb. And in the north quire aisle there were some shrines containing the bones of certain bishops of Canterbury.

Simon [*i.e. Stephen*] Langton, about whom began the schism between King John and the pope, is buried in St Anne's chapel in the south transept which stands below the chancel steps. It was Langton who translated the remains of Thomas Becket, and he also built the exceptionally high, long and wide hall in the bishop's palace, and, so I have heard, was responsible for the impressive clock in the south transept of the church. This fine chapel of St Anne was probably built originally in honour of John, earl of Somerset. In the glass in its south windows are written three names, each with the royal arms: John, earl of Somerset, Lord Percy, and Lord Mortain. Besides Earl John, and another of the Somersets, with a lady of the Clarence family, there is also buried in this chapel another bishop of Canterbury.

In the north transept between the nave and the chancel are buried bishops Pecham and Warham, and others. And there are high tombs in the church nave belonging to Bishops Simon Islip, Whittlesey, and Arundel, and ten other bishops. Bishop Whittlesey was born at Whittlesey in Huntingdonshire [*actually Cambridgeshire*], and became successively archdeacon of Huntingdon, bishop of Rochester, and finally bishop of Canterbury. Bishop Arundel, who lies beneath a pillar on the north side, was responsible with King Henry IV for building a large part of the church nave. Three bishops, Cuthbeorht, Elphege [*?Aelfsige*] and Thomas Becket, were buried in the crypts, but Elphege and Becket were later translated to behind the high altar.

Bishop Morton and Prior Goldston built the great lantern crossing tower. The earlier Prior Goldston, who held office three priors before his namesake, built the stone tower at the west end of the church. The bells within the leaded spire at the west end of the church are known as Arundel's Ring. There used to be an extremely large peal of bells called Conrad's Ring, but this was later broken up and made into a smaller peal, which was probably the one hung in the low bell-tower in the churchyard. This bell-tower has recently been demolished. The second Prior Goldston began the fine south gate into the minster precinct, and it was completed by the last prior before the dissolution, whose name was Goldwell.

Of all the priors at Christ Church the greatest builder was Thomas Chillenden, or Chislesdene, who before he became a monk was a doctor of both the laws, and according to Bishop Warham had written certain erudite commentaries on law. He was largely responsible for beginning the new work in the church nave, and he also built from new the fine cloister, the chapter house, the new water conduit, the prior's lodging and chapel, the large dormitory, the frater, bakehouse, brewhouse, and treasury, and the fine inn in Canterbury High Street. He was also responsible for most of the abbey precinct wall, and the wall separating it from the town.

Sibertswold, now generally called Seperwelle, is a village about four miles from Dover; it lies beside a wood on the left hand side as one travels from Canterbury to Dover. In the parish of Barehamdoune [*Barham*], not far from the edge of the wood and about six [*miles*] from Dover, may be seen a military camp with three ditches. It is variously described as Caesar's camp, and as a Danish camp. The church at Dale (wrongly called Dele) [*Deal*] was a prebend anciently belonging to St Martin's College, Dover. During the reign of Henry I Archbishop

Theobald of Canterbury was largely responsible for converting the College of St Martin in Dover into a [?*priory*] and for bringing Benedictine monks from Canterbury [?*to be housed in*] new buildings there [*the manuscript is defective*].

There is an ample supply of woodland in west Kent. The region of Kent beyond Canterbury is given the name east Kent, and in several parts of it there is sufficient wood; but along the coast from Reculver to the Folkestone area there is but little.

The village of Tonge is little more than half a mile from Sittingbourne. Two bowshots distant from Tonge church to the south may be seen the ditches and motte of Tonge Castle in a small wood. Tonge is a mile from the mouth of Milton Creek, and if there were a way through the marshes the shortest distance to Milton [*Regis*] would be only about a half-mile. The market town of Milton is about a half-mile from Sittingbourne. Mr Talbot thinks that Sittingbourne is so called because of the many springs that, as it were, seeth and boil out from the nearby chalk hills. The largest of the streams deriving from these springs flows in the chalk hills at the west end of Sittingbourne.

William Tilly was born in the village of Selling, about two miles from Faversham, and took the name of Celling as a monk. Of all the scholarly priors who used to be at Christ Church, Canterbury, he was the best. At Bologna he was a protégé of Poliziano, and introduced Linacre to him.

The actual manor and manor house which are still called Badlesmere lie three miles inland from Ospringe to the south, and now belong to the king. The customary burying places of the St Leger family were Ulcombe and Otterden. Their estate was divided between daughters, and one married a man named Ager [*Aucher*], who thus acquired Otterden. He was an ancestor of Anthony Aucher, who is descended, so I heard, from an ancient earl of Kent. Indeed there was an earl of Kent called Aucher before the conquest. At Leeds Priory there are buried three members of the Crevecouer family, Robert, Robert and Thomas; it is likely that each inherited the estate.

The family name of Finiox [*Fyneux*] came to Kent at around the time of Edward II, in the following way. A man called Creaulle [*Criol*], a large Kentish landowner, was held prisoner at Boulogne in France. Being very desirous of his liberty he befriended his gaoler, and promised him lands in Kent if he would help him to escape. And so they both crossed over to Kent secretly, and Criol kept his promise. As a result his gaoler or deliverer was given the name Fyneux. But the family estate was not advanced until the Fyneux who was chief judge of the king's bench. At first his land was worth £40 by the year, and he had two younger brothers who each had a share in the estate. They both increased the annual value of their holdings to £200, and when one of them died he made the other brother his heir. So that now there are two branches of the Fyneux family, the heir of Fyneux the judge, and the heir of his brother.

A portion of the estate which Fyneux was given by Criol was Swingfield, and the area around it, three miles from Folkestone on the Canterbury road.

There are two attractive timber manor houses there, but Fyneux the judge built himself a better house on land he had purchased at Herne. He did this for the sake of his health, because physicians had previously concluded that Herne was an exceptionally healthy area. Criol had owned a very fine estate in Kent, until the time when it was partitioned. Some people say that he owned Folkestone Park, which later passed to the Clintons; and Ostinghanger (now sometimes corrupted to Westenhanger) belonged to him. Until recently this belonged to Poyning, but now the king has it. Some of the Criols were buried with honours at St Radegund's [*Abbey*]; the family were great benefactors to monastic houses in east Kent, as is evident from their coat of arms in many glass windows.

Aylesford, where there is a fine stone bridge across the river, is four miles overland from Rochester. Maidstone is three miles by land from Aylesford, and this too has a good stone bridge. The river is tidal as far as Maidstone. Between Maidstone and Farleigh, which is two miles by land further upstream, and at Farleigh itself, a hard stone is extensively quarried. Farleigh has a good stone bridge. A tributary of no very great size called the Loose enters the main river about two miles beyond Farleigh. The village called Loose stands a mile inland above its confluence with the River Medway. [*The next bridge upstream on the Medway*] is Teston Bridge, of stone, and then Twyford Bridge, also of stone, a mile-and-a-half further. At this stone bridge, which crosses the main river, and at a mill a short distance above it, is the confluence of three rivers. The Medway is, as it were, the middle of the three, and rivers enter on its nearer and further banks. There is another bridge at the pleasant little town of Yalding, a quarter-mile or more above Twyford Bridge. After this going upstream there is Brambridge [*Brandbridges*], of stone, and then no important bridge up as far as Tonbridge, which is sixteen miles from Rochester by land.

Rochester Castle stands at the end of the bridge as one enters the town. The exit from Rochester in the Canterbury direction is through a remarkably strong gate, most of which survives. But no other gates survive there which are in common use. There are still six or seven towers remaining in the walls. Within the circuit of the walls at Rochester half the space is taken up by the cathedral, and its palace and other buildings.

Distances from Canterbury, in miles: Faversham, 7; Whitstable, 3; Herne, 4; Ashford, 11; Wye, 7; Chilham, 4; Ford, 5 (and another mile to Reculver); Sandwich, 8 (although it is commonly said to be 7); Dover, 12; Folkestone, 10; Hythe, 12; Lynhil [*Lympne*], 11; Appledore, 16; Cranbrook, 20 (via Ashford, 11). [*Distances along the coast:*] Sandwich to Dover, about 7 miles; Dover to Folkestone, 5; Folkestone to Hythe, 4 little miles; Hythe to Holde [?*Old*] Hythe (or West Hythe), about 2 miles. Mr Twyne says that it was on the coast here, where the ruined church survives, that there stood a town which was burnt.

[*Castles in Kent:*] Lymehille [*Lympne*] Castle is sometimes called 'Belleanow'. The castle at Thornham, now entirely in ruins, stood on a hilltop one mile east of Maidstone; it belongs at present to young Cutte. Allington Castle belonged in the thirteenth and fourteenth centuries to the Grey family, and more recently to the Savilles and Wyatts. Harte owns the site and premises of a castle near the River Cray. [*There are also castles at*] Greenwich, Woolwich, Dartford, Erith, Gravesend, Rochester, Maidstone, Aylesford and Graveney.

Maidstone is a market town with one long street of good architecture, and full of inns. Mr Talbot says that the name is a corruption of 'Medwegetoun', but it may alternatively be a corruption of 'Ailston', since, like Aylesford, it stands on the River Aile [*both in fact stand on the Medway, and Aylesford is derived from a personal name*]. The name given to Maidstone's town governor is port reeve. There is a fine college of priests in the town, and it also has the common gaol or prison for Kent, as being the shire town. The castle stands roughly in the centre of the town, and is maintained in good condition by the archbishop of Canterbury.

Sandwich, on the further bank of the River Stour, has a reasonably good wall in those places where the town stands most in jeopardy from enemies. The remainder has a ditch and earthen bank. There are four principal gates in the town and three parish churches, one of which, St Mary's, is thought once to have been a nunnery. There is a house of white friars, and outside the town is a hospital which was originally intended for diseased and injured sailors. There is also a house in which the monks of Christ Church used to stay when they owned the town. The ship which was sunk in the estuary during the time of Pope Paul [*i.e. Paul II, 1464-71*] did the estuary a great deal of harm, by causing a large bank to form. The land which extends from Sandwich to the estuary, and running inland is called Sanded Bay. Sir Edward Ringeley has a tower or fortress by the coast beyond the estuary mouth.

Stonar, which is not far from Sandwich, lies in Thanet, and was once an attractive place. But now all that is to be seen is the ruined church. In ignorance some people call it 'Old Sandwich'.

Deal is a fishing village which stands a half-mile from the coast, and three miles or more above Sandwich. Its position on the flat shore is very open to the sea, and there is an embankment, or large manmade bank, between the town and the sea. It begins near Deal, and extends much of the way to St Margaret's at Cliffe. It has led some people to believe that this was the stretch of open coastline on which Caesar landed. But it is more likely either that the ditch was built to keep out enemies, or as protection from the ravages of the sea, or (and this is my opinion) it is merely the casting-up of pebbles on the beach.

Northbourne is more than two miles inland from the sea coast almost next to Deal. A small freshwater stream flows a couple of miles or more from Northbourne to Sandwich, and into the estuary. The palace or manor house of Eadbert, Ethelbert's son, was at Northbourne, and only a few years ago, when a side wall of the hall was demolished, the bones of two children were discovered who had been walled up as a form of pagan Saxon burial. Amongst the bones of one of the children was found a rigid pin made of latten.

About a mile along the coast from Deal is Walmer, and when viewed from the further side of the harbour mouth at Dover the coastline appears low as far as Walmer, then high cliffs from Walmer right up to the point on which Dover Castle stands, then the shore flattens out again, but beyond Dover there are cliffs all the way to Folkestone. From Walmer St Margaret's [*at Cliffe*] is two miles, and Dover a further two miles. During the episcopate of Bishop Morton [1486-1500] a certain Thomas Lawrence built a pier or jetty at St Margaret's. There is a village two miles this side of Dover called Langdon, and here a house of canons regular has recently been suppressed.

The cinque ports are Sandwich, Dover, Hythe (or Hide), Romney and Hastings. The main court of the lord of the cinque ports is held on the eastern part of Lympne Hill. Near Lympne there is a place called Shipway or Shipeye [*Shepway*], which some people refer to as the old 'rode' [anchorage].

[*Distances, in miles, around the cinque ports:*] Dover to Folkestone, 5; Folkestone to Hythe, 3; Hythe to Lympne, 3; Lympne to Romney, 7; Hythe to Romney, 7; Romney to Lydd, 2; Romney to Appledore, 7; Lydd to Appledore, 7; Appledore to Lyminge, about 12; Appledore to Rye, 5; Romney to Rye, 7.

In times past Dover, which is twelve miles from Canterbury and eight miles from Sandwich, used to be a harbour. The Antonine Itinerary describes it as a harbour, and evidence of this is provided both by the discovery there of pieces of anchor and cable, and also by the fact that when the ground extending up between the hills is dug it is still found to be made of wet mud. On the seaboard side of the town there has been a very strong embattled wall, which has now been breached in part, and partly fallen down. Three gates with towers – Cow Gate, Cross Gate and Butchery Gate – stood on the seaward side, and there were also two other gates, Beeting [?*Biggin*] Gate and West Gate. So far as I could see the rest of the town never had a wall, although Mr Twyne has recently told me that it did have a wall, but without a ditch. The town is divided into six parishes, but three of them are served under one roof by St Martin's in the centre of the town. The other three stand separately, and one of them is called St James of Rudby. The more likely form of the name is 'Rodeby', after the 'rode' or anchorage for ships, but this name is insufficient evidence to prove that Dover should be regarded as the place called by the Romans 'portus Rutupi' or 'Rutupinum'. I cannot see any reason to deny that the names Ratesborough near Sandwich, otherwise called Richborough, must both be corruptions of 'Rutupinum'.

The massive, strong and famous castle of Dover stands on a hilltop almost a quarter-mile away from the town on its left hand side, and within the castle is a chapel, in the sides of which may be seen some large bricks of the British period. In the town there was a large priory of Benedictine monks, which has lately been suppressed, and also a hospital called the Maison Dieu. On top of the high cliff between the town and the pier, about a bowshot inland from the actual cliff top, may still be seen a ruined tower, which has been a lighthouse or beacon for ships out at sea. Nearby was a house of templars.

As regards the river at Dover its course is not long, and there is no notable spring or source from which it derives and flows down into its valley. They say that the main source is at a place called [Temple] Ewell, and that is not more than three or four miles from Dover. There are also freshwater springs at a place called River, and another large spring which once in every six or seven years breaks out so abundantly that, although the majority of the water resorts to the Dover stream, the rest flows to the sea between Dover and Folkestone – in fact less than two miles from Folkestone, and so nearer to Folkestone than to Dover. The position of this spring is surely such that it would not be expensive to channel the water so that it always fed the Dover stream.

St Radegund's [Abbey] stands on a hilltop three little miles west of Dover and somewhat to the south. It is a house of white canons, and its church has a fine, large quire. At present the monastery is in reasonably good condition, but it seems that in the past the buildings extended further than they do now. There is fine woodland on this hill, but fresh water is sometimes in short supply.

By water it is fifteen miles from Rochester to Queenborough in Sheppey. Queenborough stands at the westernmost point of Sheppey, and from there an arm of the Thames runs up three miles to Milton [Regis]. It is also fifteen miles from Rochester to the point opposite Queenborough where the river enters the Thames estuary, and from there it is twenty miles by water to Gravesend. There is a single parish church on Ingreyne Isle [Isle of Grain], which at high tide is surrounded by water. It lies west of Queenborough, on the nearer bank.

A certain John Warner, a Rochester merchant, made the new coping of Rochester Bridge, and the iron bars were provided by Bishop Warham. From Rochester overland it is five miles to Aylesford and six to Allington. [4/37-52]

Canterbury is a walled town, with five gates [six are listed] named as follows: Westgate; Northgate; Burgate, which is now called Mihelsgate [?Michael's Gate]; St George's Gate; Riders Gate [Ridingate], which John Brooker, the mayor of the town, lowered so much that now there is not clearance for carts to pass through it; Worth Gate, which leads to a street called Stone Street, and then to Billerica, which is now called Curtop Street [Court-at-Street]. Within the town are fourteen parish churches, as well as the cathedral church of Benedictine monks. There are also three parish churches outside the walls. St Augustine's is a Benedictine monastery, and St Gregory's is for Augustinian canons. St Sepulchre's was once a house of the Templars order, and afterwards a nunnery. St John's is a hospital for men and women, founded by the bishops of Canterbury. St Laurence's is a hospital for women only, and was founded by the abbots of St Augustine's. There is a hospital on the king's bridge within the town for poor pilgrims and travellers. There is also a hospital for poor clergy, and a small hospital within the walls, known as the Minors, which was established by the citizens. Within the walls too are houses of Dominican, Austin and Franciscan friars.

Reculver is five good miles from Canterbury, and at least two miles by water, and a mile-and-a-half by land, beyond Herne, which is its chapelry. At present the town resembles a village, and stands a quarter-mile, or perhaps a little more, from the coast. On the site of the present parish church there once stood a fine and large abbey, and Brightwald [*Beorhtweald*], archbishop of Canterbury, belonged to it. The old fabric of the abbey church survives, including two good spires. In the chancel entrance is one of the finest and oldest crosses that I have ever seen; it is nine feet, I should reckon, in height, and stands like a noble column. The large stone at its base is not carved, but the next stone, which is round, has intricate carvings, with painted effigies, as I recall, of Christ, Peter, Paul, John and James. There are Latin inscriptions, with Christ saying, 'I am the alpha and omega', and Peter saying, 'You are the Christ, the son of the living God'. The words of the other three were painted in Roman capital letters but are now obliterated. The second stone depicts the passion, and the third contains the twelve apostles. The fourth has an effigy of Christ hanging and fastened by four nails, with a support beneath his feet. At the top of the pillar there is the figure of the cross.

The church contains a very ancient book of the gospels written in Roman capitals, and in its boards is inset a crystal-stone [?*a piece of pure quartz*] with the inscription 'Claudia Atepiccus'. On the north side of the church is the figure of a bishop painted under an arch. When digging has taken place around the churchyard old belt buckles and a ring have been found. The full extent of the monastic precinct is marked by the old wall around it, and the vicarage was built from the ruins of the monastery. Outside the churchyard there is a neglected chapel, and some people say that this was a parish church before the abbey was suppressed and granted to the bishop of Canterbury. Many Roman coins have been found in the Reculver area. Although the town is no more than half a mile from the coast the sea presumably at one time came right up to it.

Gore End [*Goresend*] is two miles from Northmouth, and there is a small path called Broad Stairs which leads down the cliff at Goresend. This stretch of coast offers good fishing for mullet, and the large argosies [*merchant ships*] use Goresend as shelter from the wind. From there another bay extends along to the Foreland.

Morton planned to create a new harbour in Thanet by reclaiming his marshland. Thanet extends in length from Northmouth to Sandwich, a distance of seven miles or more by a direct route; and in breadth from the River Stour, where it flows not far from Minster, to Margate, a distance of four miles from south to north. Its circumference is therefore approximately seventeen or eighteen miles. At Northmouth, where the sea used to enter, there is still a swell of salt water up a creek for a mile or more towards a place called Sarre, and this was the usual ferrying place when Thanet was a genuine island.

Margate is about one mile on this side of the point of Sandwich estuary, and five miles up from Reculver, in the parish of St John's in Thanet. It has a village and a pier for ships, but this is now in great disrepair. Ramsgate is four miles up into Thanet, and here too is a small pier for ships.

There used to be eleven parish churches in Thanet; three of them now are derelict, but the others remain. At specific times some of the Thanet parishes attend at Reculver (a mile away from the island), as at their mother church, and others attend at Minster (lying on the island) as their superior and mother church. There are very few trees on Thanet, but both the coast and the interior of the island are full of good chalk quarries.

Ratesburgh (alias Richborough), existed before ever the River Stour altered the course of its bed within the Isle of Thanet, and it is probable that the open sea once came right up to the foot of the castle. But now the coast is a mile away from it, as a result of the mud which has built up there. The position of the old town or castle on a hill is remarkably good, and the surviving walls there are almost as great in extent as the Tower of London. They used to be very high, thick, strong and well fortified. They were made of flint, with extraordinary white and red long bricks in the British style, and set in cement made of sea sand and small pebbles. It is very likely that this good hill around the castle, especially on the side towards Sandwich, was once densely populated. Corn grows on the hill in exceptional abundance, and since time immemorial right up to the present ploughing there has uncovered a greater quantity of ancient Roman coins than any other site in England.

Common sense suggests that this place should assuredly be identified with Rutupinum. Not only are the names rather similar, but Richborough was also the genuine shortest crossing from Calais cliffs, or Calais. The crossing is now to Sandwich, about a mile from Richborough, but because of the Goodwin Sands and the decline of its harbour Sandwich is no longer important.

At least a bowshot from Richborough, in the direction of Sandwich, there is a large ditch excavated around in a circle, as if for the defence of warriors. Locally the place is called Littleborough, and it encloses an area of little more than an acre, which lies very much in a depression because of the earthwork.

Inside Richborough Castle there is a small parish church dedicated to St Augustine, and a hermitage. The hermit is an intelligent man, and I obtained some antiquities from him. Not far from the hermitage there is a cave where people have looked and dug for treasure. I saw the inside of it by candle light, and it contained rabbits; but it was so narrow that I had no intention of crawling in very far. On the north side of the castle there is a head, known locally as Queen Bertha's Head, which is set into the wall, but has now been badly weathered. Close to the wall near this spot was found a pot containing Roman coins.

Tenterden is a market town in Kent on the nearer side of the river which flows to Appledore; the river there divides Sussex and Kent. Cranbrook is in the middle of the Kentish Weald. Ashford, a market town on one side or edge of the Kentish Weald, is ten miles from Cranbrook and twelve miles from Canterbury. It is twice as large as Sittingbourne, and has in it a fine college of priests.

[Archbishop] Morton was responsible for building a large portion of Lambeth Palace. He built and transformed a large part of the house at Maidstone, and he built at Allington Park. He carried out extensive building work at Charing, and made almost the entire house at Forde. He also did work on the palace at Canterbury.

From Robertsbridge [*the River Rother flows*] to Bodiam Castle, on the further bank going towards Rye. There is a bridge over it here, and the river is a little brackish. Then I went to Bredebridge [*Brede*] in Sussex, where there is a bridge (and the river flows here [*i.e. the River Brede*]). The village is on the further bank, and in its centre is a cross which marks the boundary between Kent and Sussex. Mr Oxeney lives nearby. From there it is four or five miles to Newenden, which stands on the further bank [*of the Rother*], and there is a bridge. Then it flows to Meteham [*Maytham*], where there is a ferry but no bridge, and three houses on the far bank. From there to Smalhed [*Small Hythe*], which is a village on the nearer bank in Kent, and has a ferry across to the Isle of Oxney. Then to Reading (in Kent), which is a chapelry dependent on the parish church of Our Lady at Ebony in Oxney (in Sussex), even though this portion lies on the nearer bank. From there to Oxney [*?Stone*] Ferry, which connects Kent with Oxney, and on the further bank (in Oxney) there is a village [*Stone*]. At present part of the Isle of Oxney is in Kent, and part in Sussex. Some say, however, that now or in the past it has all been in Sussex, and others call it 'Forsworn Kent', because when its inhabitants were reckoned to be in Sussex they revolted in order to obtain the benefits of living in Kent.

From Reading it is two miles to Appledore, where there is a fine church; it is the mother church to Reading, on the Kent side, and to Our Lady's church at Ebony in the Isle of Oxney. From Appledore to the actual point where the river flows to the Black Shore and the Chaumber [*Camber*] is five miles. The true mouth of the Lyminge or Appledore River [*Rother*] is about a mile south-east of the town of Rye into Kent.

The gates which used to be on the seaward side of Dover: Beginning from the castle there was Crossgate, Seagate, Tinker's Gate, Butchery Gate, Snore [*Snare*] Gate, Bolders Gate, and then to the Wikeward. On the other side of the town were Cow Gate and Walgate, to the point where the London road enters Dover. In the reign of King John, before Hubert de Burgh obtained it, the guardian or controller of Dover was a Frenchman called Fyneux. It was about this time that the knight's service known as castle guard was inaugurated in Dover Castle. Mr Finch the knight has a list of this guard. Hubert de Burgh was the original founder of the old church of Maison Dieu at Dover, and Henry III founded the new church. The cliffs of Dover are entirely of chalk for most of the way to Folkestone, and from there to Lympne they are of a very hard stone, which in some places is of a deep blue colour.

Folkestone is five miles from Dover, and in all probability stands directly opposite Boulogne. Lord Clinton is the owner of the town, and of the parish. An attractive little stream rises in the parish, or not far beyond, and flows down to the town. It seems very likely that the town's shore has received exceptionally harsh treatment from the ravages of the sea, to such an extent that it is said that two parish churches, Our Lady's and St Paul's, have been completely destroyed and swallowed up by the sea. Close to the shore there is a place called the Castle Yard, which has a ditch along one side. It contains the substantial ruins of a solemn old nunnery, and in several places in its walls may be seen large, long British bricks. On the right hand side of the quire there is a sarcophagus of squared stone blocks. This Castle Yard has been greatly used for burials, to such an extent that when the sea erodes its edge bones can be seen half sticking out. The parish church is nearby, and incorporates some later monastic building. St Eanswith is buried there, and until recently there were traces of a priory in the area. Nearly a quarter-mile outside the town there is a chapel dedicated to St Botolph, which may at some stage be rebuilt. The town has a mayor. The present Lord Clinton's grandfather obtained from a poor man in the town a boot almost full of antiquities of pure gold and silver. A rabbit which made its burrow between Folkestone and Hythe turned up ancient coins.

The town of Hythe used to extend a great distance, and contained four parish churches which are now entirely destroyed, that is to say, the churches of St Nicholas, Our Lady, St Michael, and Our Lady of West Hythe. West Hythe is less than half a mile away from Lympne. It may well be supposed that after Lympne harbour and the large old town there failed, Hythe immediately increased and became more prosperous. The total distance from West Hythe along to the place where the main part of the town is now is a good two miles. This distance is measured along what was once the shoreline of the open sea, but which now, as a result of mudbanks and the great build up of shingle, is anything from a quarter to half a mile from the sea. During the reign of Edward II more than 160 houses were burned in an accidental fire, and this was followed immediately by a severe epidemic, which two events reduced the town. The ruins of the churches and churchyards still remain, and it is very obvious that the site of the present parish church was at one time a fine abbey. The quire contains many good marble columns, with an excellent vaulted undercroft beneath, and a good stone doorway by which the monks entered at midnight. At the top of the churchyard is a fine spring, and nearby are the ruins of the abbey's domestic buildings. Not far away there was a hospital belonging to a gentleman infected with leprosy. Saltwood Castle is not more than a half-mile away, and at the present day Hythe is merely a chapelry dependent on Saltwood parish church. The harbour offers an attractive anchorage, and its position affords a reasonably direct crossing to Boulogne. It turns so much along by the shore, and is sheltered from the open sea by the build up of shingle to such an extent, that small vessels may sail up more than a mile towards Folkestone in a dependable channel.

Lymme Hill or Lyme [*Lympne*] was at one time a renowned harbour, and good for ships which could sail up to the foot of the hill, to a place which is still called Shypwey [*Shepway*] and Old Haven. The old castle at Lympne belonged to Richard Knight of Hythe, who has recently died. Moreover the Lord of the Cinque

Ports to this day holds his chief court at a place a little to the east of Lympne. There still survive too the ruins of a strong British fortress perched on the hillside, and extending down to its very foot. This fortress appears to enclose an area of ten acres, and it probably had a wall in addition which ran right up to the top of the hill, where now are the parish church and the house of the archdeacon of Canterbury. The old walls of the [?*castle*] were made of very large British bricks and massive bricks, set almost inseparably together with mortar made of small pebbles. These walls are very thick, and at the western end of the castle may be seen the base of an old tower. Within living memory ancient Roman coins have been found in the area of this castle. There can be no doubt that an abbey once existed on the site of the present church. Graves can still be seen in the church, and the abbey lodging has been turned into the archdeacon's house, which has been built like a small fortified castle. A fine paved road ran from Lympne to Canterbury, and this is known at present as Stony [*Stone*] Street. It is the straightest road that I have ever seen, and towards the Canterbury end the paving survives continuously for four or five miles. At present a small brook flows through Lympne Castle, and other attractive streams drain the places around Lympne. But where the course of the River Limen should be I cannot say, except that it should flow from above Appledore, three miles away; but its course to the sea has now been changed and it flows by a shorter channel as a result of the extension of Romney Marsh, which was once all sea.

Court-up-streate, alias Billerica [*Court-at-Street*] belongs to a knight by the name of Mr Coluyle [?*Carlell or Carlisle*]. It is about a mile from Lympne, and at present forms a part of the parish of Lympne. Nevertheless it has a chapel to serve the buildings which remain there, which is commonly called the chapel of Our Lady of Court-up-Street, and it was here that the Canterbury nun performed all her bogus miracles [*Elizabeth Barton, the 'holy maid of Kent', hanged in 1534*]. Next to this chapel may be seen the ruins of a small castle, and it may be for this reason that the town which existed there was known as 'Bellirica', that is to say 'Bellocastrum' [*'good castle'*] in Latin, whereas the new name, Court-up-Street, began as a description of the place or court which the owner of the site held there. Local people commonly boast that it was once a large town, and they still display their civic insignia, namely a horn with brass fittings, and a mace. But it is more likely that these items belonged to Lympne, which was once indeed an important town and harbour.

Romney, four miles or more from Lympne, is one of the cinque ports, and used to be a reasonably good harbour, in so far that within living memory ships have sailed right up to the town, and cast their anchors in one of the churchyards. But the sea is now two miles away from the town, and its consequent decline has been so severe that, whereas there used to be three large parish churches, hardly one is now kept in good order.

Romney Marsh extends more than ten miles from Lympne, and at its greatest width, which I suppose is now near the town of Romney, it is about five miles wide. Its width is increasing day by day, but not evenly. In some places it is two miles wide, but in others three, four or even five miles. It is a wonderfully luxuriant feeding ground for cattle, because of the great abundance of grass growing on the mud once cast up there by the sea. But Romney itself, and an area stretching two miles around it, was probably always dry land, with the sea formerly surrounding it, as is supposed, or at least extending around the greatest part of it.

Lydd, a market town three miles beyond Romney, is reckoned to be part of Romney. The town is of an attractive size, and is all contained within a single parish, which however is very large. The townsmen are engaged in sailing boats on the sea, which at present is a mile away. Halfway or thereabouts between Romney town and Lydd the marsh begins to form an arm or ness out into the sea; this extends for a considerable distance beyond Lydd, and as it comes to a point it makes a cape, or foreland, or ness. Beyond Lydd there is a place where a large number of holly trees grow along a bank of pebbles thrown up by the sea. Birds are enticed there, and many are killed.

Appledore, which by some people is reckoned to be dependent on Romney, is a market town in Kent, and its fine church controls a territory which includes not only part of Kent but also Our Lady of Ebony in the Isle of Oxney. The freshwater river which flows to Appledore rises near Bodiam, seven miles inland up into the Weald of Sussex. Near its source is an old castle called Bodiam, and from there it flows to Tenterden, a market town in Kent, or rather it flows between the parish of Tenterden and the Isle of Oxney. Oxney is nearly ten miles in circumference, and is surrounded by salt water except where the freshwater stream separates it from the mainland. Appledore is two good miles from Tenterden, and lies in Kent on the west side of Romney Marsh. From Appledore it is six miles to the pool or open sea.

Sittingbourne (or Sidingburne) is an attractive roadside town, twelve miles from Canterbury, seven miles from Faversham, and eight long miles from Rochester. It has only one parish, and past the church flows a little brook or burn, from which perhaps the town took its name. Tonge Castle, one long mile to the side of Sittingbourne, was built, according to some people, by Hengist and the Saxons. The ditches and ruins of this castle may still be seen two bow shots from Tonge church.

Faversham is a market town with the privilege of sanctuary, and it has a large Benedictine abbey which was founded by King Stephen. The town is confined within a single parish, but that is very large. A creek extends up to the town of sufficient draught for vessels of twenty tons, and a mile from the town to the north-east there is a large quay called Thorne where large ships can unload. The creek is fed by a backwater which flows from a roadside place called Ospringe, a mile or more away. There was once a hospital here, which now belongs to St John's College, Cambridge. [*The Isle of*] Harty, which adjoins Sheppey, lies opposite Faversham and Thorne.

KENT

Whitstable is another two miles or more into Kent, beyond Faversham and along the same coast. It is a large fishing town of a single parish, which belongs to Pleshey College in Essex, and it stands on the seashore. In this area they dredge for oysters, and at Herne, three miles away, people collect good mussels which are called stake mussels. Herne lies a half-mile from the seashore, where there are good pitches for netting mullet.

The larger portion of the town of Canterbury stands on the further bank of the River Stour, and at one point the river runs through the city wall, by two or three arches made in it to take the flow of the water. The Romans called Canterbury 'Duravennum', which is a corruption of 'Dor' and 'Avona', or, as we should say, 'Doravona' or 'Doravonum'. It is my suggestion, therefore, that in all probability the River Stour was called in the British period the Avona. Canterbury is five miles from the sea, measuring directly north to near Herne. [*Archbishops*] Lanfranc and Sudbury (who was beheaded by Jack Straw) were great rebuilders of the city. Sudbury built the west gate, and repaired and renewed the wall from there to the north gate; had he lived he would have done similar work on the whole circuit of the wall around the town. The mayor and aldermen of Canterbury reverently visit his tomb once each year to pray for his soul, in memory of his good work. The oldest architecture in the town seems to be in the castle, and at Ridingate, where long British bricks may be seen. Similar bricks are visible also at St Pancras chapel and St Martin's, both outside the town. Many years ago people searched for treasure at a place called the dungeon, where Barnhale's house is now, and while they were digging they found a corpse encased in lead. There used to be some strong fortress near the castle, where the prominent hill now called Dungen Hill [*Dane John Mound*] rises.

Canterbury's river, which is now called the Stour, rises at Kingges Snode [?*Kingsnorth*], a little to west of south of Canterbury, and fourteen or fifteen miles away. Kingsnorth is three miles from the market town of Ashford, which lies on the further bank of the Stour, as does Wye, another market town, four miles downstream from Ashford. Next is Chilham, a village four miles lower, which has now been granted by the king to Cheyney, lord warden [*of the cinque ports*], for himself and his male heirs. From Chilham Canterbury is three miles, but a little above Canterbury the stream of the Stour divides into two arms, of which one passes by the west gate, and the other flows through the city and under St Thomas's Hospital. They rejoin and flow in a single course below the city. [*After Canterbury*] Fordwich lies on the further bank; it is a poor town, but it still retains its mayor. Next to Stourmouth, a good village four miles away by water, then to Richborough on the further bank, two miles or more, Sandwich on the same bank, another mile; and so within half a mile the Stour flows into the open sea. [4/59-70]

The manor of Frogenhale, which is usually called Frogenolle [*Frognal*] lies in the vicinity of Tonge Castle next to Sittingbourne, and is worth £45 in annual rent.

A knight who was a member of this very ancient family performed great feats in France, and is recorded in history.

A pleasant creek extends to Midleton [*Milton Regis*] in Kent, near Sittingbourne, and is frequented by small trading boats and other good vessels. At Bobbing, one mile from Sittingbourne, there is a fine manor, and a strong but plain house of flint next to it. This manor once belonged to the Moleyns, then to the Salvages, and now to the Cliffords. The older brother of the Cliffords of Kent sold it to Sir Thomas Neville, but the younger brother bought it back for himself and his heirs. The elder Clifford still has a manor near Boxley in Kent, which is called Sutton Valence; it used to have a park.

There was a poor hospital one mile beyond Sittingbourne called Pokeshaulle [*Puckleshall*]. Henry VII gave it to his physician, called Lynch, and he gave it to one of his sons. I imagine that by now it has been completely demolished.

Higham was a poor priory of nuns, about four miles above Gravesend in Kent, by the shore. It was suppressed at the instigation of Bishop Fisher of Rochester, and given to St John's College, Cambridge. Some people maintain that King Stephen was its founder, and that his sister was a nun there. [4/87-8]

LANCASHIRE

SIR WILLIAM LEYLAND, *of Morleys Hall near Leigh, was probably related to our author, and he seems to have been Leland's host and informant during the visit to Lancashire recorded in the itinerary. This was part of the 1538 journey from Wales to the North, which, although sketchier than some of the later accounts, includes nevertheless good brief descriptions of Manchester and Lancaster. It is supplemented by quite extensive notes which Leland arranged by the five 'shires' into which Lancashire was divided. His notes on West Derbyshire (the south-west part of the county around Liverpool) are fuller than for other areas, doubtless because of Sir William Leyland's interest; there is nothing at all noted for Blackburnshire. Some miscellaneous notes describe the Hornby area, north-east of Lancaster, and the fortunes of the Harrington family who owned it.*

THE RIVER MERSEY separates Cheshire and Lancashire all the way to the open sea. From Crossford Bridge to Manchester is about three miles, and after crossing Corn Brook on my way I passed first of all Sir Alexander Radcliffe's park and house on my left over the Irwell, and a mile or so from Manchester I skirted Mr Trafford's park and house. Then I saw Mr Prestwich's house on my left, across the Irwell, and next to it Lord Derby has a house, and a park called Alport Park. Near here I crossed the River Medlock, less than a mile before Manchester.

Manchester stands on the

south bank of the River Irwell in Salfordshire. It is the finest and busiest town in the whole of Lancashire, with the best buildings and the greatest population, yet it has only a single parish church. Not long ago this church was made collegiate, and it possesses double aisles for almost its whole length, built of very hard stone blocks derived from a good quarry next to the town. Manchester also has several stone bridges, of which the best is called Salford Bridge; it crosses the Irwell by three arches, and has an attractive small chapel on it. It separates Manchester from Salford, which is in effect a large suburb. Another bridge crosses the River Irk, and on this river there are several good mills which serve the town. On the point formed by the confluence of the Irk and the Weaver [*i.e. Irwell*] is situated the finely built college. Manchester also possesses two good market places.

Nearly two bowshot lengths below the town, on the same bank of the Irwell, can still be seen the ditches and foundations of Old Man Castle. The site has now been enclosed, and masonry from the ruined castle has been reused in building the town's bridges. Manchester is built on a site of durable rock, and had this not been the case it would have suffered damage from the Irwell, as may be well seen on the west bank. Except in certain places the Irwell is not navigable, because of shallows and rocks.

On my way from Manchester to Morleys Hall (Sir William Leyland's house) I passed enclosed land, partly used for pasture, and partly under arable cultivation. After a mile or more I encountered on my left Mr Langford's fine house, called Edgecroft. There is a very high and large timber bridge across the Irwell here, and nearby is Pilkington Park. The stonebuilt house in this park was given to Lord Derby by Henry VII after the Pilkingtons were attainted. Less than two miles from Morley, also to my left, was a house belonging to Mr Worsley of Booths. And a mile or more before arriving at Mr Leyland's house I crossed Heding Brook which marks the boundary between Salfordshire and West Derby.

Mr Leyland's house, Morleys Hall in West Derby, is surrounded by a large moat and has foundations of stone blocks rising six feet above the water; but the rest, as is the usual type of construction for all gentlemen's houses in most of Lancashire, is entirely built of timber. The orchards there, with their great variety of fruit, and the fine walks and gardens rival any house in Lancashire for the pleasure they give. Only turf and peat are used for fuel, because they are so easily obtained from the nearby peat-bogs and swamps. Chat Moss, which causes so much erosion damage to the surrounding land with its great quantity of water, rivers of creeping moss, and stagnant water, is less than a mile from Morley. And yet around Morley itself there is a reasonable supply of wood from hedgerows and small plantations; and good husbandry maintains it like a jewel. Sir John Holcroft's house, which is a mile or more from Morleys was in danger of being inundated by the moss. Morleys stands in the parish of Leigh a mile or more from the church.

As I rode on beyond Morleys I saw close by on my right after more than a mile a house belonging to Mr Atherton, and two miles further I reached Lidiate Moss. My guide told me that on the right side of this there were roots of fir wood. It was about here that I began to see a hill or hills to my right, which continued as a great long ridge on the same side all the way to Lancaster. Part of the hill where I first saw it is called Fairlocke, although local people usually call it Rivenpike [*Rivington Pike*]. One of them told me that beneath the hill near Lidiate Moss there is a village called Riven or Rivington, and that it stands on a river called Andertonford; also that a gentleman called Anderton has a house of the same name nearby, and that Mr Rivington's house is next to Rivington. The River Anderton flows into the Douglas. Near here I saw for myself that there was a ridge-like summit projecting above the rest of the hill.

I crossed the River Douglas (colloquially known as Duggels), which flows past Wigan to the sea near Latham [*Lathom*]. It is bridged at Newburgh village, a mile-and-a-half from Lathom, but I crossed it seven miles from Morley, and continued a mile-and-a-half or more to the River Yarrow. After crossing the Yarrow it was a mile or more to Chorley, a small market town in Leylandshire (the River Douglas divides West Derby from Leylandshire). It is very likely that the Douglas and the Yarrow rise in the hills towards Yorkshire.

Besides Chorley, Croston is also a market town in Leylandshire; it is three miles from both Chorley and Lathom. Leylandshire has about eight parish churches – Leyland is one, Standish, as I recall, is another, and Eccleston a third. A small brook takes a level course below Chorley, and on a hillside one-and-a-half miles away I saw a great quarry from which men dig very large and good millstones. Beyond this quarry on the right hand side, and at least a mile from Leyland church, I saw the seat of an ancient gentry family, the Faringtons. Less than a mile from Preston I crossed the River Darwen, which flows into the Ribble by Penwortham church.

This river marks the boundary between Leylandshire and Amounderness. A mile upstream from my crossing place, at Walton on Darwen, lives Mr Langton, who is lord of Newton in Makerfield, three miles from Warrington.

I passed over the great stonebuilt Ribble Bridge, which has five large arches, and is a half-mile beyond the Darwen. A further half-mile brought me to Preston, which has a single parish church and a fine market place. The Ribble nearly encircles much of the town, although it does not come within almost a half-mile of it. Penwortham, which stands on the opposite bank of the Ribble from Preston, seemed to me to be more than a half-mile from the town. The river here marks the boundary between the dioceses of Chester and York. Penwortham, a parish church and cell of Evesham Abbey, therefore lies in Chester diocese, but Preston is in York diocese.

It is ten miles from Preston to Garstang. A mile beyond Preston I crossed a large brook called Savick, which rises three or four miles in the hills to my right, and shortly below flows into the Ribble. Later I rode across the River Brock, which rises six miles away in the hills to my right, but flows into the Wyre; and likewise I rode across the Calder, which also rises in the same hills and flows to the Wyre. The River Wyre itself I rode over by a great stone bridge just before reaching the limits of Garstang town.

The source of the Wyre is some eight to ten miles from Garstang in the hills on the right hand side. More than half a mile above Garstang it flows past Greenhalgh, Lord Derby's attractive castle. Garstang, which is in Amounderness, was a market town, according to some people. Three miles further downstream the river becomes tidal, and it enters the open sea ten miles below Garstang at All Hallows chapel.

Myerscough is a large park which I left a mile-and-a-half before Garstang. Part of it is enclosed by a hedge, but towards the moor there is a park pale; on this right hand side it is stocked with red deer. The Earl of Derby possesses it as the king's tenant. Two miles downstream from Garstang is the village of St Michaels, and a mile lower on the further bank are the houses of Mr Kirkby and Mr Butler, both of Rawcliffe. Seven miles further is All Hallows village, and then the sea. Rawcliffe of Winmarleigh has his house at Winmarleigh, a mile from Garstang.

Up into the hills above Greenhalgh Castle there are three forests of red deer, Wyredale, Bowland and Bleasdale. They are partly heathland and partly wooded. The land between Morley and Preston has been

LANCASHIRE

enclosed for pasture and arable, except for the wastes of marsh and moss. In this area hedgerows and small plantations supply reasonable timber for building, and some firewood, although all the local people burn turf for the most part. Between Preston and Garstang the ground is similar, except that the majority of enclosures are for pasture. Not very much wheat is sown in this region. In the past almost the whole of Amounderness was heavily wooded, and much of the moorland was stocked with tall conifers. But now the coastal area of Amounderness has a serious shortage of wood.

My journey from Garstang took me partly through marshland, and partly through pasture with some arable. I rode across the River Cocker, which flows for no great distance before it reaches the sands less than a mile from Cockerham village. On the sands I crossed the Cocker once or twice more, not without some fear of quicksands. Where the sands end I saw several salt-houses, and here were heaps of sand taken from the salt shore. By frequent soaking with water they dissolve the salt, channel the water into a pit, and then boil it off.

About a half-mile further on I reached Cockersand Abbey, a Cistercian house founded in about the time of Henry II by a certain William of Lancaster, on a very exposed site at the mercy of all the winds. Then I rode along the sands, noting the salt-houses, and after a mile crossed the little River Conder, which flows across the sands into the sea. Then to a modest house called Ashton, on king's land which used to be occupied by a knight called Mr Leyburne, and so two or three miles to Lancaster.

Lancaster Castle is strongly built on a hill and kept in good repair. Next to Castle Hill are the ruins of an old house (of the Catfields, as I recall). What they call there the new town is built on the slope adajcent to the castle. It has one parish church, formerly an alien priory which was suppressed by Henry V, and given to Syon Abbey. The old wall which surrounded the priory extends almost to Lune Bridge, and this has led some people to believe that it was a portion of town wall. But in fact I found no evidence that the town had ever been walled. The area known as the old town lay partly beyond the black friars, and was almost completely destroyed by fire. Many Roman coins have been found in the fields and foundations in this area. The soil around Lancaster is excellent, with abundant woodland, pasture, meadow and arable.

Had I taken the main coast road from Lancaster into Cumberland I would have reached after seven miles Cartmel Sands (where a freshwater stream flows), then eight miles to Conishead Sands (with a river), and four miles to Duddon Sands (another river), with Furness Abbey four miles away up in the mountains. Cartmel and Conishead were both Augustinian priories.

But I rode over the Lune towards Warton six miles away, where Mr Kitson was born. Two miles from Lancaster the country started to become craggy, and a little mountainous. Half a mile from Warton I crossed the tidal River Keer, which rises in the hills not far away, and flows into the salt water of Lunesandes [*Morecambe Bay*]. Though a mere village Warton has a pleasant street. Around and beyond Warton, to Beetham five miles away, the landscape is very hilly and there are spectacular crags, where I saw herds of goats. cont. p. 418 [**1538:** 4/5-11]

Burscough (Briscot) in West Derby, an Augustinian priory, was founded by the earls of Derby. It is a mile from Lathom, and not far from the River Douglas. Many of the earls of Derby's family are buried there. Upholland Priory, a Benedictine house, lies two miles from Wigan, and was founded by the Wottons. Sawley Abbey stands on the River Calder [*Ribble*].

Lancashire is made up of five small shires: West Derbyshire, Salfordshire, Leylandshire, Blackburnshire, Lancastershire. Mr Leland considers Preston in Amounderness to be a small shire, in which case there are six shires or hundreds in Lancashire.

West Derbyshire, or Derbyshire: Lyrpole (or Liverpool) is a paved town, but has only a chapel of ease. Its parish church is four miles away at Walton, which is not far from the sea. The king has a small castle at Liverpool, and the earl of Derby has a stone house there. It is greatly frequented by Irish merchants because of its good harbour. Between Runcorn in Cheshire and Liverpool, five miles lower on the Lancashire side, the River Mersey loses its name, and is called in common speech the Runcorn Water. The low rate of tolls at Liverpool attracts merchants there; business is good, and a great deal of Irish yarn is bought by Manchester men there.

Warrington, on the Mersey in Cheshire, is also a paved town. It has one parish church, right at the end of the town, and an Austin friary by the bridge. The town is of considerable size, and has a better market than Manchester. Thelwall, which stands two miles upstream from Warrington, was once a small harbour and city, as is clear from the royal archives. But now fishgarths obstruct the harbour, and the old town is a poor village. It derives its name from the large theals – wooden boards or timber posts – which formed a wall around it.

Wigan, also paved, is the same size as Warrington, but its buildings are better. It has a single parish church in the middle of the town, some merchants, some craftsmen, and some tenant farmers. Mr Bradshaw has a house called Haigh a mile from Wigan. He has discovered much cannel, a substance like sea-coal, on his land, and this has proved very profitable for him. Gerard of Ince also lives in this parish. Winwick is a good benefice five miles from Wigan, and three from Warrington.

Ormskirk is four or five miles from Liverpool, and about two miles from Lathom. There is a parish church in the town. No river flows past it, but there are mosses on each side. Lathom, the principal seat of the earls of Derby, is largely built of stone.

Newton-le-Willows lies on a stream called Golborne, and is a small, poor market town. Mr Langton takes the name of his barony from it. Sir Piers Legh of Bradley has his house in a park at Bradley, two miles from Newton; and Newton is four miles from Morleys Hall.

Prescot is a small market town with no river of note, about four miles from the Mersey towards Liverpool. Mr Molyneux, a knight with a large estate two miles from Prescot, lives at a house called Croxteth. The royal park of Toxteth is nearby. Knowsley Park, with the earl of Derby's attractive house, lies within a mile of Prescot. Sir William Norris lives in a house called Speke, two or three miles from Prescot. Thomas Ireland lives at Runcorn on the River Mersey.

The River Glazebrook passes within a mile of Morleys Hall. Flete and one or two other brooks flow into it, and it flows into the Mersey. The River Douglas passes Wigan on its way alone to the sea near Lathom. There are only twelve parish churches in West Derbyshire, but their parishes are large. Winwick parsonage, two or three miles from Warrington, has a park.

Chat Moss is three or four miles wide and six miles long in one direction. It erupted within a mile of Morleys Hall, and ruined much land in the area with its moss, as well as destroying many freshwater fish there. First it polluted the Glazebrook with foul water, which was then carried, along with moss, by the Glazebrook into the River Mersey. The engulfed Mersey then carried waves of moss to the Welsh coast, the Isle of Man and Ireland. At the very top of Chat Moss, where the moss was highest and erupted, there is now a good level valley, as there used to be. A stream runs in it, and pieces of small trees can be seen on the valley floor.

There are pits for coal and cannel-coal in several parts of West Derbyshire. The large cannel mine is at Haigh, two miles from Wigan. A certain Bradshaw lives at Haigh.

Martin Mere near Lathom, four miles long and three miles wide, is the largest mere in Lancashire.

Salfordshire: Manchester. Bury, on the River Irwell, is four or five miles from Manchester, but only has a poor market. Next to the parish church is the ruin of a castle, which, with the town, once belonged to the Pilkingtons, and then to the earls of Derby. The Pilkington seat was next to Pilkington Park, three miles from Manchester.

Bolton on the Moor has a market whose main commodities are cottons and coarse yarn. Several villages on the moors around Bolton manufacture cotton. Bolton's position and surrounding lands are both inferior to Bury's. At Bolton some cannel-coal is used for fuel, but mostly sea-coal from nearby pits, and peat is burnt as well.

In the past iron used to be made at Horwich, and at one time it was made around Bury; but now, for lack of wood, the blast-furnaces are in decay.

At Blackley in the past wild boars, bulls and falcons used to breed.

Leylandshire market towns: Chorley is a surprisingly poor market, in fact no market at all. Croston, three miles from Chorley on the way to Lathom (which is six miles from Chorley), is another poor or defunct market. There are seven or eight large parishes in Leylandshire. The River Darwen flows through a part of the shire. A mile above Preston it flows past the house of Mr Langton, Baron of Newton-le-Willows (near Warrington). The Ribble rises in Ribblesdale above Sawley Abbey, and flows to Sawley. Four miles lower the Calder, which passes near Whalley, flows into it; and later the River Hodder also joins it. Whalley is ten miles from Preston.

Lancastershire: The source of the River Lune is most probably in Coterine Hill [*?Cotterdale or Cotherstone*], or not far from its foot. The Ure, Swale and Eden rivers all rise on this hill. However, Mr Moore of St Catherine's Hall in Cambridge, has given me the following information about the River Lune. It rises from three or four sources on a hill called Crosho, which is on the edge of Richmondshire. According to him it should first be called Lune in Dentdale, although the name Dent seems to suggest otherwise. North from Dentdale is Garsdale, and the stream which runs through Garsdale then flows into Sedbergh Vale, where another stream joins it. A little further downstream they flow together into the Dentdale stream, and this is what he supposes lower down to be called the Lune. In addition to these earlier tributaries it also receives at the foot of Sedbergh Vale a large brook, which flows down from the north between Westmorland and Richmondshire.

The river runs for seven miles until it reaches the end of Dentdale, having received into its valley the streams already mentioned. From here it enters Lonsdale, which is perhaps a corruption of Lunesdale, and flows south for eight or nine miles. In this valley, four miles from the end of Dentdale, is the very large and famous parish church of Kirby Lonsdale. At the end of Lonsdale, half a mile from the Lune, is Lord Mounteagle's castle of Hornby. From there it flows eight miles to Lancaster (a corruption of Lunecaster), which is situated on its south bank, and here it becomes tidal. Some people say that the main stream of the Lune is in fact the northern arm, although this is insignificant until it reaches Lonsdale. At Lancaster the ruins of old walls next to the bridge belonged only to the suppressed priory. Burrow, which lies in Lonsdale, six miles from the end of Dentdale, is now only a village, but was probably once an important town. Squared stones and many other unusual things are found by ploughmen while ploughing, and the local people talk a great deal about this place. [5/40-6]

LANCASHIRE

The college of grey friars on the north-west side of Preston in Amounderness was built on land belonging to a gentleman by the name of Preston, who lived in the town of the same name. The grant of the site of this house was confirmed by either a brother or son of Preston, and one of them later became a large landowner, and viscount of Gurmaston in Ireland, so I was told. Several members of the Preston family were buried in the friary. But the original and most important contributor to the building of this house was Edmund, earl of Lancaster (Henry III's son). Another great benefactor was Sir Robert de Holland, who accused Thomas, earl of Lancaster, of treason. Holland was buried there, although I was told that he also established a priory of Benedictine monks at Upholland near Lathom. Several members of the gentry families of Shirburn and Dalton were buried in Preston grey friars.

There was a friary at Warrington, and a black friars' house at Doncaster. The town of Preston belongs to the duchy of Lancaster.

Ribchester is seven miles upstream from Preston, and like Preston lies on the further bank of the Ribble. Although now a poor place Ribchester of old was a town. Large squared stones, vaulting, and ancient coins are found there, and the local people pretend that on one site there was a Jewish temple. Whalley Abbey lay four miles above Ribchester on the same bank, and Sawley Abbey was further upstream, but on the nearer bank. There is no bridge over the Ribble between Preston and the sea. As a rule the river is tidal up to a point between Preston and Ribchester, but the force of the spring tides takes it higher. [2/20-1]

There is a house in the town of Wigan called Briket Hall (short for Birkhead Hall). The Birkhead estate has recently descended by the female line to Tyldesley. Although some people believe that the house in Wigan was the original seat of the Birkheads, others maintain that they descended from an older family in the Kendal area, where the name Briket is still common among ordinary people. The Birkhead arms include three brooms, so it may be that the first of them to achieve gentry status had been some groom of a chamber. [4/75]

Long ago the Harrington family had a fine manor house called Tatham, less than a mile from Hornby, but the site is now more-or-less deserted. At Fyrrelande [*Thurland*], one mile from Hornby, is the ancient stone castle or manor house of the Tunstall family. The River Wenning flows through Hornby before joining the Lune; I was told that at one point the Wenning is the boundary between Yorkshire and Lancashire. The castle at Hornby stands on a hill almost in the centre of the town. [4/122]

Lord Harrington, who owned a fine estate in Lancashire and elsewhere, married the heiress of Lord Bonville of Devon, and thus acquired, among others, the manors of Winchcombe and Shute. The last lord of the genuine Harrington line was killed during the civil war between Henry VI and Edward IV. His widow married Lord Hastings, who was subsequently beheaded in the Tower of London by Richard, then duke of Gloucester. I have since heard that Hornby went to a certain Neville.

The Harrington who owned Hornby Castle had a younger brother, and one of his female descendants later married one of the Stanleys, Lord Mounteagle. He had a child by her, but it was still born, so the story goes. As a result he claimed the estate for the term of his life, and once he had possession of it he purchased the right of his heirs to inherit it.

Lord Harrington's only daughter was his heiress, and she married Thomas, first marquis of Dorset, who supported the accession of Henry VII. By her he had fourteen children, male and female, of exceptionally good bearing. The first son did not live long, but the next, Thomas, had the title Lord Harrington, and later became the second marquis of Dorset. Two miles from Cartmel there are ruins and walls of a castle which formerly belonged to Lord Harrington, and is now owned by the marquis of Dorset; it is called Gleaston. [5/221-2]

LEICESTERSHIRE

A FTER THE 1538 JOURNEY *through Wales and Northern England Leland returned to London, his route taking him down the eastern fringe of Leicestershire, via Melton Mowbray and Launde. At Burrough Hill he tells us that his archaeological curiosity led him to dig up and examine masonry around the earthwork– perhaps, therefore, this passage should be regarded as the oldest English excavation report. Then in 1541 he interrupted his outward journey to North-East England by making a detour from Deene (near Corby) into Leicestershire, probably to visit the marquis of Dorset at Bradgate. He seems to have taken this opportunity to explore Leicester, Loughborough, Lutterworth and Charnwood Forest. On his way back south he visited Belvoir Castle. Apart from a little information about some gentry families there are no notes to amplify the itinerary accounts; Market Harborough is ignored, and there is little about the western edge of the county.*

SOON AFTER I HAD CROSSED the River Smite I passed through the village of Clawson in Leicestershire. From the bank of the Trent to Melton Mowbray, and throughout Leicestershire generally, beans and peas are widely grown. At least three miles of good arable ground separate Clawson and Melton. Melton has one fine parish church, which used to be a hospital and cell of Lewes Priory in Sussex. The small Augustinian priory at Kirby [Bellars], on the River Wreake two miles below Melton, has recently been suppressed. I was told that it had been founded by a certain Bellar.

From Melton I travelled scarcely a mile to Burton Lazars, where there is a very fine hospital and collegiate church, and then more than two miles to Burrough Hill. The place which is now called Burrough Hill, which stands right on the main route from Melton to London, has a double ditch, and encloses by my estimation eighty acres. Its soil produces very good corn. At first I assumed that it was a hillfort, but then I saw clearly that a stone wall had been built around it. To make sure I pulled out some stones at its entrance, where there had been a large gate, and there I found lime between the stones. I am still not sure whether there had been any more than the one gate, but I conjecture that there had. Very often Roman coins of gold, silver and bronze, as well as pieces of foundations, have been found there during ploughing. On Whit Monday every year the local people come to Burrough Hill, to shoot, run, wrestle, dance, and perform other energetic feats. The village of Burrough is less than half a mile away from the hill, and Mr Burrough, who lives there, is the largest landowner. Leicester is about seven miles from the hill.

Note that Croxton Abbey stream, which rises at Croxton, flows to the south [i.e. north] bank of the River Eye about a mile or more above Melton.

From Burrough Hill to Launde is five miles. The Chaworths were and are [?recognised to have been] the founders of Launde Priory. Nearly half a mile before I reached Launde I passed Mr Smith's place, which has been renewed by the Mr Radcliffe who married Smith's daughter. The country in a straight line between the south bank of the Trent and Launde is devoid of woods, but fertile for arable and pasture, especially in the Launde area. But around Launde itself there is woodland, and Leigh or Leighfield Forest adjoins Launde on the east. Owston Abbey, two miles ENE, also lies in very wooded country, but there are no woods in the Pipewell direction a little beyond Launde.

From Launde I travelled about four miles to Hallaton, a pleasant little place, and then a mile to Medbourne, and almost another mile to a bridge across the Welland, which is not a large river at this point. A further three miles or so brought me to Pipewell Abbey. cont. p. 253 [**1538**: 4/19-20]

From Deene to the village of Stonton [Wyville], which belongs to Mr Brudenell, is a journey of ten miles. On my way I rode through Rockingham, and then crossed the River Welland, which here, as at many other points, forms the boundary between Northamptonshire and Leicestershire. In fact Rockingham Bridge divides these two counties and Rutland as well. Between Deene and Stonton there is fertile cornland,

and exceptionally good, large meadows on both sides of the Welland. But after Rockingham I saw little woodland, as in a landscape entirely of open fields. I rode across one or two considerable brooks between the Welland and Stonton.

From Stonton to Leicester is eight or nine miles of completely open country. As I rode from Stonton I could see two miles away the village of Noseley, which has a collegiate parish church of three priests, two clerks and four choristers. Noseley belonged to the Blaket family. Around the time of Edward III the Blaket heiress married a certain Roger Martival, and he established the little college at Noseley. With other estates nearby Noseley passed to two daughters of one of the Martivals; one became a nun and alienated much of her share, but the other married Hugh Hastings. Later Noseley passed by marriage to the Hazlerigg family, whose name is Scottish in origin, and it remains in their possession. Skeffington, which gave its name to the family, lay more than a mile beyond Noseley. On my journey from Stonton to Leicester I rode across two or three brooks.

Present-day Leicester is built entirely of timber, and Loughborough is the same. Most of the lands of St John's Hospital were given by Edward IV to Newark College, Leicester. Either Robert le Bossu, earl of Leicester, or Petronilla, a countess of Leicester, was buried in a tomb of Chalcedonian marble in the wall to the south of the high altar in St Mary's Abbey, Leicester. The perimeter wall of this abbey is three-quarters of a mile long. At the end of Mr Wigston's hospital in Leicester stood the grey friars, which I discovered was founded by Simon de Montfort; Richard III was buried there, as well as a knight called Mutton, a former mayor of Leicester. In the chancel of the Blackfriars I saw several tombs, including a flat alabaster stone with the name of Lady Isabel, the wife of Sir John Beauchamp of Holt. In the north aisle I saw another knight's tomb, without inscription, and in the north transept was a tomb with the name and arms of Roger Pointer of Leicester.

Here is a summary of what I saw at Leicester. The castle which stands near the west bridge is of no great significance, and has no trace of either high walls or ditches. I conclude therefore that the present apartments there have been built since the Barons' War in the time of Henry III; very probably the castle was badly damaged along with the town walls during Henry II's reign. Before the conquest a collegiate church of prebendaries stood within the castle precinct. But when Robert le Bossu, earl of Leicester, built the abbey for canons outside the walls, he gave the college lands to the new abbey, and built a new church for the remaining prebendaries outside the castle. This he dedicated to St Mary, as its predecessor had been. In this church of St Mary outside the castle I saw the marble tomb of Thomas Rider, the father of Master Richard of Leicester. I identify this Richard with the man of that period who, to judge from his work, was a great scholar. Apart from this grave I saw little of antiquarian interest within the church.

The collegiate church of Newark and its precinct adjoin another part of the castle site. The church is not very large, but it is exceptionally fine. To the north of the high altar is buried Henry, earl of Lancaster, with no coronet, but with two male children beneath the arch by his head. Henry, first duke of Lancaster, is buried on the south side, and in the arch next to his head is a lady, presumably his wife. Constance, who was the daughter of King Peter of Castile, and wife of John of Gaunt, lies in front of the high altar in a marble tomb surmounted by a brazen statue as of a queen. I was told that a marble tomb in the main part of the chancel belonged to a countess of Derby whom they allege (on what authority I do not know) to have been the wife of either John of Gaunt or Henry IV. It is true that during John of Gaunt's lifetime Henry IV was known as the earl of Derby. Other burials in the church are as follows: in St Mary's chapel, south of the chancel, are two knights of the Shirley family, with their wives, and an esquire called Brokesby; Lady Hungerford and her second husband Sacheverell are under a pillar in a chapel off the south transept; in the nave on the south side is a knight called Blunt, with his wife; and on the north side are three of the Wigston family, who were great benefactors of the college. One was a prebendary there, and established the free grammar school. On the south-west side of the church is a large and attractive cloister, and all the prebendal houses within the college precinct are very pleasant. The walls and gateways of the college are imposing, and a large almshouse stands within the courtyard of the precinct. All the flowers and bosses in the vaulted roof of the church were gilded by the wealthy cardinal of Winchester [?*Wolsey*].

A little above the west bridge the River Soar divides, but the branch soon rejoins the main stream. The island thus formed makes a very pleasing position for the black friars, and close to the friary is a bridge across the branch of the Soar. Downstream the whole river flows around half the town and through the north bridge, which has seven or eight stone arches. Then it divides into two once more, the larger stream flowing past St Mary's Abbey on its far bank. The other stream is called the Bishop's Water, because tenants of the bishop of Lincoln enjoy rights over it; before long it rejoins the main river, and by so doing forms an island out of a large and pleasant meadow. I assume that it is for this reason that the abbey is sometimes referred to in documents as 'St Mary of the Meadows'. Halfway along Bishop's Water is a modest stone bridge, and a little beyond it is another stone bridge, through which a small stream flows on its way from nearby villages into Bishop's Water. The Hospital of St John has a chapel, in which Mr Boucher is buried, close to Bishop's Water. Shortly beyond this the streams are united in a single valley, and the Soar flows on past the ruins of Mountsorrel Castle four miles downstream.

St Margaret's, beside the Soar, is the best parish church in Leicester; it is on the site of the former cathedral church, and nearby a small portion of the bishop of Lincoln's palace still remains. In St Margaret's is buried in an alabaster tomb John Penny, who after being abbot of Leicester later became bishop of Bangor, and then of Carlisle. He was responsible for the new brickwork in Leicester Abbey, and much of the brick walling.

Bradgate is three miles from Leicester, through well-wooded country. It has a fine park, with a lodge recently built by the father of Henry, the present marquis of Dorset, Lord Thomas Grey. A good and vigorous water supply has been channelled through the lodge by Master Brook (seemingly against the gradient) to turn a mill nearby. The park formed part of the estate of the former earls of Leicester, but passed by the female line to Lord Ferrers of Groby, and so to the Greys. The park is six miles in circumference.

Groby is three miles from Leicester, and separated from Bradgate by a mile and a half mostly of woodland. Little evidence of the former castle survives, although the hill on which the keep stood is very clearly seen. No masonry remains on it, and Thomas, the late marquis, filled the ditch with earth, intending to create a garden. The oldest work at Groby was made by the Ferrers, but the newer buildings were erected by Lord Thomas, first marquis of Dorset. They include the foundations and walls of a large brick gatehouse with a tower, which remain half-finished as he left them. He also built and nearly completed two brick towers in front of the house, which correspond to the gatehouse on either side. Next to the house is a good, substantial park six miles in circumference, as well as a poor village and a small stream. And in a valley a quarter-mile from the house is probably as fine and large a lake as any in Leicestershire. From it flows the stream which passes Groby, and turns a mill there, before it joins the River Soar.

It is about five miles from Bradgate to Loughborough, and leaving Bradgate Park I rode into Charnwood Forest, which is usually called the Waste. It is some twenty miles in circumference, and has abundant woodlands. The majority of it at present belongs to the marquis of Dorset, and the remainder is owned by the earl of Huntingdon and the king. There is no decent town in this forest, nor hardly a village. Ashby de la Zouch and Loughborough (which are market towns), Whitwick Castle and village, and Ulverscroft Priory all lie right on its borders. The marquis of Dorset has obtained by an exchange of lands the ruins of Whitwick Castle.

Almost as soon as I rode into the forest I saw two or three slate quarries in the hillside. These also belong to the marquis of Dorset. A little further on I rode past Beaumanor Park, which contains an attractive lodge and is enclosed by stone walls; it used to belong to the Belmont family. Then to Loughborough Park, which is more than a mile from the town, and which was obtained by the marquis of Dorset through an exchange of lands with the king. The marquis also owns Burleigh Park nearby. From here it is scarcely a mile to Loughborough, and here I crossed a small stream, one of whose main sources rises in Loughborough Park.

Of all the market towns in the county only Leicester itself exceeds Loughborough in size and good architecture. It has four or more fine streets with good paved surfaces, and one good parish church. There are no other chapels or churches in the town. At the south-east end of the parish church is an attractive timber house, in which Henry VII once stayed. The main stream of the River Soar passed less than a quarter-mile from where I was standing, at the left hand side of the town, and near here the Loughborough stream flowed into it.

Lutterworth is a market town ten miles from Leicestershire in the Warwickshire direction. It is scarcely half the size of Loughborough, but it has a hospital founded by two or three members of the Verdon family, ancient lords of Lutterworth. A considerable portion of the Verdons' estate has over the course of time passed to the lord marquis of Dorset; and Astley College, near Nuneaton in Warwickshire, where Lord Thomas,

LEICESTERSHIRE

former marquis of Dorset, is buried, was founded by Thomas, Lord Astley. Indeed all the land that the marquis of Dorset possesses along the borders of Leicestershire and Warwickshire used at one time to belong to the Verdons and Astleys. Certain springs rise in the hills a mile from Lutterworth, which flow into a valley and form a stream which passes the town.

Forests in Leicestershire: Leicester Forest lies right next to the town. It is five miles long but not of any great width. It is well stocked with deer. Charnwood Forest is twenty miles in circumference.

Parks in Leicestershire: The park by St Mary's Abbey. Frith Park formerly covered an extremely large area. Part of it has now been disparked, and the rest, with a good pale, is called New Park. Beaumont Leys near Leicester used to be a large park, but has now been converted to pasture. Barn Park, Towley Park and Beaumanor all belong to the king. The lord marquis of Dorset has good parks at Groby, Bradgate, Loughborough and Burleigh. Lord Huntingdon has Kirby Park, four miles from Leicester beside Leicester Forest, and Bagworth Park, where may be seen the ruins of a fortified manor house within a ditch. Lord Huntingdon also has three parks at Ashby de la Zouch. The Ashby [?estate] existed in Hastings' time, but more recently the Lord Hastings who was so important under Edward IV, obtained it partly by right and partly by purchase. The late Thomas Boleyn, earl of Wiltshire, laid claim to it through descent from Lord Rochford, Zouche's heir. From him Lord Rochford held Fulbourne and other Cambridgeshire estates. There is a good quarry for alabaster about four or five miles from Leicester, and not very far from Beaumanor.

From Bradgate I travelled through four miles of woodland and pasture to Belgrave, which is about a mile below Leicester on the River Soar. To reach it I had to cross a large stone bridge. A gentleman called Belgrave with an estate of £50 per annum lives there, and there is also another gentry family of moderate means called Belgrave living in Leicestershire. Ingarsby is four miles beyond Belgrave, across arable, pasture and wooded country. The manor of Ingarsby once belonged to a certain Algernon, and later it was given to Leicester Abbey. Its owner now is Brian Caves, who bought it from the king. It occupies a very good position, and is surrounded by very rich pasturelands. From here I rode another four miles by corn, pasture and woodland to Withcote, where Mr Ratcliffe, who married a sister of the Caves family, lives in an excellent house which he has built on Smith's land. In my opinion this is one of the most attractive houses in Leicestershire, with the finest orchards and gardens in the area; but its position is low and wet, and there is a lake in front of it. All the soil around it, however, is good for pasture. Launde Abbey is nearby.

The most reputable gentry of Leicestershire: Villiers of Brookesby, Digby of Tilton, Brooksby of Shoulby, Neville of the Holt, Shirley in the Donington area, with very fine estates, Skeffington of Skeffington, Purefey of Drayton, Vincent of Peckleton, Turville of Thurlaston, Hazlerigg of Noseley.

The ruins of Hinckley Castle, which used to belong to the earl of Leicester, but are now in royal hands, are five miles from Leicester on the edge of Leicester Forest. Hinckley has an extensive and celebrated territory. Castle Donington, which has a park, is on the edge of Charnwood Forest, towards Derbyshire. I recall that it is eight miles from Leicester, and I was told that it once belonged to the earls of Leicester, although now it is the king's. Melbourne Castle, two miles from Donington, is attractive, and in a reasonably good state of repair.

Note that the southern and eastern part of Leicestershire is open arable country, with not much woodland. Whereas the western and northern parts are well wooded. *cont. p. 302* [**1541:** *1/13-22*]

BELVOIR CASTLE is situated in the furthest part of Leicestershire in that direction, on the very crown of a high hill, which rises steeply on all sides. Its steepness is partly natural and partly man-made, as may very obviously be perceived. Whether or not there was a castle here before the conquest I am not sure, but I am inclined to believe that there was not. Its first occupant after the conquest was Toternius, from whom it passed to Albeneius, and then Rose.

Lord Rose sided with Henry VI against Edward IV, and when Edward prevailed his lands were confiscated. Belvoir Castle was entrusted to Lord Hastings, but when he came to inspect the estate and stay in the castle he was suddenly repulsed by Mr Harrington, a friend of Lord Rose, and a man of influence in the neighbourhood. Consequently Lord Hastings returned to Belvoir on another occasion with a strong force, and in great anger looted the castle, stripping the roofs and removing the lead which covered them. Much of the lead he carried away to Ashby de la Zouch for his own extensive building work. As a result the castle fell into decay, the exposed roof timbers rotted away, and eventually the ground between the walls became all overgrown with elders. The castle remained uninhabited until recently, but now the earl of Rutland has made it better than ever before. The flight of stone steps which leads up from the village to the castle is a remarkable sight, and there are two fine gates. The keep consists of a fine round tower, which has now been turned into a pleasure ground with a rail around the wall, as a place to walk in and view the surrounding countryside, and with a garden laid out in the centre. The castle has a well of great depth, fed by a very good spring.

In similar fashion Lord Hastings plundered Stoke Albany, a good manor house in Rutland belonging to Lord Rose. He carried away material to Ashby de la Zouch from there also.

The Vale of Belvoir grows abundant corn and grass but is devoid of woods. It falls in three counties, Leicestershire, Lincolnshire, and a large part in Nottinghamshire.

In exchange for other royal lands the earl of Rutland possesses Croxton Abbey, two miles away, and a commandery at Eagle near Newark which belonged to the Order of St John. Here there is a very nice manor house, although I imagine that its site is low-lying and unpleasant. *cont. p. 302* [**1541**: 1/97-8]

The Chaveney family of Leicestershire originated, as I have discovered, from the Poitiers region in France, where there are still gentry with the same name. The story goes that the first of them came from that area with Edward III's son, the Black Prince, after the battle of Poitiers, and had land given to him in Leicestershire. There is still a place called Chaveney's Leazes, now in the hands of the earl of Rutland, not very far from Belvoir Castle. The Chaveney who was the Black Prince's companion had four sons. They supported Richard II's cause, and three of them died in the quarrels between Richard II and Henry IV. Consequently old Chaveney gave portions of his estate to Croxton and Newbo Abbeys; and Jenning Chaveney, the son who survived his father, also had a share. He was the grandfather of the present Chaveney, but the estate has almost all gone. [2/7]

Sir John Grey, who married the daughter and heiress of Lord Ferrers of Groby, was killed at Northampton in the civil war, so I am told; but I am not sure about this. The Grey whose widow, the daughter of Lord Rivers, subsequently married King Edward [IV], was the father of Thomas, the first marquis of Dorset. Through the female line the marquis of Dorset inherited the Rivers family's fine manor house at Grafton; as well as good parks and lands in the area which he had by exchange for Loughborough and neighbouring parks, and other good Leicestershire estates. Loughborough had been part of the Beaumont estate, and the late old countess of Oxford held it in dower.

Lutterworth town and surrounding lands are part of the lord marquis of Dorset's inheritance from the Groby title. Beaumanor, where Leonard Grey obtained royal permission to live, also belonged to the Lords Belmont, as did the large area of pastureland between Leicester and Groby, which is called Beaumont Leys.

Ulverscroft Priory, a house of Augustinian canons about a mile from Bradgate, was the burying-place of several members of the Ferrers family of Groby. And recently the countess of Worcester, Lord Leonard Grey's wife, was also buried there.

So far as I could ascertain by questioning the former servants and staff of the marquis of Dorset, that portion of the earl of Leicester's estate which passed to Saher de Quincy, earl of Winchester, was later inherited through females to the Lords Beaumont, Ferrers and Lovell. [5/222-3]

LINCOLNSHIRE

*T*HE NORTH-EASTERN ITINERARY *in 1541, the only surviving journey to touch Lincolnshire, took Leland up the western edge of this vast county, past Stamford, and through Sleaford, Lincoln, Torksey and Gainsborough. Lincoln itself he described in some detail, and he showed his usual archaeological prowess when he encountered Ancaster; Epworth and the Isle of Axholme were treated fully, but Stamford he ignored in his itinerary account, although notes by him have survived about its interesting history.*

In fact the corpus of notes about Lincolnshire is very full and wide-ranging. This is thanks to some extent, it would appear, to Leland's informant, Richard Paynell of Boothby near Grantham, and his wide circle of Paynell relatives. Among these notes are pieces on Boston and Stamford; a series of annotations made to accompany a long extract from a history of Crowland which Leland found and copied out (the notes but not the extract are included here); a mapping exercise to describe and plot the Lincolnshire coast (a sketch map has also survived); and finally a systematic collection of notes, like those found for many other counties, which cover towns, rivers and the gentry. Leland had travelled around Lincolnshire visiting monasteries in 1534, so it is likely that some information was colllected on that occasion.

THE DISTANCE from Collyweston to Grimsthorpe is eight or nine miles across mostly flat country. There is good arable and pasture, but not much woodland, except towards Vaudey Abbey and at Grimsthorpe itself. At least a mile after I left Stamford I crossed a stone bridge over a pleasant river which I assumed to be the Gwash. I noticed here that a short distance from Stamford I entered a corner of Rutland, and continued for three miles until I reached a ford through a stream, which separates Rutland from Lincolnshire. I was told that this stream rises nearby at a place called Holywell. Two miles from here I saw Castle Bytham, where substantial walls of the building survive, and close by is the village of Little Bytham. Both are in Lincolnshire, but on the edge of the county. Lord Hussey used to own the castle. A short distance from Bytham some springs issue into a stream, which joins the county boundary stream close to the ford I mentioned earlier; and not far away is Robin Hood's Cross, also on the county boundary.

To judge from its remains Vaudey Abbey must have been a large place. It stands at least half a mile this side of Grimsthorpe, and there is a fine park between the two. In the wood beside Vaudey is a large quarry for coarse marble, of which a great deal was doubtless employed in building the abbey. The house at Grimsthorpe was of no great size until the new building around the second courtyard. Nevertheless all the old building was of stone, and there was a good, strong gatehouse, with battlemented walls on each side of it. There is also a large ditch around the house.

Between Grimsthorpe and Corby are three miles of open country, and here lives a gentleman of modest lands called Armstrong. Another three miles brought me to Boothby [*Pagnell*], and in this area there is a reasonable amount of scattered woodland. A very long time ago an heiress of the Boothby family married into the Paynells, and by this means the Paynells greatly bettered themselves. At one time the principal seat of the family possessed an estate with an annual value of £600, and this was well maintained until about Henry V's time. But then a father and son, both called Sir John Paynell, and both lecherous, began the decline. The father began selling property, and the son incestuously sired a son by his own daughter; whereupon the father sold all his land, partly outright, and partly in reversion. The son died before the father, and the daughter out of shame fled to other parts of England. Eventually she married a weaver called Dines, and bore him children. After three generations the Dines estate passed by the female line to a knight called Bosson. His property in turn was inherited by five sisters, one of whom is the wife of Richard Paynell, the present owner of Boothby. Bosson was a native of Nottinghamshire, and part of his estate lay near Newark on Trent, the rest being in Yorkshire.

Sir John Paynell senior had a second son, Geoffrey, who was in the queen of England's service, and was highly regarded. Believing that his niece was dead, he pursued his claim so forcefully with the king, that eventually the duke of Bedford agreed to sell him back all the lands which he had bought from Sir John senior, and which formed the best portion of the estate. But at about the same time as Geoffrey paid for this land, the younger Sir John's daughter, Dine's wife, returned, and obtained under false pretences the manor of Barrowby, a mile from Grantham, with an annual value of £80. Then she laid claim to the rest, so that eventually an agreement was reached that of the estate purchased from the duke of Bedford she should have Barrowby and Donington, and the rest should remain with Geoffrey Paynell. This Geoffrey was the great-grandfather of the Paynell who now lives at Boothby.

The manor of Irnham was sold by Sir John Paynell senior to Thimbleby, and the present Thimbleby has built a fine house there. The Paynells owned Newport Pagnell Castle in Buckinghamshire, but they much preferred to stay at Boothby, where they had an attractive stone house within a moat. They founded an abbey in France called Marteres. I was told that a certain Sir Ralph Paynell was vice-chamberlain to a king, and constable of Bolingbroke Castle. Sir John Paynell senior (the father), who died in 1420, lies buried on the north side of the high altar at Boothby, and his wife Elisabeth lies in the north aisle of the same church. Geoffrey Paynell was the father of the controller of customs at Boston, who possessed a manor worth £40 annually from the old Paynell estate. This Paynell was the father of Richard Paynell, who now lives at Boothby. At Somerby, a mile from Boothby, lives a gentleman of modest lands called Bawdey.

Bourne Market is three or four miles from Grimsthorpe. Near the west end of the priory but some distance from it, as if set back on the other side of a street, may be seen large ditches and the motte of an old castle. It belonged to Lord Wake, and many of those who owed allegiance to the Wake estate performed duty to this castle; each knew his rank and place of service. I recall reading once a history of Bourne Castle, and I have read that St Edmund, king of East Anglia, was crowned at Bourne, but I have no way of knowing whether it was this Bourne.

Sempringham is five miles from Grimsthorpe, and a mile to its left, more inland, is Folkingham Castle, which once belonged to Lord Bardolf, then to Lord Belmont, and now to the Duke of Norfolk. It used to be a fine house, but now it is all falling into ruin, and stands close to the edge of the fens. From Boothby it is four miles over good open arable and grassland to Heydour. A younger brother of the family of Bussey of Hougham lives in an old house at Heydour, which he and his parents rent from Lincoln Cathedral. From Heydour to Sleaford are six miles of open country. About a mile from Heydour I saw the ruins of Catley Priory [*misplaced*], which now belongs to a certain Carr of Sleaford, a gentleman in his own right, whose father was a rich merchant of the staple.

Sleaford is largely built of stone, as are all the Kesteven towns, because stone is abundant in this country. Sleaford church is large, and I noticed two very fine houses in the town. One, which stands at the east end of the church, belongs to the living, which is a prebend worth £16 in Lincoln Cathedral; the other is Carr House, which stands on the south side of it. To the WSW outside the town stands the real Sleaford Castle, in excellent condition. It is surrounded by a flowing stream derived by a channel from a small fen which lies almost directly to the west beside it. The castle gatehouse has two portcullises, and in the centre of the castle is a high tower, which does not, however, stand on a raised mound. The castle vaults at ground level are good. Lord Hussey's manor house, which has recently been almost rebuilt of stone and timber, stands to the south outside the town. The main source of the River Slea is near Rauceby village, about a mile west of Sleaford.

Gentry families of Kesteven: Bussy of Hougham; Bussy of Heydour; Thimbleby, a knight, at Irnham; Disney, or de Iseney (he lives at [Norton] Disney, six miles south-west of Lincoln, and there is a related gentry family of the same name in France. Elsham Priory near Thornton Curtis was founded by the Disneys, and several of them were buried there – others at Norton Disney); Paynell at Boothby; Armyn of Ergerby [*Osgodby*]; Leigh living at Ingoldsby (now a man of modest lands, but his forebears had a fine estate); Haulle; Grantham, a man of modest lands near Heydour; Cony at Bassingthorpe, a woolstapler who has risen through trade; Vernoun near Grantham; Porter around Grantham; Baudey a mile from Boothby; Ellis greatly risen through trade; Holland at Howell.

LINCOLNSHIRE

Four miles of open country lie between Sleaford and Ancaster, and about a mile from Ancaster I crossed Wilsford brook. Ancaster stands on Watling [Street], the main road to Lincoln, and is now just a very poor single street with a small church. An old man told me that it used to be called Oncaster or Onkaster, but gave no reason for this. In the past it was a notable town, built along a north–south alignment, although not walled so far as I could ascertain. At the south end during ploughing large squared stones from old buildings, and Roman coins of silver and bronze, are often found. And at the west end, where there are now meadows, great vaults have been found whilst digging ditches. The castle occupied a large site, and its ditches may still be seen, as well as the footings of walls in some places. On the highest part of the site there is now an old chapel dedicated to St Mary, occupied by a hermit. The site is right next to the east end of the parish church.

The little town of Ancaster is divided between two manors. The eastern side, including at its south end the castle site, lies in the manor of Wilsford. This formerly belonged to Lord Cromwell, but later, I was informed, it was sold along with other possessions in execution of the will of one of the Lords Cromwell. Then, through the intervention of Margaret, Henry VII's mother, so I was told, Bourne Priory in Kesteven obtained it. It is now the duke of Suffolk's. My informant also said that Fotheringhay once belonged to Lord Cromwell, but that I doubt.

The western side of Ancaster, including the parish church, belonged to the Vescys, who owned Caythorpe Castle in Kesteven three miles north of the town. Later it passed to Lord Belmont, and now it is the Duke of Norfolk's, who was granted Belmont land in Lincolnshire with an annual value of £400. One of the Veseys gave the patronage of Ancaster church to the priory at Malton in Ryedale, which appropriated the living. Ancaster Heath extends for some fourteen miles and comes within two miles of the fens. On either side of the town is a spring, whose streams soon join in a single valley and flow into the Wilsford brook, which then continues to Rauceby, as I recall.

An old man from Ancaster told me that near Rauceby (or Ureby) a ploughman lifted a stone, and found another stone beneath it which had a square hole containing Roman coins. He also said that in the fields of Harlaxton, two miles from Grantham, a ploughman picked up a stone, and found under it a bronze pot, and a golden helmet inlaid with precious stones. The helmet was presented to Catherine, the Princess Dowager, and in the pot were found silver beads and decayed documents.

From Ancaster I travelled across the open country of Ancaster Heath for four miles to Temple Bruer. Here there are large and massive buildings of crude construction, and the east end of the temple is built in circular fashion. The surrounding heathland is very good for sheep, as indeed is the whole of Ancaster Heath. It is ten miles from here to Lincoln, across open country.

The Foss Dyke begins a quarter-mile above Lincoln and continues for seven miles directly to the Torksey bank. Bishop Atwater started to scour the dyke, hoping to bring ships up to Lincoln. Starting from the Torksey end he reached halfway, but died, and at once the work was completely abandoned.

Grantham is eighteen miles from Lincoln, and the River Lindis [*Witham*] makes its way from there, as from a WSW direction, except for meanders on its eastward course to the sea. From Lincoln to Boston along the course of the River Lindis, including the meanders, the distance is fifty miles by water, but only twenty-four via the ferry. High Bridge has a single arch, and there is a chapel of St George built over part of it. Apart from Thorn Bridge, a little downstream from High Bridge, there are no bridges across the Lindis between Lincoln and Boston. But there are reckoned four public ferries serving different places along the river between the two towns, as follows: Short Ferry (5 miles); Tattershall Ferry (8 miles); Dogdyke Ferry (1 mile); Langrick Ferry (5 miles); to Boston (5 miles).

The gates in Lincoln city walls are as follows: Bargate at the south end of the town; Baily Gate on the south a little this side of the minster; Newport Gate directly to the north; East Gate and West Gate towards the castle. It is very likely that originally only the hilltop was walled and inhabited.

Lincoln's river divides a short distance above the town, and the two separate streams are most beneficial to the lower southern parts of the town through which they flow. Arched stone bridges carry the principal street over each of them. The smaller stream is the more southerly, and is crossed by Gowts Bridge of one arch. The larger stream bears the boats of fishermen, and is crossed by the High Bridge.

A very good house belonging to Sutton abuts the north side of St Anne's [*i.e. Andrew's*] churchyard, and a little above Gowts Bridge on the east side of the High Street is a fine guildhall, which belongs to St

Andrew's church lying opposite. It was established by two merchants, Bitlyndon [*Blyton*] and Sutton. I was told that the lower part of Lincoln used to be all marshland, but was artificially reclaimed and occupied, in order to gain advantage from the river. This area is known as Wikerford [*Wigford*], and contains eleven parish churches, as well as one which I saw to be completely in ruins. The Carmelite friars were in Wigford on the west side of the High Street. In the rest of the town, that is in the northern part on the hill, thirteen parish churches are still in use. But I saw a document which listed thirty-eight parish churches in Lincoln, and it is often said that including the suburbs there were once fifty-two.

Some people believe that there were two suburbs to the east of Lincoln. One extended towards St Beges [*?Bees*], which was formerly a cell of St Mary's Abbey, York. I assume that this was the site of Icanno, the monastery in St Botolph's time which is mentioned by Bede. It is scarcely half a mile from the minster. The other suburb stretched up towards Canwick village, half a mile from Lincoln. There was also a suburb beyond the north gate, which extended towards Burton village, or further to the west. It is said that King Stephen destroyed much of this suburb. Another suburb lay outside the Bargate, stretching south of the town towards a village called Bracebridge. A little beyond Bargate is a very fine, large cross, and on the south-west side of Bargate in this suburb stands St Catherine's.

It may readily be observed that there have been three significant periods of building at Lincoln. The first took place on the very top of the hill, where the oldest inhabited area dates from the time of the Britons. This was the northernmost part of the hill, immediately outside Newport Gate, and its ditches still survive, as well as substantial evidence of the old town walls. These were built of stone removed from the adjacent ditch, as all the top of Lincoln Hill is quarry ground. This area is now a suburb of Newport Gate, and the only notable buildings are the ruins of an Austin friary on the south side, a parish church on the east side, and the massive ruins of a tower in the old town wall, which may be discerned near the churchyard. Some people say that this old Lincoln was destroyed by King Stephen, but I think that it was actually the Danes. Many Roman coins are found in the fields to the north outside this old Lincoln. After the first town was destroyed people started to fortify the more southerly part of the hill. By making new ditches, walls and gates the Saxons created a new Lincoln out of part of old Lincoln.

Later a third period of building was undertaken at Wigford, because of the availability of water there. Except where the river and marshland provide defence this area too is walled. The River Witham broadens a little above Lincoln, and forms several pools, of which one is called Swan Pool. A stream rises beyond Carlton village, two miles or more north of Lincoln, and this flows into the upper bank of the River Witham a little above the town. With this stream, the Foss Dyke channel and the River Witham, it is not surprising that sometimes the water spreads out and overflows the surrounding meadows.

I understand that the first founder of the Carmelite friary in Lincoln was a Scotsman, Walter, Dean of Lincoln, who was known as Dorotheus. A rich merchant called Ranulph de Kyme was buried in a chapel at the friary, but his monument was taken away and placed at the south end of a new water conduit house at Wigford. There is another new conduit house beyond the River Witham. Both are served by pipes supplied from one of the friaries which were in the upper part of Lincoln. The Franciscan friary was founded by a Lincoln merchant, Reginald Miller, and two of its principal benefactors were Henry Lacy, earl of Lincoln, and his almoner, called Nunny. They were also great benefactors of the Franciscan friary at York, where Nunny was buried.

It is seven miles from Lincoln to Torksey, partly, but not entirely, over marshy ground, with very little woodland. The old settlement at Torksey lay to the south of the new town, but there is now little to see of the old buildings, except for a chapel, which people say was the parish church of old Torksey; and beside the Trent the ground has been so built up as to indicate that there were probably walls there. Nearby is piled up an earthen mound, which is called the Windmill Hill, but I think that it is the site of the keep of an old castle. To the south of Old Torksey stand the ruins of Fosse nunnery, next to the stone bridge over the Foss Dyke, which here joins the Trent. In New Torksey there are two small parish churches, and to the east stands St Leonard's Priory. The bank of the Trent on which Torksey stands is rather higher than the west bank. At this point and for a considerable distance upstream the Trent marks the boundary between Lincolnshire and Nottinghamshire. John Babington lives at Rampton village, which is at least a mile from Torksey across the Trent.

From Torksey I journeyed about a mile to Marton village over flat, sandy ground. At the northern end of this village runs the Watling Street, the public route to Doncaster. From Marton it crosses the Trent by a ferry to Littleborough village, which in consequence is generally called Littleborough Ferry; and a mile further going north it reaches Sturton on the Street, a good roadside place some fourteen or fifteen miles from Doncaster. I travelled on from Marton two miles to Knaith on the Trent, where the late Lord Darcy had a modest manor house, and then a further two miles to Gainsborough. The bank and higher ground running up from the Trent to Gainsborough on the Lincolnshire side is all sandy, but the opposite bank is low-lying meadowland.

Gainsborough is a good market town, twelve miles from Lincoln. I saw nothing much worthy of note there, apart from the parish church, where Sir Thomas Burgh, Knight of the Garter, who died in 1408, lies buried in a rich tomb with his wife, the Lady de Botreaux. Thomas was the grandfather of the present Lord Burgh, who built most of the manor house next to the west end of the churchyard. His father is buried in the chancel. Also in Gainsborough church lies Lord Edmund Cornwall, who founded three chantries there, and died in 1322. He held the large moated manor house called Thonock, which is in a wood a mile to the east of Gainsborough, and belongs to the Cornwalls. In the southern part of Gainsborough is an old stone chapel, where the townspeople say that many Danes were buried. In the same part of the town beside the Trent is a wooden chapel which has now been abandoned. Next to Gainsborough is a park belonging to Lord Burgh, and elsewhere there is another which is maintained by Mr Heneage. *cont. p. 280* [**1541**:1/23-33]

From Wrangton [?*Wroot*] to the point where I reached land on the Isle of Axholme is about a mile. From Wrangton onwards the river is called the Idle, although it is in fact the same river as the Bryer. Without doubt Idle is the original name.

The Isle of Axholme is ten miles long from south to north, and six miles wide from east to west. From the western end of Bikers Dyke as far as the great Mere fens and marshland, full of carrs, border the water. The rest is reasonably high ground, of fertile pasture and arable. The chief woodland on the island is at Belgrave [?*Belton*] Park near Epworth, and at Melwood Park not far from Epworth; there is also a pleasant wood at Crowle, a manor which formerly belonged to Selby Abbey. There are seven parish churches on the island. Epworth is the best country town there, with buildings lining one street. Haxey is a large parish, but the houses are more scattered than at Epworth. At Owston there was a castle, which used to be called Kinnard, next to the churchyard on the south side. No part of it is still standing, although the ditch and the mound on which the keep stood may still be seen. The ferry across the Trent is a quarter-mile away.

Next to Epworth and adjoining Belgrave Park still survives a large portion of the manor house of Lord Mowbray of Axholme, who until recently was the principal owner of the whole island. Beside Melwood Park stood the excellent Carthusian monastery, where one of the Mowbrays, dukes of Norfolk, was buried in an alabaster tomb. Mr Candish has now turned the monastery into a good manor house.

Many years ago there used to be a manor house at West Butterwick on the bank of the Trent. I learnt that it belonged to a gentleman called Bellethorp, and that by marriage he inherited also the lands of Burnham, another gentleman on Axholme. Bellethorp's estate later descended to Sheffield, in which family it has remained for five or six generations. In Owston churchyard, half a mile from Melwood Park, I saw five tombs of the Sheffield family. Young Sheffield's father is buried in Owston church. The Sheffield who was recorder of London is buried in the Austin friary in London. It was he who brought the family name into prominence through his marriage to the daughter and sole heir of a certain Delves, whose inheritance included also the estates of Gibthorp and Babington. Recorder Sheffield began building on a large scale at Butterwick, as evidenced by the great brick tower.

The four well-known gentry families now on the island are Sheffield, Candish, Evers and Monson. The estate of a certain Bellwood descended by marriage to the present Monson, who is a younger son of old Monson of Lincolnshire. It was old Monson who in a sense was the first to improve the family fortunes.

The fenland part of Axholme produces much of a low shrub called gall, which when burnt has a sweet aroma. The higher part of the island has productive alabaster quarries, usually known there as plaster. But the stones of this material which I saw were of no great thickness, and sold for twelve pence per load. They lie underground in smooth layers, one flake bedded under another; and beneath the alabaster layers is a rough stone suitable for building. *cont. p. 423* [**1541:** 1/37-8]

In the past there have been members of the Lincolnshire family of Dalison who were men of very substantial estates. But that was long ago, and more recently their lands have not had an annual value of any more than £70 or £100. I asked Dr Dalison, who is the brother of the present heir to the estate, but he knew little about the family or of its connections with Lincolnshire. Mr Sheffield told me that they held a portion of the Lincolnshire estate of Vere, which originated with the family of the earls of Oxford. [2/10]

Notes about certain names and information in the history of Crowland: Aswick is a farm about four miles by water from Crowland on the River Welland, in the parish of Whaplode. It belonged to the abbot. Dunesdale lies on the near bank of the Welland two-and-a-half miles above Crowland. It is a seyney [*bloodletting*] place for the monks [?]. Whaplode is nine miles from Crowland and five miles from Aswick. It stands on the Welland, which is fresh water at this point. Gedney, an attractive little town for its surroundings, is three or four miles from Whaplode. It once belonged to three sisters. One of the sisters was buried at Crowland, and her portion went to the abbey, the second portion went to Lord Wenford, and the third now belongs to Lord Pollet. Baston in Kesteven, a mile from Market Deeping, was once a market town. Langtoft adjoins it, and Bowthorpe is two miles away. Baston has only a chapel; its mother-church is at Thetford. Bukenhalle [*?Bucknall*] is near Bolingbroke. Hallington is two miles from Louth. Dunedik [*?Dowdyke*] manor borders the Wash at Fosdyke. Holbeach is less than a mile from Whaplode. Fleet, only a mile from Gedney, has had a market until within living memory, and a fair on the feast day of St Mary Magdalen. Thomas Moulton, a knight, had his castle in the fens half-a-mile from Whaplode; a small portion of it remains standing. It belongs now to Lord FitzWalter, and another part belongs to the Lord Marquis – this part is held during his lifetime by Lord Richard.

Great Postland extends about seven miles in each direction, and is fourteen miles around [? – *Leland's text is incomplete and ambiguous*]. Once it was low-lying cornland, but now, because of neglect, it is fenland and marsh. It abuts Crowland Abbey on the east, west and north sides, and its parish comprises a resident population of 160. Freiston definitely stands on the far side of the Boston estuary, along with Butterwick and Tofte [*?Fishtoft*], and three villages in Kesteven, which all pertain to the monastic cell at Freiston. All this land belonged to the de Croun family. Alan de Croun, who came over with William the Conqueror, was lord of Freiston, and gave it to Crowland Abbey; he was buried on the south side of the altar at Crowland. Watkin Rodeley Esquire, who married the duchess of Somerset, was buried in the chapel of Our Lady on the south side of the church. Some people maintain that he was a rich and important man alive during the reign of Henry VII. Also in the Lady Chapel, in a fine tomb, lay Richard Welby, an esquire of Henry VII's bodyguard. His birthplace was Moulton in Holland, where he was a man of great importance and power. His infant brother, Thomas Welby, is [*?was*] his heir, and was also buried at Crowland. Coldingham [*near Berwick on*

Tweed] was of old a cell of Crowland, given by a king of Scotland. For a long time Crowland received rents from it, but eventually Durham made an arrangement to pay Crowland £8 annually from its cell of St Leonard's near Stamford, in exchange for Coldingham. [2/146-8]

The Austin friary in the west suburb of Stamford, close to St Peter's Gate, was originally founded, it is said, by a very rich inhabitant of the town, a man named Fleming. It was completed by an archdeacon of Richmond. It should here be noted that in this suburb is a piece of land called Bread Croft, because it was in this part of the suburb that the bakers sold their bread. Even now people from Rutland resort there, and conduct their law courts there. Thus Rutland's jurisdiction extends as far as this suburb. In the southern part of Stamford, within the town walls and next to the market place, is All Saints' Hospital, which was founded by one Brown, a merchant of the town who possessed remarkable wealth. He was alive up until modern times, and some people still alive saw him.

It is probable that as many privileges have been given to Stamford (all except the privilege of treason) as to any town in England. But men from the north during the reigns of the first three Edwards badly damaged the town, and many of the documents about its history and privileges were burned.

D'Albini, the lord of Belvoir Castle (which most definitely stands in Leicestershire, in the Vale of Belvoir), was also the owner of Uffington. This lies on the further (or Lincolnshire) bank of the River Welland a half-mile below Stamford, and substantial remains of his fortified manor house survived. They have now been put into good repair by the present earl of Rutland, who succeeded to it through an heiress of the Ros family. In the days when the d'Albini family frequently lived at Uffington, one of them built a priory for canons at Newstead, and here were buried the second, third and fourth of the d'Albini line.

This Newstead Priory is less than a mile below Stamford, but is not immediately next to the river. Because Stamford has a very great reputation as having once been a place for studying the liberal sciences, there are still the names of Peterborough Hall, Sempringham and Vaudey there as lodgings for those monastic houses which sent their scholars to study there. There is however an alternative explanation as to why monasteries came and gave their names to these places.

A quarter-mile beyond Stamford in the Newstead direction there is a stone bridge over a small river called the Gwash. It rises in Leicestershire, flows past Greetham in Rutland and by Mr Harrington's house. Its total length, from its source to its confluence with the Welland just past Gwash Bridge a little below Stamford, is eighteen or twenty miles. There is a common saying that, 'the Gwash and Welland shall drown all Holland'. A number of small streams drain into the Gwash; it flows past Casterton, which once belonged to Lord Hussey. [4/88-90]

Mr Paynell, a gentleman of Boston, told me that long ago the town suffered a fire during the great and famous fair held there, and that afterwards it never really regained its former glory and wealth. But even after the fire it was many times richer than it is now. The staple hall and the steelyard house are still standing, but the steelyard is hardly ever used, or not used at all. There had been four fraternities of merchants of the steelyard, who were drawn from all over the east [i.e. the Baltic and Low Countries], and who often frequented Boston. The grey friars regarded them in a way as the founders of their friary, and many easterlings were buried there. Also in the grey friars were buried members of two gentry families, the Mountevilles and the Withams, of whom there were six or seven. A nobleman of the Huntingfield family was buried in the black friars, and when recently his body was exhumed in its entirety, there was found a leaden bull of Pope Innocent around his neck. At Boston there still remains a manor house which belonged to the Tilneys, and is named after them; it was one of them who started to build the great steeple in Boston.

From Boston it is six miles to the sands of the Wash; and then across the sands and the salt-water channel it is twelve and a further six miles to King's Lynn. Wainfleet harbour is a creek which flows inland. After some distance it throws off small side creeks on each side of the creek, which extend a short distance into the fens, and create a little marshy lake at its head.

[*Miscellaneous information from Mr Paynell:*] Lord Cromwell built a portion of Maxey Castle near Deeping. At Boston there is a certain sum paid which is called Cromwell's Fee. One member of this family built an attractive turret called 'the Tower of the Moore'. And next to it he made a fine, large pond or lake, with bricks around it; this is commonly called 'the Sinker'. Kirton takes his name from the [?*town*], or from one of the wapentakes in Low Holland. Paynell told me that in Latin his name is written 'Paganellus', and that the most important of his ancestors in the past were lords of Tickhill Castle, Bolingbroke and Newport Pagnell, as well as several other manors which have taken their family name. Holbeach in Holland is alternatively known as Oldbek. [4/114-15]

Along the coast: From Grimsby to Marsh Chapel, where there is a creek for shipping, is about four miles. (From Grimsby to Boston is reckoned to be thirty miles.) Saltfleet harbour is six miles further, then Wilegripe [?*Wold Grift, near Mablethorpe*], and so four or five miles to Skegness. This used to be a large harbour town, and Mr Paynell told me that he had proof that there was once a harbour, a walled town and a castle there. The old town was completely overwhelmed and eroded by the sea, though part of a church survived until recently, and at low water there may still be seen substantial evidence of the former buildings. The new Skegness which has replaced the old is a poor affair.

Then about five miles to Wainfleet, which has been a very good town, with two parish churches. Within living memory small boats used to come up as far as the school. But the harbour now is going to ruin. Paynell says that he recalls that there is a place at Wainfleet called Castle Hill. Two miles further is Friskney, where some people say there was once a harbour, although I am not certain about this. It lies a mile-and-a-half from the coast. Wrangle is six miles from Wainfleet, and Boston six good miles further. Freiston is on the further bank of Boston [harbour], two miles downstream from the town beside the bank. Alan de Croun, the owner of Freiston, was known as Alan Opendoor, because of his great hospitality.

Boston is reckoned to be 24 miles from Lincoln. The easterlings [i.e. Hanseatic or Baltic traders] had a large establishment and trading business at Boston until about the time of Edward IV, when one of them was killed by Humphrey Littlebury, a Boston merchant. As a result a great dispute arose, which resulted in the easterlings ceasing to trade at Boston, and since then the town has been in severe decline. A certain Maud Tilney laid the first stone of the fine tower of Boston parish church, under which she is buried. The Tilney family were believed to have founded three of the four friaries in the town. Lord Mounteville had a good, large and old manor house at Fishtoft, a mile from Boston, which is now completely in ruins. It later belonged to Lord Willoughby, and now is the duke of Suffolk's. Part of Lord Monteville's estate descended by the female line to the Beke family, and from them passed to the Willoughbys. [4/181-2]

The northern men burnt much of the town of Stamford, and it was not entirely rebuilt afterwards. Stamford's only borough privilege at the time of King Edward was that of having a seat in Parliament, although in King Edgar's time is was a borough town, and both then and at all times since it has belonged to the crown. In the town walls there were seven principal towers or wards, and to each of them were assigned certain freeholders within the town for watch and ward duty as required. [5/5]

Market towns in Kesteven: Stamford; Bourne; Market Deeping. Its church is dedicated to St Guthlac; the church of the other Deeping is dedicated to St James. A mile from Market Deeping is the ruined castle of Maxey, of which some part still stands. Very probably it was the seat of Lord Wake, but in recent times is belonged to the countess of Richmond, Henry VII's mother. Neither the town nor the market of Sleaford is of any value. Its only adornments are the bishop of Lincoln's castle, and the late Lord Hussey's house. Kyme, a good house and park, is three miles from Sleaford. Grantham.

From Stamford to Grantham is eighteen miles, entirely in Kesteven, and through quite well wooded country. From Stamford to Bitchfield, which is a modest roadside place, is twelve miles. It is mostly across flat country, except in the area around Bitchfield itself. From Bitchfield to Ancaster, a poor roadside place, is entirely flat country, much of it heathland. Then sixteen miles from Ancaster to Lincoln, across similar flat land, all in Kesteven. Note at this point that the flat heathland from Bitchfield to Lincoln is called Ancaster Heath. From Bourne in Kesteven through High Holland to Boston is a journey of twenty miles entirely across low-lying country, with much marshland and virtually no woods.

Low Holland: Crowland; Quappelode [*Whaplode*], known locally as Hoplode.

High Holland: Boston stands right on the River Lindis [*Witham*]. The majority of the town, and the most important part, lies east of the river, where there is a fine market place and a cross with a square tower. The principal parish church was St John's, and this is still a church for the town. St Botolph's used to be a chapel dependent on it. But now it has grown and been adorned to such an extent that it is the main church in Boston, and is the best and finest of all the parish churches in Lincolnshire. For singing and the cleverness of its staff it has no equal among English parish churches. This has all been achieved by the fraternity attached to the church, which is now a major landowner. The tower stands foursquare, surmounted by a lantern. It is very tall and fine, and is a landmark from every direction, both on land and at sea. There is also a good font, which is made partly of white marble, or of something very similar.

There are three friaries in Boston – Franciscans, Dominicans and Austin. There is also a hospital for poor men, and either in the town or nearby, the late Lord Hussey had a house with a stone tower. All the architecture on this side of the town is good; the merchants live in this quarter, and hold a staple for wool here. A wooden bridge over the Witham gives access to this part of the town, supported by a stone pile built in the middle of the river. At times the water seems to flow here as fast as an arrow. On the west bank of the Witham there is one long street, and the Carmelite friars are here. The open sea is six miles from Boston, and various good ships and other vessels have their anchorage there.

Lord Willoughby had a house at Eresby, and a park of black deer two miles from Spilsby, where, as I have heard say, he intends to build in lavish fashion. Spilsby is a modest market town, with buildings mostly thatched, but some roofed with reeds. There is one reasonably good house which belongs to a gentleman called Hastings, who came from Suffolk, where he owns land. Spilsby is roughly halfway between Horncastle and the coast, about five miles from each; it stands on the edge of the central marshlands of Low Lindsey. A stream flows past it, and there are many springs nearby. The soil is sandy.

Alford is sixteen miles from Boston. It is a modest market town in the Low Lindsey marshland. The town is entirely roofed with thatch and reed, and is served by a brook. In Lindsey most of the parishes in the low-lying marshland grow good wheat and beans, but little barley (as on the heavy clayland) and no woods. At Huttoft Marsh, four miles away, ships from various places enter and unload.

Wainfleet is a pleasant market town situated on a creek close to the sea. It has a fleet of small vessels. The most notable thing about the place is the school which Bishop Wainfleet of Winchester established there, and endowed with an annual income of £10 in land. Wainfleet is seven miles from Alford in the Boston direction. Louth. Market Rasen.

Caistor stands on a hillside half a mile from the River Ancholme, four miles from Langford Bridge [*Glanford Bridge, i.e. Brigg*], and nearly six miles east of Spitel [*?Hibaldstow*]. A Saturday market is held there. The town is almost all thatched, and within living memory has often been damaged by fire. Mention is made of a fortress which used to exist there. Springs issue from the hills near Caistor. Brigg. Grimsby.

Tattershall is a pleasant small market town on the River Bain, with the larger River Aye or Rhe [*Witham*] about a mile away. It is five miles from Horncastle, and three from Bardney. Horncastle, so far as I have been able to discover, is now largely built within the walls of an old town, or some huge castle. Various ruins of these walls may still be seen. It has one fine parish church, and is watered by the Bain and the Waring, which [*?join forces*] a little further on. Dr Thimbleby of the Queens College owns lands around the old walls of Horncastle. The Waring rises from several springs a few miles from the town. There is a bridge over the Waring at Horncastle. The market is very good and busy. Bolingbroke has an annual fair but no weekly market. The castle is in reasonable repair, and has a drawbridge over a surrounding moat.

Rivers and brooks in Lincolnshire: At or near Calcethorp, about three miles west of Louth, rises a large brook which is there called the Bain. It flows to a village four miles away called Baumber (presumably for Bane-burgh), and then another four miles to Horncastle, which is a market town. Its course thus far is mainly due south. Then it turns to flow directly westward, to Tattershall, or Tateshaul, a market town five miles from Horncastle. From there about another mile brings it to Dogdyke Ferry, where it joins the Ree, or Lindis [*Witham*].

The River Witham separates Lindsey to the east from Kesteven to the west, and is tidal almost up as far as Dogdyke Ferry. The brook or stream which passes to the north of Bardney Abbey, and a furlong lower flows into the main River Witham, is called Panton Brook. Its source is in High Lindsey, in Mr West's opinion not very far from the area where the Bain rises. It then flows to Hills, Mr Hansard's manor house; then Panton, a village five miles away; then Wragby village, two miles further, where it is sometimes called Wragby Beck. And so to Bardney Abbey, four miles, and then into the Witham. The monks are of the opinion that the old Bardney Abbey was not on exactly the same site as the new, but at a grange or dairy belonging to them a mile away.

The River Lud. To Ludbrook [*?Ludborough*] village, to Lude or Louth, the fine market town, via Louth Park, four miles. From Louth a mile to Grimoldby village, four miles to Saltfleet Creek, and so to the sea. Saltfleet Creek is a small harbour, which lies six miles further up the coast from Huttoft Creek. The abbeys of Bardney, Barlings, Revesby and Kirkstead all have a reasonably good supply of woodland.

[*Gentry of Lincolnshire:*] Dymoke lives at Scrivelsby, two miles from Horncastle. Sir Christopher Willoughby's son and heir now lives at Tupholme Priory, and has also inherited part of Lord Willoughby's estate. Copledyke lives at Harrington, two miles from Spilsby Market. Asschecue [*Askew*] lives in the Thornton Curtis area. Wymbish has Nocton Park Priory, and in addition a large and ancient estate. He married Lord Talboy's sister. Littlebury is at Stainsby near Hagworthingham. The Lord de Burgh lives at Gainsborough, which belongs to him, although much surrounding land is owned by Sheffield of Axholme. Dalison lives a little this side of Axholme. Heneage is at Hainton, where he owns the manor and advowson. The former Heneage estate had an annual value not exceeding £50. Hainton is less than three miles from Market Rasen, and seven miles from Horncastle. Sir Thomas Heneage has gone to great expence there in alterations and new buildings using brick and stone from the abbey. Sandon lives at Ashby [*?by Partney*], half a mile from Spilsby. Porter is near Grantham. Harrington is next to Ancaster. Bilsby lives at Bilsby, within a mile of Markby Priory. Fitzwilliams lives at Mablethorpe next to Sutton on Sea. Hastings [*lives at*] Wilksby, and Langton lives at Langton not far from Wilksby. Asterby at Bilsby is a man of modest estate. Totheby [?] is of [*South*] Thoresby near Alford. Gedney of Mavis Enderby is a gentleman of modest means. Quathering lives near Wainfleet. St Paulle. Misselden around Caistor. Luddington. Turwith [*?Tyrwhitt*] around Barton-on-Humber. Turner. Sutton at Lincoln. Dymoke of [*?South*] Carlton near Lincoln. Massingberd close to Wainfleet. Hall by Grantham. Welby at Halstead, not far from Stixwould Priory, is a man with a fine estate. [5/32-8]

Tombs in Lincoln [*Minster*]: Henry Burwash, bishop of Lincoln, is buried at the east end of the church on the north side. At his feet is buried his brother Robert, a knight of great reputation as a warrior. Also buried there is Robert's son, Bartholomew Burwash. They endowed places for five priests and five poor scholars at Lincoln Grammar School. In the chapel of Our Lady, at the east end of the church on the north side, are buried the bowels of Queen Eleanor; the arms of Castile are on the side of the tomb. In the south-east chapel next to it is buried one of the Lords Nicholas Cantilupe. He endowed a college, now incorrectly called Negem College, with a master and two or three chantry priests, later increased to seven. And nearby, at his head, is buried in a fine tall tomb one of the Wymbishes, a canon residentiary of Lincoln.

In the chapel of St Nicholas there is a remarkably fine, large psalter, with its margins full of well-drawn arms of many noblemen. St Hugh lies in the centre of the east end of the minster above the high altar. Bishop Fleming is buried in a high tomb in the wall of the north aisle in the upper part of the church; and under flat slabs nearby lie [*Bishop*] Oliver Sutton and Bishop John Chadworth. Chapels projecting from the upper part of the south wall of the church contain the tomb of Bishop Russell, and that intended for the present bishop, Longland. Next to this chapel is buried a knight called Fitzwilliam. On the south side of the sanctuary in a chapel are two separate high marble tombs, containing Catherine Swineford (the third wife of John of Gaunt, Duke of Lancaster), and Jane, Countess of Westmorland, her daughter.

Bishop Thomas is buried in the lesser north transept, and Bishop Robert Grosseteste in the uppermost south aisle in a fine marble tomb with a brass effigy over it. Bishop Repington is under a flat stone nearby. In the main north transept Bishop Thomas Weke is buried, and in the main south transept was formerly the tomb of Bishop Dalberly, but it was removed for superstitious reasons. Sir John Multon is buried in the nave, as is Bishop Gwyney. It was he who built a large chapel dedicated to St Mary Magdalene immediately outside the north wall, but affixed to the north side of the cathedral church, and endowed five chantry priests. Later this church was removed to the north side of the Exchequer, by part of the western precinct of the churchyard. The dean of Lincoln's house in the minster close occupies part of the site of a nunnery which existed before Remigius began the new minster of Lincoln; some pieces of evidence still remain of this nunnery.

The nave of Lincoln Minster as far the main crossing is of eight bays with marble pillars on each side. The first transept is longer and larger than the second. The quire between the two transepts is of four bays with marble pillars. At the north end of the lesser transept is the cloister, which has the chapter house on its eastern side. The eastern part of the chapter house is built in circular fashion, and the archway into it is supported by a marble column. There is a very fine door in the upper part of the minster on the south side which leads into the close; the bishop's palace lies opposite this, perched on the edge of the hill. The entire close is surrounded with a high strong wall, with several gates through it, of which the chief one is the Exchequer Gate. The parish church of St Margaret is within the close on the ESE side.

In Gainsborough parish church: Lord Thomas de Burgh, knight of the order of the garter, who died in 1408, is buried on the south side of the high altar with his wife, the Lady Margaret of Botreaux. Lord Edmund Cornwall, lord of Thonock, founded three chantries in the church. He died on 16th December, 1322, and is buried in the northern part of the church. [5/121-3]

LONDON AND MIDDLESEX

ALTHOUGH LELAND WAS BORN in London, lived part of his life there, suffered his illness, died and was buried there, it was left to his younger contemporary, John Stow, to offer the world a meticulous description of the Tudor capital. Stow possessed Leland's notes after his death, and there has long been a suspicion that Stow's survey may have drawn on a now lost description by Leland. But all that survives are some short notes, and thin accounts of the first leg of the journey from London to the West Country in 1542, and the returns to London from the North-East in 1541, and the West Midlands in 1543.

FROM MY CROSSING of the Thames at Staines Bridge I travelled six miles, mostly across open, arable country with pasture, to Hampton Court. Hampton village lies beside the Thames half a mile this side of the Court. [**1541**: 1/106]

NEW BRENTFORD is eight miles from London. It has a bridge of three arches across the Brent Brook, with a brick-built hospital at the far end of it. Hounslow, which is two miles further, had at the west end of the town a friary of the Trinitarian order. A land dyke of great size runs across Hounslow Heath, which acts as a drain for the whole heath, and I crossed a wooden bridge over it.

Longford is five miles from Hounslow, and a little beyond the village is a wooden bridge, where the Longford mill leat, which derives from the meadows further upstream, flows into one of the two principal streams which divide off from the River Colne. I was told that this stream leaves the Colne before it reaches the end of Uxbridge, and rejoins the mainstream not very far below Longford Bridge. The mainstream of the

Colne flows under a wooden bridge a little beyond Longford Bridge, and after more than a mile it joins the Thames near Staines church, which is a short distance upstream from the bridge over the Thames at Staines. The earl of Derby's house at Colham stands on the near side of the Colne about a mile upstream from the bridge. From this bridge to the wooden bridge at Colnbrook is about a mile.

All the land from a mile or more on this side of Longford to Colnbrook Bridge is low-lying pasture, and after heavy rainfall the river rises and overflows it. Under Colnbrook Bridge flows the second, and in my estimation the smaller, of the two principal streams deriving from the River Colne. It leaves the mainstream in a marshy area two miles above the settlement at Colnbrook and about a mile below Uxbridge. Uxbridge and Colnbrook are three miles apart. *cont. p. 19* [**1542:** *1/107-8*]

NINE MILES of good enclosed ground separate Amersham from Uxbridge. The soil is gravelly, and there are woods, meadows, pasture and arable. Uxbridge lies all along one long street, and is aligned from the west rising slightly towards the south-east. The buildings are good considering that they are of timber. Its weekly market is renowned, and there is a large annual fair on the feast of St Michael. There is a chapel of ease in the town, but the parish church is almost a mile outside, right on the main road to London, at Great Hillingdon; this is a sign that Uxbridge itself is not a very ancient town.

At the western end of Uxbridge town are two wooden bridges. The mainstream of the River Colne flows under the more westerly, and the lesser stream under the other. Each drives a large mill there. This division of the River Colne occurs barely a mile above Uxbridge, but the two arms do not rejoin. The larger flows for three miles through good meadows directly to Colnbrook, and so to the Thames. The other goes to two mills on the London road a mile and a half east of Colnbrook, and then likewise into the Thames.

From Uxbridge to the village of Southall is six miles. More than a mile before I reached Southall I passed over a bridge of six arches. This crosses a stream which flows across Hounslow Heath, or else to Brentford. From Southall to Acton, a nice roadside place, is four miles, and another four miles to Marylebone Brook and Park. The brook flows past the wall of St James's Park. Then two miles to London. [**1543:** *2/113-14*]

There was a priory in Surrey [*i.e. Middlesex*] called Ruislip. I believe it was an alien French house, and was appropriated to King's College, Cambridge. [1/329]

Next to Cripplegate inside London Wall there was a house for a few nuns, and this was acquired from the king by a London merchant called Elsing. He placed Augustinian canons there, built a hospital and endowed it with lands; henceforward the house took the name of Elsing Hospital. [2/29]

A long time ago the bishops of London used to stay sometimes at Bishop's Hall, a manor house they owned near Bethnal Green. Bishop FitzJames pulled down the old dining hall there. [4/117]

Cardinal Draper, who was archbishop of Canterbury, gave 1,000 marks [*nearly £700*] or £1,000 towards the building of London Bridge. King John donated certain empty plots in London to be built on [*so that rents from them would go*] for the building and repair of London Bridge. A mason who was in charge of the bridge house built the chapel on the bridge at his own expense from the foundations upwards. [5/6]

MONMOUTHSHIRE

ONLY ONE of Leland's five surviving itineraries across England, the first in 1538, ventured into Wales, and on that occasion he did not visit Monmouthshire. But despite the scattered and disordered nature of his notes as they have come down to us, it is possible to discern a systematic approach to his Welsh research, which must have involved him in at least one further protracted journey. He gathered information around the principality, county by county, under various heads – castles, abbeys, market towns, rivers, gentry, etc. – interspersed with eye-witness descriptions. He entered Wales on one such mission by crossing the Severn from Aust in Gloucestershire by ferry, and explored Monmouthshire and Glamorgan, probably in 1539. He rode from Chepstow to Caerwent and then Caerleon, taking a special interest in Roman evidence, then to Newport and Rhymney Bridge on the way to Cardiff. He also considered Usk and Abergavenny, though perhaps without visiting them, and he tried to document the rivers and their valleys. He described Monmouth, too, in Latin, and perhaps on a different occasion, and then made his way to Hereford. A few of his notes on abbeys and rivers are relevant to the county, and on his 1543 Midlands itinerary he diverted from Herefordshire to make a few observations about Monmouthshire castles. His usual term for the county east of the Usk was Wentland or Gwentland (the latter retained in this version); west of the Usk he referred to Wentlooge, which he identified with the Welsh cantref of Gwynllŵg.

THE FERRY from Aust in Gloucestershire to a village on the further bank of the Severn, not far from St Tereudacus's chapel [St Twrog's, on Chapel Rock] in the mouth of the River Wye, is three miles across.

Gwentland is divided into Low, Middle and High. The principal town of Low Gwentland is Chepstow, two miles from the Severn shore. Some people say that this town's old name was Strigulia, but others think that Strigulia was another place, because Lord Herbert describes himself as lord of Chepstow and Strigul, as if they were two separate places. Five or six English miles from Chepstow, in a great wooded hillside, can be seen very conspicuous ruins of a castle called Troggy, and a little brook of the same name flows past it. This castle's name somewhat resembles Strigulia, although it is claimed there that it stands in Middle Gwentland.

The town of Chepstow has been very strongly walled, and this is still quite apparent. The walls began at the end of the great bridge over the Wye, and ran to the castle, which is still standing fine and strong, not far from the ruins of the bridge. I heard it said that one tower in the castle goes by the name of Longine. There is only one parish church in the town now, a cell of one or two Benedictine monks from Bermondsey near London having recently been suppressed. Much of the land encircled by the town walls has now been converted to little meadows and gardens.

Caerwent in Low Gwentland is four miles from Chepstow on the road to Caerleon. At one time this was a fine, large city, and the sites of its four gates may still be seen. Most of its circuit of walls remain standing, though reduced and damaged. In the lower section of the wall towards a little valley are the ruins of a strong [motte], and inside and around about the walls are 16 or 17 small houses recently built for husbandmen, and St Stephen's parish church. Paving slabs of the old streets can still be seen in the town, and when digging takes place foundations are uncovered, with large bricks, tesselated pavements and coins apparently of silver and bronze. It is very likely that when Caerwent began to decline, then Chepstow began to flourish. For Chepstow occupies a far better position, as the Wye ebbs and flows with the Severn tides, so that large ships can come in there.

Portskewett, I discovered, lies between Chepstow and Caerwent, where a stream flows into the Severn. The furthest distance across Wales can be traced from here to Port-Hoyger [?] near Holyhead in Anglesey. Tintern Abbey, three miles from Chepstow beside the Wye, seems to be in Low Gwentland. Caldicot Castle, which belongs to the king, is in Low Gwentland close to the Severn shore not far from Mathern. It is said that King Henry VII was conceived at this castle. Llanvair Castle is two miles almost north from Caerwent in Low Gwentland. Mathern is a handsome residence in Low Gwentland belonging to the bishop of Llandaff.

Gwentland's soil is uniformly a dark reddish earth full of slaty stones, and larger stones of the same colour. The terrain is somewhat mountainous and well wooded. It is very fertile for growing corn, but the inhabitants are inclined rather to pastoral farming on well inclosed land.

Middle Gwentland. Opinion is divided whether or not Caerleon should be in Middle Gwentland. The Welsh say that it is only eight miles from Chepstow, but in fact it may be reckoned twelve English miles. Caerleon stands magnificently on the further bank of the Usk, one of the principal rivers of South Wales. Were it not for the obstruction of Newport bridge, very large ships might well come to the town, as they did in Roman times, but as it is big boats do indeed come. The town walls and the castle remain but in ruins. There is a theory that the old Roman church was close to the house where I stayed. Some paintings on stones were uncovered when digging there, and recently some painted encrustments were found near the castle. There is only one parish church in the town now, dedicated to St Cadoc.

There are those who maintain that Cairuske [*Usk*], otherwise called Brenbygey [*Brynbuga*], should be regarded as the principal place in Middle Gwentland. Its castle has been large, strong and fine, although the town beside it seems not to have been at all famous. Until recently it had a nunnery. The town stands on the far bank of the Usk.

The ruined Troggy Castle lies within a Welsh mile of a stretch of the River Usk on the road to Monmouth, six miles from Chepstow and almost as far from Caerleon. Tregrug Castle, also called Lan Kiby [*Llangibby*] because the parish dedication is to St Cybi, is two miles from Usk in middle Gwentland.

Newport is in Wentlugh [*Gwynllŵg*], more than a mile by a footpath from Caerleon, situated on the Usk. There is a strong and pleasant town, but I did not observe whether or not it was walled. It has a very fine castle which once belonged to the dukes of Buckingham. This great lordship, according to the Welsh, is not part of the three Gwentlands, even though its Welsh name is Guentluge [*i.e. Wentlooge*]. Because of this it might well be described

MONMOUTHSHIRE

in connection with Middle Gwentland. Newport lordship in all probability should extend to the Rhymney River, the boundary with Glamorgan.

At Goldcliff, three miles from Newport on the Severn shore, there was a monastic priory of a French order, which was suppressed and its lands given to Eton College. Raglan Castle, in Middle Gwentland, is very fine and pleasant, but the settlement next to it is deserted. It is eight miles from Chepstow and seven from Abergavenny. Two good parks adjoin the castle. Llantarnam Abbey, a Cistercian monastery two miles from Caerleon, has recently been suppressed.

The lordship of Abergavenny is coterminous with High Gwentland. The town of Abergavenny itself is handsome and walled, moderately well inhabited, with a parish church and a fine castle. The Bergavenny lordship is one of the most ancient baronies of the kingdom. [**1539**: 3/42-5]

W ENTLLUG [*Gwynllŵg*] is divided from Gwentland on the east by the River Usk. To the south is the Severn Sea, on the west the Rhymney River along its whole length, and to the NNE lie the hills of High Gwentland. From south to north, that is from the Severn Sea to the head of Meredith lordship, is about twenty miles. At its widest from east to west it is not estimated to be more than eight miles, and in various places less than that.

In the south, towards the Severn, the ground is rather low-lying and full of dykes for draining it. Beans grow in great abundance, and in various places all sort of corn are grown. This low ground extends southwards to the Severn Sea from the causeway or highway that leads from Newport to Rhymney Bridge. North of the highway the land rises and is still higher further north. In the Gwynllŵg lowlands there is very little woodland, except at Parke Bahan [*Castleton Park*], three miles from Newport along the Cardiff road which passes through it. Castelle Behan [*Wentllooge Castle*] is a short distance outside the park to the south, and is in ruins. It belonged to the Duke of Buckingham. There are no deer in the park and no park pale now, and it is in the king's hands by virtue of Newport lordship. At Tredegar Mr William Morgan, who owns land worth £200 annually, has a very fine stone residence. It is a mile and a half south-west of Newport on the east bank of the Ebbw River.

The area of Gwynllŵg up towards Caerleon has good pasture and woodland. The six miles of land from Rhymney Bridge along the east bank of the Rhymney to Bedwas parish is very well wooded, and there is fairly good arable in some places in between, firstly in Llanuihengle [*Michaelstow-y-Fedw*] parish, and then in the adjoining Machen parish. Rhymney Bridge is two miles from the Severn Sea, and there is a village nearby called Rhymney in English, but Tredelerch in Welsh. Thence a mile further up the Rhymney flows in a fair valley called Dyffryn Risca, which extends three or four miles upstream. It has abundant woods, as if it was forest land, mixed with open ground but not much arable. From the head of this valley it is another four miles up the Rhymney to Eggluis Tider uab Hohele [*Eglwys Tudur ab Hywel, i.e. Ynysddu, Mynyddislwyn, near Blackwood*], by rugged hills, wide valleys and abundant woodland. The head of the Rhymney River is three or four miles above this in the hills of High Gwentland. Many springs issue from there and flowing into a single valley the brook is called Kayach [*Nant Caiach*]. From there it flows into Dyffryn Risca, where it is augmented by a brook called Risca entering it from a parish called Eglwysilan, and then it is called Risca. Eglwysilan is in Senghenydd in Glamorganshire, four miles distant from Dyffryn Risca. And when it comes into Bedwas parish it is called Rhymney, and goes under that name to the Severn Sea. The watershed between the Rhymney and Ebbw rivers, north of the highway to Rhymney Bridge, is mostly hilly, so better for cattle than for corn. And there is a very high hill called Twmbarlwm.

The Ebbw River rises in the wide mountains of north High Gwentland, and flows directly into a valley called Dyffryn Sirhowey. It enters the Usk a mile and a half below Newport, and a half-mile from the Usk harbour mouth. There is a wooden bridge over the Ebbw called Pont Bassaleg two miles above the confluence of the Ebbw and Usk, which carries the highway between Newport and Cardiff. This bridge is scarcely two miles from Newport town.

Newport is only two miles from Caerleon. From Newport to the place where the Ebbw flows into Usk harbour is at least a mile and a half. And then it is more than a half-mile to the harbour mouth. Caerleon and Newport bridges are both constructed of wood.

From Usk harbour mouth to the mouth of the Rhymney, where there is no harbour or entrance suitable for ships, is six miles. There is nothing very noteworthy along this shore. Its banks are raised up sufficiently to fend off the sea from overflowing into the low lands of Gwentland.

Newport is a large town, and the part where the church stands is on a hill. The church is dedicated to St Guntle [*Gwynlliw, now Woolos*], which in English is Olave. There is a great stone gate by the bridge at the east end of the town, another in the middle of the town through which the High Street passes, and a third at the west end of the town, just beyond which is the parish church. The most handsome part of the town is a single street, but the town is in ruins. There was a religious house by the quay below the bridge, and the castle is on the east side of the town above the bridge.

Gentry in Gwynllŵg: Morgan, the principal landowner, has a very handsome residence at Tredegar, and a town house in Newport. Another of the Morgan family is of moderate means living at Newport. And another Morgan lives beside the Rhymney at Machen in a fine house. Had his father not divided the landholding partly to his other sons he would have held a handsome estate. John Morgan at Lampeder [*Peterstone*] parish in Low Gwynllŵg. Roger Kemeys, with land worth £26 annually, lives in Newport. Henry Kemeys lives at Maes Glâs, three miles west of Newport [*in fact close to Tredegar*], a man of means. Davy Kemys, with land worth £40, lives a mile above Rhymney Bridge. Thomas Lewis dwells at Mairin [*Marshfield*], two miles from the Severn shore. [**1539**: 3/12-15]

MONMOUTH IS A WALLED TOWN, and lies within Hereford diocese because it is situated between the rivers Wye and Monnow, from which it derives its name. Of these two rivers it seems to us the Wye stands lower and the Monnow higher. The town is surrounded by its wall, except where the river forms the town defence, that is along the southern part, from the abbey gate, eastwards almost to the bank of the Wye. But because through age the wall's masonry has crumbled, a great part of the defences has collapsed, although great ruins and deep ditches remain. By contrast from the abbey gate the wall extends to the western part of the Monnow. There are four gates in the wall, that is to say, the abbey gate, east gate, Wye gate (so called from the river) and the Monnow gate, which was built on the bridge across the river from which it derives its name. On the far side of the bridge is a suburb which lies in Llandaff diocese, where once there was a parish church of St Thomas, but now a chapel said to have the same dedication. In the town there is only one parish church, which adjoins the Benedictine monastery. The old castle, where Henry V was born, was built on a small hill near the market place. Monmouth town is separated solely by its bridge over the Wye from the Forest of Dean and the county of Gloucestershire. It is a free town, not subject to government by the neighbouring authority. Apart from where they are protected by the rivers, all Monmouth's suburbs are surrounded by a very deep ditch. Troy [*Mitchell Troy*], an ancient seat of the Herberts, is only about 500 yards distant from Monmouth's suburb. Beyond the south (that is the abbey) gate is Herchenfield [*Archenfield*], which means the hedgehog district; it is regarded as a constituent of the lordship of Shrewsbury. Tintern, a Cistercian monastery on the farther bank of the Wye, five miles distant from Monmouth. [**1539 (?)**: 3/45-6]

The Severn Sea surrounds more than half of Gwentland. The Wye is also a very large and well-known river which passes through Gwentland, and flows into the Severn at St Twrog's chapel. There are other small brooks in Low Gwentland which flow into the Wye. The River Usk impinges on Gwentland and forms the border with Brecknockshire. The Rhymney is the boundary between Middle Gwentland and Glamorganshire. The River Monnow rises in the land of Ewyas and flows in a pleasant valley at Trewyn, a gentry residence ten miles from Monmouth. It reaches the Wye not far from the town that shares its name.

Castles in Monmouth lordship: Monmouth, royal, once under the jurisdiction of Lancaster. Skenfrith Castle, on the Monnow three miles above Monmouth. White Castle, four miles from Monmouth and a mile above the Monnow. Grosmont Castle, five miles from Monmouth and not far from the bank of the Monnow. Those who live in the area around these castles owe their allegiance to Monmouth.

Archenfield is a great lordship belonging to the Earl of Shrewsbury. It lies between Monmouth and Hereford, about two miles distant from each, and on one side is drained by the Wye. A small river called Garan [*?Gwyrne Fawr*] rises in a wood called Grege [*?Crug*] six miles north-west of Monmouth, so a husbandman told me, and flows into the Wye [*if correctly identified this river flows into the Usk*]. Prisoners are taken to Goodrich Castle, which is somewhat outside Archenfield, although it belongs to the Earl of Shrewsbury. A gentry family called Minos are large landowners in Archenfield. Kilpeck Castle next to Archenfield belongs to the Earl of Ormond. Archenfield is full of inclosures with much corn and woodland. [3/46-7]

[*In a list of South Wales abbeys and* priories] At Chepstow a little priory of a few Benedictine monks, a cell of Bermondsey at London. Tintern, a Cistercian abbey on the banks of the Wye, about five miles from Chepstow. Monmouth, a Benedictine priory. Abergavenny, a Benedictine priory of the French order. It was founded by a Norman, Hamelin de Barham, and formerly stood in the suburb by the east gate. Usk, a nunnery beside the river an arrow shot from the castle, five miles upstream from Caerleon. Grace Dieu, a Cistercian abbey standing in a wood with a stream running by, and with very good pastures around it. It stands between Usk, three miles away, and Raglan, four miles. Llantarnam, a Cistercian abbey standing in a wood three miles from Caerleon. [3/50]

There is a wooden bridge to cross the Wye from Monmouth to the Forest of Dean, but no other bridge below Monmouth right down to the river's actual mouth. There was a timber bridge at Chepstow…

  River Monnow rises at a place called Foresthene [?] about twenty miles west of Monmouth. Skenfrith Castle stands five miles upstream from Monmouth town right on the bank of the Monnow, and in the past it is quite likely that the river flowed into the castle moat. Much of the outer ward of the castle remains standing, though it is somewhat low-lying. There is a stone bridge over the Monnow a little above the castle. Hubert de Burgh, Earl of Kent, was the lord of Skenfrith, and the noble Edmund, Earl of Kent, possessed it.

  Grosmont Castle stands three miles above Skenfrith, on the right bank (as the river flows) of the Monnow, and about a half-mile away from it. It occupies a strong site on a rocky hill with a dry ditch, and there is a village of the same name nearby. Most of the castle walls are still standing.

  The third castle of Tirtre, or Three Towns, lordship is called White Castle, and is three miles directly south of Grosmont. It stands on a hill, with a dry moat, and is constructed almost entirely of great slaty stone. It is the largest of the three castles. The terrain hereabouts is open farmland, with no large woodland nearby, although Grosmont forest lies to the north. There is good arable and pasture around this and both the other castles.

  The town of Monmouth, beside the confluence of the Monnow and the Wye, is on the left bank of the Monnow, which is crossed by a stone bridge by the town. A certain John of Monmouth, a knight, was lord of the town, and founded Grace Dieu (or Trothy) Abbey on the right bank two miles WNW of Monmouth. [2/69-71]

Llanthony, an Augustinian priory, which is there called Honddu Slade, stands in the Vale of Ewyas fourteen miles from Brecon. But it is another Honddu that flows to Brecon. It was a fine priory, and stood between two great hills. [3/106]

NORFOLK

NO PORTION *of itinerary survives for Norfolk, and we are left only with the scrappiest and most meagre of notes, of more genealogical than topographical interest.*

John Heydon's father began to acquire land, and lived at Baconsthorpe, where presumably the Bacon family had at one time been men of some standing. John's attainments were all in the field of the law. He purchased land, and began to build the façade or gatehouse of the new manor house at Baconsthorpe; but he died before any further building work was done there. John's son, Henry, devoted all the gains made from the law and from office-holding towards improving his home, but still managed to distinguish himself. First he completed at very great expense the rest of the house, of which his father had only begun the façade. Also he purchased land with an annual value in rent of £200, £100 of which is at [West] Wickham near Lewisham in Surrey (towards Croydon); here he built an excellent manor house and a fine church. To each of his two younger sons he left land worth annually £40. The eldest son, who is still alive, is John Heydon, knight. All three were men of good age, all of whose lands were acquired by purchase. [2/11-12]

Philip Tilney of Norfolk had much of the Thorpe estate, including the fine manor of Ashwellthorpe near Wymondham in Norfolk. He also owned Thetford in the Isle of Ely [*Little Thetford, near Ely*], and I believe that this had been Thorpe land also. I was told that there were two members of the Thorpe family who were brothers. One was chancellor of England, and the other chief justice.

Philip [*Tilney*] had three sons, Frederick, Robert and Hugh, and twelve daughters. He left Frederick an estate worth nearly £500 annually. Before he died Philip was a priest, and prebendary of Lincoln. He is buried in Lincoln Minster, in front of the west door.

Massingham in Norfolk belonged to Philip Tilney, and he also owned much land in Lincolnshire. I imagine that this is part of the reason why the family name rose to prominence in Lincolnshire. Mr Framlingham, who recently married Sir Philip's widow, told me that the Tilneys had a house close to Boston, and that one of the family is buried near the tower in Boston church, which he had been largely responsible for building.

Frederick Tilney had only a daughter, and she married Lord Barnes, the father of the last Lord Barnes. That is how the last Lord Barnes became the son and heir of the Tilney estate. But after his death his mother married Thomas, duke of Norfolk, and they had three distinguished sons. The last Lord Barnes sold off the majority of the estate, but his daughter married Knyvet, the king's servant porter, who thus acquired some of it. His children now have some of the Barnes's land, especially Ashwellthorpe near Wymondham.

Philip Tilney's second son, Robert, was given by his father land in Cambridgeshire with an annual value of £100, and his heir lives there still. Hugh, the third son, also had £100 worth of land, in Boston and areas of Lincolnshire. He had a son, Sir Philip Tilney of Suffolk, and a daughter, who became the duchess of Norfolk. Old Philip also looked after his twelve daughters so well, that even the youngest was married to a man with an estate worth £40. [4/95-7]

Swaffham is a town with only a single parish church, but it has one of the busiest markets in the whole of Norfolk. It belongs to the Richmond estate, and is only three miles from Castle Acre. It owes its livelihood mostly to craftsmen and grain dealers. The nearest river is the Acre [*River Nar*], but the town itself is short of water, and has many wells of a great depth. Many of the surrounding villages, including Pickenham, Wade [?] and Litcham, are included in the privileged liberty of Swaffham. [4/116]

The prinicpal houses of the Albany family of Norfolk were at Buckenham Castle and Wymondham, and they held their estate through performing an office called the king's butler. This office still belongs to the direct heir of the family. Three of the last of the Albanys were named Guliam, William and Hugh. Hugh had four daughters, and as I recall they married Dunevet (now usually called Knyvet), another Tattershall, a third Monthaut, and the fourth FitzAlan of Sussex. I have more recently been told that the partition of the estate was thus: Tattershall had Buckenham Castle, Monthaut had Castle Rising, Somery had Barrow Castle; and FitzAlan had Arundel. [4/119]

Sir John Dicons [*Dickon*] told me that when a baulk or boundary was being dug in the parish of Kenninghall in Norfolk a large number of earthernware pots were found intact containing cremated human remains. Not far from the duke of Norfolk's new house at Kenninghall may be seen a large moat, which formerly enclosed a fine house. Local people have a story that a queen, or some great lady, stayed there, and died there. [4/120]

The river that flows from Coxford, where there is a house of Augustinian canons twenty-five miles from Norwich, rises in the WNW; but I was told that another headwater flows into it from a source to the south. In old grants to Christ Church, Norwich, the river that flows through the town is called the Wensum. There are notices at Norwich, Yarmouth and King's Lynn which record great epidemics which have afflicted those towns. The precinct of Christ Church Minster in Norwich extended all the way to Bigod's castle. [4/122]

NORTHAMPTONSHIRE

THREE OF THE SURVIVING ITINERARIES touch on Northamptonshire. Leland passed through Rockingham and its forest on his return from Cumbria in 1538, but his account is brief, and its value is far outweighed by the description he has left us of his journey to the North-East three years later. He seems to have been in no hurry to reach his destination, as he took time to explore Northamptonshire quite thoroughly – meandering through the county from Oundle and Fotheringhay down to Northampton, Weedon and Towcester, before striking north again to Kettering and the Rockingham area on his way to Stamford. And if that was not enough, he revisited several of these places on his return later in the year.

The third itinerary description, although less wide-ranging, is in fact the most impressive of all. It comes as Leland made his way in 1543 across the South Midlands towards Shropshire, and the Northamptonshire portion consists of a description of Brackley. This is perhaps the best and most complete portrait of a small town to be found anywhere in his work. After this the brief notes and scraps which follow seem unimportant.

FROM MEDBOURNE I rode almost a mile to a bridge, and here I crossed the River Welland, which at this point has no great flow. This bridge and river, which are about three miles from Pipewell Abbey, mark the boundary between Leicestershire and Northamptonshire. All the country from Medbourne to within a mile of Pipewell is remarkably good meadow land.

About a mile after I had crossed the Welland I saw Rockingham Castle standing on the brow of a rocky hill. It was about two miles away to my left, on the opposite side of Rockingham Forest. Almost a mile before I reached Pipewell I entered the woodlands of Rockingham Forest. Pipewell Abbey stands within the forest, right at one end of it; and yet I had been told that most abbeys do not, nor used to, lie within forests [? *meaning unclear*]. The founder of Pipewell was a Northamptonshire knight called Butville [*Batevileyn*]. Mowbray, Lord of Rutland, and Lord Zouche enlarged it.

Rockingham Forest is two miles wide in some places, only a mile in others, and roughly fourteen miles long. Rockingham Castle is falling into ruin. There are no red deer, only fallow, in the forest, and the finest game in the forest is to be seen at a place called the Laund of Benefield. Several gentlemen with excellent estates live in villages close to Pipewell. In fact there is a gentleman living in almost all the villages of Northamptonshire.

From Pipewell it is a good three miles to Kettering market, over pasture and arable. The manor house of the Tresham family is a mile from Pipewell at Barton [*?Rushton*]. Higham Ferrers is seven miles from Kettering, and nearly a quarter-mile before reaching Higham I crossed the River Nene. Higham Ferrers has a mayor, a collegiate church and a grammar school. The castle has recently fallen down and been completely demolished. *cont. p.* 1[**1538**: 4/21-2]

I TRAVELLED ACROSS six miles of exceptionally good arable and pasture country from Leighton Bromswold to Barnwell. Here four strong towers remain of Berengar le Moyne's castle, which later belonged to Ramsey Abbey, and now to Montagu. Inside the castle ruins there is now a meagre house for a tenant. Oundle is a mile away, and on the far bank as I approached it from Barnwell. The bridge across the Avon [*Nene*] is set on a causeway and consists of sixteen arches, great and small. A small channel or brook flows into the river among the arches of the bridge, on my left hand side as I approached the town.

Oundle is all built of stone, and has a very good market. The parish church is very fine. It has a good south porch built by a certain Robert Wyatt, a merchant of the town, and Joan his wife. They were also responsible for an attractive almshouse of squared stone masonry on the south side of the churchyard, which has a good large hall above it for the fraternity of the church. In addition they built lodgings at the west end of

NORTHAMPTONSHIRE

the churchyard for two priests to serve the chantry which they established. As I recall, the date inscribed on brass on the almshouse door is the year of Our Lord 1485. At the WNW end of Oundle churchyard is the grange or house of the parsonage appropriated by Peterborough Abbey, with an annual value of £50. Peterborough also owned the town, and this has now been granted by the king to the queen for her dower.

As I entered Oundle I saw another church or chapel, dedicated formerly to St Thomas, but now to Our Lady. The River Nene meanders to such an extent around Oundle that it almost makes the town into an island, except for a short piece to the WNW. As I rode out of the town towards Fotheringhay I crossed a stone bridge over the Nene, called the North Bridge. It is of great length, and is carried across very flat meadows all around by a causeway of I should guess some thirty large and small arches, and this enables travellers to pass when the river overflows. Fotheringhay is two miles from Oundle, over remarkably fine cornland and pasture, but few trees.

The settlement at Fotheringhay lies along a single street, and all the buildings are stone. Its showpiece is the fine architecture of its collegiate parish church. Edward IV loved Fotheringhay, and it was his intention to grant it market privileges, and by demolishing weirs and mills to make it accessible for small barges. The church and the building which now houses the college used to be a nunnery. The nuns were transferred from there to Delapre next to Northampton, and in recognition of this the establishment at Fotheringhay paid an allowance to Delapre. The son of Edward III, Edmund of Langley, obtained permission to build a college at Fotheringhay, according to some people, but death prevented him from carrying out his plan. He left two sons, Edward and Richard, and Edward began the college with a reasonable endowment.

It so happened that Richard was suspected of treason, and was put to death at Southampton at about the time that Henry V went to France. Richard had a son who became Edward IV's father. When the battle of Agincourt was imminent Edward was granted his wish by King Henry to command the vanguard into battle. But he was a fat man, and in the great heat and crush he died of suffocation. His body was later brought to Fotheringhay and buried with honour in the centre of the chancel. His tomb is covered by a flat marble slab with his portrait in brass. After Edward's death and out of consideration for his good service, Henry V confirmed the college's rights, and endowed it with some of the lands of alien priories, including Newent Priory near Lea Market on the borders of Gloucestershire.

Later Edward IV was somewhat envious of Henry V's fame, and so re-established the college in his own name. He was responsible for some of the present buildings, and he had the body of his father brought there from Pontefract, to be buried on the north side of the high altar, where his mother is also buried, in a vault with an attractive chapel over it. During Edward IV's reign the fine college cloister was built, when a certain Field was the master of the college. Field set passages from the book called 'The Lands of the Ethiopians' in the glass windows with figures drawn most skilfully. Sir Richard Sapcote, who established his family in Huntingdonshire, was buried at Fotheringhay in the year 1477.

There are exceptionally good meadows next to Fotheringhay, and approaching from Oundle the settlement stands on the far bank, with a wooden bridge across the Nene. The fine castle is reasonably strong, with double ditches, and a very old, strong keep. The castle apartments are excellent. I understand that Catherine of Spain [*of Aragon*] spent a large sum on refurbishing it in recent years. The castle descended until recently to the dukes of York, from Edmund of Langley, son of Edward III.

The River Nene forms the boundary with Huntingdonshire as far along as Mr Sapcote's house at Elton, less than a mile from Fotheringhay. A knight by the name of Kirkham also lives a mile or so from Fotheringhay, although his house is some distance from the river.

Next I travelled back from Fotheringhay via Oundle to Lilford, where a gentleman called Elmes has an attractive manor house. The village lies beside the Nene, and I was told that there used to be a bridge across the river here. From there it was a mile upstream to Thorpe Waterville, and here I saw the ruined outer wall of the Watervilles' castle. Thrapston was more than a mile further; it belongs to Lord Mordaunt, so I was told, by joint inheritance with Brown the serjeant-at-law, and the son of Sir Wistan Brown. The bridge of eight arches across the Nene is a quarter-mile beyond Thrapston. On my journey from Fotheringhay to this point I kept the River Nene on my right hand side, but from here to Northampton it lay on my left hand, some distance away.

Right at the end of Thrapston Bridge stand the ruins of a very large hermitage, which was originally well built but has recently been closed

NORTHAMPTONSHIRE

down and had its roof removed. Close by, on the further bank from Thrapston, is a place called Islip, and about a mile beyond, though not beside the river, is the village and castle of Drayton, the most attractive house in this neighbourhood. Islip and Drayton both passed to Lord Mordaunt when the inheritance was divided. Drayton Castle was largely built by a man called Green, who came to prominence at the time of Richard II. The majority of his estate, including Green's Norton, he gave to his elder son, but Drayton and the rest of his lands went to the younger son. Later, Green's estate passed to two daughters, one of whom bequeathed her share to her own three daughters. Drayton passed by the female line to Stafford, earl of Wiltshire, and here he kept his household; he was the uncle of Edward, the late duke of Buckingham.

A ride of more than six miles brought me from Drayton to Finedon Bridge. This is a stone bridge across the attractive Kettering stream [*River Ise*], which a mile lower flows into the Nene near the valley below Wellingborough. About five miles further up [i.e. down] the Nene is another stone bridge, called Higham Bridge. The town of Higham Ferrers stands close by, five miles from Wellingborough. Wellingborough itself is a good, busy, market town about a quarter-mile from the Nene. In common with almost all the towns in Northamptonshire it is built of stone.

Wellingborough and Northampton are eight miles apart, and the country between them is entirely arable and pasture in open fields, with little or no woodland. The land between Oundle and Wellingborough is similar. On my way from Wellingborough I crossed two pleasant brooks, which flow down to the Nene in separate valleys. Almost half-way to Northampton I passed Castle Ashby more than a mile away on my left hand side. The castle which used to be here has been demolished entirely, and turned into an enclosure for cattle.

The town of Northampton stands on the north side of the River Nene, on the brow of a modest hill, which rises steadily from south to north. All the old buildings were of stone, but the new are of timber. The town wall has four gates, east, west, north and south; the east gate is the finest of them all. Outside the south gate is a good suburb, and another, smaller suburb outside the west gate. This contains a very attractive house, built of polished stone blocks. The castle stands next to the west gate. It has a large keep, and the rest of the precinct is very large, with earthen bulwarks in front of the castle gate.

There are seven parish churches within the walls of Northampton. The principal church is All Hallows, which is large and well built, and stands in the heart of the town. Dependent on it is a chapel of St Catharine, which lies in a graveyard within the town used by All Hallows parish for burial. I saw also the ruins of a large chapel outside the north gate; and in addition there are two parish churches in the suburbs. I saw the one in the west suburb as I rode over the west bridge. This bridge is well arched in stone, and crosses the River Nene before the Weedon stream has combined with it.

St Andrews, the former house of black monks, stood in the northern part of the town, close to the north gate. It was founded by Simon St Liz, the first earl of Northampton and Huntingdon. But he is not buried there, because he died and was buried in France. However, the second Earl Simon, and his son the third Earl Simon, were both buried at St Andrews, as well as a certain Verney, who was knighted at the battle of Northampton, and also an archbishop, who was buried under a flat slab in the chancel. The house of St James stands at the furthermost part of the western suburb, and is entirely surrounded by a fine, high, massive wall of stone blocks.

In the time of Henry VI a great battle was fought at Northampton, on the hill outside the south gate; and here there is an excellent cross, which, as I recall, is called the Queen's Cross. Many Welshmen were drowned in the Nene during the battle, and the casualties were buried either at Delapre or at St John's Hospital. This hospital was originally founded by an archdeacon of Northampton called William St Clare. At St John's they say that he was the brother of one of the Earls Simon, whom they call St Clair, but in documents I have always seen them called St Liz, not St Clair. This hospital stands inside the town wall, just up from the south gate. In the north side of the church is buried the Lady Margaret in a high tomb; and on the south side lies Elis Pouger, with an epitaph in French. The hospital of St Thomas lies outside the town, adjoining the west gate. The citizens of Northampton built it less than a century ago, and endowed it with some lands.

Of all the friaries that of the grey friars was the best built and the largest. It stood just beyond the principal market place, due almost directly north. Its site and precinct were city property, and so it was assumed that the citizens had founded it. Two members of the Salisbury family were buried in the grey friars; and I recall that someone told me that the daughter of one of them was the mother of Sir William Parr and his older brother. The black friars stood in the street where the horse market is kept each week. The white friars stood a little above the grey friars. The house of the Austin Friars stood on the west side of the street by the south gate, right next to St John's Hospital. It was believed that the Langfelds [*Longevilles*] of Buckinghamshire were its founders, and old Sir [?] Longeville was recently thought to be their descendant. Various members of the family were buried in its church, but I did not hear of any other noblemen buried there.

The headwater of the Nene rises a little above and to one side of the village of Guilsborough, and first forms itself into a valley there. Guilsborough is six miles almost directly due north of Northampton. The river touches a few villages on its way to Northampton.

The source of the Weedon stream, so far as I could gather from the inhabitants of Weedon, is at Fawsley, in Mr Knightley's pools; but it is also fed by springs in Badby pools, and by a brook which enters the stream a short distance below Weedon, on the further bank from where I was standing. Mr Knightley is a man of great possessions, and Fawsley is his principal house, although it is not on a particularly grand scale. Mr Newenham, who is a knight, lives a mile away from it. Fawsley pools are only about a mile from Charwelton, the source of the River Cherwell which flows to Banbury, and only a hill separates the sources of these two rivers. After Weedon the stream flows to Flore, a neighbouring village; then to Heyford village, two miles further, where is the principal seat of the Mantell family; and then another three miles to St Thomas's Bridge at Northampton, where it joins the Nene. Just as the Nene rises almost due north of the town, so the Weedon stream rises due west.

Weedon is a pleasant roadside place, on a level site, and is well known to carriers because it stands next to the famous road, which is commonly known by the local people as Watling Street. On this account the place is called Weedon on the Street. It has no market, and its parish church is as modest as the little town itself. But near the south side of the churchyard there is a fine chapel dedicated to St Werburgh, who had once been a nun at Weedon. The monastery which existed there in Bede's time was later destroyed by the Danes, and I could not easily find out when I was there whether there had been a monastery at Weedon since the conquest. The vicar told me that the place once belonged to the monastery of Bekharwik [*Bec-Hellouin*] in Normandy; and that after the alien priories of this French order lost their possessions in England, Henry VI granted the lordship of Weedon to Eton College near Windsor. Within living memory there was a courtyard surrounded by good buildings and St Werburgh's chapel within it; but now all that are to be seen on the south side of the chapel are large barns belonging to the lessee.

Towcester is seven miles from Weedon, and seven miles from Northampton, and the country between is flat cornland and pasture. John Farmer told me that certain ruins or ditches of a castle at Towcester are still visible. I must make further enquiries about this.

From Northampton I travelled a mile to Kingsthorpe; this is only a chapelry of St Peter's, Northampton, which is now a very poor church next to the castle – but Kingsthorpe is a well-endowed benefice. Beyond Kingsthorpe I rode past Moulton Park, which used to belong to Lord Vaulx, but now is the king's. It is enclosed by a stone wall, and provides a reasonable supply of wood. The only building in the park is a modest lodge. The earl of Warwick held three manors in Northamptonshire, of which two were Hanslope and Moulton.

My journey then took me across nine miles of open country, which produces good grass and corn, to the pleasant market town of Kettering. A quarter-mile before Kettering I rode across a wooden bridge over a small stream which originates and takes its name from a village a few miles away. And a little further I crossed by another wooden bridge a brook which takes its name from the village of Skerford [?], five miles away, from where it flows. This brook runs along the foot of the sloping ground on which Kettering stands. A little beyond the town in the Geddington direction I crossed another brook, which flows from Arthingworth, some six miles off; both sides of Kettering, therefore, are well watered. All three brooks meet in the meadows a little below Kettering.

Geddington is a pleasant but remote place two miles from Kettering. Through its centre flows the Arthingworth brook, which I crossed again here over a stone bridge. Then I continued a further four miles to another remote place called Weldon. The countryside here, in addition to a good supply of corn and grass, has a reasonable quantity of wood. Next to the main road and a short distance to the south of Weldon there is a good stone quarry, where large-scale excavations may be seen. Just outside Weldon I crossed a small brook, and saw there a fine chapel. Then I continued for two miles, past cornland, pasture and woods, to Deene.

NORTHAMPTONSHIRE

About the time of King John the lord of Deene manor was a man called Yve, and he paid a fixed rent to the abbot of Westminster for an estate which had formerly belonged to a priory there. This priory had been a cell of Westminster before its suppression. From Deene to Benefield is two long miles; here the ditch and ruins of an old castle are visible next to the west end of the parish church. Mr Brudenell told me that he had once read in an old royal document that its owner had been Bassingburn, or a similar name ending in -burn. The present owner is Zouche of Codnor. There is another castle at Braybrooke, on the River Welland. Its builder was a nobleman of the period named Braybrooke, and he obtained licence to fortify it. The present owner, who possesses a fine estate, is Mr Griffin.

From Deene I travelled three miles to Rockingham, mostly through woodland, though with some arable and pasture. Rockingham Castle occupies a commanding position on top of a hill, with a massive ditch, and further bulwarks outside the ditch. The castle's outer walls are still standing, including some strong towers. The keep is exceptionally fine and strong, but the apartments that lay within the castle bailey have been unroofed and are falling to ruin. One very notable feature of the castle walls is that they have battlements on both sides. If, therefore, the bailey were to be taken by attackers entering by either of the two great castle gates, the sentries on the walls could still defend the castle. I noticed that there is a strong tower in the bailey, which connects by a drawbridge across the dungeon ditch with the tower of the keep.

Below Rockingham Castle lies a large valley, which produces abundant corn and grass. According to the old perambulation Rockingham Forest is about twenty miles long, and in some places its width extends to four or five miles, although elsewhere it is less. There are several lodges for the keepers of its fallow deer. It is well-wooded, but contains also good arable and pasture land. Benefield Laund is extensive, and provides good coursing. It lies within the forest, three miles from Benefield itself, and does not belong to the village.

Three miles of woodland and pasture separate Rockingham from Pipewell, where the abbey used to be. There are good buildings here. Four miles from Pipewell is a large royal park where the king hunted.

Harringworth is three miles from Deene, over arable, grass and some woodland. Lord Zouche has an excellent manor house there, built in the village like a castle, next to the parish church. Its outer court is completely ruined, except for a large portion of the gatehouse and adjacent front wall, which are still standing. The inner part of the house is reasonably well maintained, and is surrounded by a ditch. The walls of the inner courtyard are battlemented in some places. Within this courtyard is a fine chapel, which contains the body of one of the Zouche family, a large flat slab marking the place of his burial. Beside the manor house is a park, which contains a fine lodge. I heard it said that the Zouche family have possessed this house for a long time, and reckon it to be one of their foremost seats. *cont. p. 212* [**1541:** *1/3-13*]

KING'S CLIFFE PARK is enclosed in part by a stone wall, and in part by a pale; it is three miles from Deene. I travelled from Deene for five or six miles, through partly open and partly wooded country, to Collyweston. Almost half-way along, and four miles from Stamford, I passed on my right hand side the former priory of black canons called Fineshade. There used to be a castle here known as Hely [*Hymel*], which belonged to the Engayne family. They lived in this castle until it happened that one of the family, having no children of his own, founded a priory there, to which he granted land in the vicinity. As a result the castle was demolished in order to build the priory, so that now almost no evidence survives that there was ever a castle on the site.

A house at Collyweston was begun by Lord Cromwell, but most of it has been built anew by Lady Margaret, the mother of Henry VII. Moneybags still survive there in the chapel and elsewhere. *cont. p. 221* [**1541:** *1/22*]

FROM STAMFORD TO COLLYWESTON two-and-a-half miles over open country. From Collyweston to Deene six miles, mostly over open arable and grassland. From Deene to Fotheringhay six miles, mostly through woodland in part of Rockingham Forest. From Fotheringhay to Oundle (a market town) two miles. From there through Thorpe Waterville to the village, where the king dined in a modest house, four or five miles, entirely over open ground, with good arable, and grassland. From there across similar country, nine miles to Leighton [*Bromswold*] in Huntingdonshire, a further eight miles to Higham Ferrers, and six miles to the place where Mr St John lives, in an extremely pleasant moated manor house; and it was here that I saw an old tomb with an effigy in the chancel wall of the parish church. Some people think that it was a member of the Breusis or Brewsis family, who were once owners of that manor. *cont. p. 2* [**1541:** 1/99]

From Bicester I rode the seven miles to Brackley. My journey took me through very fertile country, with good arable and grass, and some woodland, many rabbits, but little enclosed ground. I entered Brackley across a small stone bridge in a valley. It had one arch, and through this flows the River Ouse – here only a small stream. From this bridge the main street of the town climbs up on to a pleasant hill, and at the top another street turns eastwards to St Peter's, the principal church of the town.

To judge from the old ruins Brackley used to have many streets in it, of considerable size. From St James's church at the south end to St Leonard's chapel the town was built up for half a mile. The circuit of the town must have been almost two miles. It flourished during the Saxon period but was destroyed by the Danes. It flourished again after the conquest, when it became a staple for wool and was granted mayoral privileges; these the present poor town still retains.

There used to be a fine castle at the south-west end of the town on the left bank of the stream. Its site and the hill on which it stood are still plainly visible, and indeed are called Castle Hill. But no portion of standing masonry can now be seen. Close to this hill on its western side are two small but pleasant low-lying meadows known as the Fish Weirs, and it is very likely that they were once fishponds. There used to be several rows of houses in the vicinity of the castle, but they are now completely demolished.

Of the three fine stone crosses in the town, the one near the south end has recently been thrown down by thieves in search of treasure. There is another at the west end of St James's church. And the third, which is very old, beautiful and lavish, stands in the middle part of the High Street. It includes several niches, which contain effigies of ladies, and men in armour, and it is said by some that it was made by the staplers of Brackley; but I am inclined to believe that it was the work of some noble landowner in the town.

At the south end of the town there stands an ancient church, which is a chapel of ease to St James's. It has a fine chapel or aisle on the south side of the chancel, and the window surrounds of this chapel contain stone effigies of figures holding woolsacks in their hands, as a sign that it was built by the staplers.

The church of St James and St John stands in the centre of the town. It was formerly collegiate, with an almshouse or hospital, but this has been suppressed, and given with its lands to Magdalen College. There are a number of noblemen and noblewomen's tombs in the sanctuary of this church, as follows: two noblemen in one tomb, with a lion rampant and fleurs-de-lys on their shields; on the south side in the wall a nobleman whose arms are ten golden besants on a red field; and at his feet another with a lion rampant on his shield; Robert Holland, who died in the year 1373, lies there also, alongside his wife Maud; and another nobleman and his wife, whose arms are variegated gold and red. Someone told me that one of the Lords Lovell has recently been identified as the founder of this house, and that it was he who granted it to Magdalen College.

St Peter's church, the principal church of the town, and the mother church of the whole Brackley deanery, is situated on the eastern side of the town. I saw no tomb or great antiquity in the church, but in the churchyard there is the effigy of a priest in his vestments. This priest was a vicar of Brackley who had been buried alive there on the orders of one of the lords of the town. This vicar, it is said, incurred the lord's displeasure because he exacted a horse as payment for a burial. The lord, however, so the story goes, went to Rome for absolution, and showed great remorse. The living of St Peter's was appropriated by Leicester Abbey, who endowed it with a vicarage.

There are two good springs a little to the WNW of St Peter's church. One is called St Rumold's Well, because it is said that within a few days of his birth the saint preached there. The other is just called Well. These two springs are less than a stone's throw apart, and a small stream flows from each of them, which immediately combine into one. The flow of water is not so strong as it has been, since it is said that in the past it used to drive a cutler's mill which was there. There is also a good spring in the town's high street, out of which a trickle of water flows.

During Richard III's reign Lord Lovell was the owner of Brackley, but his estate was confiscated by Henry VII, and the manor of Brackley, as well as half the land around it, was given to Stanley, earl of Derby, or to his son.

The River Ise, or Ouse, which flows past the south end of Brackley, rises just above Steane, a mile-and-a-half west of the town. Here Lord Sannes has a manor house, which was once Lord Morley's.

Distances from Brackley: Buckingham, 5 miles; Northampton, 14 miles

(7 to Towcester and 7 on to Northampton); Chipping Norton, 14 long miles (6 to Deddington and 8 on to Chipping Norton – there used to be a castle at Deddington, which is in Oxfordshire); Banbury, 7 miles. Seven miles to Brackley [?*Banbury*], seven miles to Brailes, seven miles to Campden and seven miles to Hailes (Campden is a market town in Gloucestershire).

Brackley market, which used to be kept on Wednesdays, has been abandoned. The town lies in the county of Northamptonshire, which extends one mile further south as far as Aynho, Aynho is the last village in Northamptonshire in this direction. Two miles from Brackley there used to be a house of white monks.

Leaving Brackley I rode to King's Sutton, entirely across open arable and grassland. The spire of Sutton church is a fine piece of work. St Rumold was born in this parish, but the chapel dedicated to him, which stood in the meadows about a mile from the village, has recently been robbed of its stone and demolished. A certain Westhaul, who provided a new roof for Sutton church, is buried there in a tomb in a chapel on the south side. *cont. p. 294* [**1543:** 2/35-8]

Malory told me that there used to be a collegiate church at Cotterstock, which is almost halfway between Fotheringhay and Oundle, a short way off to the right when coming from Fotheringhay. The college consisted of a master, three priests and three other clergy. The living of Cotterstock was appropriated to it, as well as a nice estate. I heard that it was originally founded by a certain Gifford, but someone called Nores, who claimed to be its founder, has recently taken its lands away from it, leaving only the benefice in its possession. [2/30]

Sir Davy Philippes, who is buried in a parish church near the bridge gate at Stanford on the Hille [*Stamford Baron, the portion of Stamford formerly in Northamptonshire*], had an attractive manor house, so I am told, at Thorne [?*Thornhaugh*], two or three miles from Stamford. A number of protégés and gentlemen of the Lady Margaret's retinue (the present king's grandmother) used to stay there with him at various times.

The house at Collyweston, it is sometimes said, was originally started by a gentleman whose coat of arms included three silver bells on a black field; and he, so they say, was at first a parish priest, either of Collyweston itself or somewhere nearby. Lord Cromwell and Lady Margaret, Henry VII's mother, both added to the house.

I have heard that Edmund of Langley, the son of Edward [*III*], spent a large sum on Fotheringhay Castle, and that his son enlarged the college there which he had started. [4/91-2]

At the present time there are two branches of the Tresham family in Northamptonshire. The seat of the elder brother is now usually at Rushton near Kettering, although he generally calls himself Tresham of Lyveden. Lyveden is two miles from Oundle, and Tresham owns an estate there worth £200 annually; part of the old manor house is still standing, amid fine meadowland. He also owns a manor and house at Sywell, three or four miles north of Northampton. On one occasion a certain William Tresham, who owned this estate, was on his way from Northampton to Sywell, and while saying his mattins he was cruelly killed by two servants of Lord Grey of Ruthin, named Salisbury and Glyn of Wales, with a group of accomplices. By chance William had his own retinue of servants following a half-mile behind him, who, when they heard the commotion, came and cut off both ends of the spear lodged in his body, and took him back to Northampton. But when the shaft had been pulled out there he died.

The other Tresham, of Newton, two miles from Rushton, is descended from a younger brother called Henry, who married the heiress of Mulshos. This Henry was either the grandfather or the great-grandfather of the present Tresham of Newton, and also of Doctor Tresham of Oxford. Tresham of Newton's estate has an annual value of about £100. [4/97-8]

There are the ruins of a castle, or some important house, in Lord Zouche's park in Northamptonshire. The town of Oundle is virtually surrounded by the River Nene, and there are two bridges there. In the meadows next to the town of Northampton there is a large round hill which appears to be a military earthwork; the name Clifford is associated with it. Benefield Castle, which was never particularly large, has been entirely razed to the ground. I gather that it belonged to the Bassingbournes, and then passed to one of the Zouche family. [4/118, 122, 123]

Mr Paynell told me that on the Buckinghamshire side of Brackley he saw clear evidence that the town had once been walled, and that there were remains of the foundations of semi-circular gates and towers in the wall. (I searched carefully, but could find no sign of either walls or ditches.) He also said that there had been a castle, and that its ditches and mounds are still visible. (I did see the castle site.) Furthermore he said that there had been several churches in it, and that until recently there was a house of crutched friars, in which was buried an important gentleman named Neville. He also told me that one of the Nevilles once killed a priest in Brackley church, and buried him still in his clerical robes; and that then Neville captured another priest there and buried him alive. Much information about occurrences in that church, according to Mr Paynell, were to be found in an old book which he saw in the quire or vestry of Brackley church. [5/224]

NORTHUMBERLAND

No part of Leland's account of Northumberland can be recognised as proper itinerary, and so we have no idea of the route which he followed when he visited the county. It is likely, however, that he passed through in 1538 – the description of this journey is missing after Kendal and before Byland Abbey, but there are substantial notes on Cumbria and Hadrian's Wall, as well as on Northumberland, to suggest that he explored the northern counties at this time. He may have returned to Newcastle in 1541, but the itinerary as we have it ventures no further north than Gateshead. What has survived are substantial notes on the county, organised by type of monument and feature, and in part derived from two informants, Dr Robert Davell and the vicar of Corbridge. These notes, although less detailed than we might wish, nevertheless are quite wide-ranging geographically, and cover most topics of interest to Leland on his travels. We may spot the perceptive fieldworker reaching a very sensible conclusion when he noted that Hadrian's Wall had been robbed and destroyed more in populous places than in areas of wasteland.

The walls of Newcastle were completed during the reign of Edward III. The principal parish church of Newcastle, St Nicholas, is built right on the Pictish wall [Hadrian's Wall] itself. The house of grey friars in Newcastle was founded by the Cairluelle [Carlell] family, who were originally merchants in the town, but later acquired property. Their estates have now passed by the female line to the Thirgills [?Thirkilde] of the Yorkshire Wolds.

The black friars' house was founded by two knights, Sir Peter and Sir Nicholas Scott, father and son; but the site was given by three sisters. The lands of the Scotts, who also began as merchants, passed by daughters to Heron of Ford, to Denton, and to another. Eshott Castle, near Felton, belonged to the Scotts, but now it is almost demolished.

The house of white friars was founded by Thornton, who was first a merchant and then a man of property. His lands descended to Lord Lumley, and practically all the fine Lumley estate came from Thornton. Whitton in Northumberland, the Isle in the bishopric of Durham, and also Lulworth all belonged to Thornton. Lumley's rise to the peerage came about through his marriage to an illegitimate daughter of Edward IV. Thomas Lumley, the later Lord Lumley, killed the wealthy Thornton's bastard son in the ditch at Windsor Castle. The Thornton who was mayor of Newcastle was born at Whitton. He purchased land with an annual value of nearly £600 and died a remarkably rich man. One theory about his wealth was that it was derived from capturing silver ore on the high sea.

The Austin friary was founded by Lord Ross; there are three or four fine towers in their building. The Crutched friars' house, also known as Wall Knoll, was founded by Laurence Acton, a former mayor of Newcastle. The Acton estate passed to Lumley along with that of the Thorntons. [4/117-18]

I learned from Dr Davell that the mouths of the Rivers Blyth and Wansbeck are not much more than three miles apart, and that the land which separates them is sometimes called Bedlingtonshire. Bedlington is the name of the parish church there, which has a number of dependent villages and hamlets. Coquet Island stands on a very good seam of sea-coal, and at low tide men dig for it on the seashore by the cliffs, with very good reward. Certain islands adjoin the Farne Islands which are larger than Farne itself, but they are uninhabited. A kind of large bird, called St Cuthbert's birds, breed on them, and puffins may be found there breeding in the rocky cliffs. Puffins have grey feathers like ducks, and a ring around their necks, but they are smaller than ducks and do not have coloured feathers. [4/123]

The earl of Northumberland's [titles and estates:] Lord of the honours of Cockermouth and Petworth; Lords Percy, Lucy, Poyninges, Fitzpayne, Brian. Cockermouth came via Lucy, Petworth through a royal grant. Fitzpayne's and Brian's estates passed to Poyninges, and all three were inherited by Percy. He has castles and manors at Cockermouth in Cumberland (worth annually £700); Alnwick, Warkworth, Langley and Prudhoe Castles in Northumberland; the manor of Rothbury on the Coquet seven miles above Alnwick, and here there is a town similar to Corbridge; the manor of Corbridge also, where may still be seen much evidence of buildings of squared masonry; the manor of Chatton on the River Till one mile from Chillingham. [5/49]

At Kyloe, which is a manor of the bishop of Durham not far from Norham, in the early years of Henry VIII's reign, was found between two stones the buckles of a military belt, with tips and bars of pure gold, a pommel and cross for a golden sword, and golden buckles and tips for spurs. Dr Ruthall had some of them. [5/55]

The following information I learned from the vicar or parson of Corbridge at Newcastle.

Corbridge is about eleven miles from Newcastle. But from Durham by the most direct route it is not more than sixteen or eighteen miles. The town, which at present is very modestly built up, lies on the same bank of the Tyne as Newcastle. Corbridge church is dedicated to St Andrew, and the living, which was once appropriated by Tynemouth Priory, later passed by exchange to Carlisle. The names survive of several streets which formerly existed in the town, and are recalled by the older inhabitants; much evidence of old buildings may still be found there, as well as Roman coins.

The stone bridge which now crosses the Tyne at Corbridge is large, but has been built a little downstream of the old bridge. Clear evidence of the site of the old bridge is still visible, and nearby a pleasant stream flows down into the Tyne close to the town and on the same bank. It is my belief that this stream is called the Corve, even though the name is not used locally, and that the town is named after it. Beside this stream and among the ruins of the old town is a place called Colecester, on the site of a former fortress or castle. Local people tell a story about a giant called Yoton, who they say used to live there. In the book called the Life of St Oswin the Martyr, so far as I can make out, Corbridge is always written as Colebridge.

As I recall, there is no bridge over the Tyne between Newcastle and Corbridge. But at the earl of Westmorland's castle at [Bywell], three miles downstream from Corbridge, the ruins of stone arches of a bridge across the Tyne may still be seen. There is a bridge on the Tyne at Chipchase.

A man named Monboucher had a large estate in Northumberland, and Dr Davell told me that the hospital in Newcastle still owns lands given by him. The Rudhams, too, had extensive estates in Northumberland, around the River Till, until a certain member of the family, who had married one of Humframville's [Umfraville's] daughters, killed a man of standing, and in consequence forfeited land with an annual value of £400. As a result the present Rudham of Northumberland is a man of moderate means. The Northamptonshire family of Hazlerigg also has an estate in Northumberland, with an annual value of £50. It includes an attractive tower at Eslington, and this at present is occupied by one of the Collingwoods, who manages the Haslerigg lands.

The River Team rises in the south-west, ten miles inland, and flows into the Tyne about a mile above Gateshead, not far below Ravensworth Castle. The ruins of Tarset Castle, which are close to the North Tyne in Northumberland, now belong to Lord Borow.

During Edward IV's reign a particularly uncouth member of the Gray family of Northumberland was suspected of having committed adultery with the queen of Scotland. When a Scots gentleman made this accusation Gray is said to have gone to Edinburgh with a band of one thousand men, and thrown down his gauntlet to challenge his accuser to fight in the tilting-lists. Although he left without the contest taking place, it was nevertheless assumed that the accusation against him had been well-founded.

The estate of the Harbottle family in Northumberland, which had an annual value of £200, has recently passed to two daughters. One married Sir Thomas Percy, who was hanged at Tyburn for treason. The other married into the Cheshire family of Fitton. Dr Davell told me that the boundary of the see of Durham extends up the Tyne [he says Trent] above the confluence of the Derwent, as far as the parish of Ryton.

There is a tower or small castle at Bowes, on Watling Street.

The Davells descend from a Norman family, and have been great landowners in northern England. But during Edward II's reign their fortunes declined and fell to ruin. This was because the two heads of the family, Sir Loson Davell and Sir Hugh Davell (whom Dr Davell told me were both barons, although I was not convinced by his evidence), sided with Thomas, duke of Lancaster and the barons, against Edward II and Piers Gaveston. As a result the Davell estate was confiscated and split up. Four or five younger brothers survived, and later obtained moderate estates; indeed one of their descendants spent £100 a year from his Nottinghamshire estate merely on falconry and hunting. But the present-day Davell gentry are of modest means. Their principal seat and estate used to be in the Pontefract area of Yorkshire, but the lands of the Gascoignes, and the Truewhit or Tyrwhitt family of Lincolnshire, also belonged to them. I understand that the name of the Davell's original seat in Normandy still survives, in the Alençon region.

Roger Thornton was the richest merchant ever to dwell in Newcastle. He lived in the time of Edward IV, and built St Katharine's Chapel, the town hall, and an almshouse for poor men, which he sited next to Sandhill Gate within the town, a little below Newcastle Bridge and right on the bank of the Tyne. His daughter and heiress married into the Lumley family, and greatly increased their possessions; the island [?] and almost all the land they own in Yorkshire and Northumberland, was inherited from Thornton.

Another rich Newcastle merchant, John Ward, established a hospital for twelve poor men and twelve poor women next to the Austin friars in Newcastle. And a certain Christopher Brigham, also a Newcastle merchant, has recently built a small hospital by the grey friars in the town.

The walls of Newcastle are said to have been started during the reign of Edward I, and the reason for their building has been reported as follows: A rich and important Newcastle man was captured by the Scots in the town itself. He was taken prisoner and ransomed for a large sum of money. On his return home he started to build a wall along the bank of the River Tyne from Sandhill Gate to

Pandon Gate, and continued it further to the tower next to the Austin friary. The remaining merchants of the town, seeing how much progress this one man had made, set their helping hands to the task; they continued until the entire town was protected by a strong wall, and it was finished, I was told, during the reign of Edward III. The strength and magnificence of Newcastle's wall far exceeds all the city walls of England, and of most of the towns of Europe.

The penultimate prior of Durham, Prior Castle, built up from the foundations the defensive tower on Lindisfarne. The site had previously been occupied by a chapel and poorhouse. At Ovingham, on the Tyne opposite Prudhoe, there was a canonry, occupied by a master and three canons, as a cell of Hexham. Umfraville granted the living of Ovingham to Hexham on condition that they should place canons there.

Morley of Morpeth was once the owner of Warkworth Castle, at the mouth of the River Coquet. Dr Davell told me that Anthony Bek either built or rebuilt Kensington, and gave it to a king or prince. He also built Durham Place in London.

[*Hadrian's Wall:*] ... from there it passes within less than a mile of Newcastle, and then turns upwards towards Tynemouth. Dr Davell told me that the church of St Nicholas, Newcastle, stands on the Pictish Wall. On the waste ground between Thirlwall and the North Tyne substantial portions of the wall are still standing. It was built of squared stone blocks, and these can still be seen. But notice that in those areas along the wall which are most thickly populated, there it survives least of all, because the stone from the wall has been used in buildings. On the further side, facing the Picts, the wall was strengthened with a ditch. In addition to the stone wall traces survive in very many places of a wall built of turf which lay a bow-shot on this side of the stone wall; but there is no good evidence that it was made in as complete a fashion as the stone wall.

[*The course of Hadrian's Wall:*] From Bowness to Burgh by Sands about four miles, and from there it goes within a half-mile of Carlisle, and even less on the north side. It crosses the Eden three-quarters of a mile below Carlisle, and continues to Tarraby, a small village one mile from Carlisle. Then it runs through the barony of Linstock, and through Gilsland along the northern side of the River Irthing. It passes a quarter-mile from Lanercost Abbey [*i.e. Priory*], then three miles above Lanercost it crosses the Irthing, and then a small stream called Polt Ross – this marks the boundary between Gilsland in Cumberland and South Tynedale in Northumberland. Next it comes to Thirlwall Castle on the South Tyne, and from there straight along South Tynedale, not far from the great ruined castle of Carvoran, which is near Thirlwall. Then it crosses the North Tyne, and so runs directly eastwards through the head [?] of Northumberland.

There is a legend that Oswald won a battle at Hazeldean, which is two miles east of St Oswald's Ash; and that Hazeldean is the place which Bede calls Heavenfield. The local people still find small wooden crosses in the ground there.

In South Tynedale, apart from the part next to Hexhamshire and part in the south or south-east of Tynedale, there is only one parish church, and that is called Haltwhistle. There are also some chapels-of-ease, including one called Whitechapel which is not far from Willington. One of the holy men called Aidan is buried there, along with other holy men in the chapel-yard. In North Tynedale likewise there is a single parish church. It is called Simonsburn, and it too has several chapels. I have since been told that Simonsburn itself lies in South Tynedale, and that in North Tynedale there is only a chapel at Bellingham, dependent on Simonsburn.

In Redesdale there are only three parish churches. Elsdon is the most important, and the others are Holystone [*actually in Coquetdale*] and Corsenside. These parishes are frequented by the outriding men or thieves of the English border country. The source of the River Rede lies within three miles of the Scottish border. It rises in the north, and flows to the south-west through Redesdale until it joins the northern arm of the Tyne a little below Bellingham. Bellingham itself is situated a little distance from the North Tyne, and is ten miles from Hexham. The River North Tyne rises directly due north and flows almost straight to the north [*i.e. south*] until it joins the South Tyne. Some people are of the belief that either at Holystone, or in the area of the River Coquet, three thousand christenings took place on a single day, in the time of the early Saxon church. The River Coquet, which for a distance of several miles divides Coquetdale and Redesdale, flows past Harbottle, where there is a good castle, and then to the former stone bridge, now fallen, called Linne Briggs. There have been many buildings in that area, but now it is deserted.

[*Market towns in Northumberland:*] Newcastle; Hexham; Alnwick; Berwick. Bamburgh is no longer a market town. Morpeth is a market town twelve long miles from Newcastle. A pleasant river called the Wansbeck flows beside the town, and its principal church stands on the nearer side. Also on this side is the fine castle sited on a hill, which like the town belongs to Lord Dacres of Gilsland. Morpeth is a long town with paved streets and reasonably well-built low houses. It is a far more attractive place than Alnwick.

Castles in Northumberland: Newcastle. Chipchase is a pleasant place with a castle, close to the east bank of the River North Tyne. This bank marks the boundary between Tynedale and Northumberland, for although in some respects Tynedale belongs to Northumberland, in other ways it is autonomous. Tynemouth Abbey was at one time used as a castle. [*?Seaton*] Delaval Castle is four miles from Tynemouth and less than a mile from the coast. Otterburn Castle stands on the Otter Burn in Redesdale, which lies close to North Tynedale. There are the ruins of a castle belonging to Lord Borow at Mitford, on the south bank of the Wansbeck, four miles above Morpeth. It was broken down by the king, because a certain Sir Gilbert Middleton had robbed a cardinal on his way from Scotland, and had fled to his castle at Mitford.

Morpeth Castle stands next to the town, and is well maintained by its owner, Lord Dacres, to whom the town also belongs. The castle is set on a high hill surrounded by dense woodland. Widdrington Castle, which belongs to the Widdrington family, stands less than a half-mile from the coast, quite close to

NORTHUMBERLAND

Coquet Island. A small stream flows on the north side of the castle, and then into the sea on its own. There is also a small village called Widdrington.

Warkworth Castle stands on the south bank of the River Coquet. It is well maintained and large. It used to belong to the Earl of Northumberland. It is built on a high hill about a mile from the sea, and is for the most past surrounded by the river. There is a pleasant town at Warkworth, with a stone bridge at the end of it on which a tower is built. Beyond the bridge is Bamburghshire.

Alnwick Castle. Howick is a small tower belonging to the [?Grey family] a mile from the coast. Two miles beyond Howick and right on the coast is Dunstanburgh. It stands on a high crag, and is more than a half-mile in circumference. It used to contain many buildings, and nearby is a strong [?tower, i.e. Lilburn Tower]. Embleton lies between Dunstanburgh and Bamburgh; it is a mile from the coast and a mile from Dunstanburgh. Bamburgh has been a great castle of massive size, and one of the strongest in the region. Haggerston is a tower on the south bank of the River Lindis [South Low]. Chillingham Castle belongs to Sir Edward Grey, whose wife was formerly married to Sir Robert Heldercar. Ford Castle in Glendale stands on the east bank of the Till. It is quite strong, but in disrepair. Etal Castle occupies a flat site close to the east bank of the Till; it belongs to the earl of Rutland. Castle Heaton, two miles downstream from Etal, lies on the west side of the Till. It belongs to Sir Edward Grey, and was badly damaged by the Scots at the battle of Flodden Field. Wark Castle, with a pleasant town, lies on the south side of the Tweed. Norham Castle is also on the south side, and Berwick is on the north side.

Hutton is a fine castle in the centre of Northumberland reckoned across its width. It is four or five miles due north of the tower at Fenwick, and is the oldest house of the Swinburne family. Wallington Castle is two miles east of Houghton. It is the principal seat of the Fenwicks, and now belongs to Sir John Fenwick.

Religious houses in Northumberland: Bolton, a house of canons in Coquetdale [actually on the Aln], which is usually called Glendale; it was founded by Lord Rose. Holystone, a nunnery in Redesdale between Haydon Bridge and Hexham [actually Holystone is in Coquetdale, nowhere near Hexham]. Hexham. Lambley, a nunnery on the South Tyne. Brinkburn Priory on the Coquet, for Augustinian canons; the Lisles were the most likely founders, or the Feltons before the Lisles. Holy Island, for monks. Bamburgh, a cell of St Oswald's. Newminster. Farne. Coquet, a cell of Tynemouth. Tynemouth. Blanchland, for white canons. Because it stands on the further side of the Derwent it falls in Northumberland. The low-lying country between the mouths of the Wear and the Derwent is known as Wyralshire. The larger portion of Chester-le-Street lies in Wyrale. On the site of St Edmund's Hospital at Gateshead in Wyrale there used to be a monastery, I have been told; in all probability it is the one mentioned by Bede.

Rivers of Northumberland: Derwent; Tyne; Pont; Wansbeck; Aln; Wreigh. The Team is a small river which flows into the Tyne on its south bank a mile above Newcastle. The Cong Burn passes Lanchester before it reaches Chester-le-Street. Lanchester is six miles west of Chester. At or close to Chester the Heddle Brook [*?Humble Burn*] joins Cong Burn. The Coquet, or Conke, rises in somewhat marshy, heather-covered country. The mainstream of the Till is really the River Breamish; and it is called this at its source and for a certain distance. But further downstream it loses this name and is known as the Till. The River Glen rises in the Cheviot Hills, and flows in Glendale as far as Newton village [*Kirknewton*], where there is a tower. There is a small brook called the Boubent [*Bowmont*] Water, which flows nine miles from Scotland to the Glen at Lanton village; a ruined tower lies a mile from Lanton. At Coupland, one mile downstream the Glen, the river divides and forms islets; but it is soon reunited, and flows into the Till two miles above Ford Castle.

The course of the Till is thus: it rises in the Cheviot Hills, flows into Glendale to a castle called Chillingham, which is six miles from Cheviot; then eight miles to Ford Castle; then a mile downstream to Etal Castle, which lies on a stone bridge on the east bank; three-and-a-half miles to Castle Heaton on the west bank; two miles to Twizel Bridge, which is of a single arch, but large and strong, and here is a small settlement and a tower; and so not a half-mile to a small village on the east bank called Horncliffe, where the Till flows into the Tweed. Horncliffe is a half-mile above Norham [*Horncliffe lies below Norham, and not at the Till's confluence*].

The River Tweed rises in Tweeddale in Scotland, so I am told, at a town called Peebles, and flows through Ettrick Forest and Tynedale [*?Tweeddale*], both in Scotland; the inhabitants of this area continually plunder and rob Glendale and Bamburghshire. At the point where a small stream called the Redden Burn, which divides England on the east from Scotland on the west, flows into it, the Tweed first touches English soil and begins to mark the boundary with Scotland. A good mile below this point is a small village called Carham, where two canons occupy a cell of Kirkham Priory in Yorkshire. Carham has a small tower for defence against the Scots. Then a mile or more to Wark Castle, which is a reasonably strong fortress; then to a peel tower at Cornhill, two miles further. This lies opposite Coldstream on the Scottish bank, where there is a nunnery. Then it is three miles to Norham Castle, where there is also quite a good town. From here it is six miles to Berwick, which stands a little way to the north side of the Tweed. On the southern bank of the river by the bridge lies Tweedmouth, like a suburb to Berwick.

[*Woodland in Northumberland:*] I have been told that the only forest in Northumberland is the Cheviot, and this, it is said, extends for twenty miles. It has a great deal of small wood, and some oak, but the ground is overgrown with heather, and in places with moss. It has a great abundance of red and roe deer. The forest of Loughes lies in Tyndale, on the west side of the North Tyne, in fact between the two Tyne rivers. There is little woodland between Newcastle and Tynemouth, or between Newcastle and Morpeth, but between Morpeth

NORTHUMBERLAND 275

and Alnwick there is a good supply of wood in some places and many parks. [*The route from Newcastle to Berwick is as follows:*] Newcastle to Morpeth, twelve miles; Morpeth to Alnwick, twelve long miles; Alnwick to Berwick, twenty miles. Wood is in short supply between Alnwick and Berwick.

Hexham is fourteen miles from Newcastle, and in that direction there is little woodland, except in a few places. Hexham, which is the market town for South Tynedale, is a liberty in its own right, and is not considered to lie within Tynedale. Hexham liberty extends ten miles in a south-westerly direction.

In Bamburghshire, which is part of Northumberland, there is little or no woodland; and in Redesdale wood is not abundant. Glendale has woodland here and there, and the inhabitants have a good supply from Cheviot. But the great wood of Cheviot has now been plundered, and only crooked old trees and shrubs remain. From Redden Burn along the Tweed to Berwick there is virtually no woodland, but coal is dug for fuel at Murton, a small village in Glendale, two miles from Berwick. Glendale extends along the Tweed from Redden Burn to Tweedmouth, which lies within it. Holy Islandshire includes all the coastline from Haggerston to Beal, and so down to Bamburgh. [5/56-68]

Tyne Bridge at Newcastle has ten arches, with strong defences, a tower on the bridge and a gate at the end of the bridge. Turning right over the bridge towards the quay there is a town chapel with a poorhouse. Then there are some houses with a water gate, a square building which serves as a town hall, and a chapel, as I recall. Then an extremely strong wall runs along the harbour side to Sandgate on the Tynemouth road, and from there to Pandon Gate the wall has five towers. Close to this gate a mill is worked by the Deene Water, which flows through the wall and is crossed by a small arched bridge. In this area the Trinitarian friary stood. Between Pandon Gate and Pilgrim Gate there are fifteen towers, and a further eight round to Newgate. The house of the Observant friars stood next to Pandon Gate, and was a very fine building. Further down the same street and on the opposite side, a little way up a lane, stood the Austin friary.

After Newgate comes Westgate, which is exceptionally strong, with four guardhouses and an iron gate with thirteen towers. The fine house of the black friars stood between Newgate and Westgate, and outside their house and the town wall is a walled park with a lodge. The water of both the Deene streams derives from the coal pits at Cowhill or Cowmore [?*Cow Moor, part of Town Moor*] a half-mile outside Newcastle. The Nuns' Deene is crossed by two bridges, and flows towards Pilgrim Gate on its way down to the Tyne. From Westgate to the bank of the Tyne the town wall has sixteen [*towers*], some almost round, the others square. In this area I saw a hospital, and then the white friars, whose garden extended almost to the Tyne. Five conduit heads supply Newcastle with fresh water. [5/126]

There used to be a house of Trinitarian friars at Berwick, but Anthony Bek, bishop of Durham, destroyed it. The master of this house at the time of its destruction was a certain William Wakefield, and he came to Newcastle where, with help from the two brothers, William and Lawrence Acton, he built a house of the Trinitarian order within the town of Newcastle, and himself became its first master. [5/145]

NOTTINGHAMSHIRE

*L*ELAND EXPLORED *north Nottinghamshire on his way back from his 1538 tour of the northern counties. The account of this journey is more jumbled and less of a travelogue than the later itineraries, but the Nottinghamshire portion includes some interesting material, such as the method of crossing the Trent at Hoveringham – Leland went in the ferry-boat, but his horse had to wade across the ford. Three years later, on the north-eastern itinerary, he returned to the county, clipping the northern tip on his outward journey, and travelling back down from Blyth to Worksop, and through Sherwood Forest to Nottingham. The description of Nottingham, which obviously impressed him, is quite long and detailed, and might have been longer if the 'small piece of paper' to which he refers had survived.*

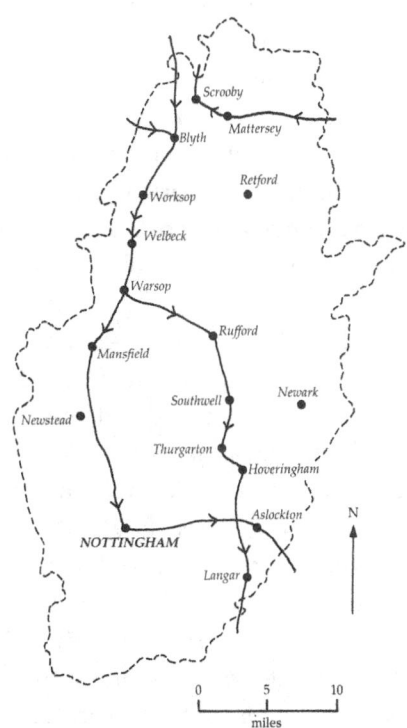

BLYTH IS A MARKET TOWN on the small River Blyth, four miles beyond Worksop on the way to Doncaster. The source of the River Blyth is a marsh five miles from Worksop, to which it then flows, then to Blyth the market town, and then into the River Don [*i.e. Idle*]. It is not called the Blyth along the whole length from its source, but only in the central portion, between Radford (or Worksop) and Blyth town. Before this little river reaches Worksop it is joined by a pleasant brook. Three miles beyond the town of Blyth, and within its parish, is the market town of Bawtry; so there are two market towns in the one parish. Not far beyond Bawtry in the Doncaster direction lies the boundary between Nottinghamshire and Yorkshire, as there is a market town called Tickhill with a friary and a ruinous castle two miles beyond Bawtry, and this lies in Yorkshire. Documents at Blyth Abbey suggest that at about the time of William the Conqueror there was a castle at Blyth, which was called in Latin 'Blida'. I think that it stood near the abbey, or else the abbey was built on the actual castle site. A Norman by the name of Roger de Builli founded Blyth Abbey around the time of William the Conqueror.

Mansfield is a Nottinghamshire market town in the king's possession. It lies in Sherwood Forest on the highway from Rotherham to Nottingham. Nottingham is a large market town, and the town of Newark upon Trent also has a good market. Worksop was made a market town more than thirty years ago. At Retford a good house, or More Hall, has recently been built; it is a good market town, sometimes called Redford, which lies within five miles of the bank of the River Trent. In fact there are two Retfords. The smaller is called West Retford, and East Retford is the other, which is a market town as large as Rotherham, and has a church which is almost as attractive. There is only one bridge across the river, and this divides the two towns. Retford has suffered a fire, but both parts of it have subsequently been rebuilt.

The distance from Rotherham to Warsop is ten long miles, and the terrain is partly woodland (especially within three miles of Warsop), partly pasture, and partly arable. Less than a good mile before I reached Warsop I rode through a park belonging to a knight called Mr Townlea, who lives for the most part in Lancashire. There is a very attractive small house in this park.

Next to Worksop there is a park measuring six or seven miles around, and this belongs to the Earl of Shrewsbury. In some old documents Worksop is called Radford, and the river which flows through it goes on to Blyth. [*Worksop Priory*] was established by William de Lovetot during the reign of Henry I, when Anselm was bishop of Canterbury and Gerard was bishop of York. Lovetot's lineage and inheritance descended by a daughter to a man named Furnivall, and then again by marriage to one of the Nevilles. Neville's daughter by his wife married Talbot, the first earl of Shrewsbury, and their children included Talbot, known as Lord de Lisle. The first prior of Radford or Worksop was William Huntingdon. Many members of the Lovetot, Furnivall and Talbot families were buried at Worksop. One of the Lovetots was earl of Huntingdon and founder of Huntingdon Priory.

Worksop is a market town, and there is an area now surrounded by trees which is called Castle Hill; here the Lovetofts at one time had a castle. The stone from the castle, according to some people, was taken away to build the fine lodge in Worksop Park which remains unfinished. The father of the present earl of Shrewsbury intended to finish it, as is clear from the large quantity of dressed stone lying there. But it is my opinion that the canons took the stones from the ruined castle to build the large walls which enclose the priory. On the south side of the priory courtyard there is a very fine large gate of dressed stone. All the country from Worksop to East Retford, apart from a little near Worksop, is fertile arable in enclosed fields, but there are few trees.

From Worksop I rode for a mile beside dense woodland to Newhagg [*Hagg Hill*], which is a park belonging to the king, and lay on my right hand side as I travelled. A mile further on, still by woodland, I crossed Carburton brook, and then after another mile, of flat heathland, I rode across Budby brook. The heathland continued for a mile further, and then after two miles of fine woodland I crossed the Rume Water [*Rainworth Water*]. The name of the village on the far bank is generally shortened from Rumford to Rufford. The former Rufford Abbey, a house of Cistercian monks, lay a quarter-mile beyond the village. It now belongs to the earl of Shrewsbury, who obtained it from the king in exchange for land he owned in Ireland.

Rainworth Water rises south of Mansfield, five miles from Rufford Abbey. As the river approaches the abbey it forms a fine lake of the same name in the valley there, but then resumes its narrow course and flows to Rufford village. I discovered that further downstream both the Budby stream and the Carburton stream run into it, and then after a considerable distance it flows to Bawtry (sometimes called Vowtre), and then, so I was told, into the Trent. Bawtry is a market town in Nottinghamshire, five miles from Doncaster. I must find out the course of the River Blyth.

From Rufford Abbey I rode for four miles through flat arable and pastureland until I reached a village where I crossed a stream. It was called the Girt [*Greet*] if I remember correctly. Nearly a mile before I reached this village I passed close on my right hand side to Hexgreave Park, and a little beyond it on the left hand side I saw close by the park a pleasant manor house of a knight called Mr Newnam. It lies in the parish of Kirklington. The stream flows to the mills at Southwell, and then into the Trent. Southwell was only two miles further from this place, across very fertile cornfields.

Southwell lies in Nottinghamshire. The town which adjoins the minster has reasonably good buildings, but no public market. Our Lady's minster is large, but the architecture is too severe to be agreeable. An archbishop of York is buried in the chancel. There is an attractive palace belonging to the bishop of York, and the clergy, especially the prebendaries, have good dwellings. The archbishop has three parks: the little park, which is also known as New Park, Norwood Park, and Hexgreave, which is the principal park.

Next I travelled across two miles of cornland to the village of Thurgarton, where an Augustinian priory has recently been suppressed. From there it was a good mile to Oringgam [*Hoveringham*] ferry, where my horse crossed the Trent by the ford, but I went in the boat. I have never seen finer meadows than here, on both banks of the Trent. At this crossing place Nottingham is six miles away to the right, and Newark four miles to the left. Newark lies on the nearer bank of the Trent from us.

After I had left the Trent a short distance behind me there were open fields in every direction for as far as I could see, with very few trees, but the abundance of the harvest was quite incalculable. I rode four miles to Langar, where next to the church is a stone house battlemented like a castle, which belongs to Lord Scrope. And two miles beyond Langar I caught sight of Belvoir Castle in the distance on a high peaked hill. Half-a-mile before I reached Langar I passed the manor house of a knight called Sir John Chaworth, and around it I saw large and wonderfully fine meadows. This Chaworth Place is called Warton [*Wiverton*] Hall. After Langar I travelled four miles past excellent meadowland and arable until I reached a stream called the Smite, which defines the boundary between Nottinghamshire and Leicestershire. *cont. p. 211* [**1538**: 4/15-19]

From Gainsborough I crossed the Trent into Nottinghamshire and rode five miles to the village of Mattersey. For the first two miles I passed low-lying meadows, and for the next three there was arable and pasture land. Two miles before I reached Mattersey I passed a park on my right hand side, and a mile further I saw on my left the course of the River

[*Idle*], which I crossed by a bridge as I entered Mattersey village. From here I rode across a mile of low-lying watery and rather marshy country, and a further mile or more of higher ground as far as Scrooby.

Scrooby is a modest little place, but I did notice two things there. First was the parish church which, although not large, was very well built of polished squared stone. Second was the archbishop of York's great manor house, which stands within a moat. The buildings are arranged around two courts, of which the first is very spacious, and all built of timber except for the front of the hall. This is of brick, and is approached by a flight of stone steps. The building of the inner court was also timber, so far as I could see, and its total circuit was less than a quarter that of the outer court. Not very far beyond Scrooby manor house I rode by a ford across the River [*Ryton*], and continued between the pales of two parks attached to Scrooby until I reached Bawtry, a mile or more from Scrooby. *cont. p. 420* [**1541:** 1/33-4]

MOST OF MY FIVE-MILE JOURNEY from Rossington to Blyth was past woodland, but also some arable, pasture and meadow. As I approached the town of Blyth itself there were flowing two streams. The one I crossed first was the larger, and flows from the west; the other, which they told me was called the Blyth, runs close to the houses on the edge of the town. As I recall, it was actually the same stream as that which flows from Worksop, or else the Worksop stream flows into it. These two streams join in the meadows just below Blyth, and flow to Scrooby, two miles downstream. Blyth is a market town with attractive buildings, and at the east end of the priory church tombs of noblemen are to be seen. I had heard that there was once a castle at Blyth, and I enquired about this; but I could discover nothing about it, except that shortly before I reached the town traces of an ancient building were visible beside a wood.

About a mile beyond Blyth I went past a park called Hodsock, where Mr Clifton has a fine house. And two miles further, after riding over much heathland and then through woods I crossed a small brook with a little stone bridge over it; and this took me straight into Worksop, which is a pleasant market town with two streets, and reasonably good buildings. It has a fine park close by, and within it a good manor house of squared stone has been begun. The old castle on a hill next to the town has been completely demolished, and the site virtually forgotten. The town, castle and large park originally belonged to the Lovetots, and then, according to some people, one of the Nevilles. The Furnivall family definitely owned it, and after them the Talbots. The Augustinian priory at Worksop had extensive buildings, and was the burial place for the aforesaid noblemen.

After Worksop I rode alongside the pale which surrounds the great wood, known as Roomwood for a distance of two miles or more, and crossed a small bridge over the Welbeck stream. This stream derives from two springs, of which one issues not far above Welbeck Abbey; but the larger stream rises further away to the west, and the two flow into one valley near Welbeck. Welbeck Abbey lies on the right hand side about a half-mile upstream from the bridge where I crossed. I was told that the wood had belonged to Worksop Priory, and had been bought from the king by a man named Whalley. From the bridge I rode about a mile to the village of Cuckney, where the Welbeck stream is joined by a brook flowing down from the west. From there I travelled two miles through arable, woodland and pasture to Warsop village. Here there was another brook, which, like the other, flows into the Rufford Stream [*River Maun*]. Another three miles riding through similar countryside brought me to Mansfield, which is an attractive market town of a single parish with a stream flowing through its centre. Soon after I had left the town I crossed a pleasant stream which runs in the nearby valley. It rises three miles to the west above Mansfield, and I was told that it then flows to Clipstone three miles lower down, and into the River Maun.

Within the space of a mile or less I rode into the heart of the thickly-wooded Sherwood Forest, where there are abundant deer for game. I continued in the dense woodland for five miles, until I came to a poor roadside place [*?Papplewick*] at the far side of the wood. But just before I left the wood I passed about a quarter-mile on my right hand side the ruins of Newstead, an Augustinian priory. The River Leen passes by Newstead, and flows on to Lenton Abbey, then to Nottingham, and shortly below into the Trent. From the roadside village I crossed low-lying marsh-like ground for a distance of half a mile, and then I reached a rather prominent spur of high land. After a mile of this I reached an enormous park, which I rode alongside for almost three miles. It is called Bestwood Park, and belongs to the manor and castle of Nottingham. Then for a total distance of two miles I passed two or three hills, until I reached Nottingham.

Nottingham is a large town which occupies an imposing site on the slope of a hill; its buildings are of timber and plaster, but are well built. Not only becuase of its buildings, but also the very great width of its street and its even paved surface, make Nottingham's market place and street the finest without exception in the whole of England. There are three parish churches, dedicated to St Mary, St Peter and St Nicholas. St Mary's church is excellent, its modern architecture all in one style, and with so many fine windows that no craftsman could contrive to add to them. On the south side of the town towards the river there are great cliffs and outcrops of large stones which are excellent for building. Many houses have been built on the tops of these cliffs, and at their foot are large caves formed by digging out building stone for use in the town. Some of these caves are used as dwellings, and some as cellars and for storage.

There were three friaries in Nottingham, if I remember correctly, two of which stood in the western part of the town not far from the castle. There used to be quite a good town wall built of stone, with several gates; much of the wall is down now, and all the gates except two or three. There is an arched stone bridge across the River Leen on the south side of the town, but no suburb beyond it. It is very noticeable that whereas the site of the town itself and the land next to it on the north stand high, so all the ground to the south outside the town is flat, low-lying meadowland, through which flow only the Trent and the little River Leen.

(I have written some other interesting things about Nottingham on a small piece of paper.)

Nottingham Castle stands on a rocky hill to the west of the town, and the River Leen flows around its foot. In all probability the castle was built of stone won from this rock, and from its great ditches. The outer courtyard is large and of reasonable strength. From it an imposing bridge on pillars carved with beasts and giants leads over the ditch into the second ward, and the façade of this inner ward by its entrance is exceptionally strong with towers and portcullises. Most of its western parts, including the hall and other buildings, are in ruins, but the eastern and southern sides are strong with good towers.

But the most beautiful and ornate of the buildings are the apartments on the north side. Edward IV began the building work in stone on a most lavish scale, and entirely completed one excellent tower three stories high, as well as erecting its counterpart in stone from the foundations to the first sill of the chambers, including wonderful semi-circular bay windows. But at that point he left off, and it was his brother Richard III, so they told me there, who imposed upon that building an upper floor of timber. This also had round bay windows, which he made of wood, but to the same proportions as the stone ones beneath, so that they would provide a good support for the wooden windows above. As a result this northern range is without doubt an exceptionally fine piece of architecture.

The dungeon or keep of the castle stands on the south-east side, and is extremely strong by virtue both of its position and its workmanship. In the same area is an attractive old chapel and a very deep well. There is also a spiral staircase with a turret over it, which, according to the castle caretakers, Edward III's men used when they came up through the rock and took Earl Mortimer prisoner. A good stairway still leads down beside the rock to the bank of the Leen. And there are several buildings between the keep and the inner court of the castle, as well as steps leading down below ground, where the castellans say that King David of Scotland was imprisoned. Altogether I noted three chapels in the castle precinct and three wells.

The confluence of the little River Leen with the great mainstream of the Trent occurs in the meadows on the south side of the town, and when any water is carried down off the land much of the valley and the meadows become flooded. The main stream of the Trent and the great stone-arched bridge across it are not more than two bow-shots' distance from the Leen bridge adjoining the southern edge of Nottingham. Derby is twelve miles from Nottingham, and almost halfway between them at Sawley Ferry there is a stone bridge and causeway with many arches, partly to straddle the channel of the Trent itself, and partly as a bridge over the meadows when the Trent is in spate. From the Trent Bridge next to Nottingham right up to Newark, twelve miles away, there are no bridges, nor are there any beyond Newark to the mouth of the Trent; all crossings are by ferries. Nottingham is sixteen miles from Leicester, and twelve long miles from Belvoir.

Leaving Nottingham I first rode for a distance of three miles across meadows and some marshy land, and then a further three miles over ground which was higher but not hilly. At the end of this I reached an attractive brook or small river called the Myte [*Smite*], which rises six miles or more further west and flows another eight miles down before reaching the Trent not far above Newark. Approaching this River Smite I passed about a mile to my left the Nottinghamshire village of Aslockton, the birthplace of Thomas Cranmer, archbishop of Canterbury. The heir to the Cranmers still lives there, a man with lands of an annual value of less than £30. From here I rode across two miles of reasonably high, good land, and came to a village. Then it was four good miles to Belvoir, over marshland, meadow, pasture and arable. Open-field country was within sight my whole way from Nottingham to Belvoir. *cont. p. 218* [**1541**: *1/88-90, 93-7*]

Robert English and Thomas Thirland, rich merchants who were mayors of Nottingham, are buried in St Mary's church. Of the six or seven gates formerly in the town wall all are demolished except for three. St John's Hospital, outside the town, has been virtually demolished. Grey and white friars. [*5/147*]

OXFORDSHIRE

LELAND SET OUT from London in May 1542 on his West Country itinerary four weeks after he had been appointed rector of Great Haseley in Oxfordshire. This appointment doubtless influenced his route, and explains his detailed treatment of Haseley itself, its leading family, the Barentines, and the nearby towns and villages, such as Ewelme, Dorchester and Thame. For a spell during the 1540s he was perhaps resident at Haseley, as his West Midlands tour in 1543 began there, and he was also very familiar with Oxford, where he was a canon of what was then known as King's College. It is hardly surprising, therefore, that his treatment of Oxfordshire is wide-ranging and well-informed; our only slight disappointment is his rather peremptory description of the west of the county, which he visited in 1544 on his way from Oxford to the Bristol area.

BEYOND CAVERSHAM BRIDGE lies Caversham village, which is in Oxfordshire. My journey from there took me through a large area of woodland for five miles or more, and then a further four miles across hilly open country to a remote village called Ewelme. Ewelme was the inheritance of the Chaucer family, and the last male of the line to own it, Thomas Chaucer, lies buried in a tall marble tomb in Ewelme parish church, in a fine chapel on the south side of the chancel. His epitaph runs thus: 'Here lies Thomas Chaucer Esquire, sometime lord of this manor and patron of this church, who died on the 18th day of November, AD 1434; and of Matilda his wife, who died on the 28th day of April, AD 1436'.

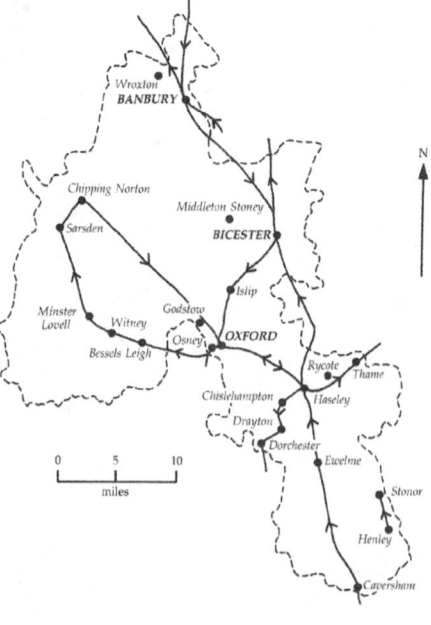

According to some people this Chaucer was a merchant, who purchased land with an annual value of £1,000, and that there are woolsacks in Ewelme symbolising his business. The story runs also that it was his intention to found the hospital at Ewelme, and also the hospital at Castle Donnington. But both were actually built by William, duke of Suffolk, with an allowance of fourteen pence per week for each poor man living there. The heiress of Thomas and Matilda Chaucer was their daughter Alice, and she married William de la Pole, duke of Suffolk. Because of his love for her and the convenience of her estates William took to spending much of his time in Oxfordshire and Berkshire, where her estates lay. At Ewelme he removed and enlarged the manor house, and with his wife Alice he built the beautiful new parish church which stands on the hill. I believe that Ewelme took its name from a large lake in front of the manor house, and from the elm trees growing around it.

William was killed, but Alice outlived him, and was eventually buried in Ewelme parish church on the south side of the high altar in a rich alabaster tomb, with a crowned effigy lying on it wearing the dress of a vowess [*a widow who has taken a vow of chastity*]. The epitaph runs as follows: 'Pray for the soul of her most serene highness Alice, duchess of Suffolk, patroness of this church, and original founder of this hospital, who died on the 20th day of May, AD 1475, Dominical Letter A'.

The attractive hospital for thirteen poor men adjoins the west end of Ewelme parish church; its design is circular, rather after the fashion of the vicars' houses at Windsor. There is a very good well in the centre of the hospital precinct. The master or provost of the foundation has pleasant apartments, and every inmate has fourteen pence per week.

On a tablet in Ewelme church I read the following: 'Pray for the souls of John, duke of Suffolk, and Elizabeth his wife. This John was the son and heir of William and Alice.' John de la Pole, duke of Suffolk, had by his wife Elizabeth these sons: John, earl of Lincoln; Edmund, later duke of Suffolk; Richard; William; and another son who was a scholar at Gonville Hall in Cambridge, and lies buried at Babraham.

The manor house of Ewelme lies in the hollow at the foot of the village. It has a fine outer courtyard, built of brick and timber. The inner part of the house stands within a good moat, and is lavishly built of brick and stone. There is a fine hall, which has large iron bars instead of cross beams running across it. The adjoining parlour is exceptionally fine and well-lit, as are all the apartments in the house. It is usually said that Duke John was responsible for most of the good buildings within the moat at about the beginning of Henry VII's reign. Next to the manor house is a most attractive park.

From Ewelme it was five miles to Haseley, across open country largely devoted to pasture, but with a reasonable supply of corn. Haseley is divided into four: Great Haseley, Little Haseley, Latchford and Rycote. Great Haseley in former times was a manor of the Pypard family, and it descended through many generations of them. The present farmhouse, which belongs to Windsor College, next to the church is on the site of the Pypard manor house. The family had fine possessions, and their name is found as lords of the principal manor until the reign of Edward III; but sometime around this period the Pypard manor house, together with the patronage of the living of Haseley, was given to Windsor College. The Pypard arms may be seen in the east window of the fine chancel of Haseley church.

Little Haseley is held by Mr Barentine, as I was told, by knight service of the Pypard manor. He has a most attractive mansion house there, with ornamental gardens including remarkably fine walks, as well as orchards and lakes. At the start of Edward III's reign Latchford was still part of the Pypard estate. But then it so happened that a younger son of the Pypards of Haseley fought so bravely in battle against the Scots that he was knighted. Because he had no land (his elder brother being heir) he was anxious to possess a small portion of the estate, and so his father gave him Latchford to hold by knight service of the Pypard's manor in Great Haseley. The descendants of this young knight of the Pypard family stayed on at Latchford until eighty years ago, when the last of them left a daughter as his heir, and she married a certain Herefordshire gentleman named Lenthall, whose son lives at Latchford now.

Rycote belonged to a man named Fulco of Rycote, and later passed to one of the Quartermaynes. The Oxfordshire house of Quartermayne has been famous, and owned extremely fine property. Their principal seat was at Weston near Rycote, where Mr Clark lives now. The tower or small castle at Shirburn, which is less than a mile from the town of Watlington, also belonged to the Quatermaynes, before passing to Fowler, and now by exchange to the Oxfordshire family of Chamberlain.

Around the time of Henry VI several Quatermayne brothers died one after the other, and the whole estate quite unexpectedly descended to the youngest brother, whose name was Richard. He was a merchant in London, and later became the controller of customs there. Richard employed as his clerk a certain Thomas Fowler, a gifted character who later became chancellor of the duchy of Lancaster. Thomas was a great favourite of Richard Quartermayne, and Richard acted as godfather to his son, who was given the name Richard Quartemayne Fowler. Richard lived at Rycote, and arranged for Thomas Fowler to live at Weston. Because Richard had no children of his own he made Thomas Fowler's son Richard the heir to the greater portion of his estate.

Richard Quartermayne (Richard Fowler's godfather) built an extremely good and large chapel of ease just outside his manor house at Rycote, and established a chantry there for two priests to sing perpetually for his soul. He endowed the chantry with a good estate, and built the priests a fine house next to the chantry. This project commenced in the reign of Henry VI, and was completed in that of Edward IV. The same Richard also established a chantry in the parish church at Thame, two miles from Rycote, and it is here that he lies buried in a chapel under a marble slab. In addition he founded, and endowed with land, a hospital next to Thame church. His heir, Richard Fowler, was a spendthrift who sold the whole estate and left his children very meagre allowances. Sir John Heron, treasurer of the household under both Henry VII and Henry VIII, bought the reversion of Rycote manor, and for a while it belonged to his son Giles. But Giles Heron, just as Sir Richard Fowler had been, was wise in words but foolish in deeds, and he sold Rycote to John Williams who is now a knight.

From Haseley it was a half-mile to the village of Great Milton, and I heard it said that here, many years ago, there had been a priory for monks. One informant told me it had been a cell of Abingdon. The priory buildings were probably on the site of the lessee's house right next to the churchyard, as the foundations of large buildings may still be seen there. Some people maintain that the house of Monsieur de Louches was also on this site. In Milton church there is a tall tomb of freestone with the effigies of a knight and a lady, and an inscription in French to the effect that Richard de Louches, knight, and his wife Helen lie buried there. Popular opinion there is that Louches was granted the priory land. From him it passed by the female line, and in more recent times one Danvers acquired the manor. Sir Reginald Bray bought it from Danvers, and the late Lord Bray sold it to Dormer, who was mayor of London. In Milton there is an estate attached to a prebend at Lincoln, and the bishop of Lincoln is patron of the church. Attached to Great Milton is Little Milton, and here there is a chapel of ease dedicated to St James.

It is three miles from Haseley to Chislehampton (or Chisiltun, as it is commonly known) across flat country. Good corn and grass is produced here, but, as in all this corner of Oxfordshire, there is no woodland. At Chislehampton I crossed three small wooden bridges over pools of shallow water caused by the River Thame in spate, and then immediately I rode across a large bridge under which the main stream of the Thame flows. It was a timber bridge, but supported by five large stone pillars. From there I continued to Drayton village, which until recently belonged to Dorchester Abbey, and then a further mile brought me to Dorchester. In Dorchester I saw the following points of interest.

The abbey for canons. Before the conquest there was a bishop's see here, but it was transferred to Lincoln by Remigius. Bishop Alexander of Lincoln built an abbey for Augustinian canons on the site, although the church continued to be called the prebendal church. It is said that the body of St Birinus the bishop was buried there, and an effigy in freestone still survives which formerly lay on the tomb of Bishop Aeschwine [?*Aescwig*], according to the inscription. In the quire beside several abbots a knight lies buried, with an effigy of him lying cross-legged, but his name has been forgotten. At this knight's feet lies a man named Stonor who, from the style of his dress, must have been a judge during Edward III's reign. On the north side of the quire there lies another knight, whose effigy was of alabaster, and whom the former abbot thought to be one of the Segrave family; but later the abbot told me that he had recently heard that a knight by the name of Holcum was buried there. In the chancel, in front of the door into the quire, a gentleman called Wace was buried; and in the south quire aisle, close together under plain marble slabs, lie three members of the gentry family of Drayton. Mr Barentine now owns a portion of the Drayton estate. At the head of these Draytons a gentleman named Gilbert Segrave lies buried under a flat marble slab.

The nave of the abbey church was used until recently as the parish church. But since the suppression a certain [*Beauforest*], a very rich inhabitant of Dorchester, bought the eastern portion of the church for £140, and gave it to augment the parish church.

The town of Dorchester, which was badly damaged by the Danes, used in the past to have many more buildings extending southwards and towards the Thames. There used to be three parish churches, one a short distance south of the abbey church, a second further up to the south, and a third to the south-west. In the open and enclosed fields which lie south of the site of the present town Roman coins are found of gold, silver and bronze. The bishop's palace, so they say there, lay at the north-western end of the town. Foundations of old buildings can still be seen in the area, and courts are still held on the site.

The River Thame approaches the town first at its east end, and then around to the south it passes under a very fine stone bridge, which lies just outside the town. If you approach Dorchester from Wallingford the town lies on the further bank of the Thame. The bridge is of considerable length, and is linked to a large stone causeway. There are five main arches in the bridge, and in the causeway joined to its southern end. The Thame and the Isis join in the meadows about a half-mile below Dorchester Bridge, and the distance from Dorchester to the Thames ferry is about a mile. In this area the nearer, or northern, bank is low-lying meadow land, but the south bank is high up all the way along, like the long ridge of a hill. *cont. p. 11* [**1542: 1/112-18**]

I TRAVELLED FROM ABINGDON about a mile to the fine rabbit warren which belonged to the abbey, and then four miles to Chislehampton Bridge, a further three miles to Haseley, and then about seven miles to Oxford.

Robert d'Oilly came to England with William the Conqueror, and was granted the baronies of Oxford and St Waleries. He it was who built Oxford Castle, and it is my guess that he either built the town walls, or at least repaired them. He also built the Chapel of St George within the castle, and established a prebendal college there. Robert died without issue, and the place of his burial is not known with any certainty. But he had a very close friend called John de Einerio. They had fought in the wars together as sworn brothers, and John had sworn to share whatever fortune befell Robert. And so Robert enriched him with property, and this included, in the opinion of some, giving him St Waleries.

Robert d'Oilly also had a brother called Nigel, but nothing outstanding is recorded about him. However, Nigel's son Robert turned out to be a very distinguished man. This second Robert had a wife called Edith Forne, a woman whose reputation was highly esteemed by Henry I; indeed it was through the king's influence that Robert married her. Robert was the founder of the priory for Augustinian canons at Osney, which is close to Oxford among the islands formed by the River Isis. The circumstances of its foundation are related by some sources as follows:

Edith was accustomed to take frequent walks out of Oxford Castle for recreation with her lady companions. Whenever she reached a certain point magpies always used to congregate in a particular tree, and chatter there as if they were speaking to her. Edith observed this behaviour with great fascination, and for some time was very apprehensive about what seemed to be a miracle. And so she sent for her confessor, a man of virtuous life named Radulph, who was a canon of St Frideswide; and she sought his advice. He observed the way in which the magpies only chattered when she arrived, and he advised her that she should build some church or monastery on the spot. She therefore persuaded her husband to build a priory, which he did, and he made Radulph its first prior. On the wall of the arch above Edith's tomb in Osney Priory there is a painting of Edith coming to Osney, with Radulph accompanying her, and the tree with the chattering magpies. A stone effigy of Edith, wearing the apparel of a vowess, and holding a heart in her right hand, lies on the north side of the high altar.

Robert d'Oilly (the second), the founder of Osney Priory, was buried at Eynsham Abbey three miles from Oxford. He and his wife Edith had a handsome family, including Henry, who was their heir; and he was buried in the very centre of the sanctuary of the church of Osney Priory, under a flat marble slab which has a cross tipped with fleurs-de-lys depicted on it. Henry's son was also Henry, and from him descended other heirs; but in course of time the d'Oilly estates were dispersed. At the present day there is a member of the family alive with an estate worth annually £140, and he is married to the daughter of Lady Williams of Rycote. In common parlance his name has been shortened from de Oilleio to Doilley.

At the head of Henry d'Oilly's tomb lies Ela, countess of Warwick, who was a woman of very great wealth and nobility. She is buried under a very fine marble slab, with her likeness engraved on a copper plate wearing the dress of a vowess. She did not give lands to Osney, but she did give many rich jewels; and she gave some land to Rewley Abbey near Osney, as well as rich gifts to Reading Abbey. John St John was a well-known man, whose tall large marble tomb is under a canopy on the north side of the sanctuary of the church at Osney. His wife lies under a marble slab beside her husband's tomb.

A knight by the name of Beaufort is buried in the quire at the head of Countess Ela. Along with an abbot of Osney he built the nave of the church there as it now stands, and both of their portraits are depicted in the vaulting. On either side of the nave there are very fine double aisles. And on the north side of the sanctuary there is a lady chapel, which was built many years ago by a certain abbot of Osney called Thomas Kidlington, who was born at Kidlington in Oxfordshire. In this lady chapel, in a good tomb with an effigy, is buried a nobleman of the Plackett family.

To begin with a number of priors were in charge of Osney, but then the priory estate was increased and in part granted along with a certain spiritual peculiar jurisdiction in Gloucestershire; and henceforth they became abbots. Mr James Bayllie, an inhabitant of Oxford, possesses part of a book of the acts of the abbots of Osney. *cont. p. 14* [**1542:** *1/122-5*]

I CKFORD BRIDGE is two miles from Haseley, and in the meadows at this point the River Thame separates into two arms, but shortly afterwards they join up and form a single stream. Over the left arm (looking downstream) is a stone bridge of two arches, and close by is a wooden bridge over the other arm. The bridges at Shonington [*Shabbington*] are a mile above these on the Thame, and Thame Bridge in the town of Thame is two miles further, if the distance is reckoned by the course of the river. Three miles by river below the bridges at Ickford is Wheatley Bridge, which has eight stone arches.

From Ickford Bridge it is three miles to Welstreme [*?Oakley*] in Buckinghamshire. This is a pleasant, elongated village, and contains a fine old house belonging to the Rede family in a good moat, and with a square stone gatehouse at the entrance. All around Welstreme are fine woods which serve as coverts for the deer of Bernwood Forest. The village of Arncote is three-and-a-half miles further, and here there is a wooden bridge called Blackthorn Bridge. It crosses a stream which rises not far away and drains, I imagine, into the River Cherwell. Then a mile-and-a-half brought me from Arncote to Bicester.

There are good meadows and pastureland around Bicester, and in some places also good woodland. A public market is held in the town weekly. Close to Bicester is the source of a small stream, which flows through part of the town and then through the priory, before joining the Cherwell four miles lower in the Otmoor area.

Bicester belonged to the Bassett family, then to the Lestranges, and now to the earl of Derby. Some people maintain that the site of the Bassett mansion house is where the common pound is now, in the centre of the town; but others say that it was where the former Bicester Priory stood. This priory, for Augustinian canons, was originally founded by Gilbert Bassett and his wife Aeglean Courtney. Gilbert was merely a knight, but he was a close companion in arms to a nobleman knight called Giffard. Gilbert, according to some people, was buried overseas, but Aeglean Courtney was buried in Bicester Priory. Several members of the ancient gentry family of Damory, as well as one of the last of the Lords Lestrange, were also buried in the priory. The priory church was dedicated to St Eadburga the virgin.

The parish church is also dedicated to her, and in its quire is buried one William Standley [*Staveley*] Esquire, owner of Bignell, which is a mile from Bicester and within the parish. He married Alice, the daughter and heiress of Sir John Francis, and died in 1498. Three miles south of Bicester there is a wooded hill called Earls' Hill, which some people believe is the site of a manor house.

Distances from Bicester: Oxford 10 miles; Thame 9 miles; Buckingham 10 miles; Banbury 10 miles; Brackley 7 miles; Studley Priory 3 miles, on the Oxford road.

Middleton [*Stoney*] village and castle lie two miles west of Bicester in Oxfordshire. The castle stood close to the church, and its site is almost entirely overgrown with bushes, although some fragments of its walls are still visible. According to some people this castle belonged to the Bassetts, then the Lestranges, and now the earl of Derby. The manor has an annual value of £50. Someone listed for me the earl of Derby's lands in Oxfordshire which had come to him from the Bassetts through the Lestranges, as follows: Bicester; Middleton; Whichford and Long Compton near Chipping Norton; and King's Sutton, which lies close to the road from Brackley to Banbury. But I assume that some of these manors came to Stanley, earl of Derby, through the attainder of Lord Lovell. *cont. p. 263* [**1543:** *2/33-5*]

From King's Sutton to Banbury extend three miles of open, treeless country. Scarcely a mile below King's Sutton I crossed the River Cherwell by a one-arched stone bridge.

For the most part the town of Banbury stands in a valley, which is confined on its northern and eastern sides by low-lying ground, partly meadow and partly marsh; on the south and south-west the land is rather more hilly compared with the site of the town itself. Banbury's best street is that which runs east–west down to the River Cherwell. At the western end of this street is a large open area surrounded by quite good architecture, and with a fine cross on a plinth of many steps. A very notable market is held in this area every Thursday, and it is watered by a stream of fresh water.

Another good street runs from south to north, and at either end of it is a stone gate. These are not the only gates in the town; but there is no definite evidence, or even probability, that Banbury ever had a ditch or town wall. On the northern side of the market place is a castle with two ditched wards. There is a fearful prison for convicts in the outer ward, and in the northern part of the inner ward is a nice piece of new stone building. I can find no evidence that there was any castle or fortress at Banbury before the conquest. This castle was built by Bishop Alexander of Lincoln during Henry I's reign.

Banbury has only one parish church, and it is dedicated to Our Lady. It is a large building, especially in its width. I only saw one notable tomb there, and that was of black marble; William Cooper, Henry VII's cofferer, is buried there. In the churchyard are houses for chantry priests. The living of Banbury is a prebend of Lincoln, and there is an endowment for a vicar. In the centre of the town is a chapel dedicated to the Trinity.

At the eastern end of Banbury is a bridge over the Cherwell of four fine stone arches, and this marks the boundary between Oxfordshire and Northamptonshire. But going north from Banbury Oxfordshire extends for another three miles. The bishop of Lincoln is the lord of Banbury, and for a long time the bishops have also held at fee-farm of the king the entire hundred of Banbury. These possessions are worth £180 to the bishop.

The River Cherwell rises at a spring or small pool in the village of Charlton [*Charwelton*], some seven miles above Banbury to the NNE. So fast does it gush out from the source that it immediately forms a small stream.

Distances from Banbury: Coventry, 20 miles, via the market town of Southam, which is ten miles from each; Northampton, 14 miles; Daventry, 10 miles; Oxford, 20 miles; Warwick, 14 miles.

Wroxton, a priory for canons, is two miles from Banbury, and now belongs to Mr Pope. One mile north of Banbury is an old manor house called Hardwick, from which a family name derives. It belongs to Mr Cope, and he also owns a manor house at Hanwell, two miles north-west of Banbury, and still in Oxfordshire. This is a very appealing and elegant house. *cont. p. 367* [**1543**: 2/38-40]

I TRAVELLED three or four miles from Banbury across open country to a small roadside place called [?*Aynho*]; most of the following seven miles to Burghchester (otherwise Bicester) were also over open ground. But before I came within two miles of Bicester I passed through a clearing in a valley between two fine stands of trees on the hillsides. After Bicester I left Otmoor on my right hand side and rode eight miles to Islip. My shortest route, had it not been flooded, would have taken me across Otmoor. Thame Abbey was originally founded in Otmoor.

Islip is a pleasant roadside place on the left bank of the River Cherwell. Close by is a fine bridge over the river, with a good stone arch. Going upstream from Islip the bridges over the Cherwell are Gosford Bridge, one-and-a-half miles; Emmeley [?] Bridge, two miles; Heyford Bridge, two miles. The distance from Islip to Oxford is three miles, if you go through the meadows beside the Cherwell, but four miles on the left bank where it is more hilly and wooded. From Oxford Haseley is four miles, and Thame is four miles beyond Haseley.

When Alexander was bishop of Lincoln the town of Thame, which belonged to the king, was given at fee-farm for an annual rent to the see of Lincoln, for the bishop and his successors. And Bishop Alexander built a Cistercian abbey in his park there. This abbey is called Thame not because it was built beside the river, but because it is not very far from the town of Thame. *cont. p. 20* [**1543**: 2/109-10]

APPROACHING HENLEY I could see Hurley Priory in the valley; it was a cell of Westminster, and stands on the right bank of the Thames. Henley Bridge, like the majority of bridges in that area, is entirely made of wood, although it used to be of stone, as is shown by the foundations revealed at low water. The principal owners of Henley are the Hastings family, earls of Huntingdon. It descended to the them from Lord Moleyns, through the Peverel and Hungerford families. There is abundant wood and corn around Henley. The terrain is undulating chalkland.

Rotherfield, with its park, is about a mile from Henley. It is usually known as Rotherfield Greys, because it came into the possession of one of the Greys of Ruthin. Some people affix the name Grey Murdoch, explaining that Murdoch was a bishop, and this view is supported by the various mitres to be seen in the hall at Rotherfield. As you enter the manor house you see on your right hand three or four very old stone towers, a clear indication that it was at one time a castle. It has a very large courtyard paved with brick and surrounded with timber buildings; but this is of a later period. It may not yet be forgotten in Henley that it used to belong to Lord Lovell, and that as a result of his attainder it was granted to Knollys.

Stonor is three miles outside Henley, with its fine park and woodland, and its rabbit warren. The mansion house has been built up against the hillside, with two courts of timber, brick and flint. The present owner, Sir Walter Stonor, has enlarged and strengthened the house, which has for a long time been in the possession of his family. At one time it was usurped by a man named Fortescue, who married a Stonor heiress, but he was later dispossessed.

It is a quarter-mile or more from Oxford to Hinksey Ferry. A stone causeway leads from Osney to the ferry, and several wooden bridges built into the causeway carry it over the many small channels into which the Isis divides at this point. The ferry itself crosses the main stream of the river.

Bessels Leigh is a small village three miles from Hinksey Ferry on the main road from Oxford to Ferendune (otherwise Faringdon). The pasture and woodland there is excellent. The Blessell [?Bessel] family had owned Leigh since Edward I's time or earlier, and they used to live there. The house is built entirely of stone and stands at the western end of the parish church. They also owned Radcot, which lies on the River Isis near Faringdon; this used to be a strong tower and is now a mansion house. The Bessel family originated in Provence, in France, and were active participants in armed combat. From monuments at Leigh it is clear that one of them jousted with a stranger knight who had challenged him, and killed the knight in the presence of the then king and queen of England. It was estimated that the Bessels owned property worth annually nearly £300. The last male heir lived until within living memory, but then Leigh and Radcot passed by marrying a Bessel heiress to the Fettiplace family.

From Leigh I rode on, and after a half-mile I came to Towkey [*?Tubney*], where once had been a village. The church or chapel still survives, and nearby in a wood was a manor house which is now completely demolished. It belongs to Magdalen College, Oxford, and is let.

My journey took me two-and-a-half miles across fine, open, fertile cornland to Newbridge on the Isis. The country all about is low-lying, and the meadows are frequently flooded after severe rainfall. The bridge itself has six large stone arches, and at each end there is a long stone causeway. A furlong after I had crossed it I passed a fine mill, and it appeared that a brook flowed down there to join the Isis near Newbridge. Another four miles or more brought me to Witney, where a market is held, and there is a fine church with a good stone spire. From there it was a mile to Crawley Bridge, with Crawley village next to the bridge. The bridge has two stone arches and crosses the River Windrush, which flows through Witney.

From there it was about a mile to the village of Minster, which takes the name Lovell from a former owner. Next to the church there is an old house of the Lovell family. But now the manor is leased from the king by Mr Vinton of Wadley near Faringdon. My next three or four miles took me through the king's forest of Wychwood. Like the town of Burford, it used to belong to the Beauchamps, earls of Warwick. It has abundant woodland and fallow deer. I emerged from the forest into country which was open on every side, but with some narrow strips of woodland and attractive groves. At Beckington [*Bledington, Gloucestershire*] there is a manor house with a fine mill, and the River Bruerne [*Evenlode*] flowing past it.

I had scarcely gone two miles further when I came to a place called Borow [*?Knollbury*] on top of a slight hill. Here I could see a large ditch a quarter-mile in circuit, and excellent corn growing inside. I assumed when I first saw it that it was a hillfort; but then I noticed that in some places at the top of the ditch there had been a wall built along it, and at its east end I could make out the site of a gate. But in fact it was nothing more than a hillfort, and there is another one on the same area of downland. Half a good mile further I came to Cerceden [*Sarsden*].

Mr Barentine's manor and village of Churchill is close to Sarsden. The manor of Sarsden belonged originally to Golafer, then, as I recall, to Browning. Recently a man named Horne has built the fine house there of squared stone. Bruern Abbey is a mile away, close to the right bank of the river. It has good pasture, arable and woods. Stow on the Wold is about three miles from Bruern, as is also the market town of Burford, where there is an important quarry of superior stone. The Beauchamp family, Earls of Warwick, owned Burford and Wychwood Forest, but some people maintain that the Spencers and the Lovells also had some interests there. There was a house at Burford called the Priory, and this estate now belongs to Horman, the king's barber. One mile from Burford is Langley, and here remain traces of an old manor house built on the edge of Wychwood Forest.

From Sarsden it is three good miles to Chipping Norton. The Croft family used to own it, then Rodney, and then Compton, who purchased it. Hook Norton is three miles across open country from Chipping Norton. The fine park and old manor house there used to belong to the Chaucer family, then it passed by marriage to the Poles, dukes of Suffolk, and now it is in the king's hand, by an exchange with Brandon. Cold Norton Priory lay about a mile from Chipping Norton, and has been appropriated by Brasenose College, Oxford. Mr Ashley's manor house stands about a mile beyond the priory. Tew, where Mr Rainsford lives, is three miles away. From Sarsden to Oxford is fifteen miles. *cont. p. 14* [**1544**: 5/71-5]

When Rosamund's tomb at Godstow nunnery was taken up recently, it was found to have been inscribed in Latin, 'The tomb of Rosamund'; her bones were wrapped in leather and encased in lead. When the coffin was opened a very sweet smell emanated from it. Close to Godstow there is a cross with the Latin inscription, 'May he who passes by this symbol of salvation make a prayer, and beseech Rosamund to grant pardon for his sin'. [1/328-9]

The senior branch of the Greville family has its seat at Drayton, an Oxfordshire village two miles from Banbury, and some people believe that the family came over at the conquest. The first important enlargement of their estate came when Lewis Greville married Margaret, daughter and heiress of a nobleman called Sir Giles Arden. Sir Giles's wife Philippa also possessed substantial property in her own right, and so the estates of both Giles and Philippa descended to Lewis Greville. His tomb may still be seen in Drayton parish church. Lewis's son married an heiress, the daughter of a man named Corbet, and their son married another, the daughter of Poyntz. Court rolls which survive at Drayton show that at one time the Greville estate realised an annual income of £2,200.

One of the Grevilles of Drayton, after they had amassed this great estate, travelled much overseas, and died in battle. He left his property in the hands of a minor gentleman of Drayton, whose name was Somerton, with no instruction as to its disposal. This Somerton (part of the gate from whose house still survives) sold much of the estate, and diverted some to his own heirs, and the name still remained until recently. This is how the Greville estate began to decline. [2/12-13]

A stone marking the boundary of four counties: Three miles west of the Rollright Stones there is a large stone. It stands on Barton Heath, which is named after Mr Palmer's vilage nearby This stone marks the actual point where Gloucestershire, Worcestershire, Warwickshire and Oxfordshire all meet. Mr Palmer's son affirmed that this stone, and not the Rollright Stones, is the true boundary. [4/81]

The town of Thame is divided into three parts. Old Thame lies along the road from the church towards the market place, but not right up to it. The market place and the finest part of the town in the direction of the London road is called New Thame. The third part is called Priest's End, and comprises the area around the church and the bridge towards Haseley. Thame has two bailiffs and four constables: two in the new town, and one each in the old town and Priest's End. [4/34-5]

The fine manor of Harpsden and its grand old large manor house with double courts, which stands half a mile from Henley on Thames, belonged to the well-known gentry family of Harpsden, and passed to the Fosters of Berkshire. Sir Humphrey Foster's father sired twenty-one children. [4/101]

The stone-arched bridge at Dorchester is relatively new, and before that a ferry was used to cross the Thames when the water was high. [5/2]

Quatermayne established a hospital at Thame in Oxfordshire, and one member of the family is buried in Thame church. They had a considerable estate in the Oxfordshire, Berkshire and Buckinghamshire region. The last of the Quartermaines left most of his property to a certain Fowler, whose son later became chancellor of the duchy of Lancaster, but his son sold it all off. Rycote was one of the Quatermaines' manor houses. Young Chamberlain of Oxfordshire told me that the manor of Coates near Northampton anciently belonged to the Chamberlains. He also said that the family had acquired through marriage the lands of a knight called Helke. [5/124]

The rebuilding of the university church in Oxford, known as St Mary's church, began during the time of Dr FitzJames, who was later bishop of London. He secured a large sum towards the building work. Its parapets included very many pinnacles, but in a single night the majority of them were blown down in a storm.
Long ago there were within the town of Oxford more than 800 houses of burgesses, and another 400 outside in the suburbs. It is sometimes said that there used also to be more than twenty-four parish churches in the town and

suburbs. Oxford's seal includes an ox within a castle or walled town, and the Latin inscription around it is, 'Seal of the city of Oxford', etc.

The Oxford burgesses claim Vortimer as the founder of their town. Henry I was partly responsible for the rebuilding of Oxford, but it reached its peak, in the numbers both of its students and of its other inhabitants, during Henry III's reign. They were so numerous then that a special provision was made for victualling within a two-mile radius of the city. At this time too there was an infinite number of scribes and parchment-makers in Oxford.

Bridges on the Cherwell: East Bridge at Oxford; upstream to Islip Bridge, of stone, three miles overland; Gosford Bridge, a mile or more; Emmeley [?] Bridge, two miles further; Heywood Bridge, two miles further, etc. Where the bridge over the Cherwell now stands next to Magdalen College there used, in Henry III's time, to be a crossing or ferry called Steneford.

A younger brother of the senior branch of the Barentine family was a London goldsmith, who became remarkably wealthy and purchased a fine estate. It is said that he died without heirs, and gave a portion of his land to another younger brother of the Barentine's called Drew. Drew had numerous children, but in due course they died, and the portion reverted to the senior branch of the family. The parcel of land left by Drew to his descendants was Little Haseley in Oxfordshire, the home now of Sir William Barentine. Barentine the goldsmith built the manor house at Little Haseley, and donated fine lands to the company of goldsmiths in London. In return they kept a very solemn obit for him every year. He lived in the fine house right next to the goldsmith's hall, and I believe that he built not only the house, but also part of the hall. He is buried in the church of St Zacharias next to the goldsmith's hall.

The senior branch of the Barentines was most prominent during the reigns of Henry I, Henry III and Edward III. Since the time of Edward III the line has descended through nephews. The grandfather of the present Mr Barentine married the daughter of the countess of Hainault; she was fathered by William, duke of Suffolk, who married the countess, then divorced her, and married Chaucer's heiress. [5/231-3]

RUTLAND

THE TWO BRIEF itinerary accounts are both taken from the 1541 journey to North-East England, on the outward and return journeys, and should be read in conjunction with the entries for neighbouring counties. Leland's notes on Rutland are largely concerned with the course of rivers, although he also mentions, not without scepticism, the tradition of Rutter and the wooden horse.

I RODE FROM WITHCOTE, partly through the wooded country of Leighfield Forest, and then into Rutland; it was still wooded to begin with, but then the land opened out and became exceptionally fertile arable and pasture. After four miles I arrived in Uppingham. Uppingham is a market town, with only one modest street and a very modest church; even so it is reckoned to be the best town in Rutland. Lyddington, where the bishop of Lincoln has an old manor house, is a mile away; and Harringworth is three short miles, all across open country.

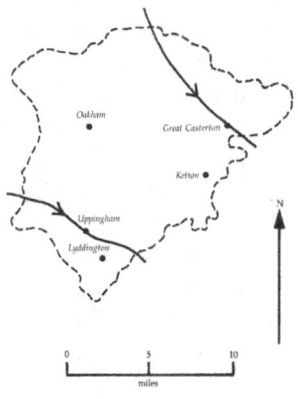

About a mile before I reached Harringworth I passed through a Rutland village. Harringworth is actually in Northamptonshire, and stands on the River Welland. The county of Rutland is approximately circular in shape, and the River Welland forms part of its border, from Stamford right along to the bridge at Rockingham. *cont. p. 221* [**1541:** 1/22]

I RODE FROM BELVOIR CASTLE to Croxton [*Kerrial*], which is two miles, and from there another six miles to a small roadside place. My journey was all across open country, with good pasture and arable, but little woodland. Six miles further of similar terrain brought me to the causeway along Watling Street [*Ermine Street*] on the stretch between Ancaster and Stamford. I kept to the great ridge of Watling Street for three miles, passing open country of corn and grass, but little or no woodland, as far as Great Casterton Bridge. A pleasant brook flows under Casterton Bridge, and I assume that it can be none other than the River Gwash, on its course from Rutland to join the River Welland not far below Stamford. I remained on the ridge of Watling Street for another mile as far as Stamford, but as I left Stamford I had difficulty in finding the ridge again. In fact it runs on to Weedon-in-the-Street and Towcester, and then I assume to Stony Stratford, Dunstable and St Albans. *cont. p. 262* [**1541:** *1/98-9*]

The River Chater flows into the Welland about two miles above Stamford on the upper bank. It rises in Rutland or the edge of Leicestershire, sixteen miles west of the confluence; then flows within a mile of Uppingham (which is in Stamford [*i.e. Rutland*]) on the nearer bank; then six miles down to Oakham, which is a mile away on the further bank; then only five miles to Ketton (in Rutland) on the nearer bank, where there is a stone bridge of six arches across the Chater; then a half-mile lower into the River Welland. In Ketton live two gentlemen with attractive estates; one is called Kingston. Water from several springs is channelled in lead conduits to the Stamford friaries. One fine spring is channelled a quarter-mile right into the centre of the town, where there are two or three castellated conduit houses. [*4/90*]

There is a popular tradition in Rutland that there was a man called Rutter who stood in great favour with his prince. For a reward he asked to be given as much land as he could ride over in a day on a wooden horse. By magic powers he rode over all the land that is now Rutland, but afterwards he was swallowed up into the ground. I believe that this tradition is probably mistaken, and it is more likely that it referred to Rotherland or Rutherland, which is abbreviated to Rutland.

    The present earl of Rutland, I discovered, is descended on his mother's side from the last duke of Exeter, who married St Leger. [*4/124*]

Several small brooks flow into the further bank of the Welland before it reaches Rockingham. The Little Eye, which forms the boundary between Leicestershire and Rutland, flows into the further bank of the Welland a half-mile below Rockingham Bridge. The River Wrete or Wrek [*Chater*] enters by the upper bank of the Welland a half-mile below Collyweston Bridge; a mile upstream from its confluence with the Welland, at Ketton, there is a bridge across it, arched with stone. The River Gwash flows from a little above Oakham in Rutland, then eight miles to Byry [*Great*] Casterton, where there is a three-arched bridge, then a mile or more to Newstead Bridge, and soon after into the Welland. Bridges on the River Welland below Rockingham Bridge are at Collyweston, Stamford, Uffington, West Deeping, East Deeping and Crowland. [*5/145*]

SHROPSHIRE

THE 1538 TOUR of the northern counties explored parts of west and mid Wales before returning into England, and the English itinerary begins near the Welsh border at Alberbury. The Shropshire portion of this early journey, via Moreton Corbet and Prees to Whitchurch, is brief and sketchy, but we are treated to a much fuller description five years later. The West Midlands itinerary took Leland through the county, from Ludlow via Church Stretton to Shrewsbury (the furthest point on this journey) and then back via Much Wenlock to Bridgnorth.

Apart from the itinerary accounts substantial notes on Shropshire have survived. There are systematic lists of towns, castles, monasteries and other features, as well as interesting descriptions of Oswestry, Pontesbury and the Clee Hills. For some Shropshire places along the Welsh border see pp. 469-70.

NEXT TO ALBERBURY CHURCH in Shropshire may be seen the ruined castle of Fulk Fitz-Warine, the noble warrior, and less than a mile away was the White Abbey, where he is buried; it was suppressed and granted to Chicheley College [All Souls], Oxford. Between Alberbury and Shrewsbury are six miles of fertile arable, woodland and pasture.

I rode two miles from Shrewsbury to the Augustinian abbey at Haughmond. No more than three-quarters of a mile after I had left the Severn on my right hand I entered a wood, and soon afterwards crossed a brook, whose source is in Penleighs Mere, and which shortly after enters the

SHROPSHIRE

Severn. From there I rode across a mixture of pasture and marshy ground to Moreton Corbet, where I saw Mr Corbet's fine castle. Two miles further I crossed the River Roden, which rises not far above Wem, a mile away.

From there it was five [*or seven, Leland has both*] miles to a little roadside place called Prees. My road took me through rather flat country, with some heathland and some good arable. Mr Sanford has a house beside a fine lake on the edge of a wood, a mile-and-a-half from Prees. Then I went another three miles, over reasonably fertile sandy ground, to Whitchurch. Approaching Whitchurch I passed a most attractive lake, stocked with bream, pike, tench, perch and dace. Apart from the bream all these fish are generally found in all the lakes of Shropshire, Cheshire and Lancashire; in some of them trout are found as well.

The town of Whitchurch in Shropshire has a very good market. Sir Gilbert Talbot is buried in the parish church. A mile-and-a-half beyond Whitchurch I rode past the pale of the earl of Shrewsbury's large park of Black Mere. This park contains both red and fallow deer, and there is an excellent house or lodge within it. I was told that there were three good lakes in the park, and the largest of these, which I could see from the pale, is called Blakein [*Black Mere*], and so gives the park its name.

One imagines that these lakes, which are found mostly in marshy areas and rather low-lying places, derive their water from their boggy surroundings, and stagnate because there is nowhere for the water to go. It is most likely that some of them originated as marl pits, since the sandy soil of parts of Shropshire, and more particularly of Cheshire and Lancashire, will not produce good corn harvests unless it is marled. Other lakes have perhaps formed where large quantities of turf and peat have been dug. *cont. p. 26* [**1538:** *4/1-2*]

TEME BRIDGE AT LUDLOW, and the river downstream from it, form the boundary between Herefordshire and Shropshire. The town of Ludlow is on the left bank of the Teme and so lies in Shropshire. It stands on a hill, so that from whichever direction you approach it you have to climb. It has a good wall, which I would reckon to be about a mile in circuit. The wall has five gates. Broad Gate, and the area leading to Broad Street, is the most attractive part of the town. Old Gate, like Broad Gate, leads out to the Teme, but is not so close to it. Corve Gate leads to the left bank of the River Corve; and there are also Galfride

[*Galford*] Gate and Mill Gate. One part of the town is enclosed by the castle, which stands between Corve Gate and Mill Gate on a strong, well-ditched crag of rock.

There is only one parish church in the town, but that is very fine, and large, and richly adorned, and is regarded as the best in the whole region. It stands on the highest ground in the very centre of the town, and on the north side its churchyard is confined by the town wall. This church has been greatly improved by a guild founded in it and named after St John the Evangelist. Local people assert that this was founded during the reign of Edward the Confessor, and they always maintain that the pilgrims who carried the ring from over the sea as a sign from St John the Evangelist to King Edward were in fact inhabitants of Ludlow.

The guild appoints a guardian each year from among the burgesses, and at present there are ten priests who are members of this college. They are supported partly by endowed lands, and partly by charity collections from the local people. These priests have a good house at the west end of the churchyard, and next to it is a hospital or almshouse to accommodate thirty poor people, and sometimes more. The almshouse is maintained partly by the guild, but also from money given as obits for men buried in the church.

Not long ago there was a very rich merchant in Ludlow by the name of Hosier, and he is buried in the parish church. He established a chantry in part of the college just described, and he endowed it with an annual income from land of £10 or £12. This stipend now pays for a schoolmaster.

I noted the tombs of several men of renown in Ludlow church, as follows: Beaupie, once Edward IV's cofferer, whose coat of arms includes a leg; Cox, a gentleman servant to Prince Arthur; Dr Denton, Master of St John's, Ludlow; Sulyard, justiciar in the Welsh Marches; Hosier, the merchant.

Ludlow has two castellated conduit houses, both supplied with water from the same source. There were also two good colleges of friars in the town. The white friars was a fine, expensive building, which stood on the north side, almost at the far end of the suburb beyond Corve Gate. It was established by a knight named Ludlow, who was the owner of Stokesay, a castle or tower on the way to Bishop's Castle. Vernon, the present owner of Stokesay, who acquired it by marriage, has recently been credited with founding the friary. The Austin friary stood outside Galford Gate.

I saw suburbs beyond all Ludlow's gates except Mill Gate, which I did not visit. The suburb across Teme Bridge to the south is called Ludford, and has its own small parish church. Teme Bridge is of stone, and has three fine arches and a chapel on it dedicated to St Catherine. Until it was built, about a hundred years ago, people had to cross the river by a ford a little further downstream. On the left bank of the river, and the north side of Teme Bridge, there stands outside Broad Gate a church of St John, which used to be a college with a dean and fellows. It was founded by a certain Jordan.

There is a good stone bridge across the Teme at Leintwardine, a village five miles upstream from Ludlow. At Brampton [Bryan], two miles from Leintwardine, is a tower or castle, and five miles above Leintwardine on the Teme is a pleasant town called Knighton. Four miles below Ludlow there is a stone bridge of two arches over the Teme at Tenbury. Tenbury is a market town on the right bank of the Teme in Herefordshire; I have since been told by Thomas Evan that he is certain that Tenbury is actually in the furthest part of Worcestershire. There is a house called Burford a little upstream from Tenbury on the left bank in Shropshire; this is the principal seat of Baron Burford. The Ledwyche Brook flows into the Teme on its left bank near Tenbury.

The River Onny rises at Shelve in the Bishop's Castle area, and flows for fifteen miles before it joins the Teme a little below Bromfield. Bromfield Priory was a cell of monks dependent on Gloucester Abbey. Giffard gave it to Gloucester, and at one time there were prebendaries there. The priory stood between the Onny and the Teme. The buildings themselves lay on the left bank of the Teme, and close to the river; the Onny's right bank adjoined the far side of the priory orchard, and not far below the priory is the confluence of the rivers. This is two miles above Ludlow. There is an attractive stone bridge over the Onny a little above Bromfield, and another two miles upstream at Wistanstow [?]; Mr Vernon has a house close to the river further up. It is probable that the Earl of Oxford's moated farmhouse at Bromfield occupies the site of the castle which belonged to Giffard, and which was destroyed by force. Caynham Castle, now demolished, stood three miles from Ludlow; it is sometimes called Caiholme.

Distances from Ludlow: Clee Hills, 3 miles ENE; Worcester, 20 miles; Bridgnorth, 15 miles; Presteigne, 5 miles; Knighton, 10 miles; Bishop's Castle, 20 miles; Shrewsbury, 20 miles; Gloucester, via Bromyard, 30 miles.

My exit from Ludlow was by Corve Gate, and I immediately came to Corve Bridge, which has five fine stone arches. From this bridge the River Corve flows straight past Ludlow Castle, and shortly below flows into the Teme on its left bank. I noted here that whereas the Teme flows from the WNW out of Wales, the Corve flows from ENE through Corvedale in Shropshire.

From Corve Bridge at Ludlow I rode for six miles partly across quite good arable and partly through patches of woodland, until I came to a poor village called Strefford. Here there was a small brook which a half-mile lower flows into the River Onny on its left bank. Next I passed on my right hand side two large woods stocked with roe deer, the Edge and the Long Forest; and from there I rode on three miles past well-wooded country until I reached Stretton. This is a pleasant, remote little town, and a lawyer named Brooke has a nice house here next to the church. The brook which runs here is the same, so I was told, as the one which I encountered at Strefford. Great [Church] Stretton has the most important buildings in Stretton Dale, but there are also two other settlements, Little Stretton and Old [All] Stretton. Stretton Dale, which belongs to the earl of Arundel, is only three miles long, and is surrounded by great hills, well-wooded in some places.

After Stretton I rode past hilly, wooded country for three miles to a roadside place called Leebotwood. A mile or more later I passed Mr Corbet's park close to my left hand. Then for four miles I crossed flat country which grew some corn, and a further two miles of better arable soil, which brought me to Shrewsbury. About a half-mile before I reached Shrewsbury I rode by a ford across the Meole Brook [Rea Brook], at a point where there was also a long narrow wooden bridge which took its name from the brook. A mile above Meole Bridge there is another wooden bridge across the Meole called Dagge Bridge. And as I entered Shrewsbury close to the abbey there was a three-arched stone bridge over the Meole; just below this bridge is the confluence of the Rivers Meole and Severn.

By the bridge too a sidestream breaks out of the River Severn, but in summer when the river is at its lowest this branch scarcely trickles over its bed. A bridge of eight low arches crosses this branch, and as soon as it has flowed under the bridge it rejoins the mainstream again. There are two large and important bridges at Shrewsbury which cross the Severn in its entirety. The greater and more attractive is the Welsh Bridge, which lies upstream of the other, and is so called because it is the way from the town towards Wales. It stands on the western side of Shrewsbury, and at one end of it is a large gate which allows access to the town; at the other end, facing Wales, is a mighty strong tower which prevents enemies from getting on to the bridge. The other bridge is lower down the Severn, and this has four large arches as well as a drawbridge.

The town of Shrewsbury stands on a rocky outcrop of stiff red earth, and the River Severn encircles it to such an extent that were it not for a little neck of land it would be an island. Its usual Welsh name now is Moythik, but the Welsh writers refer to it as Penguern, which means 'the alder peak'. The correct spelling of its proper English name is 'Schrobbesbyri', which does not much disagree with 'Penguern', although the Latin version, 'Salapia', is very different from the Welsh name.

Shrewsbury has a strong wall of more than a mile in circuit, and is well defended by water, which may be regarded as taking the place of a town ditch. There are three gates in the town. The castle, which stands in the northern part of the town, has been a strong building, but is now largely in ruins.

The town has four parish churches. The main one, dedicated to St Chad, is collegiate, with a dean and ten prebendaries under the bishop of Lichfield's patronage. Next to it is a hospital maintained by the Shrewsbury guild of merchants. The second church, which is also collegiate, is St Mary's; it has a dean and nine poor prebendaries, and the king is its patron. Within living memory a Shrewsbury merchant, one Diggory Walter, built a hospital at the west end of St Mary's church. St Alkmund's parish church was appropriated by Lilleshall Priory, and close to St Alkmund's is St Julian's parish church; this was appropriated by Battlefield Chapel, one mile north of Shrewsbury.

The house of grey friars in Shrewsbury was founded by the Charltons, and Lady Charlton, whom they regarded as their foundress, was buried there. The friary stood on the Severn bank just upstream from the five-arched bridge. In recent times a friar by the name of Father Francis rebuilt a large portion of this friary. The house of black friars was established by Lady Geneville, and stood a little way outside the town wall at the end of Marwall Street beside the Severn. Many gentlemen casualties at Battlefield were buried in the black friars' church. The Austin friars, founded by the Stafford family, stood a little below Welsh Bridge.

Owen Glendower promised Percy that he would join him at the Battle of Shrewsbury. Battlefield chapel is a mile away to the north of Shrewsbury. It was founded as a small college and endowed by Henry IV, but the patronage was granted to the gentleman and his heirs on whose land it was built.

There is a fine stone bridge over the Severn four miles above Shrewsbury called Montford Bridge, and it has recently been renewed. Shrawardine Castle is on the left bank of the Severn two miles further upstream, and a mile above the castle is another bridge over the Severn, Buttington Bridge. There is also a bridge over the Severn near Welshpool.

A fine long bridge of stone crosses the Severn at Atcham to give access to the village of Wroxeter, which is a mile-and-a-half lower than Atcham on the left bank. Roughly halfway between Atcham and Wroxeter the River Tern enters the Severn. It is very likely that the destruction of Wroxeter was the cause of the building of Shrewsbury; for Wroxeter was a good walled town until it was destroyed by the Danes.

Not more than a mile below Wroxeter on the left bank of the Severn is the foot of the Wrekin Hill, which is also known as Mount Gilbert. The Wrekin is the highest point in all the surrounding region, and stands up treeless like a beacon. On top of this hill is a delightful flat piece of ground, on which grows good fine grass, and there is a pleasant spring.

Sir Rowland Hill, a London merchant, has recently built a new bridge over the Tern, a little above its confluence with the Severn. Crowlington [*?Crudgington or Rowton*] Bridge, of stone and timber, is five miles or more up the Tern; and Stoke Bridge, of timber, is three miles higher. Stoke upon Tern is a pleasant little place on the left bank, and about a mile away on the right bank is another small place called Hodnet. Drayton, a market town two miles further upstream, also has a small bridge.

The only bridge over the Severn between Atcham and Bridgnorth is a stone one at Buildwas, where the Cistercian monastery was built on the right bank. Thomas Cleobury, the former abbot of Dore, told me that in the reign of Offa, King of Mercia, when the robe of office of the archbishop of Lichfield was taken from Lichfield and restored to Canterbury, one of the old bishops of Lichfield went to Buildwas to live the life of a hermit.

Distances from Shrewsbury: Chester, 30 miles; Oswestry, 12 miles; Wroxeter, 4 miles, but often reckoned to be 3 miles; Wenlock, 8 miles; Whitchurch, 15 miles; Montgomery, 16 miles; Bridgnorth, 16 miles.

SHROPSHIRE

I travelled from Shrewsbury for four miles across reasonably good country for corn and grass, although there was not much woodland in view, until I came to a poor village called Cound. A pleasant stream called the Rhe [Row] Brook flows down from the south through this village, and into the Severn a little further downstream. At Cound it is crossed by a narrow wooden bridge. I continued for two miles to the village of Harley, and from there a further two miles of rough going, as I passed over a high rocky hill called Wenlock Edge. This brought me to the market town of Wenlock, which lies in Shropshire surrounded by hills, and where there used to be an abbey. A small stream flows from the hills to the west of Wenlock and passes through the centre of the town. It flows into the Severn on its right bank, which is about two miles away. I have heard this stream called the Rhe.

I rode on past some arable, pasture and woodland for six miles until I reached a village called Morville. I saw a small priory or monastic cell, also called Morville, on my right hand as I entered the village. Bridgnorth was two miles further. The town occupies a prominent position on the right bank of the Severn (as the river flows downstream). It used to be strongly walled, but the walls are now all in ruins. There are four gates through the walls. There is a ditch beside the walls, except near the Severn; in this area nature has made its own fearful ditch, as the Severn runs in a deep valley between two steep hills.

The name Bridgnorth has only recently become prevalent, and all the old records call it Bridge. One theory supposes that the ending refers to a forest called Morthe, lying directly opposite the town across the Severn.

The castle stands in the southern part of the town, and on its eastern side the sheer-sided valley fortifies it instead of a ditch. Its walls rise to a great height, and there used to be two or three strong wards in the castle, which have now fallen into complete ruin. I estimate that the castle accounts for more than a third of the circuit of the town, which in its entirety is barely a mile. On the north side of the castle there is one mighty gate, but this has been blocked up, and a small postern gate has been forced through the wall next to it as the castle entrance. The castle precinct, and especially the outer courtyard, has recently had many new wooden dwellings built in it.

Bridgnorth has only one parish church, which is a fine building dedicated to St Leonard. It also has one most attractive street which runs from north to south. The houses on each side of this street have galleries, like those in some of the city streets in Chester, and these enable people to pass along in the dry when it rains. The town depends on the cloth industry, but this has declined there, and the town has very badly declined along with it.

Within the castle there is a collegiate church dedicated to St Mary Magdalene for a dean and six prebendaries. This church, which is now a rather rough building, was originally built and endowed with lands by Robert de Belleme, earl of Shrewsbury, as a chapel for the castle alone. Robert had earlier established a similar chapel to St Mary Magdalene at Quatford, on the request of his wife who had made a vow to this effect when caught up in a storm at sea. Quatford lies north-east [*i.e. south-east*] of Bridgnorth on the Severn, and there are still many traces of the tower or manor house there which once belonged to Robert de Belleme.

The bridge which stands to the east of Bridgnorth has eight large arches and a chapel dedicated to St Sythe [*Sitha or Zita*]. Over the bridge is an attractive long street of modest buildings called the Low Town; it has a chapel of St John. Right next to Low Town, due east from Bridgnorth, is a hilly and well-wooded area called Morthe. It used to be a forest or chase for deer, but there are no deer there now. It is frequently maintained by some people that in a cliff within this forest or wood King Athelstan's brother spent some time leading the life of a hermit. The spot may still be seen, and is called the Hermitage.

Bridgnorth's spectacular walls and strong castle have been in decline since the occasion when one of the Mortimers held it by force during a rebellion. cont. p. 407 [**1543**: 2/76-86]

Pontesbury is merely a small country town, and lies four miles south-west of Shrewsbury. A brook rises in a nearby hill just above the town, called Ponslithe [?*Pontesford Hill*], and from there flows down to the Severn about a half-mile above Shrewsbury. Like Shrewsbury Pontesbury lies beyond the Severn, but is three miles from the riverbank.

Attached to Pontesbury church are a dean and three prebendaries. Cole, who was subdean of the King's Chapel, used to be dean of Pontesbury, and he went to great expense on the dwelling house there. Two other good houses belong to the prebendaries, and Lord Powys is the patron.

On the south side of the churchyard may be seen substantial evidence, including fallen masonry, of a large manor house or castle, and this area still has the name of 'Castle Pavement'. A quarter-mile or more from Pontesbury church is

SHROPSHIRE

a wood called Hogstow Forest, which belongs to the manor of Caus, and halfway between the church and this wood the ruins of a castle or tower belonging to Lord Powys are visible on top of [*a hill*]. From this hill it is possible to see Shrewsbury and many other places in the area. The wooded forest of Hogstow is large and has deer; it extends in one direction almost as far as Caus Castle, which now belongs to Lord Stafford. [2/26-7]

Certainly two brooks, the Teme and the Corve, flow past Ludlow in Shropshire. The Teme flows into the Severn between Powick and Worcester.

Ludlow is a very handsome town with good walls and gates, and on every side it rises proud from a valley. A fine castle stands to one side, but within part of the wall encircling the town. There is one parish church right in the centre of the town, and outside the walls are several chapels, as well as two friaries, Austin and Carmelite. Corve Gate and Galford Gate, among others, are the names of town gates.

The bishop of Hereford has a castle of considerable strength in the Shropshire area of the Marches. It is called Bishop's Castle, and beside it stands a town called Bishop's Town, in which a very good weekly market is held. [3/50]

Sir John Talbot, who married Troutbeck's heiress, lives in a good lodge right at the top of Albrighton Park, which lies on the very edge of Shropshire three miles from Tong.

Corbet of Moreton Corbet owns land around Shropshire worth annually over £500; he also owns a manor near Leighton Buzzard in Buckinghamshire [*i.e. Bedfordshire*]. His younger brother owns Leigh, two miles from Caus Castle. He acquired it partly by marriage, and it is worth £70 per year. According to some people the Corbets owned Caus Castle until recently. Another Corbet branch is at Longnor, four miles from Shrewsbury on the way to Ludlow. The estate includes a park and has an annual value of £40.

Sir Richard Mainwaring of Ightfield, two miles from Whitchurch. John Dodd of Cloverley, which is a mile from Ightfield, is worth £70 per year, and Sir Robert Needham of Sheinton £270. Grosvenor of Bellaport, three miles from Market Drayton, and Grosvenor of Eaton Bote [*?Buerton*] in Cheshire, are both descended from younger brothers of Grosvenor of Houme [*?Hulme*], whose five daughters and heiresses all married. The eldest married Shackerley of Lancaster, who thereby acquired the manor of Houme.

Newport of [*High*] Ercall, a manor worth £100 with a park; he also has land nearby worth a further £100. Together with Mitton, of Cotton near Shrewsbury, this man acquired the Shropshire and Warwickshire estates of Sir John Borrow. Mitton's principal house is at Moor Hall in Warwickshire. His house at Cotton, which is a quarter-mile from Shrewsbury, has an annual value of £130. He is also referred to as lord of Mouthey [*?Mowthwy, Powys*], but I believe that he is only the king's steward there.

There are branches of the Leighton family at Leighton itself, Wattlesborough, Plaish (which is a mile or two from Acton Burnell), and Roden Mere (on the River Rodden two miles from Charlton Castle).

Trentam of Shropshire used to live in the town itself [?i.e. *Shrewsbury*], where his best house was. Now he has sold his Shropshire properties, which had an annual value of £50, and has bought Rocester Priory in Staffordshire on the River Dove. Thornes of Shrewsbury, land worth £50. Onslow of Onslow, two miles from Shrewsbury, land worth £40. Otley of Pitchford, four miles from Shrewsbury and a mile from Acton Burnell, land worth £100. Scriven of Frodesley, a mile from Acton Burnell, land worth £70. Lee of Longnor, where there is a fine manor [?*house*] and park a mile from Acton Burnell, land worth £100. This Lee is the elder brother of the Lee who married Leighton of Wattlesborough's wife.

Laken of Willey, where there is a park three miles from Bridgnorth, £200. Gatacre of Gatacre, three miles from Bridgnorth, £70. Woolridge of Dudmaston on the bank of the Severn, £70. Haughton of Beckbury, four miles from Bridgnorth, £40. Young of Caynton, £70. Vernon, son of Sir Henry Vernon, of Hodnet, £130 by marriage to one of the heiresses of Ludlow. Cotton of Cotton, £50. Chorlton of Apley close to Wellington. Chorlton of Wombridge. [3/65-7]

Oswestry is twelve miles north-west of Shrewsbury. Distances from Oswestry: Trallwng, or the Welshpool, twelve miles; Wrexham, ten miles; Whitchurch in Shropshire, twelve miles; Chester, ten miles to Wrexham, and then eight by the highway to Chester; Ruthin, fifteen miles, and Denbigh five miles further; Flint Castle, twenty miles.

There used to be a castle at Ellesmere, and there are still very fine lakes. The town has four reasonably well-built streets, and is permitted to hold two fairs, but there is no public market at present.

Croes Oswald [*Oswestry*] occupies a flat site in a valley, and lies twelve long miles north-west of Shrewsbury across open, almost treeless country. The circuit of the town within its wall is about a mile. There are four gates: New Gate (Porth Newydd) to the south; Black Gate (Porth Du) to the south-east, towards Shrewsbury; Beatrice Gate, from which the street leading into the town takes its name, to the north-east, towards Chester; Wallia or Mountain Gate (so-called because it is the way to the mountains, only a quarter-mile distant), to the north-west, towards Penllyn Mountain in Merioneth. Apart from at these gates there are no towers in the town walls, but there is a ditch around the town which is fed by streams.

St Oswald's Church is a very fine building, with a leaded roof and a large tower and spire; however, it stands outside New Gate, so that there is in fact no church within the town. St Oswald's was at one time a minster called the White Minster. Later it was turned into the parish church, and the living was appropriated by Shrewsbury Abbey. Its cloister stood where the monks' tombs are until within living memory. The street and area around the church are called

Stretllan [*Strad y Llan*]. All the town's chapels are out in the suburbs. There is a chapel dedicated to St John the Baptist between Strad y Llan and Black Gate. A second lies in the same suburb and is within a bowshot of St Oswald's; it is called the Chapel of St Oswald, and is at Oswald's Well. A third, dedicated to St Edith, lies to the north-east on the way to Chester.

Within the town are ten notable streets, and the most important are Cross Street (where there is a stone cross), Bailey Street (where there is the largest market and the traders), and Newgate Street. The wooden Booth Hall, or town house, is a fine building, and stands near the castle. It is said that Madoc, son of Meredoc, prince of Powys, built the castle, and there is a tower still standing in the castle which is named after him. There is also a chamber built by Richard II after Arundel had been condemned to death for treason.

Oswestry [*is governed by*] a bailiff and serjeants. The houses within the town are built of timber and roofed with slate. Its main livelihood is derived from selling cloth made in Wales. It has a castle which stands on a mound (probably artificial) surrounded by a ditch, which adjoins the town wall, on the south-west side of the town between Beatrice Gate and Wallia Gate. A certain David Holbache, who was a lawyer and steward of the town and manor, built a free school on the south-west side of the church, and gave land worth £10 to support it. Some people say that David Inn in London was also built by him.

There are four suburbs. The largest consists of four streets, and is called Strad y Llan. The second suburb is the street called Wallia. The third, which is called Beatrice, has as many as 140 different barns for corn and hay. Blackgate Street, which is the fourth suburb, also has thirty barns for the townspeople's corn, in addition to other buildings.

A brook flows through the town and past the cross. It derives from a place called Simon's Well, which lies a bowshot outside the wall to the north-west, and then flows in through the wall between Wallia Gate and New Gate, through the town, and out under Black Gate. St Oswald's Well lies a bowshot from St Oswald's Church, in the fields to the south-west. The story goes that an eagle snatched the arm of Oswald from the tree, but the bird fell to earth, and where it fell the spring which has been made famous by the legend now issues forth. A wooden chapel has been built over the spring, which has been enclosed within a stone wall. There is also a stream called Beatrice, because it flows through a small wooden bridge at Beatrice Gate. The three streams pass under stone bridges at Wallia Gate, New Gate and Black Gate, and then flow with the Cross Brook a mile downstream to the south-west, where they enter the River Morda. This river rises on Llanfarda Hill. There used to be a church on this hill, which some people believe used to be the parish church of Oswestry; it is now ruined.

The country around Oswestry is flat, and produces good corn and grass crops, except over to the north-west into Merionethshire. In the Whittington direction there are woods in the manor of Llwyn hen dinas, in Whittington Park and in Whittington Moor.

The settlement or castle of Hen Dinas stands a quarter-mile north-west of Oswestry on a small rounded hill about a half-mile in circumference. At the foot of the hill it is surrounded by three large ditches, and on the top great oak trees are now growing. It is a common belief that there was once a city within the ditches, but I am inclined to think that it was a hillfort, and perhaps the place mentioned in connection with the battle between Penda and Oswald. There is another earthwork mound close to Hen Dinas, between it and Oswestry.

Whittington lies in a valley one long mile north-east of Hen Dinas. It contains a hundred houses, with a round castle of no great size enclosed by a ditch in the centre of the village. [3/73-6]

Market towns in Shropshire: Shrewsbury; Bridgnorth, 14 miles from Shrewsbury; Wellington, 7 miles from Shrewsbury on the London road; Drayton on the River Tern, 12 miles from Shrewsbury; Whitchurch, 14 or 15 miles from Shrewsbury; Newport, on a brook, 12 or 13 miles from Shrewsbury (less than a mile from Newport is a fine large mere or lake); Bishop's Castle, a very famous market; Ludlow. Peter Undergod, a gentleman in the retinue of an English Prince of Wales, built St John's Hospital outside [Teme] Gate at Ludlow, and later endowed it with lands.

At Bloreheath above Market Drayton, a mile to the north of the town, a battle was fought between King Edward's men and Henry VI. The earl of Salisbury and the northerners on King Edward's side defeated Lord Audley (killed) and Lord Dudley (wounded), thereby winning the battle against Queen Margaret, Henry VI's wife, and the men of Cheshire. Bishop Hall of Chester, who was the queen's chaplain, arranged for her to stay at Eccleshall, and she went there after the battle.

Castles in Shropshire: Shrewsbury. Bridgnorth is thirteen miles from Shrewsbury down the River Severn. Caus Castle stands on a hill five miles south-west of Shrewsbury. It was formerly the duke of Buckingham's, but now belongs to Lord Stafford. The royal castle of Montgomery is twelve miles from Shrewsbury. It was once a large walled town called 'Cairovalduine'. It lies within Shropshire, although is reckoned not to be part of the county. The hundred of Chirbury was annexed to Montgomery, so that men from the hundred might help to defend it. Ludlow is twenty miles from Shrewsbury. Newport stands on a brook, or waste, fourteen miles east of Shrewsbury, and Whitchurch on a stream sixteen miles west of Shrewsbury. Drayton lies on the River Tern fourteen miles from Shrewsbury, and Wigmore Castle twenty miles from Shrewsbury stands on a stream which is sometimes almost dry. Whittington is a castle owned by Lord Fitzwarin; it is six miles upstream from Shrewsbury and close to the Severn, and the course of Offa's Dyke runs nearby. Shrawardine belongs to the earl of Arundel, and lies between Shrewsbury and Whittington, four miles from the former, two from the latter. Red Castle near Whitchurch used to belong to Lord Audley. It lies eight miles directly north of Shrewsbury and is completely ruined. It used to be a strong castle, but has been derelict for a long time. Myddle Castle, three miles from Shrewsbury, belonged to Lord Derby, but is very ruinous. Moreton Corbet stands in marshland four miles north of Shrewsbury, and belongs to the Corbet family. Knockin Castle in Shropshire belonged to Lord Le Strange, but is now the earl of Derby's; the building is now in ruins. Charlton Castle belongs to Lord Powys, and stands on the River Tern six miles from Shrewsbury and a mile from the village of Tern. Tern means 'lake' or 'pool'. Corfham Castle is fourteen miles south of Shrewsbury, and stands on the River Corve (which gives its name also to Corvedale).

Acton Burnell was a good manor house or castle, and a Parliament was held there in a large barn. It is four miles from Shrewsbury, and its owners have included Lord Lovell, then the duke of Norfolk, and now Sir John Dudley. Lovell acquired Acton Burnell by virtue of marrying Burnell's daughter, which augmented the Lovell estate. Later he was created Viscount Lovell.

Some of these castles, although lying within Shropshire, are not subject to county jurisdiction. They have their own laws and courts, and other privileges, apart from restriction imposed on them by the recent statute.

Oswestry Castle now lies in Shropshire. Caynham Castle stood on a hilltop within two miles of Ludlow, but is now completely demolished. Holdgate Castle, which once belonged to Lord Lovell, stands under the Clee Hills close to Corvedale, and six miles from Ludlow. The duke of Norfolk exchanged it with Mr Dudley for other lands. Broncroft is a very good fortified house owned by the earl of Shrewsbury. It stands in or close to the Clee Hills.

Stokesay is built like a castle and stands five miles away from Ludlow. It used to belong to the Ludlow family, but now to the Vernons. Sir Richard Ludlow had two daughters, and they married Humphrey Vernon and Thomas Vernon, the brothers of the late Sir Henry Vernon of the Peak. Henry's third son married a Montgomery heiress.

Shepeton Corbet [*Sibdon Carwood*] Castle is six or seven miles from Ludlow, close to the Bishop's Castle road. Hopton Castle is halfway between Bishop's Castle and Wigmore, and three miles from Sibdon. Bishop's Castle itself stands on a crag which is strong, but not very high, and is in good condition.

Abbeys and Priories in Shropshire: Shrewsbury Abbey. White Abbey, near Alberbury, was suppressed long ago. An Augustinian house at Wombridge on the London road, two miles beyond both the town of Wellington and Lilleshall Abbey. Brewood [*White Ladies*] Priory for Cistercian nuns, has recently been suppressed; it stands right on the border between Shropshire and Derbyshire [i.e. *Staffordshire*]. Buildwas, for Cistercian monks. Haughmond, for Augustinian canons. Wenlock, for Benedictine monks. At Tong, which is a small roadside place in Shropshire, between Wolverhampton (seven miles) and Newport (five miles), there is a community and warden, with an almshouse founded long ago by the Vernons of Haddon in the Peak. Almost all the prominent members of this family who have lived since the almshouse was founded are buried there. Tong Castle stands a half-mile from the town on a bank overlooking the brook which flows to Tong from Weston, which is two miles away, and lies in Staffordshire. The old castle was built of stone, but recently Sir Henry Vernon has rebuilt it entirely of brick.

Rivers in Shropshire: Severn. The Tern rises near Maer in Staffordshire, and flows through the villages of Drayton, Ternhill, Besford [*actually on the Roden*] and Sleap, before entering the Severn at Atcham, two miles from Shrewsbury. Elsewhere I was told that it entered the Severn near Tern Bridge. The Corve rises in Corvedale and flows into the Teme at Ludlow; Corvedale is fertile cornland which extends from the Wenlock area to Ludlow. The Rea flows past Wenlock. The source of the Roden is in Combermere Lake [*no*], and it then flows past Whitchurch (a good market town), and the villages of Lee [*Brockhurst*] and Shawbury, entering the Tern at Walcot. Combermere is stocked with very large bream and other good fish. The Onny enters the Teme near Bromfield (a cell of Gloucester). Harmer Pool [?*Haughmond*] is a mile from Shrewsbury. The River Teme enters the Severn on its further bank not far from Powick Mill, a mile-and-a-half downstream from Worcester.

Terrain and land use in Shropshire: In boggy, waterlogged ground seven miles from Shrewsbury, and elsewhere in the county, are found the roots of fir trees, and of whole trees cut down long ago; but by whom, and for what reason, no-one there can tell. They are found below the surface, sometimes a foot or two deep, sometimes five or six feet. Many of them are of great length, without any forks. When burnt they have a good smell.

Cleobury Mortimer is a village in Shropshire with a park next to Wyre Forest, on the road from Ludlow to Bewdley. The Clee Hills are divided into three parts: the hills nearest to Wenlock are called the Brown Clee, and are frequented by deer; those towards Ludlow are called St Margaret's Clee; and between Wyre Forest, which has fine timber, and Ludlow is Titterstone Clee. The Clee Hills begin four miles from Tenbury and extend to within four miles of Wenlock; so my guess is that they run for eight or ten miles. The Ledwyche Brook has its source in the Clee Hills, and flows for seven miles until it enters the Teme at Burford, where Mr Cornwall who owns the barony of Burford has his house. The River Rea also rises in these hills, and flows into the Teme at Newton [*Newnham*] Mills in Worcestershire, three miles below Tenbury.

The boundaries of Shropshire: I have heard it said that Blackmere [Black Park], which is a very large park close to Whitchurch, forms the boundary between Shropshire and Cheshire for some distance. There is a fine manor house in the park. At Monkbridge, a mile below Tenbury, local people told me that there was the meeting point of Worcestershire, Shropshire and Herefordshire. Langfield Dale. Stretton Dale.

[*Gentry of Shropshire:*] Sir Richard Mainwaring, the head of the family of that name, lives three miles east of Prees in a village called Ightfield; his house is surrounded by a park and a large area of woodland. Sandford lives at Sandford, three miles south of Whitchurch; Sandford consists only of his house and park.

Newport lives in a house called [*High*] Ercall, which lies between the Rivers Roden and Tern, near their confluence. Sir John Talbot lives on the London road sixteen miles from Shrewsbury towards the village of Hampton [*?Wolverhampton*]. His house stands in a park called Pepperhill.

The principal seat of the Charlton family is now at Apley, a half-mile from Wellington, and a mile from the Wrekin Hills. However, it appears that in former times Charlton Castle was their main house. There are several Shropshire gentry called Charlton. The Charlton at Charlton Castle married the heiress of Lord Powys, and Grey. Later Lord Powys married Charlton's heiress. Arthur Newton has sold off nearly all his estate.

Iron is manufactured in some parts of Shropshire, particularly in the woods between Buildwas and Wenlock. Coal is dug close to Wombridge, where the priory was. [5/12-18]

The Clee Hills lie wholly in Shropshire. Part of Worcestershire lies on the opposite bank of the River Teme, which marks the boundary, but along most of the river it is Shropshire on the far bank as well. There is not a great deal of wood on the Clee Hills, although there is enough brushwood; and there are abundant stocks of coal, soil, stone, and nitre – this makes exceptionally good lime, and a great deal is made to supply the surrounding country. The Clee Hills extend to within three good miles of Ludlow; and to the east, seven miles from Ludlow on the Bewdley road, the village of Cleobury [*Mortimer*] stands at their foot. There was a castle at Cleobury, and its site, near the church on its northern side, is still called the castle ditch. There are no market towns in the Clee Hills.

The highest portion of the Clee Hills is called Titterstone, and here there is a fine, flat green area with a spring. Three miles away there is another hill called the Brown Clee, and here there is a chase for deer. Another is called Catherton Clee, which is frequented by grouse; it is the source of a stream called Mill Brook, which later flows into the Rea Brook, and this joins the Teme below Teme Bridge. Along the banks of the Mill Brook there are some smelting shops for the manufacture of iron brought from Catherton Clee or Casset Wood. [5/189-90]

Some say that the source of the River Roden is in a large lake called Hurmer [*?Hawk Lake*], six miles north of Shrewsbury. A brook derives from this lake, and flows to another lake called Wibbemere [?]; this is most frequently described as the source of the Roden. After six or seven miles the river flows into the Tern, two miles above Tern Bridge. [5/231]

SOMERSET

SOMERSET IS ONE *of the best-described counties, and it held a particular importance for Leland because of its Arthurian connections. But for all its length his account of Somerset has some notable and surprising omissions – Taunton is not described, there is nothing about Shepton Mallet, Chard or Wincanton, and he seems not to have visited the Bristol Channel, or Severn Sea, coast between Avonmouth and Burnham. What we have are descriptions of two journeys, the West Country tour of 1542, and the 1544 visit to the Bristol area, as well as supplementary notes about Glastonbury and Wells (some of which have here been omitted), and odd scraps of information.*

The 1542 itinerary through Somerset took a meandering course. Leland entered the county from Trowbridge, and after visiting Farleigh Hungerford he explored Bath with his astute antiquarian eye. From there to Wells, which he also described in detail, and after an excursion to Glastonbury he headed into Selwood Forest, through Bruton to South Cadbury, Arthurian Camelot. Ilchester he found in a bad way, and after Montacute he crossed the Somerset Levels to Bridgwater (another good description), and so around the Quantocks to the coast. We leave him on Exmoor.

The later itinerary, which gives the impression that Leland was filling gaps in the knowledge gained from his earlier visit, was mostly concerned with the Mendips and the northern corner of the former Somerset. Two landowning families, the Newtons and the St Loes, seem to have given him hospitality and information, and he also ventured south, to explore Frome, Nunney, Mells and Yeovil.

FROM TROWBRIDGE to Farleigh Castle is about three miles, past good pasture and cornland, and the area near Farleigh itself is well-wooded. Before I reached the castle I descended into a rocky valley, where I crossed the River Frome. For a short distance here streams break away from the river and form little islands between them, before rejoining the main river again; consequently the causeway across the river is made up of several small bridges. The water flows close to the foot of the castle, which is set on a craggy hill, and turns a mill there. In the outer courtyard of the castle

SOMERSET

there are several attractive towers, as well as an old chapel with a new chapel attached to it. Under the arch of this new chapel, but close to the older building, is buried one of the Hungerford family with his wife, and they have two escutcheons on brass plates with the following Latin epitaphs:

'Here lies Thomas Hungerford, knight, lord of Farleigh, Wellow and Heytesbury, who died on 3rd December, A.D. 1398. May God have mercy on his soul, Amen.'

'Here lies the Lady Joanna, wife of the aforesaid Thomas Hungerford, daughter of Sir Edmund Hussey, who died on 1st March A.D. 1412.'

There is also a notice in the chapel, on which is written the following information: 'Thomas Hungerford, knight, and the Lady Joanna, his wife. Sir Walter Hungerford, Lord Hungerford, knight of the Garter and high treasurer of England. Catherine, Walter's wife, heiress of Peverel. Sir Robert, Lord Hungerford. Margaret, wife of Robert, earl of Hungerford, heiress of Botreaux. Eleanor Molynes, wife of Robert, heiress of Molynes.' Note by Leland: I heard it said that this earl and his wife were buried in Salisbury Cathedral.

The ancestry of the late Lord Hungerford: Walter Hungerford, knight. Joanna, Walter's wife. Edward, Walter's son. Jane, his wife. Sir Walter, Lord Hungerford. His wives were: Susan, daughter of Danvers, of Dauntsey near Bradenstoke; Alice, Lord Sannes' daughter; Elizabeth, Lord Hussey's daughter. Walter and Edward, sons of Walter, late Lord Hungerford.

There were two chantry priests attached to this chapel, and they had a pleasant dwelling-house at its eastern end. There is a fine gatehouse into the inner courtyard, with the Hungerford arms ornately carved on it in stone. Within this second court are an imposing hall and three chambers. There is a popular saying that one of the Hungerfords took the duke of Orleans prisoner, and paid for this part of the castle out of the ransom money.

Farleigh Hungerford stands in Somerset, and the River Frome marks the boundary between Somerset and Wiltshire, not only here, but all the way down to the point where it enters the Avon, about a mile-and-a-half downstream. Bradford on Avon I estimate to be at least two miles further up the Avon from this confluence. A park adjoins Farleigh Castle, and a short distance up from the castle is a village.

Norton St Philip is an attractive market town in Somerset about a mile from Farleigh Castle. Its name is derived from the dedication of its church to St Philip and St Jacob, and there is a fair held in the town on the feast day of these saints.

From Farleigh Hungerford I rode through woodland for a mile until I came to a large, well-built grange that had belonged to Hinton Charterhouse. The priory itself stands not very far away from this grange on the brow of a hill about a quarter-mile from the further bank of the Frome, near the confluence of the Frome and the Avon. After I had ridden another mile or more past woods and hills I arrived at a spot where I could see a rough stone wall close to me on my right hand side, which from its great length looked to have been a park wall. Someone told me later that Hinton Priory originally stood there; if this is true, then it must have been the manor of Hatherop, which the monks were given for their first residence.

About a mile further on I arrived at a village, where I crossed by a stone bridge a small brook which local people call Midford Brook. Its source is at the foot of the Mendip Hills, seven miles or more due WSW of this bridge, and about a mile lower it flows into the Avon. From this bridge Bath is two good miles away, over hilly country with quarries, and little woodland within sight. About a mile before reaching Bath I left the Bristol road, which is taken by those who travel regularly between Salisbury and Bristol.

Before I arrived at Bath Bridge over the Avon I descended past a craggy hill full of fine springs of water; and on this craggy hill a long street has been built as a suburb of Bath, with a chapel dedicated to St Mary Magdalene. A large gate with a stone arch gives access to the bridge, and the bridge itself is of five fine stone arches. Between the bridge and the south gate of Bath I noticed good meadows on both sides, but especially on the left hand, which lie due south-west of the town.

The city of Bath is built in a valley which is both fertile and delightful, surrounded on every side by large hills, from which flow many springs of pure water. These are brought by several routes to supply the city, and since lead is manufactured in the area many houses in the town have lead pipes to take the water from place to place.

Bath has four gates, east, west, north and south; and it is only at these gates that there are now any towers on the town wall. From inside the town the wall appears to be of no great height, but from outside the height from ground level is considerable. Nearly all of it, apart from a section near Gascoyne's Tower, is still standing. Gascoyne's Tower is the name generally given to a corner portion of the wall which stands higher than the rest; it was built within living memory by an inhabitant of the town called Gascoyne who, as his fine for committing some wrong in the city, had to repair a ruined section of the wall.

Between the south and west gates in the walls of Bath, and also between the west and north gates, may still be seen a number of important ancient stone carvings. First I saw the ancient flattened head of a man with great locks of hair, similar to a coin I have of Gaius Antius. The second carving which I noticed between the south and north [i.e. west] gates was a statue which I assumed to be of Hercules, since he held a snake in each hand. Then I saw a statue of an infantryman brandishing a sword, and with his shield held out in front of him. Next was a branch with intertwining leaves folded into circles. Then a statue of two naked figures lying in an embrace. And then two ancient heads with the locks of their hair dishevelled. Next a running greyhound, and at his tail was a stone inscribed with large Roman letters from which I could construe no sense. Then I saw another inscription, but all except a few letters had been completely weathered away. And as I approached the west gate I saw a statue of a man entwined by two snakes; I assume that he was Laocoon.

The following I saw between the west and north gates: Two inscriptions which had some words clearly legible, but the rest completely defaced. A statue of a naked man. A stone with cupids intertwined with vines. A tablet carved at each end with a lively figure, embellished above and below. On the tablet an epitaph was inscribed, and I could clearly make out the Latin words for 'lived for thirty years'. The inscription was reasonably complete, but I found the manner in which it was written confusing, since letters stood for whole words, or one letter was used in place of two or three. Then I saw two statues, one of a naked man grasping what I took to be a snake in each hand; this statue was not far from the north gate.

Whatever antiquities had been in the walls between the north and east, and east and south gates, had been destroyed by the construction of the abbey, and by building new walls. I have great doubts as to whether these ancient works were put in their present positions in the walls of Bath during the Roman occupation of Britain; or whether they were collected from old ruins in the town, and later set up in the walls when they were rebuilt, as proof of the town's antiquity.

There are two springs of hot water in the WSW part of the town. The larger of them is called the Cross Bath, because it has a cross erected in the centre of it. This bath is much frequented by people suffering from diseases such as leprosy, pox, skin complaints, and severe pain. It is pleasantly warm, and there are eleven or twelve stone arches along the sides where people may shelter from the rain. This bath has alleviated many skin conditions and pains. Two hundred feet away there is another bath, called the Hot Bath, because when people first encounter it they think that it will scald them, but once their bodies have become acclimatised to it is more bearable and agreeable. It covers a smaller area than the Cross Bath, and has only seven arches along the wall. These two baths adjoin St John's Hospital, in the centre of a small street; it would be reasonable to suppose, therefore, that Bishop Reginald of Bath positioned the hospital close to these two public baths so as to assist poor people who visited them.

The King's Bath is very fine and large. It stands almost in the centre of the town, and at the west end of the cathedral church. The bath and its precinct are surrounded by a high stone wall. Around the edge of the bath itself is a low wall, into which are built an arcade of 32 niches, in which men and women can stand privately. It is to this bath that the gentry resort. A sluice carries water from this bath, and in the past it supplied two buildings used as baths in Bath Priory. These had no springs of their own, and so would otherwise have been empty.

The water in the baths is the colour of deep blue seawater, and it churns continually like a boiling pot, giving off a somewhat unpleasant and sulphurous odour. The water from the two smaller baths flows out westward along a channel into the Avon downstream from the bridge. But the water from the King's Bath turns a mill, and enters the Avon upstream from the bridge. In all three baths it is plainly visible how the water bubbles up from the springs.

Within the walls of Bath there are [number omitted] parish churches, and among these the tower of the church at the north gate has the appearance of being ancient. There is also a parish church and suburb outside the north gate. Right next to the Cross Bath is a hospital dedicated to St John; it was founded by Bishop Reginald of Bath. For a long time the principal livelihood of the town has always been the making of cloth. Within living memory there were three clothiers, all contemporaries, named Style, Kent and Chapman, and they brought prosperity to Bath. But since they died the trade has fallen off to some extent.

According to the chronicle of the former monastery of Bath, in the year of our Lord 676, when Theodore was archbishop of Canterbury, King Osric established a nunnery at Bath, and Bertane was its first abbess. There is also a charter from the time of Archbishop Theodoric which records that a great man by the name of Ethelmod was given leave by King Aethelred to grant land to a certain Bernguid, abbess of Bath, and to a certain Foulcburc. The chronicle of Bath Abbey does not refer at length to any important activity of King Offa of Mercia at Bath. The prior of Bath told me that, after the time of the nunnery, St Peter's church at Bath had secular canons; possibly King Offa of Mercia established them there, as I have read that Offa was responsible for something of note at St Peter's. Alternatively the canons may have arrived after the nunnery had been destroyed by the Danes.

Edgar was very active as a benefactor to St Peter's at Bath, and during his time, and ever since, there were monks in the town; except that for a time they were expelled by Alfarus, earl of Mercia, who was a scourge of monks. John, who was a physician born at Tours in France, was installed as bishop of Wells, and won permission from Henry I to establish the see at Bath. As a result the abbey lands were granted to him, and he appointed a monk to be prior there, dividing the property of the old monastery between the prior and himself. This John pulled down the old church of St

Peter at Bath, and built a much better one from new. He was buried in the middle of its sanctuary, and I saw his effigy still lying there nine years ago. At that time the entire church which he built had been laid waste, without a roof, and weeds were growing around the tomb of John of Tours. He also built a palace at Bath on the south-west side of St Peter's Abbey; of this one large square tower and some other ruins are still visible. While I was there nine years ago I also saw a fine large marble tomb of a bishop of Bath, from which they said that oil trickled; this is quite probable, for a generous quantity was used to embalm his body. Several other bishops were also buried there.

Oliver King, bishop of Bath, in recent years began an excellent new church at the western portion of the old church of St Peter's, and he completed a good deal of it. The remainder was later finished off by the priors of Bath, especially the last prior, Gibbs, who spent a large sum of money on the fabric. Oliver King left almost all the old church of St Peter's to fall into ruin. However, the walls are still standing.

King Edgar was crowned with much rejoicing and honour at St Peter's in Bath; and as a result he felt a great affection for the town, and accorded its inhabitants valuable exemptions and privileges. In recognition of this at all their ceremonies they pray for the soul of King Edgar. And every Whitsun, which is the reputed anniversary of Edgar's coronation, they appoint from among the townspeople a king of Bath, in joyful memory of King Edgar and the privileges granted by him to the town. This king and his attendants are regaled by even the wealthiest inhabitants.

From Bath I travelled eight miles to Paulton and two further miles to Chewton Mendip, where a fine church tower has been newly built. Although it is hilly the whole way this is nevertheless fertile country for corn and grass; but less so for the five miles between Chewton and Wells, because here the land lies partly in Mendip.

Wells is built at the foot of the Mendip Hills, on a stony site which is full of springs, and hence its name. The most important of the springs, which is known as Andrew's Well, rises in a piece of meadow not far above the east end of the cathedral church, and after running directly westwards enters the Croscombe Stream [*River Sheppey*] rather more to the south.

Wells is a large town, and almost entirely built of stone. I estimate its circumference to be little short of two miles. Virtually all its streets are watered by little streams which derive from the springs. Its industry is clothmaking, and there used to be a great clothier in Wells by the name of Mawdelyne, who has now been succeeded by his son. For the most part the town lies east and west, but an area with a street projects to the south, and at the far end there used to be a chapel, said to have been dedicated to Thomas Becket.

Wells has a single parish church, but it is large, and stands in the western part of the town. It is dedicated to St Cuthbert. On its north side there is a hospital for twenty-four pauper men and women, with a chantry priest. This hospital and its chapel were built as a single elevation under one roof running from west to east. It was founded and almost completed by Nicholas Bubwith, bishop of Bath; what remained to be done was finished off by a certain John Storthwayt, one of the executors of Bubwith's will. There used to be another hospital in the town, which was dedicated to St John. It stood close to the south bank of St Andrew's stream, and had been founded by Bishop Hugh, and another bishop. However the king has recently granted this building to Bishop Clerk of Bath in exchange for the manor of Dogmersfield.

In the market place there is a conduit which draws its water from the bishop's conduit. Permission for this was granted by a former bishop of Bath, Thomas Beckington, and in return the burgesses solemnly visit his tomb once each year to pray for his soul.

Along the northern side of the market place, adjoining the northwest corner of the bishop's palace, there are twelve tall and exceptionally attractive stone houses, with fine windows, and all exactly the same. This beautiful building work was undertaken by Bishop Beckington, and it was his intention, had he lived longer, to build a corresponding row of twelve on the south side of the market square. Had he accomplished it Wells would have set an example to all the market places in the west country.

William Knight, the present bishop of Bath, is building a cross in the market place on a very lavish scale. It has seven fine pillars surrounding another six pillars, which in turn surround a single pillar. These will be vaulted, and above will be a town hall.

The precinct in front of the bishop's palace lies on the east side of the market square, and is divided from it by a fine high wall, incorporating an excellent gatehouse. This must have been built by Bishop Beckington, as it displays his arms. On the south side of the precinct is the bishop's palace, which has a wide moat supplied by water channelled into it from St

Andrew's stream. This palace has a strong wall, and battlements like those of a castle. In the centre of its principal front is a good gatehouse, and at each end of this façade a round tower. There are probably two similar round towers on the south side of the palace, so that there is one at each corner. The palace hall is exceptionally beautiful, and the rest of the house too is large and fine. Many bishops have contributed to the fabric, as it stands now.

Before the see was translated to Bath the canons of Wells had their houses on the site of the bishop's palace. John of Tours, the first bishop of Bath, displaced them, and they have since built themselves twelve excellent houses, which lie partly inside and partly outside the cathedral churchyard on the north side. The dean's house also lies on the north side of the churchyard. Bishop Beckington built the gatehouse at the west end of the cemetery, and was also responsible for the vaulted gate with a gallery above, which lies at the east end of the churchyard.

Travelling from the north Glastonbury lies about five miles from Wells in a south-westerly direction. Next to St John's in Wells I crossed St Andrew's stream, and then about a quarter-mile from the town I encountered a small stream, which was an arm of the St Andrew's or Wells Water. As I crossed it I could see nearby to the left a one-arched stone bridge. This arm combines with the main stream of the Wells Water a little lower in the meadows. About a half-mile beyond this bridge I crossed another brook, larger than Wells Water, which is called Croscombe Water [River Sheppey]. I was told there that the confluence of the two streams lay not far from the causeway on the right hand side, and that they flow together in one valley down to the Meare. Near the Croscombe Brook in this meadow there is a castle, known as Fenny Castle, which is set on a hill; its ruins are still visible. Croscombe Brook rises a mile above Shepton Mallet, through which it then passes. It continues for a mile to Croscombe, then three miles to Dulcote Bridge, and about a mile-and-a-half to the bridges along the road from Wells to Glastonbury.

Continuing for a mile or more I reached a stone bridge of one arch. A pleasant stream flowed down from my left hand side, and just above the bridge broke into two courses, which I crossed by two small stone bridges. About a half-mile further on I came to a few houses, and then arrived at a large flat meadow, which I reckoned to measure six or seven miles around the edge. For a mile the road across this meadow was carried on a causeway, up to Hartlake Bridge, which has one stone arch. All this flat marsh or meadowland which lies west of the causeway as far as Hartlake Bridge is called Crannel Moor, and the part lying to the east is Sedge Moor.

Through this stone bridge flows the River Sowey [*Whitelake River*], which rises at the foot of the Mendip Hills; its source is a spring named after St Aldhelm, which lies east of the village of Doulting. Before the river arrives at Hartlake Bridge, one mile to the east, a channel has been made to divert part of the flow from it, and an artificial marsh wall has been built to separate this channel from the main stream of the river. This wall stretches down to Hartlake Bridge, and continues for a mile beyond, until both streams flow into the Meare. If this embankment were not maintained, and the two channels of the River Sowey were not kept clear of weed, the whole of the flat marshland would be inundated after a downpour, and the meadow's value would be lost.

After Hartlake Bridge a small bridge took me across this arm of the Sowey, and I continued across the low-lying ground for about a quarter-mile. Then I climbed a little on to slightly hilly ground, and rode for a whole mile before arriving at Glastonbury. All the meadow which lies beyond Hartlake Bridge to the WSW is called Glastonbury Moor.

The principal street, and also the longest, in Glastonbury runs east and west, and at the market cross at the western end there is another street which leads directly south and approximately north. A market is held in the town every Wednesday. Glastonbury has two parish churches. On the north side of the main street is the church of St John the Baptist, which is most attractive and light. The eastern part of it has aisles, and is very elegant. The nave has arcades on each side, and the quire has arcades of three arches. The square bell tower at the west end is very tall and fine. On the north side of the quire is buried a certain Richard Atwell (called 'Ad Fontem' in Latin), who died in about the year 1472. He spent large sums of money on this church, and granted to it some fine houses which he had built in the town. His wife Joanna lies in a similar marble tomb on the south side of the quire. In the south transept a gentleman by the name of Camel is buried in a good tomb.

The River Brue flows to the western part of Glastonbury from Bruton ten miles away, and continues for another two miles into the Meare. A mile before it reaches Glastonbury it comes to a bridge of four stone arches which is known as Pontperlus [*Pomparles*], and it was here, according to legend, that King Arthur cast his sword into it. At this bridge the river divides in two, and the main stream flows to Glastonbury. The other passes through low-lying marshy land, and joins up with the main stream again before they flow into the Meare.

When the water is at its highest in winter the Meare is four miles in circumference, and when at its lowest two-and-a-half miles. The average is three miles. This lake or Meare is a good mile long, and at its western end it forms into a hollow for about a mile. Then the water divides into two arms, one flowing to Highbridge and the other to Rooksbridge, going their separate ways to the [*sea*] by creeks.

From Wells I rode south to the stone bridge at Dulcote, under which the Croscombe Water flows. The distance was about a mile, and the road was very rocky and difficult. The next mile was similar, and at this point I saw an elm wood of reasonable size. For the next three miles I crossed flat open downland with stony soil, and then a mile of low-lying pasture. This brought me to the village of Evercreech, where Clerk, the previous bishop of Bath had a manor house. It was already in a poor state, and during his time it was demolished completely.

From Evercreech I rode to Golafre Bridge [*Milton Bridge*], which is of stone, and crosses a tributary of the River Brue. This brook rises three miles away to the north-east, and about a mile downstream enters the Brue two miles below Bruton. The village of Milton overlooks Golafre Bridge, and consequently the brook is sometimes called Milton Water. There is considerable woodland about Milton and the bridge. Then from Milton to Bruton is about a mile-and-a-half.

As I approached Bruton from the north-west the whole town stood on the nearer bank of the River Brue. One street runs from north to south, but a much finer street runs east and west. At present clothmaking is the major occupation in the town. The eastern bridge has three stone arches, and Bruton parish church and the abbey stand together on the further bank next to it. In the market place there is a new cross of six arches, with a pillar in the centre for the market traders to stand in. It was begun and brought up to roof level by Ely, the last abbot of Bruton.

The original abbey was for monks, and was established by Algar, earl of Cornwall. But after the conquest it was refounded as a house of canons by Mohun, and several of his family were buried there. More recently a

SOMERSET

prior of Bruton whose name was William Gilbert travelled to Rome, and secured permission to change the designation of the house from a priory to an abbey. This Gilbert became abbot, and spent a large sum of money on the fabric of Bruton Abbey, practically rebuilding it.

The town of Bruton, as far as the market cross, and also the abbey on the further bank of the river, lie within Selwood Forest. The River Brue rises three miles away at a place called Brewham, and this also is in Selwood. In the same area, that is to say within two or three miles of the source of the Brue, the Stour and the Wylye also rise. The market town of Mere is about eight miles from Bruton, and Castle Cary is two miles.

As I took my leave of Bruton I crossed a stone bridge of three arches at the WSW end of the town, and at that point a small stream enters the Brue from the north-east. I am told that there is another stone bridge across the Brue five miles below Bruton called Lydford, and Pomparles Bridge is two miles lower. After the bridge I rode up a stony hill to an expanse of very fine and fertile open country with few trees, and continued for five miles. After four miles of this I crossed a brook by a stone bridge, which brought me immediately to North Cadbury, and about a mile further to South Cadbury. Beyond them is a great ridge of hills.

The River Cadbury [Cam] has two sources. About a half-mile before I reached Cadbury I crossed a stream which rises at a pond in Mr FitzJames's park, and joins the Cam about a half-mile after the bridge by which I crossed it. The other headwater rises three miles above North Cadbury to the north-east. From North Cadbury the Cam flows to a bridge one mile west of South Cadbury, with the other stream by now sharing the same valley, and then about five miles downstream, and within a quarter-mile of Ilchester, it enters the River Ivel.

Right at the south end of South Cadbury church stands Camelot. This was once a noted town or castle, set on a real peak of a hill, and with marvellously strong natural defences. It has just two entrances up very steep tracks, one on the north-east, the other on the south-west. The distance around the foot of the hill on which this fortress stands is more than a mile. Near its summit there are four ditches or trenches, each separated by an earthen rampart. Above these ditches right on the hilltop is a large open space which I would reckon to be twenty acres or more; in various parts of it one may observe the foundations and rubble of walls.

There used to be a quantity of blue-grey stone which has been removed by the inhabitants of the nearby villages. This area has often been ploughed, and has produced very good yields.

Roman coins of gold, silver and copper have been turned up in large quantities during ploughing there, and also in the fields at the foot of the hill, especially on the east side. Many other antiquities have also been found, including at Camelot, within living memory, a silver horseshoe. The only information local people can offer is that they have heard that Arthur frequently came to Camelot. The old Lord Hungerford owned this Camelot, but now it has passed to Hastings, earl of Huntingdon, by his mother. Several villages in that area have the name Camelot as an affix, such as Queen Camel, and others. The hill and ditches are now good for rearing sheep. The land on the south-west and west sides of Camelot all lies in a vale, so that from one or two directions it may be seen from a great distance. Sherborne is three miles from Camelot, across open fertile country. A gentleman called Mr Gilbert has a poor mansion house right at the foot of Camelot on the south-east side. *cont. p. 94* [**1542**: 1/137-52]

From Sherborne I went back to South Cadbury, which was three good miles away. Shortly after passing Cadbury I turned directly westward by a small chapel, and when I had gone a good mile further I crossed a stone bridge. The river here had been joined by the brook which rises in Mr FitzJames's pond, which somewhat increased its flow. From here I travelled across low-lying ground as far as the eye could see, to Ilchester four miles away. All along my route the pasture grounds and fields were largely enclosed with hedgerows of elm trees.

By my reckoning the confluence of the Rivers Cam and Ivel occurred a mile before I reached Ilchester. One of the furthest sources of the River Ivel is located by some people at Corscombe, two miles above Yeovil. Its course takes the river down past Yeovil, and then three miles downstream it reaches the village of Yeovilton. I was told that here for a short distance the river breaks into two and is then reunited. From here it flows straight to Limington, where I saw a water channel cut long ago by hand to divert the water to turn a mill in Limington. Then the whole river flows scarcely a mile to Ilchester.

My entry into Ilchester from the south-west was over a large stone bridge of seven arches, in the middle of which were two small stone buildings. That on the right hand was the common gaol for prisoners in Somerset; that on the left was smaller and looked to me as if it had been a chapel. The town of Ilchester used to be a very large affair, and one of the oldest towns in the whole region. But now it has fallen into spectacular decay, almost as if it had been devastated by an army.

Within living memory there have been four parish churches in the town, but only one of them now is still used. Remains of two of the others are still standing, but the fourth has been completely destroyed. Ilchester has a free chapel, and its rear premises extend to the river bank right below the bridge, where a most attractive dwelling house adjoins the chapel. I have heard it said that a long time ago there was a nunnery on the site of this chapel. There was also until recently a friary in the town. But the most substantial example of ancient architecture which I saw in the whole town was an arched and vaulted stone gate with a chapel or church over it; it was dedicated to St Michael, if I remember correctly.

The River Ivel flows from Ilchester to Langport, which is four miles downstream, and then to Michelboro [*Burrow Bridge*], where it is crossed by a wooden bridge. The river is tidal for some distance above this bridge. From there to Ilminster (I must find out more, as I have since discovered that Ilminster is only a mile from Whitelackington, where Mr Speke lives, and this is not the River Ivel). And so to Bridgwater. Were it not for the wetlands a journey from Ilchester to Bridgwater would be less than ten miles, but as it is, the distance is twelve miles.

From Ilchester I rode for about a mile to the village of Limington. This settlement and manor belonged to a certain Gyvernay, who lies in a lavish tomb in a fine chapel on the north side of Limington parish church. At his feet in a low tomb lies a woman who is depicted by her stone effigy as wearing a veil. Also in this chapel, beneath the south arch, are buried a gentleman and his wife, whom I think were also members of the Gyvernay family. A chantry priest is attached to this chapel. Gyvernay lived, it is thought by some, in the farmhouse at the north-east side of the church, and the family's estate passed by inheritance to the Bonvilles of Devon. Only one of the Bonvilles was a baron, and that was Sir William Bonville. His son married an heiress of Lord Harington, and Cecily, his heiress, married Thomas, marquis of Dorset. Lord Bonville had many bastard children, and one of them he settled in the west country with an estate worth annually about £70. This family is still living there.

From Limington I rode for four miles to Montacute, beside good pasture and arable land, which was enclosed and reasonably supplied with woods. Montacute is a town with a poor market, and is built of stone – as is usual in all the towns of this region. In the Glastonbury chronicle I read that in Saxon times the place was called Logaresburch. Some people believe that there was a large castle and fortress in the town during the Saxon period, and some that the count of Mortain built the castle there shortly after the conquest. But what is not in question is that there has been a castle at Montacute, and that the count of Mortain stayed in it. It was this count who changed its name to Montacute, because it stood on the sharp peak of a hill, and ever since that name has been preferred. The count of Mortain also established a priory for three or four Benedictine monks at the foot of Montacute Hill, and endowed it with three good manors. These were Montacute itself, and the adjacent Tintinhull, and Criche [*actually East Chinnock*], ten miles WSW of Montacute.

The count of Mortain sided with Robert Curthose against Henry I, and was later captured, imprisoned, and his lands confiscated. It was then that the three manors he had granted to Montacute Priory were taken away, and the monks were forced to go begging for a time. Eventually Henry I took pity on them, and offered them back the lands they had owned, and more besides, if they would leave Montacute and move to Langport, where it was his intention then to have founded an important monastery. But the monks entreated him to be allowed to keep their old premises, and as a result he restored their three manors to them, and transferred the intended abbey from Langport to Reading. Then a certain Reginald Chancellor appeared (probably named after his office), who was a man of great influence with Henry I. He turned to religion, became prior of Montacute, and enlarged both the fabric and the estates of the priory. As the priory prospered, and became owner of the entire manor of Montacute, the important castle partly fell into ruin, and was partly demolished for materials to build the priory. As a result for many years now none of its buildings have survived, except a chapel which was built right on the top of the keep, and that is still there.

After Montacute I rode for about a mile to Stoke sub Hamdon. Here, in a valley close to the village, I saw the substantial ruins of a manor house or castle, including a very ancient chapel, which is still standing, and which contains the tombs of several noble men and women. Along the south-west side of the chapel are five effigies on tombs, each one adjoining the next. Three are of men in armour with their shields, two are of women. The inscriptions which used to be on each have become so worn that they are now illegible. I saw two shields emblazoned in blue and white, in vairy pattern. In this part of the chapel there are also two tombs without effigies.

On the north side of the chapel nave there is a tomb set in the wall with neither effigy nor inscription. And on the north side of the quire is another tomb, which has a good effigy of an armed man, with a shield in vairy pattern all over, as I recall. Also there is a very large flat marble slab just in front of the quire door, with a figure engraved on a brass plate, and around it the following inscription in French:

'Here lies the noble and valiant knight Maheu de Gurney, formerly seneschal of Landes and commander of Castel Daques for Our Lord the King in the Duchy of Guyene. During his life he fought at the battle of Beuamazin, and later took part in the siege of Dalgezire against the Saracens, also the battles of Le Scluse, Crecy, Ingenesse, Poitiers, Nazarre, Dozrey, and many other battles and sieges, in which he honourably won great praise and credit over a period of 56 years. He died on the 26th day of September in the year of Our Lord Jesus Christ 1406. May God have mercy on his soul. Amen.'

In addition to this grave there is another at the western end of the chapel nave which has a large flat stone slab without inscription. In the windows I noticed three distinct coats of arms, one variegated blue and white, another with three vertical red stripes to the right on a gold background, and the third of one crosslet made up of many on a red background, if I remember correctly. Although this collegiate chapel, once well served by priests, is in poor condition, and mass is only said there now three times each week, it still has attached to it a provost, who has a large house nearby in Stoke village.

Also nearby, at Hamdon, is the famous stone quarry, from which for a long time stone has been taken for all the high quality buildings in the entire region.

From Stoke I travelled south-west to a modest market town called Crewkerne; it is five miles from Montacute, and four from Stoke, over hilly country. Crewkerne is sited at the foot of a hill. There is nothing particularly remarkable to see there, although its cross, surrounded with small pillars, is attractive, as is the town hall in the market place. Its church stands on the hill, and next to it there is a grammar school, which is endowed with lands which pay an annual salary. About a mile from Crewkerne is the place called Haselbury [*Plucknett*], where the saintly hermit and prophet Wulfric lived during Henry I's reign. The manor now belongs to the earl of Derby.

I set off across hilly country, which nevertheless produces good corn and grass crops, as well as the elms which make up the hedgerows of enclosures almost everywhere in Somerset, and had ridden scarcely two miles before I came to the village of Hinton St George, which is so called because the parish church is dedicated to St George. There used to be a very old manor house at Hinton, but all that is to be seen there now is the very fine manor house of freestone, which has in the inner courtyard two good tall castellated towers. It was built by Sir Amias Poulett, the father of the present owner, Sir Hugh Poulett, who has recently constructed a park on a hillside not far from his house.

After another two-and-a-half miles of hilly and enclosed ground I reached Kingstone, and about a mile further on I passed Whitelackington a half-mile away on my right. This is where Mr Speke has his chief seat, and a park; but after about another mile I passed another of his manor houses on my left. Next I rode three miles to Curry Mallet, where Chambernoun of Devon has a park. Leaving this park a short distance away on my left I soon reached a large brook, which rises to the WSW, and flows ENE until it joins the River Ivel, I should think about two miles above Michelborow [*Burrow Bridge*]. At this point I left the hill country and arrived at the Somerset Levels and marshlands.

Keeping on this flat ground for two miles or more I came to North Curry. Wells Cathedral has a good estate here, as well as property at Stoke Gregory nearby. After about another mile I reached the River Tone, and rode along its bank for a distance of half a mile, until I came to a wooden bridge across it. Half a mile further down the Tone is Athelney, which has a wooden bridge giving access to the abbey, and there is yet another wooden bridge over the Tone downstream, almost at the confluence of the Tone and the Ivel. Taunton (or Toneton) lies five miles south-west of Athelney, and about seven miles from Bridgwater. There is a large bridge across the Tone a mile below Taunton at Basford [*?Bathpool*].

From the bridge near Athelney I rode for two miles across low-lying marshland to Petherton Park, where the ground begins to rise again towards the west and south-west and is not wetland. The park is stocked with a large number of deer, but almost the only barriers to stop the cattle on the common land from entering it are the dikes. The deer prance across these dikes and feed all over the marshes before returning to the park again. In the park there is a nice lodge surrounded by a moat, and a pleasant brook flows through the park, which enters the Ivel half a mile lower. It is called the Peder, and it rises in the hills about two miles away to the WSW. First it flows past North Petherton, an attractive country town with a fine church, the living of which was appropriated to Minchin Buckland. Then it impinges on South Petherton, the parish in which the park lies, and so to the River Ivel. The distance from the lodge in Petherton Park to North Petherton is a mile, and Bridgwater is two miles further. As I approached Bridgwater the road for more than a half-mile was carried on a stone causeway.

On my entry to Bridgwater I passed a chapel dedicated to St Saviour, which stood on the bank of the estuary. Then I came to a suburb, where I crossed a bridge. The brook running under it rises at Broomfield, four miles to the west. The town's south gate adjoins this bridge. Bridgwater has no town wall, nor did I see any evidence that there ever was one. But there are four town gates which are named from their positions, east, west, north and south; and the walls of the stonebuilt houses within the town serve in place of a town wall.

From the south gate I rode along a pleasant street for a while, and then turned east and came to the market place. The finest street and the best prospect of the town runs from the west gate to the east gate, where the River Ivel joins the salt water creek. This arm of the sea runs from south to north, and the street crosses it by an extremely old, strong and high bridge of three stone arches. It was begun by William Brewer, the town's first owner, in the reigns of Richard I and John; and I was told that a gentleman from Devon or Cornwall by the name of Triveth completed it. On the coping of the bridge parapets there is a shield emblazoned with trivets, which are the arms of Triveth. The portion of the town which lies west of the bridge and estuary is three times as large as that lying to the east. The castle, which used to be an extremely fine and strong piece of architecture, but is now falling into total ruin, stands on the west bank of the estuary immediately downstream from the bridge. It was built originally by William Brewer.

In the western part of the town I noted the following: One large parish church. A good building which used to house a college of grey friars, and which was erected by William Brewer, son of the first William Brewer. Particular benefactors of this house were one of the Lords Botreaux and his wife, and so his heart, and his wife's body, were buried there. The Bridgwater customs officer has now turned the building into an extremely good and agreeable dwelling house. In the same area of the town there is a hospital which was established and built by the townspeople, but it is endowed with little or no land. St Saviour's Chapel, which lies outside the town to the south, was built within living memory by a Bridgwater merchant called William Poel or Pole.

The only building of note in the eastern part of the town is the house or former college of St John, and this lies partly outside the east gate. The priests attached to this college wore habits like those of secular priests, but with a cross on their breasts; a pauper hospital adjoined the building. The college was established by the first William Brewer, and he provided it with a good endowment. He was buried at the Cistercian monastery which he had founded at Dunkeswell in Devon, and his wife was buried at Mottisfont Priory, another of her husband's foundations. Within living memory more than two hundred houses in Bridgwater have fallen into utter ruin.

From Bridgwater to Cannington is two miles, and as I approached it I crossed a large brook which rises not far away in the hills to the west, and after passing Cannington it flows into the estuary by my reckoning two miles or more below Bridgwater. Cannington is a pleasant country town, with a very fine and well adorned parish church. It had a priory of nuns, and their church abutted the east end of the parish church. The priory now belongs to the Rogers who is at court [*Edward Rogers*], and he was also granted Minchin Buckland.

[*Nether*] Stowey, a poor village situated in a valley among hills, is three good miles from Cannington. Here Lord Audley has a good manor house in an exceptionally pleasing position overlooking pastureland, with separate parks for red and fallow deer next to it, and a fine brook which supplies all the domestic needs of the manor house. The Lord Audley who rebelled during the reign of Henry VII started to enlarge the house, and the stone foundations on a large scale are still to be seen half-finished. The River Stowey flows along through Nether Stowey village on its way from its source in the hills nearby on the west to the sea, which lies about four miles from the village.

After Nether Stowey I travelled five miles and passed the village of St Audrie's a short distance to my right; it lies about a mile inland. In this parish I saw a fine park and manor house which belong to the Luttrells. They are called Quantoxhead because they lie at the head of the Quantock hills towards the coast. These hills run in ridges from Quantoxhead in the north towards Taunton in the south-east. Between Stowey and St Audrie's I crossed two substantial brooks which flow down the hillsides to the sea.

Williton is two miles from St Audrie's, and on my way I crossed a large brook which rises to the south, and runs north to the sea. A quarter-mile from Williton I came to Mr John Wyndham's house at Orchard. For four generations the manor belonged to the Sydenham family, and it was the second owner, a younger brother of the family, who built virtually all the worthwhile portion of Orchard manor house. He married an heiress of a certain Gamon or Gambon, who had estates in Devon and Cornwall with an annual value of £130; the Gambon arms are three black legs on a silver background. The third Sydenham died, leaving a son and two daughters, but the son died before he reached the age of 22. One of the daughters married John Wyndham, a younger brother of Wyndham of Felbrigg in Norfolk. The senior branch of the Sydenham family is settled at Brympton [d'Evercy] near Montacute, but the elderly Sydenham of Brympton now lives at a small manor house which he owns called Combe [Sydenham[, less than a mile from Orchard. And another member of the Brympton branch resides at Nettlecombe, which is a mile or a little more from Orchard. His estate may be worth £50 annually. At Mr Wyndham's house I noticed in stained glass the arms of John and Thomas Wyndham, both knights. One married the daughter of Howard, duke of Norfolk, and the other the daughter of Lord Scrope of Bolton.

Orchard lies in the parish of St Decun, or Decumans, which is a mile or more from the coast, and two miles from the chapel of Our Lady of Cleeve. I rode three miles or more from Orchard to Cleeve Chapel, and nearly a mile before I reached the chapel I crossed a brook which flows from Cleeve Abbey. At this point the abbey was scarcely a quarter mile away to the south on my left hand; and close by on the north, or left hand side, I saw a fine stone bridge with a single arch. Cleeve Chapel, where offerings were made to Our Lady, is well built on a craggy site, but not particularly high. To the south of it there is a good inn built entirely of stone, which used to serve the pilgrims. The chapel is about a half-mile from the sea, and two miles from Dunster.

Marshwood Park lies between Our Lady of Cleeve and Dunster, and on my way I crossed a brook which flows through Dunster Park. The town stands in a valley, but the parish church occupies a more elevated site. A very important market is held in Dunster every week, and on Whit Monday the town has the right to hold a fair. It is a clothmaking town, and rose to fame as a result of the Mohuns, who were later earls of Somerset. The Mohuns held royal jurisdiction at Dunster, and built the excellent strong castle there. The keep of Dunster Castle used to have an abundance of fine architecture, but now there is only a chapel still in good condition, and this has recently been repaired by Sir Hugh Luttrell. The north-east portion of the courtyard is now the best preserved part of the castle. During the lifetime of his wife Dame Margaret, who was the sister of the elder Lord Daubeney, Sir Hugh Luttrell built a good tower at the northern approach to the castle. He had another wife, whose name was Guinllean, and she was the daughter of a certain York of Devon. Sir Hugh's son, Sir Andrew Luttrell, renewed part of the castle wall on the east side. Castle Hill is surrounded on every side except the north-east by large hills, and there is an attractive park adjoining the eastern part of the castle. Many privileges belong to this castle and many knight's services are due to it.

There used to be a priory of Benedictine monks which was a cell of Bath situated at the foot of the castle hill on the north-west side. The entire priory church is now used as the parish church, although formerly the monks closed off the eastern part for their own use. In this part, on the north side near the high altar, one of the Luttrells or Mohuns was buried under an arch. I am inclined to think that he was a Mohun, since his helmet is garlanded, and in former times this was how lords were buried. Two effigies, of one of the Mohuns and his wife, lie on the south side of the chancel, and nearby there used to be an effigy of a gentleman of the Everard family. This was placed here by the Mohuns, in return for an obligation on the part of the Everards to defend part of the castle, but this statue now lies in the churchyard between two arches or buttresses. The Everards' manor house was, and still is, at Aller, a mile from Dunster Castle in the parish of Carnetun [*Carhampton*]. This name is an abbreviated form of Carantoc's town, and a chapel dedicated to this saint, which was once the parish church, still exists there. A certain Elizabeth, the wife of one of the Luttrells, lies buried in front of the high altar there under a plain stone slab. A pleasant brook flows down nearby from the hills to the west.

From Dunster I rode two miles to Minehead, where a pleasant market is held once a week. The most attractive part of the town lies at the foot of a hill. The remainder runs steeply up the hillside, and at the top there is a fine parish church. The town is extremely full of Irishmen. The pier lies at the north-east point of the hill. There used to be a good park next to Minehead, but Sir Andrew Luttrell recently destroyed it.

The shortest crossing from Minehead to Wales is eighteen miles, to Aberthaw in Glamorgan. Stogursey, where there is a good village, is seventeen miles from Minehead, going up the Severn Sea coastline; and from there it is another three miles to Steart, at the mouth of the Bridgwater estuary. Going three miles down the coast from Minehead there is a place called Hurlstone. This is the start of the anchorage generally known as Porlock Bay, which is a reasonably good anchorage for ships. It extends for three miles to Comban [*Culbone*], which may be an abbreviation of Columbane. I was assured that Somerset continued this far, or further. Most of the shoreline from Culbone to Steart is hilly ground, and there is no supply of wood near the coast. What wood exists is all in the hedgerows of the enclosures. However, there is a great abundance of beans in this coastal region and running inland. At Bridgwater a kind of staple for these beans exists at times when corn is dear overseas. This region also has a plentiful supply of wheat and cattle.

From Dunster I rode seven miles to the village of Exford. For the first three or four miles the going was all hilly and rocky, with some woodland, and everywhere brooks in the valleys between the hills. I imagine that these brooks flow towards the Severn Sea. The remainder of my ride to Exford took me partly over moorland, with something of a dearth of cornland, and partly over hilly ground, where many brooks come together to the nearer bank of the River Exe. At Exford the river is still small, no more than a brook, and it is crossed by a little wooden bridge.

The Exe rises on Exmoor at a place called Excross, three miles northwest of Exford, and flows towards Tiverton, twelve miles downstream, and from there ten miles to Exeter. My way from Exford to Simonsbath Bridge was entirely across forest, waste and moorland, where young cattle are bred and reared, but there are virtually no cornfields or dwellings. At this place called Simonsbath a river flows in a deep valley between two great moorland hills, and a wooden bridge affords a crossing. In summer the river usually flows evenly over stones which can be easily used to cross over, but when rains and the storms of winter come it turns into a deep torrent. At all points this stream is a great deal larger than the Exe is at Exford, even though it is a tributary of the River Exe.

The boundary of Somerset to the north-west lies two miles or more beyond this stream to a place called the Spanne, and the Tourres. Here there are earthen mounds thrown up long ago as boundary markers between Somerset and Devon; and in this area too is the boundary and limit of the forest of Exmoor. cont. p. 72 [**1542:** 1/155-68]

TWO SPRINGS RISE near Westbury, one to the south, and the other to the south-west. They soon join and flow together around [*North*] Bradley, until a mile-and-a-half further they enter the Biss Brook (which flows past Brook Hall), and so to Trowbridge and then the River Avon. The pleasant clothmaking town of Bradstock or Bradford is two miles [*?from Trowbridge*].

My route from Trowbridge to Bath, a ride of seven miles, was very hilly. After leaving the woodland and the castle and park of Farleigh to my left I rode across Freshford Bridge, which was of two or three fine new stone arches. This was three miles from Trowbridge, and two miles further, at the very bottom of a steep-sided valley I crossed a wild stream flowing over stones. A mile beyond this there was a considerable quarry beside the road, then a level area, then about a mile down a steep valley to Bath. From here I rode across three miles of open country to Kelston, a good village in Wiltshire [*Somerset*], and here the Avon flows some distance away, on the left hand side of its valley.

Information given me by Sir John Newton: The true family name of Newton is Caradoc. Newton was mistakenly applied to the family because Sir John's grandfather lived, or was born, at Trenewydd in Powysland.

Stoke-sub-Hamdon belonged to Gurney, and he is buried there in a collegiate chapel next to the ruins of his castle. Some people maintain that he was principally responsible for founding Gaunt's house in Bristol. He established a priory for nuns at Barrow Gurney in Somerset, and he owned Widcombe, and Richmont Castle beside Mendip, five miles from Wells. All the buildings of this castle are completely demolished. After Gurney it belonged to Hampton, then to Caradoc, alias Newton. Kingswood Forest extends as far as Mr Newton's house at Barr's Court.

Anciently Mendip was reckoned to have four principal owners. First the king, and his share passed to the bishop of Bath as lessee. Glastonbury had the second share. The third was Bonville, Lord Bonville, and now is Lord Grey's, the marquis of Dorset. Fourth was Gurney, and now Caradoc, alias Newton. The estimated length of Mendip from east to west is twenty miles. At its broadest it is six miles wide, but in many places it is less. On the top of one of the Mendip Hills, two miles from Banwell, is a camp called Dolbury, and there is a well-known popular saying that, 'If Dolbury digged were, Of gold should be the share'.

Gurney used to spend much of his time at Richmont Castle. Its site is at the foot of Mendip due east from Bristol, in the parish of East Harptree and close to the parish church. A portion of the keep is still standing. Sir John Newton dug up many of the old castle foundations for use in building a new house called Eastwood close to the site. Near East Harptree is another village called West Harptree Gurney, and the glass windows there display his coat of arms, and the varieties of arms that the Gurney family bore. During Gurney's time Lord Fitzwarren had inherited the wardenship of Mendip Forest, and it was well stocked with deer; but some time later as a result of riots and trespasses caused by hunting it was disafforested, and still is.

It was by this means that the Gurney estate passed to Newton: There was a man named Newton living at Wick near Banwell, who had a good estate, and his younger brother, Sir John's father, married the youngest daughter of Hampton, who had previously been married to one of the Choke family, but had died without issue. Although she was the youngest of Hampton's three daughters, it chanced that she inherited all three portions of the estate. The Newton estate at Wick, however, passed by the female line to Sir Henry Chappell, son of Sir Giles Chappell, who had lived at Wick, and to Mr Griffiths of Northamptonshire, owner of Braybrooke Castle. This means that Newton of Barr's Court has no share in the Wick estate. *cont. p. 132* [**1544:** 5/84-6]

From Brook to Frome Selwood in Somerset is four miles, largely through woodland and pasture until I came within a mile of the town, and there it is open. Frome has quite a good market, and stands on the steep side of a rocky hill. It has a good, large parish church, and a very fine spring in the churchyard, from which by pipes and channels water is carried to several parts of the town. The town depends largely on clothmaking, and there are several fine stone houses. At the foot of the town flows the River Frome. The town lies on the left bank, and there is a stone bridge of five arches, with a mill beside it. A side stream flows past the mill and through a two-arched bridge. Two tributaries of the Frome, one from Maiden Bradley five miles away, and the other from Hindon [?Horningsham], join about a mile upstream from the town. Bruerne [?Bruton] lies eight miles from Frome.

    I rode two miles, past fertile open arable land all the way, from Frome to Nunney Delamare, which is a good village. At the west end of Nunney parish church there is an attractive castle, which has at each end, north and south, a pair of good round towers of such diameter that they adjoin and form a single structure. The castle walls are very strong and thick, the stairs narrow, and the accommodation inside is rather dark. It stands on the left bank of the brook, which divides it from the churchyard. The castle is surrounded by a moat, which derives its water from the brook. Except on the east side, where the brook provides defence, there is a strong wall around the outside of the moat. The castle was built by Delamare and his wife, who lie buried in the north side of Nunney church, and after them it belonged to Poulet, Lord St John. The Nunney Brook flows down, as I saw for myself, from the SSW, and three miles lower it enters the River Frome. Then I rode back from Nunney to Frome town.

    Two miles further I reached a valley, where another brook ran down to the Frome. In this valley a number of good clothiers live, with fine houses and fulling mills. From here it was two good miles to Norton St Philip, a small town largely dependent on clothing, and with a modest market. Next I rode to Farleigh Castle, two miles, and Bradford on Avon, two more miles. King Aethelred granted the lordship and the living of Bradford to the nunnery at Shaftesbury, in atonement for the murder of his brother, St Edward. A certain De La Sale, or Halle, of a gentry family whose descent is traced from the time of Edward I, lives at one end of Bradford.

    Bath is five miles from Bradford, and for the first two miles or more I followed the right [*i.e. left*] bank of the Avon, through hilly, wooded country, until at Freshford I crossed the River Frome by a stone bridge. A mile or more further I came to a new stone bridge which took me over a small brook a little above the point where it enters the Avon by the left bank. To the south-east a mile before I reached Bath I saw two parks surrounded by a stone wall which had become ruined, and there were now no deer. One belonged to the bishop, and one to the prior, of Bath. *cont. p. 139* [**1544: 5/97-8**]

After Pucklechurch I rode to Keynsham in Somerset, which used to be a good market town, but is now poor and in ruins. At Keynsham there are two stone bridges. One of them, of six large arches, stands entirely in Gloucestershire, but is now completely derelict. The other is close to it, and spans the River Avon with three large stone arches; the river is here the boundary between Somerset and Gloucestershire. Just outside Keynsham, on the Somerset side, there is a royal park enclosed by a stone wall. And in the quarries of the Keynsham area are found stones shaped like coiled snakes.

Next I rode three miles to Pensford, partly by open, and partly by enclosed, fields. This is a pleasant little clothmaking town, with a market, and a stream which flows down to it and drives several fulling mills. Its present owner is one Browne of Lime Street in London.

From Pensford it was two long miles through hilly country, with enclosures and considerable woodland, to the village of [*Bishop*] Sutton. Sir John St Loe, who descends from a younger brother of the Lords St Loe, has an old manor house here. In fact little of the St Loe possessions passed to him, since the last Lord St Loe lacked a male heir, and his estate descended through daughters to Lord Hungerford and Lord Botreaux. Much of Sir John St Loe's estate came to him from the De La Riviere family by the female line, either his father's wife or mother. At Newton St Loe, beside the Avon two miles from Bath, there is a fine manor house built like a castle, and although it now belongs to Lord Hastings, earl of Huntingdon, it was one of the principal seats of the Lords St Loe.

Chute [*Chew Magna*] is a mile-and-a-half from Sutton, across good enclosed land. This is a pleasant place which has had a good clothmaking industry, and a fine manor house belonging to the bishop of Bath on the south side of the church. The church is attractive, and is the mother church of several parish churches in the area, which once a year pay homage to it. On the north side of the church lies buried Sir John St Loe's grandfather in a good marble tomb. Three miles south of Chew lies Ubley, where there is a modest old manor house with a fortified gatehouse and a park beside it. It belonged to Lord Cheddar, whose large estate passed by heiresses to the Lords Lisle, Daubeney and Newton.

Then I rode eight long miles from Sutton to Wick [?*Aldwick near Butcombe*], where there is a large manor house built, for the most part, by Newton, chief judge of England. The manor belonged to Lord Cheddar, and was then Newton's, whose two daughters married Griffith of Braybrooke and Sir Giles Capel. Consequently Ubley and Wick and several other manors are still divided between the two.

Two or three miles from Wick is Banwell, where the bishop of Bath has a good estate. In the reign of King Alfred of Wessex there was an important monastery at Banwell. The position of Banwell, with the wetlands close by, is not very salubrious, and Wick is worse, although there is quite good woodland in the area. About a mile from Wick is the village of Kenn, and here lives Mr Kenn, whose estate is worth £130 annually. And three miles from Wick in the Bristol direction is Wraxall, where Sir William Gorges has a modest old manor house set in a valley, with an attractive park extending up the hills on either side. Between Wraxall and Bristol, two miles from the former, four from the latter, is Barrow Gurney, where Drew of Bristol has created a fine dwelling-house out of the former nunnery.

Sutton is seven miles from Bristol, and from Sutton I rode over the hills for three miles to Eastwood, at the foot of the Mendips. There used to be a good castle called Richmont at this Eastwood, where the nobleman Gurney spent much time. It has now been completely razed to the ground, and the present owner, Sir John Newton, has taken material from the ruins for the house he has built close by, on the very spot where Richmont Castle grange stood in Gurney's time. Eastwood is five miles from Wells.

The land between Sutton and Midsomer Norton, which are five miles apart, is quite hilly, with enclosures. Two miles before I reached Norton I crossed a pleasant brook which flowed down to my left as I rode. Midsomer Norton is five miles from Norton St Philip, and five miles, across open country, from Mells.

Mells is built on something of a slope, and used to be an attractive little clothmaking place belonging to Glastonbury. It was the plan of Abbot Selwood of Glastonbury, who observed the wealth of the inhabitants of Mells, to rebuild it with modest houses of stone blocks, in the shape of an Anthony Cross; but of this plan he only built one small street. It has a fine church, which was built of squared stone by the whole parish within living memory. The vestry, an elaborate piece of fine craftsmanship, was generously funded by a London draper named Garland; and a gentleman living in the parish built a fine chapel on the north side of the church. There is also an attractive stone manor house close to the west end of the church, which was probably built in part by Abbot Selwood of Glastonbury. Later it was used by the lessee of the manor, and now Mr Horner has purchased the manor from the king.

A stream flows down from the coal pits on Mendip and turns south in the valley at Mells. It then runs into the River Frome, and so to the market town of Frome Selwood, which is three miles from Mells. One portion of Selwood Forest is also three miles from Mells, and in this forest is a chapel containing the buried bones of St Algar, which not long ago were foolishly searched for by the common people out of superstition. In its present form the bounds of Selwood Forest extend for thirty miles; it stretches in one direction almost to Warminster, and in another approximately ten miles to the Shaftesbury area.

From Mells I rode for two miles past some hills and enclosures to Nunney Delamare, and then about another mile over similar ground to a long village callled Tut... [?*Trudoxhill*], with a parish church dependent on Nunney. A half-mile further I entered Selwood Forest proper, and after another half-mile I passed on my right hand side the former Carthusian priory of Witham. This is not within the forest, but adjoins the edge. From here I travelled four miles, partly in the forest and partly over open ground, until I reached Stourton. *cont. p. 403* [**1544**: 5/102-6]

F ROM CLIFTON it was a mile or more to Yeovil. This is a good market town, occupying a pleasing position on a rocky hill, and its buildings are quite good. It stands in Somerset on the left bank of the River Ivel [*Yeo*]. The town enjoys great borough privileges, and law courts are held there. It has a fine, light parish church, which contains four or five chantries endowed with land. One of the chantry chapels, at the west end of the church, is large and fine, and seems to be older than the rest of the building.

Not far from the town is a bridge across the Ivel, of three large stone arches. It carries the main road running westwards from Sherborne, which is three miles or more from Yeovil. A little above Ivel Bridge the river divides, but reunites close to the bridge, thus forming an island of fine meadowland. After Ivel Bridge the river flows three miles to Ilchester, then turns north to Mychelborow [?*Burrow Bridge, or possible Muchelney*], leaving Athelney some distance away to the left. Then it passes Langport, and so to Bridgwater, which lies close to its left bank.

Langport used to be a very attractive town, with a good market and many fine houses. But now it is in decline. From Sherborne it is about two miles to Milborne Port, which used to have a market, and still retains borough privileges. A stream flows down past the town, before entering Sherborne Water. *cont. p. 107* [**1544**: *5/109-10*]

Notes on Glastonbury Abbey:] Abbot Walter Fromont [*i.e. Geoffrey de Fromond*] began the great hall, and his successor, Walter of Monington, completed it. Walter of Monington built the chapter house as far as the central portion, and the next abbot, John Chinnock, completed it, as well as building the cloister, the dormitory and the frater. He is buried in a tomb with an effigy in alabaster. Abbot Adam [*of Sudbury*] gave seven large bells.

Abbot Richard Beere built the new apartments by the great chamber in the gallery, which is called the king's lodging. He also built new apartments for secular priests and the priests of Our Lady. He built Edgar's chapel at the east end of the church (although a portion of it was the work of Abbot Whiting). Bere buttressed the walls on both sides of the church's east end which had begun to spread; he also vaulted the crossing tower, and created beneath it the two strainer arches, like those of a St Andrew's cross, to prevent it from falling. He made a lavish altar of silver and gold, which he set in front of the high altar. There are six good windows along the top of each side of the east end. There used to be four, but two were added, and the sanctuary enlarged, by Abbot Walter of Monington.

After he had returned from his mission as ambassador in Italy Abbot Beere built a chapel of Our Lady of Loretta, which adjoins the north side of the church nave. He also built a chapel of the sepulchre at the south end of the nave, and nearby, in the nave south aisle, he is buried under a marble slab. He founded an almshouse with a chapel for seven or ten poor women in the northern part of the abbey, and he also built a manor house to replace the poor lodge in the park at Sharpham, two miles west of Glastonbury.

[*Other Glastonbury possessions include:*] Wirrall Park close to Glastonbury on the western side. Norwood Park, where Abbot John Selwood built a house, a mile east of the town. Pilton Park about six miles east of Glastonbury – here Abbot John Chinnok built a manor house. Weston, a small manor house due west of Glastonbury. Meare, a fine old manor house two miles north of Glastonbury. Damerham, a modest manor house seven miles WSW of Salisbury in Wiltshire. East Brent, a fine manor house ten miles NNW of Glastonbury. Sturminster Newton Castle, which was given to Glastonbury by Edmund Ironside, in Dorset, four miles from Shaftesbury.

[*Notes on Wells Cathedral:*] Thomas Beckington built the west range of the cloister with its vault, as well as a good school, with an apartment for a schoolmaster and a treasury above it, with twenty-five windows facing the precinct. He also began the south range of the cloister, but this was completed within living memory by a certain Thomas Henry, treasurer of Wells and archdeacon of Cornwall. This side has no buildings above it. Thomas Beckington died on 14th January 1464 [1465]. Thomas Bubwith built the east range, with the small chapel below and the great library above, which has twenty-five windows on each side. On the north side there is no cloister range for walking in, as the nave south aisle encroaches on this area; the only building on this side of the cloister garth is a chapel built by a certain Cookham. On the eastern side of the cloister an exceptionally fine chapel is set into the transept, which is the work of Bishops Stillington and King. [1/289-92]

Castle Cary in Selwood once belonged to Lord Seymour, and then passed by the female line to the De La Zouche family. On the death of Richard III it was confiscated and granted to Lord Willoughby of Brook. [4/131]

Cheddar, which lies at the foot of the Mendip Hills, is a good agricultural township dependent on Axbridge. [4/143]

There is a great hill, or ridge, extending from Glastonbury to within two miles of Bridgwater. It makes a true highway for travellers between the two places. This ridge is of virtually no width at all [?], and on both sides of it are low-lying wetlands. As you go from Glastonbury it is Brent Marsh away to your right. [5/5]

STAFFORDSHIRE

GOOD DESCRIPTIONS of Lichfield and Tamworth compensate for an otherwise meagre account of Staffordshire. This small corner of the county was visited on Leland's way back from Shropshire during the West Midlands itinerary in 1543, but for the rest we have only his tabulated notes which he compiled for many of the northern and midland counties. These describe towns, castles, monasteries, rivers and forests; but they include a number of inaccuracies, suggesting that Staffordshire was a county which Leland never explored very thoroughly. An annotated list of Staffordshire families, of biographical interest only, has been omitted from the following pages.

SUTTON COLDFIELD and Lichfield are five miles apart, and the country between them has quite good woodland and pasture, but it is not really suitable for growing good corn, since in many places it is infested with heather and bracken. The direct road passes through Shenstone, two miles from Sutton, and from there it is exactly three miles to Lichfield. At Shenstone there is a royal park well stocked with deer, and three miles in extent around its perimeter. A brook called the Black Water flows from the north, and crosses the road from Sutton to Lichfield, before it enters the River Tame on the left bank, as one faces downstream.

For all its stature the town of Lichfield is built on a low-lying, flat site, and it is only the close and the cathedral church, with a long street to the north of the town bridge, that occupy rather higher ground. There is no evidence that that there was ever a town wall, although Bishop Langton of Lichfield did construct a ditch in part of the town. A long time ago there was a castle at the southern end of the town, but no portion of it is now standing. The site with ditches is visible, and is still known as Castle Field. However, it is my guess that a more likely site for the original castle would actually have been the enclosure of the palace, which occupies a rather castle-like position.

The town itself is large and attractive, with three parish churches. St Mary's is an extremely beautiful piece of architecture, which stands right in the market place. St Michael's is at the south-east end of the town; and Stow Church at the east end. Here also is St Chad's Well, of pure water, on the floor of which may be seen the stone where it is said that St Chad used to stand naked in the water to pray. Here Chad had his oratory at the time of Wulfhere, King of Mercia, when all the country around Lichfield was forest and wilderness.

Attached to St Mary's Church in the market place is a guild or society established in about the time of Edward III, and greatly improved within living memory by Dean Heywood of Lichfield. The fraternity consists of five priests, and they officiate in St Mary's Church. There was also a religious house in Lichfield dedicated to St John, right on the southern edge of the town, which comprised a master and fellows, who were men of religion; but I was unable to discover who was its original founder. It was refounded by Bishop Smith of Coventry (and later of Lincoln) during Henry VII's reign. He reorganised it as a hospital, with a master, two priests and ten pauper men. He also established there a school, with a schoolmaster and usher to teach grammar, at an annual salary of £10, and an under-schoolmaster at £5. Henry VII gave the new foundation great support. He granted it an old hospital called Denhall in the Wirral, along with lands and the living of Burton church, also in the Wirral. There was also a house of grey friars in the south-west quarter of Lichfield; it was established by Bishop Alexander of Lichfield, who granted it certain free burgage plots in the town for its site.

Water is supplied to the town from a hill by a lead conduit, which has two conduit houses; one faces the street on the east wall of the grey friars' close, and the other is close to the market place. Another conduit supplies water to the close, where there is also a conduit house; and from there water is carried to the prebendal houses, and the houses of the vicars choral and choristers.

There used to be a fine old cross with steps around it in Lichfield market place. But Dean Denton of Lichfield has recently spent £160 in enclosing this cross within a structure of eight fine arches surmounted by a round vault, so as to enable poor market traders to stand in the dry.

The northern part of Lichfield is divided from the southern part by three pools or lakes. Two of these lie on the western side, and are not nearly as large as the third, which lies on the eastern side. Several springs rise in these pools, but the main source is a brook which flows into them and supplies them with water. It flows from Pipe, about a mile-and-a-half west of Lichfield.

The two western pools are divided by a large and extremely long causeway with stone walls on either side. Stone arches are incorporated into this causeway to enable water to flow from the first to the second pool. The causeway provides access between the southern and northern parts of the town, and was last rebuilt at great expense by Walter de Langton, bishop of Lichfield. There is another good stone causeway, little more than one-quarter as long as the other, between the second and third pools; it too has a channel for water to pass through it. This causeway leads out of Lichfield past the south gate of the cathedral close, and on its eastern side is a fine mill. I do not know who was the last to rebuild this causeway, but I think that it was Bishop Langton.

The third pool, which lies on the eastern side, is a most attractive feature, well stocked with fish, and extending, I would reckon, for about a half-mile to a place where all the water is confined into a narrow valley. From there the water flows down for three miles to the right bank of the Trent, in the vicinity of Mr Griffith's house called Wychnor. This house of Mr Griffith's is built in a low-lying position, and is very vulnerable to flooding when the Trent rises. Long ago there was a manor house at Wychnor built on a higher site, but that is completely derelict.

The cathedral church at Lichfield was originally dedicated in honour of St Mary and St Peter, and elevated to the seat of a bishop by King Oswy of Northumbria, who became king also of Mercia after he had killed the pagan Mercian king, Penda. After Oswy's death the sons of Penda, who had adopted the Christian faith, promoted this church, and supported Chad. At a much later period the church was renovated and rededicated to St Mary and St Chad. Bishop Langton built a new dike and an extremely strong wall around the entire cathedral close, and at its western end he erected a magnificent gate of great strength; he also built a smaller gate at the south-eastern end of the close, and the bishop's palace at the eastern end, besides many other worthy deeds.

There are very fine prebendal houses in the close built by several different men, and there is a good house for the choristers recently erected by Bishop Blythe. Fairwell Priory, a small nunnery suppressed by Thomas Wolsey, bishop of York, was granted to Lichfield by him to compensate the cathedral for a pension which it should have been receiving from his Oxford college. It was appropriated for the benefit of the Lichfield choristers. Thomas Heywood, dean of Lichfield, built the library in the north-western quarter of Lichfield Cathedral. The pride of the cathedral church is the architecture of its west front, which is exceptionally lavish and beautiful. It has three stone spires, two at the west end and one in the centre.

That portion of the town of Lichfield lying north of the great causeway or bridge is all laid out along a single fine street; at one time this included some of the prebendal houses, and also the vicars' college.

Distances from Lichfield: Stafford, 12 miles; Derby, 16 miles; Warwick, 20 miles; Tamworth, 5 miles, and Nuneaton, 9 miles beyond, straight along the road; Burton upon Trent, 8 miles.

The forest or chase of Cannock (or Cank) Wood, or at least the foremost part of it, still survives within four miles of Lichfield, and from there it extends to within a mile of Stafford. There are many springs, and the sources of many streams, in this forest. Long ago all the countryside in the neighbourhood of Lichfield was like a forest and wilderness, and by nature rather poor soil; now by contrast, through the passage of time and by cultivation it has become reasonably fertile, and in many places so much woodland has been felled that there is no indication that the area was ever wooded. As a result wood has become an expensive commodity in Lichfield compared with the price charged within living memory.

The direct road from Lichfield to Coventry takes you five miles to Bassett's Cross, where there are no buildings, and then a further seven miles to Coleshill. Canwell Priory, established by the Bassetts, and later by the Lisles, stood about a half-mile from Bassett's Cross. It was a cell with only one monk. A mile towards Lichfield from the cross is Weeford, where a brook crosses the highway. A fight took place at Weeford Bridge between Lord Lisle and Sir Henry Willoughby, and Willoughby was badly injured (Purefoy had earlier been killed there by Willoughby during the dispute between Edward IV and Henry VI).

I travelled four miles from Lichfield to Hopwas, across sandy soil, with heathland in many places, but also some wood, pasture and corn. At the far end of Hopwas village, as I left it, I crossed the River Tame by a stone bridge of sixteen arches, which takes its name from the village. From there I rode for a mile between arable land on my left and meadows on my right until I reached the town of Tamworth. The River Tame divides to form two islands between Tamworth and Hopwas Bridge, but reunites a little upstream from the bridge, by which point the whole river has resumed its single course. Salter's Bridge over the River Tame is four or five miles further downstream.

Some people calculate that the confluence of the Tame with the Trent occurs ten miles below the town of Tamworth. The Tame enters the Trent by its right bank three miles or more below Mr Griphin's [*Griffith's*] house, between Burton and Repton, a mile above Repton [*no*]. I noticed that when the Tame approaches Tamworth it is flowing from the south-west; but its source in fact lies due WNW of the town.

Tamworth has an important market, and a very long history, since it was rebuilt by Ethelfleda, Lady of Mercia and sister of Edward the Elder, after it had been rased and sacked by the Danes. Taking its name from the valley in which the River Tame, and also the River Anker, flow, Tamworth is built on the slope of a small hillside, and its main street and buildings run from east to west. The north side of this high street, where the parish church is situated, and the northern part of the town lie in Warwickshire. The south side of the street, and this part of the town running down to the right bank of the Anker, are in Staffordshire, including the castle, which stands in this area at the very point where the Tame and Anker flow together. I only saw three buildings of note in the town: the parish church, the castle and the bridges.

The church is collegiate, with a dean and six prebendaries, although each of them employs a substitute to perform his duties there. Nobody there could tell me who had built the college. Some thought that it had been a college since before the conquest, although others believed that it had been founded by the Marmion family; and this opinion is more likely to be correct, since successive generations of the Marmion family were owners of Tamworth Castle. At the present time the king is reckoned to be the patron of this college. There are several fine tombs of noble men and women in the eastern part of this collegiate church. One was a member of the Freville family, Baldwin Freville according to some, who owned Tamworth Castle. Also there are buried the parents and grandparents of Ferrers, the castle's present owner. Tamworth has a guild of St George, which had property with an annual value of £5, but recently a certain John Bailey added another £5 worth of land to its endowment, and with this a grammar school has now been built.

Tamworth Castle stands on a reasonably high site in the southern quarter of the town, right next to the bank of the River Anker, and at its confluence. The outer courtyard and great ward of the castle have been completely ruined, and the walls fallen down. Only some insignificant domestic buildings remain. However, the motte is still there, and a large round stone tower surmounting it. Mr Ferrars keeps this in good repair, and lives there. The castle's owners since the conquest have been the Marmions, Frevilles and Ferrars.

Of Tamworth's two bridges, Bowbridge is the finer, even though it spans the Anker, which is a lesser river than the Tame, and it is away at the ENE edge of the town on the road to Polesworth and Nuneaton. This River Anker flows from the Leicestershire border in the east. The other bridge is called St Mary's; it has twelve large arches, and carries the road to Coventry. It lies on the Tame just below the confluence, and a short distance downstream from the castle. I deduce from a large stone on the bridge, inscribed with the Bassett arms, that it was built by Lord Bassett of Drayton.

Tamworth has three annual fairs. Two are town fairs, but the third, as I recall, belongs to the college. The town is entirely built of timber. *cont. p. 378* [**1543:** 2/99-105]

The market towns of Staffordshire are as follows: Stafford, Lichfield, Newcastle-under-Lyme, Burton upon Trent, Uttoxeter, Tutbury, Wolverhampton, Tamworth. At Stafford there is a free grammar school established by Sir Thomas Countre, parson of Ingestre near Haywood, and Sir Randol, who was a chantry priest in Stafford. They were also responsible for the fine square tower and the bells of St Chad's Church, Stafford. The parish church which serves Newcastle-under-Lyme is a good mile away at Stoke-on-Trent, but the townspeople generally worship at St Sonday's [*i.e. St Dominic's – the name arises from confusion with the Latin for Sunday, 'dies dominica'*] Chapel near the castle. All the castle except one tower has been demolished. On the southern side of the town there used to be a house of Dominican friars. Burton upon Trent has a single parish church, but there is also a chapel at the end of the bridge. The River Trent meanders around a large part of the town. Many marble-carvers work there in alabaster. Uttoxeter also has a single parish church. The inhabitants are graziers, because there are marvellous pasture grounds there beside the Dove. The town belongs to the duchy of Lancaster, and lies on the road from Derby to Stafford, nine miles ENE of Stafford. Wolverhampton is a very good market town. It has a free school established by Sir Stephen Jennings, mayor of London, [*and its collegiate church*] is served by prebendaries from the College of Windsor, whose dean is also dean of Wolverhampton. About a mile away there is a college in the village of Tettenhall.

Castles in Staffordshire: Stafford Castle is not far from the town, on the River Sow. There is a castle or attractive fortress at Caverswell, four miles north of Stone. At Stone there was a priory of canons, which once belonged to the Montgomery family, and now to the Giffards. Lichfield at one time had a castle, which occupied a low-lying site in the middle of a pool, like an island. This pool is in some places a quarter-mile wide, but elsewhere it is less, and the castle site is approached by a causeway, which has several bridges in it to permit the spring water to flow through.

Newcastle-under-Lyme is so called either because of a brook which flows in the area, or a nearby hill or wood. The castle belonged to the duke of Lancaster. A brook flows past the town from a pool near the castle. Heighley Castle belongs to Lord Audley, and is only two miles from the village of Audley. Consequently some people believe that Heighley is a corruption of Audley. The tenants of Audley attend this castle. Tutbury Castle used to be the castle of Ferrières, earl of Derby, but now it has passed to the crown through the duchy of Lancaster. Eccleshall Castle belongs to the bishop of Chester; it has five large pools, through which a brook passes before it flows out.

Sturseley, or Stourton, Castle is undoubtedly in Staffordshire [*actually Worcestershire, east of Stourbridge*], and I have heard that there was a Lord Stourton who was baron of this Stourton. It belongs to the king, but the Pole family were permitted to live there, and it was there that Cardinal Pole was born. Tamworth Castle belongs to one of the Ferri[gr]eres family, and stands on the River Anker. The town lies partly in Staffordshire and partly in Warwickshire; but the whole of the castle definitely falls into Warwickshire. Not very far from Stone Priory may be seen the site of King Wulfhere's castle or manor house. It is called Bury Bank and is a mile from Stone in the direction of the moorland. The castle stood on a crag beside a brook, and there are still large ditches and masonry to be seen there. Dudley Castle stands close to the Worcestershire border, although the castle itself is in Staffordshire.

The rivers of Staffordshire: Sow (this river flows past Stafford, St Thomas's monastery a good mile away, and Shugborough, before entering the Trent at Haywood Bridge); Trent (I have already plotted the course of the Trent as far as Newark); Dove; Penk (a small river which flows through Penkridge, and enters the

Sow near Stafford); Churnet (I already have its complete course); Blith (its source is on Wetley Moor, and it flows past the villages of Draycott in the Moors and Tean, and joins the Dove near Uttoxeter [*no*]); Tame (flows through Tame Bridge, the Handsworth district, Aston, Birmingham, Curdworth Bridge, Kingsbury, the Fazeley district and Tamworth, and enters the Trent at Wychnor Bridge – Kingsbury, in Warwickshire, has a fine manor house and an estate worth annually £140, belonging to a certain Bracebridge).

Abbeys and priories in Staffordshire: At Stone Priory there were several tombs of the earls of Stafford which were made of alabaster. After the house was suppressed the effigies which lay on these tombs were taken to the Austin friary at Ford Bridge, or Stafford Green, on the near side of the river. In this friary was hung up a pedigree of the Stafford family. On Stafford Green, close to the River Sow, there was also a free chapel dedicated to St John. The grey friars' house lay at the other end of Stafford, across the river. Mr Stretey of Lichfield told me that Bishop Langton of Lichfield, who was treasurer to Edward I, built the fine palace and the close wall at Lichfield, as well as Eccleshall Castle, the manor house at Shugborough, and the palace near Stroud.

Forests, parks and chases in Staffordshire: Between Lichfield and Wolverhampton there is a chase stocked with deer called the Seven Hayes. Near Penkridge there is an attractive royal chase [*Teddesley*], whose hereditary forester is Littleton of Pillenhaul [*Pillaton Hall*]. Needwood Forest is next to Tutbury, and between Tutbury and Lichfield – although it comes no nearer to Lichfield than five miles. Four parks belong to the Honour of Tutbury: Castle Hay, Hanbury, Barton, and the New Park. This forest is amazingly well stocked with deer.

Cannock Forest is large, and is partly owned by the bishop of Lichfield. His house and park of Beaudesert are in the forest, and lie in the parish of Longdon, as indeed does much of the forest. He also has a house, with a park now stocked with red deer, at Shugborough on the edge of Cannock Wood. This Shugborough once belonged to a certain Suchborough, who had a long beard; and it was he who gave it to the Lichfield bishopric – although I cannot be certain of this. Shugborough is sometimes called Haywood, because it stands close by. Between Shugborough and Cannock Wood there is a fine pool.

Next to Eccleshall Castle there are five nice pools, and two miles away in the same manor is Blore Park, which belongs to the bishop, and measures five or six miles in circuit, stocked with remarkably fine wood. Sutton Chase was five miles from Lichfield, partly in Staffordshire and partly in Warwickshire. It has now been completely felled, and Bishop Veysey of Exeter has planted houses of stone and brick there, with many good inhabitants. A knight called Mountford had his possessions confiscated during Henry VII's reign. He had owned a manor house here called Sutton, near Sutton Coldfield, and he also had Coleshill Hall in Warwickshire, and a park which was granted to Sir Simon Digby, lieutenant of the Tower of London.

The position of Staffordshire, and its mineral resources: Coal is found at Wednesbury, a village five miles WSW of Lichfield. And at Walsall, a mile north of Wednesbury, there are coal pits, lime pits that also supply Sutton Coldfield four miles away, and iron ore. Walsall is a small Staffordshire market town inhabited by many smiths and bit-makers. It now belongs to the king, and there is a park of the same name scarcely a half-mile from the town on the road to Wolverhampton. [5/18-23]

SUFFOLK

NOT EVEN THE GHOST *of an itinerary through Suffolk may be reconstructed from the meagre fragments about the county which survive among Leland's notes.*

I noticed in a grant made by Henry IV that the site of the black friars' last premises at Thetford, on the Suffolk side of Thetford Bridge, had previously been occupied by a hospital called Maison Dieu. At the foot of the document making the grant there are references to John, earl of Warwick, and Henry, duke of Lancaster, who was Henry IV's maternal grandfather. The grant singles out Edmund Gundeville as a particular object of the friars' prayers. [1/325]

Mr Hopton of Blythburgh told me that at a small village called Wenhaston, which is about a half-mile upstream from Blythburgh on the same bank of the river, may be seen ditches and other earthworks signifying the site of an important building. One theory is that the East Anglian kings had some large premises here, and that nearby was the ancient abbey which Bede mentions in his history. But another version says that the castle and abbey recorded by Bede lay on the opposite bank of the Blyth, at the point where a creek enters it, one mile from Dunwich [*?error* *for Southwold*] and about a mile-and-a-half from Blythburgh. The place is called ... [*?Wangford*] Hill, and ditches and mounds are visible there, including one of considerable size. This is the more likely site of the place referred to by Bede.

I was told by Mr Sheffield that, until the time of the earl of Oxford (the one who came in with Henry VII), Henham Castle was very dilapidated, so that, apart from the gatehouse and the massive keep, all the present buildings were the work of this former earl.

Burgh Castle stands in Suffolk in the Lowestoft region; substantial ruined walls of the castle may still be seen. [2/25].

George Ferrars told me that the inhabitants of Dunwich, in pleading for help for their town against the ravages of the sea, affirm that a large area of forest which used to stand in the neighbourhood has been swallowed up, and the sea now covers the site. [2/28]

There was a man named Henry Framlingham, who was often called after the office he held, Henry Surveyor. He was a hearty fellow who owned a good estate in and around the town of Framlingham. Later along came one Jenkin Framlingham, who purchased a fine manor, with a manor house, near the market town of Debenham in Suffolk, one mile from Soham. This manor house stands on an attractive hill surrounded by woodland, a short distance from Debenham. It is called Crows Hall, after a gentleman called Crow who had owned it before Jenkin Framlingham bought it. Jenkin is buried in Debenham church, and from then on the Framlinghams have been lords of the town of Debenham. Recently they entered into an exchange of lands with owners at Wingfield and in Norfolk, in return for their property in Framlingham itself, and in some other nearby places. Apart from the Framlinghams of Debenham there are no other landed families with that surname. [4/101]

SURREY

*L*IKE *LONDON AND MIDDLESEX*, *perhaps, Leland was too familiar with Surrey to compile detailed notes or write up visits in preparation for the books he intended to write. Thus only scraps survive – but one of these, describing Kingston, is as interesting as anything he wrote about more exotic towns in the west and north.*

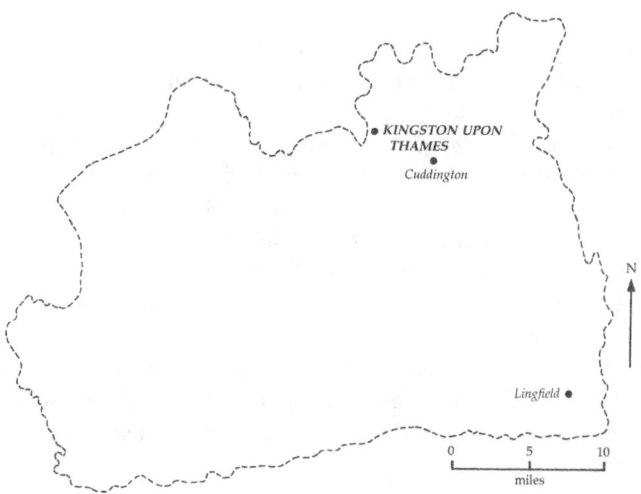

I have heard Mr Garter say that the manner in which the coronations of kings was conducted at Kingston upon Thames before the conquest, was to perform the ceremony on platforms erected in the market place. [1/328]

Kingston upon Thames: The antiquities of the town are found where the land slopes down from Coombe Park towards the gallows. Very frequently, whilst ploughing or digging, people have found the footings of the walls of buildings, various coins of bronze, silver and gold with Latin inscriptions, and painted pottery. During Cardinal Wolsey's time one such vessel was found to contain a large number of silver Roman coins, sheets of silver for coining, ingots to beat into sheets for coin, and silver chains.

There is a popular belief that long ago the bridge at old Kingston, which was the usual crossing-point of the Thames, was further down the river than it is now;

but that when the new town was built in the Saxon period soil was excavated from the steep side of Coombe Park itself in order to build beside the river, and then a new bridge was sited next to it.

The townspeople of Kingston maintain that their town church is on the site of a former abbey. But I believe that to be unlikely, because Henry II appropriated their church to Merton Abbey [*Priory*] in Surrey, and then it was a parish church, not an abbey, priory or dependent cell. The townspeople also have definite information about a few kings who were crowned there before the conquest, and they argue that two or three of them were buried in the parish church, although of this they can show neither proof nor evidence.

In the new town beside the Thames there is a building which is still called the Bishop's Hall, although it has now been converted into an ordinary dwelling house for an inhabitant of Kingston. It used to belong to the bishops of Winchester, and it is my guess that one of the bishops grew tired of it and neglected it, building instead beside the Thames at Esher, two or three miles upstream.

Several kings have granted Kingston important privileges, and these it retains to the present. It is the best market town in the whole of Surrey. There was and is a chapel called Magdalene's, and attached to it is a hospital which had a master, two priests and some pauper men. I was told that its founder was one Lovekyn, who was mayor of London. I also learned that Lovekyn was a native of Kingston, who lived in Thames Street near New Fish Street, and was the founder of the college in St Michael's church by Crooked Lane. It is my guess that this Lovekin dwelt in the house where Mr Finkel lived, and he was buried in the nave of St Michael's church.

Kingston has three dependent chapelries or hamlets lying alongside the Thames towards London; they are Petersham, Richmond or Sheen, and Kew. Kingston's liberty extends from almost as far as Mortlake upstream almost to Cobham. [4/85-6]

At Lingfield, on the edge of Surrey, about a mile from Starborough Castle, there is a college within the parish church, which was founded by one of the Cobhams. Some of the Cobham family are buried there. [4/118]

Crompton of London owns a field near Cuddington in Surrey (where the king is building). In this field a fine clay outcrops, which is unlike anything found elsewhere in England. It is used by goldsmiths and metal founders to make moulds, and is sold for two gold crowns per load. [4/121]

SUSSEX

ANOTHER POORLY REPRESENTED COUNTY, Sussex does not figure in any of the surviving itineraries. The detailed accounts of Petworth and Winchelsea, however, may be fragments of lost itineraries. In the case of Petworth Leland's preliminary notes have also survived, much after the fashion of counties explored on the 1542 visit to the West Country. This journey peters out in the Winchester or Portsmouth area, and so it may be that he went to Petworth at the same time. The account of Winchelsea probably resulted from a visit during Leland's ramblings in Kent; it is clear that he visited Tenterden and the Kent–Sussex borderland to the south, and this provides the likely context for his interesting description of the rise and fall of a medieval new town.

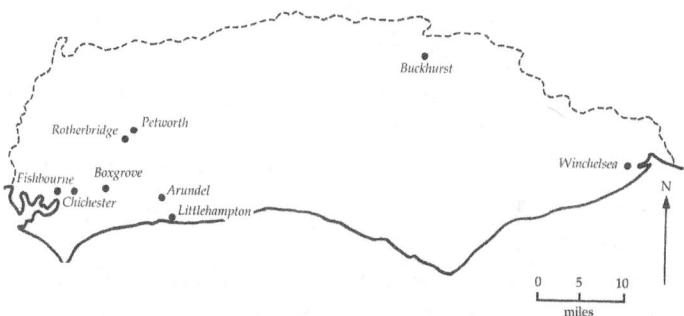

THE MARKET TOWN of Petworth in the Sussex Weald has greatly increased since the time when the earls of Northumberland used to stay there occasionally. Good clothmaking is carried on there now. The town's parson enjoys great privileges, and holds his own court leet in respect of certain tenements that he possesses. A parson named Acon built the spire on the fine church tower in the town, and was also responsible for making the good stone bridge called Rotherbridge, which crosses the water flowing down from Cowdray barely a mile from Petworth. Another parson, called Edmunds, realised that Petworth suffered from a serious water shortage, and diverted a large spring which issues a mile from the town, bringing it in a lead [?pipe] into Petworth, with supplies to the manor house, the parsonage, and two or three places in the town street.

In Petworth church are buried some of the children of the Percy family, but none of the lords. But Sir William Redmille lies there; he was a knight who lived, so I was told, in one of the lodges belonging to the great park at Petworth. One or two of the Scropes are buried there also, and I have heard that others are buried at Boxgrove Priory, which is near Lord De La Warre's former house at [?Halnaker]. Also buried in Petworth church are some of the Dauterey [*Dawtrey*] family; in Latin their name is written 'de alta ripe' ['*of the high bank*']. Their principal house is called the Moor, and lies in Petworth parish, half-a-mile from the town. They also own another house in Petworth near the church.

About a mile below Rotherbridge near Petworth on the nearer bank can be seen the moat and other remains of an old manor house called Baienet [*Bewgenet*], and this, I discovered, used to be the home of a gentleman named Dyke, who possessed a good estate. On the further bank of the river opposite it is a rabbit warren. The Dyke estate has passed by marriage to Mr Goring and Mr Dering. Some people say that there was also a third sister, and that she married Shirley, the cofferer of the king's household, but that his share passed to the other two. As I recall, Rivers Park [*?Riverhill near Egdean*] was also part of the Dikes' property.

At the mouth of the River Arun on the seashore are two small settlements four miles from Arundel. The nearer is called Cudlow, and its harbour is Cudlow Haven; the further is called Littlehampton. Close to the road between Arundel and Chichester, on the right hand side, there is a fine wood, with a park and an old house in it called Slindon, which belongs to the bishop of Canterbury. Two or three miles below Chichester on the far side of the creek there is a small place called Fishbourne, and some people call its harbour Fishbourne Haven. The stream which passes Chichester flows into this creek. [4/92-3]

THE OLD TOWN of Winchelsea became very severely and obviously damaged by the ravages of the sea. This devastation all occurred over a period of six or seven consecutive years. During this time the inhabitants of Winchelsea appealed for help to Edward I, and asked him for a site on which to build a new town. And so the king dispatched John of Kirkby, bishop of Ely and treasurer of England, to Winchelsea to inspect a site for the new town. The place chosen was at the time partly in use as a rabbit warren, and its principal owner was a knight called Sir John Tregoze, although Battle Abbey and a certain Maurice also owned portions. The king negotiated with them, and an area of 150 acres was assigned for the new town, including a portion outside the town in the king's meadow, and another on the steep hillside.

And so during the period of years already described the king gave his help towards founding and walling New Winchelsea, and the inhabitants of Old Winchelsea gradually made progress with building work at the new town. So that by the end of the six- or seven-year period the new town was fairly well equipped, and for a few years afterwards it daily continued to grow.

But within the first twenty years since its establishment New Winchelsea was twice invaded by enemies, first by Frenchmen who caused a great deal of damage in the town, and secondly by Spaniards. They landed by night at Fareley [*Fairlight*], where the tall tower is, three miles from Winchelsea, and about halfway to Hastings. During this invasion the town of Winchelsea was terribly ransacked, and since then has scarcely recovered its earlier position of wealth. It is often said that at the time of the raid there had been twenty aldermen in the town, all merchants of great substance. Winchelsea has two parish churches within the town walls, and there used to be two colleges of friars. There is another parish church just outside the town, but that is dependent on the liberty of Hastings.

For a long time there has been an important family in the Winchelsea area of Sussex called Finch, and it is very likely that they owed their prominence through a successful Winchelsea merchant. Documents record that the commanders at the battle of le Trade [*?le Goulet, Brest*] were Alard and Finch Herbert, and that Finch was badly wounded there. The present generation of the Finch family say that their real name is Herbert, and that the two names were joined when a Herbert married the heiress of the Finch family and added her name to his. There was a Vincent Finch at the time of Henry IV who sued the king in order to recover a manor in the Winchelsea area. Alard of Winchelsea was a man of importance, and he is buried there; his descendant, who has inherited his coat of arms, is Oxenbridge of Sussex. [4/113-14]

Knepp Castle, Bewbush Park and other estates in Sussex belonged at one time to the Braose family, but were inherited by the Grevilles from their ancestors. More recently, after a great deal of dispute and bargaining, they have passed to the Howards, dukes of Norfolk. [2/12-13]

Dawtrey told me that three women, perhaps sisters, divided between them the lands of the honour of Petworth. They married into three families – Percy, Dawtrey and Aske – which I assume all originated in the north of England. Aske is a northern family, and Aske the traitor was a younger brother. This original partition between three families has not been entirely maintained, and the estate has been dispersed. It is probable, in fact, since so much of it remained Percy property until recently, that Dawtrey and Aske never had equal shares, but were merely Percy's vassals. All three families have a mill-pick on their arms, but with different backgrounds.

Dyke (whose lands have now descended to Mr Goring) and other gentry in the area were vassals of the honour of Petworth. Dawtrey the knight who lived in Southampton was the uncle of old Mr Dawtrey of Petworth, who is still alive. All the property of Dawtrey of Southampton was acquired by purchase. Lightster, chief baron of the exchequer had as his second wife the widow of this Dawtrey. The house at ... [?Burton] was built by the father of Goring who lives there now. Previously he and his ancestors had lived at Bewgenet, which is a mile or more away beside the Petworth River [Rother]. The ruins of the house of the Dikes family, which later descended to the Gorings, may still be seen there.

Rivers [Riverhill] Park, in the neighbourhood of Petworth, belonged to someone called Rivers, although the manor house lay some distance outside the park, as may still be seen. Its site is still called Rivers church, and a member of the family is buried in this parish church. Bolney is a gentleman. Arundel is seven miles from Petworth, and Chichester is ten. [4/77-8]

The oldest branch of the Sackville family still extant has its seat at Buckhurst in Sussex, which is next to Waterdown forest, and two or three miles from Rotherfield. This Sackville owns land with an annual value of £300. Sackville of Bedford, who was groom-porter, descended from this house, and so too did Sackville of Bletchingley in the Reigate area, and Sackville of Calais. The Bletchingley Sackville owns an estate worth nearly £30 annually. [4/82]

WARWICKSHIRE

A*PART FROM A FEW NOTES about towns, rivers, castles and boundaries, and a brief paragraph about Rugby, all Leland's information about Warwickshire (or at least, all that has survived) seems to have been gleaned from a single itinerary, the journey through the West Midlands to Shropshire and back again in 1543. His outward route explored the south of the county, yielding an excellent account of Warwick, and good descriptions of Stratford and Alcester. On his return he explored what is now the Birmingham conurbation and Coventry. Modern Birmingham, as might be expected, is quite unrecognisable from Leland's description; in his day it was of less importance than Sutton Coldfield, to which he devoted more space. After exploring Coventry he headed south again and returned via Southam to Banbury, from where his journey through Warwickshire had begun. In addition (although not included here) there have survived preliminary accounts of both Warwick and Stratford, which embody a few differences from these itinerary descriptions. From comments in his notes it appears that he also wrote descriptions of Henley in Arden, Nuneaton and Atherstone, but these appear to have perished.*

Leland's interests, as explained in the introduction, were not confined to topography. He was also an accomplished Latin poet, and several hundreds of his poems survive. But throughout the itineraries there is scarcely a hint that he was also gathering material to be one day turned into poems. Almost the only poetic description in the work relates to Guy's Cliffe near Warwick. He began his account in English, but as the muse took over he lapsed into Latin to describe the beauty of the place, and my translation hardly does his words justice.

MY RIDE FROM BANBURY to Warwick took me past twelve miles of openfield country, producing good corn and grass, but with no woodland, and then two miles where there were some enclosures and woods. About half a mile before I reached Warwick I crossed a stone bridge of one arch, under which a pleasant stream runs towards the River Avon.

Warwick had an extremely strong town wall and ditch, and the distance around inside the walls is a good mile. The most spectacular remains of the ditch lie between the castle and the west gate, and along this section the great earthen bank on which the wall stood still survives. Near the gates portions of the walls are still visible. The east and west gates survive, but the north gate has been demolished. On the south side the strong bridge next to the castle served in place of a south gate.

Warwick Castle is magnificent and strong. It lies at the WSW edge of the town, close to the right bank of the Avon, and is built on a lofty crag of rock. There are three good towers on its eastern face and a fine tower on the north. On this side of the castle Richard III demolished part of the wall so as to insert a massive tower or stronghold from which to fire off cannon. He began and half-built this tower, but it remains unfinished as he left it. The keep is situated in the WNW part of the castle, and is now in ruins. On this same side is a tower, with an iron postern gate leading through it. All the main apartments, as well as the hall and chapel, lie on the south side of the castle, and here the king has incurred great expenditure in consolidating the castle foundations in the rock, for large pieces had fallen away from the rock beneath the foundations. A collegiate church has existed within the castle since the conquest.

The town of Warwick stands on a great rocky crag, which rises from east to west. The pride of the town is its two beautiful streets. One is called the High Street, and this runs from the east gate to the west, with an excellent cross in its centre. The other street, which runs from north to south, forms a cross-roads with it in the middle.

Within the town itself there is only one parish church, and this is a fine, large building which stands in the centre and is dedicated to St Mary.

Roger Beaumont, earl of Warwick, transferred the college to it from within the castle, and endowed it with a good estate. Thomas Beauchamp, earl of Warwick, who was the grandfather of Earl Richard, Henry VI's lieutenant in France, decreed in his will, so I was told, that his executors should completely rebuild the chancel, or eastern part of St Mary's church. This they did, and he is buried there with his wife. Richard, earl of Warwick, the lieutenant of France, planned a very large, fine and lavish chapel on the south side of the quire. This grand piece of work was in due course built by the executors of his will, and he lies there entombed like a prince, his likeness portrayed in an effigy of copper and gilt, beneath staves of copper and gilt like the hoops of a cart.

Noblemen buried in the nave of St Mary's church, Warwick: Sir John Tunstall, of the household of one of the former earls of Warwick. William Bareswell, dean of Warwick. He was one of the executors of earl Richard's will, who oversaw the erection of the lady chapel and the completion of the collegiate house begun by earl Richard himself. John Rous, chantry priest of the Guycliffe chapel, who built a library over the south porch, and adorned it with books. He died 14th January 1491. This Rous was an expert mathematician in his day, and a great historian; it is assumed that he was related to the Rouses of Ragley near Alcester.

In the south aisle is an esquire named Power, three members of the Hungerford family settled at Edmundscote on the Avon, about half a mile above Warwick, and another esquire named Beaufort who inherited part of the Hungerford estate. In the transept, between nave and quire, lie Thomas Beauchamp, the father of earl Richard, lieutenant of France, in a good marble tomb; William Peito, lord of Chesterton, and his wife; Mr Haly, a man of great learning who died recently; Haseley, dean of Warwick, who was once Henry VII's schoolmaster; and Alester, dean of Warwick. His tomb lies at the west end of the lady chapel, in the place where earl Richard was buried before his tomb was moved into the lady chapel. In the quire are Thomas Beauchamp (Earl Richard's grandfather) and his wife; and Catherine, Earl Thomas's eldest daughter. She is buried under a flat marble slab at the head of her father's tomb.

In the lady chapel lies Richard, earl of Warwick, who died on 30th April 1439, in the 17th year of Henry VI. His epitaph runs as follows: 'Pray devoutly for the soul (to whom God grant absolution) of one of the most respected knights of his time, for his manliness and skill, Richard

Beauchamp, late earl of Warwick, Lord Despenser, of Abergavenny and many other great estates, whose body lies here under this tomb, in a stone vault most fair set in the bare rock. He died in the proper Christian manner on 30th April 1439 at Rohan Castle after a long illness, while he was lieutenant of France and of the duchy of Normandy with the full authority of our sovereign King Henry VI. His body was conveyed with the utmost care and reverence by land and sea to Warwick on the 4th October in the same year, and was laid to rest with solemn rites in a fine stone chest at the west door of this chapel. There his body remained until this chapel, which had been planned during his lifetime, was built in accordance with his last will and testament. The chapel was built on the solid rock, and all its parts were completed and furnished by his executors according to the instructions in his will; and then, by the same authority, they reverently translated his body to the vault described above. Honoured be God therefore.'

Information extracted from the glass of the east window in the lady chapel: Elizabeth, daughter and heiress of Thomas, Lord Berkeley and Lisle, was the first wife of Richard Beauchamp, earl of Warwick. They had three daughters – Margaret, who married John, earl of Shrewsbury; Eleanor, who married Edmund Beaufort, earl of Somerset; and Elizabeth, who married George Neville, Lord Latimer. Earl Richard married a second wife, Isabel, Lady Spenser of Glamorgan and Morgannock. Henry, duke of Warwick, the son and heir of Earl Richard and Isabel, married Cecily, the daughter of Richard Neville, earl of Salisbury. Anne, the daughter of Earl Richard and Isabel, married Richard Neville, son and heir of Richard Neville, second earl of Salisbury.

Some people maintain that one of the Nevilles, Lords Latimer, whom they suppose to have been killed at the Battle of Edgecote near Banbury, is buried at the west end of the lady chapel. But there is no sign of a tomb nor an inscription, and the story must refer to Sir Henry Neville, who was son and heir of George Neville, Lord Latimer; but this Henry (the present Lord Latimer's grandfather) never became a lord, as he died before his father.

The former residence of the college and deanery of St Mary's in Warwick lay in what is now the ESE part of the churchyard. The new lodgings of the college, just outside the east end of the churchyard, were built by the executors of Earl Richard's will. Most of the prebendal houses lie on the street to the west of the church. The college has a dean and five prebendaries.

There is a fine chapel over the east gate dedicated to St Peter, and over the west gate is a good chapel of St James. Four priests sing in St James's Chapel, and they belong to a fraternity of Our Lady and St George, which some people believe was started in Earl Richard's time, and of which he was a benefactor. They have an attractive college building on the north side of St James's Chapel, and they are governed by the burgesses of Warwick.

The suburb outside the east gate is called Smiths Street. I was told there that Jews once lived in it; it also had a college dedicated to St John, and a hospital. On the south-east side of the town is a suburb with a parish church of St Nicholas, appropriated to St Mary's college in Warwick. The suburb which lies to the south beyond the bridge is called Bridge End, and this has a chapel of St John which once belonged to the prior of St John in London. Its property passed to the commandery at [Temple] Balsall near Warwick.

West End, the suburb outside the west gate, is a very large street. There was a college of black friars in the northern part of this suburb which also was large, and founded, so I was told, by the Butler family, Lords Sudeley, and by the Montforts. This is the only post-conquest foundation in Warwick of any importance which I have so far come across, which was not the work of the earls of Warwick. There is also a suburb on the north side of Warwick, and here there is a chapel of St Michael, which was once collegiate, with a master and brethren. But now it is regarded as a free chapel and royal donative, and the fabric of the college building is in poor condition.

There is an excellent chapel of St Mary Magdalene on the right bank of the River Avon scarcely a mile upstream from Warwick, which some call Gibclif and others Guy-clif [*Guy's Cliffe*]. An old story is still recalled by the local people that Guido, earl of Warwick during the reign of Athelstan, was very much attached to this place and built an oratory there. The legend is sometimes continued that after Guido had won great victories in distant places, and had been away for so long that he was given up for dead, he came back and lived here as a hermit, unknown to his wife Felicia until right at the moment of his death he revealed his true identity. A cave in the rock next to the bank of the Avon there is pointed out as the place where he used to sleep, and pleasant springs in a good meadow nearby are still claimed as having supplied Earl Guido's drinking water.

Until Earl Richard's time there was only a small chapel and a cottage inhabited by a hermit at the spot; but Earl Richard felt a great affection for the place, and built a good new chapel, which he dedicated to St Mary Magdalene, as well as establishing two chantry priests there in the service of God. He erected a a gigantic statue of Earl Guido, enclosed the silvery springs in the meadow with pure white stone as smooth as marble, and constructed an attractive building like a roofed cage, which was specifically to protect visitors from the rain. For the chantry priests he built a nice stone house next to the chapel, and endowed it with the surrounding land. It is a place of pleasure, a house fit for the muses. Silence may be found there, a charming wood, caves in the living rock, the happy sound of the river rolling across the stones, little shady groves, clear sparkling springs, meadows strewn with flowers, moss-lined caves, ribbons of water swiftly flowing between the boulders, a solitary place as well, enjoying silence, which of all things the muses love the best.

There are three parks close to Warwick on its northern side. Wedgnock is the nearest, and another called Grove practically adjoins it; the name of the third is Haseley. There is a priory of nuns called Wroxall about three miles north of Warwick.

The course of the Avon, and its important bridges: ... then to Edmundscote Bridge, and about a half-mile lower to the good stone bridge of twelve arches at Warwick. Then two miles to Barford Bridge of eight fine arches. A half-mile downstream it passes Fulbrook Park and fortlet on the right bank, and then a mile-and-a-half lower it passes Mr Lucy's manor house of Charlecote on the left bank. Behind Mr Lucy's house a stream which rises three miles away to the south-east enters the left bank of the Avon. From here it is three miles to Stratford Bridge, which has fourteen large and five smaller arches. Bidford Bridge, five miles lower, is stonebuilt, and has recently been repaired using some of the stone from Alcester Priory. Below this the Rivers Arrow and Alne both enter the Avon in a single valley. Salford is an attractive roadside place. At Offenham, four miles below Bidford, there is a narrow stone bridge across the Avon for pedestrians. Evesham Bridge, one mile lower, has eight good large arches, and then three miles downstream, at Fleodanbury or Fladbury, the Piddle Brook flows into the Avon by the right bank. An attractive bridge has recently been built across the Piddle Brook a short distance above this confluence. Two miles further downstream the Avon flows under Pershore Bridge.

At Warwick I discovered that the larger part of Warwickshire, which lies on the right hand side of the Avon as one goes downstream, is in Arden (the old name for this portion of the county). Much of the land in Arden, which produces good grass but is not fertile cornland, has been enclosed. By contrast the other, more southerly, part of Warwickshire, on the left bank of the River Avon, is largely composed of very fertile open fields, with something of a shortage of woodland.

I rode two miles from Warwick to Barford Bridge, which has eight fine arches. From here I could see a good park called Fulbrook, which lay a half-mile further down the Avon on the right or northern bank. In the park was an attractive castle built of stone and brick, and I was told that an earl of Bedford had lived there. There is a small lodge or building of some kind in the park which is called Bergenny; it is my guess that it was constructed by one of the Lords or Ladies Bergavenny. The earls who lived in Warwick Castle regarded Fulbrook Castle as an eyesore, and it was a source of bad feeling between the respective owners. Sir William Compton, the keeper of Fulbrook Park and the castle, saw that it was becoming derelict and hastened its demise. Some of the materials, according to one report, he took for his house at Compton [*Wynyates*] near Brailes in Warwickshire, and he allowed others to take portions of it down.

From Barford Bridge I visited Thelsford, a mile away. Here was a priory of Maturins, also known as the order of the Holy Trinity, which held very few possessions. It is said that the Lucy family founded the priory, and that several of them were buried there. Next I rode a mile to Charlecote, where Mr Lucy has an ancient manor house on the left bank of the Avon. Right next to the Lucy's house itself, and also on the left bank, a stream flows into the Avon from Wellesbourne, one mile away. About a mile after Charlecote I crossed another, smaller, stream on its way down to the Avon. Charlecote and Stratford lie three miles apart, separated by good open fields of corn and grass.

The town of Stratford occupies a level site on the right bank or side of the Avon, as one goes downstream. It has two or three very large streets, and back lanes besides. Of the main streets one leads from east to west, and another from south to north. The buildings are timber, and of reasonable quality. The town belongs to the bishop of Worcester. On Holy Rood Day, 14th September, each year a great fair is held. The large parish church, which stands at the south end of the town, is a fine piece of architecture. It has been suggested that it occupies the site of a monastery called Stratford, which was granted for the enlargement of Evesham when St Egwin was bishop of Worcester, but there is no firm evidence for this idea.

The present church at Stratford is thought to have been rebuilt by John of Stratford, who was archbishop of Canterbury at the beginning of Edward III's reign, and who took the name Stratford because he was born here. He made the ordinary parish church collegiate, and added some lands to its possessions. Attached to this college were a guardian, four priests, three clerks, four choristers, with their old dwelling house of squared stone blocks next to the churchyard. The church is dedicated to the Trinity. In more recent years the quire was rebuilt by a certain Thomas Balsall, doctor of divinity, who was the college guardian. He died in the year 1490, and is buried in a fine tomb on the north side of the sanctuary.

Near the south end of the town in a fine street there is an excellent chapel of the Trinity. It was built anew within living memory by one Hugh Clopton, mayor of London. (Around the nave of this chapel there was carefully painted the dance of death, popularly known as the dance of Pauls, because there was a similar painting at St Paul's [*Cathedral, London*], around the cloisters on its north-west side, which were demolished by the duke of Somerset during Edward VI's reign. [*added later*]) This Clopton also built an attractive house of brick and timber by the north side of this chapel, where he spent his last years and died. On the south side of the chapel there is a grammar school. It was established by a university teacher named Jolliffe, who was born in Stratford, and inherited property there which he gave to the school. In addition there is an almshouse for ten paupers on the south side of Trinity chapel, which is maintained by a fraternity of the Holy Cross.

The same Hugh Clopton also built the large, lavish bridge across the Avon at the east end of the town. It has fourteen large stone arches, and at the western end is a long stone causeway which now has a parapet on each side. Until Clopton's time there was only a poor wooden bridge with no causeway leading up to it. Consequently many poor people and others refused to visit Stratford when the Avon was in spate, or if they did come they had to risk their lives. Clopton came of a gentry family from the village of Clopton near Stratford. Hugh Clopton never married, but he greatly improved the house, a half-mile north of Stratford, which is still occupied by someone of the same name. Grevill, of an old gentry family, lives at Milcote, which is barely a mile below Stratford close to the right bank of the Avon. Another member of an old gentry family, Mr Trussell, lives three miles from Stratford at Billesley. There is little woodland to be seen near Stratford.

Distances from Stratford: Warwick, 7 miles; Bidford-on-Avon, a roadside place, 5 miles; Evesham, 10 miles; Alcester, 5 miles; Henley [in Arden], 5 miles.

From Stratford I rode for five miles past open fields, with abundant crops of corn and grass, until I reached a ford and small wooden bridge across the River Alne, flowing down from the north as far as I could make out. After another two miles of open fields I reached Coughton, and here I crossed the River Arrow by a wooden bridge. Mr Throckmorton has a fine moated manor house at Coughton. The parish church here is excellent, with exceptionally good glass and decoration, which are partly the work of Sir George Throckmorton's father, and partly Sir George himself. In the church nave there is a good tomb made by Sir George's father, who died whilst on pilgrimage to Jerusalem. The two miles from Coughton to Alcester took me past enclosed ground, and I noticed that the surrounding countryside was quite well wooded. Part of Feckenham Forest in Worcestershire comes within three miles of Coughton. The bishop of Worcester has a fine manor house at Alvechurch, six miles from Coughton.

Alcester is a pleasant Warwickshire market town, which once was very large; and some people maintain that there used to be thirteen parish churches in it. The market is held there on Tuesdays. It is sometimes said that Alcester Priory, which now lies a short distance outside the town to the ENE, used to be in the town centre. Much evidence of buildings and many human bones have been found at sites outside the town, especially in Black Field. Local people often talk of St Chad, bishop of Lichfield, and tell a story about the injuries which he received there.

Long ago Alcester Priory was a great monastery, but later it became dependent on Evesham. The Beauchamp family owned the town, and had a house near Alcester Priory which was called Beauchamps Hall. This subsequently passed by marriage to the Lords Broke, and has now, again by marriage, come into the possession of Fulk Grevill. He is at present taking building stone from Alcester Priory, which he has also acquired, for work on Beauchamps Hall.

The modern town of Alcester stands on the bank of the River Arrow. But its name, which includes Alne, is a clear indication that the earlier town stood mainly by the River Alne. The confluence of the two rivers, Alne and Arrow, is near the east end of the town. The Alne flows down from Henley in Arden, a market town five miles upstream from the confluence, and is crossed by several wooden bridges. The Arrow, I was told, flows from the Black Hills some seven or eight miles, or more, above Coughton, and it too passes under several wooden bridges on its way to Alcester. East of the town there is a bridge over the Arrow which has stone foundations and a superstructure of planks.

Half a mile below Alcester the River Arrow passes a manor house called Arrow, which belongs to Mr Conway, and two-and-a-half miles further downstream at Salford it enters the Avon by the right bank. A knight by the name of Browne has a fine manor house a mile or more SSW of Alcester. Coukefeild [Cook Hill] nunnery lay about a mile south-west of Alcester; it belongs now to Fortescue, the groom-porter at court. At one point the boundary with Worcestershire comes within a mile of Alcester.

Three generations of the Tankervill family, father, son and grandson, are buried in the chapter house of Kenilworth Priory.

Distances from Alcester: Henley in Arden, 5 miles; Worcester, 10 miles; Stratford upon Avon, 5 good miles; Evesham, 7 long miles. *cont. p. 405* [**1543:** 2/40-52]

[K]ING'S] NORTON is an attractive country town in Warwickshire. It contains some good houses belonging to woolstaplers, and has a fine church with a good stone spire over the bell frame. A small brook flows past the eastern side of the town. Between Alvechurch and King's Norton there are good areas of woodland and pasture, and reasonably good arable. The land is similar between King's Norton and Bremischam [Birmingham], which are five miles apart.

Before I arrived in Birmingham I came through an attractive street of houses inhabited by smiths and cutlers which, as I remember, was called Dyrtey [Deritend]. It is a hamlet or chapelry of [Aston] parish, and is completely separate from the parish of Birmingham; a brook marks the

WARWICKSHIRE 377

boundary between them. At one end of Deritend is a private chapel and timber dwelling house, close to the bank of the brook. This flows down towards the right as one crosses the ford next to the bridge, and a few miles lower it enters the Tame by its right bank. Its source, according to some, is four or five miles above Birmingham towards the Black [*Clent*] Hills in Worcestershire. Above Deritend the brook divides into two streams, which rejoin a short distance below the bridge.

Birmingham's beauty lies in a single street, which runs for a quarter-mile up the side of a modest hill, beginning almost at the left bank of the brook. It is a good market town, right on the border of Warwickshire in this direction, and so far as I could see it has only one parish church. In the town are many smiths who makes knives and all kinds of cutting tools for a living, also many lorimers who make bits, and a great many nailers. Thus a great part of Birmingham's livelihood derives from its smiths. They receive their iron from Staffordshire and Warwickshire, and their coal from Staffordshire.

A mile beyond Birmingham I crossed Sharford [*Salford*] Bridge, which has four stone arches. The River Tame flows under this bridge, and there are fine meadows around it. Dudley Castle stands on the River Tame six miles upstream from Sharford Bridge. I rode on for four miles to Sutton Coldfield across sandy ground, which is more suitable for trees than for wheat-growing. The usual crops in this area are rye, barley and oats, and because the soil is sandy and dry it is also good for rabbits. In Sutton Chase there are four lodges – Coldfield, Bearwood, Lindridge and Hillwood.

The town of Sutton Coldfield stands on Coldfield Heath, and belonged to the Spenser family before it passed to the Beauchamps. It was an important town in the earl of Warwick's time, and the inhabitants say that it then had market privileges. The earls of Warwick had a modest manor house there, with a park and a chase. According to some people Richard Beauchamp, an earl of Warwick during Henry V's reign, constructed five good pools there with large and expensive stone dams. All these pools lay in the park, and were called Mill Pool, Cross Pool, Wyndley Pool, Keepers Pool and Bracebridge Pool. One of them, close to the west end of Sutton parish church, may still be seen, and its dam serves as a road into the town. It is a strong stone wall with an arch through it, from which a stream issues out of the pool and turns a mill. The other pools have now been deliberately turned into dry land, and where they were are now good meadows.

In Earl Richard's time there was only a lodge or modest manor house at Sutton, on a hill to the west of the parish church, and within this manor house was a free chapel dedicated to St Blase, with an annual value of £3. Neville, earl of Warwick, according to one report, built an attractive timber hall there; but after the earldom of Warwick was attainted and passed to the crown, the town of Sutton, lying as it does on poor soils, began day-by-day to fall into ruin, and the market was completely abandoned. Wingston was authorised to sell off the timber from the manor house, and kept part of it for himself. In fact the hall was actually rebuilt at Broadgate, the house of the marquis of Dorset near Leicester, and it is still standing there.

A native of Sutton, John Harman alias Voysey, bishop of Exeter, was greatly distressed to see its decline, and obtained from Henry VIII a new charter to reopen its market. He started to rebuild the houses or build from new, and in addition to this he obtained permission to disafforest Sutton Chase. Having done this he built several attractive stone houses in the forest, and installed his poorer relatives in them. Each house has a useful plot of land attached to it, and for this the tenants pay the king a modest rent. Besides this he reused the site of the former house of the earls of Warwick as the house for his tenant, and one of the bishop's relatives lives there now. He has also established a grammar school in the town, and endowed it with property. For himself he has built an attractive brick house, and he stays there sometimes. It is built in a grove about a half-mile north of Sutton church. He has planted some good fruit trees there, and they are growing, though with some difficulty. In addition he added north and south aisles to the church and a steeple, and has erected an elegant memorial for himself in the wall of the north aisle. And so Sutton Coldfield has been placed on a sound footing by Bishop Harman, and is growing daily. *cont. p. 350* [**1543**: 2/96-9]

From Tamworth it was about three miles to Fazeley, and on my way I passed a park on my left hand side. The soil here is sandy, and better for woodland and pasture than for corn. Next I crossed the Tame by Fazeley Bridge, which has sixteen stone arches. About a mile after Fazeley I rode past Middleton Park, and here Sir John Willoughby has a fine manor house, which he inherited from his father, Sir Henry Willoughby, an old knight of the Holy Sepulchre. The oldest and principal branch of the Willoughby family has its seat at Willowgtowne [*Wollaton*] near Nottingham. Sir John Willoughby married one of the last Lord Lisle's two sisters and heiresses, but has no issue; Dudley married the other sister. Sir John's heir is his brother, Sir Edward Willoughby, and he has a son who will inherit both Sir Edward's and Sir John's estates; this son is married to the sister of the marquis of Dorset.

Two miles further I crossed a six-arch stone bridge over a river which flows from the east and enters the Birmingham Water to the west. Birmingham Water flows into the Tame a mile above Curdworth Bridge. After another mile I reached Coleshill Bridge, which has stone arches; this crosses a brook called the Cole. Coleshill is an attractive roadside town in Warwickshire. It has only the one long street, running from north to south along a hill, and with a parish church at the southern end. It is regarded as about halfway between Tamworth and Coventry.

Next I rode for four miles to Meriden, across enclosed land, with some arable, pasture and woodland. At the far end of this village a brook runs down on the left hand side, and I saw a park beside it. I then rode for another three miles across similar country until I crossed a brook. I had to cross this same brook again a mile further on, as I approached Coventry from the west. Here the brook flows down on the left hand side, then under a two-arch bridge within the town of Coventry itself. The stream still flows on the left hand side, and when it reaches the meadows by Coventry Abbey it turns again to the left and so meets a bridge one mile lower on the London road.

The western side of Coventry is low-lying, but to the east it rises somewhat. The town wall was begun in Edward II's time, and the names of the gates in the wall include Bishop Gate, Gosford Gate, Greyfriars Gate, Little Park Street Gate, Spon Street Gate, and Cook Street Gate. The wall has many fine towers. The stone of which it is built contains particles of a dark reddish hue, like the colour of ferruginous rock. This indeed is the colour of the stone in this whole region. Most of the stone for the walls was taken from the adjacent ditches, which surround the majority of the town wall. It is only recently that this wall at Coventry was completed.

Coventry only obtained the privilege and honour of having a mayor 180 years ago. There are many fine streets of good timber buildings, but the most important in the whole town is the one which leads from the west up to the ESE. There were three handsome churches right in the very centre of Coventry, which all stood, along with a charnel chapel, in the same churchyard. First was the abbey church. This was originally built as a nunnery by King Canute the Dane, but during the reign of Edward the Confessor Leofric, earl of Mercia, converted it into a house for monks, and adorned it with an unbelievable quantity of gold and silver. It has now been suppressed. Second is St Michael's, a grand parish church of exceptionally fine architecture. The third is Holy Trinity, also an extremely fine building.

There are no other parish churches in the town. But there is a church or college dedicated to St John the Baptist, which had a master and religious brethren, as well as a hospital. Its church still stands, and a priest still sings there; but the club-footed Hales [*John Hales*] has acquired a share of this college (and none but the devil can shift him [*added later*]). There is another collegiate church at Bablake, which is dedicated to St John and another, just inside the West Gate (or Bablake Gate – the name probably derives from a nearby conduit). This college was established by the Coventry burgesses, and is attached to a guild or fraternity which has great privileges. At present there is a master and eight ministers, although until recently there were twelve ministers. A very wealthy merchant of Coventry, by the name of Bond, recently added to Bablake a well built hospital to accommodate ten pauper men and women. Bond also set up a foundation to pay an annual salary of £10 to a preacher there.

There were two very good friaries in Coventry, the grey friars and the white friars. The latter was founded in 1342, the 17th year of Edward III, by Sir John Poultney, who was four times mayor of London. There was a charterhouse founded principally by a queen, which lay outside the town; and there are several fine suburbs outside the town wall. The king has a palace in Coventry, although it is in rather poor condition. A parliament was held here, and there is still a mint for coins. The bishop of Coventry and Lichfield has an old palace here. The town grew because of its cloth and cap manufacturing industry, but now that these are in decline Coventry's glory is waning.

Distances from Coventry: Lichfield, 12 miles; Leicester, 14 miles; Daventry, 14 miles; Southam, 10 miles; Killingworthe [*Kenilworth*], 4 miles, and then another 4 miles to Warwick.

The brook which comes from the west end of Coventry flows under a stone bridge of three arches a mile below the town on the London road. As I rode over this bridge the water flowed to my right, and a short distance downstream this brook enters the River Sow by the right bank beneath Wynnell [*Willenhall*] Bridge. This bridge over the Sow has five stone arches, and also carries the road from London to Coventry; it is about a half-mile from the three-arched bridge mentioned above.

One-and-a-half miles further down the London road I crossed Finford [*Finham*] Bridge over the River Avon. This bridge, which has eight stone arches, is six miles or more upstream from Warwick. Thelford [*Chesford*] Bridge is about three miles lower on the Avon, and is the means of crossing the river in order to reach Kenilworth. Kenilworth itself stands nearly a mile from the Avon's right bank.

In recent years King Henry VIII has gone to great expense in repairing Kenilworth Castle. Among the renovations was the dismantling of the attractive wooden banqueting house known as the pleasance which stood next to the lake, and the re-erection of part of it in the outer courtyard of the castle.

From Finford Bridge I rode three miles to Marton Bridge, which is of three stone arches and has a good stone causeway at each end. The River Leam flows directly from the east, under this bridge, and continues westwards to enter the River Avon about a mile above Warwick. Warwick is reckoned to be about six miles downstream from this bridge. As I crossed the bridge I saw a village called Marton close by on the south side. From here it was four miles to Southam. On my journey there was almost no woodland on either side between Willenhall Bridge and Southam; but there was good pasture and arable, all in open fields.

Southam is a modest market town of a single street, which occupies a somewhat sloping position on the side of a small ridge of land. Along with several other small manors in the area it belonged to the prior of Coventry, then at the suppression passed to the crown, and has now come by exchange to Knightley. South of Southam a small stream runs down from the right, which I crossed by a small bridge on the road to Banbury. The distance from Southam to Banbury is ten good miles, all by open field country, with no woodland, but exceptionally good pasture and arable. *cont. p. 296* [**1543:** 2/105-9]

Market towns in Warwickshire: Warwick; Coventry; Henley in Arden (which I have described); Monks Kirby (I know where this is); Alcester; Rugby; Tamworth on the Anker; Nuneaton; Atherstone (all these three I have described); Birmingham, which is on the Chester road, twelve miles beyond Coventry (I have described it); Southam, six miles from Warwick.

Castles in Warwickshire: Warwick; Kenilworth; Astley; Brandon, five miles north of Coventry, and Brinklow, five miles east of Coventry: both of these are derelict, and both, so I was told, once belonged to the Lords Mortimer. Baginton Castle, two miles from Coventry, is also now derelict; it belonged to the Bagots.

Rivers: Avon; Anker; Sowe. This river rises near Hawkesbury, three miles north-east of Coventry, and flows through Sowe Common, past Whitley, and enters the Tame [*i.e. Avon*] near the village of Stoneleigh. The River Leam enters the county from Northamptonshire, and passes close to Grandborough, Leamington [*Hastings*], Marton, and Offchurch, entering the Avon at Edmund Coote Bridge. The River Cole rises in Yardley Wood near King's Norton, and flows into the Tame after passing Coleshill. The Blythe rises in Warwickshire near Routon [?*Rowington*] by Temple Balsall, and flows to Hampton in Arden, Packington, and between Coleshill and Maxstoke, before joining the Tame near Shustoke.

[*Warwickshire boundaries:*] From the Oxfordshire border at the Rollright Stones near Chipping Norton, to the Staffordshire border at Tamworth, the length of the county may be estimated at 36 miles. In the direction of Rugby the boundary with Leicestershire runs along Watling Street. A border with Staffordshire runs a mile beyond Birmingham. [5/10-12]

Certain ditches are visible at Hall Place, Rugby. Rugby is a market town in Warwickshire which was the home of the noted gentry family called Rugby; this family included the famous Sir Henry Rugby. The duke of Buckingham used to own the town. [4/118]

WESTMORLAND

LELAND'S TREK to the far north in 1538 can be traced only as far as Kendal. Thereafter the narrative itinerary breaks down, and we cannot pick it up again until we find him in Yorkshire on his way back south. Much of his Westmorland material, therefore, takes the form of notes about his usual topics of interest – rivers, towns and castles – rounded off with a page or two of hearsay.

NEAR BEETHAM there is a large park which contains a good house belonging to the earl of Derby. An attractive river called the Byth [*Beela*] flows past it, and in all probability runs down to the Kent. From Beetham my ride took me across a large stream called the Stainton Beck, and after two miles I reached less craggy ground which was better for growing crops. There was some wheat, but much more oats and four-rowed barley. Then I crossed the River Kent and arrived in Kendal. In this area there are a number of fine woods, including Mr Parr's park, and many others. Kendal is regarded as a barony, in the possession of Mr Parr. [**1538:** 4/12]

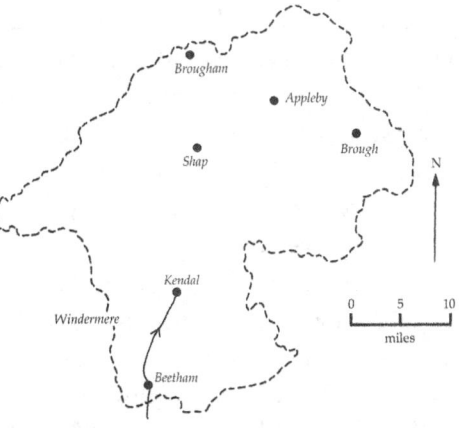

THERE IS ONLY ONE good market town in Westmorland, and that is called Kendal, also I believe, Kirkby Kendal. It is named after its river, the Kent, and is very well known for its woollen cloth market. There is only one church in the town, although the countryside within the surrounding parish has many chapels, and there are several also in the town itself. On a hill about half a mile east of Kendal is a park which belongs to young Mr Parr, the head of that family, and in the park there is a fortified house.

The River Kent has good depth, but it cannot easily be used by boats because of the rocks which are rolled about in it, and other obstructions. It derives from many sources, probably all within the county, and seven or eight miles from Kendal is a lake called Kentmere. All these headwaters flow into one good valley two miles above Kendal, and then past the town, which stands on the west side of the river.

The source of the Kent: It rises at Kentmere, in a lake which is quite large – about a mile in circumference – and well stocked with fish. The headquarters of the whole barony of Kendal is in Westmorland. The shire courts, with responsibility for the whole of Westmorland, are held at Appleby. Kentmere village and lake are eight miles directly due north of Kendal on the Penrith road, and Kentmere chapel is dependent on the parish of Kendal. Gilpin's house is Kentmere Hall. At first the river descends between two hills, and after two miles is crossed by a wooden bridge, New Bridge. Then in the hamlet of Staveley, a mile lower, is a small stone bridge called Barley Bridge. There are other stone bridges at Bowston, two miles downstream, and Burneside, a further mile. Here is the seat of the Bellingham family. From Burneside Kendal is one-and-a-half miles lower, and here the river flows under a stone bridge of eight or nine arches called Stramongate Bridge, then clips the parish church on its east bank; then, after a little more than a quarter-mile, it encounters another stone bridge, Nether Bridge, of three or four arches, which carries the York road running due east. After this it is four or five miles to the stone bridge at Levens. Kendal's streets, or gates, are important routeways, but cannot be defended. Strickland Gate leads northwards to Strickland village; Stramangate is named after the bridge; Kirkgate is the principal street, and runs north–south. The River Pronte [Sprint] enters the Kent a mile above Stramangate Bridge. There are about thirty chapelries and hamlets dependent on the mother church at Kendal, whose living was appropriated by York Minster. The castle stands a furlong east of the town.

Appleby is the county town, but now it is only a poor village, with a ruined castle in which the prisoners are kept. There is an old castle beside the River Eden called Brough Castle, and about a half-mile away is the village of Brough, where many pilgrims come to visit a shrine of Our Lady. There is also an old castle at Brougham, which local people claim to be sinking. Around Brougham the many worked stones turned up by the plough are evidence of former buildings. The castle occupies a strong site by virtue of the rivers which enclose the surrounding country.

There is a very large lake, or mere, which lies partly beneath the edge of the Furness Fells. It is called Wynermerewath [*Windermere*], and contains an unusual fish called a char, which they told me does not occur anywhere else in the region. There are many dales in the border country of Westmorland and Lancashire, and in each one flows a brook which gives its name to the dale. It is said that there exists in Westmorland a famous inscribed stone, which at one time served as a boundary marker.

Less than a mile from Penrith, but in Westmorland, are the ruins of what is supposed to have been a castle. In stands on what is virtually an island, less than a bowshot from the River Lowther on one side and the River Eamont on the other. This ruin is called by some the Round Table, and by others Arthur's Castle. A mile below it, at Brougham Castle, is the confluence of the Eamont and Lowther rivers. [**1538**: 5/46-8]

Information from a Westmorland man: There is a large brook called the Owse Water [*Hawes Waterbeck*] in Westmorland. It rises about a mile west of the source of the Lowther, which flows past Shap Priory. The place where it rises is called Mardale, and at first it flows in a narrow valley for about half a mile. Then it broadens out into a lake two miles long [*Haweswater*], before turning into a river again and flowing for another half-mile, where it joins the Lowther next to the village of Bampton. Between the point at which the lake narrows to form a river valley again and the confluence with the Lowther there is a stone bridge across it. There are no stone bridges on the Lowther this side of Brougham apart from Shap Bridge. Shap is three miles downstream from Bampton.

On the west bank of the River Eamont, half a mile below Brougham, there are some caves formed in the rock, close to the riverbank, which are like halls and chambers, and other domestic rooms.

Pendragon Castle stands on the far bank of the River Swale, not far from its source. Much of it is still standing. In this area the river defines the boundary between Westmorland and Richmondshire.

Important Westmorland gentry families include Loder, Musgrove, Thwarton, Sandford and Sawkill.

The course of Watling Street from Boroughbridge to Carlisle (note that the road runs about a mile from Gilling [*West*], and three miles from Richmond). From Boroughbridge to Catterick is sixteen miles, twelve to Leeming (a poor village) and a further six [*sic*] to Catterick. From there it is ten good miles to Greta Bridge, five miles to Bowes (a dreadfully poverty-stricken roadside place), eight miles to Brough on Stainmore, about four miles to Appleby and five to Brougham. Here Watling Street passes through Whinfell Park, over the bridges across the Eamont and Lowther, and past Penrith a quarter-mile or more away on its western side. From Brougham it continues seventeen miles to Carlisle.

The settlement at Brougham used to be of some considerable importance, but now it is very empty and its buildings are in poor condition. The River Eden runs within a quarter-mile of Brough. Maiden Castle, where now nothing survives except a hill with ditches around it, is close to the east side of Watling Street, five miles this side of Brough. [5/146-7]

WILTSHIRE

THE FIRST WILTSHIRE PLACE encountered by Leland on the journey to Cornwall in 1542 was Malmesbury, and his description of this hilltop town is among the best he ever wrote. After Malmesbury he explored Bradford on Avon and the western edge of the county; later in the year his return journey took him to Salisbury, which resulted in another long and useful description. Leland returned to Wiltshire two years later, on his last itinerary, the 1544 visit to Bristol. This time he travelled across the centre of the county, and explored Marlborough and Devizes on his way, it appears, to stay with the Willoughby family at Brooke Hall near Westbury. Later during this itinerary we find him straying into Wiltshire again to visit Stourton.

Among his notes are paragraphs about Marlborough (here largely omitted as most is duplicated in the account of his itinerary), Edington Priory, Ludgershall, and other places, together adding up to an interesting and reasonably comprehensive portrait of the county.

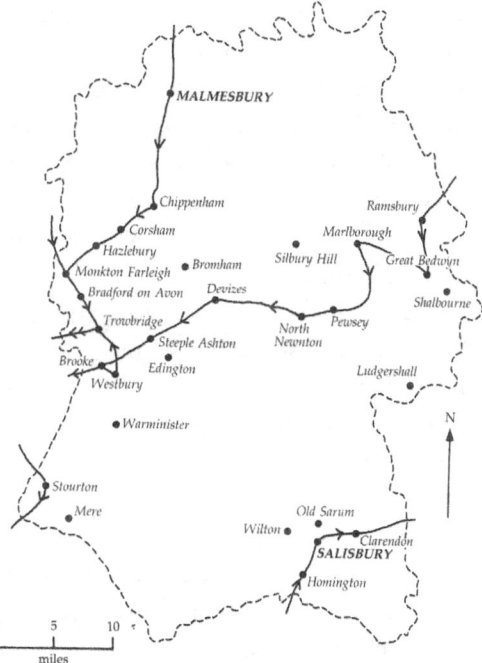

FROM CIRENCESTER it is eight miles to Malmesbury. I rode for the first mile or so along the Fosse Way, and then turned off to the left, which took me past open-field country all the way; although it produces good corn and grass, there is very little woodland. Directly below Malmesbury is a valley, in which what I took to be the Newnton Water flows, and here I crossed by a stone bridge and entered the town by the east gate.

Malmesbury stands right on the top of a large, slate-like crag, in a marvellous naturally defended position. The Newnton Water flows to the town from two miles to the north, and the Avon Water from Luckington village four miles to the west, and they meet near a bridge on the south-east side of the town. Here, as the Avon, they flow south for a while, and then turn directly west towards Bristol. The conduit which served Malmesbury Abbey was fed by the Newnton Water. So close together are the Newnton and Avon rivers in the valley by Malmesbury's western suburb, that less than the distance of a bird-bolt shot prevents the town from standing on an island.

The town has four gates – called east, west, north and south – and all are in ruins. In many places the town walls still stand to their full height, but they are now very weak. However, nature has supplied the town with a mighty ditch. At one time there was a castle here of great renown, which the Britons called Caer-Bladon, and the Saxons at first called Ingleburne. The town must have been built later within this castle, since, so far as I can discover, there was no town of Malmesbury at the beginning of the Saxon era. The name derives from a certain Scot named Maildulphus, a successful teacher of literature in the place who later secured the foundation of an abbey there; and so it became Maildulphsbury, the place of Maildulph. The actual founders of the abbey were the king of Wessex and a bishop of Winchester. Aldhelm succeeded Maildulph as abbot, and later became bishop of Sherborne. He has become the town's patron saint.

Malmesbury is permitted a large fair around the feast of St Aldhelm, and during this period the town maintains a body of armed men to keep the peace. Consequently one of Malmesbury's boasts is that it has its own supply of arms.

There were formerly three churches in the abbey churchyard. The abbey church itself is a very magnificent building, and the townspeople have recently purchased it from the king, and have turned it into their parish church. It used to have two towers, but one, which stood at the crossing of the church, had an enormously high spire, and this fell down dangerously within living memory and was not rebuilt afterwards. It was a landmark for all the surrounding country. The other tower, large and square, still stands at the west end of the church. The nave of the old parish church, at the western edge of the churchyard, has been completely demolished, and the east end has been converted into the town hall. Its fine square tower at the west end has been retained as a dwelling house.

In addition there used to be a small church adjoining the south transept of the abbey church; and the story is told that John the Scot, a great churchman during the reign of Alfred, king of Wessex, was killed in this church by his own followers, who stabbed and skewered him with their writing styluses. Weavers have now set up their looms in this little church, but it is still standing, and the fabric is very old. A statue was erected in the abbey church in honour of this John the Scot, who was the translator of Dionysius from Greek into Latin.

Malmesbury holds a good and busy market every Saturday. In the market place there is a very fine and elaborate structure built entirely of stone, which is to shelter the poor market traders when it rains. It has eight large columns and eight open arches, and in the centre is a single large column which supports an intricate vault. It was built by the townspeople within living memory.

All the abbey buildings are now the property of a man named Stumpe, who bought them from the king. He is an exceptionally rich clothier, whose son has married Sir Edward Bayntun's daughter. Stumpe was largely responsible for turning the abbey church into a parish church, and its main benefactor. At the present time every corner of the enormous domestic buildings which belonged to the abbey is full of looms for weaving cloth, and it is Stumpe's intention to build one or two streets for clothmakers in the open ground at the back of the abbey inside the town walls. At present three thousand cloths are made annually in Malmesbury.

Some people believe that at one time a nunnery existed where the hermitage now stands, in the town ditch at the west end of the former parish church. And there is a rumour that there was another nunnery on the way to the abbot's park, which lies just outside the town on the Chippenham road. I have also read that the poor hospital by the south bridge, outside the town on the Chippenham road, stands on the site of a nunnery.

I left Malmesbury by the south gate, and turning left I crossed the Avon by a fine stone bridge with three arches. Next climbing a small hill I passed a chapel or parish church on my left, and then I skirted the park with the former abbot's manor house, also on my left. I arrived after about a mile at a village called Fosse [*Corston*], where there was a bridge with a good stream flowing under it. Then I rode six miles to Chippenham.

All the land was open on the side of the river which I rode along from Malmesbury to Chippenham, with fertile arable and grassland, but few trees. The course of the River Avon lay about two miles to my left as I rode, and I noticed two important buildings between Malmesbury and Chippenham. The first was Draycot [*Cerne*], where Sir Henry Long has a fine manor house and park about a mile from the Avon. This is five miles from Malmesbury, and two from Chippenham. Looking across the river I could see the ruins of Bradenstoke Priory on top of a hill one-and-a-half miles from the river on the other side. Bradenstoke is about four miles from Malmesbury. All sections of Bradon Forest are well-wooded, stretching right from Malmesbury towards Chippenham. Someone told me that there were no significant bridges across the Avon between Malmesbury and Chippenham. I crossed two streams on this leg of my journey. Mr Pye lives at ... [*?Rowden*], which is not far from Chippenham and within the parish.

Leaving Chippenham a mile away to my left I went on about a mile to the village of Allington, and then three miles to Corsham, a good country town, where there are the remains of an old manor house. It is the custom for the park next to this house to be given in dower to the queens of England. In the time of Queen Anne Mr Bayntun obtained permission to take down part of the house to reuse in his building work at Bromham. Old Mr Bonham told me that Corsham was connected with the earldom of Cornwall, and that the earls owned the dwelling house and sometimes stayed there. All the inhabitants of this little town were bond tenants; and when on a certain occasion one of the earls of Cornwall heard them secretly bemoaning their lot, he sold them their freedom, and granted them the manor of Corsham in copyhold, for which they pay a chief rent.

From Corsham it is about two miles to Haselbury, and not far before I turned down to Hazelbury I passed on top of a small hill a hermitage [*Chapel Plaister*] on my left hand side. The manor house at Hazelbury stands in a slight valley, and until old Mr Bonham's father began building work there it was a house of simple construction. Up until then the Bonhams lived at Lacock, next to the Avon. Near Lacock there is a field, called Silver Field, where people find many Roman coins.

After Hazelbury I rode a-mile-and-a-half to the village of Monkton

Farleigh, near which a priory of black monks stood on a small hill, which once had a prior and a community of twelve. It was one of the properties recently granted to the earl of Hertford. Between Hazelbury and Monkton Farleigh, and also for about the next two miles to Bradford on Avon, the country begins to become more wooded, and to be broken up into hills and valleys.

Sir Henry Long has a small manor house about a mile from Monkton Farleigh, at South Wraxall. Mr Bonham told me how this family of Longs originally came to be established. Apparently a certain robust character known as Long Thomas received the patronage of one of the old Lords Hungerford. And because this Thomas was nicknamed 'Long' so Long was later taken over for use as the family surname. Long Thomas owned some land which Hungerford had secured for him, and this was inherited by Robert and Henry Long. After them a certain Thomas Long, a descendant of the younger brother, who was clever in legal matters, managed to secure the inheritances of both Robert and Henry. Sir Henry and Sir Richard Long were the sons of this Thomas.

The town itself of Bradford on Avon is situated on the slope of a slate-like crag, and has a moderately good weekly market. The town is all stone-built, and stands on the nearer bank of the Avon as I approached it. In the highest part of the town as I entered it there is a chapel, but the fine, large parish church stands below the bridge on the bank of the Avon. The living has an annual value of £50, and was appropriated by Shaftesbury Abbey; the vicarage is at the west end of the church.

Halle, or de la Salle, a man of property worth £100 annually, lives in an attractive stone house at the east end of the town, on the right bank of the Avon. Near the church, in the north-east part of the town, there is a very fine house which was built by a rich clothier named Horton. He also built a commodious church house, of squared stone blocks, outside the east end of the churchyard, as well as several fine stone houses in Trowbridge. Horton's wife is still alive, but he left no children, and another clothier, by the name of Lucas, now lives in his Bradford house. The town's entire economy depends on clothmaking.

Bradford Bridge has nine good stone arches. Bath is five miles downstream from Bradford. The principal stone bridges over the Avon between Malmesbury and Bradford are as follows: Malmesbury Bridge; Christian Malford Bridge, about five miles lower; Caisway [*Kellaways*]

Bridge, about two miles lower; Chippenham, a very fine bridge, about a mile lower (the town of Chippenham stands on the opposite bank, towards London, so that anyone coming from London to Chippenham does not have to cross the bridge); Rey Bridge, about a mile-and-a-half lower; Staverton Bridge, about four miles lower, and here the Thrugh-bridge Water [*River Biss*] enters the Avon; Bradford Bridge, two miles lower; Bath Bridge, of five fine arches, five miles lower; Bristol Bridge, ten miles lower. Two miles upstream from Bristol there was a public ferry across the river, and here, on the same bank of the river as Bath, was a chapel dedicated to St Anne, which was a great place of pilgrimage.

On the far side of Bradford Bridge there is a small street, with a hospital of royal foundation at the end of it. At the end of this street as I turned up towards Trowbridge, there was a good stone quarry in a field on my right hand side. Bradford and Trowbridge are separated by about two miles of good arable, pasture and woodland. I entered the town across a stone bridge of three arches.

Trowbridge stands on a small craggy hill, has very good stone buildings, and prospers on account of its trade in draperies. In recent years one James Terumber, a very rich clothier, built a fine impressive house in the town, which at his death he gave with other property as an endowment for two chantry priests in Trowbridge church. He also built a small almshouse next to the church, where six paupers live, and receive threepence per week towards their keep. Horton, a Bradford clothier, has built several fine houses in Trowbridge recently. Another rich clothier, by the name of Bailey, also erected buildings here not long ago; his son carries on the drapery business now, both in Trowbridge and at a place two miles outside on the road to Farleigh Castle. There is another large clothier in Trowbridge by the name of Alexander [*?Langford*].

Trowbridge church is a light and attractive building, and its parson, whose name is Molines, is a well educated man. The castle stood in the southern part of the town, but has now been completely demolished. It had seven large towers, of which portions of two are still standing. The River [*Biss*] runs close to the castle. It rises away to the south-east, about a-mile-and-a-half from Warminster, and after Trowbridge it flows to Staverton, a hamlet dependent on Trowbridge, where it enters the Avon. At the confluence there is a stone bridge over the Avon. Staverton stands on the same side of the Biss as Trowbridge. In the centre of Trowbridge there is a good stand for the market men to shelter in; like the one at Malmesbury, which is much more attractive, it is eight sided and has a column in the middle. The earls of Salisbury owned Trowbridge, then the dukes of Lancaster, and now the earl of Hertford. *cont. p. 320* [**1542:** *1/130-7*]

A LARGE STREAM flows along the valley at Homington, and I crossed it here by a three-arched bridge, on my way to Salisbury two miles beyond, across wholly open country. This stream or river is called the Chalkbourne [*River Ebble*]. It rises six miles from Shaftesbury in a valley, which is a mile away on the left hand side as you travel along the highway from Salisbury to Shaftesbury. From its source it flows about twelve miles to Homington, and two-and-a-half miles below Homington it enters the Avon, about a mile downstream from Harnham Bridge. I seem to recall that Mr Bayntun has a house by this river, where his father used to live.

Salisbury, including the suburbs of Harnham Bridge and Fisherton, is two good miles in circumference. There are many fine streets in the city, especially the High Street, and Castle Street, which is so called because it serves as the road to the castle at Old Sarum. All Salisbury streets are similar in having little streamlets and channels of water drawn from the Avon flowing through them. The site of Salisbury itself, and much of the land around it, is flat and low-lying, and forms a basin which receives the majority of the water flowing from Wiltshire.

Salisbury market place is very fine and large, and has a good supply of running water from a streamlet. In one corner is the council house, which is not a very elegant building but is solidly built of stone. Salisbury market is well supplied with meat, but far better with fish; in fact the majority of the main varieties of fish caught between the Tamar and Southampton are sent to Salisbury.

There are only two parish churches in the city. One stands next to the market place in the centre of the town, and is dedicated to St Thomas. The other is St Edmund's, and is a collegiate church established by Bishop de la Wyle of Salisbury. It stands at the north-west [*north-east*] edge of the town close to the town ditch. This ditch was dug by the inhabitants at a time when Bishop Simon of Salisbury granted the burgesses permission to strengthen the town with a battlemented wall. Where the main stream of the River Avon did not provide sufficient defence this ditch was excavated in its entirety. But the wall was never begun; although I do recall seeing one or two stone gates in the town.

Harnham Bridge was a village long before New Salisbury was built up, and there was a church of St Martin attached to it. All that remains standing of this old church is a barn in a very low-lying meadow on the north side of St Nicholas's Hospital. The reason for it being abandoned was the wetness of the site, which is frequently inundated. In its place a new church dedicated to St Martin was built on a different site, and this still stands. One of the bishops of Salisbury obtained royal permission to divert the king's highway to pass through New Salisbury, and to build a major bridge across the Avon at Harnham. The diversion of this road was the sole reason for the ruin of Old Sarum and Wilton. Before this was done Wilton had twelve or more parish churches and was the principal town in Wiltshire.

There was a village at Fisherton across the Avon before New Salisbury was built, and it had its own parish church there, as indeed it still does. In Fisherton, which since the new town was built has become a suburb of Salisbury, a house of black friars was built not far from Fisherton Bridge. There was also a house of grey friars inside the town, which was founded by a bishop of Salisbury.

The city of Old Sarum stands on a hill one mile north-west of the new city, and its perimeter is half a mile or more around. It is an old place and has been exceptionally strong, but after New Salisbury was established it went totally to ruin. One explanation for this is that shortage of water caused the inhabitants to leave the place, although in fact there were many wells of sweet water. Another reason that is given is that when castles and town walls were kept in good repair after the civil wars, there was a disagreement between the keepers of Old Sarum Castle and the canons; to the extent that on one occasion the castellans prevented them from re-entering the town when they were coming home from a rogationtide procession. As a result the bishop and the canons conferred with each other, and eventually began to build a church on a site which they themselves owned. Consequently the inhabitants immediately started to move to New Salisbury and set up buildings, so that as a result a large number of houses at Old Sarum were pulled down and rebuilt in the new city.

Osmund, who was earl of Dorchester and later bishop of Salisbury, built his cathedral church, and also his palace, in the western part of the town of Old Sarum. The only sign of them there now is a chapel of

Our Lady, which is still standing and kept in repair. There used to be a parish church of the Holy Rood at Old Sarum, and another over the east gate; there are still some remains of this visible. I saw no evidence that there had ever been more than two gates at Old Salisbury, east and west. There was a good suburb outside each of these gates, and that on the east contained a parish church dedicated to St John. A chapel still stands in this area. Within living memory people have lived in houses in the east suburb of Old Sarum, but now there is not a single house inhabited, either within Old Sarum, or outside it. There was a very fine and strong castle within Old Sarum which belonged to the earls of Salisbury, especially the Longspees – although I have read that the first earl after the conquest was called Walter. Substantial ruined buildings of this castle still remain. The ditch which surrounded the old town was a very deep and strong structure. Even at its nearest point, which is Stratford [sub Castle] village, south of Old Sarum, the river is a good quarter-mile away, or more.

The course of the River Avon: The Avon rises in the north-east not far from Wolfhall in Wiltshire, but the first important bridge which it comes to is at Upavon. From there it is four miles to Amesbury, where there is a bridge, and another four miles to the villages of Woodford, on the right bank, and Netton, on the left bank. The bishops of Salisbury had their own manor house at Woodford, but Bishop Shaxton pulled it down because it was already somewhat in ruins. From here it is three miles to Fisherton Bridge, of six stone arches, and then a very short distance to Crane Bridge, also of six stone arches; then a furlong downstream there is Harnham Bridge, a large and substantial structure with six great stone arches. Here, at the western end of this bridge, and divided from it by only the distance of a small island, is another bridge of four attractive arches. A good flow of water runs under this bridge, which I assume to be either an arm of the River Avon, which leaves the mainstream a little above the bridge, and soon afterwards rejoins it; or else this is the Wilton Water [*River Wylye, in fact the Nadder*], which here joins the Avon. From Harnham Bridge it is four miles to a fine stone bridge at Downton, then another four miles to Fordingbridge, which is stone, five miles to Ringwood Bridge, and five miles to Christchurch Twyneham, where it flows directly into the sea. Christchurch and Salisbury are eighteen miles apart.

The course of the River Wylye: The Wylye rises three miles or more above Warminster, and flows ten miles down to Hanging Langford, which stands on the right bank as one faces downstream. Then three miles to the village of Stapleford, which is on the same side; here a stream called the Winterbourne [*Till*] enters the Wylye from the north-west. Two miles further the Wylye divides into arms and flows through the town of Wilton. At this point it is joined by a river called the Nadder, or the Fovant Water, so-called because it rises near the village of Fovant, five miles west of Wilton. From Wilton it is two miles to Salisbury, and here, near Harnham Bridge, is the confluence of the Wylye [*Nadder*] and the Avon.

The following is written, in Latin, on a tablet in the Lady Chapel of Salisbury Cathedral: 'Pray for the soul of Richard Poor, sometime bishop of Salisbury, who laid the foundations of this church on its present site in a field anciently known as Miryfield, in honour of the Blessed Virgin Mary, on the feast of St Vitalis the Martyr, 29th April, in the year of Our Lord 1219, during the reign of King Richard I. This church was built over a period of forty years, spanning the reigns of three kings, namely the aforesaid Richard, John, and Henry III; and it was completed on 25th March 1260. The same Bishop Richard ordained that a mass should be solemnly celebrated every day in this chapel to Our Blessed Virgin Mary, and he appropriated the rectory of Laverstock as an endowment for this mass. This Bishop Richard was afterwards translated to the bishopric of Durham. He established a monastery at Tarrant in the county of Dorset, where he was born and given the name of Richard Poore. His heart is buried there, but his body is interred at Durham. He died 15th April in the year of Our Lord 1237, the 21st year of Henry III's reign.'

Robert, Lord Hungerford died 18th May 1459, and is buried in a chapel which he founded on the north side of the Lady Chapel altar. His wife Margaret, the daughter of William, Lord Botreaux, is buried in the middle of the same chapel in a high tomb.

Another epitaph: 'Under this marble tomb with inscribed top lies buried the body of the reverend father Nicholas Longespee, sometime bishop of Salisbury, who contributed greatly to this church. He died 18th May 1291. To his south lies Robert Wickhampton and to his north Henry Brandeston.'

Under a canopy in the north wall of the Lady Chapel lie two noblemen of the Longespee family. Richard Beauchamp, bishop of Salisbury, lies in a flat marble tomb in the centre of a chapel to the south of the Lady Chapel altar. His parents also lie in marble tombs in this chapel, and Sir John Cheyney, late knight of the garter, is buried there as well. Prior to this Bishop Beauchamp had constructed a lavish tomb with a chapel over it at the west end of the Lady Chapel, and it is said that he once asked a sister of ... [?] whether she liked it. However another bishop of Salisbury, John Blythe, was subsequently buried under it. St Osmund's first tomb lay on the south side of the Lady Chapel while the shrine was being constructed.

Other burials: In the sanctuary, north side: Bishop Audley of Salisbury; Roger Mortival, bishop of Salisbury, who was a great benefactor of the cathedral, and died 14th March, 1302 [*actually 1330*]. In the sanctuary, south side: Simon of Ghent, bishop of Salisbury, died 2nd April 1297 [*actually 1315*]. In the centre of the sanctuary: Robert Wyvil, bishop of Salisbury. In the south aisle: Giles of Bridport, bishop of Salisbury; Richard Mitford, bishop of Salisbury. In the north aisle: Wytte [?], bishop of Salisbury, with a gilt brass effigy. In the nave of the church: John Chaundler, first treasurer, then dean, then bishop of Salisbury, died 1426; another bishop of Salisbury is also buried there. In the north aisle of the nave: two tombs claiming to be of former bishops of Salisbury; a Latin inscription on one of them runs, 'If you offer help, you will receive help in turn'. Besides these there is the tomb of Walter Hungerford, knight, who was captured by the French and ransomed by his own side. There is also a tomb with an effigy of a bishop only four feet long. On the south side too there are old tombs, and one has a marble effigy of a man in armour. Another bishop is buried next to the wall of the south aisle and close to the high altar, but the burial is on the outside, as if in the churchyard where the vergers are buried. Near this burial is a somewhat weathered Latin inscription on one of the cathedral's great buttresses.

The nave arcade of Salisbury Cathedral consists of ten arches on each side, very lavishly constructed with marble. The first transepts (which run north and south from the west end of the quire) each have three arches, but the west walls of these transepts are solid vertical walls with no arches. The quire arcades (including the sanctuary) consist of seven arches on each side. Between the quire and the sanctuary is a second pair of transepts, which provide light and serve as a division, and these have two arches each. In the fine, large Lady Chapel to the east of the high altar are three marble columns on each side. The vestry stands on the north side of the nave. The stone tower, surmounted by its tall stone spire, is a noble and memorable piece of architecture. The chapter house is large and fine; it is eight-sided in design, with a central column. The cloister on the south side of the church is one of the largest and most magnificent in England.

On the north side of the cathedral church, in the churchyard, is a substantial and sturdy square tower for the great bells, with a spire on it. The great hall, parlour and chamber of the bishop's palace, which stands on the south-east side of the churchyard, were built by Bishop Beauchamp. There is a large and mighty wall around the palace [*i.e. close*] with three gates through it. The chief one leads north into the town, and is named the Close Gate; St Ann's Gate is to the east, and Harnham Gate leads south towards Harnham Bridge. This close wall was never entirely finished, as may be clearly seen at one point. I seem to remember reading that Bishop Roger and the Salisbury canons entered into an agreement about the close wall. The vicars choral of Salisbury have an attractive college and living quarters.

Bishop Giles of Salisbury was known as Bridport, because he was born at Bridport in Dorset. It was he who roofed the whole of the new cathedral church at Salisbury with lead. He also founded De Vaux College for students on a site between the palace wall and Harnham Bridge. Some of these students remain at the college in Salisbury, and have two chaplains to take services in their church there, which is dedicated to St Nicholas; the remainder study at Oxford. These De Vaux students are obliged to celebrate the anniversary of Giles their founder, at the parish church in his birthplace, Bridport.

Richard Poore, bishop of Salisbury, and the first builder of the cathedral church at New Salisbury, also established a hospital of St Nicholas close to Harnham Bridge. He installed a master, eight pauper women and four pauper men into it, and endowed the hospital with lands. To the south of this hospital, standing on an island, is a chapel dedicated to St [*John*]. And on the north side of the hospital is an old barn, where at one time was the parish church of St Martin. This church was deconsecrated and a new church, also dedicated to St Martin, was built in Salisbury in its place. The reason for this move was because the old church stood on an exceptionally low-lying and cold site, and in spate the river flooded it. But this church of St Martin, and the hamlet or village of Harnham, were in existence before any part of New Salisbury was built.

During the reign of Henry VI there was a bishop of Salisbury named Aschue or Aiscough who was beheaded on a hill close to Edington by a mob which, it is claimed, were enraged at a money tax levied on them. There is a chapel and a hermitage on the site now. The victim's body was buried in the monastery of Bonshommes at Edington. Aiscough was a master of arts [?*university teacher*].

Bishop Simon granted the burgesses of his town of New Salisbury permission to surround the town with a ditch and a wall. The great long ditch is still to be seen there, but the wall was never begun.

Clarendon Park and manor house lie about a mile south-east of Salisbury. The park is very large, and is maintained by many keepers. There used to be a priory at Clarendon called Ivychurch. From Salisbury to Romsey is fourteen miles, and from there the road goes to Southampton. From Salisbury to St Thomas Becket's Bridge, which has two stone arches, is a mile wholly across open country. A pleasant brook flows under this bridge, which rises three miles above it to the north-east, and enters the Avon about a mile below Harnham Bridge. I continued for three miles, and here I passed a large wood called Buckholt, a mile away on my right hand side. In the past this has probably been a chase for deer. *cont. p. 151* [**1542**: 1/258-69]

From Lambourn I rode on to the town of Ramsbury, a distance of about five miles. At first my journey took me across good open cornland, and then past hills which produced good corn and woods. The left bank of the Kennet borders the town, and the river itself sweeps along in a low-lying valley. Ramsbury has a fine and large old church, and half a mile further upstream on the left bank the bishop of Salisbury has a fine old house. An arm of the Kennet branches from the mainstream just above this house and rejoins it a short distance below, so that the meadows to the south of the house lie in a kind of island. Also close to the south side of the house is an excellent large park, overhanging the Kennet on the steep side of a high and well-wooded hill. Littlecote, the principal seat of the Darrell family, stands one mile from Ramsbury. Salisbury is twenty good miles from Ramsbury.

After Ramsbury I rode on for three miles to Great Bedwyn, travelling through Savernake Forest for most of the way. This town has the right to send a burgess to Parliament, but it is only a poor thing to look at. In the south aisle of the church lies buried a famous man, one Adam Stokke, and nearby is another member of his family, buried under a flat slab. The Stokkes owned Stokke Hall nearby, and their estate then descended to the

Lords Hungerford. I had once been told that there was a castle at Great Bedwyn, but no-one in the town could tell me anything about it. A mile below Great Bedwyn, on the right bank of the stream which flows past it, is Little Bedwyn. This stream flows to the Kennet. Hungerford is three miles from Great Bedwyn.

From Bedwyn it was a good mile to the village of Shalbourne, which I would guess should really be called Chalkbourne, because the bourne there rises and flows on chalky soil. This brook, which gives Shalbourne its name, rises a short distance above the village. After passing Shalbourne on its right bank it flows on for about two miles until it reaches the Bedwyn Brook, or else it runs into the Kennet by itself. Shalbourne is three miles from Hungerford.

The Choke family rose to much greater prominence under Choke, Chief Justice of England. He acquired estates with a total annual value of £400, and made his principal seat at Long Ashton near Bristol, which he fitted out with quantities of silver.

From Ramsbury to Marlborough was a journey of three miles, across fertile but hilly arable and woodland. About a half-mile before I reached Marlborough I crossed a brook which flowed down from the hills to the north-west, and then ran down south-east into the Kennet about a half-mile below Marlborough.

The town of Marlborough extends from a hilltop lying due east to a valley lying due west. Right at the west end of the town there are the ruins of a great castle, and part of the tower of the keep is still standing. King Edward stayed there at the time of a Parliament. At the east end of the town there is a chapel dedicated to St Martin, and in the centre is a parish church of Our Lady. Its nave is a very old piece of architecture, and there is a legend that it was once a nunnery. But Marlborough's principal parish church stands at the very west end, and is dedicated to St Peter. White canons had a priory called St Margaret's across the Kennet a short distance to the south of the town, but Mr Daniell lives there now; there was also a friary on the south side of the town.

The River Kennet flows down from the north at the west end of Marlborough, and then along a valley to the south, so that it leaves the town on its left bank. From here it flows directly eastwards. Its source is to the NNW, at the valley by Silbury Hill. Both here and at Avebury one mile away, as well as at several other places on the downs, there are the burials and camps of warriors. Silbury Hill is about five miles from Marlborough.

Leaving Marlborough I crossed the Kennet and rode into Savernake ('the sweet oak') Forest, and after four miles or more I came to Pewsey, which is a good village. Here I crossed the River Avon, and continued through flat open-field country, which produces abundant grass and corn, and exceptional wheat and barley, to a village called Manningford, and then to [North] Newnton village, which is two miles or more from Pewsey. The River Avon flows past both these villages, leaving North Newnton on its left bank, and then it continues to Upavon, a good village, two miles downstream. A small brook flows into the Avon from the north-west at the east end of North Newnton church. Its course has recently been altered, and this has greatly benefited the village, which occupies a low site and in the past has been badly troubled with flooding in the winter.

From North Newnton I rode a half-mile to the hamlet of Hilcott, which lies in the same parish; and from there seven miles to the Vyes [Devizes], across open-field country. On my approach to Devizes I passed near a brook which flows into the Avon near the village of Upavon.

The town of Devizes occupies a site which is somewhat sloping, and most of its inhabitants are involved in clothmaking. Its beauty lies all in one street, and it has a very famous market. On the south-west side of the town there is an imposing castle raised up on a lofty site, which is defended partly by nature and partly with ditches, the spoil from which has been cast up the slope to a great height, so as to defend the walls. This castle was built in the reign of Henry I by a certain Bishop Roger of Salisbury, the king's chancellor and treasurer. No English bishop, before or since, has ever erected so strong or expensive a piece of military architecture. To construct its keep or dungeon, which stands on an artificial mound, cost an unbelievable sum. In the gate may still be seen six or seven places made for portcullises, and some fine masonry went into it. But now it is in ruins, and a portion of the front of the towers to the keep gate and its chapel were taken away quite uneconomically for use in building Mr Bayntun's house at Bromham, scarcely three miles away. Several good towers still remain in the castle's outer wall, but everything is going to ruin. The principal gate which leads from the castle to the town is still very strong, and has places for seven or eight portcullises. There is a fine park next to the castle.

Blackmore Forest lies in a valley towards the north-west, not far from Devizes. As I left the town I was able to see Bromham Hall situated in a valley about three miles away. I rode six miles to Steeple Ashton across fertile open country, with abundant woodland in some places. Steeple Ashton is a pleasant little market town which depends largely on its cloth trade; it has attractive buildings and a very fine church, built within living memory. The pinnacled stone steeple is very tall and fine, and it is because of this that it is called Steeple Ashton. Two clothiers, Robert Long and Walter Lucas, built the north and south aisles respectively at their own expense. Romsey Abbey in Hampshire held both the living and the entire manor. Sir Thomas Seymour has acquired it from the king, along with nearly all the hundred of Horwell, alias Whorwellsdown, and a large area of good woodland.

From Steeple Ashton it is about two miles through wooded country to Brook Hall. In the distant past there was an old manor house on the site of the present Brooke Hall, and part of it can still be seen, but the new building work was erected by Henry VII's lord steward. The window glass is full of rudders, which was possibly his personal badge, or the symbol of the admiralty. It has a good, but not very large, park, which does, however, contain a great number of excellent fine-grained oak trees, such as are used for the ceilings of houses.

Westbury, which gives its name to the hundred for that area, is a small market town one mile away. An important market for corn is held at Warminster, which is four miles from Brooke Hall – one mile to Westbury, and three miles beyond. The real name of the brook which flows past Brooke Hall is the Biss. It rises at a place called Bismouth [*Biss Bottom*] a hamlet dependent on Westbury parish, two miles above the village of Brooke. Then it flows to Brooke village, and a mile downstream to Brooke Hall, which it passes close to its right bank, and about two miles lower it reaches [?*Trowbridge*]. Edington village and priory are about two miles from Brooke Hall.

From Brooke Hall I went to Westbury, a mile-and-a-half away, across low-lying country with woods, pasture and arable. It is the chief town of the hundred and gives it its name. A small weekly market is held there, and it has a large church. The town depends largely on clothmaking. *cont. p. 342* [**1544**: 5/79-83]

From Marshfield I rode across four miles of hilly country, and arrived at a stone bridge over a brook which I could see not far below entered the River Avon by its right bank. I continued another three miles, over hilly, rocky, and wooded terrain, to Bradford, on the right bank of the Avon. Then two miles to Trowbridge, a market town, and another two miles through wooded country to Brooke. *cont. p. 343* [**1544:** 5/96-7]

THE VILLAGE OF STOURTON lies at the foot of a hill on the left bank of the River Stour. Lord Stourton's house stands on a slight hill composed of stony ground. This manor house has two courtyards, and the façade of the inner courtyard is magnificent, with high battlements like a castle. There is a park which adjoins the manor house and extends into the hills. The source of the River Stour is six fountains or springs which all lie on the north side of the park. Three are just within the park pale, but the other three are outside the park. Lord Stourton, whose family name is of great antiquity in this region, has the six fountains on his coat of arms.

There are four hillforts near Stourton. One lies to the north-west, within the park, and has a double ditch. I surmise that a manor house or castle stood here, although Lord Stourton disagrees. One-and-a-half miles from Stourton there is a second double-ditched hillfort, on top of a high hill which is popularly known as Whitesheet Hill. The other two hillforts lie in different parts of the manor.

Not far outside Stourton, in a grove on a hill, there is a very attractive house called Bonhams, which Lord Stourton has recently built. The senior branch of the Bonham family of Wiltshire is its owner.

From Stourton I rode for four miles, largely through wooded country, until I crossed the River Cale at a large ford. Then for scarcely a mile I crossed wasteland, and after another mile I passed Mr Carent's house and park on my left hand. *cont. p. 106* [**1544:** 5/106-7]

There is a hospital of St Giles on the edge of the town of Wilton, which is endowed with lands. The body of Etheldred, saint and martyr, and king of the West Saxons, is buried there; he was killed at the hands of the pagan Danes on 13th April, AD 827. There is also a tomb of a certain Barwik or Barok.

There is a place in Wiltshire called Castle Combe, four miles east [*west*] of Chippenham. Various knights' services and liberties are attached to it, and the manor now belongs to someone called Scrope.

Harnham Bridge [*Salisbury*] consists of six large arches over the main stream of the Avon, and four smaller arches over the lesser stream. [1/304]

Edington long ago was a prebend belonging to Romsey Abbey, a nunnery in Hampshire, and was worth £70 or more annually. Bishop Edington of Winchester was born at Edington. He became the chancellor or England, and accompanied Edward III and Edward the Black Prince to the war in France. He built a fine new church at Edington, and created a college there with a dean and twelve priests, some of whom were prebendaries. He also, at about the time that King Edward won Calais, effected the removal of Edington prebend from Romsey's possessions, and appropriated it to his new college, at the same time procuring an additional annual income from land of £130 for the college.

Edward the Black Prince held in very high esteem the Bonshommes overseas. And so when he returned home he earnestly requested Bishop Edington to turn the priests of his college into Bonshommes. According to his wishes Edington asked his collegiate priests to subscribe to that order, and all except the dean did so. Edington therefore sent for two of the Bonshommes at Ashridge to take charge of the other twelve at his college. The elder of the two who came from Ashridge was called John Aylesbury, and he became the first rector of Edington.

Bishop Edington himself donated a large sum of money and plate to his college. The executor of his will, a Salisbury prebendary by the name of Blewbury, arranged that a large benefice under the patronage of Shaftesbury should be appropriated to Edington. I was told that Blewbury was buried at Edington. Sir Richard Penleigh, a knight, spent much time at Edington, and died and was buried there. He gave to the college the manor of [West] Ilsley, two miles from Wantage in Berkshire. Another knight, called Rous, who also is buried at Edington, donated his fine manor of Baynton, which is about half a mile from Edington. [2/23-4]

At [Great] Bedwyn in Wiltshire there used to be a castle or fortress, and its ruins and site may still be seen. The town's burgesses have the privilege of returning members to Parliament. [2/27]

There is a newly built market house at Marlborough, and a mill on the River Kennet outside the town. [4/130]

There used to be a castle at Ludgershall in Wiltshire, close to the road from Marlborough (ten miles away) to Andover (four miles away). It stood in a park, and has now been completely demolished, although an attractive lodge has recently been constructed out of its ruins, and belongs to the king. [5/6]

The site and ditches where Mere Castle stood may be seen close to the market town of Mere. The excellent gatehouse and façade of Lord Stourton's house at Stourton were built from spoils taken during the war with France. [5/223]

WORCESTERSHIRE

ON HIS JOURNEY INTO WALES in 1538 Leland had occasion to cross Worcestershire, but most of his description dates from five years later, when he explored the West Midlands in 1543. This itinerary took him first to Evesham, on his way into Gloucestershire, and then later he explored the northern and central parts of the county. From Bridgnorth he travelled to Kidderminster and Bewdley, which impressed him greatly, and then to Worcester. A good account of Worcester is followed by an even longer and more detailed description of Droitwich. The salt-making processes seem to have fascinated Leland, and he took the trouble to visit and refer to wiches and salterns in various parts of the country. From Droitwich he made his way back north to Bromsgrove and Alvechurch, before crossing into Warwickshire. In addition to the itinerary accounts there have also survived notes on the Bredon and Upton area, a passage of tabulated information about rivers, forests, towns and castles, and a description of the course of the Stour.

THE COUNTRY was reasonably well-wooded in places all the way as I rode from Hailes to Pershore. Then from Pershore to Worcester, and on almost as far as Tenbury, there was more woodland, although in valleys and on hillsides there were good crops of corn. And as for good meadowland and pasture Worcester lacks nothing. cont. p. 468 [**1538**: 3/40]

FROM ALCESTER I rode towards Evesham. For the first two miles the country-side was wooded, with enclosed fields, and then for the next mile there were fewer enclosures, and more arable than woodland. The last four miles were across completely open country, although near Evesham there was some woodland on the right bank of the Avon.

The town of Evesham is reasonably large with quite good timber buildings. It has a fine, large market place, and several attractive streets. Evesham market is very well-known. But there are no hospitals or other pious foundations of note in the town apart from the former abbey. Evesham did not exist as a town before the abbey was established, and its present site was originally called Hetheholme by the Saxons.

The abbey was founded by King Kenred of Mercia and Bishop Ecgwine of Worcester, and the abbey buildings were the work of many hands over a long period. Clement Litchfield, the penultimate abbot, went to great expense on the fabric of Evesham Abbey itself, and on its properties. He beautified the quire with much new work, and he built in the churchyard a really lavish and tall square tower of stone. It had a large bell in it, and a good clock, and it served as a gatehouse for one part of the abbey. The same abbot also carried out building work on his manor at Offenham, which is about a mile upstream from Evesham on the right bank of the Avon. Within the churchyard wall of Evesham Abbey are two parish churches attended by the townspeople; but all the profits from them, apart from one of the vicarages, were appropriated by the abbey.

Long ago there used to be an abbey at 'Fleodan byrig', now generally known as Fladbury, in Worcestershire, three miles below Evesham on the right bank of the Avon. In Ecgwine's time it was appropriated to Evesham. The living now has an annual value of £80. The abbey also held a grange or manor house called Ombersley, six miles from Evesham, and this is where the last abbot is now living.

Distances from Evesham: Hailes, 6 miles; Winchcombe, 7 miles; Pershore, 5 miles; Tewkesbury, 9 miles; Worcester, 12 miles.

From Evesham I rode across six or seven miles of open country through the Vale of Evesham, remaining in Worcestershire all or nearly all the time, until I came to the village of Stanway, which lies at the foot of the Cotswold Hills. Although it lies away in one corner of the county the Vale of Evesham is, as it were, the granary of Worcestershire, so fertile are its cornfields. It extends from the left bank of the Avon right to the foot of the Cotswolds. *cont. p. 125* [**1543:** 2/52-3]

WORCESTERSHIRE

MY TWELVE-MILE RIDE from Bridgnorth to Kidderminster took me mostly through rather undulating and hilly enclosed country, with the River Severn away to my right. In places the land was overgrown, but elsewhere there was good corn and grass; and after I had passed the halfway point there was a plentiful supply of wood growing along both banks of the Severn, much of which is brought down the river to serve the area around Gloucester. As I approached Kidderminster, a Worcestershire market town, I passed through a suburb, and then across a bridge of two or three arches over the River Stour. The source of this river is near the pools of the former Halesowen Priory six miles away.

The larger and better part of Kidderminster stands on hilly ground on the left bank of the Stour. In the market place there is an attractive cross, which is encased by six columns and stone arches, with a seventh column in the centre to carry the vault. The town, which depends mostly on the cloth industry, has a very fine church, which contains in its quire the rich burial of a knight by the name of Cony [*Sir Hugh Cooksey*]. At some time in the past the town belonged to the ancient gentry family of Bissett, from whom it later passed to three Bissett heiresses. Two-thirds of the inheritance descended to Lord Bergavenny, whose family is still the owner, but the third heiress had leprosy, so it is said, and she built a hospital at Maiden Bradley in Wiltshire, which later became a priory of canons. Her share she gave to charitable purposes, and the living of Kidderminster was appropriated to Maiden Bradley.

About four miles below Kidderminster the River Stour flows into the Severn on its left bank. The confluence is at a place called Rockstone [*Redstone Rock*], which is three miles below Bewdley on the Severn. I travelled from Kidderminster to Bewdley, a journey of only two miles, over a fine piece of downland; in common with the soil on every side immediately around Bewdley, however, it is not very fertile.

My entrance into Bewdley was by a very fine bridge across the Severn with great stone arches which had just been rebuilt. There is no other bridge on the Severn below this until Worcester. Many long, flat craft come to this bridge carrying all kinds of merchandise up and down the river, to Bewdley and above. The eastern part of the bridge and the left bank of the Severn lie in Worcestershire, but it is said and maintained by many that the west end of the bridge and the right bank of the Severn, together with the town of Bewdley, are in Shropshire. The Shropshire forest of Wyre adjoins Tickenhill Park.

Bewdley itself is built on a hillside, so skilfully that no-one could wish for a better site. With the riverbank to its east it climbs westward up the hill, so that anyone standing on the opposite hill across the bridge has a view of nearly every house in the town. At sunrise, when the town is lit from the east, it glitters as if it were gold, for all its buildings are new. It has only three memorable streets. The first runs north and south, keeping to the bank of the Severn; the second is the fine, spacious market place adorned with good buildings; the third is the counterpart of the first, running north and south along the hillside.

Within the town there is only a chapel-of-ease, and this is a timber building in the town centre. The parish church stands a mile further down the Severn, like Bewdley on the right bank as one goes downstream. It is at Ripley [?*Ribbesford*], where Mr Acton has a good manor house. Judging by its distance from the parish church I imagine that Bewdley is a very new town, and that previously there was only a poor hamlet on the site. But that when a bridge was built across the Severn there, the concourse of people using it, and the appeal of such a convenient site, encouraged settlers to live there. And because its site seemed so picturesque it was given the French name, Bewdley, or 'beautiful place'. I asked a merchant there how old the town was, and he confirmed that it was in fact new, adding that its charter had been granted by King Edward [IV]. Its privileges used to include that of sanctuary, but that has been revoked and annulled.

West of Bewdley, on the very top of the hill on which the town is built, a fine manor house stands among trees in a good park. It is called Tickenhill. I am not certain whether or not an older house occupied the site in the past, but the present building appears to be modern, and I was told that in fact it was built in its entirety by King Henry VII for Prince Arthur, and repaired for the Lady Mary. Subsequently I have learned that in fact Richard earl of the Marches and duke of York built it; the land belonged to Mortimer, earl of the Marches.

From Bewdley I travelled about four miles through wooded country, with some enclosed cornfields, until I reached Mitton. Here the River Stour divides into two or three streams and drives mills. Not far below Mitton the whole river enters the Severn, at a place called Rockstone [*Redstone Rock*]. Two miles beyond Mitton, over enclosed and wooded sandy country somewhat lacking in arable, I passed on my left the castle of Hartlebury about half a mile away. This castle belongs to the bishop of Worcester, and several bishops have been responsible for its fine architecture. It has good ponds, a deer park and a rabbit warren; but the soil around the castle is poor.

From here I rode for five miles past enclosed fields with reasonably good grass and arable, and ample woodland, until I reached a stone bridge. The brook which flows under it comes from Droitwich, where the salt is made, and then a little lower to a village called Salwarpe. Consequently when it reaches the bridge it is known as Salwarpe Brook. From there it runs down to Ombersley, a good manor worth £180 annually which formerly belonged to Evesham Abbey, and soon afterwards it enters the Severn by its left bank. Beyond the Salwarpe Brook the land is enclosed and fertile, and the distance to Worcester is three miles. By my reckoning, therefore, Worcester is fourteen miles from Bewdley, although the total mileage usually given is only twelve.

The town of Worcester, which is called Cair Angon in Welsh, stands on the left bank of the Severn on a site which slopes up from the river. It has a fairly good wall, which is kept in good repair. This wall has six gates: Bridge Gate by the Severn, which has a good square tower over it; a postern gate by St Clement's Church close to the north side of the bridge over the Severn; Fore Gate, a fine piece of architecture, which leads to the north; Sudbury Gate, which leads east on the road from Worcester to London; St Martin's Gate; Trinity Gate, which is only a postern.

The castle stood adjacent to the south side of the cathedral, almost next to the Severn. It has now been completely demolished, and half of its outer courtyard or precinct now lies within the close wall of Worcester cathedral church. The motte of the castle keep is very large, but now is overgrown with brushwood. This castle became ruinous soon after the conquest, and half its site was given to the priory to enlarge its close.

There are several fine streets in the town lined with good timber buildings; the best known and the finest of all runs from the gate of the bishop's palace northwards to Fore Gate. Markets are usually held in two places in Worcester, a short distance in from St Martin's Gate, and a short distance in from Fore Gate. The cathedral church stands on the south side of the town, and there are also eight parish churches. St Helen's is reckoned to be the oldest, since before the time of King Edgar it had already been granted as a prebend to Worcester Cathedral; another prebend, so I have heard, was Bloxham [*i.e. Blockley*] in Worcestershire. I was also told that, until Edgar established monks in the cathedral, all Worcester's churches were chapels dependent on the cathedral. The house of the black friars, which was founded by the Beauchamps of Powick, stood in the northern part of Worcester, next to the wall but just inside. It occupied the highest site in the town, with a fine view.

Beyond the bridge over the Severn there is a good suburb, many of whose inhabitants cross the bridge to attend St Clement's church. The bridge is a majestic piece of architecture, tall, strong, and with six great stone arches. Outside Fore Gate extends a long, fine suburb northwards, and at its far end, to the north-east, is a fine old and large chapel dedicated to St Oswald. I discovered that this chapel had been originally built for monks who had become or were likely to become infected with leprosy. Then it was converted to a hospital, with a master, fellows and paupers, but later it was turned into a free chapel, named after St Oswald, as if it had previously been dedicated to him. During outbreaks of epidemics it served as a common graveyard for Worcester, and corpses were buried there. This chapel of St Oswald is still standing, and there is a good dwelling house next to it which has recently been repaired by Parker, the bishop of Worcester's chancellor. But its land has been sold and taken away from it. Right by the north side of St Oswald's graveyard there was a nunnery called Whistones. Since it was suppressed its church has been completely demolished, and the remaining buildings have been turned into a farmhouse.

Outside Sudbury Gate also there is a good suburb, in which stood a hospital called St Wulstans. It was sometimes known as the commandery, and it had a master, priests and pauper men. Some people say that it was originally founded by a queen. Later it received land from a Worcester merchant by the name of Carter, who thus re-established it, and thereafter the almshouse supported a number of old or frail Worcester merchant men. The house was suppressed by Morison, and is now occupied by a clothier. Also in this suburb is a chapel dedicated to St Godwald, but my enquiries were unable to discover who Godwald was – some said that he was a bishop.

The suburb beyond St Martin's Gate contained a house of grey friars, which was established on low-lying, marshy ground by the earls of Warwick. A short distance to the south of the castle precinct there is a chapel dedicated to St Ursula. The mainstay of Worcester's wealth is its drapery trade, and there is no town in England at the present day which makes so many cloths per year as Worcester.

I observed at Worcester that the high peaks of the Malvern Hills appear to be quite close to the town, but in fact the distance from Worcester to Great Malvern Priory, which lies at the foot of the hills, is six miles. The Malvern Hills extend a great distance from south to north, and their highest point is at the north-east. A certain Gilbert de Clare, earl of Gloucester, and his wife Joanna of Acres, the daughter of Edward I, caused a ditch to be dug on the top of the Malvern Hills, which infringed the rights and boundaries of the bishops of Hereford and Worcester. The River Teme flows into the Severn on the right bank at Powick Mills, one mile below Worcester.

Distances from Worcester: Hereford, 20 miles; Ludlow, 20 miles; Bewdley, 12 long miles, Gloucester, 19 miles (12 to Tewkesbury, and 7 on to Gloucester); Evesham, 10 miles; Bromsgrove, 12 miles; Alcester, 12 miles; Winchcombe, 18 miles; Bridgnorth, 24 miles (12 to Kidderminster, 12 to Bridgnorth).

From Worcester I rode about six miles to Droitwich, through enclosed countryside, with quite good arable, enough wood and good pasture. Droitwich occupies a rather low-lying position in a kind of valley between two hills. It stands on the left bank of a pleasant river, which is known a little further downstream as the Salwarpe Brook. The town's main attraction is a single street, although there are many lanes there in addition. In the main street is a modest church, and the weekly market held in the town has a reasonable reputation. The town itself is rather unpleasant and dirty when any rain falls, as the streets which carry most of the traffic are either badly paved or not paved at all.

The town owes its pre-eminence to the manufacture of salt. But although the profits from this industry are unusually large, yet in the main the townspeople themselves are poor. This is because the majority of the income goes to the gentry, whilst the townspeople do all the work. On a small hill close to Droitwich shortly before I arrived I saw a parish church; and there was another church on another small hill beyond the wooden bridge, a short distance outside the town on the right bank of the river, and a little above the main salt spring.

At present there are three salt springs in the town of Droitwich, and the main one is less than a bowshot from the right bank of the river which flows down there. This spring produces twice as much salt water as the other two put together. There is a popular belief that when Richard Wich was bishop of Chichester this salt spring failed, but that intercession by him restored it to its former yield. On this account, or simply from the respect with which the Droitwich people and the salters regarded this Richard, their fellow-countryman, they used until recently to decorate the salt spring or well with tapestry on his anniversary, and to hold drinking parties and revels. There are a large number of salt-houses or furnaces near the well, where the salt water is evaporated to leave a residue of pure white salt.

The other two salt springs are on the left bank of the river, at a considerably lower level than the large spring, and right on the edge of the town. At these springs too are several furnaces for making salt, but the income and yield from these two springs stands no comparison with the large spring.

I asked one of the salters how many furnaces they had altogether at the three springs, and he reckoned eighteen score, or 360, adding that each one paid 6s.8d. per year to the king. But the truth is that long ago they received permission for 300 furnaces, or more, for which they paid a rent or tax to the crown of a total of £100. This total has remained the same, but the number of furnaces has now increased to 400.

Recently a gentleman living in Droitwich by the name of Mr Newport organised a search for another salt spring which had existed there. It site was indeed discovered, along with the timber shoring that had been set up to prevent the earth from falling into it. But since its discovery this pit has not been exploited, either because the salt spring was not sufficiently strong, or because it might have reduced the profits of the other three springs. There is an opinion that if there were the market for it, and if sufficient wood were available, it might be worth finding and digging out more salt springs in the Droitwich area. I did hear that in recent years a salt spring was found in another part of Worcestershire, but that the Droitwich men are entitled to keep their monopoly of salt-making in the region.

The Droitwich salters take advantage of their salt springs to draw off and evaporate the water for only six months each year, from midsummer to Christmas. I imagine that this is partly to maintain a good price for their salt, but also, and I think that this is the principal reason, so as to conserve wood. For salt-making has been a large and significant destroyer of woodlands in the past, and will be in the future, unless the coppicing of young trees is practised to a greater extent. This shortage of wood can now be seen in the Droitwich area. For the nearby places from which the salters were accustomed to buy and obtain their wood have been stripped of their woodland, and they are forced to look for wood from as far afield as Worcester, and the country around Bromsgrove, Alvechurch and Alcester. I asked a salter how much wood he supposed was consumed by the furnaces each year, and he answered that he reckoned 6,000 loads annually. And most of this is young pole wood, because it can be easily chopped up. The people you see around the furnaces have very bad complexions. The correct output of each furnace is four loads of salt per year. If the furnace-men exceed this quota in one furnace then, so it is said, that is their profit.

Leaving the edge of the town I saw on my right hand a fine new timber house, which belongs to Mr Newport. And on my left was a bridge of four stone arches across the brook which runs past Droitwich, and at the nearer end of this bridge was a fine new timber chapel. My ride of four miles to Bromsgrove took me past enclosed country which had some good arable, reasonable woodlands, and well-kept pastures. Two or three times along the road I crossed the stream that flows past Droitwich, and as far as I could make out, either the Bromsgrove stream flows into this just below Bromsgrove itself, or in fact they are one and the same stream – yes, this is the case.

The town of Bromsgrove is really just one long street, and occupies a level site. It has quite a good weekly market, and depends to some extent on its cloth trade. The town centre is reasonably well paved. About a mile before I reached Bromsgrove I passed a park called Grafton on my left hand side. Before the Battle of Bosworth Field it belonged to the noble family of knights, the Staffords. But it was confiscated by the crown, and Henry VII granted it to Sir Gilbert Talbot, in whose family it has remained to the present. There is a fine manor house in this park, and one of the Talbots now lives there.

Approaching Bromsgrove I crossed a brook which flowed down away to my right; and then just as I was leaving the far end of the town I crossed this same brook again, this time flowing away to my left. Riding half-a-mile further I saw the brook once more, and another stream flowing into it, but this time after I had crossed it my way took me by hills, valleys and woods, leaving the brook entirely away to my left. After three or four miles I reached Alvechurch, a pleasant country town which belongs to the bishop of Worcester.

Alvechurch is an attractive roadside place, which stands on the right bank of a brook in a valley. This brook rises a few miles away to the west, and soon after Alvechurch it flows into the Arrow, and so down to Coughton where Sir George Throckmorton lives. The bishop of Worcester has a fine manor house set on a hill beyond the left bank of the stream, and a little to the north-east of the town. His house is made entirely of timber, and does not appear to be very old. Not long ago it was in a poor state, but then Bishop Latimer repaired it. It has a park, and all the countryside around Alvechurch is well-wooded. After wet weather the ground becomes very unpleasant. About half a mile beyond Alvechurch as I rode towards [*King's*] Norton I crossed the River Arrow, which flows out of the Black Hills about four miles away to the north-west. *cont. p. 376* [**1543:** 2/86-96]

John Throckmorton was the first to establish his family as of any standing in the village of Throckmorton, which at the time he had neither inherited nor purchased. He merely leased it from the bishop of Worcester because the manor and village had his name. He became under-treasurer of England at about the time of Henry V, and is buried in the parish church at Fladbury. Fladbury, six miles from Evesham, was one of his manors, and other members of his family are buried in the same church. [2/14-15]

Hanley is a remote country town which lies a bow-shot length away from the right bank of the Severn, one mile above Upton. The castle stands in a park on the western side of the town. Sir John Savage, and his father and grandfather, spent much time in the Hanley and Tewkesbury area when they were keepers of Hanley Castle. The earls of Gloucester owned it and often stayed there. Mr Compton was the keeper after the Savages, and during his time there he removed all its masonry.

Tetbyri [*Towbury*] Castle is two miles upstream from Tewkesbury on the left bank of the Severn in the parish of Twyning [*Gloucestershire*]. It stands on a hillside with double ditches, and is now overgrown with trees and juniper bushes. It belonged to Winchcombe Abbey. Perhaps it was a residence of King Offa, or King Kenwulf.

Upton stands as a cluster [*?of buildings*] on the right bank of the Severn four miles above Tewkesbury, and at this point there is a wooden bridge over the river. At Upton, and also at Tewkesbury, are large royal stables which were until recently used for great horses.

Arley is a good country town on the left bank of the Severn, about five miles above Bewdley. At Alveley there was a fine house of the Mortimer family beside the River Teme; this now belongs to Mr Cometon.

Bredon in Worcestershire is a large, remote, scattered community, standing on the left bank of the Severn about halfway between Pershore and Tewkesbury. Directly east of the town there is a large hill also called Bredon, and on the slope of the hillside near its foot lies Elmley Castle, two miles from Bredon town, and overlooking the Vale of Evesham. Dr Guente [*?Dr Richard Gwent*] was incumbent of Bredon. Maybe it was here stood the noble monastery of Bredon mentioned by Bede. Bredon and Cleeve [*Gloucestershire*] both belong to the bishop of Worcester. The countryside at Bredon itself is not wooded. [4/135-6]

Market towns in Worcestershire: Worcester, on the Severn; Evesham, on the River Avon twelve miles from Worcester; Bromsgrove, ten miles north of Worcester; Pershore, on the Avon six miles from Worcester; Kidderminster, on the River Stour, twelve miles north-east of Worcester; Bewdley, the sanctuary town, has on a hill right next to it the king's manor house of Tickenhill.

Castles in Worcestershire: Worcester; Hanley Castle, in ruins, seven miles downstream from Worcester on the further bank of the Severn; Abberley, also known as Abbatsley, which formerly belonged to the earl of Warwick; Hartlebury Castle, the bishop of Worcester's property, set on a strong crag seven miles from Worcester; Helmelege [*Elmley*], where there is a castle belonging to the king. Only one tower of the castle is still standing, and part of that is broken down. As I went past I saw carts carrying stone away from it to mend Pershore Bridge, about two miles away. The site is on top of a thickly wooded hill, with a small settlement next to it; the Vale of Evesham lies at the foot of this hill.

Rivers in Worcestershire: The Severn rises on a hill called Plynlimon and flows to Caersws (which although a well-known name is in fact only a poor roadside place); from there to Mahenclift [*?Machynlleth, but if so Leland is mistaken*] and Llanidloes [*on the Severn but above Caersws*], which is a good village; then to Newtown and on to Welshpool, passing within a mile of Montgomery. From Welshpool it flows within half-a-mile of Pontesbury College to Shrewsbury, then to Wroxeter (alias Rokecester), Bridgnorth, Worcester, Tewkesbury, Gloucester, etc. Other rivers are the Avon, the Arrow, and the Dowles Brook; this, I discovered, rises on Clee Hill in Shropshire, flows past a poor village called Cleobury [*Mortimer*], and joins the Severn not far above Bewdley.

Forests and Chases in Worcestershire: Wyre Forest, which is more than twenty miles in circuit, lies partly in Worcestershire, although most of it is in Shropshire. It extends from Holt on the Severn up as far as Bridgnorth, and from Bewdley, which stands on the fringes of the forest, as far as a river called the [?Rea]. Feckenham Forest, I have been told, lies entirely in Worcestershire, and is smaller in extent than Wyre. Malvern Chase is larger than either Wyre or Feckenham, and includes a large part of the Malvern Hills, as well as Great and Little Malvern. At one point, so I am told, Malvern Chase is twenty miles long, although it does not embrace the whole of the Malvern Hills.

Droitwich is six miles north of Worcester. Of its three salt springs two are close together, but the third is a quarter-mile away. The finest salt in England is made here. Alcester lies less than a mile from the county boundary. Dudley Castle lies in Staffordshire, but very close to the Worcestershire border. A knight called Sir Gilbert Talbot has a good house called Grafton near Bromsgrove; and Pakington has an excellent new brick-built house called Hampton [Lovett] Court, which lies six miles from Worcester in a northerly direction. [5/8-10]

The course of the River Dour (or Stour) in Worcestershire. The Dour (or Stour) derives from the ponds at Halesowen, a priory [abbey] of white canons, and from other springs nearby. Then it flows to the small town of Halesowen, which is about a mile away on the upper bank; and from there about four miles to the Worcestershire market town of Stourbridge. Kinver is a roadside place two miles further on the upper bank, and a mile from Kinver stands Stourton Castle (in Staffordshire, as I recall) on a hill not far from the nearer bank. From there the Stour flows to Kidderminster (two miles from Bewdley). Kidderminster is a good market town, with one large parish church. The river runs through the middle of the town, and when in spate it floods part of it. The living was appropriated to the canons of Maiden Bradley in Wiltshire. A short distance below Kidderminster there is a fine manor house on the Stour called Candalewel [*Caldwall*]. It formerly belonged to the Conxeys [*Cookseys*] and now to a family with good lands called the Winters. The Stour enters the Severn by its nearer bank at Stourmouth not far below Mitton, which is two miles from Kidderminster. Clent in Cowbage [?Cowbach], the site of St Cenelm's martyrdom, is two miles from Halesowen Priory. [5/220]

Premises belonging to the bishop of Worcester: The palace at Worcester. Hartlebury Castle, which is seven miles from Worcester –the route is via Ombersley, four miles, Hartlebury, three miles, and a further four miles to Kidderminster (Ombersley is on the Severn and belongs to Evesham). Alvechurch, which was repaired by Latimer, is two miles from Bordesley Abbey. Northwick in the manor of Claines, two miles from Worcester. Until living memory Northwick belonged to John of Wodds, but was bought by a bishop because he had no house in Claines. It has a moat, and there used to be a park. Whittington in the Cotswolds, now in ruins. Hillingdon, where the parish church of Uxbridge is situated, fifteen miles from London. Stroud Place in London.

Premises belonging to the prior [*of Worcester*]: Battenhall, a mile from Worcester, with a park and lakes. Grimley, three miles upstream from Worcester, close to the right bank of the Severn and opposite Ombersley. Hallow, a park with no house, two miles from Worcester. Crowle, four miles from Worcester. Moor, near the River Teme and the Herefordshire border, ten miles from Worcester. [5/228-9]

YORKSHIRE

LELAND'S JOURNEY back from the Lake District in 1538 brought him through Yorkshire, and he has left us a brief account, foreshadowing the more detailed itinerary of three years' later. He visited Nostell Priory near Pontefract, then on the point of dissolution, and continued to Rotherham and the Sheffield area, omitted from his later journey. This account is also notable for his mention of Robin Hood, whom he located to Barnsdale Forest.

When Leland returned to Yorkshire in 1541 on his north-eastern itinerary to Durham and the Tyne, all the monasteries had been dissolved, and his references to them are in the past tense. Yorkshire in fact occupies about forty per cent of the text of this itinerary, and it is clear that he was not simply passing through, but making excursions to specific places and areas. Arriving from north Nottinghamshire he first of all explored the Doncaster and Pontefract area, including a visit to Wakefield. From there he rode to York, but before describing the city he made a journey into the East Riding, to see Beverley and Hull, and returned via Howden and Wressle Castle (which impressed him greatly). After a short exploration of York itself he set off again via Malton and the Vale of Pickering to Scarborough, and then seems to have explored the coast down to Spurn Head and Holderness. His comments on Hedon's decline as Hull prospered are especially perceptive. From Scarborough he returned through Pickering to York again, and then resumed his journey northwards, via Northallerton, crossing the Tees into Durham at Sockburn.

The return journey, from Barnard Castle, brought him to Richmond, which at this point in his account he did not describe in detail. However, a substantial note about Richmondshire exists separately, and contains a great deal of interesting material. From Richmond and Wensleydale he followed the Ure down to Ripon, and then across to Knaresborough, leaving us good descriptions of both towns. Then, in more cursory fashion, the description continues southwards, via Wetherby and Ferrybridge out of Yorkshire and back towards Nottingham.

This lengthy itinerary is complemented by extensive notes. Richmondshire, including the Yorkshire Dales, is described, and there are separate brief portraits of Wakefield, Bradford, Beverley and Leeds, with other notes on Ripon and the

Cleveland area. The most serious omissions from his narrative lie in the West Riding – no information has survived about the Halifax and Huddersfield area, nor about Craven. In the notes section printed below considerable portions of text of purely genealogical or epigraphic interest have been omitted.

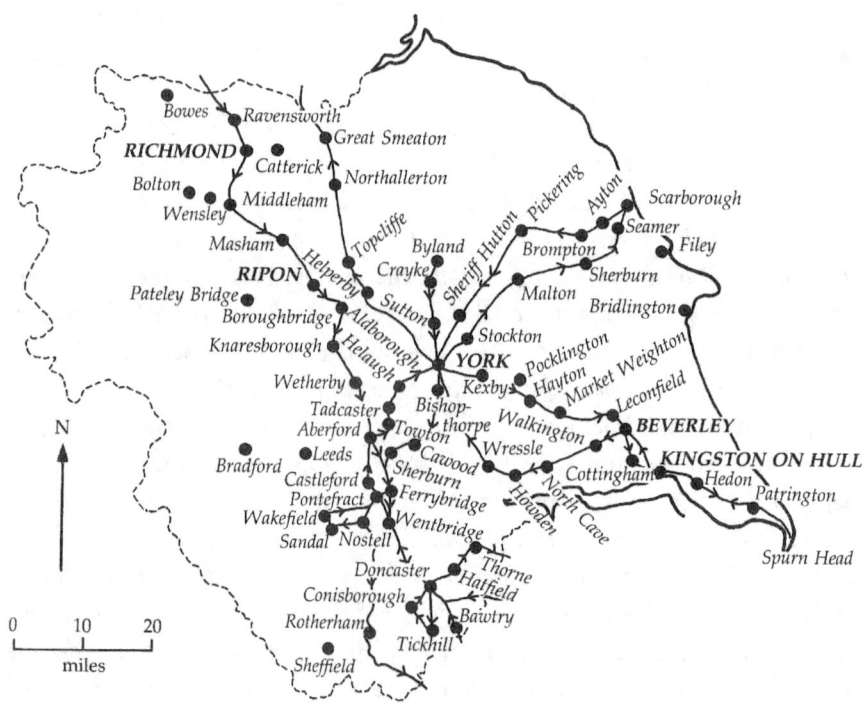

From Byland I rode largely through woods for a mile to reach Newburgh, a roadside place with an Augustinian priory. From there to Crayke Castle, which is set on a hill two miles away. According to some this castle was given to the Cuthbert who is still living. Then three miles to Sutton [-*on-the-Forest*], and six miles on to York. For four miles between Sutton and York I crossed a large area of flat common land, which was used both for grazing cattle and for digging turves.

For almost three miles after leaving York I crossed remarkably good arable land, but with few trees to be seen nearby. Halfway along I saw close to my right hand an excellent large estate called Bishopthorpe, which belongs to the bishops of York. After these three miles the terrain grows rather more wooded, and at about the fourth mile I passed close to Mr Aclam's park [*Moreby*], which contains an attractive dwelling house. After another four miles alongside the River Ouse, where the soil was good for pasture, corn and woodland, I crossed the river and arrived at Cawood. The archbishop of York has a very fine castle here, and there is an attractive village. From there it was five miles to Sherburn [*in Elmet*], a market town employing many pinmakers. The road from Cawood to Sherburn, which crosses well-wooded country, follows for almost its whole length a stream called Bishop Dike. This rises a little this side of Sherburn and flows into the Ouse. On this stage of my journey I rode close to a park which I think belongs to the bishops of York.

After Sherburn it was a mile to the village of Milburne [*South Milford*], and from there I continued for four miles or more to Ferrybridge. Here there is a village, and an eight-arched stone bridge across the River Aire. So far as I could see this stretch of country was flat, with good cornland but few trees. Between Milford and Ferrybridge, three miles away to my left, I could see the woodland of the renowned Barnsdale Forest, where it is said that Robin Hood lived as an outlaw [*Leland misplaces this forest, which lay further south, closer to Doncaster*].

Pontefract was only a mile after Ferrybridge. It is a fine, large market town, with good trade, and an excellent castle standing on a craggy rock – also an abbey of black monks, a parish church, a college of priests, a house of grey friars and a fine chapel. There is also a fine church outside the town on the hill where the good Duke of Lancaster was beheaded. From Pontefract I travelled for three miles, through heavily wooded country, to St Oswald's [*Nostell*], an excellent house of canons with good buildings. Here there is a remarkably good conduit of water with a conduit house against the front of the priory. The soil in this area is fertile, for wood, pasture and corn. More than a mile beyond Nostell I passed close to a park containing a fine mansion house, which belonged to a Mr Burton, a knight who has recently died. And from there it was four miles, past woodland and arable, to Howton or Haulston [*Great Houghton*], where there is a ruined manor house which they said belonged to the Tempest family. A mile or more from Houghton I passed Brierley Park close to my right hand, and this contains a fine manor house belonging to Lord Mounteagle. Two miles beyond this I rode over a stone bridge which spans the River Dearne, and from here it was four miles to Rotherham . The Dearne is a small river which, so they say, enters the River Don between Rotherham and Doncaster.

I entered Rotherham by a fine stone bridge of four arches, which has a well made stone chapel on it. Rotherham is a reasonably large market town, with a large and fine collegiate church. The college was inaugurated by an archbishop of York called Scot, and also known as Rotherham, on the same site as the present excellent and lavishly built brick college; it has a provost, five priests, a schoolmaster who teaches singing, with six choristers, another who teaches grammar, and a third who teaches writing. Although between Cawood and Rotherham there is a good supply of wood, yet the inhabitants burn predominantly coal, which is found in great abundance there, and is sold very cheaply. There are excellent coal pits a mile from Rotherham. The town has very good smiths manufacturing all kinds of edged tools.

Hallamshire begins two miles from Rotherham. Sheffield, its principal market town and the site of Lord Shrewsbury's castle, is three miles from Rotherham. In one direction Hallamshire extends six or seven miles above Sheffield to the west, but in another direction, I am told, the next village to Sheffield lies in Derbyshire. The whole of Hallamshire is reckoned to lie within Yorkshire, and attends the sessions at York. There are many smiths and cutlers in Hallamshire. In Sheffield Park on a hilltop there is a good lodge or manor house. Sheffield Castle is far surpassed by Winfeld or Wenfeld [*South Wingfield*] in Derbyshire, even though this is only a manor house. The two villages or small towns of Ecclesfield and Bradfield share the same parish church. Consequently, so I was informed, there are strictly speaking only three parish churches in Hallamshire, and one large chapel. The shire has abundant wood, but coal is the principal fuel. It has quite good pasture, but the arable is only fair. The Earl of Shrewsbury now owns not only the market town of Sheffield, but also Worksop in Nottinghamshire and Rotherham, which formerly belonged to Rufford Abbey. He has a park with a manor house or lodge in it called Hardwick upon Line [?*Leen*], four miles from Newstead Abbey. cont. p. 277 [**1538**: 4/12-15]

BAWTRY IS A VERY POOR and destitute market town. It stands in Yorkshire, according to its inhabitants, and so it would appear that the county boundary must follow the Scrooby Water [*River Ryton*] in some places. Doncaster is seven miles from Bawtry, across a large flat expanse of sandy ground called Blithelow; the name is derived from the River Blyth. Three miles before I reached Doncaster I crossed a brook by a ford, and here, as I recall, is Rossington Bridge.

In the town of Doncaster I noted in particular the following: The fine, large parish church of St George stands precisely on the site of the town's castle. This castle fell into total ruin long ago, although its ditches are still partly visible, as well as the foundations of some of the walls. It is likely that much of the castle ruins were robbed for the foundations and filling of the walls when the church was built. An old stone house, which is now used as the town hall, stands at the east end of St George's Church. There is a theory that this is either part of the old castle buildings, or else was built out of its ruins. Where the land slopes away within the castle precinct there is an attractive little timber-built house, which serves as a college for the town's priests. There used to be another parish church in the town, and it is still standing, although now it functions merely as a chapel of ease.

There was an excellent house of white friars in the centre of Doncaster, but this has now been damaged. It used to contain a fine tomb of white marble, which I was told belonged to Margaret Cobham, Countess of Westmorland. The effigy from the tomb has been moved into St George's Church, but the coronet is depicted in such a way as to denote a duchess. There was also a house of grey friars, and this stood at the north end of the bridge of three stone arches, which is commonly called Friars' Bridge. And from here I could see that the northern part of Doncaster, which contains only a few undistinguished buildings, is in effect an island. For at the west side of the town a branch derives from the River Don, and after a short distance rejoins the main-stream again at the east side. At the northern end of this island is a large bridge with five stone arches, and a great stone gate with towers at the southern end of this bridge. It is called St Mary's Gate because there is a fine chapel dedicated to Our Lady on its west side. And on the east side next to the water are two or three large mills. So far as I could discover or see there is no evidence that Doncaster ever had a town wall. There are, however, three or four gates, including an attractive stone tower on the west side; but the finest is St Mary's Gate. In spite of the abundance of stone in the area the entire town is built of wood, and the buildings have slate roofs. The surrounding countryside has good meadowland and arable, and some woods.

I travelled five miles due south-west from Doncaster to Tickhill, partly over low-lying pastureland, and partly across stony ground with fertile arable. Tickhill is a very impoverished market town, although it has a fine, large church. This contains a stone tomb to someone named Eastfield, once steward of Tickhill and Hatfield, who died in 1386. The castle is well defended by a ditch, and a wall built from masonry of a very hard and dark stone. The keep is the finest portion of the castle, and apart from an old hall all the buildings within the castle precinct have been demolished. A stream which rises no great distance away flows past the town towards Rossington Bridge.

A short distance to the west of Tickhill there was a friary, which contained the burials of several members of the FitzWilliam family, including the Lord Privy Seal's father and grandfather. Their tombs have now been translated to Tickhill parish church, along with that of Purefoy. Several members of the Clarel family were also buried in Tickhill Priory, and there is still a house near Tickhill called Clarel's Hall. South of the town is a wood called Toorne Wood, five miles in circumference. In former times the manor of Tickhill was of such importance that it was known as the honour of Tickhill.

From Tickhill I travelled along a stony road past enclosures for four miles until I reached Conisbrough. The only noteworthy thing which I saw here was the castle. This stands on a rocky eminence with a ditch, and it has had strong walls with numerous towers. The River Don flows past the town. From Conisbrough I returned across fertile ground the three miles to Doncaster, and then rode to Hatfield across open sandy country, a journey of five miles. In Hatfield village there is a fine parish church, with a park nearby. But the lodge or manor house is only a modest wooden building. Hatfield is surrounded by forest land, and although there are very few trees yet red deer in large numbers haunt the fenland and large moors extending towards Axholme and the village of Thorne. The manor of Hatfield formerly belonged to Lord Mowbray.

Between Hatfield and Thorne, which are two miles apart, I crossed a branch of the River Don. Next to Thorne churchyard there is an attractive little tower or small castle with a good ditch. Like Thorne itself this once belonged to the Mowbrays, but now it is used to imprison offenders against the forest law. All around Thorne the ground is flat, with fens and moors. From Thorne it is a mile or more by water to a large lake called the Mere, and this itself is nearly a mile across, and stocked with good fish and waterfowl. A small watercourse or drain, which is known by the name of the Brier, extends three miles from the Mere to Wrangton [?*Wroot*] Cote, and on both sides the land is very waterlogged. *cont. p. 229* [**1541:** 1/34-7]

From Doncaster I rode more than a mile to Causeby [*Scawsby*] Leazes, where the Yorkshire rebels recently gathered, and two miles further I saw on my left hand an old manor house where the king dined. After another five miles I came to Wentbridge, a poor roadside place where the River Went flows under an attractive five-arched stone bridge, and from there it was three miles to Pontefract. The countryside between Doncaster and Pontefract is everywhere quite fertile for corn and pasture, and in some places has reasonable woodland and enclosed land.

These are the things which I took most notice of in Pontefract: Some of the older people repeatedly assert that the embankment of Watling Street runs through Pontefract Park. As far as I can make out Pontefract may be identified with the town called Legeolium, and later on it was called Brokenbridge. Indeed, ruins of such a bridge are still visible barely half a mile outside old Pontefract to the east, but in all honesty I cannot say that this bridge stood precisely on Watling Street. The name Pontefract is French, and was introduced by a Norman family, the Lacys, as a substitute for the English Brokenbridge. The site of the best part of present-day Pontefract, on top of the hill, was occupied after the Conquest by just a chapel and a few scattered buildings. This chapel was called St Leonard's in the Frith, and so far as I can discover this part of the new town was called Kirkby.

Edmund Lacy built the college of white friars in this part of the town, and in the same area Sir Robert Knollys, who had a distinguished military career in France, built Trinity College, with a hospital adjoining. The college has a master and six or seven priests, and the hospital contains thirteen pauper men and women. It was Sir Robert's original intention to have established this college at his manor of Sculthorpe [*Norfolk*], three miles from Walsingham; but he altered this plan at the desire of his wife Constance, a woman of low birth and a dissolute career for a time before her marriage, and built it instead on the very spot in Pontefract where she had been born, and endowed this college with land yielding an annual income of £180.

Pontefract Castle, which some people call Snorre Castle, contains eight towers, and of these the keep is very fine, with a good spring. This keep takes the form of three large and three small round turrets. In the ditch on the north side is the constable's tower. William the Conqueror granted this castle, along with the town of Brokenbridge and a very large tract of the surrounding countryside, to a Norman nobleman by the name of Hilbert de Lacy. It was he who founded the college of St Clement within the castle, although there had been a college and hospital at Brokenbridge before the Conquest. The monks lived in this college until the priory was erected, and it survives as a hospital. Hilbert de Lacy's son, Robert, appropriated both this hospital and St Clement's within the castle to the new priory, upon certain conditions. St Clement's still has a dean and three priests. Recently St Nicholas's Hospital came under the rule of St Oswald's [Nostell] Priory.

Before the conquest the castle, town and area around Brokenbridge belonged to a certain Richard Aschenald. His son was Aelric and his grandson was Swane; Swane's son was Adam. Adam had two daughters, and they married Geoffrey Neville and Thomas Burge. But neither of these acquired any share in the Brokenbridge region. Pontefract Priory was established at the suggestion of [Archbishop] Thurston by Robert, Hilbert de Lacy's son, and Cluniac monks were introduced from the house of La Charité.

I travelled past enclosures and reasonably wooded country for three miles or more from Pontefract to Nostell. Until Henry I's time the site now occupied by the newly erected parish church of St Oswald's contained a building and church for poor hermits, surrounded by woodland. But then a certain Ralph Aldlaver, Henry I's confessor, began the new monastery for canons, and himself became its first prior. The architecture of this priory is exceptionally fine and grand. It has the best supply of piped water in the whole of this part of England. The penultimate prior was responsible for channelling this water by conduit from a source one and a half miles away; and he also built an exceptionally fine kitchen in the monastery. An attractive lake lies at the west end of the buildings.

The three miles or so from Nostell to Sandal village consist of enclosed countryside very agreeable to the eye, with abundant woodland, pasture and arable. Mr Waterton, who has a fine estate, owns an attractive manor house in the parish of Sandal. The parish church is appropriated by St Stephen's College, Westminster. At the eastern [*western*] end of this village there is an attractive little castle on an eminence with a ditch around it. It formerly belonged to Warren, Earl of Surrey, but now to the Crown. Sandal is only about a mile from Wakefield.

The main points of interest which I noticed in Wakefield were these: There is a fine stone bridge of nine arches, under which flows the River Calder. On the east side of this bridge is an excellent chapel of Our Lady, with a foundation for two chantry priests attached to it. Some claim that it was the townspeople who founded this chantry, although it is also attributed to the Dukes of York, since they obtained the licence of mortmain [*royal permission to set up a charity*]. I also heard a report that one of the instigators was a servant, either of Edward IV's father, or of his brother, the Earl of Rutland. A fearful battle was fought in the fields to the south of this bridge. When the Duke of York's men turned to flight, either the duke himself, or his son the Earl of Rutland, was killed just up from the bars beyond the bridge leading up the slope to the town of Wakefield, which is built in a very fine position at the top. A cross to commemorate the event has been erected on the spot. The popular version of the story in Wakefield is that the Earl was trying to take refuge in the house of a poor woman, but in fright she shut her door, and immediately the Earl was killed. Because of the slaughter of men which occurred in this battle Lord Clifford was dubbed 'the butcher'.

Wakefield's principal church at the present day is a recent building, but is exceptionally fine and large. There is a theory that the old parish church used to be at the other end of the town, where now is a chapel of ease. The vicarage at the east end of the churchyard is also a fine, large building. It cannot have been the parsonage house for all that many years, as its present incumbent is only the fourth or fifth vicar to have lived there. Before the benefice was appropriated by St Stephen's College, Westminster, it was a very considerable living. So much so that one of the Earls Warren, owners of Wakefield and much of the surrounding country, presented a son or near relative to it; and it was he who built most of the house which is now the vicarage.

A quarter-mile outside Wakefield may be seen a man-made earthen mound, which is said by some to be where one of the Earls Warren started a building, but that as fast as he could build the force of the wind destroyed the work. But this is merely an idle story, and others say that it was nothing but the mound for a windmill. The place is now called Lowe Hill.

The town of Wakefield extends entirely from east and west, and there is a fine open area as the market place. The architecture of the town is reasonably good, largely of timber but with some stone. The entire economy of the town depends on its coarse cloth industry. There are few inland towns in Yorkshire that can boast a better site or surroundings. And there are abundant seams of coal to be found in the Wakefield area.

From Wakefield I returned the six miles to Pontefract. I passed enclosed land for part of the journey, but elsewhere, especially half-way along at a place which I remember was called Wakefield Moor, there were open fields. About halfway along I passed coal pits a short distance away to my right. These pits lie close to the main source of the River Went, although it has one or two other sources as well.

From Pontefract I rode for two miles, mostly past enclosed ground, to Castleford. Next to the churchyard there I was shown a garden in which many curious building foundations have been discovered. My informant said that it was the site of a castle, but I think rather that it had been some manor house. Castleford Bridge has seven arches, and crosses the River Aire. Three miles upstream and inland to the west Swillington Bridge crosses the same river, and two miles below Castleford is Ferrybridge. The village of Whitwood is a mile from Castleford, and here, close to the bank of the River Calder in an enclosed field of pasture land I saw the banks and ditches of a former castle. It is now called the Castle Hill, and belongs to a certain Archibald Giseland of Lincolnshire.

Watling Street lies immediately opposite Castleford Bridge, and I travelled along it for five miles to Aberford, at first over low-lying meadowland, but for most of the way on flat but higher ground, which produced good crops. To the east of Aberford survive two or three long ditches which have the appearance of military earthworks. In no other part of England have I seen such obvious remains as here of the massive man-made embankment on which Watling Street runs.

Aberford is only a poor roadside place on Watling Street. The Cock Beck rises about a mile to its west and then flows through Aberford; it continues a tortuous course to a hamlet called Lead, where Scargell had a fine timber manor house. When he died this knight left two daughters as his heiresses; one married a man called Tunstall, the other Gascoyne of

Bedfordshire. The Cock Beck then twists round past the fields of Saxton and Towton villages, before entering the River Wharfe below Tadcaster. Saxton village lies a mile away from Lead, and here Mr Hundesgate [?*Hungate*] lives. In Saxton churchyard were buried the bones of many of the casualties of the Palm Sunday battle [*Towton Field*], which had previously lain in five pits, still visible half a mile away to the north in Saxton's fields. Towton village, a mile from Saxton, has a large unfinished chapel begun by Richard III. The father of Sir John Moulton laid the first stone of the chapel, and here too were buried many of the battle casualties. The battle was fought as much in the parish of Saxton as of Towton, yet it is named after the latter place.

From Towton it is about a mile to the village of Ulleskelf, and here one of the prebends of York owns a good house, which includes a good orchard containing walks laid out with topiary work. Much of this house was built by Higdon, the former Dean of York. Around Ulleskelf itself the countryside is rather low lying and meadowish, and this continues downstream towards the confluence of rivers near Nun Appleton. Ryther parish church is only a mile from Ulleskelf.

I rode for three miles from Ulleskelf to Tadcaster, past good arable and pasture grounds with some woodland. Tadcaster stands on the nearer bank of the River Wharfe, and is a good roadside town. Tadcaster Bridge, which crosses the Wharfe by eight fine stone arches, was last rebuilt, according to some people, using part of the ruined masonry of the old castle at Tadcaster. A massive hill, with ditches and the enclosure of this castle, may still be seen beside the Wharfe a little above the bridge. From its site it seems that it must have been a most imposing structure.

Tadcaster stands more than a mile from Watling Street, which veers more in the Carlisle direction, and crosses the Wharfe at a place called St Helen's Ford. This is a mile and a half upstream from Tadcaster, and on the opposite bank is St Helen's Chapel. Three and a half miles above St Helen's Ford is the village of Wetherby, which has a stone bridge over the Wharfe, and two miles further upstream is Harewood, another village with a stone bridge across the river. Otley, also with a stone bridge over the Wharfe, is another seven miles up the river.

From Tadcaster I rode about two miles across enclosed fields to Healaugh Priory. This was originally founded by a nobleman called Geoffrey Haget, who was lord of the manor of Healaugh, and a large landowner in the area known by Yorkshiremen as Ainsty, which is bounded by the Rivers Ouse, Nidd, Wharfe and Aire. Some members of two gentry families, the Deepdales and the Stapletons, were buried in Healaugh Priory, including a certain Sir Brian Stapleton, a valiant knight who is much spoken of. From the priory it is barely a mile to Healaugh village, and there I saw substantial ruins of an old stone manor house which, along with the fine wooded park beside it, belonged to the Earl of Northumberland. At one time, so far as I can make out, it was part of the Haget estate. From Healaugh village I rode the seven miles to York. For the first two miles I passed reasonably wooded and enclosed country, but then there were four miles of fertile corn and grassland in flat open fields.

Kexby Bridge is five miles from York, across reasonably fertile open country. This bridge, which has three fine stone arches, spans the attractive River Derwent, which flows past Malton and enters the Ouse near Wressle. I should think that the bridge lies about halfway between. There are the following bridges on the Derwent upstream from Kexby: Stamford Bridge, two miles; Buttercrambe Bridge, one mile; Howsham Bridge, two miles; Kirkham Bridge, two miles or more; Malton; Yedingham, seven miles; Hay Bridge, three miles; Ayton Bridge, two miles; and the source of the river two miles further. There is still a common belief that a portion of the Derwent once flowed to Scarborough, but that by downcutting into both sides of the hills large quantities of stone and earth fell down and blocked its course. Apart from a stone bridge at Sutton, two miles downstream, there are no bridges across the Derwent below Kexby, and people cross by ferries instead.

After Kexby I rode one and a half miles to the village of Wilberfoss, where there used to be a priory for nuns; and not far away to the left was Catton Park, which used to belong to the Percys, but is now the king's. From Wilberfoss it was three miles to Barmby village, and a further three miles to Hayton. In this village I was told that the pleasant brook which runs through it rises a mile away in the hills and flows into the Derwent. On my way to Hayton I crossed Pocklington Beck, but left Pocklington itself about a mile away on my left. After Hayton I rode through four villages, each a mile apart: Thorpe [le Street], Shiptonthorpe, [Market] Weighton (a large country village), and Sancton, where Mr Langdale lives. From here I journeyed a further six miles to Leconfield.

All this tract of land between York and Leconfield produces quite good yields of corn and grass. but there are few trees. I discovered that the whole of this part of the East Riding lies in a hundred or wapentake called Harthill. Some people say that Harthill extends to Wressle in one direction, and elsewhere borders the Wold in many places, although the Wold itself lies outside the hundred. The market town of Pocklington certainly lies within this hundred, and in ignorance some people claim that Beverley does too; but the inhabitants of Beverley regard themselves as outside hundredal jurisdiction.

Leconfield is a large building which stands in one very spacious courtyard within a large moat. Three-quarters of the house is constructed of timber, apart from an insignificant brick gateway; the other quarter is well built of stone with some brick. In a small room used as a study there, which is called Paradise, I saw the genealogy of the Percy family. The park next to the house is very good and large, and reasonably well wooded. A nice brick tower in the park serves as a lodge. Beverley is only two miles from Leconfield.

Among the buildings which I noticed in Beverley was the collegiate church of St John. It is a fine church, all in one style, and it contains, in addition to the tombs of saints, three very noteworthy tombs on the north side of the quire. In one of them, within a vaulted chapel, is buried Percy, Earl of Northumberland, and his son, the last earl's father. In another is Eleanor, the wife of one of the Lords Percy, and in the third, which is of white alabaster, is Idonea, Lady Percy, the wife of another Lord Percy. Under Eleanor's tomb is buried one of the Percy family who was a priest. The houses of the prebendaries are built around St John's churchyard, and one of them, which has a moat but is all in ruins, belongs to the bishop of York. The finest portion of the provost's house is the gate and the façade.

Next to the meadows, where the canal for ketches runs, is a church dedicated to St Nicholas, which is dependent on St Mary's. It stands at the north end of the town, and is large and fine, with transepts. Until recently there were two friaries in Beverley. According to some people the Dominican house was founded by a man named Goldsmith, and therefore belonged to the town; but Lord Darcy recently contested the patronage with the town. The Franciscan friary was founded by the Huthome family of Scorborough near Leconfield, but the last but one Earl of Northumberland contested its patronage. The town also had four hospitals. St Giles's was thought to have been founded before the conquest by a certain Wulfe, and it belonged to the bishops of York until Bishop Giffard granted it to Warter Priory, an Augustinian house in Yorkshire. It recently passed to the Earl of Rutland, and he closed it. Trinity Hospital was allegedly founded by someone called Ake; it is still standing, in the town centre. Near the black friars was a hospital of St Nicholas, but that is in ruins. But right outside the north bargate a hospital survives which was founded by two merchants, Akeborow and Hodgkin Overshal. I recall that there is a statue of Our Lady over the hospital's gate. In addition there is a house of the Trinity towards the eastern side of the town, which belonged to the knights of the Order of St John.

Beverley is a large town, with good timber buildings. The best part of it is its northern end, where the market is held. There used to be a good cloth industry in the town, but that has now greatly declined. The town has no wall, but it retains three good brick-built gates, the North Bar, Newbiggin Bar (to the west) and Kellgate Bar (also to the west).

Cottingham is three miles from Beverley. For the first two miles the countryside was well wooded, and at the end of two miles I passed the great park of Beverley on my left-hand side. From there it was a mile across low-lying meadow ground to Cottingham. All the area around Cottingham as far as Meaux Abbey, and on all sides in the Kingston upon Hull direction, is low-lying, very fertile meadowland and pasture.

As I entered the southern part of Cottingham, which is a large country town, I saw the site of Stuteville's castle. It had a double ditch and moat, but nothing now remains of this castle. The property of this lordship and manor, with all its substantial rights, was later divided into four portions, and until recently they belonged to the king, the Countess of Salisbury, the Earl of Westmorland and the Lord Powis. But now the king has three-quarters, and Lord Powis the fourth. And at present there are four modest houses for tenant farmers within the castle precinct, each separate and corresponding to the four owners.

The town of Cottingham extends southwards and eastwards. Its parish church is old and quite large, but the parsonage house for such a large benefice is not very good. It lies on the north side of the churchyard. The parish of Cottingham is very large. A stream flows past the east end of the town, rising in a wood one mile to the north, and after Cottingham continuing for a mile and a half into the River Hull at a place, as I recall, known as Newland. From Cottingham it is four miles across low-lying ground to Kingston upon Hull; two miles of this consists of a causeway with ditches on both sides. But Cottingham does not lie on the direct road from Beverley to Kingston, because by the shortest route the distance between the two towns is reckoned to be only six miles.

In the time of Edward III the settlement at Kingston was merely a modest fishing community, and dependent on the village of Hessle, which lies two or three miles further upstream the Humber. The first great expansion of the town was as a result of voyages to Iceland for fish, and the town enjoyed the entire trade in Icelandic cod imported into England, and part of the trade in other fish. During the reign of Richard II the town grew very wealthy. A Hull merchant by the name of Michael de la Pole, who had been apprenticed, so the story goes, to one Rotenhering, also of Hull, attained such popularity for his cleverness, energy and wealth that he was created Earl of Suffolk. This enabled him to procure from Richard II many grants and privileges for the town. It was during his lifetime that new building took place in Hull to a remarkable extent; and in addition the town was enclosed with ditches and a town wall was begun. This wall was completed, and was built entirely of brick, as indeed most of the buildings in the town were at that period.

This wall has four main gates, all brick-built. The north gate is of four wards, and along the wall between this gate and Beverley Gate are twelve brick towers, with a postern in one of them. Between Beverley Gate and Myton Gate, as I recall, are five brick towers, also with a postern in one of them; and then a further three brick towers from Myton Gate to Hessle Gate, which has three wards. After Hessle Gate the wall runs straight as a die to the harbour entrance, where it meets the Humber estuary, and along this stretch there are five brick towers, including one with a postern to the shore. Because the wall is so straight it is used a great deal for making cables, and for winding hemp to make smaller ropes. From the mouth of the River Hull up into the harbour there is no wall, but each merchant has his own steps, right up as far as the north gate. There are no suburbs outside the town.

Next to the west end of St Mary's Church Michael de la Pole built a grand brick house of palace-like proportions, with a good orchard and a full-scale garden, enclosed by a brick wall. He also built three other houses in the town, each with a brick tower. Two of them stand in the town centre, and the third is on the bank of the River Hull beside the harbour.

Hull has two churches, Holy Trinity and St Mary's, but neither is a parish church in its own right. Trinity Church, which is built of brick, is by far the larger and finer of the two. There are four important chapels on the south side of the church, arranged as a transept. One was founded by two merchants, named Hanby, and Richard Haynson. Next to it is a chapel which some say was built by a Chancellor of Lincoln. The third chapel is stone-built, and was built by Bishop Alcock, who was born in Beverley; it is a chantry chapel, and in it are buried the bishop's parents, William and Joanna Alcock. The last of the four chapels is known as the Mariners' Chapel. There is a chantry chapel in the nave also. This was made by a priest called Ripplingham, and his father, a Hull merchant, is buried there. And in the north transept there is the chapel of a certain Robert Frost, a merchant. The church's crossing bell-tower is large and fine . On the south side of the churchyard is the free school erected by Bishop Alcock, and at the west end of the churchyard is the fine row of dwelling-houses built for priests of the town by a mayor of Hull, one John Gregg, who also built the hospital next to it. Nearby is the Mariners' Hospital. Selby's Hospital stands on the north side of the churchyard, and Selby himself, and his wife, lie buried in the wall of the south quire aisle, with excellent effigies.

The white friars' college, which the Percy family were credited with founding, stood near Beverley Gate, and the Austin friary stood at the east end of Trinity Church. The town hall, which has a brick tower used as a prison, is nearby. The majority of the bricks used in building the houses and town walls of Kingston were made at a place called the Tilery, which lies outside the town to the south. During the period when all the imports of cod into England from Iceland came through the town, the ships used to bring back with them as ballast from Iceland large cobble stones, because their cargo of fish was too light, and as a result these cobbles were used to pave the whole of Kingston from one end to the other.

Kingston's first charter gave it a warden, later it was governed by bailiffs, and later still by a mayor and bailiffs. Then in Henry VI's reign the town was accorded the status of a county in its own right, with a mayor and sheriff. I was told that the first charter of incorporation dates from 180 years ago.

Outside the north gate there was a charterhouse established by the de la Pole family, and a hospital which they also founded, and which is still standing. Certain members of the family were buried in this Carthusian monastery, and during its recent suppression several lead coffins containing bones were discovered in a vault beneath the high altar. Like the majority of other buildings in Hull, most of this monastery was built in brick.

The shortest crossing of the Humber to the Lincolnshire shore is from Kingston to Golflete [*Goxhill Fleet*], a distance of about three miles. But the more usual crossing is from Kingston to Barton-on-Humber; although this is seven miles away, the passage is reckoned as good as that to Golflete on account of the force of the tide.

Places along the coast from Kingston: Patrington, where there is a small harbour or creek, is ten miles, on the Yorkshire shore of the Humber; and from there it is a further ten miles right to the point of land on the Yorkshire side of the estuary, at Ravensburgh; then up the coast eighteen miles to Hornsea, where there is a small creek; twelve miles to Bridlington harbour; three miles further to Flamborough Head, which juts out into the sea; and nine miles to Scarborough (in fact taking the shortest route by road Bridlington and Flamborough are the same distance from Scarborough); from Scarborough eight miles to a little fishing settlement of twenty boats called Robin Hood's Bay, with a haven or bay a mile long; then four miles to Whitby, where there is a large fishing town and a harbour reinforced by a pier; from here it is fifteen miles to the mouth of the Tees.

From Kingston I took the direct road back to Beverley, a distance of six miles. For the first five miles I crossed low-lying pasture and marshy land, followed by a mile of quite well-wooded enclosures. After Beverley I rode past another mile of enclosed ground and another past good open arable, which brought me to Walkington. This fine open-field cornland continued for the next five miles, as far as North Cave, where a brook flows down to the Humber. But all the following three miles to Scalby were over low-lying marshland and meadows, with one arm of the Humber visible on my left. This area of marshland has many carrs of water, and is known as Walling Fen. It is so large that fifty-eight villages stand in or abutting it, the majority of them lying within the bishop of Durham's manor of Howden; the rest are in Harthill hundred. The fen itself, which is sixteen miles around its perimeter, lies wholly in Howdenshire. And the twelve miles of country between Walkington and Howden likewise fall all into Howdenshire, which extends along the bank of the estuary almost the whole way from the mouth of the Derwent to the edge of Ferriby. From Scalby I continued the four miles to Howden, across enclosed pasture ground for nearly a mile, and the other three across marshy fenlands.

Howden is the only market town in Howdenshire, and is not very highly regarded. It has a collegiate church which is old and quite attractive, and has five prebends attached to it, called Howden, Thorpe, Saltmarsh, Barnby and Skelton. It is said that one of the first prebendaries was John of Howden, whom they call a saint, and who is buried in the quire. According to an inscription on a very fine marble-like stone the entrails of Walter Skirlaw, bishop of Durham, are buried in Howden church. There is also a tomb belonging to one of the Methams in a chapel in the church's south aisle. The bishop of Durham has his palace on the south side of the church; the first portion of this by the entrance is made of timber, but the other three parts are mostly of stone with some brick. Certain churches in Howdenshire pay homage to Howden church. The park next to Howden on the road to Wressle belongs to the bishop of Durham. The pre-eminent gentry families in Howdenshire are the Methams of Metham, half a mile from the Humber shore, the Mountetons, and the Portingtons of Portington. About two miles along the York road from Howden is Hemingbrough, where there are three small prebends belonging to Durham in the little collegiate church.

I rode the three miles from Howden to Wressle across low-lying meadow and pasture all the way, part of which has been enclosed with hedges. By comparison with this very low ground all around it the site of Wressle castle appears quite high. The majority of the outer court of this castle is timber built, and the castle itself has a moat on three sides. The fourth side, where the entrance is, is dry. The whole castle, inside and out, is built of very fine large square stone blocks, and some people believe that most of it was brought from France. Of the castle's five towers four, which stand in the four corners, are of approximately equal size. The fifth is the gatehouse, and its apartments are five storeys high, whereas three of the others have four storeys of apartments, and the other one contains the buttery, pantry, pastry-room, larder and kitchen. The hall and the main bedrooms are fine, as are the chapel and closets.

My verdict on this house is that it is one of the most perfect on this side of the Trent. It has the appearance of being new, although in fact it was built by a younger brother of the Percys, Earls of Worcester, who was held in high favour by Richard II. He purchased the manor of Wressle, which had an annual value then of not much more than £30; but having no heir, the estate passed, with the king's permission, to the Earls of Northumberland. The outer court, however, is newer than the rest. And the last but one Earl of Northumberland constructed the stone brewhouse, outside the castle wall, but adjoining its kitchen.

One thing that I particularly liked was a study in one of the towers, which was called Paradise. It contained in its centre an eight-sided lattice-work cabinet, which had on each side a desk with ledges so that books could be placed on cupboards within them. These desks appeared to be firmly fixed to the top of the cabinet, and yet each one of them, or all of them, could be pulled down to fit into a chest-high groove, and thus form a desk on which to place books.

The castle wardrobe was exceptionally fine, as were the gardens inside the moat and the orchards outside. In the orchards were mounds with topiary hedges and a spiral flight of steps cut into them like the helix of a cockleshell, so that they could be climbed to the top without effort. The River Derwent flows almost right beside the castle, and about a mile lower enters the Ouse. After heavy rain this river in spate overflows the land around the castle, which is low-lying meadow. There is a park close to the castle.

From Wressle I rode about a mile, mostly over meadowland, to [?*Breighton* or ?*Menthorpe*] Ferry, and from there eleven miles to York. For most of this journey all I saw was meadowland and marshy ground, with little arable, although towards York the soil and corn were better.

The town of York stands on both east and west banks of the River Ouse, which runs through it; the built-up area east of the river is twice as large as that on the other side. This is the course of the wall from the bank of the Ouse around the eastern part of the city: First there is a large tower with an iron chain to cast across the river; then one more tower, and so to Bootham Gate or Bar; between here and Goodram Gate or Bar are ten towers; then four towers to Layerthorpe, a postern gate; from here, for the space of two bow-shots, the deep and obscure River Fosse which flows out of Galtres Forest defends this part of the city without a wall; then three towers to Walmgate, and so to Fishergate, which has been blocked up ever since the mob burned it during Henry VII's reign. It is sometimes said that Walmgate was built when Fishergate was blocked, but I doubt that.

In the wall near this gate is an inscribed stone which reads, 'Sixty yards long, AD 1445, at the expense of William Todd, mayor of York'. From here to the bank of the Fosse three towers, with a postern in the third; and from there across the river by a bridge to the castle. The five-arched Fosse Bridge is upstream from it, and there is also Layerthorpe Bridge, of three arches over the Fosse, and Monk Bridge, a five-arched bridge over the Fosse outside Goodramgate. The castle precinct is not of any great size. It contains five ruined towers, and a keep entirely in ruins. A channel of water derived from the River Fosse flows around the hill that it stands on.

Within the wall of the part of York east of the Ouse the following places are noteworthy: The cathedral church and its palace stand between Bootham Gate and Goodram Gate. The nave arcade in York cathedral church consists of eight bays on each side, four bays on each side of the transepts, and nine on each side of the chancel. The Austin friary lay between the tower beside the River Ouse and the six-arched Ouse Bridge. The site of the white friars was not far from Layerthorpe Gate. There was a house just within Layerthorpe Gate which belonged to the Bigot family, and a hospital next to it which they had founded. But Sir Francis Bigot allowed both the hospital and his house to go all to ruin. There is a hospital of St Anthony which was founded about a century ago by a Yorkshire knight called John Langton. Some say that he was mayor of York. The grey friars is not far from the castle. The former Augustinian priory had a hospital of St Leonard. There is a chapel on Fosse Bridge, and going north from the bridge there is a hospital dedicated to the Trinity, which was established by the city merchants.

There were the foundations of a hospital outside Micklegate, and close to the side of the gate itself. It was begun by Sir Richard of York, a mayor of York, whom the Yorkshire mob wished to have beheaded when they entered York by burning Fisher Gate during Henry VII's reign. The hospital was never completed. St Mary's Abbey lay outside Bootham Gate. St Andrew's, a house of Gilbertine Canons, stood near the Ouse outside Fishergate. There was another religious house near one of the York bars which I heard someone say had been a Cistercian monastery. It was here that several people were killed when the citizens of York engaged the Henawdes [*Hainaults*], who took arms to support Edward III. There is a chapel and a town hall, with a hospital, on the east bank of the Ouse upstream from Ousebridge. Ouse Bridge has six arches, and there is a chapel or church on it. From York it is a distance of twenty-four miles by water down the Ouse to Airmyn, and another twenty-four miles to Hull. Up the Ouse it is sixteen miles by water to Boroughbridge.

The western part of York is enclosed in the following way: First there is a turret, and then the wall runs over the side of the keep belonging to the castle which stood on the west bank of the Ouse corresponding to the castle on the east bank. The site of this western castle is now called the Old Bailey, and its precinct and ditches are clearly visible. From the start of this west wall to Micklegate there are nine towers, and round to the bank of the Ouse again another eleven towers. At the lowest of these eleven towers is a postern gate, and its tower is right opposite the east tower, so that the chain can be drawn across the Ouse between them.

In this western part of the city there was a priory of black monks called the Trinity. The nunnery of Clement Thorpe stood outside the wall of this western part adjoining St Andrew's. Not far from Micklegate there was a house of black friars. York's liberties and territories extend for a great distance around the city, especially since the channelling of several rivers in the area. In one direction they extend as far as Tadcaster Bridge on the Wharfe.

My three-mile journey from York to Stockton yn the moore [*Stockton-on-the-Forest*] took me across low-lying pasture and wasteland. The next five miles crossed similar terrain, until I came to a brook which flows from the region of Sheriff Hutton Castle. The crossing-point is generally called the Spittle, which is a corruption of 'Hospital' . A half-mile further is the village of Whitwell [*-on-the-Hill*], and Kirkham is a mile away on the right hand side by a wood. For the space of about a mile in this area the fields are enclosed, and there is some woodland. For the next two miles the ground was gorse-covered, and then I reached a stream called Crambeck; this flows from Hinderskelfe Castle, which stands on a site full of springs. Not far away the stream flows into the Derwent. From Crambeck I rode to Malton, three miles away. Hinderskelfe is also three miles from Malton, and Malton is twenty miles from Beverley and a further six from Hull, thus twenty-six miles in total.

The town of Malton stands on the nearer bank of the Derwent as I approached it, and is surrounded by hills and dales which produce abundant corn and pasture. Malton has a good market, and two chapels of ease which are dependent on the parish church still standing at Old

Malton. This is a quarter-mile upstream from Malton on the same bank of the Derwent, and is where the former priory stood. Judging by the surviving ruins Malton Castle was a large structure, but at present the only dwelling within it is a modest farmhouse.

The manor of Malton is divided between three owners, Lord Clifford, Yevers [*Eure*], and one of the Conyers. Eure is also the sole owner of the Old Malton manor. Lord William Vescy and several of the Eure family were buried at Malton. The ancient seat of the Eure family is Wotton [*Witton*] Castle within the bishopric [*i.e. of Durham*], and they also own a good manor called Berwick-on-the-Hill near Metford in Northumberland. Lord Vescy left a daughter, who married Aiton, and their daughter married Lord Bromfeld; he had three daughters, who married Clifford, Eure, and Conyers of Sockburn.

The River Rye rises on Black Moor and flows past Rievaulx Abbey. Four streams flow into its left bank: the River Riccal, the River Seven, the Costa Beck and the Pickering Beck. So far as I could make out the River Seven also rises on the side of Black Moor, and from there flows past Sinnington, where Lord Latimer has a fine manor house, four miles from the town of Pickering. It enters the Rye about a mile upstream from [*?Habton*] Bridge. The Costa Beck derives from a spring at a place called Keld Head right on the edge of Pickering itself, and flows into the Rye near Kirby Misperton, two miles below Pickering. The Pickering Beck rises in Black Moor and joins the Costa Beck a half-mile below Pickering.

Mount Ferrant Castle stood two miles from Malton in the manor and parish of Birdsall. Its stone has now been completely robbed, and bushes grow on the site. At one time the castle belonged to Lord Mauley, of whose line eight generations, all called Peter, succeeded to it. The last Peter Mauley left two daughters, and they married Bigot and Salwaine [*?Salvin*]. Bigot's share of the estate included Mulgrave, with Seaton and seven other dependent townships around it close to the coast, as well as Mount Ferrant and Birdsall, Suadale [*?Swaledale*] in Richmondshire, and other manors. For his part of Mauley's estate Salwaine received the barony of Egton, on the Esk not far from Whitby, Lockington, Brough (which lies close to Watton on the River Hull, and which once included a fine manor house of the Mauley family), Nesswick, and the manor of Doncaster. He exchanged Doncaster with Lord Percy for another manor, and when one of the Percys was attainted Doncaster passed to the Crown. Subsequently the Percys' inheritance was restored to them, but not Doncaster, because they had acquired it by exchange or purchase.

The single house and manor of Ceterington [*Settrington*] was the Yorkshire Bigots' first inheritance in the county. It had previously belonged to Bigot, Earl Marshal, and through an entail to the male heir passed to a younger brother of the Bigot family. Several members of the family are buried in Settrington parish church.

A story goes that the destruction of Mount Ferrant occurred in the following way: Two generations after the death of Bigot, Earl Marshal, a Bigot of Settrington secretly courted and won the affection of a daughter of Albemarle, Earl of Holderness. Albemarle was extremely angry at this, and when Bigot was away he attacked Mount Ferrant, captured and demolished it. But later the two men were reconciled, and Bigot married Albemarle's daughter, largely through the intercession of the Prior of Watton. In consequence Bigot favoured Watton by allowing it to appropriate the living of Birdsall; and it is also claimed that he converted the manor house at Mulgrave into a castle to replace Mount Ferrant.

Mulgrave Castle stands on a craggy hilltop, but with much higher hills on both sides of it. On the summit of the hill to its north is a beacon, and nearby are several stones commonly known as Wade's Grave; the local people say that Wade was a giant, and that he owned Mulgrave. There are many springs on the moorland near Mulgrave, and from them issue two becks, Sandbeck and Eastbeck. They flow in the valleys between the great hills, one on each side of the castle, and before long enter the sea, which is not far away.

From Malton I rode for about eight miles to the village of Sherburn. My journey took me through open-field country, which produces good corn and grass, but little or no wood. The Earl of Salisbury owned Sherburn, but it passed to King Richard through his wife, Anne. After Sherburn I kept the hills on my right hand, and low-lying ground with carrs on my left, until after five miles I reached the large isolated town of Seamer, which takes its name from the large lake adjoining it on the south-west side. Seamer has a modest parish church, and in the quire I saw a flat marble slab with an epitaph in French, marking the burials of John Percy and Joanna de Aiton. At the west end of the churchyard is the Percys' manor house. It is large, but the architecture is poor, and only its chapel is well built. From here I travelled one mile across fairly flat ground, and two miles further in a valley hemmed in by steep hills on both sides, and so I came to Scarborough.

Although it has a charter, the town of Scarborough appears to lie in the wapentake of Pickering Lythe, since Scarborough Castle is reckoned to fall under Pickering's jurisdiction, and the shore from Scarborough right along to the headland of Philaw [*Filey*] Brigg, which is some six miles in the Bridlington direction, comes under the control of Pickering Lythe. Where it is not defended by the sea and the shoreline the town is protected for a short distance by a stone wall, but mostly by ditches and earthen banks. Only two gates give access to the town from the landward side; Newburgh Gate is reasonably good, but Aldburgh Gate is very poor. Scarborough is built entirely on a slaty cliff, which offers a very fine prospect from out at sea. The only parish church in the town is dedicated to Our Lady, and virtually adjoins the castle. It is a beautiful building, with aisles on both sides and transepts. Two of the three old bell towers with spires are at the west end of the church; the third is over the crossing. There is a large chapel next to Newburgh Gate, and there were formerly three friaries in the town, grey, black and white.

To the east of the town there is a single point of land which juts out into the bay, and here is the harbour for ships. An exceptionally good castle, strong and large, stands on a sheer crag on this headland. The only approach to the castle is by this steep, slate crag, and even before the castle precinct is reached there are two towers. Both have drawbridges between them, with sheer cliffs on either side. The first court contains the keep, which is the oldest and strongest part of the castle, and three towers in a row. A wall adjoins them, which runs down from this first court to the edge of the sea cliff. This wall contains six towers, the second of which is square and full of apartments; it is called the Queen's tower or lodging. Outside this first courtyard is a large green, enclosing sixteen acres if reckoned to extend to the shore. In it is a chapel, and the remains of old walls of domestic buildings which stood there. The castle entrance between the drawbridges is such that money could be spent on bringing the sea right around the castle, since its situation is as a small foreland or point between two bays.

At the south-east corner of the town, on the shore, there is a bulwark which the buffeting of the sea has thrown into ruins. It was constructed by Richard III, who stayed at Scarborough Castle for a while, and who also began a wall of squared stone blocks around part of the town. A freshwater stream flows into the sea past the bulwark on its south-east side. An old Scarborough seafarer told me that Henry I endowed the town with great privileges. The pier which was constructed to provide shelter for ships is now badly damaged almost half-way along it.

Distances from Scarborough: Beverley, thirty miles, and a further six to Hull; Robin Hood's Bay, eight miles, and from there to Whitby, where a new quay and port is being built out of stone won from nearby rockfalls. There are cliffs all along this coast, and they continue for all but the last six miles of the sixteen-mile stretch of coast from there to the mouth of the Tees.

[*In the other direction*] from Scarborough: Bridlington is nine miles, all by cliffs as far as Flamborough Head, and so to the mouth of Bridlington harbour. Flamborough is now considered to be a manor house rather than a castle, and its position is such that the distance from Scarborough to Bridlington is the same as that from Scarborough to Flamborough. Hornsea is twelve miles along the coast from Bridlington, and from Hornsea Ravensburgh [*Spurn Head*] is eighteen miles, and Patrington ten. Patrington is a town with a small harbour, but no market. From there it is four miles to Hull, and six to Hedon harbour.

Hedon used to be a fine harbour town. It stands more than a mile inland up a creek of the River Humber. Near the town this salt-water creek divides and encircles it, so that ships used to berth around the town. But now it is approached by three bridges, and some of the places where the ships berthed can be clearly seen to be overgrown with rushes and reeds. The harbour has very badly declined. Within living memory there were three parish churches, but now there is only one, St Augustine's, a very attractive building. Near its churchyard may be seen evidence of the site of a former tower or castle, built for the town's defence. Hedon retains its borough privileges, with a mayor and bailiffs, but whereas in Edward III's time it attracted many good ships and rich merchants, now there are only a few boats, and no merchants of any standing. Its downfall has been the diverting and sanding-up of the harbour channel, and a fire which damaged much of the town. According to some people the wool staple for the north of England was once held at Hedon, but the truth is that when Hull began to prosper, so Hedon went into decline.

The owner of Hedon was the Earl of Albemarle and Holderness; he also possessed Skipton in Craven at the same time. He had a large manor house at Newton, which is a mile below Hedon in the direction of the Humber; its site is on the lower side of the creek, whereas Hedon is on the upper side. At Newton the Albemarles established a chantry with two priests. In addition the family owned a castle or large manor house at Skipsea, which lies in Holderness, not far from the coast, and six or seven miles from Bridlington.

The boundaries of Holderness are as follows: The boundary strikes the coast between Bridlington and Skipsea; then to the Earl's Dike, built by one of the Albemarles, Earls of Holderness. This dike is three or four miles from Bridlington, and extends almost to Frodingham Bridge. This is a wooden bridge, and the only bridge over the River Hull. The dike and the water in it join the River Hull a little upstream from this bridge, but when the springs are high the water flows as far as the bridge. From Frodingham Bridge, which is two miles or more below [Great] Driffield, the River Hull marks the boundary all the way to its estuary. From there the limit of Holderness extends to Spurn Head at the very mouth of the Humber, and from there up the sea coast as far as the shore between Skipsea and Bridlington.

I rode from Scarborough to Ayton, and as I crossed the River Derwent I saw a manor house which had once belonged to a knight whose name was Ayton, but now to the principal branch of the Eures. This manor house includes a tower or fortress. Three or four miles further I passed Brunston [*Brompton*], and after another three miles came to Wilton, where there is a manor house with a tower which belongs to Cholmeley. He inherited much of the estate of a knight named Hastings, and he has another house at Rollesley [?]. The father of the present Cholmeley established the family name in the region around Pickering, where he held high office. From Wilton I rode on to Pickering. Most of my journey from Scarborough to Pickering took me past hill and dale, through country with a reasonable supply of corn and grass, but little woodland visible.

Pickering is a large town, but the buildings do not stand close together. The larger part of the town, including the parish church and the castle, lies on a large slaty hillside, to the south-east of the brook which separates it from the smaller part. This brook, which a mile below Pickering runs into the Costa Beck, sometimes flows as a torrent, but it soon becomes placid again. I saw in Pickering Church two or three tombs of the Bruce family. One had a garland around his helmet, and was lying with his wife in a chapel on the south side of the quire; another, after whom a chantry was named, was buried under an arch in a chapel on the north side of the main part of the quire. The living of Pickering, to which several of the churches in Pickering Lythe pay allegiance, is held by appropriation by the Dean of York.

The castle stands not far from the parish church at one end of the town, on the brow of the hill under which the brook flows. There are four towers in its outer court, including one which is called Rosamund's Tower. In the inner court there are also four towers, if the keep be included. The castle walls and towers are in reasonably good condition, but the timber apartments in the inner court are in ruins. This inner court also contains a chapel with a chantry priest. This castle, together with the town and manor of Pickering, has for a long period of time belonged to the Lancaster family, but I was unable to discover there who had built the castle, or to whom it had belonged before the Lancasters. What remains of the castle walls do not seem to have been built all that long ago. I recall hearing it said that Richard III at one time stayed at this castle, and on another occasion at Scarborough Castle.

I crossed the brook by a stone bridge of five arches in order to reach the other part of the town, and here were two notable sights, the ruins of a manor house called Bruce's Hall, and the Lascelles manor house at Keld Head.

The parish boundary of Pickering is twenty miles in total length, and extends right up to the peaks of Blakmore [*Black Rigg*]. Beside the castle there is a park which is more than seven miles around its perimeter, but it is not very well wooded. The liberties of Pickering Lythe extend as far as Filey Brigg, which stands on the coast six miles from Scarborough towards Bridlington; and from there along the coast to Scarborough Castle, and beyond towards Whitby. In the direction of the Wolds they extend as far as Normanby Bridge, and in another direction right up to the peaks of Black Rigg. So I estimate that their total extent is twenty miles in length, but their breadth is not so great. And although in the Ayton area this territory crosses the River Derwent, yet around Malton the Derwent forms the boundary. Mr Constable informed me there that the country which lies to the north-east of the Derwent from Sherburn parish church to Stamford Bridge (which is on the Derwent) belongs to a hundred called Hercrosse, which lies between the Wolds and Ryedale.

There were religious houses along the Derwent in Pickering Lythe at Wykeham, and at Yedingham two miles lower; both were priories for nuns. Further down the Derwent, but not in Pickering Lythe, were Malton and Kirkham Priories.

From Pickering it is three miles to Thornton Bridge on the River Rye. As I rode down from the town of Pickering I crossed a flat, low-lying meadow, by estimation about four miles in circumference, which lies in Pickering parish. And before I reached the Rye I had to cross the Costa Beck, which receives Pickering Beck (a larger stream than itself) a mile below Pickering. From the River Rye I travelled more than a mile to Appleton, and two and a half miles from there to Henderskelfe, partly over low-lying, but mostly high, ground.

At Henderskelfe is a good stone structure built four-square like a castle with four towers, but its dimensions are small. The more recent building work seems to have been undertaken by the Greystock family, whose estate now belongs to Lord Dacre. I estimate that its park is four miles in circumference, and includes much fine young woodland. From Henderskelfe I travelled mostly over high ground to Shirhuten [*Sheriff Hutton*] Castle, and a mile before I arrived I passed Mr Gower's old manor house on my right hand.

I discovered at Sheriff Hutton that the castle was built by Ralph of Raby, the first of the Neville Earls of Westmorland; and I further learnt that during his lifetime he built or substantially enlarged or repaired three other castles also. In front of the castle entrance there is a base court with service buildings. The front of the castle itself has no ditch, but then it occupies a high position. I noted that the façade of the castle's first precinct has three large high towers, including the gatehouse in the centre. In the second precinct there are five or six towers. The imposing stairway up to the hall is very magnificent, as is the hall itself, and all the rest of the house; in fact I saw no house in the north so much like the palace of a prince. I was told there that the castle was built of stone brought from a quarry at Terrington two miles away. There is a park beside the castle. The reason for the castle's good condition is that the late Duke of Norfolk lived there for ten years, and after him the Duke of Richmond.

From Sheriff Hutton I travelled the seven miles back to York, in the Forest of Galtres the whole way. At least four miles of this journey was over low-lying meadowland and marshy terrain full of carrs; the rest was better ground, but not very high. The River Fosse, which serves to drain the forest, emerges from this side of it and flows to York. I saw very little woodland in this part of the forest. In York there is a building called David Hall, which is designated as the place where offences committed in Galtres are punished.

Leaving York I journeyed for eight miles to Tollerton, a manor and village which are perquisites of the treasurer of York Minster. My way took me over higher ground than elsewhere in Galtres, with reasonable amounts of woodland. At Tollerton I could see four miles away to my right Crayke Castle, which King Egbert granted to St Cuthbert. At the present time there are few signs of any ancient castle on the site. There is a hall of some antiquity, with other buildings, including a large stonevaulted stable. But the large square tower next to them, which provides additional accommodation on the hilltop, and which is very fine, was built entirely by Bishop Neville of Durham. Crayke has a park, and the boundary of the manor, which has an annual value of £40, extends to seven miles.

After Tollerton I travelled for a further two miles within the Forest of Galtres, but then reached its edge. And near here I could see away to my left the village of Myton, which is ten miles north-west of York. It was here that the Scots defeated an English army in the time of Edward II. A mile further, past reasonably good arable, pasture and meadowland, with some woods, I reached Helperby, and after another mile arrived at Thornton Bridge, a three-arched bridge across the deep and fast-flowing River Swale. I crossed the Swale again, by a wooden bridge, three miles further on at a remote place called Topcliffe. There is an attractive manor house at Topcliffe, on which the last Earl of Northumberland expended money; it stands on a hill about a half-mile from the town, almost on the river bank of the Swale. The manor is divided into two portions, of which the larger is well wooded, and extends six or seven miles in circumference.

Breckenbrough, where Mr Lascelles has built a very attractive house, lies four miles beyond Topcliffe, and next to it flows the River Wiske, which divides Breckenbrough manor from that of Kirby Wiske. To my right about a mile from Breckenbrough I could see the small market town of Thirsk, where the Lords Mowbray had a large castle. There is a park with attractive woodland around this castle, and a brook called the Cod Beck, which rises among the peaks of Black Moor, flows past Thirsk before joining the Willow Beck.

After Kirby Wiske I rode on for four miles over pasture and arable land to Northallerton, and I noticed that for much of my journey from Tollerton as far as Wiske Bridge (which is generally called Smeaton Bridge) I was passing along quite a fertile valley, between the Black Moor hills on the east, and the Richmondshire hills on the west, which lie a fair distance apart.

The town of Northallerton extends north and south along a single fine street. It has a large parish church, but I did not see any noblemen's tombs in it. A friary stood on the east side of the town, and on the same side, a mile before I reached Northallerton, I saw a hospital which had been established by a bishop of Durham. On the west side of the town, not far from the church, is the palace of the bishop of Durham, and this is strongly built with a good moat. And two bow-shots WNW of it a motte and ditches mark the site of the former Northallerton Castle, of which no portion of the masonry is now visible. A very small beck, commonly called Sunnebeck, flows through the town from east to west, and a little to the north outside the town is a single-arched stone bridge. This crosses a larger brook than Sunnebeck, which rises partly to the east, and flows westwards through the meadows between Castle Hills and the bishop's palace. Near here Sunnebeck flows into it, and less than half a mile downstream it joins the Wiske.

Northallertonshire falls wholly within the jurisdiction of the bishop of Durham, and those gentlemen with estates there hold them from the bishop. The most prominent gentry are the following: Malory; Conyers; Strangeways, of [*East*] Harlsey, where Judge Strangeways built an attractive castle; Vincent, of Smeaton parish, which lies just beyond Smeaton Bridge; Thwaites, whose house I saw on my left-hand side a little before Smeaton Bridge. There is very little woodland in Northallertonshire, and the only park is at Hutton, and now with no deer. This shire extends in one direction from within a short distance of Ripon to a point close to the bank of the Tees; on the east its boundary is the Black Moor hills, and on the west Richmondshire. I discovered that the reputed site of the Battle of the Standard, between the men of England and Scotland, is at a place called Cowton Moor, four miles north-west of Northallerton. Although there is good arable in Northallerton, yet the majority of the land which I saw at first hand between the town and Smeaton Bridge consisted of low-lying pasture and waste, partly overgrown with bracken.

I travelled the six miles from Northallerton to Smeaton Bridge over the Wiske, which flows from six miles away to the east of Smeaton. From there it is three miles to the crossing-point of the Tees over to Sockburn. There are important bridges over the Tees at Croft, Piercebridge, and Yarm, which is a stone bridge three miles above Stockton, and I have heard was built by Bishop Skirlaw. *cont. p. 110* [**1541**: 1/38-69]

I LEFT BARNARD CASTLE by crossing the very fine three-arched bridge over the Tees, and this brought me immediately into Richmondshire, which extends along this bank of the Tees right up to its source. There is quite reasonable woodland on both sides of the Tees in the Barnard Castle area. From the bridge I rode for a mile along the stony and craggy bank of the Tees to a beck called Thorsgill, one mile from Barnard Castle. This beck is crossed by a one-arched bridge just before it flows into the Tees, and Eggleston Priory overhangs the high bank of the Tees right at the beck's confluence. In the nave of Eggleston Church I saw two very fine tombs of grey marble; in the larger was buried a certain Sir Ralph Bowes, so I was told, and in the smaller was one of the Rokesbys. Immediately beneath the cliffs on both banks of the Tees next to Eggleston are outcrops of very fine marble. Marblers from both Barnard Castle and Eggleston take marble from here, some of which they dress, and some sell on elsewhere undressed.

Leaving Eggleston I rode past arable, woodland and pasture for two miles to Greta Bridge, which has two or three arches. The village of Greta stands on Watling Street, and derives its name from the River Greta which flows through it, and then enters the Tees next to Mr Rokesby's house. Nearby is a park enclosed with a stone wall; it is called Brignall Park and belongs to Lord Scrope. After Greta another five miles brought me to Ravensworth, but before arriving at the village and castle I had to cross the attractive River Ravensworth. This river rises seven or eight miles above the castle in the hills to the WNW, and three miles lower it flows into the River Swale, which at its closest point is three miles from Ravensworth Castle. There is nothing memorable about this castle, apart from two or three square towers, and a fine stable which has a conduit leading to the side of the hall. There is also a park three miles in circumference.

From Ravensworth it is three long miles to Richmond, and for one of these miles I was riding through a large wood on a hill, which had several raging streams running through it between stones down to the Swale. The tract of country between Ravensworth and Richmond is very hilly, with some good arable land but much waste. At Richmond I passed along a great long street before reaching the best part of the town at the top of the hill, known as the bailey and the castle. Some people are of the opinion that the area known as the bailey was once the castle's outer courtyard, and later was built over with houses. It had a wall, but this is now in ruins. Portions of four or five named gates still survive. In the town there is a chapel with unusual carvings on the walls, and local people imagine that it was once a temple of idols. Two miles from Richmond is Gilling, and here it is believed by some was the pre-conquest seat of the manorial lord.

I crossed the four-arched Richmond Bridge, and after a mile of difficult rocky terrain I rode for a further seven miles across moorland with few trees within sight, until I reached Middleham. Just before I entered the town I crossed the River Ure by a ford. Middleham is an attractive market town built on a craggy hill, at the top of which is the castle. This has reasonably good ditches, and the inner portion consisted of ancient work of the FitzRandolphs; but all the outer part of the castle is of very recent.construction, by the Lord Neville known as Daraby.

From Middleham it is only about a mile to Wensley, and three miles further to Bolton. The large stone bridge at Wensley was built across the river many years ago by a good inhabitant of the place, called Alwyn. Bolton is a very rough place, but its castle, which is not a large building and is all compressed within four or five towers, has an attractive park next to it. From there I went to the site two miles away of Lord Scrope's exploration for lead in a great rockface; and from there back to Middleham.

The next two miles, to Jervaulx Abbey, took me mostly past enclosed pasture land, and not far from Middleham I crossed the River Cover just before its confluence with the Ure away to my left. Masham, a pleasant bustling market town with a fine church, was four miles further, past woodland, pasture and some good arable land. At the far end of this little town a bridge took me across an attractive river called the Bourne, which joins the Ure a little further downstream. As I crossed the Bourne I saw the manor of one of the Aldboroughs lying on the opposite bank of the Ure near its confluence with this river.

From there I rode three or four miles to Grewelthorpe over hilly heathland, with some waste, and another three miles of similar terrain to Ripon. On my way, a half-mile after Thorpe, I passed close to Kirkby Malzeard, on my left hand side. This is a large parish, and the manor now belongs to the Earl of Derby, but Mowbray once had a large castle here. The countryside between Middleham and Ripon, and around Ripon itself, has plenty of woodland.

The older portion of Ripon was built largely to the north and east, as far as I could gather by looking at it, but the best parts of the town now are to the south and west. The old Ripon Abbey stood in a valley, one field distant from the later minster, and there is now a chapel dedicated to Our Lady on the site. Abbot Marmaduke of Fountains obtained this chapel from Archbishop Salvage of York, whose protégé he was, and from the prebendaries of Ripon. Once it belonged to him and his abbey he pulled down the east end, which was a piece of extremely ancient architecture, and replaced it with a fine new structure of squared masonry, but he left the very old fabric of the west end standing. He also began and completed an excellent high wall of squared masonry at the eastern end of the precinct in which the chapel stands; it had been his intention to continue the wall right around this precinct, and to establish a cell of Cistercian monks there. A member of the Engleby family is buried at the east end of this chapel, and there is another buried outside in the precinct. A chantry priest officiates in the chapel. But what struck me most of all was a row of three crosses standing at the eastern end of the chapel precinct. They must have commemorated the burials of some important men there, and they were of extremely ancient workmanship. These crosses, and the walls of this chapel of Our Lady, were probably the only surviving evidence left for me to see of the original town and monastery of Ripon, prior to its depopulation by the Danes.

The new minster, which now serves as the parish church, is a fine and large piece of architecture, and stands on the hill. In recent years its nave has been enlarged to a great width by the treasurer of the church, assisted by the gentry of the surrounding country. It has three towers surmounted by spires, two at the west end, and one over the crossing. The popular belief is that Archbishop Odo of Canterbury, when he accompanied the king into northern England, took pity on the devastated church at Ripon, and began a new building on the site of the present minster, or at least arranged for it to be built. Be that as it may there can be no doubt that the entire church now standing has been built since the conquest. Close to the minster were built the houses for the prebendaries, including also a fine palace for the archbishop. Next to this, built of squared masonry and arranged in an attractive quadrangle, are the houses for the vicars choral, which were built by Henry Bouet, archbishop of York.

The parish of Ripon is of very great extent, stretching in one direction as far as Pateley Bridge, seven miles away. This parish includes some chapels of ease, and there used to be a parish church called Allhallows near the northern part of the old town. But the true heart of the town now, and the place where the market square is, was at one time called Holly Hill, because holly trees grew there. The name suggests that this part of the town was built up more recently.

On the edge of Ripon, on its ENE side, may be seen a large artificial earthen mound thrown up in a flat field. This is now called Ilshow [*Ailcy*] Hill, and in all probability was an important fortress during the British period. Allhallows Hill is the name given to another mound, like the motte of a castle keep. This stands on the edge of a field behind the bishop's palace, right at the northern end of the town. Their positions mean that each mound is sited opposite the field of view of the other.

Ripon stands entirely on the nearer bank (as I approached it) of an attractive river called the Skell, which derives from the west and flows around the south of the town. It passes first under a stone bridge, then under a wooden bridge, and about a quarter-mile lower flows into the Ure; this is at a point roughly half-way between two stone bridges, North Bridge and Hewick Bridge, which cross the Ure about three-quarters of a mile apart.

Within the town of Ripon are three hospitals. Two of these, St Mary Magdalene and St John, were founded by the archbishops of York. Magdalene Hospital was on the nearer bank of the Skell, as I approached, and close to the river. St John's was on the further bank, and also quite near the river. The third hospital, St Anne's, was established by a gentleman in the locality, whose estate was inherited by several men through marriage, and has now been dispersed. St Anne's stands close to the nearer bank of the Skell, near the point where for a short distance the river is divided into two streams by weirs for mills. On the further bank of the Skell there used to be a large number of tentering-frames for the woollen cloths formerly manufactured in the town; but now the clothmaking industry has declined almost to nothing, and unemployment has increased severely. There is, however, still a fair held at Ripon around the feast of St Wilfrid, and this has a great reputation as a horse sale.

I rode from Ripon for about four miles, partly through woodland and partly beside arable and pasture, towards West Tanfield. On my way out of Ripon I passed a large park, six miles in circumference, which belongs to the archbishops of York. Because there is no bridge I had to cross by ferry in order to reach West Tanfield.

The small town of West Tanfield stands on a sloping site close to the Ure. The river water usually has a peaty colour, resulting from the type of moorland soil in Wensleydale, from which it flows. In the church there are several tombs to members of the Marmion family in a chapel on the north side. The oldest seems to be the one which lies beneath a canopy in the wall, but there is also one of a lady lying alone and dressed as a vowess, and another lady wearing a coronet on her head. In the centre of the chapel is a tall alabaster tomb which I was told belongs to one Lord John Marmion, and on the south side is another of the Marmions buried alone. There is a chantry at West Tanfield, which was founded by one of the Marmions, with a master and two priests; and in addition there is another chantry.

The castle at Tanfield – or rather, in its present state the mere manor house, stands close to the bank of the Ure. The only significant architecture which I saw there was a fine gatehouse with towers, and a hall of squared masonry. The bailiff or caretaker at Tanfield, whose name is Claregenet, has an old book about the Earls of Richmond and the Marmions. There are two fine parks there, and a reasonable amount of woodland. East Tanfield lies about a mile further downstream the River Ure. Somebody at West Tanfield told me that Marmion married one of three daughters who were the heiresses [*of the estate*]; but I must ascertain whether in fact there were not three Marmion daughters who were heiresses, and that Lord Fitzhugh did not marry one of them.

Leaving Ripon I crossed the River Skell, and shortly afterwards forded the Ure downstream from Hewick Bridge. On one side I could see the manor of Hutton Conyers, which is now owned by Malory. There used to be a park here, but now there are few trees in it. Although surrounded by areas of Richmondshire, this manor forms part of the territory and liberty of Northallerton. Richmondshire extends in one direction right up to the north bridge over the Ure by Ripon, and in another direction as far as Boroughbridge.

At the far end of Hewick Bridge, on the bank of the Ure, there is a fine chapel built of freestone by a hermit who was a stonemason; it is not entirely finished. On the other side of the road, opposite Hutton Conyers, I saw a manor which, as I remember, was called Gindene [*Givendale*]. There is a fine stone manor house here, which used to belong to Ward. The estate was inherited by three daughters, two of whom married Musgrove (of Cumberland and Westmorland) and Neville (of Thornton Bridge). From Givendale I crossed three miles of arable and pasture land to reach Boroughbridge, and here I crossed the Ure by a large stone bridge.

Boroughbridge stands on Watling Street, and is an impoverished place. A small brook called Tudlad [*River Tutt*], which rises about four or five miles to the west, flows through the town near one end of it, and shortly afterwards enters the Ure below Boroughbridge. Just outside the town, on the west side of Watling Street, stand four massive stones, their tops formed by human workmanship into points. At the present time they stand in three separate fields. I estimate that the first is twenty feet high and eighteen feet in circumference. From ground level up to about half its height it is approximately square, but above this it has been roughly fluted up to a point. But the topmost three or four feet (I should guess) have been ·broken off. Two more of similar shape stand together, within six or eight feet of each other, in a different field at least a bow-shot away; one is bigger than the other. The fourth is the largest and tallest of them all – I should estimate that it weighs the equivalent of five waggon loads. It stands in another field a good stone's throw away from the two together. On none of these stones could I find any inscription, but they have been very badly battered by the weather, and so it may be that they had inscriptions, which have been worn away. I assume that they were monuments placed here next to Watling Street by the Romans, where there was the most traffic, and so where they would be seen most often. They are all aligned from west to east.

Aldborough is about a quarter-mile from Boroughbridge. During the Roman period this was a great city on Watling Street, and stood on the south-west side of the River Ure. It was called 'Isuria Brigantum', and had a wall about a mile in circuit, of which I could still see some fragments, although nothing substantial. Aldborough now is a small village. In its parish church two or three knights of the Aldborough family are buried (induding Sir William and Sir Richard). They used to live in the parish, and their descendants still live there, although in reduced circumstances. The actual sites of the buildings of the Roman town are now large, fertile, arable fields, and every year in these fields ploughing turns up many Roman coins of silver and bronze. Burials, watercourses, mosaic pavements, spurs inlaid with jewels, and many other exotic things have also been found. At the edge of the field where the old town lay is a hill called Stodart [*Studforth Hill*], which looks like a castle motte.

Knaresborough is three or four miles from Aldborough, and my journey took me through pasture and arable, with some woodland. A mile before I reached Knaresborough I passed a park on my left hand; and there are two other parks belonging to the town. All are reasonably well wooded. The town itself, which takes its name from the craggy hill on which it is built, is not very large, nor very well built, but it has a busy market. The magnificent castle occupies a strong position on a crag, and on the sides where it is not defended by the River Nidd (which here runs in a barren stony valley) it has a very deep ditch hewn out of the rock. I counted eleven or twelve towers in the castle wall, in addition to a very fine tower in the second court.

March Bridge is one of Knaresborough's two stone bridges, and a short distance upstream from it, on the further bank as I approached, is a well with a remarkable property, which is called Dropping Well. Water continually seeps into it from the great rocks next to it, and this water is so cold and of such a composition that whenever anything falls from the rocks into the well, or is thrown in, or grows nearby on the rocks and is splashed by this water, it turns into stone. Or at any rate it takes on the appearance of stone, perhaps as a result of some sand or mineral property of the rocks being continually washed out by the springs trickling through them, and gradually adhering to such objects. I heard it said that at one time a stone conduit was built to carry water from this well across the Nidd to Knaresborough Priory, but that it fell into decay before the priory was dissolved. A little downstream from March Bridge, on the nearer bank of the Ure [*i.e. Nidd*] as I approached, I saw an old chapel in the cliff cut out of the solid rock.

Knaresborough Priory itself stands three-quarters of a mile below March Bridge on the nearer bank (before I crossed the Nidd). It was first established by a certain Robert Flower, who was the son of Tok Flower, twice mayor of York. He had previously spent a short period as a monk at

Newminster Abbey, Morpeth, having abandoned the estate and property of his father which, as the eldest son, he would have inherited. But desiring a life of solitude as a hermit he retired to the rocks beside the River Nidd, and when his holiness became known others went to join him there. So he affiliated his group with the order of friars whose purpose was the ransom of prisoners, known as the Trinitarian friars. Stoteville, when he was living at Knaresborough, gave lands to this house, but I cannot yet be sure whether he actually owned Knaresborough, or merely held custody of it for the king. The present owner is the duchy of Lancaster. I did hear that at one time King John was badly disposed towards Robert Flower, but that later he became a benefactor to him and his venture. Part of the Flower estate at York was granted to this priory, and the name Flower has only in recent years disappeared from York.

For the first two or three miles above Knaresborough the banks of the River Nidd are well wooded, but further up, right to the source, nearly all the land is devoid of wood and corn, and is merely forest ground, full of heather, moorland and bogs, with rocky hills. This forest extends about twenty miles in length from a mile below Knaresborough right up to Bolton in Craven, and in some places it is as much as eight miles wide. The forest's main woodland has decayed. Knaresborough is twelve miles from York, and fourteen miles, as the river flows, above the confluence of the Nidd with the Ure (there inaccurately called the Ouse) at Nun Monkton.

I left Knaresborough and crossed the Nidd, riding a mile (almost all through woodland) to Plompton, where there is a park, and a fine stone house which incorporates two towers. Its present owner is a man called Plompton, and he has recently increased his fine landholdings by marrying the daughter and heiress of the Babthorpe family. After Plompton the ground was stony for two miles, although reasonably fertile for corn and grass, and then I saw Spofforth a half-mile away to my left. The Earl of Northumberland had an excellent manor here, and a manor house with a park. But the house was badly damaged during the civil war between Henry VI and Edward IV by the Earl of Warwick and his brother the Marquis Montacute, to whom, as I recall, the Percy lands were granted.

Another three or four miles journey, through arable, pasture and some woodland, brought me to Wetherby, a small market town on a hill, where I saw a cross of ancient workmanship. Then I crossed the River Wharfe by a stone bridge and continued for six miles to Aberford, which is on Watling Street. In fact from a distance of two or three miles before I reached the main road I could see the level embankment on which Watling Street runs. I rode straight along this embankment for three miles or more, but then turned off to the left to visit Brotherton, three miles away. This was where Edward I's son Thomas was born, because the queen happened to go into labour here whilst out hunting. From Brotherton I took the stone causeway which runs about a mile to Ferrybridge, and which has several bridges under it to drain off water into the river from the low-lying meadows along the left bank of the Aire. Ferrybridge was where the first Lord FitzWalter of the Radcliffes was killed, as he fled from the Battle of Cock Beck. It is a roadside town about a half-mile from Pontefract, and although not large has quite good buildings. The bridge itself crosses the Aire and has seven arches.

From Ferrybridge I travelled to Doncaster via Wentbridge, and several miles before I arrived I observed again the very substantial embankment of Watling Street. After Doncaster I crossed three miles of open field country to reach Rossington Bridge. This is a wooden bridge spanning an attractive brook which derives from several springs to the west. The church and village of Rossington are a quarter-mile away on a small hill. *cont. p. 281* [1/77-88]

Lord Menel was the principal owner of the whole of Cleveland, and nearly all the landowning gentry families there were tenants of the Menel estate. Lord Menel held land as tenant of the archbishop of Canterbury, and at the present time the archbishop owns two estates consisting of lands in the north which were held by the Menels during the minority of the present Lord Conyers. The main seat of Lord Menel was at Whorlton in Cleveland, and since the estate was partitioned it passed to Mr Strangeways. Besides other manors in Cleveland Lord Menel owned Yarm, Seamer, Middleton and Greenhaw on the edge of Blackmore. He also owned the whole of Cheviot in Northumberland, and two other manors there. Lord Fauconberg's estate, which included Skelton Castle in Cleveland, has been divided between Mr Strangeways and Mr Conyers, and the castle has fallen to Conyers' share. [2/6-7]

A certain Ecmundeton, of an ancient gentry family, married one of Lord Davell's heiresses, and as a result he and his heirs retain one of the Davell manor houses in the Marshland area of Yorkshire, at Fockerby in the parish of Adlingfleet. There is an arm here of the River Ure [*i.e. Ouse - the arm is actually the River Trent*]. Fockerby is about a half-mile from Adlingfleet, which, although only a remote place, is the best town in the whole of Marshland. It lies six miles beyond Butterwick, and I am told that in the church there one or two members of the Davell family are buried. Ecmundeton's estate, now with a total yearly value of £140, includes lands of the Spain and Stapleton families. [2/15]

Sir Arthur Hopton told me that the majority of his estate formerly belonged to the Swillington family, who at one time owned land with an annual value in excess of £1,400. Their principal seat was at Swillington in Yorkshire, which is four miles from Pontefract Castle, in the neighbourhood of the River Aire. This Swillington still belongs to Sir Arthur Hopton, and in fact is the main portion of land that he owns ([*later note by Leland:*] It has recently been sold to Mr North, who then exchanged it with Sir George Darcy for Eynsham). [2/19]

The town of Richmond is paved and has a wall. The castle, beside the River Swale, forms as it were the nub of the encircling wall, which has three gates. Frenchgate is in the northern, most populous, part of the town, and there are also Finkle Street Gate and Bargate. All three gates have been destroyed, but traces of them remain. The wall, now ruinous, is not more than a half-mile around its perimeter, so that it encloses little more than the market place, the houses which surround it and the gardens behind them. Finkle Street suburb extends directly westward from the market place, and there is also a suburb outside Bargate. However, Frenchgate suburb is almost as large as the other two suburbs combined, and includes the parish church which serves the whole town. There is a large chapel dedicated to the Trinity in the market place, and a little beyond the limit of Frenchgate suburb is, or at least was until recently, the chapel of a woman hermit. Bargate suburb, with its chapel dedicated to St James, extends as far as the end of the bridge over the Swale, which is sometimes closed by a chain. Across the bridge there are no buildings. Behind Frenchgate is the grey friars, not far outside the wall, and their house, with meadow, orchard and a small wood, are also enclosed by a wall, through which a postern gate gives access from the market place. At the grey friars is the only conduit of water in the whole of Richmond. Not far from the friary wall is a chapel dedicated to St Anthony. The perimeter of the castle, which is now mere ruins, is almost as large as that of the town wall. The whole town and its suburbs lie on the further bank of the Swale, but on the nearer bank, not much more than 1,000 feet from Frenchgate suburb, is the cell of St Martin.

Middleham, on the nearer bank of the River Ure, has a market, which is held on Tuesday. The town itself is small, and has only one parish church. At one time, however, this was collegiate, and the incumbent is still known as the Dean of Middleham. In fact Richard III was responsible for making the church collegiate, because Middleham belonged to the Earl of Warwick, and the king stayed there. But Henry VII took away the lands with which the new college had been endowed. The town stands on a hillside, and Penhill, the great hill above it more than a mile away, is considered to be the highest hill in Richmondshire. Middleham

Castle adjoins the town on one side, and excepting Bolton is the finest castle in Richmondshire. The castle has two parks, Sonskue and Westpark, close to it, and a third, called Gaunless, a half-mile away. Westpark and Gaunless are well wooded. At the east end of Middleham there is a small hospital with a Jesus chapel.

Vensela [Wensley] is a small, poor market town beside the Ure, upstream from Middleham. It is not far from the edge of Middleham's Westpark. Grinton is a small market town on the nearer bank of the Swale, six miles west above Richmond. Like Wensley, some of its houses are roofed with slate, and some with thatch. Grinton market supplies corn and linen cloth for the population of Swaledale, whose principal occupation is the digging of lead ore. There are large hills on both sides of the dale, and from these the ore is extracted. Little corn is grown in Swaledale. At Catterick Bridge the only building is an inn, but the town of Catterick is a mile downstream, on the nearer bank of the Swale, and a furlong's distance from the river side. It is now a very poor town, and no longer has a market. Near Catterick church is an area called Catterick Swart or Sands, and here there is some indication of former buildings, as well as ancient squared stones dug up there.

Apart from Richmond Castle and Middleham Castle on the Ure, there are the following castles in Richmondshire. Killerby Castle, which belonged to the Conyers family, lies in ruins on the nearer bank of the Swale about three miles below Catterick Bridge. Hornby Castle, the principal seat of Lord Conyers, is three miles from the Swale; it is two miles south of Catterick and three miles north-west of Bedale. Lord Latimer has as his principal seat a fine castle at Snape. It stands in a valley, and around it are two or three well-wooded parks with lakes. Two miles away is Great [West] Tanfield, and here, on the banks of the Ure, stands Tanfield Castle, which passed from Lord Marmion into the FitzHugh family, and now belongs to Lord Parr.

Bolton is a very fine castle in Swaledale [*in fact Wensleydale*]. It stands on an earthwork, beneath which a small brook flows, less than a mile from the further bank of the Ure and, as I discovered, four miles from the River Swale. It is the principal seat of Lord Scrope. There is no town next to it, but the little market town of Wensley is two miles away to the east. Ravensworth Castle, three miles north-west of Richmond, is situated on marshy ground, with a park on slightly rising land beside it, an attractive village nearby, and a beck called Ravensworth [*Holme*] Beck flowing past it. It belongs to Lord Parr.

In the valley at Aldbrough, two miles south of Piercebridge on the Tees, may be seen substantial ruins of a house or small castle, next to a beck. Similar ruined buildings may be observed also at Caldwell, two miles west of Aldbrough. Caldwell takes its name from a small source or spring next to the ruins of the ancient house, water from which flows into a beck a furlong away. This beck rises in a bog about two miles to the south-west above Caldwell, flows away to Aldbrough, and then to the nearer bank of the Tees five miles downstream. In between Caldwell and Aldbrough are visible several artificial mounds and numerous ditches, some now full of water. Some of these ditches may be seen near St John's, which is the parish church serving both the aforesaid villages. Although there is a belief that they are the ruins of some ancient town, it is more likely that they were a military camp.

Sir James Metcalf has an excellent house in Wensleydale called Nappa, or colloquially 'No Castle'. It lies about seven miles west of Wensley or Vensela Market, the town which stands on the nearer bank of the Ure at the very point at which Wensleydale, to which it is said to give its name, begins. Inhabitants of Wensleydale are known as 'Vennones'. The Wensleydale area is very hilly, so that few crops are grown but many cattle are pastured.

Adjoining the nearer bank of the Ure, within a quarter-mile of Nappa, is Bishopdale. It runs up to the west between the higher reaches of Uredale and Swaledale [*i.e. Wensleydale and Wharfedale*]. Bishopdale belongs to the king, and includes a great expanse of wild moorland. There are red deer in the surrounding hills, and in mild winters the deer remain there, but in severe winters they move away from this extremely cold and exposed place.

Mr Bowes has a small house four miles north of Catterick. Mr Conyers of Marske has a good house in the village of Marske, which is less than a quarter-mile from the further bank of the Swale, and two miles west of Richmond. Sir Henry Gascoyne lives in an attractive house three miles north of Richmond called Sedbury, with a nice park containing a small lake. Mr Pudsey has a house a bowshot from the nearer bank of the Tees at Barforth, six miles downstream from Barnard Castle. A little below Greta Bridge, almost at the Greta's confluence with the Tees, Mr Rokesby has a house called Mortham. Mr Frank's attractive house at Kneeton is five miles north of Richmond. A modest gentleman called Wycliffe lives in a small village of the same name; but it is said that John Wycliffe the heretic was born at Hipswell, which is a poor village a good mile from Richmond.

Abbeys and priories on the Swale: Marrick, a priory of Benedictine nuns, was founded by the Aske family. It stands on the further bank five miles above Richmond. Sir Ralph Bowmer has a house in the village of Marrick, which stands on a hillside a half-mile away from the priory in a valley. Grinton is a mile upstream from Marrick, and in the valley on the nearer bank a mile downstream is a Cistercian nunnery called Ellerton Priory, which takes its name from the elder trees. A short distance below Richmond on the nearer bank is St Martin's Priory, a cell of St Mary's Abbey, York. On the further bank, a little lower, is an abbey of Premonstratensian canons dedicated to St Agatha [*Easby Abbey*]. It was founded by Lord Scrope.

On the Ure is Jervaulx (or Urivallis) Abbey, a house of Cistercian monks on the near bank, two miles below Middleham. It was originally founded by Lord Marmion, whose estate passed to the FitzHughs, and then the Parrs. Coverham, where there was good singing, lies on the further bank of the River Cover less than two miles west of Middleham; it was a Premonstratensian house. Fountains Abbey, a Cistercian monastery, lies in Richmondshire on the River Skell. Eggleston Priory, for Premonstratensian canons, lies on the nearer bank of the River Tees a mile downstream from Barnard Castle (which is on the further bank). About a quarter-mile below Eggleston, right on the riverbank, is a fine quarry of black marble mottled with white. Nun Monkton is on the River Nidd. There are no collegiate churches in Richmondshire, which is divided into two deaneries, Catterick and Richmond. The Archdeaconry of Richmond enjoys a good income, and exercises peculiar jurisdiction in Richmondshire, over which the bishop has no control.

Notable rivers in Richmondshire: The River Greta flows past a village called Barningham, which stands on its nearer bank. A gentry family of the same name, which in the past had a large estate but is now of modest means, lives at Barningham. Greta Bridge, where there are some inns, is about two miles away, and after that Mr Rokesby's house at Mortham, which stands on the nearer bank barely a quarter-mile from Greta Bridge. Less than a quarter-mile lower the Greta flows into the Tees. Lord Scrope has a park next to Greta Bridge, which is called Brignall Park, or in Latin 'Bellus Mons' ['*beautiful hill*'].

The River Wiske flows under Wiske Bridge, where there are no buildings, and then four miles to an attractive little Richmondshire settlement on the nearer bank called Danby, or (from the river name) Danby Wiske. Northallerton is about two miles downstream on the further bank, and then it passes the village of Kirby, before joining the Swale. There is a brook in this area called Leeming Beck. This flows from Bedale, which stands on the nearer bank, and is a fine market town, second only to Richmond itself in the shire. From Bedale it flows to Leeming village, which lies on the road from Richmond to York, five miles on this side of Catterick Bridge.

Above Grinton the Swale flows in a single valley for a number of miles, but in the upper reaches it is fed by many springs which flow into Swaledale. A little below Marske, Mr Conyers' house at the end of Swaledale, an attractive stream flows through Applegarthdale into the further bank of the Swale.

I am told that in Richmondshire the name Uredale is not used, and the valley in which the upper reaches of the Ure flows is called Wensleydale. Some people maintain that the source of the Ure is Mossdale Moor, which is in Richmondshire. After it has flowed through Wensleydale (also in Richmondshire) it comes to Middleham, and then two miles to Jervaulx Abbey. From here it is six miles to [*West*] Tanfield village, on the further bank, where Lord Parr has a castle and a large wooded park. Then one mile further on the same bank is Little [*East*] Tanfield, the home of Workcop the herald. Up to this point, I am told, both banks of the Ure lie in Richmondshire. Three miles below Little Tanfield the Ure flows around one side of Ripon (the River Skell flows around the other), and then continues to Boroughbridge.

The River Cover, I have heard it said, rises near Scale Park beside Craven, and descends after two or three miles to a place called Coverdale [?]; it then flows past St Si[mon]'s chapel to Coverham, and so into the Ure.

Mr Place lives at a place called Halnaby, seven miles north-east of Richmond. Mr Lascelles lives in a fine house next to the little town of Danby Wiske. Mr

Catterick also lives in an attractive house, at Stanwick. This is a half-mile east of the village of Caldwell, which is where the military camp is still visible.

[*Boundaries:*] Almost from its sources the River Tees forms the northern boundary, dividing Richmondshire (on the nearer bank) from the bishopric [*of Durham*] for a distance, at a guess, of some eighteen miles. Wiske Bridge, which lies three miles away from the nearer bank of the Tees, marks the boundary between Richmondshire and Cleveland. The borders of the land of Craven march with that of Richmondshire, portions of both Yorkshire and Craven lying southwest of Richmondshire.

Bowes is a roadside settlement in Richmondshire, which lies eight miles almost directly due west of Richmond, and eight miles further to the west there is a place called Maiden Castle. Here is a great round pile of rough stones, some small and some large, arranged in the shape of a cairn, some sixty feet in circumference. Surmounting them all and forming the apex is a single stone one and a half yards tall, so that, including this stone, the whole structure is approximately eighteen feet high. It stands on a hill right on the edge of Stainmore, and marks the boundary between Richmondshire and Westmorland. A quarter-mile north of Maiden Castle there is a beck which flows into the Tees.

Arkengarthdale runs predominantly up towards north, and is separated from Swaledale by a beck named after it. It produces some bigg-barley and oats, but little or no wood. Swaledale grows little corn and no woodland, but much grass, as well as heather and some nut trees. The wood they burn for smelting their lead is brought from other parts of Richmondshire and from County Durham. Uredale produces very little corn except bigg-barley and oats, but it has abundant grassland commons. Coverdale is even worse off for arable than Swaledale or Uredale, and it has no woodland except around Coverham Abbey. Bishopdale runs up to the west into Westmorland from the top of Coverdale [*Carlton*] Moor. It has no corn, but deer live there, and there is a very attractive carr or lake in the dale. In these dales and the mountainous country between them there is very little woodland, or none at all. However, all the rest of Richmondshire to the east of the hills and dales is well supplied with arable land, on which is grown abundant wheat and rye, and it has reasonably good meadowland and woods. The best woods lie to the east of the Rivers Swale and Ure.

In the dales of Richmondshire they use heather, peat and turves for fuel. And in the areas where they clear the heather good grassland springs up, sufficient to feed cattle for a year or two, until the heather infests it again. There are good supplies of building stone in very many places in Richmondshire. The shire has no coal pits, although the eastern parts burn a great deal of sea-coal brought from County Durham.

Lord Conyers generally dwells at Horneby [*Halnaby*], his castle in Richmondshire. Lord Latimer has a good house at Sinnington in Black Moor, not far from Ripon [*i.e. Pickering*]. The Strickland family has a fine manor house at Thornton Bridge, two miles from Ripon. Stamford Bridge, the site of the battle against the Danes, lies five or six miles due east of York in the direction of Kirkham Priory. Wressle, on the Derwent, was once a very fine and favourite castle of the Percy family. Mulgrave Castle, not far from Whitby, used to belong to the Bigot family, but Mr Bigot's seat now is Mount Ferrant Castle not far from Settrington. The principal seat of the Metcalf family is called Nappa Castle in Richmondshire. Myllam [*Middleham*] Castle, also in Richmondshire, enjoys a very good supply of red and fallow deer. [4/25-33]

The battle of Towton, where Edward IV's father was killed, took place three miles from Sherburn [*in Elmet*] in Yorkshire. The Cock Beck flows near the battlefield, and runs into the Wharfe this side of Tadcaster. On the battlefield itself a vast number of men died and were buried there. Mr Hungate, grandfather of the court, collected a large number of their bones, and arranged for them to be buried in the churchyard at Saxton, a mile and a half from Sherburn. Hungate, clerk of the queen's stable, is one of the younger sons of the Hungate who now lives at Saxton. Lord Dacors and the Earl of Westmorland, both killed at Towton, are buried at Saxton; Westmorland is buried inside the church, but Dakers has a modest grave in the churchyard. At the site of the battle there is a chapel or hermitage to commemorate and pray for the men who died there. [4/77]

Knappey [*Nappa Hall*] in Yorkshire, now the principal house of the Metcalfs, was bought by one Thomas Metcalf (son of James Metcalf) from one of the Lords Scrope of Bolton. At the time it was a piece of land worth £4 per annum, and the house there was little better than a cottage. But Thomas began building work there, including two very fine towers and other apartments. Thomas had a son James, and his son is the present heir. The first three Metcalfs all lived to a great age, and Thomas was an important official in the region, being steward, caretaker or receiver of the Richmond estate. As a result of this he grew rich and could afford both to build and to purchase. At the present day many other small pieces of land are annexed to Nappa, and in the country town called [? *Askrigg*] and other nearby places three hundred men can show that they are related to the Metcalfs. [4/86]

The estate of the Mallett family of Yorkshire has been utterly dispersed as a result of sales and female descendants, so that only one of them now owns land, and that is worth a mere £30 per annum. His best house is at Normanton, three miles downstream from Wakefield, but a mile from the nearer bank of the River Calder. He also owns land on this side of the Calder three miles above Wakefield in the parish of Altoft. It is clear from the ruins that there was a manor house there, and the place is now named Malleting, after the family name. [4/91]

The Church of St Nicholas, Beverley, commonly called Holme Church, is where there is a canal for small boats; the distance from the River Hull to the bridge at Holme on this canal is about a half-mile.

South Burton, or Bishop's Burton, is two miles from Beverley on the York road. Walkington is two miles west of Beverley. North Burton is a half-mile south-west of Leconfield, and Scorborough a mile north-east of Leconfield. Dalton is four miles north-west of Beverley; the provost has an attractive house there. There were several crosses, each one a mile from Beverley, which marked the limit of the town's sanctuary; one was Molescroft Cross, close to the entrance to Leconfield Park, and there were others on the way to North Burton, on the way to Kilnwick Green, and going south towards the Humber. Sigglesthorne is in Holderness. [4/180]

Wakefield on the Calder is a very busy market town, and reasonably large. It has a good supply of meat, and also of fish, both from the sea and from the several nearby rivers. Consequently all foodstuffs are very cheap there. An honest man will feed well there for twopence a meal. The town has only one principal church, but there is also a chapel, and here lived a female hermit up until the time when she was discovered to be pregnant. In addition there is a chapel dedicated to Our Lady on Calder Bridge, where many pilgrims are accustomed to go to worship. A furlong or more outside the town can be seen ditches and banks, as well as an artificial earthen mound marking the position of a watch tower. From these it seems that there was a castle there. I have read that the de Warennes, Earls of Surrey, once owned this town. It now depends entirely on the cloth trade. The Duke of York, Edward IV's father, was killed in battle at Wakefield.

Bradford is a smart, busy market town, about half the size of Wakefield, or a little more. It has one parish church, and a chapel dedicated to St Sitha. Its mainstay is the cloth industry, and it lies six miles from Halifax and four miles from Christestal [*Kirkstall*] Abbey. Three brooks meet in the town. One rises above Bowling Hall, which would make its source a mile and a half from the town, and when it reaches the town there is a one-arched bridge over it. The second rises two miles away, and has a mill as well as a bridge. The third rises four miles away. Bowling Hall used to belong to the Bowling family, but now it is owned by the Tempests.

Beverley is a very large town, but I could see no sign that it had ever been walled, even though it had certain stone gates built with portcullises for defence. The town contains three parish churches; the minster church in which St John, once bishop of York, is buried; and one chapel. There are also houses of grey friars and black friars, and a commandery of the order of St John. A large channel has been cut from Beverley to the bank of the River Hull, which enables attractive boats to visit the town. A small freshwater brook flows to the town from the nearby Westwood Park, which belongs to the bishop. Many old and important privileges belong to Beverley, as to a place of sanctuary. The common seal of the town includes the figure of a beaver. Bede gave the name 'Wood of Deira' or in Old English 'Deirewauld' to the place where Beverley now stands. Long ago there was an abbey of monks and nuns, which was virtually destroyed by the Danes, and this stood in place of the minster. Brithung, who was St John's deacon, was once the Abbot at Beverley, and both he and St Winwaldus are buried there.

Leeds, two miles below Kirkstall Abbey on the River Aire, is an attractive market town, as large as Bradford, but not so busy. It has a single parish church, of quite good architecture. Cloth is its main industry. [5/38-9]

Richard, Lord Scrope was Chancellor of England during the reign of Richard II, and it was he who built Bolton Castle from its foundations up. It has four large and strong towers, and these contain all the important apartments; it took eighteen years to build, at an annual cost of nearly £700. It stands on a craggy hillside alongside Bolton village, four miles from Middleham, and it was completed before the death of Richard II. One thing which I was very much struck by in the hall at Bolton, was the way in which the chimneys are built in cavities along the sides of the walls separating the hall windows. Through these cavities, and without the use of louvres, smoke is very cleverly drawn off from the hall fireplace. The majority of the timber used in building Bolton Castle was fetched from Engleby Forest in Cumberland, and in order to transport it Richard, Lord Scrope, had stationed along the route teams of oxen to relay it from place to place until it reached Bolton. There is a very fine clock at Bolton, which marks the movement of the sun and the moon, and other predictions. The park at Bolton has a stone wall, and two miles beyond Bolton there is a hill containing a lead mine.

The same Richard, Lord Scrope purchased the inheritance of the St Quintin family, owners of Hornby Castle in Richmondshire. But he was content that a servant of his, whose name was Conyers, should take precedence over him as ward of the estate, and so he acquired Hornby Castle. William Conyers, the first Lord Conyers, who was the present lord's grandfather, spent a large sum on the castle, which had previously been only a mediocre building.

The inner portion of Middleham Castle had been built before it came into the possession of the Neville family. The ruins of a small castle, or tower, stand on a hilltop, called Penhill, which is two miles from Middleham. Like Middleham itself, this belonged to Ralph Fitzrandolf. Around Middleham, and belonging to it, are four or five parks, some of which are reasonably well wooded. There is also quite good woodland around Jervaulx Abbey.

There is a fine bridge of three or four arches across the Ure at Wensley, a mile or more above Middleham. It was built over two hundred years ago by the parson of Wensley, whose name was Alwyn. There are no very significant bridges over the Ure above Wensley, although there is Bainbridge, and further up is Aysgarth Bridge, where the river falls a great distance between two precipitous rocks. The bridge across the Ure near Middleham is merely a wooden construction. About a mile below Jervaulx Abbey there is a large old bridge over the Ure, called Kilgram Bridge. From there it is almost four miles downstream to Masham Bridge. This is a timber bridge, and lies a little below Masham. Six miles lower, on the nearer side of Ripon, is North Bridge, with seven stone arches. Bridge Hewick is a quarter-mile lower, or less, and this has three arches. The River Skell enters the Ure between these two bridges.

There are five wapentakes in Richmondshire, and in delineating Yorkshire this whole area is reckoned to lie in the North Riding. Bishopdale abuts the Craven region, and the Ure, which flows through Wensleydale, adjoins Bishopdale. The upper end of Wensleydale is a royal forest of red deer. The Ure rises in a moss about a mile above Coteren Hill [*Cotter End*], some fourteen miles west of Middleham. The whole summit of Cotter End, and a little beyond, lies in Richmondshire, but on the far side of the hill there is a beck called Hell Gill, because it flows in such a deathly place. This beck is a tributary of the Ure, and defines the boundary between Richmondshire and Westmorland.

Swaledale lies beyond Wensleydale, and from the hills and crags on each side many brooks flow into the River Swale. Bridges on the Swale: A fine bridge at Grinton, five miles above Richmond; then Richmond Bridge; three miles lower Catterick Bridge, of four stone arches; then five miles lower Morton Bridge, which is wooden; five miles to Skipton Bridge, also wooden; three miles to Topcliffe Bridge (wooden); three miles to Thornton (stone); then to Myton, which is near its confluence with the Ure.

Some seams of coal have been discovered high up in the mountainous western part of Richmondshire, but they are not exploited because of the difficulty of transporting the coal to the lowland part. Most of the coal which is used in the area around Richmond town is brought from Rayle Pits in the Auckland region. Coal seams are exposed in some places in the cliffs along the coast, as around Coquet Island and elsewhere; and some people prefer to restrict the expression 'sea-coal' to such seams. But they are not so good as the coal which is dug inland.

Seams of coal are sometimes three feet thick, sometimes as much as almost four feet, and the principal seams can be as thick as the height of a man. The skill lies in reaching the coal with the least effort expended in deep digging. Some seams lie beneath overburdens of rocks and stones; indeed there is a theory that coal actually lies under the rock that Durham Cathedral is built on.

In a book at Lord Scrope's I read that the heirs to Lord Egremont's estate were Lucy, Fitzwalter, Haverington and Multon. The book also described the privileges which John of Brittany, Earl of Richmond, claimed for both his shire and town of Richmond. They included the right to legislate for his own courts, liberties for his borough including two annual fairs to be held there, exclusive right to maintain a gaol for the shire, and free warren on his own land, forest land in Wensleydale, and several other places. I read in the same book that, together with Beatrice his wife, John of Brittany, Earl of Richmond agreed with the prior of Eggleston that six canons should be resident permanently at Richmond Castle to sing the offices.

Noblemen's tombs in the church at Ripon: In the north transept there are two tombs with effigies of members of the Markenfeld family and their wives. In a chapel in the south transept is a tomb of one of the Malorys; several others, I was told, are buried outside under flat slabs. On the north side of the quire is a Latin epitaph: 'Ranulph Picot died A.D. 1503'. The relics of St Wilfrid which were buried under an arch near the high altar have recently been removed. There are five fine arches between the nave and the side aisles. The nave itself is very wide, and has lately been built anew, especially by a prebendary of the church (although I later heard that he was merely the paymaster for the work). There are two or three arches in each of the transepts.

The Latin inscription on the new wall of St Mary's Chapel, Ripon: 'St Cuthbert, bishop of Lindisfarne, was a monk here. St Eata, archbishop of York, was a monk here. St Wilfrid, archbishop of York, was a monk here, and the first abbot. St Willibrord, archbishop of Walretensis [*Utrecht*], was a monk here'.

The River Nidd rises five miles above Pateley Bridge towards the west, a short distance this side of a chapel called Middlesmoor, which, so far as I could discover, lies in the parish of Kirkby Malzeard. From Pateley Bridge (wooden) and village, which are in Ripon parish, its course is as follows: Newbridge (wooden), three miles; Killinghall Bridge (one large stone arch), three miles; a further three miles to Knaresborough (west bridge of three stone arches, and a little lower March Bridge of three arches – both serve the town of Knaresborough); Gribololbridge [?*Goldsborough Bridge*] (a very large bridge of a single span), about a mile; Walshford Bridge (four arches), four miles; Cattal Bridge (wooden), two miles; Skip Bridge (wooden, with a large causeway). Skip Bridge is the last and lowest bridge on the River Nidd. Its causeway has nineteen small bridges to overcome and carry the road across carrs which flow from the surrounding marshland. It was constructed by a man named Blackburn, who was twice Mayor of York, and he also built a causeway outside one of York's suburbs. He has a solemn obit in York Minster, and a chantry at Richmond. Because his children were very extravagant he established four chantries at All Hallows in North Street, York, and a further four at All Hallows, Pavement. The River Cover rises six miles to the west of Coverham Priory. There is a bridge across it a short distance upstream from the priory, and barely two miles lower it flows into the Ure, a little below Middleham Bridge. Between its source and Coverham Priory there is nothing worth recording. The River Burn rises in the western hills at a place called Moor Head, and it flows from the west into the Ure a little below the town and bridge of Masham. By its confluence, on the opposite bank, stands the village of Aldburgh. A mile further east stands a house called Thorp [? *Perrow*], which belongs to Mr Danby. But he has another house at Farnby, two miles from Leeds, and lives there more of the time.

There are two manors not very far from Ripon, called Norton Conyers and Hutton Conyers. The former belongs to Norton, the latter to Malory, and they were inherited by their ancestors through two daughters, heiresses of Conyers. Malory has another house not far from Fountains, called High Studley. There are three Studleys adjacent to each other – High, Middle and Low. Plompton's seat is at Plompton, a mile from Knaresborough; he has also inherited by marriage a large part of the Babthorpe estate, although the lawyer of that name retains Babthorpe itself, which, as I recall, is in Holderness [*actually at Hemingbrough, east of Selby*]. Markingfield lives in his manor house at Markingfield, which is named after him. Wyville lives on the further bank of the Ure, a little above Masham. Lord Lovell had a castle at Killerby, which lies within a quarter-mile of the nearer bank of the River Swale, a mile below Catterick Bridge. Mr Metcalf now rents this manor from the king. Substantial ruins of the castle are still visible, and some people say that a water supply was fed by conduits to the tops of some of the towers. [5/133-45]

APPENDIX
THE WELSH ITINERARY

THERE ARE THREE DIFFICULTIES *facing anyone attempting to work on Leland's surviving notes on Wales. In the first place they are even more diverse and scattered than the English equivalent. Secondly, most of his material takes the form of lists or random notes, rather than journeys, so that it is hard to make out where he went or in what order, or indeed whether he ever visited many of the places he described. And thirdly, for a non-Welsh speaker, the nomenclature of place-names as received through the prism of Leland's Tudor English creates uncertainty and confusion. Miss Toulmin Smith encountered these problems, so swept all the notes relating to Wales into volume 3 of her five-volume set, but struggled to present them in any coherent order. In my first edition I dodged the issue by omitting Wales entirely, and sub-titling my book, 'Travels in Tudor England'.*

For this edition I have grasped some of the nettle. There are the vestiges of a journey (which can be dated to 1539 – see p. xlviii) that Leland made through Monmouthshire and into Glamorgan (and perhaps beyond). I have excluded the Glamorgan material, which takes the form of notes on the different commotes, but I have added a chapter on Monmouthshire to the main text in its alphabetical place, and treated it in the same way as the English counties – of which it was one for several centuries after Leland. But there is also a more extended journey, from Montgomery, Hay and Brecon to Pembrokeshire and then through mid-Wales to Shropshire, which is written as itinerary (mostly), and forms the prelude to Leland's 1538 expedition to Lancashire and the north. Rather than segment it, Welsh county by county, I present it in this appendix as a narrative, as it is found in Leland's manuscript – and transcribed by Toulmin Smith in her volume 3, pp. 38-42, 110-26.

I have however made one rearrangement and two omissions. I have transferred Leland's description of Brecon to its appropriate position, but omitted descriptive passages about places in Brecknock which he appears not to have visited on this journey (and perhaps not at all). I have also omitted the descriptions of rivers, lakes, mountains and other landscape features in a part of mid-Wales centred on Strata Florida, Leland evidently stayed there for some time, and collected information either by taking excursions in various directions, or from interrogating the abbot and his monks. I have noted these omissions below where they occur.

The account of the 1538 journey, so much as survives, begins at Hailes in Gloucestershire, and the stages before Leland reaches Montgomery will be found on pp. 142 and 405. Leland leaves Wales between Welshpool and Alberbury, and the next stage of his journey will be found on pp. 304-5.

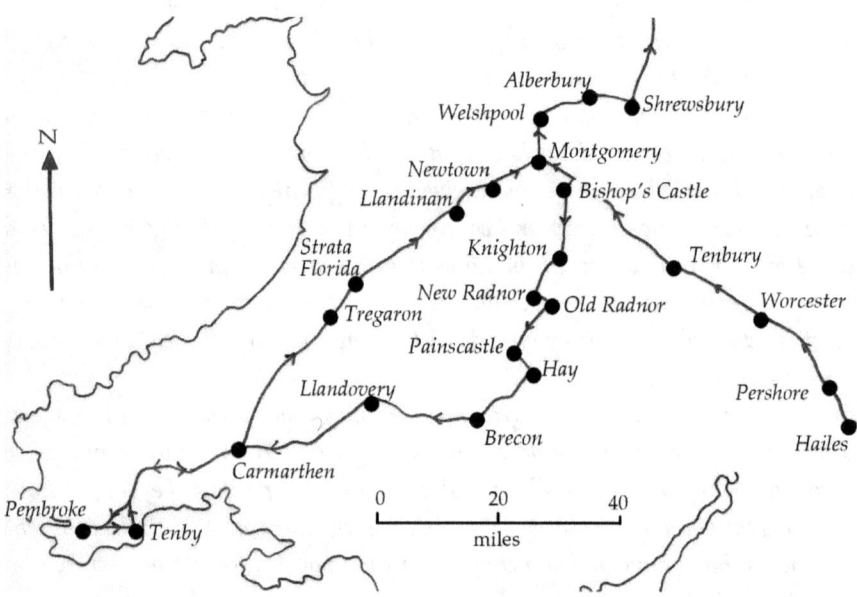

TWO MILES on this side of Montgomery on the way from there to Bishop's Castle, is a river which flows out of the nearby hills called the Taidbrooke [? *Caebitra*]. It rises from a hillside within a mile of Bisshops Toune [*Bishop's Castle*] and flows into the Kenlet [*Camlad*] in the valley by Montgomery. Marton Pool, quite large and well stocked with fish, is three miles from Montgomery and two miles from Chirbury Priory, which was recently suppressed.

Halfway between Bishop's Castle and Montgomery is a pleasant stream which divides the lordship of Caus, a notable part of Shropshire, from Chirbury hundred. Caus, which at one time belonged to the Duke of Buckingham, wraps itself in an extraordinary fashion around the upper parts of Shropshire.

Offa's Dyke is clearly visible for a distance of two miles almost halfway between Bishop's Castle and Montgomery. It is not very far from the motte on a hilltop, and it marks the boundary between Caus lordship, or Montgomery, and Herefordshire; and again not far along it slightly impinges on Chirbury hundred, and then passes a little way by Caus again. I was told at Montgomery that Offa's Dike is visible to some extent in the Radnor area, and also within three miles of Oswestry.

On the way from Bishop's Castle to Clun lordship there is a large wood which grows down the hillside, and beneath the hill within a mile and a half of Bishop's Castle is a small river called the Unk. It flows past this wooded hill, and a quarter-mile on this side of Clun Castle it flows into the Clun. The Clun flows into the Teme at Leintwardine. Between Clun and Knighton there is a river called Cluideford [?], which flows for a short distance before entering the Teme. The River Teme at Knighton is the boundary between Maelienydd and Clun lordships, and Knighton, as I recall, stands between two rivers. It is the Teme that flows down from Knighton, having risen five or six miles above the town in the Maelienydd hills, a half-mile above a chapel called, as I remember, Bostel.

About halfway between Knighton and [New] Radnor the Lugg flows out of Maelienydd and then down to Presteigne, which is a good market town. Nearby is the boundary between Presteigne lordship and Lug Harneis [? *Richard's Castle*] lordship, belonging to the barony of Burford. Steple-Castelle [? *Castell Foel Allt*] on the Lugg is in Lug Harneis in Burford barony. Presteigne town (which in Welsh is called Llanandras) serves as the market for corn for most of Maelienydd. Welshpool, a market town, takes its name from a nearby pool, which is quite large and well stocked with fish.

Montgomery was ravished by Owain Glyndŵr, and he partially destroyed Radnor. There is a tradition there that after he had gained the castle he took its garrison of sixty men and caused them to be beheaded on the edge of the castle yard; and that where their blood was shed a certain plant called bloodwort has since grown. At Radnor there is a chapel beside the church in the churchyard. Radnor wool is much praised. The valley around Radnor, which extends in one direction to Leominster, grows very abundant corn and grass. Some people say that the Welsh name for Leominster, Llanllieni, derives from the flax or hemp that grows thereabouts. But this is false, as the name refers to 'lion'. The Vale of

Radnor goes in one direction towards Chester and in the other towards Shrewsbury. There is a hill next to Old Radnor called Pencraig.

As I came from Radnor to Hay I passed Old Radnor on my left hand set on a hill two miles from New Radnor. Some people say that a market used to be held at Old Radnor. It still has a very fine church which is well maintained. Within two miles from Radnor I crossed a brook called Wadele [Cynon] that flows into the Lugg, and a mile or two further on I passed on my left Huntington Castle, which had belonged to the Duke of Buckingham. And a mile or more beyond this I crossed at Newchurch the River Arrow that flows to Leominster. The Arrow rises not far from Glascŵm, where there is a church but few houses. From there it is at least a mile before it reaches Newchurch, and then it flows through the fine park of Huntington Castle. Two miles or more beyond Newchurch I could see Painscastle at least a mile away on my right as I passed by.

Approaching Hay, as I began to descend I could see on the other side of the Wye, a good mile away from Hay, the castle of Clyro. After crossing the River Wye, which sorely troubled my horse because I did not have good information about the ford, I arrived at Hay as night was falling.

Hay stands close against the Wye, and still shows evidence of a really strong wall, with three gates and a postern in it. There is a castle, too, which at one time must have been really imposing. There is only one poor parish church within the town, but in the suburb close to the Wye is quite a fine parish church. Also in the suburb is a chapel where on a Sunday I heard mass. Not far from the parish church in the suburb is a large man-made mound of earth, either for a windmill to stand on, or for some military purpose.

There is still a market held in Hay, but inside the walls the town is remarkably decayed, and this destruction is attributed to Owen Glyndŵr. In the town I was shown the ruins of a house that had belonged to a gentleman named Walwyn, who was responsible for Prince Llewelyn's sudden capture at Builth Castle, where he was beheaded and his head sent to the king.

The Dulas is a pleasant river which rises in the mountains about three miles from Hay and flows right down to the town and into the Wye by the east gate. When the fields nearby are ploughed Roman coins are very often found, and the common expression there is that they are Jews' money. The town belonged to the Duke of Buckingham, and his son Lord

THE WELSH ITINERARY 471

Stafford now owns it. When one looks out of the west gate of Hay, Arthur's Hill is clearly visible and some other peaks along the ridge.

When I came halfway between Hay and Brecon I passed on my left side the great ruins of Bronllys in Cantreceli [*the Cantref Selyf*], and I also saw, two miles from Bronllys on the left the ruins of Dinas Castle on top of a hill. So then to Brecon, where as I came downhill close to the town I could see the River Honddu below me, and I entered the suburb by Porte Hene [*the old gate*].

Brecon has a wall with four gates. The upper gates are Old Gate and High Gate to the north, and the West Gate is by the Dominican friary. These are in the suburbs. Welsh names for these gates are Porthene hichca [*Porth hen ucha*], the upper or old gate; Portbont, the Bridgate, also known as West Gate; Portissa, the lower gate, also known as East Gate; Portdoure, the water gate, also known as Portwiske. In addition to these gates there is another at the start of a suburb, which is also called Porthene [*the old gate*].

In the town is a mighty great chapel of St Mary with a large bell tower. It is built of expensive hard squared masonry and cost £1,000. The parish church [*i.e. now Brecon Cathedral*] was on the site of the priory. It existed before the priory, and is still there, outside the town wall to the north on the bank of the Honddu. There is also a parish church called Llanvaes, which means outside, that is to say, outside the walls. It stands between the River Usk and the Taranell brook at the lower end of Brecon town. And in the east suburb there is a hospital with a chapel.

The castle stands outside the town, separated from it by the River Honddu, over which is a two-arched high bridge giving access to the castle. The castle is very large, strong and well maintained, with a very large, fine keep. There is evidence of an excavation which was an attempt to divert part of the Honddu around Brecon to the Usk and thus make it into an island.

A market is held twice a week, on Wednesdays and Saturdays. Roman millstones have been found in the fields around the town. Immediately downstream from the great bridge, at the end of the lower part of the castle, the Honddu flows into the Usk. But Usk Bridge at Brecon was thrown down by the Usk in spate on 16 November 1534, not as a result of rain, but of snow that melted off the mountains. The water flowed three feet above the top of the high bridge, and the circle mark [*?flood marker*] can be seen almost halfway up the cloister wall of the Blackfriars.

Only the market belongs to the manor of Brecon, and the only priory in the manor within living memory was the Benedictine house, a cell of Battle Abbey, founded by Bernard de Neufmarché. [*passages omitted here, see p. 468*]

On my way from Brecon to Llanameueri [*Llandovery*] before I had gone three miles I entered the great forest of Brecknock, where until recently one could not pass without paying a toll, and through there for three miles to the little forest. I kept the River Usk on the right side all the time, and about the end of the little forest I saw a construction by the river strongly built as a lodge. Local people say it was built by a lady, Malt Walbere [*Maud de Braose*], who also built much of Brecon Castle. She is known by some people as Matabrune, and many stories are told of her being a witch or hag. About a mile further I came to Trecastle, which was once a large borough and market, but now much of it is in ruins, and the ruined castle may be seen nearby. In the valley below the town flows Luggan brook [*Logyn*], which rises two miles away in a marsh on a hillside and joins the Usk by Trecastle. On the far side of this river, close to Trecastle, is being built a place called the Bishop's Town, which is governed from Llanddew manor a mile from Brecon (Trecastle is governed by Brecon).

I travelled uphill for more than a mile, leaving on my right hand Mynydd Du, the Black Mountain, and two miles further on I saw on my left the source of the River Usk, from a fountain or spring called Blaen Usk. The terrain between Trecastle and Llandovery is hilly and largely devoid of woodland, but towards the valley where Llandovery sits there is quite abundant pasture and arable. It should be noted here that less than thirty years ago no barley was sown in either Brecon or Llandovery lordships, and the inhabitants bought their barley, and much of their other grain, from places in Herefordshire. But now they have enough for their own use and also to sell.

About three miles on this side of Llandovery is the course of a very slight stream, and this forms the boundary between the lordships of Brecon and Llandovery. Trecastle is nine miles from Brecon, and Llandovery six miles further on. Shortly before I reached Llandovery I passed over a brook called Gwydderig, which flowed a little further on into the Towy, not far from Llandovery. And not far from this brook I crossed the River Brân, which rises twelve miles away and flows close to the foot of Llandovery Castle. Almost by it I then crossed a little brook called Euery [*?Nant Bawddwr*], which flows through the middle of Llandovery town. So the castle has the River Brân on one side of it, and on the other Nant Bawddwr, which also flows into the great Towy river.

Llandovery is a poor market town, which relies heavily on visits from traders who carry fish from the Carmarthen area to the lower parts of Wales. There is only one street, and that is poorly built of thatched houses. Belonging to the town is one church within it, and another a quarter-mile outside.

Less than two furlongs after I had left Llandovery I rode across the River Towy, which in winter often drowns people here because it lacks a bridge, and then before I arrived at Aber-Marlais four miles further I crossed two brooks – one was called Mynys. The Marlais brook flows through the park to which it gives its name, for no great distance before it enters the Towy. In Marlais Park is a moated stone house of fine appearance, which has recently been repaired and enlarged by Sir Rhys ap Thomas. Thomas ap Jones esquire lives there now.

The land between Llandovery and Aber-Marlais is well wooded. I learned at Llandovery that the Towy flows past Llangurig in Powysland in the lordship of Arustle [*Arwystli*], and that its source is not far from there [*Leland has added 'false' against this sentence*]. Two miles beyond Aber-Marlais on my way to Carmarthen I could see about three miles away on my right hand the deserted priory of white canons [*Premonstratensian*] commonly called Talley. And further on at least two miles I rode down into a large valley where the pleasant River Dulas flowed down to enter the Towy. But before I came down into this valley I could see on my right hand, on this side of the Towy, Dynevor Castle three miles away by my estimation.

From this River Dulas I crossed another brook about two miles further on, and three or four miles beyond that I rode over another also called Dulas which falls into the Towy right next to Dryslwyn Castle. I discovered that the name Dryslwyn means a place full of difficulty and encumbrance to pass through. After another three miles I crossed over a large bridge under which flows the fine River Cothi not far before it enters the Towy. Then through a little valley between high hills on both sides for three miles or more to Abergwili, where there is a fine collegiate church of prebendaries attached to St David's. From there it was a mile on to Carmarthen.

From Carmarthen to Cywyn Bridge. The Cywyn rises at Blaen-Cowin two miles or more above the bridge, and flows afterwards into the Taff. From Cywyn Bridge to Duddey stream [*Dewi Fawr*] and from there a bowshot to Garthkiny River [*Cynin*] that runs beneath St Clears village. From there to Whitland on the Taff is four miles, but before I arrived at Whitland I crossed the Fenni brook. I am told that there is a forest by Llandovery, but between Carmarthen and Whitland nowhere has such an abundance of woodland as Whitland, which stands by itself in a vast wood as if in a wilderness. But much of the land elsewhere and the surrounding hills are unwooded.

From Whitland I travelled towards Lamphrey. A half-mile after Whitland I crossed Marlais stream, and then continued my journey past moderate hills and valleys until I reached Lamphrey, where the bishop of St David's has a castle-like stone residence standing by a brook that flows into the salt water by Pembroke. It is twelve Welsh miles, about eighteen English miles, from Whitland to Lamphrey.

All along the highway between Whitland and Lamphrey it is mostly heathland, although on both sides at some distance I could see good cornland in the valleys and on the hillsides. But the land is rather devoid of woodland, as is most of Pembrokeshire, except where there are a few parks. But in various parts of Pembrokeshire the land is coal-bearing, which the inhabitants commonly use to make their fires, and they also burn furze, as they do also around Carmarthen, although wood is in greater abundance there. I passed one of these coal pits about four miles from Lamphrey. Also about halfway between Whitland and Lamphrey I saw on my right hand what appeared to be a castle about three miles away. And then on within two miles of Lamphrey on my right I saw Carew Castle, which was repaired or rebuilt in magnificent style by Sir Rhys ap Thomas. It stands on a creek of Milford Haven. From Lamphrey to Pembroke is only a mile or so.

Pembroke stands on a very strong crag on one arm of the Milford Haven, which makes a creek about a mile beyond the town so as almost to surround it. The town has a good wall with three gates – east, west and north – of which the east gate is finest and strongest. It has in front of it a circular tower with no roof, and in its entrance is a portcullis of solid iron. The castle stands close to the wall on a hard rock, and is very large and strong, with two wards. In the outer ward I saw the chamber where King Henry VII was born, and in recognition of this a chimney has been newly built with the arms and badges of Henry VII. Underneath the great strong round tower in the inner ward is a marvellous vault called the Hogan [*the Wogan*]. This round tower is surmounted by a stone roof of almost conical shape, and its top is covered with a flat millstone. There are two parish churches in the town and another in the suburb. Monkton, a cell of Benedictine monks in the suburb, has been suppressed. The town has been well built, and the eastern suburb was almost as large as the town, but now is totally ruined.

Coming from Lamphrey towards Tenby I rode past the ruinous wall of a park which had formerly belonged to Sir Rhys, but is now devoid of deer. In the park are very few mature trees, or none at all, but only shrubs and conifers, as is the case in the two stone-walled parks around Carew. The church and hamlet of St Florence sit in a valley by the park. A little further on, and more than halfway between Pembroke and Tenby, Mainorpirrhe [*Manorbier*] castle was visible a mile away on the right hand. It stands in effect between two small pointed hills, and between them the Severn Sea has formed a gulf almost a quarter-mile long. From there to Tenby.

The town of Tenby stands on a mighty rock, but of no great height, and the Severn Sea engulfs around it to such an extent that at high tide almost one third of the town is surrounded by water. It is strongly walled, and has good gates, each with a portcullis of solid iron. But the gate that leads towards Carmarthen is the most handsome, since it is encircled outside by an open-roofed tower, after the fashion of Pembroke's east gate. Outside this gate is a pleasant suburb, and in the middle of the town is a fine parish church. The town itself lacks fresh water, so that it has to be brought in.

From Tenby I went to the coal pits on a hilltop two miles away, not far from the Severn shore. And a good mile beyond them I rode through a wood which, although not very large, was the finest that I remember seeing in Pembrokeshire. Then I came again to the way to Whitland.

The nearest crossing to Caldey [*Island*], which is a little more than a mile, is almost halfway between Manorbier and Tenby from a small point. When I was opposite Manorbier I could see Lundy [*Island*] lying far off in the Severn Sea.

A mile beyond Carmarthen on my journey to Llandewi Brefi I crossed the River Gwili, and then followed its course keeping it in sight as I rode for the next four or five miles. And I noticed various little brooks going into it in the lowest part of the valley. Then riding several miles further I began to see the River Teifi, and it remained in my view as I rode among stony hills and valleys and through an oak wood. After that I passed a pleasant lake called Gogurne [?] on my right hand, and also close by on the right Pencragan [?*Crugiau Rhos Wen*], a rock so-called because it is a round-capped hill of stones. A little further I came to a wretched cottage in a valley by the Teifi where I baited.

From there I rode to Llandewi Brefi five miles further on (some people say that Llandewi is called Brefi because it stands on the Brefi brook). Between these two places I saw a pleasant lake not far from the bank of the Teifi called Llinpeder [?*Llyn Pencarreg*], which was somewhat bigger than Llyn Gogurne, but I did not see any substantial discharge of water from either of them. I also saw one or two bridges over the Teifi.

Llandewi Brefi is only a simple or poor village, and I passed over a little brook to enter it. It is set among mountains on every side except the west, where the Teifi river flows a half-mile away in its valley. The collegiate church of prebendaries, roughly built, stands on a somewhat elevated site. From there it is two miles to Tregaron, where there is a church standing on a round earthen embankment. Beside it runs a brook called the [*Brennig*].

So, as I passed beneath a lofty hillside, I could see close by on my left a large boggy wetland, out of which the local inhabitants dig turves for fuel, and beside this same bog is a pleasant lake called Llinridde [?], two miles from Strata Florida.

Except on the west, where there is the Dyffryn Tyve [*Teifi valley*], Strata Florida is surrounded not far away by mountains. From the old tree-roots that can still be seen it is evident that the hills thereabout have been well wooded, but there is almost no woodland on them now. This is for three reasons. First, the wood was cut down and never coppiced, and this has been a major cause of woodland destruction throughout Wales. Second, after the woodland was felled goats grazed on the new shoots so that they only developed as shrubs. Third, people destroyed the large woods specifically so that they should not be a refuge for thieves.

Strata Florida church is large, with side aisles and transepts, and beside it is a large cloister, but the frater and infirmary are now mere ruins. The cemetery used for burial by the surrounding countrymen is very large, and surrounded by a small stone wall. There are 39 large yew trees in it. The courtyard or forecourt in front of the abbey is very large, and the foundations of the church's nave were set out to have been 60 feet longer than it is now.

Thence I went at least a half-mile up the Teifi valley, and then a mile and a half up the craggy and stony mountains to Llyn Teifi, and two miles further, past Claerddu, to Craig Naw Llyn. Had I gone a mile further to a high hill I might have seen Plynlimmon, five miles distant from there. The hills between Llyn Teifi and Craig Naw Llyn did not appear as stony as those between Strata Florida and Llyn Teifi. When I stood on Craig Naw Llyn there was nowhere visible any woodland, only hill-pastures.

From Strata Florida I rode two Welsh miles past rough pasture in hill and vale and then crossed a wild brook running through rocks, called Mochnant, then another whose name I cannot remember, to a third, called Nant-Llys, and there on my right I saw a hill called Crag John. Then I crossed Milwyn river, which I could see flowed into the River Ystwyth. Before I reached the Milwyn I had ridden for the space of three miles in Comeustwith [*Cwmystwyth*]. From the Milwyn I entered the Ystwyth valley, which is hemmed in so narrowly with rocky mountains that in winter the stream occupies the whole valley bottom. As I first entered this valley I could see on my right hand a hill called Mynydd [i.e. *Craig*] Ddu. [*passages omitted here, see p. 468*]

So, about the middle of this Ystwyth valley that I was riding in, I guess four miles in length, I saw on the right hand on a hillside Clo . . moyne [? *Cwm-tinwen*], where there has been a great deal of digging for lead. Smelting it has destroyed the woods that used to grow plentifully thereabout. I heard a wonderful story of a crow that was fed by one of the diggers there. The crow took away the digger's purse, and while he was pursuing the crow after his purse, the pit collapsed and his fellow diggers were crushed.

Taking my leave of the Ystwyth valley and climbing a high hill I came a mile further to a place where I could see a large green area in a valley, and out of this boggy place the Ystwyth rises. And less than the distance of a bowshot away from it I saw another similar place, and from this issued a small headwater stream of the Wye, which flowed at least a mile below in a valley.

Having crossed the Wye I climbed up a hill, from where I looked back and saw Pumlumon [*Plynlimon*], the source of the Wye. It seemed to me a very high mountain, and my guess was that it was about six miles away. All the way from Strata Florida to here I saw almost no woodland or arable, but from here onwards the soil grew more fertile, with fine meadows, cornfields and woods.

So I came to Llangurig on the Wye, more than a mile further, and then two miles past arable, woodland and meadows, to Llanidloes on the Severn. The distance between the rivers Wye and Severn is less than two miles, and there are only small insignificant streams between them. Then it was four miles down the Severn to Llandinam past good corn country and meadows with a great abundance of woodland. And it was similar the five miles further to Newtown, where on one side of the town a small brook flows into the Severn; and the same for the six miles to Montgomery. Between Newtown and Montgomery on a wooded hilltop on the left side I saw the ruined walls of [*Dolforwyn*] castle.

Going the five miles from Montgomery to Welshpool I crossed the Severn by a ford. The terrain between these two towns has no shortage of corn nor wood, but it is the land in the valley and along the Severn riverbanks that is the most pleasant. Welshpool itself is a town with a single parish church, well built after the Welsh fashion. Gledding [*Lledan*] brook flows almost next to the church, and so into the Severn.

Castell Coch [*Powis Castle*], in English 'Red Castle', stands on an outcrop of dark red-coloured stone. It has two separate wards, of which one used to belong to Lord Dudley, but now both belong to Lord Powis. Beside the castle is a fine park with a pale, and between the town and Castell Coch is a pleasant lake or pool, from which the town derives its name.

It is seven hilly miles from Welshpool to Alberbury. The land is wooded and the valley arable. Passing the hills I crossed over three or four pleasant streams, but I do not know their names. On my way less than three miles from Welshpool I saw a very notable hill beyond the valley on my left, which had three peaks, like three heads rising out of one body. I first saw these peaks in front of me near Newtown some fourteen miles away, and after I had passed Shrewsbury and Whitchurch, I saw them again sixteen miles away behind me. It took me three miles to ride past these hills. The highest of the three peaks is called Moel y Golfa, and this is reckoned the furthest limit of Powysland in this direction. The second is called Breidden, and this is in Caus lordship. I do not know the name of the third, but they are usually called the Breidden hills. Not far away from these hills one enters Shropshire. So they form the boundary between Powys, Caus and Shropshire. *cont. p. 304* [**1538:** *3/40-2, 110-126*]

INDEX OF NAMES

This is an index of surnames, but also includes Anglo–Saxon names, kings, queens, saints, nobility (by title), bishops (by see) and other ecclesiastics. Readers approaching Leland for biographical and genealogical information should be aware that much material of this kind is omitted from the present edition, and are advised to use the Toulmin Smith edition, which has a detailed index of persons and landowners in volume 5, pp. 245–80.

Aben 15
Abergavenny 174
Achard 18
Aclam 419
Acon 363
Acres 411
Acton 268, 276, 408
Aelfsige 186–7
Aescwig 290
Aidan (St) 272
Aiscough 398–9
Aiton 438–9
Ake 430
Akeborow 430
Alard 365
Albany 219, 251-2
Albemarle 439, 441–2
Albeneius 218
Albine 41
Alcock 432
Aldborough 448
Aldhelm (St) 329, 388
Aldlaver 424
Aldun 118
Alester 369
Alfarus 325
Alfred (father of Judhael) 73
Alfred (King) 108, 153, 346, 389
Algar (son of Leofric) 168
Algar (St) 347
Algernon 217
Alwyn 448, 463
Anderton 203
Anne (Queen) xi, 390, 439
Anselm 186, 278

Antius, Gaius 323
Archdeacon 41, 49, 85
Arden 299
Arilda (St) 129, 150
Armstrong 222
Armyn 224
Arthur (King) xiv–xvi, 58, 330, 332
Arthur (Prince) 306, 408
Arundel (Arundale, Arundell) 34, 37, 40, 44, 51, 53, 65, 97, 162, 177, 187, 308, 315–16
Aschenald 424
Ashendon 13, 16
Ashley 33, 105, 299
Askaperius 150
Aske 366, 458
Askew 237
Asterby 237
Astley 217
Athelstan (King) 39, 42, 65, 74, 92, 312, 371
Atherton 203
Aton 110; see also Ayton
Atwater 226
Atwell 329
Aucher 188
Auckland (Dean) 115
Audeleys 30
Audley 30, 150, 316, 338, 356, 397
Aveling 124
Avery 150
Aylesbury 404
Ayton 442; see also Aton

Babington 228, 230
Babthorpe 454, 466
Bache 168, 175
Bachelar 14
Bacon 250
Bagers 147
Bagots 382
Bailey 355, 392; see also Bayllie
Baldwin 21
Bale xvii–xviii, xxxiii, xlii
Balliol 117
Balsall 374
Balthasar 184
Barbour 16
Bardolf 224
Barentine 286, 288, 290, 298, 301
Bareswell 369
Barham 248
Barnes 251
Barnhale 199
Barningham 459
Barok (Berwike) 105, 403
Barret 52
Barricus (St) 45
Barton 184, 197
Barwik 403
Bassett 43, 294, 353, 355
Bassingburn 261
Batevileyn 254
Bath (Bp) 142, 325–8, 330, 343, 345–6
Bath (Earl) 75, 92
Bath (Prior) 325–6, 345
Baudey 224
Bayllie 293; see also Bailey

Baynard 162
Baynham 132
Bayntun 390, 393
Bayntun's 389, 401
Beatrice (wife of John of Brittany) 464
Beauchamp 1, 3, 4, 142, 146, 168, 176, 213, 298–9, 369–70, 375–7, 396–8, 410; see also Warwick (Earl)
Beauforest 290
Beaufort 116, 293, 369–70; see also Somerset (Earl)
Beaumont 118, 217, 220, 369
Beaupie 306
Becheton 32
Becket, Thomas (St) 73, 79, 96, 108, 187, 327
Beckington 298, 327–8, 349
Bede 68, 118, 147, 227, 271, 273, 359–60, 415, 462
Bedford (Duke) 117, 127, 223, 373
Bedlaw 75
Beere 348
Beeston 32
Bek 111, 118, 271, 275
Beke 234
Belasyse 117
Belgrave 217, 229–30
Bell xlvi, 128
Bellar 211
Belleme 312
Bellethorp 230
Bellingham 272, 384
Bellwood 230
Belmont 216, 220, 224–5
Beorhtweald 193
Beornstan (St) 152
Beornwulf (King) 129
Bergavenny 110, 116, 168, 176, 245, 373, 407
Berkeley 128–9, 134, 137–9, 141, 145–6, 370
Berners 179
Bernguid 325
Bertane 325
Berwike (Barok) 105
Bessel 297
Bethune 169
Beville (Boville) 40, 65
Bigot 436, 438–9, 461
Bigrame 182–3
Bilsby 237
Birinus (St) 290
Birkhead 209
Bissett 407
Blackburn 465
Blake 124
Blaket 213
Blakston 174
Blessells 16
Blewbury 404
Blewett 162
Blois 136
Blunt 45, 137, 214
Blythe 353, 382, 397
Blyton 227
Bodrugan 50
Bodulcan 56
Bohun 120, 167, 182; see also Hereford (Earl)
Bointon 118
Boleyn xi, 22, 217; see also Anne (Queen); Wiltshire (Earl)
Bolney 366
Bond 380, 390
Bonham 390–1, 403
Bonville 55, 91, 209, 333, 343
Booth 31, 113, 315
Boothby 222
Borow 269, 272, 298
Borrow 313
Bosel 129
Bosson 222–3
Bossu 213
Bostock 32
Boteler 125–6; see also Butler
Botolph (St) 196, 227
Botreaux 36, 37, 64, 229, 238, 321, 338, 345, 396
Boucher 215
Bouet 450
Bourchier 179; see also Bath
Bourgchier 186
Boville (Beville) 40, 65
Bowes 117, 270, 385, 447, 458, 460
Bowling 462
Bowmer 458
Bracebridge 227, 357, 377
Brackenbury 116, 138
Bradenstoke (Prior) 124
Bradford 95–6
Bradshaw 206–7
Bradstone 137
Brandeston 396
Brandon 299
Braose 366, 472
Bray 3, 7, 161, 289
Braybrooke 261
Breauté 3
Breinton 165
Brendan 175
Brentingham 88
Brereton 28, 31, 33
Breton 31–2, 177
Breusis 263
Brewer 84, 93, 337–8
Brian 108, 268; see also Brien
Brictric 148
Bridges 124, 143, 146, 170
Bridport 397–8
Brien 83; see also Brian
Brigham 270
Brin 33
Brithung 463
Brittany 464
Broke 77, 375; see also Brooke
Brokesby 214
Bromfeld 438
Bromflete 110
Bromley 33
Bronescombe 48
Brook 215
Brooke 42, 80, 308, 387, 402–3; see also Broke
Brooker 192
Brooksby 218
Brooks's 161

INDEX OF NAMES

Broughton 23
Brown 232, 256
Browne 345, 376
Browning 99, 298
Broy 2
Bruce 442
Bruce's 443
Brudenell xxiii, 23, 212, 261
Bubwith 327, 349
Buckingham (Duke) 140, 165, 244–5, 257, 316, 382, 468, 470; *see also* Stafford
Buckingham (Earl) 120; *see also* Giffard
Budé xi
Budock 77
Budock (St) 47
Builli 278
Bulkley 32
Bulmer 115
Bunbury 31, 33
Burford 170, 173, 469
Burge 424
Burgh 195, 229, 237–8, 249
Buriana (St) 43
Burley 168
Burnell 314, 317
Burnham 115, 230
Burrough 212
Burrow 97
Burton 137, 419
Burwash 237
Bury 118
Bussy 224
Butler 146, 204, 371; *see also* Boteler
Byfield 2
Bytten 87

Cadurcis 130
Caesar, Julius 190
Calvacante 14
Calveley 27, 32–3
Camden vii, xxxiv, xxxvi
Camel 329
Campernulph (Chambernoun) 51, 80

Candish 230
Canterbury (Abp) 186–7, 190, 193, 241, 278, 285, 310, 325, 364, 374, 449, 455
Canterbury (Archdeacon) 197
Cantilupe 147–8, 164, 175–7, 237
Canute (King) 129, 380
Capel 346
Caradoc 342–3
Carantoc (St) 340
Cardinham 51, 53
Carent 107, 403
Carew 41, 72, 83–5, 90, 93, 474, 475
Carlell (Carlisle) 197, 267
Carley viii, xiv, xvii, xviii, xxxviii, xli, xlii, xliv,
Carlisle (Bp) 69
Carnbull 183
Carniovies (Carnsey) 38–9, 64
Carnsew 44
Carnsey 38–9, 64
Carow 36, 64
Carpenter 160
Carr 224
Carteis 52
Carter 410
Cary 92
Castile 80, 83, 214, 237
Catfields 205
Catharine (Dowager Princess) 77, 226
Catherine (Queen) 256
Catterick 460
Cavel (Cavelle) 41, 44
Caves 217
Caxton xxx
Cayle 54
Celling (Tilly) 188
Cenelm (King) 125
Cenelm (St) 150, 416
Cenwulf (King) 125, 150
Chad (St) 309, 351–2, 375
Chadworth 237
Chalcedon 98
Chamberlain 288, 300

Chambernoun 41, 336
Champion 185
Chancellor 334
Chandos 168, 170, 176
Chapman 325
Chappell 343
Charlemagne liii
Charlton 309, 319
Chaucer 286–7, 299, 301
Chaumbre 76
Chaumburne 80
Chaumon 37
Chauncy 138
Chaundler 397
Chaveney 219
Chaworth 212, 280
Cheddar 146, 346
Cheltenham 147
Cheney 14, 184; *see also* Cheyney
Chester (Bp) 33, 356
Chester (Earl) 30
Cheyne 20
Cheyney 199, 397; *see also* Cheney
Chichele 186
Chideock 107
Childerleigh 80
Chillenden (Chislesden) 187
Chinnock 348
Choke 343, 400
Cholmeley 442
Cholmondeley 26, 27, 33
Chorlton 314
Cirencester (Abbot) 144
Cissa (King) 12–13, 15
Clare 142, 147, 149, 168, 258, 411; *see also* Gloucester (Earl)
Claregenet 451
Clarel 422
Clarence 187
Clarence (Duke) 121, 148
Clarivaulx 117
Clark 288; *see also* Clerk
Claxton 115
Cleobury 310
Clerk 327, 330; *see also* Clark

483

Clifford 111, 200, 266, 425, 438; see also Cumberland (Earl)
Clifton 281
Clinton 189, 195–6
Clopton 374–5
Clusilla 54
Cobham 362, 421
Code 55
Codrington 137
Cole 312
Colebrande the Dane 153
Collingwood 269
Columbariis 74
Cometon 415
Compton 53, 299, 373, 414
Conan 42
Coningsby 170
Conomor 54
Constable 443
Constance (wife of John of Gaunt) 214
Conway 376
Cony 224, 407
Conyers 110, 183, 438, 446, 451–2, 455, 457–60, 463, 465
Cookham 349
Cooksey 407, 416
Cooper 295
Cope 296
Copeland 66
Copestan 80, 83; see also Copston
Cophin 75
Copledyke 236
Copston 77; see also Copestan
Corbet 299, 304–5, 308, 313, 317
Corbete 49
Cornwall 168, 173, 229, 238, 318
Cornwall (Duke) 62
Cornwall (Earl) 11–12, 40, 42, 53, 55, 65, 124, 180, 330, 390; see also Richard, King of the Romans
Cotton 314

Countre 355
Court 12
Courtenay 15, 79–80, 83, 86, 89, 186; see also Exeter (Marquis)
Coventry (Prior) 380–1
Cowlin 41
Cox 306
Cranmer 285
Crevecouer 188
Croft 173, 299
Crompton 362
Cromwell xiv–xv, 225, 233, 262, 265
Croun 231, 234
Crow 360
Culwyn 68
Cumberland (Earl) 68; see also Clifford
Curthose 129, 334
Curtis 130
Cusance 162
Cuthbeorht 187
Cuthberga (St) 105
Cuthbert (St) 67, 115, 118, 167, 268, 327, 418, 445, 465
Cutte 185, 189
Cwenthryth 150

Dacers (Dacors, Dacre, Dacres) 69, 272, 444, 461
Dalberly 238
d'Albini 232
Dalison 231, 237
Dalton 209, 462
Damory 294
Danby 465
Daniel 31–2, 168, 175
Daniell xlvii, 400
Danvers 44, 289, 321
Daraby 448
Darcy 229, 429, 456
Darrell 399
Daubeney 340, 346
Davell 267–71, 455, 456
Davenport 31–2
David (King of Scotland) 284

Dawney 84
Dawtrey 364, 366
Deepdale 428
Delaber 168
Delabont 81
Delamare 344
Delaware xlix, 139
Delves 33, 230
Dene 10
Denmark (King) 134
Dennis 137–9
Denny xi
Denton 268, 306, 351
Derby (Countess) 214
Derby (Earl) 179, 201–2, 204, 206–7, 240, 264, 294, 317, 336, 383, 449; see also Stanley
Dering 364
Despenser xxxv, 150, 370
Devereux 169
Dickon (Dicon) 252
Digby 218, 357
Dinan 45
Dines 222–3
Dinham 44
Diocletian 144
Dionysius 389
Disney (de Iseney) 224
Dodd 313
Dodo (Duke) 148
Dogget 96
d'Oilly 291–2; see also Oilleio
Dorchester 394
Dormer 290
Dorotheus 228
Dorset (Marquis) 55, 90–1, 145, 210–11, 215–17, 219–20, 333, 343, 378–9; see also Grey
Downe 27, 31
Doyley 22
Draper 241
Drayton 290
Drew 346
Dudley 316–17, 379, 478
Dunstan 186
Durham (Bp) 111, 116–19, 124, 268–9, 276, 396,

INDEX OF NAMES

433-4, 438, 445-6, 460
Durham (Chancellor) 119
Durham (Dean) 119
Durham (Prior) 271
Dutton 32
Dyke 364, 366
Dymoke 236-7

Eadbert 190
Eadburga (St) 294
Eadmund 118
Eadred 118
Ealdred 129
Eanswith (St) 196
Eanus 15
Eastfield 422
Eata (St) 465
Ecgwine 406
Ecmundeton 455-6
Edburge 129
Edgar (King) 13, 15, 325-6, 409-10
Edgecumbe 35, 50, 78, 81
Edington 404
Edmund the Elder (King) 142
Edmund (St) 223
Edmunds 363
Edward (Black Prince) 12, 404
Edward the Elder (King) 131, 153, 354
Edward (King and Martyr) 9, 16, 344
Edward the Confessor (King) 123, 164, 167, 306, 380
Edward I (King) 67, 148, 357, 364, 400, 411, 455
Edward II (King) 129-30, 137, 175
Edward III (King) 6, 17-18, 51-2, 66, 83, 120, 150, 168, 219, 265, 284, 404, 436
Edward IV (King) 5, 13, 51-2, 81, 83, 126-7, 142, 145, 150, 160, 186, 209, 213, 217-18, 255-6, 268, 283, 353,

408, 425, 454, 461-2
Edward VI (King) xv-xvi, xlvii, liv, 374
Egbert (King) 129, 445
Egerton 27, 31-2
Eggleston (Prior) 464
Egra 156
Egremont 464
Egwin (St) 374
Einerio 291
Eleanor (Queen) 6, 237
Elizabeth (Queen) xlvii
Elizabeth of Hungary (St) 152
Ellesforde 168
Ellis 224
Elmes 256
Elsing 241
Elwine 45
Ely 330
Ely (Bp) 31, 183, 364
Engayne 183, 262
Engleby 449
English 285
Erasmus xi
Erisey 41
Espec 4, 6
Especs 4
Essex 17
Essex (Earl) 149, 182
Ethelbert (King) 163-4, 166, 190
Ethelfleda 131, 142, 354
Ethelmod 325
Ethelmund (King) 172
Ethelred (Earl) 131
Ethelred (King) 105, 129
Ethelwold 13, 15
Ethelwulf 95
Eure 111, 438
Eva 129
Evan 307
Everard 340
Evers 230
Evreux (Countess) 177
Ewyas 176
Exeter (Bp) 36, 48, 62, 65, 78-9, 82, 88-9, 357, 378
Exeter (Duchess) 5, 82; see also Holland

Exeter (Duke) 74, 82, 303; see also Holland
Exeter (Marquis) 91; see also Courtenay

Falconbridge 116
Fanhope 4-6
Faricius 15
Faringtons 203
Farley 130
Farmer 260
Farnham 118
Fauconberg 455
Felicia (wife of Guido) 371
Felton 273
Fenwick 273
Fercher 175
Ferrars 183, 355, 360
Ferrers 174, 215, 219-20, 355
Fettiplace 297
Field 256
Fimbarrus (St) 51
Finch 195, 365
Finkel 362
Fisher 200
Fitton 32, 270
FitzAlan 251-2; see also Arundel (Earl)
Fitzhamon 149
Fitzharding 134
Fitzhugh 451, 457-8
FitzJames 241, 300, 331-2
Fitzneele 6
Fitzpayne 95, 268
Fitzrandolf 448, 463
Fitzwalter 69, 231, 455, 464
Fitzwarin, Fitzwarren 17, 304, 316, 343; see also Bath (Earl)
Fitzwilliam 51, 76, 237, 422
Fleming 90, 93, 232, 237
Flower 453, 454
Fogge 186
Fontaine 40
Force 42
Forne 291
Fortescue 41, 80, 297, 376

Fortibus 79, 86
Foster 300
Foulcburc 325
Fouleshurst 33
Fowler 288-9, 300
Fox 114, 152-3, 160
Foye 130
Framlingham 251, 360
Francis 294, 309, 436
Frank 458
Fremund 6
Freville 355
Frithe 96
Frithwald 21
Frobenius l
Fromond 348
Frost 432
Froucester 130
Fulford 41
Fuller xviii
Furnivall 278, 282
Fyneux 184, 188-9, 195
Fyton 9

Gallor 95
Gamage 130
Gambon 339
Garland 347
Garter 361
Gascoyne 113, 118, 323, 426, 458
Gatacre 314
Gaunt 135, 214
Gaveston 270
Gedney 237
Geneville 309
Gerald 33
Gerard 207, 278
Germoe (St) 42
Gervase 156
Ghent 397
Gibbs 326
Giffard 129, 294, 307, 430; see also Buckingham (Earl)
Gilbert 331-2
Gilpin 384
Giseland 426
Glastonbury (Abbot) 106
Glendower 310

Gloucester (Abbot) 130
Gloucester (Duke) 150, 210
Gloucester (Earl) 106, 121, 133, 136, 142, 145, 147-50, 411, 414; see also Clare
Gloucestershire (Count) 134
Glyn, Glynne 41, 45, 266
Glyndŵr 469-70
Godolphin xxiii, 34, 41-2, 44-5
Godric (St) 119
Godwald (St) 410
Golafer 298
Goldsmith 429
Goldston 187
Goldwell 187
Gonson x
Goodman 127
Gorges 346
Goring 364, 366
Gorings 366
Gostwick 1, 4, 7
Gower 444
Graineville, Granville 40-1, 44, 65
Grandisson 87-8, 176
Grantham 224
Graystanes 118
Green 257
Grevill xlvi, 299-300, 366, 375-6
Grey 5, 70, 171, 190, 215, 219-20, 266, 273, 297, 319, 343; see also Dorset (Marquis)
Greystock 444
Griffin 261
Griffin (Prince) 167-8
Griffith 346, 352, 354
Griffiths 343
Grimbald 153
Grosseteste 238
Grosvenor 313
Guidotti 156
Gundeville 359
Gurney 335, 342-3, 346
Gwalo 136
Gwent 415

Gwyney 238
Gyvernay 333

Haget 427-8
Hainault 436
Hainault (Countess) 301
Hakluyt xlvi, 172-3
Hales 380
Hall 183, 237, 316
Halle 344, 391
Haly 369
Hampton 343
Hanby 432
Hanford 31
Hansard 236
Harbottle 270, 272
Harding 135-6
Harington 333
Harman (Voysey) 378
Harnhill 128
Harold (King) 167, 176
Harper 33
Harrington 201, 209-10, 218, 232, 237
Harrison xxxiii
Harte 190
Haseley 369
Haslerigg 269
Hastings 6, 37, 53, 168, 210, 213, 217-19, 235, 237, 296, 332, 345, 442; see also Huntingdon (Earl)
Hatfield 118
Haughton 314
Hauley 130
Haulle 224
Hawley 82-3
Haynson 432
Hazlerigg 213, 218, 269
Hearne viii, xxxii
Heath xlvi
Heldercar 273
Heling 55
Helke 300
Heneage 229, 237
Hengist 198
Henry 349
Henry I (King) 6, 9, 18, 123-4, 136, 144, 149,

INDEX OF NAMES

172, 292, 301, 325, 334, 424, 441
Henry II (King) 134, 362
Henry III (King) 3, 11, 128, 136, 176, 195, 209
Henry IV (King) 115, 150, 170, 186–7, 214, 219, 310, 359, 365
Henry V (King) 18, 117, 173, 205, 247, 255–6
Henry VI (King) 5, 110, 117, 126, 145, 218, 260, 316, 353, 369–70, 454
Henry VII (King) lii, 10, 13, 27, 32, 50, 80, 83, 105, 145, 147, 160, 175, 186, 200, 202, 210, 216, 225, 231, 234, 244, 262, 264–5, 289, 295, 351, 360, 402, 408, 413, 456, 475
Henry VIII (King) ix–xii, xv–xviii, xx, xxiii, xxv, xxx, xliv, xlv, 4, 12, 21, 23, 34, 47, 49, 63, 65, 70, 74, 75–6, 79, 98, 102, 127, 131, 173–4, 178, 180, 184, 188–9, 199, 206, 216–17, 244, 255, 279, 282, 289, 298, 309, 327, 347, 354, 356, 358, 362, 368, 378, 381, 389, 402, 412, 415, 423, 430, 449, 458, 466
Herbert xlvi, 41, 68, 242, 248, 365; *see also* Pembroke (Earl)
Hereford (Bp) 31, 147, 164, 168, 174, 176–7, 313, 411
Hereford (Earl) 120, 129–31, 140, 149–50, 167, 182; *see also* Bohun
Heron 268, 289
Hertford 391, 393; *see also* Seymour
Heydon 250–1
Heywood 301, 351, 353
Hiatte 146
Higden xxix–xxx
Higdon 427
Hill 80, 310
Hinmar 118
Holbache 315
Holcroft 203
Holcum 290
Holinshed xxxiii
Holland 209, 224, 264; *see also* Exeter (Duke)
Holman 73
Hood, Robin 417, 419
Hopton 317, 359, 456
Horman 299
Horne 145, 298
Horner 347
Horsey 97, 107
Horton 36, 64, 130, 391–2
Hosier 306
Howard x, 339, 366; *see also* Arundel (Earl), Norfolk (Duke)
Howden 434
Huddleston 127
Hudelstan 69
Hugh (St) 237
Humfrevill 118, 269
Hungate 427, 461
Hungerford 37, 64, 123, 214, 296, 321–2, 332, 345, 369, 391, 396–7, 400
Huntingdon 278
Huntingdon (Earl) 20, 37, 64, 95, 187, 216–17, 258, 279, 296, 332, 345; *see also* Hastings, St Liz
Huntingfield 233
Hussey 137, 221, 224, 232, 234–5, 321
Huthome 429
Huttoft 156, 235–6

Ia (St) 45
Icanno 227
Inkepen 152
Ireland 207
Irencester 6
Ironside 348
Iseney 224
Islip 187

Jane (sister of Henry IV) 115
Jennings 356
John (King) 81, 83, 148–9, 186, 195, 241, 261, 454
John (Treasurer of Exeter) 87
Jolliffe 374
Jones 473
Jordan 307
Jordanus (St) 143
Judhael 73
Judoce (St) 153
Julers 98

Kemeys, Kemys 247
Kempe 186
Kendal 55
Kendrick xxvi
Kenn 346
Kenred (King) 406
Kent 325
Kent (Earl) 5, 249
Keverne (Piran) (St) 46, 60
Kidderminster 125
Kidlington 293
Kiligrew 41, 44, 47
Kineburge 129
King 326, 349
Kingston 303
Kirkby 204, 364
Kirkham 256
Kirton 233
Kite 69
Kitson 206
Kiwartun 44
Knight xlv, 184, 196, 327
Knightley 259, 381
Knolles 32
Knollys 297, 423
Knyvet 251
Kylligrin 45
Kyme 228, 234

Lacy 25, 88, 104–5, 129–30, 167, 169, 174–5, 228, 423–4; *see also* Lincoln (Earl)
Laken 314

Lambarde xxxiii
Lamelin 54
Lancaster 175, 205, 443
Lancaster (Duchy) 209, 248, 289, 300, 356, 454
Lancaster (Duke) 67, 105, 214, 237, 270, 359, 393, 419
Lancaster (Earl) 109, 209, 214
Lanfranc 199
Langdale 428
Langdon 41, 191
Langford 236, 396
Langley xxxv, 118, 150, 255–6, 265
Langton 96, 161, 186–7, 204, 207–8, 237, 350, 352, 357, 436
Lanthony (Prior) 128
Lascelles 443, 445, 459
Latimer 3, 116, 370, 414, 416, 438, 457, 460
Latimer 370
Launceston (Prior) 36
Lawrence 191
Leader 182
Lee 20–1, 31, 314
Legh 207
Leicester 31, 118
Leicester (Countess) 213
Leicester (Earl) 213, 215, 218, 220
Leigh 224
Leighton 314
Leinthall 170–1
Lenthall 288
Leofgar 168
Leofric 88, 168, 380
Lereve 129
Lestrange 3, 294
Lestwick 32
Levelis 44
Leweston 109
Lewis 247
Leyburne 205
Leyland ix, xxi, 201–2
Lichfield (Abp) 310
Lichfield (Bp) 309, 351–3, 357, 375

Lightster 366
Lily x, xxxi
Linacre 188
Lincoln (Bp) 21, 23, 131, 183, 215, 237, 290, 295–6, 302, 351
Lincoln (Chancellor) 432
Lincoln (Dean) 228, 238
Lincoln (Earl) 25, 105, 287; see also Lacy
Lingain, Lingham 165, 175
Lisle 67, 138, 145–6, 273, 278, 346, 353, 370, 379
Litchfield 406
Littlebury 234, 237
Littleton 357
Llandaff (Bp) 244
Llewellyn (Prince) 173, 470
Loder 385
London 12, 40, 65
London (Bp) 241
Long 390–1, 402
'Long Thomas' 391
Longespee 396
Longeville 259
Longland 237
Loring 6
Losinga 168
Louches 289
Lovebone 38, 64
Lovekyn 362
Lovell 220, 264, 294, 297–9, 317, 466
Lovetot 183, 278–9, 281
Lower 53–4
Lucas 391, 402
Lucy 268, 372–3, 464
Luddington 237
Ludlow 306, 314, 317
Lumley 268, 270
Luttrell 339–41
Lynch 200
Lynes 109
Lyster 156

Mabilia (Countess) 36, 64, 168
Madoc 315
Magason 147
Magdalens 137

Maildulphus 388
Mainwaring 313, 318
Mallett 461
Malmesbury 108
Malory 265, 446, 451, 464–5
Malvern 130
Mandeville 120, 182
Mannock 25
Manoring 32
Mantell 259
Marbury 26, 169
Margaret (mother of Henry VII) 105, 225, 262, 265; see also Beaufort
Margaret (Queen) 316
Markenfeld 464
Markingfield 466
Marmaduke 449
Marmion 354, 451, 457–8
Marney 102
Marsh 118
Martin 79, 172
Martins 109
Martival 213; see also Mortival
Massey 31, 33
Massingberd 237
Matabrune 472
Matilda (Empress) 14
Matilda (Queen) 148–9, 155
Mauley 438
Mauley's 438
Maungeant 129
Maurice 365
Maurice (St) 79
Mawdelyne 327
Maxwell 67
Maybank 107
Mean 136
Menel 455
Mepham 186
Mere 31, 96, 108
Meredoc (Prince) 315
Meredydd 168, 175
Merewald (King) 168, 172–3
Metcalf 458, 461, 466
Metcalfs 461

INDEX OF NAMES

Metham 434
Mewis 42
Middleton 272
Milatun 41
Mille 156
Miller 228
Minos 248
Minshull 33
Misselden 237
Mitford 397
Mitton 313
Mohun 44, 54–5, 90, 92, 330, 340
Mohuns 90, 340
Moleyns 12, 200, 296, 321
Molines 392
Molyneux 207
Monboucher 269
Monington 348
Monjoy 45
Monk 76
Monmouth 249
Monson 230
Montacute 23, 454
Montagu 254
Montfort 118, 213, 371
Montgomery 90, 317, 356
Monthaut 251–2
Moore 208
Mordaunt 7, 256–7
Morgan 247
Morison 410
Morley 264, 271
Mortain (Count) 42, 187, 334
Mortimer 173, 284, 318–19, 382, 408, 415
Mortival 397; see also Martival
Morton 187, 191, 193–4
Morville 67, 311
Morwent 130
Moulton 231, 260, 427
Mounteagle 208, 210, 419
Mountetons 434
Mounteville 233–4
Mountford 357
Mowbray 4, 6, 146, 230, 254, 422, 445, 449; see also Norfolk (Duke)

Moyne 477
Mulshos 266
Multon 238, 464
Muncius 150
Murdoch 297
Musgrove 385, 452
Mutton 213
Myles x

Neckam 124
Needham 32–3, 313
Neufmarché 472
Neville 88, 112–13, 115–16, 118, 200, 210, 218, 266, 278, 282, 370, 378, 424, 444–5, 448, 452, 463; see also Warwick (Earl), Westmorland (Earl)
Newborough 102
Newmarket 130
Newnam 280
Newport 313, 319, 412–13
Newton 121, 132, 266, 320, 342–3, 346
Nores 265
Norfolk (Duchess) 251
Norfolk (Duke) x, 4, 224, 230, 251–2, 317, 366, 444; see also Howard, Mowbray
Norris 29, 207
North 456
Northumberland (Earl) 153, 268, 273, 363, 428–9, 435, 445, 454; see also Percy
Norton 465
Noteres 116
Nowell xxxiii
Nunny 228

Odo 148, 449
Offa (King) 164, 166, 174–5, 310, 325, 414
Oilleio 292; see also d'Oilly
Oldcastle 168
Oldford 33
Oldham 82, 88
Onslow 314

Orleans (Duke) 322
Ormonde 22–3, 107, 248
Osborne 130
Osmund (St) 394, 397
Osney (Prior) 293
Osric (King) 129–30, 325
Oswald (King) 131
Oswald (St) 271, 315–16, 410
Oswin (St) 269
Oswy (King) 352
Osyth (St) 21
Otley 314
Overshal 430
Oxenbridge 365
Oxeney 195
Oxford (Countess) 220
Oxford (Earl) 29, 120, 231, 307, 360
Oxton 80–1

Page 179
Painter 77
Pakington 416
Palmer 300
Pancefoot 128
Pandonia 24–5
Parker 130, 410
Parr 258, 383, 457–9
Patishull 3
Paynell 221–4, 233, 266
Pecham 185, 187
Peito 369
Pembroke (Countess) 130
Pembroke (Earl) 130, 168; see also Herbert
Pembrugge 168
Penda (King) 316, 352
Penny 215
Percy 187, 268, 270, 310, 364, 366, 428–9, 432, 434, 438–9, 454, 461; see also Northumberland (Earl)
Peter of Castile (King) 214
Petite 41, 44
Peverel 296, 321
Peverelle 40, 65
Philippa (Queen) 98, 299
Philippes 265

Phillips 168
Philpot 154
Picot 465
Pighius xv, li
Pigot 3
Pilkington 202, 207
Place 459
Placetes 120
Plackett 293
Plompton 454, 465
Plympton (Prior) 77
Poel 338; *see also* Pole
Pointer 213
Pole xxxi, 33, 287, 338, 356, 413, 431–2
Poliziano 188
Pollard 17
Pollet 231; *see also* Poulet
Pontoise 152
Poore 96, 396, 398
Pope 174, 178, 296
Port 129
Porter 224, 237, 251
Portington 434
Potmare 126
Pouger 258
Poulet 45, 336, 344; *see also* Pollet
Poultney 380
Power 369
Powis (Powys) 312–13, 317, 319, 430, 478
Poyning(es) 102, 189, 268
Poyntz xlvii, 138, 299
Prestland 32
Preston 209
Prestwich 201
Prideaux 80
Prise xxxiii
Protasius 156
Ptolemy 143
Pudsey 118–19, 458
Purefoy 218, 353, 422
Pye 390
Pypard 288

Quarre 169
Quartemayne 288–9, 300
Quathering 237
Quenburg (Queen) 168

Quincy 220
Quinil 88

Raby 116, 444
Radcliffe 201, 212, 455
Radclyf 68
Rainsford 299
Ramsam 96, 108
Ramsey (Abbot) 183
Randol 355
Ratcliffe 217
Rawcliffe 204
Rede 146, 272, 293
Redmille 364
Redvers 79
Rehan 168
Reinhelm 168
Remigius 238, 290
Repington 238
Rese 87
Reskymer 46–7
Richard I (King) 123, 149, 396
Richard II (King) 17, 22, 150, 169, 219, 315, 431, 435, 463
Richard III (King) 23, 50, 83, 103, 145, 160, 186, 213, 283, 349, 368, 427, 439–40, 443, 456
Richard, King of the Romans 53, 55, 124; *see also* Cornwall (Earl)
Richmond (Archdeacon) 232, 459
Richmond (Countess) 74, 234
Richmond (Duke) 74, 444
Richmond (Earl) 175, 451, 464
Rider 214
Ringeley 184, 190
Ripplingham 432
Rivere 139
Rivers 219, 366
Rivington 203
Robin Hood 417, 419
Roches 160
Rochford 6, 217
Rodeley 231

Rodney 299
Rogers 17, 100, 137, 338
Rokesby 447, 458–9
Rollo 149
Rolls 76
Roodes 185
Ros 4, 232
Rosamund, Fair 299
Rose 218–19, 273
Roskymer 41
Ross 268
Rotenhering 431
Rotherham 183
Rous xxx, 24, 369, 404
Ruan 80
Rudham 269
Rugby 382
Rumbald 123, 144
Rumold 265
Rumold (St) 264
Russell 20, 23, 87, 139, 237
Ruthall 124, 269
Rutland (Earl) 161, 219, 232, 273, 303, 425, 430
Rutter 302–3
Rycote 288
Ryves 109

Sackville 366
St Albine 41
St Amande 124
St Asaph (Bp) 168, 175
St Carilef 118
St Clare 82, 258
St David's (Bp) 474
St Etheldred 183, 403
St George 173
St Helen's 18
St John 2–3, 6, 96, 110, 262, 292, 344
St Leger 82, 188, 303
St Liz 183, 258; *see also* Huntingdon (Earl)
St Loe 139, 320, 345
St Paulle 237
St Quintin 463
St Winnow 53
Sale 344
Salisbury 258, 266
Salisbury (Bp) 9, 94–6,

INDEX OF NAMES

394–9, 401
Salisbury (Countess) 430
Salisbury (Dean) 9
Salisbury (Earl) 21, 52, 54, 116, 316, 370, 393, 395, 439
Salle 391
Salvage 32, 449
Salvin 438
Sanchia (wife of Earl of Cornwall) 124
Sandford 318, 385
Sandon 237
Sandys 161
Sanford 305
Sannes 264, 321
Sante 13
Sapcote 256
Savage 414
Savaric 142
Saville 185
Savilles 190
Sawkill 385
Scargell 426
Saxton xxxiii
Scot 389, 420
Scott 268
Scriven 314
Scrope 280, 339, 364, 403, 447–8, 457–9, 461, 463–4
Scylley 89
Sebroke 130
Segrave 290
Selby 66, 432
Selwood 346–8
Serlo 124, 129, 130
Seymour 123, 349, 402; *see also* Hertford (Earl), Somerset (Duke)
Shaxton 395
Sheffield 120, 230–1, 237, 360
Sheppard 137
Sherborne (Abbot) 91, 95, 96
Shirburn 209
Shirley 214, 218, 364
Shrewsbury (Earl) 248, 278–9, 305, 312, 317,

370, 420
Sidwell (St) 87
Simon (of Prestbury) 147
Skeffington 213, 218
Skirlaw 111, 118–19, 434, 447
Smith vii–viii, xxxii, xxxvii–xxxix, 29, 212, 218, 351, 467
Smyth 183
Snew 148
Somerset (Duchess) 231
Somerset (Duke) 105, 374; *see also* Fitzroy, Seymour
Somerset (Earl) 90, 92, 105, 187, 340, 370; *see also* Beaufort
Somerton 299–300
Somery 252
Southampton x, xlv
Spain 456
Speke 333, 336
Spencer 20, 147, 299
Spenser 370, 377
Spenser 23
Spofford 177
Spurstow 27, 32
Stafford 108, 120, 140, 145, 257, 309, 313, 357, 413, 471; *see also* Buckingham (Duke)
Standeley, Standley 27, 31, 294
Stanley 32–3, 131, 210, 264, 294; *see also* Derby (Earl)
Stapleton 88, 428, 456
Starkey 31–2
Staveley 294, 384
Stawford 74
Stephen (King) 14, 136, 176, 198, 200, 227
Stillington 349
Stockport 30
Stokke 399
Stonnard 54
Stonor 290, 297
Storthwayt 327
Stoteville 454
Stour 81

Stourton 107, 356, 403–4
Stow xxxiv, xxxix, 239, 351
Stradel 175
Strange 317
Strangeways 92, 99, 108, 446, 455
Stratford 182, 186, 374
Straw 186, 199
Stretey 357
Strickland 2, 68, 384, 460
Strode 41
Strongbow 130
Stumpe 389
Stuteville 430
Style 325
Suchborough 357
Sudbury 186, 199, 348
Sudeley 126–7, 146, 371
Suffolk (Duke) 225, 234, 287, 299, 301, 431
Sulyard 306
Sutton 227, 237
Swillington 456
Swinburne 141, 273
Swineford 116, 237
Sydenham 339

Talbot xxxiii, 146, 188, 190, 278, 282, 305, 313, 319, 413, 416; *see also* Shrewsbury (Earl)
Talboy 237
Tame 121–2, 124, 142, 145
Tankervill 376
Tattershall 251-2
Tavistock (Abbot) 56
Taylor 136, 164
Tempest 419, 462
Terumber 392
Tewkesbury (Abbot) 125, 146–7
Theobald 188
Theodore 43, 325
Theodoric 41, 325
Thimbleby 223–4, 236
Thirkilde 267
Thirland 285
Thomas 473–5
Thorne 10
Thornes 314

Thornhill 106
Thornhull 109
Thornhulls 109
Thornton 268, 270
Thorpe 251
Throckmorton 375, 414
Throgmorton 139
Thurston 424
Thwaites 446
Thwarton 385
Tilly (Celling) 188
Tilney 233–4, 251
Todd 436
Tonmers (Toomer) 107
Torrington 76
Toternius 218
Totheby 237
Tours 326, 328
Townlea 278
Tracy 73–75, 125–6, 148
Trafford 201
Trecarrel 44
Trederth 47
Treffry 34, 51–2, 54, 65
Trefusis 47–8
Tregoze 170, 176, 365
Tregyon 49
Trelawny 54–6
Tremayne 46–7
Trentam 314
Tresham 254, 266
Tresinny 41
Trevanion 40, 50
Treviliane 37
Trewinard 44
Triveth 337
Troutbeck 313
Trussell 375
Tudor 168, 175
Tuke xi
Tunstall 114, 209, 369, 426
Turgot 118
Turner 237
Turville 218
Twyne 189, 191
Tyrrell 162
Tyrwhitt 237, 270

Umfraville 269, 271
Undergod 316

Underwood 121
Uvedale 160

Valletorte 56, 77, 79
Vaughan 164
Vaux, Vaulx 6, 49, 174, 178, 260
Venables 32–3
Verdon 216–17
Vere 177, 231; *see also* Oxford (Earl)
Vergil, Polydore xiv, xxxi
Verney 258
Vernon 306, 307, 314, 317–18
Vernoun 224
Vescy 110, 225, 438
Vesey 74, 78, 225
Veysey 357
Villiers 218
Vincent 135, 218, 365, 446
Vinton 298
Vivian 40–1, 65
Vortimer 301

Wace 290
Wade 439
Wadham 139
Wainfleet 235
Wake 223, 234
Wakefield 276
Walbere 472
Walch 137
Waldavus 153
Walker 118
Walsh 144
Walter 309
Walwyn 470
Ward 270, 452
Ware 107
Warelwast 36, 65, 78
Warenne 462
Warham 187, 192
Warmecombe 170
Warner 192
Warre xlix, 176
warren 30, 425
Warrens 30, 364
Warwick (Countess) 292
Warwick (Earl) xxx, 120,
138–9, 142, 153, 260, 298–9, 359, 369–71, 377–8, 410, 415, 454, 456; *see also* Beauchamp, Neville
Waterton 424
Waterville 256
Watton (Prior) 439
Weke 238
Welby 231, 237
Wenford 231
Werburgh (St) 133, 259–60
Werstan 147
West 236
Westhaul 265
Westmorland (Countess) 113, 237, 421
Westmorland (Earl) 110, 112–13, 115–16, 269, 430, 444, 461; *see also* Neville
Weston 2
Whalley 282
Whiting 348
Whitney 129
Whittington 44
Whittlesey 187
Wich 412
Wickhampton 396
Wicks 134, 137–9, 146
Widdrington 272
Wigston 213–14
Wilfrid (St) 465
William I (King) 129, 148–9, 162, 231, 278, 287, 291, 424
William II (King) 162
Williams 289, 292
William's 3, 45, 148
Willibrord (St) 465
Willoughby 234–6, 349, 353, 378–9, 387
Willow (St) 54
Wiltshire (Earl) 107, 120; *see also* Boleyn
Winchcombe 125
Winchcombe (Prior) 125
Winchelsey 186
Winchester (Bp) 13, 15, 102, 152, 154, 156–7,

INDEX OF NAMES

160–1, 235, 362, 388, 404
Winchester (Earl) 150, 220
Wingfield 182
Wingston 378
Winter 416
Winwaldus (St) 463
Wise 77
Witham 233
Wodds 416
Wolfe xviii
Wolsey x–xi, 11, 153, 214, 353, 361
Wood xii
Woodstock 150
Woolridge 314
Worcester (Bp) xlvi, 128–9, 131, 136, 177, 374–5, 406, 409, 413–16, 434

Worcester (Countess) 220
Worcester (Earl) lii, 434; see also Percy
Worcester (Prior) 416
Worcestre xxx
Workcop 459
Worsley 202
Worth 42
Wotton 438
Wriothesley x, 158
Wulfe 429
Wulfhere (King) 351, 356
Wulfric 336
Wulfstan 129
Wyatt xvi, xlv, 190, 254
Wycliffe 458
Wyle 393
Wymbish 237
Wyndham 339

Wytte 397
Wyvil 397
Wyville 212, 466

Yogge 77
York 340
York (Abp) 113, 129, 131, 186, 278, 280, 353, 418–20, 429–30, 449–51, 462, 465
York (Dean) 427, 443
York (Duke) 121, 150, 256, 408, 421
Yoton 269
Young 314
Yve 261

Zouch, Zouche 7, 53, 81, 123, 217–19, 254, 261–2, 266, 349

INDEX OF SUBJECTS

This is a selective index of certain topics, especially in the fields of archaeology, trades and industries, plants and animals, which may be of special interest to users of this volume. Many topographical features and buildings, such as churches, bridges, woods and rivers, are mentioned on almost every page, and it would be pointless to index these. References to Leland's life and career are included in this index.

admiral 126
admiralty 402
adultery 270
alabaster 116, 213, 215, 217, 230, 287, 290, 348, 356-7, 429, 451
anchorages xxxvi, 29, 46, 48, 59, 78, 86, 135, 157, 191, 196, 235, 341
antlers 84, 115
archaeological sites xxvii-xxviii, xxxi, xlix, 112, 151, 211, 221; *see also* barrows; burials; coins and coin hoards; cremation urns; cropmarks; defended sites and hill-forts; linear earthworks; mosaics; Roman artefacts; settlements; standing stones
Arthurian connections xiv-xvi, xxiii, 34, 58, 320, 330, 332, 385, 471

barley, bigg- 460; four-rowed 383
barrows 50
baths 324-5
beacons and lighthouses 45, 191, 310, 439
beans 21, 211, 235, 245, 341
bells and bell towers 81, 95, 187, 265, 329, 348, 355, 376, 398, 406, 432, 440, 471

bigg-barley 460
birds 50, 58, 60-2, 198, 268, 315, 477
bloodletting (seyney) 231
boundary mounds and stones 300, 342, 385
breweries 128, 160
brickmaking 432
burials (archaeological discoveries) 6, 13, 67, 144, 163, 190, 199, 375

cannel 207-8
cap-making 380
carriers 259
carts 153, 192, 415
caves 50, 194, 283, 371-2, 385
chains (for defence) 48, 52, 54, 78, 83, 159, 435, 437, 456
cheese 131
chimneys 43, 463, 475
clocks 187, 406, 463
coal; see mining
cobble paving 432
coins and coin hoards 12, 112, 144-5, 165, 174-5, 193-4, 196-7, 205, 209, 212, 225, 227, 243, 269, 291, 323, 332, 361, 380, 390, 453, 470
conduits and conduit houses 55, 63, 67, 81-2, 96, 128, 136, 156, 158, 187, 228, 275, 303, 306, 327, 351, 360, 368, 419, 424, 447, 453, 456, 466

cotton manufacturing 207-8
coursing 141, 261
cow-dung (as fuel) 102
cremation urns 252
cropmarks (on archaeological sites) xxviii, 151, 162, 194, 212, 298
crops (less usual): *see* beans; bigg-barley; four-rowed barley; flax; garlic; hemp; peas; *see also* plants (less usual)
crops, liming or marling 30, 305, 319, 358
crosses 16, 54, 114, 144, 175, 193, 195, 222, 227, 258, 263, 271, 299, 315, 324, 335, 353, 368, 449, 454, 462
crosses, market 13, 16, 148, 235, 295, 327, 329-31, 351-2, 407, 425
cutlery 264, 376, 420

daggers 94, 109
'Dance of Death', painting 374
deer 27, 31-2, 59, 111-12, 115-16, 140, 160, 174, 177, 183, 204, 217, 235, 245, 254, 261, 274, 282, 293, 298, 305, 308, 312-13, 318-19, 337-8, 343, 345, 350, 357, 399, 409, 422, 446, 458, 460-1, 464, 475; *see also* antlers;

INDEX OF SUBJECTS

hunting
defended sites and hillforts
(not medieval castles) 12,
14, 17, 27, 42, 50, 137-8,
141, 144, 187, 194, 211-
12, 266, 271, 298, 316,
331-2, 343, 359-60, 382,
386, 395, 401, 403, 414,
426, 457-8, 460
drought 143
ducks 117
dyeing 10

elder, stinking 59
epidemic disease 17, 196,
252, 410
etymology 66, 72-3, 164,
166, 175, 188, 269, 309,
400, 423

fairs 6, 64, 74, 76, 79, 86,
107, 147, 186, 231, 233,
236, 240, 314, 322, 340,
355, 374, 388, 451, 464
ferries xxiii, 11, 16, 18, 29,
38, 44, 46, 54, 62, 70,
84, 100, 103-4, 117, 132,
135, 157-8, 169, 193,
195, 226, 229-30, 236,
242, 277, 280, 284, 291,
297, 300-1, 392, 428,
435, 451
festivities and games 173,
212, 326, 412
fires (destructive) 95-6,
105, 125, 136, 147, 196,
205, 233, 236, 278, 441
fir-roots (in meres, etc, used
as fuel) 26, 28, 30, 60,
203, 318
fish, fishing 28, 37-9, 45,
49-52, 54-62, 64, 68-9,
77, 82-6, 90-1, 97, 102-
4, 110, 119, 154, 156-9,
190, 193, 199, 207, 226,
263, 305, 318, 352, 384-
5, 393, 423, 431-3, 462,
468-9, 473
fishgarths 206
flax 469
flooding 14-15, 60, 128-9,

146, 148, 171, 181, 203,
233, 284, 296, 298, 329,
352, 394, 398, 401, 416,
471
fossils 138, 184, 345
fowling 198
four-rowed barley 383
fruit and orchards 2, 15, 21,
68, 202, 218, 288, 307,
378, 427, 431, 435, 456
fuels (less usual) xxvii; *see
also* cannel; coal; cow-
dung; fir-roots; gall;
gorse; heather; peat; turf
fulling 89, 124, 134, 139,
181, 344-5
furniture (desks and
cabinets) 435

gall 230
games and festivities 173,
212, 326, 412
gaols and prisons 21, 56,
63, 133, 155, 177, 181,
188, 190, 248, 295, 333,
384, 422, 432, 464
gardens 2, 58, 60, 68, 103,
202, 215, 218-19, 275,
288, 426, 431, 435, 456
garlic 43, 103
goats 206, 476
gorse (as fuel) 36, 64, 474
grain dealers 252, 472
guide xxii, 203

hazel 166
health resorts 189, 324
heather (as fuel) 36, 64
hemp 469
hermits and hermitages
13, 15, 96, 104, 119,
184, 194, 225, 256, 310,
312, 336, 371-2, 389-90,
399, 424, 452, 454, 456,
461-2
holly 198, 450
hunting 16, 150, 270, 343,
455; *see also* coursing;
deer; fowling

illnesses 190, 324, 370; *see

also* epidemic disease;
leprosy; madness;
physicians
incest 222
inns 108, 174, 187, 190,
315, 340, 459

Jews 133, 136-7, 152, 209,
371, 470
jousting (tilting) 270, 297
juniper 414

Leland, John:
bibliographical work
xii-xiv, xix; clerical
livings xvi; education
x-xi; influence xix, xxxi-
xxxiv; insanity xvii-xviii;
itineraries xv, xvii, xx-
xxxi, xli-xlix; language
xxxiv-xxxvii; monastic
visits xii-xiv; poetry xi,
xvi, xix
leprosy (and Lazar houses)
40, 65, 81, 98, 168, 196,
324, 407, 410
lighthouses and beacons 45,
191, 310, 439
liming and marling (crops)
30, 305, 319, 358
linear earthworks 2, 190,
426

madness xviii, xxxiii,
xxxviii, 9
magic and miracles 6, 129,
150, 184, 197, 292, 303
mammals 3, 41, 59, 61,
111, 208; *see also* deer,
goats; rabbits, seals,
sheep
maps xvii, xxvii, xxx-xxxi,
xxxiii-xxxiv, 49, 109, 221
marble carvers 356, 447
market crosses 13, 16, 148,
235, 295, 327, 329-31,
351-2, 407, 425
market houses and town
halls 14, 21, 103, 270,
275, 327, 336, 389, 404,
421, 432, 436

marling and liming (crops) 30, 305, 319, 358
mining: coal 115, 119, 207-8, 268, 275, 319, 347, 358, 377, 420, 426, 460, 464, 474-5; copper 50, 61; iron ore 119, 132, 358; lead 58, 119, 448, 457, 463, 477; tin: *see* tinworking
miracles and magic 6, 129, 150, 184, 197, 292, 303
moneybags 262
mosaics 144, 166, 243, 453; *see also* Roman artefacts

'New Year's Gift' xv, xvii, xx, xxiii, xxv, xxx-xxxi, xxxiii, xxxvii-xxxviii, xlii, xlviii, xlix-liv
nut trees 460

orchards and fruit 2, 15, 21, 68, 202, 218, 288, 307, 378, 427, 431, 435, 456

parchment makers 301
paving, cobbles 197, 243, 432
peas 211
peat (as fuel) 26, 202, 208, 305, 460
physicians 15, 189, 200, 325
piracy 51, 155-6
plants (less usual): *see* hazel; holly; juniper; stinking elder; *see also* crops (less usual)
pound, common 55, 294
prisons and gaols 21, 56, 63, 133, 155, 177, 181, 188, 190, 248, 295, 333, 384, 422, 432, 464
punishment, capital 94, 137, 150, 153, 166, 175, 186, 197, 199, 210, 270, 398, 419, 436, 469-70

quarrying, 50, 108, 113, 119, 139, 145, 147, 189, 202-3, 227, 260, 299, 322, 335, 342, 345, 392, 444; alabaster 217, 230; chalk 194; marble 119, 176, 222, 447, 459; millstones 203; slate 58, 216
quicksands 205

rabbits 29, 43, 58, 60, 62, 104, 194, 196, 263, 377; *see also* warrens
ransoms 126, 171, 270, 322, 397, 454
relics (of saints) 6, 16, 129, 136, 164, 172, 465
resorts, health 189, 324
riots and revolts 16, 95, 145, 195, 343, 365, 398-9, 423, 435-6
road conditions, adverse 22, 127, 296, 330, 333, 414
roads 16, 124, 144, 197, 205, 259, 322, 328-9, 353, 377, 394, 431, 455, 465
Roman artefacts 12, 41, 87, 112, 144-5, 165-6, 174-5, 193-4, 205, 212, 225, 227, 242, 244, 269, 291, 323-4, 332, 361, 390, 452-3, 470-1; *see also* coins and coin hoards; mosaics; settlements
ropemaking 94, 431

saltmaking 26, 28-30, 205, 405, 409, 411-13, 416
sanctuary, places of 46, 59-60, 158, 198, 408, 462
scribes 301
seals (animals) 61
seals (on documents) 68, 186, 301, 462
settlements (archaeological remains, pre-medieval) 12, 68-9, 165, 194, 208, 291, 360, 361, 453; *see also* Roman artefacts
seyney (bloodletting) 231
sheep 38, 58, 62, 99-101, 143, 226, 332
shipbuilding 84
shipwrecks 83, 190
smithing and metalworking 75, 358, 376-7, 420; bits 358; cutlery 376-7, 420; gold 301, 362; nails 377; pins 419
standing stones 439, 452-3, 460
stinking elder 59
stonemasons 241, 452
storms 44, 51, 83, 91, 101, 300, 312, 342

tentering frames 450
tide-mills 49
tilting (jousting) 270, 297
tinworking 42, 44-5, 48, 53, 57-63, 78-9, 82
town halls and market houses 14, 21, 103, 270, 275, 327, 336, 389, 404, 421, 432, 436
turf (as fuel) 26, 202, 205, 305, 418, 460, 476

underground passage 117
unemployment 140, 450

warrens (rabbit) 17, 79, 144, 291, 297, 364-5, 409; *see also* rabbits
water supply 4, 13, 15, 36, 45, 55, 63, 67, 81-3, 96, 136, 141, 152, 154, 156, 166-71, 171, 192, 215, 275, 323, 393, 424, 466; *see also* conduits and conduit houses; wells
weavers 128, 134, 222, 389
wells 23, 25, 42, 49, 58, 71, 96, 142, 163, 252, 264, 284, 287, 315, 326, 351, 394, 412, 453
wildlife: *see* birds, deer, ducks, fish, mammals, rabbits, seals
windmills 144, 228, 426, 470
witches 472

INDEX OF PLACES

All places mentioned in the text, including battlefields, islands, foreign countries and rivers, are indexed, but buildings, suburbs and localities within towns are excluded. Homonyms are distinguished by county or area. Leland's variant spellings are given in italics. Abbreviations include R(iver), I(sland), Is(lands).

Abbatsley 415
Abberley Castle 415
Abbey Dore 164, 169, 174–7, 310
Abbotsbury xiii, 101
Aberford 426, 454
Abergavenny 169, 174, 176–7, 242, 245, 248, 370
Abergwili 473
Aber-Marlais 473
Abertaw 72
Aberthaw 341
Aberystwyth xx
Abingdon xiii, xlvii, 8, 12–18, 124, 289, 291
Abson 146
Acle 177
Aconbury 164, 168, 175, 177
Acre, Castle xiii, 251
Acton, Iron 140–1
Acton, R 138
Acton (Ches) 30
Acton (Middx) 240
Acton Burnell 314, 317
Adderley 137
Adelstow 39
Adinggreves 5, 7
Adlestrop 142
Adlingfleet 455
Adlington 31
Agincourt, battle xxxv, xlvi, 171, 173, 255
Ailcy Hill 450
Aile, R 190
Ailston 190
Ailstone Bridge 169
Ainsty 428

Aire, R 419, 426, 428, 455–6, 463
Airmyn 437
Alaune, R 38, 58
Albans, St xiii, xliii, xlv, 2, 11, 180, 185, 303
Alberbury 177, 304, 317, 468, 478
Albrighton Park 313
Alcester xlvi, 367, 369, 372, 375–6, 381, 405, 411, 413, 416
Aldborough 452–3
Aldbrough 457
Aldburgh 440, 465
Alderley xlvii, 137–8
Alderley, stream 145
Aldermaston 18
Aldersey 30
Aldwick 346
Alençon 270
Alford 235, 237
Alingtre 168
All Hallows (Lancs) 204
All Stretton 308
Allen, R 39
Allen Bridge 104–5
Allen, St 40, 65
Aller 340
Aller, R 86
Allhallows Hill 450
Allington (Kent) 189, 192, 195
Allington (Wilts) 390
Almondsbury 146
Aln, R 273
Alne, R 372, 375–6
Alney I 142
Alnwick 268, 272–3, 275

Alport Park 201
Alre, R 152–4
Alresford 153–4
Alresford R 157
Alscote 75
Alsford Pond 153
Altoft 461
Alton 154
Altrincham 31
Alvechurch 375–6, 405, 413–14, 416
Alveley 415
Alverdiscott 75
Alveston 140
Alvington 131
Amber, R 70
Amberbridge 70
Amersham 22–3, 181, 240
Amesbury 395
Amounderness 204–6, 209
Ampney, brook 123
Ampney Crucis 123
Ampthill xlv, xlvii, 1, 4–6
Ancaster xxviii, 221, 225–6, 234, 237, 302
Ancaster Heath 225–6, 234
Ancholme, R 236
Andersey I 15
Anderton 203
Anderton, R 203
Andertonford, R 203
Andover 151, 161, 404
Anglesey 243
Angon, Cair 409
Anker, R 354–6, 381–2
Ankerwyke Priory 19–20
Anton, R 151
Antony 41, 50, 57

Antony Creek 57, 61
Apley 314, 319
Appleby xxxvi, 384–5
Appledore (Devon) 75
Appledore (Kent) 189, 191, 194–5, 197–8
Applegarthdale 459
Appleton 444
Appleton, Nun 427
Archenfield 248
Ardaverameur 44
Arden 373
Ardeveraman 44
Ardevora 44, 49
Arkengarthdale 460
Arley 415
Arncote 293
Arrow, R (Herefs) 165, 171, 174, 470
Arrow, R (War) 372, 375–6, 414–15
Arrow Bridge 171
Arthingworth, brook 260
Arthur's Hill (Round Table) 385, 471
Arun, R 364
Arundel xlix, 252, 364, 366
Arustle 473
Arwennak 47
Arwystli 473
Asaph, St 168, 175
Ashbourne 70
Ashby, Castle 257
Ashby by Partney 237
Ashby de la Zouch 216–19
Ashford 186, 189, 194, 199
Ashley 33
Ashprington 81–2
Ashridge Priory 180, 404
Ashton (Lancs) 205
Ashton, Long 400
Ashton, Steeple 402
Ashwellthorpe 251
Askrigg 461
Aslockton 284
Aspebyri 30
Astley Castle 382
Astley College 216
Aston 357, 376
Aswick 231

Atcham 310, 318
Athelney 336, 348
Atherstone 367, 381
Auckland, Bishop 111–12, 114–15, 117–19, 464
Auckland, St Andrews 111, 115
Auckland, West 111
Auckland Castle 111–12
Audley 356
Audrie's, St 339
Aust xlviii, 132, 169, 242
Aust Cliff 132, 169
Austell, St 50, 61
Austerson 33
Avebury 400
Avon, R (Bristol) 132–5, 143, 322, 325, 342, 344–5, 388–92, 403–4
Avon, R (Christchurch) 393–6, 399, 401
Avon, R (Devon) 81, 84
Avon, R (Warw) xxiv, 126, 142, 143, 147–8, 150, 367–9, 371–6, 381–2, 406, 415
Avon, R 2, 254
Avon, stream (Glos) 138
Avona 199
Avonmouth 320
Avon's 135, 381
Axbridge 349
Axe, R 91–2, 99
Axe Bay 92
Axe Bridge 91 Axe Bridge 91
Axholme 4, 30, 221, 229–30, 237, 422
Axminster 92
Axmouth 91–2, 97, 99
Axnoller 99
Aylesbury 19, 21–3
Aylesbury, Vale of 20–1
Aylesford 189–90, 192
Aynho 265, 296
Aysgarth Bridge 463
Ayton 442, 443
Ayton Bridge 428

Babington 230

Bablake 380
Babraham 287
Babthorpe 466
Baconsthorpe 250
Badbury 104
Badby 259
Baddiley 32
Baddiley Mere 32
Baddington 32
Badlesmere 188
Badminton 146
Baginton Castle 382
Bagley Wood 12–13
Bagworth Park 217
Bahan, Parke 245
Baienet 364
Bain, R 236
Bainbridge 463
Bakewell 70–1
Balsall, Temple 371, 382
Bamburgh 272–3, 275
Bamburghshire 273–5
Bampton (Devon) 92
Bampton (Westmor) 385
Banbury 21–2, 259, 265, 294–6, 299, 367, 370, 381
Banbury, hundred 295
Bane-burgh 236
Bangor 215
Banka, St 41
Banwell 343, 346
Bar, stream 32
Barbridge 32
Bardney xiii, 131, 236
Barehamdoune 187
Barford, Great 5
Barford Bridge 372–3
Barforth 458
Barham 187
Barley Bridge 384
Barlings Abbey 236
Barmby 428
Barn Park 217
Barnard Castle 116–18, 417, 447, 458–9
Barnby 434
Barnet 2
Barningham 459
Barnsdale Forest 417, 419

INDEX OF PLACES

Barnstaple xiii, 72–5, 92
Barnstaple's 73
Barnwell xiii, 254
Barow 17
Barrington 131
Barrow Castle 252
Barrow Gurney 342, 346
Barrowby 223
Barr's Court 121, 132, 343
Barton 254
Barton, hundred 149
Barton (Lancs) 31
Barton (Staffs) 357
Barton Heath 300
Barton-on-Humber 237, 433
Basford 336
Basingstoke 161
Basingwerk 29
Bassaleg 246
Bassett's Cross 353
Bassingthorpe 224
Baston 231
Bath xiii, xxv, 75, 92, 139, 142–4, 320, 322–8, 330, 340, 342–6, 391–2
Bathan Wood 105
Bathpool 336
Battenhall 416
Battle Abbey 365, 472
Battlefield 309–10
Baumber 236
Bawddwr, Nant 473
Bawtry 277–9, 281, 420
Baynton 404
Bayworth 13
Beachley 169
Beal 275
Beaminster 91, 98–9
Bearwood 377
Beauchamps Hall 375–6
Beaudesert 357
Beaulieu xiii, 46, 158
Beaumanor 220
Beaumanor Park 216–17
Beaumont Leys 217, 220
Beaurepaire Park 113
Bec-Hellouin 259
Beckbury 314
Becketbury 138

Beckington 298
Bedale 457, 459
Bedenham Creek 159
Bedford xxi, xxii, xliv, 1–7, 366, 373
Bedfordshire **1–7**, 11, 23, 182, 313, 427
Bedlington 268
Bedlingtonshire 268
Bedminster 135
Bedwas 246
Bedwyn, brook 400
Bedwyn, Great 399–400, 404
Bedwyn, Lit Beechwood 179
Beela, R 383
Beer 91
Beeston 30, 32–3
Beetham 206, 383
Bekharwik 259
Belcastle 69
Belgrave 217
Belgrave Park 229–30
Bellaport 313
Bellingham 272, 384
Bellirica 197
Bellocastrum 197
Belton Park 229
Belvoir, Vale of 219, 232
Belvoir Castle 211, 218–19, 232, 284–5, 302
Benefield 261
Benefield Castle 266
Benefield Laund 254
Bere (Berks) 10
Bere (Devon) 41, 51, 63, 80
Bere Ferrers 77
Bere Forest 160
Bergenny 373
Berkeley 132, 138–9, 141, 146
Berkhamsted xliv, 179–81
Berkshire **8–18**, 287, 300, 404
Bermondsey 243, 248
Bernwood Forest 293
Berrington Hall 173
Berry Head 84–5
Berry Pomeroy 82

Berwick-on-the-Hill 438
Berwick on Tweed 231, 272–5
Besford 318
Bessels Leigh 297
Bestwood Park 282
Bethnal Green 241
Beuamazin, battle 335
Beverley xiii, xxiii, 417, 429–33, 437, 441, 461–3
Beverstone Castle 146
Bewbush Park 366
Bewcastle 69
Bewdley 318–19, 405, 407–9, 411, 415–16
Bewgenet 364, 366
Bewpray 41
Bicester 263, 293–4, 296
Bickleigh Bridge 78
Bickley 26
Bicknor 174
Bideford 75–6, 92
Bidford Bridge 372
Bidford-on-Avon 375
Bidwell Brook 82
Bierton 21, 23
Biggleswade 6
Bignell 294
Bikers Dyke 229
Billerica (Court at Street) 192, 197
Billesley 375
Bilsby 237
Binchester 112
Bindon 100, 102
Birdsall 438–9
Birkenhead Priory 29
Birkhead Hall 209
Birmingham xxv, 357, 367, 376–7, 381–2
Birmingham Water 379
Bisham Priory 11
Bishop Auckland 111–12, 114–15, 117–19, 464
Bishop Dike 419
Bishop Sutton 345
Bishopdale 458, 460, 464
Bishop's Burton 462
Bishop's Castle 177, 306–7, 313, 316–17, 468–9

Bishop's Cleeve 148, 177
Bishop's Hall 241, 362
Bishop's Stones 119
Bishop's Stortford 181
Bishop's Town 313, 472
Bishop's Waltham 157, 160
Bishop's Water 215
Bishopthorpe 418
Bismouth 402
Biss Bottom 402
Biss, R 342, 392, 402
Bitchfield 234
Bitlyndon 227
Bitterne 157
Bitton 132
Black Bridge 154
Black Head 50
Black Hills (Clent Hills) 376–7, 414
Black Mere 26, 305, 318
Black Moor (Cleveland Hills) 438, 445–6, 460
Black Mountains 472
Black Park 318
Black Rigg 443
Black Rock 85
Black Shore 195
Black Water 350
Blackburn 465
Blackburnshire 201, 206
Blackheath, battle 161
Blackley 208
Blackmere 318
Blackmore (Yorks) 455
Blackmore Forest (Dorset) 94, 106, 109
Blackmore Forest (Wilts) 401
Blackmore Vale 94
Blackthorn Bridge 293
Blackwater, R 157
Blackwood 246
Blacon Head 29
Blaen Usk 472
Blaen-Cowin 474
Blagdon 106
Blakein 305
Blakmore 443
Blakwel 70
Blanchland 273

Blandford Forum 104, 106, 109
Blazey, St 51
Bleaklow 70
Bleasdale Forest 204
Bledington 298
Bletchingley 366
Bletsoe 1–2, 6
Blith, R 357
Blithelow 421
Blockley 410
Blore Park 357
Bloreheath 316
Bloughan Pool 52
Bloxham 410
Blyth 277–8, 281
Blyth, R (Northumb) 268
Blyth, R (Notts) 277, 279, 281, 421
Blyth, R (Suffolk) 359
Blythburgh 359–60
Blythe, R (Warws) 382
Bobbing 200
Boddington 146
Bodiam Castle 195, 198
Bodinnick 54–5, 62
Bodmin 36, 39–40, 52, 55, 57–8, 63–5
Bodmin Pool 52
Bodrugan Park 50
Bokelly 44
Bolingbroke 223, 231, 233, 236
Bollin, R 28
Bologna 188
Bolsover 70
Bolton (Lancs) 207–8
Bolton (Northumb) 273
Bolton (Yorks, Wensleydale) 339, 448, 457, 461, 463
Bolton (Yorks, Craven) 454
Bonhams 403
Booth 31, 315
Boothby Pagnell 221–4
Booths 202
Bordesley Abbey 416
Bordford 16
Boroughbridge 385, 437, 451–2, 459

Borrowdale 68
Bosbury 177
Boscastle 36–7, 64
Bosham 79
Bossiney 37–8, 64
Bostock 32
Boston xiii, 221, 223, 226, 231, 233–5, 251
Bosworth Field, battle 23, 27, 413
Bothom 105
Botley 157–8, 161
Boubent 274
Boulogne xvi, 188, 195–6
Bourne xiii, 223, 225, 234
Bourne, R 448
Bourton-on-the-Water 142
Bourton Water 142
Bovy I 59
Bow Bridge 81
Bowes 117, 270, 385, 447, 458, 460
Bowland Forest 204
Bowling Hall 462
Bowmont Water 274
Bowness 66–7, 271
Bowston 384
Bowthorpe 231
Boxgrove Priory 364
Boxley 200
Boxwell 146
Bracebridge 227
Brackenbury 116, 138
Brackley xxvii, 253, 263–6, 294
Bradenstoke Priory 124, 321, 390
Bradfield 420
Bradford 417, 462–3
Bradford Abbas 107
Bradford on Avon 322, 342, 344, 387, 391–2, 403
Bradford Peverell 99–100
Bradgate 211, 215–17, 220
Bradley (Lancs) 207
Bradley, Maiden 344, 407, 416
Bradley, North 342

INDEX OF PLACES

Bradon Forest 123, 390
Bradstock 342
Brailes 265, 373
Brambridge 189
Bramhall 31
Brampton Bryan 307
Brân, R 473
Brancepeth 110, 112–13
Brandbridges 189
Brandon Castle 382
Brandon Hill 134–5, 382
Bray 9
Braybrooke 261, 343, 346
Brayford 72
Brea, Carn 43
Breage 34, 41
Breamish, R 274
Breckenbrough 445
Brecknockshire 131, 248, 467, 472
Brecon xliii, xliv, 166, 169, 249, 467, 471–2
Brede 195
Brede, R 195
Bredebridge 195
Bredon 148, 405, 415
Bredwardine 164, 174
Breidden 479
Breighton 435
Breinton 165
Bremischam 376
Brenbygey 244
Brennig, brook 476
Brent, East 348
Brent, South 81
Brent Brook 239
Brent Marsh 349
Brentford 239–40
Brereton Hall 28, 31, 33
Brest 365
Brewham 331
Brewood Priory 317
Bridford Bridge 86
Bridgnorth 304, 307, 310–12, 314, 316, 405, 407, 411, 415
Bridgwater 107, 320, 333, 336–8, 341, 348–9
Bridlington xiii, 433, 440–3

Bridport 94, 98–9, 109, 397–8
Brier, The 423
Brierley Park 419
Brigg 236, 440, 443
Briggs, Linne 272
Brignall Park 447, 459
Briket Hall 209
Brinkburn Priory 273
Brinklow 382
Briscot 206
Bristol xiii, xxvi, xxx, xli, xlvii, 8, 94, 121, 124, 132–8, 141–6, 149, 169, 286, 320, 322, 342–3, 346, 387–8, 392, 400
Bristol Channel (Severn Sea) 37, 64, 75, 320
Brittany 39, 50, 97, 464
Brixham 84
Broad Stairs 193
Broadgate 378
Broadward Bridge 171
Brock, R 204
Brockhurst 318
Brockworth 131
Brokenbridge (*see also* Pontefract) 423–4
Bromfield 130, 165, 177, 307, 318
Bromham 390, 401
Bromley 33
Bromley, Gerrard's 33
Brompton 442
Bromsgrove 146, 405, 411, 413, 415–16
Bromswold 183, 254, 262
Bromyard 165, 169, 177, 307
Broncroft 317
Bronllys 471
Bronsil 146
Brooke Hall 42, 80, 308, 387, 402–3
Brookesby 218
Broomfield 337
Broomhall 32
Brotherton 455
Brough (Westmor) 384–6
Brough (Yorks) 438

Brougham 68, 384–6
Broughton 23, 183
Brown Clee 318–19
Browney, R 113
Brownsea I 104
Bruce's Hall 443
Brue, R 329–31
Bruer, Temple 226
Bruern 142, 298–9
Bruerne 298, 344
Brunsdown 92
Brunston 442
Bruteport 98
Bruton 320, 329–31, 344
Bryan, Brampton 307
Bryer, R 229
Brympton d'Evercy 339
Brynbuga 244
Buckden 183
Buckenham Castle 251–2
Buckfast xiii
Buckholt Wood 151, 399
Buckhurst 366
Buckingham 1, 19, 21–3, 181, 264, 294
Buckinghamshire 9, 11, **19–23**, 181, 223, 259, 266, 293, 300, 313
Buckland xiii, 77
Buckland, Minchin 337–8
Bucknall 231
Budby, brook 279
Buddel, stream 97
Budleigh, East 90
Budley 157
Budock 47, 77
Budworth 30
Buerton 313
Buildwas 310, 317, 319
Builth 169–70, 470
Bukenhalle 231
Bulbourne, R 181
Bulkeley Hill 32
Bunbury 27, 31–3
Burford (Oxon) 298–9
Burford (Salop) 173, 307, 318, 469
Burgh by Sands 66–7, 271
Burgh Castle, 360
Burghchester 296

Burleigh 217
Burleigh Park 216
Burn, R (Bucks) 19
Burn, R (Yorks) 465
Burnell, Acton 314, 317
Burneside 384
Burnham (Bucks) 20
Burnham (Som) 320
Burnhope Burn 112
Burrough Hill xxviii, 211–12
Burrow (Lancs) 208

Burrow Bridge (Som) 333, 336, 348
Burscough Priory 206
Burston 21, 23
Burton (Chesh) 351
Burton (Lincs) 227
Burton (Sussex) 366
Burton, North 462
Burton, South 462
Burton Head 29
Burton Lazars 211
Burton upon Trent 353–5
Bury 118, 207–8
Bury Bank 356
Bury St Edmunds xiii, xxiii, xlix
Butcombe 346
Buttercrambe Bridge 428
Butterwick 230–1, 456
Butterwick, West 230
Buttington Bridge 310
Buxton 71
Byland xiii, 66, 267, 418
Byry 303
Byth 383
Bytham, Castle 221
Bytham, Little 221
Bywell Castle 269

Cablan 58
Cadbury, North 331
Cadbury, South xxiii, 320, 331–2
Caebitra 468
Caen 133, 149
Caer-Bladon 388
Caerhays 40

Caerleon 242–6, 248–9
Caernarvon 130
Caerwent 242–4
Caiach, Nant 246
Caiholme 307
Cair Angon 409
Cair Kenin 42
Cairdine 41
Cairovalduine 316
Cairuske 244
Caistor 236–7
Caisway 391
Calais xi, 194, 366, 404
Calamansack 46
Calcethorp 236
Calder, R (Lancs) 204, 206, 208
Calder, R (Yorks) 425–6, 461–2
Calder Abbey 69
Caldey I 475
Caldicot 244
Caldshore 156
Caldwall 416
Caldwell 457, 460
Caldwell Priory 3
Cale, R 106, 108, 403
Cale Bridge 108
Calshot 157–8
Calstock Bridge 35, 56–7
Calveley 27, 32–3
Cam, R 331–2
Camber 195
Cambridge x, xii, xiii, xxiii, xliv, 1, **24–5**, 42, 182, 198, 200, 208, 241, 287
Cambridgeshire xlix, 24–5, 180, 183, 185, 187, 217, 251
Camel, R 38–40, 329
Camel, Queen 332
Camelford 39, 53, 58, 64–5
Camelot xxiii, 320, 331–2
Camlad 468
Campden, Chipping 142, 265
Cank Wood 353
Cannington 338
Cannock Chase 353, 357
Canterbury xiii, 6, 184–95,

197–9, 241, 278, 285, 310, 325, 364, 374, 449, 455
Cantreceli 471
Canwell Priory 353
Canwick 227
Carburton, brook 279
Cardiff xlviii, 242, 245–6
Cardinham Castle 51, 53
Caregroyne 61
Cargreen 57, 61, 63
Carham 274
Carhampton 340
Carleton 68
Carlisle 26, 66–9, 197, 215, 269, 271, 385–6, 427
Carlton 228
Carlton, South 237
Carlton Moor 460
Carmarthen xliii, xlviii, 166, 473–6
Carmarthenshire xlviii
Carn Brea 43
Carne Godolphin 42
Carne Gotholghan 57
Carnetun 340
Carnhangibes 44
Carr Bridge 48
Carrick Roads 61
Cartmel 210
Cartmel Sands 206
Cartuther 55
Carvoran Castle 271
Cary, Castle 331, 349
Casset Wood 319
Castel Luen 69
Castel Daques 335
Castel de Placeto 120
Castell Coch 478
Castell Foel Allt 469
Casterton 232
Casterton, Great 302–3
Castle Acre xiii, 251
Castle an Dinas 40, 65
Castle Ashby 257
Castle Bytham 221
Castle Cary 331, 349
Castle Combe 403
Castle Donington 218, 287
Castle Dore 54

INDEX OF PLACES 503

Castle Eaton 123
Castle Frome 177
Castle Hay 357
Castle Heaton 273
Castle Hill 234, 279
Castle Mills 4, 7
Castle Park 7
Castle Rising 252
Castleford 426
Castleton Park 245
Castrencis 168
Catherton Clee 319
Catley Priory 224
Cattal Bridge 465
Catterick 385, 457–60
Catterick Bridge 457, 464, 466
Catton Park 428
Caullons Creek 46
Caundle 97, 107
Caus 313, 316, 468–9, 479
Causeby 423
Causham 10
Cave, North 433
Caversham 10–11, 286
Caverswell Castle 356
Cawood 419–20
Cawshot 156
Cayl Castle 43
Caynham Castle 307, 317
Caynton 314
Caythorpe Castl*Cerceden* 298
Cerne Abbas xiii, 99, 104, 390
Ceterington 439
Chagford 86
Chagha Mill Pool 52
Chalfont 20
Chalkbourne 393, 400
Char, R 97, 385
Chard 320
Charing 195
Charlecote 372–3
Charlton Castle 295, 314, 317, 319
Charmouth 97
Charnwood Forest 211, 216–18
Charterhouse, Hinton 322

Charwelton 259, 295
Chat Moss 202, 207
Chater, R 303
Chatton 268
Chaveney's Leazes 219
Cheddar 349
Cheilow Creek 46
Chelsea 161
Cheltenham 127, 142, 147
Chenies 20, 23, 180
Cheping Lanburne 17
Chepstow 131, 169–70, 242–5, 248–9
Chertsey 20
Cherwell, R 259, 293–6, 301
Chesford 381
Cheshire xvi, xx, xxxviii, **26–33**, 201, 206, 270, 305, 313, 316, 318
Cheshunt 179, 181
Chesil Beach 98, 101
Chess, R 181
Chester xxix, 26, 29–30, 32–3, 114, 175, 274, 310, 312, 314–16, 356, 382, 470
Chester, diocese 204
Chester Bar 29
Chesterfield 70
Chester-le-Street 114, 118, 273–4
Chesterton 143, 369
Cheviot Forest 274–5, 455
Cheviot Hills 274, 455
Chew Magna 345
Chewton Mendip 326
Chich 21
Chicheley 304
Chichester 186, 364, 366, 412
Chicksands Priory 3, 6
Chideock 97, 107
Childerley 185
Chilham 189, 199
Chillingham 268, 273–4
Chilswell 15
Chiltern Hills 21–3, 179–80
Chinnock, East 334, 348

Chipchase 269, 272
Chippenham 389–90, 392, 403
Chipping Campden 142, 265
Chipping-Faringdon 14
Chipping Norton 265, 294, 299, 382
Chipping Sodbury 124, 138–9, 141–2
Chirbury, hundred 316, 468–9
Chirbury Priory xliii, 177, 468
Chisiltun 290
Chislehampton 290–1
Cholderton, East 161
Cholmondeley Hall 26–7, 33
Cholmondeston 33
Chorley 203, 208
Christchurch xiii, 104, 157–8, 395
Christian Malford 391
Chudleigh Bridge 86
Church Stretton 304, 308
Churchill 298
Churn, R 123–4, 143
Churncester 143
Churne, Rt 357
Churntown 143
Chute 345
Cinque Ports 14, 184, 191, 196–7, 199
Cirencester xiii, xxiii, 121, 123–4, 127, 132, 142–4, 387
Claerddu 477
Claines 416
Clarel's Hall 422
Clarendon Park 399
Clawson 211
Clee Hills 304, 307, 317–19, 415
Cleeve, Bishop's 148, 177, 415
Cleeve Abbey xiii, 74, 339
Cleeve Chapel 339–40
Cleeve Hill 148
Clent 416

Clent Hills 377
Cleobury Mortimer 310, 318–19, 415
Cleveland Hills 418, 455, 460
Cliffe, St Margaret's at 190–1, 262, 367, 371
Clifford 174, 266
Clifford Bridge 86
Clifford Priory 177
Clifton Maybank 97, 107, 281, 347
Clipstone 282
Clobham Bridge 53
Clopton 375
Clovelly 92
Cloverley 313
Cluideford 469
Clun 469
Clwyd Forest 173
Clyro 470
Clyst 89
Coates 300
Cobb 97
Coberley 124, 143, 146
Cobham 362, 421
Coch, Castell 478
Coche 15
Cock Beck 426–7, 455, 461
Cocker, R 67, 205
Cockerham 205
Cockermouth 67–9, 268
Cockersand Abbey 205
Cod Beck 445
Codde Fowey 65
Codnor 70, 171, 261
Codrington 137
Coker, West, stream 97
Colcombe Park 91
Cold Norton Priory 299
Coldfield 377
Coldfield Heath 377
Coldfield, Sutton xxxiii, 350, 357–8, 367, 377–8
Coldingham 231–2
Coldstream 274
Cole, brook 379
Cole, R 382
Colebridge 269
Colecester 269

Coleshill 353, 379, 382
Coleshill Hall 357
Colham 240
Collyweston 221, 262, 265, 303
Coln, R 123
Colnbrook 9, 19, 240
Colne Priory 120
Colne, R 9, 19–20, 23, 180, 239–40
Columb St John 40, 65, 80
Colwall Park 177
Coly, R 90–1
Colyford 91
Colyton 90–1, 97
Comban 341
Combe Sydenham 339
Combe, Castle 403
Combeinteignhead 86
Combermere Abbey 28, 30, 32
Combermere Lake 318
Comeustwith 477
Compton, Long 294
Compton Valence 99
Compton Wynyates 373
Conarton 58
Conder, R 205
Cong Burn 115, 274
Congleton 28, 30–1
Conin 42
Conisbrough 422
Conishead Sands 206
Conke, R 274
Connor 43
Connor Downs 58
Conor, Dour, R 58
Constantine 47
Cook Hill Priory 376
Cookham 9, 349
Coombe Castle 43
Coombe Park 361–2
Copplestone 41
Coquet, R 268, 271–4
Coquet I, 268, 273, 464
Coquetdale 272–3
Corbek 103
Corbridge 267–9
Corby (Lincs) 222
Corby (Northants) 211

Corfham Castle 317
Coriminum 123, 143
Corn Brook 201
Corndean Farm 150
Cornhill 274
Cornwall xvi, xx, xxiii, xxiv, xxxiv, 11–12, **34–65**, 72, 79, 97, 124, 168, 173, 180, 229, 238, 318, 330, 337, 339, 349, 387, 390
Cornworthy 81–2
Corscombe 332
Corsenside 272
Corsham 390
Corston 389
Corve, R 306, 308, 313, 317–18
Corve, stream 269
Corvedale 177, 308, 317–18
Costa Beck 438, 442, 444
Coteren 464
Coterine 208
Cotherstone 208
Cothi, R 473
Cotswolds 8, 124, 131, 142–4, 150, 406, 416
Cotter End 464
Cotterdale 208
Cotterstock 265
Cottingham 430–1
Cotton 313–14
Coughton 375–6, 414
Coukefeild 376
Cound 311
Coupland 69, 274
Court-at (up)–Street 192, 197
Couwhath 51
Coventry xxv, 295, 351, 353, 355, 367, 379–82
Cover, R 448, 458–9, 465
Coverdale 459–60
Coverham 458–60, 465
Cowbach 416
Cowbage 416
Cowdray 363
Cowes, East and West 158
Cowhill 275
Cowley Bridge 88–9

INDEX OF PLACES 505

Cowmore 275
Cowton Moor, battle 446
Cowwath 65
Coxford 252
Crabwall 29
Craig Ddu 477
Craig Naw Llyn 477
Crambeck, stream 437
Cranage 32
Cranborne 94, 105–6, 148–9
Cranbrook 189, 194
Crannel Moor 329
Crantock 45, 58
Craven 418, 441, 454, 459–60, 464
Crawford Bridge 109
Crawley 298
Cray, R 190
Crayke Castle 418, 445
Crecy, battle 335
Crediton 72, 89
Creedy, R 88–9
Crendon Bridge 20
Crewkerne 98, 335–6
Crich Chase 70
Criche 334
Cricklade 123, 143, 145
Croes Oswald 314
Croft (Herefs) 173
Croft (Yorks) 447
Croft Bridge 117
Cromford 70
Croscombe 326, 328, 330
Crosho 208
Crossford 28, 201
Croston 203, 208
Crowland xiii, 221, 231–2, 235, 303
Crowle 229, 416
Crowlington 310
Crows Hall 360
Croxteth 207
Croxton (Cambs) 25
Croxton (Leics) 212, 219
Croxton Kerrial 302
Croydon 250
Crudgington Bridge 310
Crug 248
Crugiau Rhos Wen 476

Cuckney 282
Cudden-Beck 62
Cuddington 362
Cudlow 364
Culbone 341
Culham 15
Culham Water 15
Culhamford 16
Culy Castle 40
Cumberland xxi, **66–9**, 205, 268, 271, 452, 463
Cumbermere 32
Cumbria 253, 267
Cumwhitton 67
Curdworth Bridge 357, 379
Curry, North 336
Curry Mallet 336
Curtop Street 192
Cwm-tinwen 477
Cwmystwyth 477
Cybi, St 244
Cynin, R 474
Cynon, brook 470
Cywyn Bridge 474
Cywyn, R 474

Dagge Bridge 308
Dalgezire, siege 335
Dalton 462
Damerham 348
Danby Wiske 459, 465
Dane, R 28, 30, 199
Darley 31, 70
Darlington 111, 117–19
Dart, R 81–2, 84
Dartford 190
Dartington Park 82
Dartmoor 82, 86
Dartmouth 52, 82–5, 90, 93
Darwen, R 203–4, 208
Dauntsey 44, 321
Daven, R 30
Davenham 32
Davenport 31
Daventry 295, 380
David's, St 172, 474
Ddu, Craig 477
Deal 187, 190–1
Dean, Forest of 132, 145–6, 150, 170, 177–8
Dearne, R 419
Debenham 360
Decumans, St 339
Decun, St 339
Deddington 265
Dee, R 29–30
Deene xxiii, 150, 211–12, 260–2
Deene Water 275
Deep Hatch, R 59
Deepdales 428
Deeping 231, 233–4
Deeping, East 303
Deeping, Market 231, 233–4, 303
Deeping, West 303
Deerhurst 121, 142, 146–7
Deerness, R 113
Deira, Wood of 462
Deirewauld 462
Delamere Forest 27, 31
Delapre Abbey 255, 258
Delapre Park 258
Delaval 272
Dele 187
Delph, The 183
Denbigh 314
Denhall 29, 351
Denhall Roads 29
Denney Abbey 25
Dent 208
Dentdale 208
Denys, St 157
Derby 70, 284, 353, 356,
Derby, West 202–3, 206
Derbyshire 30–1, **70–1**, 218, 317, 420
Derbyshire, West 201, 206–7
Deritend 376–7
Dertwiche 28, 30
Derwent, R (Cumb) 67–8
Derwent, R (Derbs) 70–1
Derwent, R (Durham) 118, 270, 273
Derwent, R (Yorks) 428, 434–5, 437–8, 442–4, 461
Devernesse 113

Devizes 387, 401
Devonshire xii, xxiii, xxiv, 6, 35, 41–2, 47, 54, 57, 63, **72-93**, 209, 333, 336–40, 342
Dewi Fawr, stream 474
Didbrook 125, 148
Didcot 148
Diddlebury 177
Dieppe 48
Diffrin Risca 246
Diffrin Tyve 476
Dinas Castle 471
Dinas, Castle an 40, 65
Dinas, Hen xxxvi, 315–16
Dinmore Hill 170
Dipperford 76, 92
Disney, Norton 224
Divelish, R 107
Dodington 137–8, 145–6
Dodman Point 50, 61
Dogdyke Ferry 226, 236
Dogmersfield 327
Dolbury 343
Dolforwyn 478
Don, R 277, 420–2
Doncaster 209, 229, 277–9, 417, 419–23, 438–9, 455
Donington (Lincs) 218
Donington, Castle 218
Donnington 17, 287
Doravona 199
Doravonum 199
Dorchester (Dorset) 94, 100, 108, 394
Dorchester (Oxon) 12, 16, 18, 124, 286, 290–1, 300,
Dore, Abbey 164, 169, 174–7, 310
Dore, Castle 54
Dore, R 175–6
Dorset xxiii, xxiv, xxvi, xlix, 41, 55, 72, 91, **94-109**, 148, 158, 396, 398
Dorstone 174, 176
Douglas, R 203, 206–7
Doulting 329
Doune 84

Dounevet 57
Dour Conor 58, 416
Doure, R 186
Dove, R 314, 356–7
Dover xiii, 184, 187–9, 191–2, 195
Dover, stream 192
Dowdyke 231
Dowles Brook 415
Down Ampney 123
Downesend 84
Downton 395
Dozmary Pool 57–8
Dozrey, battle 335
Draycot Cerne 390
Draycott in the Moors 357
Draynes Bridge 53
Drayton (Leics) 218
Drayton (Northants) 257
Drayton (Oxon – north) 299
Drayton (Oxon – south) 290
Drayton (Salop) 318
Drayton (Staffs) 355
Drayton, Market 310, 313, 316
Driffield, Great 442
Drisilega 145
Droitwich 405, 409, 411–13, 416
Drumburgh 67
Dryslwyn Castle 473
Duddey, stream 474
Duddon Sands 68–9, 206
Dudley Castle 316–17, 356, 377, 379, 416, 478
Dudmaston 314
Duffield 70–1
Duggels, R 203
Dulas, R 175–6, 470, 473
Dulcote 328, 330
Dunedik 231
Dunesdale 231
Dunestaple 6
Dunevet 63, 252
Dungen 199
Dunham Massey 28, 31
Dunkeswell xiii, 93, 338
Dunmere 39, 58, 64

Dunstable xiii, 1, 5–6, 21–3, 303
Dunstanburgh Castle 273
Dunster 340–1
Dunwich 359–60
Duravennum 199
Durham (City) xiii, 66, 112–19, 269, 417, 464
Durham (County) xxiii, xli, xliv, xlv, **110-19**
Durham (Diocese) 268, 270, 396, 438, 460
Dursley 121, 139, 145–6
Dutton 32
Dyffryn Dore 175
Dyffryn Dulas 175
Dyffryn Sirhowey 246
Dynevor Castle 473
Dyrham 137–40
Dyrtey 376

Eagle 219, 315
Eamont, R 68, 385
Eamont Bridge 385
Earl's Dike 442
Earls' Hill 294
Easby Abbey xiii, 458
East Anglia xxiii, xxxii, xlviii
East Brent 348
East Budleigh 90
East Chinnock 334, 348
East Cholderton 161
East Cowes 158
East Deeping 303
East Hanney 17
East Harlsey 446
East Harptree 343
East Looe 55, 62–3
East Lulworth 102–4
East Meon 158
East Retford 278–9
East Tanfield 451, 459
East Wivelshire, hundred 63
Eastbeck 439
Eastgate 111
Eastleach 121
Eastnor 146
Easton 153

INDEX OF PLACES 507

Eastwood (Glos) 141
Eastwood (Som) 343, 346
Eaton (Chesh) 32, 313
Eaton Socon 5–6
Eaton, Castle 123
Eaton, Water 123
Ebbingford 37
Ebble, R 393
Ebbw, R 245–6
Ebony 195, 198
EcclesbouEcclesbourne Mouth 71
Ecclesfield 420
Eccleshall 33, 316, 356–7
Eccleston 203
Eden, R 66–9, 208, 271, 384, 386
Edge 308
Edgecote, battle 370
Edgecroft 202
Edinburgh 270
Edington 387, 398–9, 402, 404
Edmundscote 369, 372
Efford 37
Egdean 364
Egerton 31–2
Eggleston 117, 119, 447, 458–9, 464
Eggluis Tider uab Hohele 246
Eglwys Tudur ab Hywel 246
Eglwysilan 246
Egremont 69
Egton 438
Ellerton Priory 458
Ellesborough 21, 23
Ellesmere 314
Elmet, Sherburn in 419, 461
Elmley Castle xlvi, 415
Elnig 25
Elsdon 272
Elsham Priory 224
Eltisley 24–5, 182
Elton 256
Elvethland 165
Ely xiii
Ely, I 251

Ely (diocese) 180
Embleton Castle 273
Emmeley Bridge 296, 301
Enderby, Mavis 237
Enfield Chase 2
Engleby Forest 463
Ennerdale Forest 67
Enulphesbury 182
Epworth 221, 229–30
Ercall, High 313, 319
Eresby 235
Erisey 41
Erith 190
Erme, R 80–1, 83
Ermine Street 302
Ermington 80
Erth, St 44
Eseburne 126
Esher 362
Eshott Castle 268
Esk, R 66–8, 438
Eslington 269
Essex 17, 102, **120**, 149, 162, 181–2, 185, 199
Estbrenton 81
Etal Castle 273–4
Ethy 54
Eton College 20, 81, 147, 245, 260
Ettrick Forest 274
Euery 473
Evenlode, R 298
Evercreech 330
Evershot 99
Evesham xiii, 126–7, 150, 204, 372, 374–6, 405–6, 409, 411, 414–16
Evreux 177
Ewell, Temple 192
Ewelme 286–8
Ewenny xlviii
Ewyas Castle 170
Ewyas Harold 164, 174–6, 248–9
Ewyas Lacy 174
Excross 341
Exe, R 72, 86, 88–9, 341–2
Exeter xiii, 5, 36, 41, 48, 62, 65, 72, 74, 78–82, 86–91, 303, 341, 357,

378
Exford 341–2
Exminster 86
Exmoor 72, 75, 82, 320, 341–2
Exmouth 85–6
Eye xiii
Eye, R 212
Eye, Little 303
Eyford Bridge 106
Eynesbury 182–3
Eynsham xiii, 16, 292, 456
Eyton xlvi, 173

Fairford 121–4, 142, 145
Fairlight 365
Fairwell Priory 353
Fal, R 49–50, 61
Falmouth 40, 44, 46–7, 61
Fareham 159
Fareley 365
Faringdon 8, 12, 14, 17, 124, 297–8
Farleigh 189
Farleigh Hungerford 320–2, 342, 344, 391–2
Farnby 465
Farne Is 268, 273
Farnham 118, 154
Faversham xiii, 188–9, 198–9
Fawathe 65
Fawsley 259
Fazeley 357, 378
Feckenham Forest 375, 416
Felbrigg 339
Felton 268
Fenni, brook 474
Fenny Bridges 89–90
Fenny Castle 328
Fenwick 273
Feock Creek 48
Ferendune 297
Ferrant, Mount 438–9, 461
Ferriby 434
Ferrybridge 417, 419, 426, 455
Feverleigh 164
Filey Brigg 440, 443

Filleigh 41
Finchale Bridge 119
Finchale Priory 118
Finedon Bridge 257
Fineshade Priory 262
Finford Bridge 381
Finham 381
Fishbourne 364
Fisherton 393–5
Fishtoft 231, 234
Five Bridges 108
Fladbury 372, 406, 414
Flamborough Head 433, 441
Flamstead Priory 179
Flaxley Abbey 132, 150, 177
Fleet 231
Fleet, Goxhill 433
Fleodan 406
Fleodanbury 372
Flete, brook 207
Flint 29, 314
Flodden Field, battle 273
Flokars Brook 29
Flore 259
Florida, Strata xx, xxxiv, xxxviii, xliii, 467, 476–8
Fockerby 455
Foel Allt, Castell 469
Folkestone 188–9, 191–2, 195–6
Folkingham Castle 224
Ford (Kent) 189, 268
Ford Bridge (Herefs) 170
Ford Bridge (Staffs) 357
Ford Castle 273–4
Forde Abbey 92, 195
Fordingbridge 12, 395
Fordington 100
Fordwich 199
Foreland 193
Forest, Long 308
Foresthene 249
Forne 50
Forthampton 147
Forton 159
Fosdyke 231
Foss Dyke 226, 228
Fosse Priory 228

Fosse Way 124, 143–4, 387, 389
Fosse, R 435–6, 445
Fotheringhay xxxv, 147, 225, 253, 255–6, 262, 265–6
Fountains Abbey xiii, 449, 458, 465
Four, Le 50
Fovant 396
Fowey 34, 51–5, 61–2, 65
Framlingham 360
Frampton 99–100, 109
France 5, 52, 65, 88, 117, 126, 146, 188, 200, 219, 223–4, 255, 258, 297, 325, 369–70, 404, 423, 434
Fraw, R 99, 103, 132
Freiston 231, 234
Fremington 75
Freshford 342, 344
Friskney 234
Frith Park 217
Frith, The (Berks) 8–9, 217
Frith, The (Yorks) 423
Frithaw 181
Frithelstock Priory 76
Frocester 131
Frodesley 314
Frodingham Bridge 442
Frodsham 30
Frogenhale 199
Frogenolle 199
Frognal 199
Frome 320, 322, 343–4, 347
Frome, brook 165
Frome, R (Bristol) 132–5, 138
Frome, R (Dorset) 99, 103, 108–9
Frome, R (Herefs) 169, 174, 177
Frome, R (Som) 320, 322, 344, 347
Frome, Castle 177
Frosterley 111
Froward Point 84
Fulbourne 217

Fulbrook Park 372–3
Fulford 41
Furness 66, 68
Furness Abbey 206
Furness Fells 385
Fyrrelande 209

Gaddesden, Great 179, 181
Gade, R 179–81
Gainford 116
Gainsborough 221, 229, 237–8, 280
Galmpton 84
Galtres Forest 435, 444–5
Ganarew Castle 174
Gara Bridge 81
Garan, R 248
Garsdale 208
Garstang 204–5
Garthkiny, R 474
Gatacre 314
Gateshead xxiii, 115, 118, 267, 269, 273
Gaunless, R 111
Gaunless Park 457
Gawsworth 32
Gear Bridge 46
Gear Creek 46
Geddington 260
Gedney 231, 237
Germans, St 41, 55–7, 62
Germany xiv, 1
Germoe, St 42
Gerrans 50
Gerrard's Bromley 33
Gersick 42
Gibclif 371
Gibthorp 230
Gifford, Stoke 137
Gillan Harbour 46
Gilling 448
Gilling, West 385
Gillingham Forest xxvi, 94, 108–9
Gilsland 67, 271–2
Gindene 452
Givendale 452
Glamorganshire xxiii, xlviii, 242, 245–6, 248, 341, 370, 467

INDEX OF PLACES

Glanford Bridge 236
Glâs, Maes 247
Glascŵm 470
Glassiney College 47–8
Glastonbury xiii, xxiii,
    106–8, 142, 320, 328–
    30, 334, 343, 346–9
Glastonbury Moor 329
Glazebrook, R 207
Gleaston 210
Gledding 478
Glen, R 274
Glendale 273–5
Gloucester xiii, xxiv, xlvi,
    16, 106, 121, 127–33,
    136, 138, 141–50, 164,
    167, 169, 176–7, 210,
    307, 318, 407, 411,
    414–15
Gloucestershire xx, xliii,
    xlviii, 14, 18, 44, **121–
    50**, 174, 178, 242, 248,
    256, 265, 293, 298, 300,
    345, 405, 414–15, 468
Gluvias, St 48
Godmanchester xiii
Godolgan Castle 41
Godrevy Rock 58
Godstow Abbey 123, 299
Gogurne, Llyn 476
Golafre Bridge 330
Golant 52, 62
Golborne, stream 207
Goldcliff Priory 147, 245
Golden Valley 163
Goldoun 49
Goldsborough Bridge 465
Golfa, Moel y 479
Golflete 433
Gonyn 42
Goodrich Castle 174, 248
Goodwin Sands 194
Goonhilly 60
Gore End 193
Goresend 193
Gosford Bridge 296, 301,
    379
Gosport 158–9
Gotholghan, Carne 57
Goudhurst 185

Goulet, Le 365
Goxhill Fleet 433
Grafton 146, 219, 416
Grafton Park 413
Grampound 49
Grandborough 382
Grantchester 24–5
Grantebridg 25
Grantham 6, 221, 223–6,
    234, 237
Graveney 190
Gravesend 185, 190, 192,
    200
Great Barford 5
Great Bedwyn 399–400,
    404
Great Casterton 302–3
Great Driffield 442
Great Gaddesden 179, 181
Great Haseley 286, 288–
    91, 293, 296, 300
Great Houghton 419
Great Malvern 411
Great Marlow 11
Great Milton 289–90
Great Missenden 22–3
Great Postland 231
Great Smeaton 446–7
Great Staughton 2, 182
Great Torrington 75–6, 92
Greatham Hospital 118
Greenhalgh 204
Greenhaw 455
Greenhithe 185
Greenwich xvi, xxxiv, 190
Greet, R 279
Greetham 232
Gref I 50
Grefe 61
Grege 248
Grekelade 123
Greta 385, 447
Greta Bridge 385, 447,
    458–9
Greta, R 447, 458–9
Grewelthorpe 448
Greystoke Castle 69
Greystone Bridge 35, 56,
    63
Gribbin Head 51

Gribololbridge 465
Grimley 416
Grimoldby 236
Grimsby 233, 236
Grimsthorpe 221–4
Grinton 457–9, 464
Groby 215–17, 219–20
Grosmont Castle 174,
    248–9
Grove Park 372
Guentluge 244
Guildford xiii, 154
Guilsborough 259
Guisborough xiii
Gull Rock 50, 61
Gulle 82
Gunbyri 31
Guntle, St 247
Gurmaston (Ireland) 209
Gurney, Barrow 346
Guy-clif 371
Guycliffe 369
Guyn Castle 174
Guy's Cliffe 367, 371
Gwarnick 34–5, 40, 65
Gwash Bridge 232
Gwash, R 221, 232, 303
Gwavas Lake 42, 59
Gweek 45–6
Gweek Water 46
Gwent 415
Gwentland 242–6, 248
Gwili, R 476
Gwithian 43
Gwynlliw, St 247
Gwynllŵg 242, 244–5, 247
Gwyrne Fawr 248

Habton Bridge 438
Haccombe 41, 85
Haddon 71, 317
Hadrian's Wall xxi, 66–7,
    267, 271
Haggerston 273, 275
Hagmondesham 22
Hagworthingham 237
Haigh 206–7
Hailes xx, xliii, 44, 125,
    142, 150, 265, 405–6,
    468

Hainton 237
Halesowen 407, 416
Halifax 418, 462
Hall Park 141
Hall Place (Essex) 120
Hall Place (Warwicks) 382
Hallamshire 420
Hallaton 212
Hallington 231
Hallow Park 416
Halnaby 459–60
Halnaker xlix, 364
Halstead 237
Halton Castle 30
Haltwhistle 272
Hamble 157–8
Hamble Creek 157, 161
Hamble Hook 156–7
Hamdon 108, 334–5
Hampshire x, xlix, 12, 46, **151–62**, 402, 404
Hampton (Herefs) 170–1
Hampton (Middx) 20, 239
Hampton (Worcs) 150
Hampton Court (Herefs) 170
Hampton Court (Middx) xxiii, xlv, 20, 179, 239
Hampton in Arden 382
Hampton Lovett 416
Hams, South 85
Hanbury 357
Handforth 31
Handley 148
Handsworth 357
Hanging Langford 396
Hanham 132
Hanley 414
Hanley Castle 148, 414–15
Hanney, East 17
Hanslope 260
Hanwell 296
Harborough, Market 211
Harbottle 270, 272
Harbourne Water 81–2
Hardnesse 82
Hardwick 296
Hardwick upon Leen 420
Harewood 427
Harlaxton 225

Harley 311
Harlsey, East 446
Harmer 318
Harnham Bridge 393–6, 398–9, 403
Harnhill 128
Harpsden 300
Harptree, East 343
Harptree Gurney, West 343
Harrington 237
Harringworth 261, 302
Harrold Priory 7
Harthill, wapentake 429, 433
Hartlake Bridge 329
Hartland xiii, 35, 64, 75–6, 92
Hartland Point 37, 64, 75, 92
Hartlebury 408, 415–16
Hartlepool 117–18
Hartpury 130
Harty, I 198
Haselbury Plucknett 336
Haseley, Great xvi, xxiii–xxv, xlii, xlv, xlvi, 286, 288–91, 293, 296, 300
Haseley, Little 288, 301
Hastings 191, 365
Hastings, Leamington 382
Hatfield 422
Hatfield Forest 422
Hatherop 322
Hatton 32
Haughmond 304, 317–18
Haulston 419
Hauxton Mills 24
Haverfordwest xlviii
Hawes Waterbeck 385
Haweswater 385
Hawk Lake 319
Hawkesbury 382
Hawley's Hall 82
Haxey 230
Hay Bridge 428
Hay on Wye xxii, xliii, 166, 169–70, 174, 467, 470–1
Hay Wood 176
Hay, Castle 357
Haydon Bridge 273

Hayes, Seven 357
Hayle 44
Hayle, R 41, 43–4, 58, 60
Hayton 428
Hayward Bridge 106
Haywood 355–7
Hazelbury 390–1
Hazeldean, battle 271
Healaugh 427–8
Heaton, Castle 273–4
Heavenfield 271
Heddle Brook 274
Heding Brook 202
Hedon 23, 417, 441–2
Heighley Castle 356
Helford 60–1
Helford 46–7, 60–1
Hell Gill 464
Hell Kettles 117
Hellandbridge 39, 64
Hellas 45
Helmelege 415
Helperby 445
Helston xxiii, 34, 45, 60
Hely 262
Hemel Hempstead 180–1
Hemingbrough 434, 466
Hempstead, Hemel 180–1
Hemyock Castle 72, 93
Hen Dinas 316
Henford 167
Henbury 31
Henderskelfe 444
Henham Castle 360
Henley in Arden 367, 37Henley on Thames 9, 11, 23, 124, 296–7, 300
Herchenfield 248
Hercrosse, hundred 443
Hereford xxiv, xxxv, 31, 120, 129–32, 140, 143, 147–50, 163–70, 172, 174–8, 182, 242, 247–8, 313, 411
Herefordshire xlvi, **163–78**, 242, 288, 305, 307, 318, 416, 469, 472
Herne 184, 189, 193, 199
Hertfordshire xxiii, xlix, **179–81**

INDEX OF PLACES 511

Hessle 431
Hetheholme 406
Hewick Bridge 450-2, 463
Hexgreave Park 279-80
Hexham 271-3, 275
Hexhamshire 271
Heydour 224
Heyford 259
Heyford Bridge 296
Heytesbury 321
Heywood Bridge 301
Hibaldstow 236
Hichingbrook 24
High Ercall 313, 319
High Holland 234-5
High Leigh 31
High Lindsey 236
High Wycombe 23
Higham Ferrers 1, 254, 257, 262
Higham Park 2
Higham Priory 200
Highbridge 330
Higher Wych 28
Highworth 14
Hilborough 23
Hilbre 29
Hilcott 401
Hill Castle 183
Hillingdon 240, 416
Hills (Lincs) 236
Hillwood 377
Hinchwick 142
Hinckley Castle 218
Hincksey Hill 14
Hinderskelfe Castle 437
Hindon 344
Hingston 57
Hinksey Ferry 297
Hinton Charterhouse 322
Hinton St George 336
Hipswell 458
Hodder, R 208
Hodnet 310, 314
Hodsock 281
Hogan 475
Hogstow Forest 313
Holbeach 231, 233
Holderness 119, 417, 439, 441-2, 462, 466

Holdgate Castle 317
Holland 231-5
Holland, High 234-5
Holland, Low 233, 235
Holmcultram Abbey 68
Holme (Dorset) 100, 103
Holme (Glos) 147-8
Holme (Yorks) 461
Holme Beck 457
Holme St Benets xiii
Holmebridge 100, 103
Holt (Leics) 213, 218
Holt (Worcs) 415
Holy I 273
Holy Islandshire 275
Holyfield 181
Holyhead 243
Holystone 272-3
Holywell 221
Homington 106, 393
Honddu, R 249, 471
Honiton 72, 89-90
Hook Norton 299
Hook Park 109
Hooke Park 98-9, 109
Hook's Ditch 181
Hoplode 235
Hopton Castle 317
Hopwas 354
Horeston 70
Horethorne 97
Horham Hall 185
Hornby (Lancs) 201, 208-10,
Hornby Castle (Yorks) 113, 457, 463
Horncastle 235-7
Horncliffe 274
Horneby 460
Horningsham 344
Hornsea 433, 441
Horse Bridge (Devon) 35
Horse Bridge (Glos) 142
Horsley Castle 70
Horwel Stream 151
Horwell hundred 402
Horwich 208
Horwood 145
Hougham 224
Houghton 273

Houghton Regis 5-6
Houghton, Great 419
Houghtoun 6
Houme 313
Hounslow 22, 239
Hounslow Heath 20, 239-40
Hoveringham xxiii, 277, 280
How End 2
How Water 2
Howden 417, 433-4
Howdenshire 433-4
Howell 224
Howick 273
Howsham Bridge 428
Howton 419
Hubley 146
Huddersfield 418
Hughenden Brook 23
Hull, Kingston upon xxiii, 417, 430-3, 437-8, 441-2
Hull, R 430-3, 437-8, 461-2
Hulme 313
Humber, R xxiii, xxx, 431, 433-4, 441-2, 462
Humber, Thornton on xiii
Humble Burn 274
Hung Road 135
Hungerford 8, 400
Hungerford, Farleigh 320, 322, 342, 344, 391-2
Huntingdon xiii, 1, 24, 183, 279
Huntingdonshire xliv, 2, 25, **182-3**, 187, 256, 262
Huntingford 145
Huntington 165, 470
Hurbertoun 81
Hurley Priory 11, 296
Hurlstone 341
Hurmer 319
Hursley 154
Hurst Castle 158
Hurstingstone, hundred 183
Huttoft Creek 236

Huttoft Marsh 235
Hutton Castle 273
Hutton Conyers 451–2, 465
Hutton Park 446
Hutton, Sheriff 437, 444
Hyde Abbey 153
Hymel Castle 262
Hythe 184, 189, 191, 195–6
Hythe, West 189, 196

Icanno 227
Iceland 431–2
Ickford Bridge 293
Idle, R 229, 277, 281
Idridgehay 71
Iford Bridge 104
Ightfield 313, 318
Ilchester 320, 331–3, 347
Ilminster 333
Ilshow 450
Ilsley, West 404
Ilton Castle 83
Ince 207
Ingarsby 217
Ingenesse, battle 335
Ingestre 355
Ingleburne 388
Inglewood Forest 67–9
Ingmer Meadow 68
Ingoldsby 224
Ingreyne 192
Iniscaw 43
Inispriuen 60
Innisschawe, I 59
Ipswich xiii
Ireland 43, 50, 65, 74, 131, 207, 209, 279
Irk, R 202
Irnham 223–4
Iron Acton 138, 140–1
Irthing, R 68, 271
Irwell, R 201–2, 207
Isaac, Port 38, 64
Isbourne, stream 126–7
Ise, R 23, 257, 264
Isebroke Bridges 105
Isis, R 7, 12–16, 18, 121, 123–4, 142–3, 291–2, 297–8
Isleston 85
Islip (Northants) 257
Islip (Oxon) 296, 301
Isuria 452
Italy x, xxxi, 348
Itchen 157–8
Itchen Stoke 153
Itchen, R 157
Ive, R 69
Ivel, R 97, 99, 107, 109, 331–3, 336–7, 347
Ives, St 44–5, 58, 182
Ivington 171
Ivybridge 80
Ivy-castle 125
Ivychurch Priory 399

Jarrow xiii, 118
Jerusalem 375
Jervaulx Abbey xiii, 448, 458–9, 463
Julian Bridge 104, 156
Justinian, St 57–8

Kaine Place Creek 77
Kayach 246
Kea Creek 48
Keer, R 206
Keld Head 438, 443
Kellaways 391
Kelston 132, 342
Kemble 143
Kenbrook, R 165, 174
Kenchester xxviii, 163–6, 174
Kendal xxi, 55, 66, 209, 267, 383–4
Kenford 99
Kenilworth 376, 380–2
Kenin, Cair 42
Kenlet, R 468
Kenn 346
Kennet, R 10, 17, 399–401, 404
Kennet Valley 8
Kenninghall 252
Kensdale 142
Kensey Brook 36
Kensington 271

Kent xxxiii, 5, 98, **184–200**, 249, 325, 363
Kent, R 383–4
Kentish Weald 194
Kentmere 384
Kenton 86
Kenwater 171
Kerrial, Croxton 302
Kerrier, hundred 63
Kestel, Pen 46
Kesteven 224–5, 231, 234, 236
Keswick 68
Kettering xliv, 253–4, 257, 260, 266
Kettles, Hell 117
Ketton 303
Keveral 41
Keverne, St 46, 60
Kew 38, 44, 362
Kexby 428
Key, R 123, 184
Keynsham xiii, 135–6, 139, 149, 345
Kiby, Lan 244
Kidderminster 125, 405, 407, 411, 415–16
Kidlington 293
Kidwelly xlviii
Kilgram Bridge 463
Killerby 457, 466
Killhope Burn 112
Killinghall Bridge 465
Killingworthe 380
Kilmington 92
Kilnwick Green 462
Kilpeck 175, 177, 248
Kimbolton 182–3
Kinderton 33
Kingges Snode 199
King Road 135, 143
King's Cliffe Park 262
King's Langley 179
King's Lynn xiii, 233, 252
King's Norton 376, 382, 414
King's Sutton 265, 294
Kingsbridge 83
Kingsbury 357
Kingsland 171–4

INDEX OF PLACES 513

Kingsnorth 199
Kingsteignton 86
Kingsthorpe 260
Kingston Lacy 104–5
Kingston upon Hull 417, 430–3, 437–8, 441–2
Kingston upon Thames xlix, 361–2
Kingstone 336
Kingswear 84
Kingswood 138, 145
Kingswood Forest 137–8, 140, 145, 149, 343
Kington 129, 150
Kinnard Castle 230
Kinver 416
Kirby, Monks 381
Kirby, West 29
Kirby Bellars xliii, 211
Kirby Lonsdale 208
Kirby Misperton 438
Kirby Park 217
Kirby Wiske 445–6, 459
Kirkby Malzeard 449, 465
Kirkham xiii, 256, 274, 428, 437, 444, 461
Kirklington 280
Kirknewton 274
Kirkoswald 68–9
Kirkstall Abbey xiii, 462–3
Kirkstead Abbey xiii, 236
Kirton 233
Kismeldon Bridge 76
Knaith 229
Knappey 461
Knaresborough 417, 453–4, 465
Kneeton 458
Knepp Castle 366
Knighton 307, 469
Knockin Castle 317
Knollbury xxviii, 298
Knowsley Park 207
Knoyle, West xvi, xxvi, xlii
Knutsford 30–1, 33
Kyloe 269
Kyme 228, 234

La Charité Abbey 424
Lacock 390
Laine 39
Lambeth x
Lambeth Palace 194
Lambley Priory 273
Lambourn xlvii, 17, 399
Lambourn, R 17
Lamelin 54
Lamorran Creek 49
Lampeder 247
Lamphrey 474–5
Lan Kiby 244
Lanant 58
Lanburne, Cheping 17
Lancashire ix, x, xxii, xliii, 29–31, 33, **201–10**, 278, 305, 385, 467
Lancaster 66, 201, 203, 205–6, 208–9, 248, 313
Lancastershire 206, 208
Lanchester 274
Landamas Castle 174
Landes, seneshcal 335
Lanercost Priory 68, 271
Langar 280
Langdale 428
Langdon 191
Langfield Dale 318
Langford, Hanging 396
Langley 115–18, 145, 150, 179, 255–6, 265, 268, 299
Langley (Durham) 116
Langley (Oxon) 145, 299
Langley, King's 179
Langley Beck 116
Langley Castle 268
Langley Chase 115, 117
Langport 333–4, 348
Langrick Ferry 226
Langstone Harbour 160
Langthorne, Stratford xiii
Langtoft 231
Langton 237
Lanherne 40, 51, 53, 97
Lanihorne Castle 49
Lanihorne Creek 49
Lanlivery 53
Lansdown 145
Lanteglos-by-Fowey 54
Lanton 274
Lantyan Pool 52
Laprin Bridge 53
Largin Bridge 53
Latchford 288
Latham 203
Lathom 203, 206–9
Latinelad 143
Latton 143
Launceston 35–6, 44, 55–7, 63, 72, 76
Laund of Benefield 254, 261
Launde xiii, 211–12, 218
Lavendon 7
Laverstock 396
Lea 169, 174, 256
Lea, R 179, 181
Leach, R 121
Lead 427
Leadon, R 177
Leam, R 381–2
Leamington Hastings 382
Lechlade 121–3
Leconfield 428–9, 462
Leconfield Park 462
Ledbury 146, 177
Ledwyche Brook 307, 318
Lee 318
Lee Mill Bridge 80
Leebotwood 308
Leeds (Yorks) 188, 417, 463, 465
Leeds Priory (Kent) 118
Leeming 385, 459
Leeming Beck 459
Leen, R 282–4
Leen, Hardwick upon 420
Leftwich 33
Legeolium 423
Leicester xiii, 31, 118, 211–18, 220, 264, 284, 378, 380
Leicester Forest 217–18
Leicestershire xxviii, **211–20**, 232, 253, 280, 303, 355, 382
Leigh (Chesh) 33
Leigh (Lancs) ix, xxi, 201, 203
Leigh (Salop) 313

Leigh (Som) 135
Leigh, Bessels 297–8
Leigh, High 31
Leigh Forest 212
Leighfield Forest 212, 302
Leighton (Salop) 314
Leighton Bromswold 183, 254, 262
Leighton Buzzard 313
Leintwardine 307, 469
Lelant 44, 57–60
Lemon, R 86
Lemster 171
Lenton Abbey 282
Leominster xlvi, 163–5, 169–74, 177, 469–70
Leonard Stanley 131
Lerryn Bridge 54
Lesnewth, hundred 63
Letelege 157
Levens 384
Levine Pool 47
Lewes Priory 211
Leweston 109
Lewisham 250
Leyland x, 203
Leylandshire 203–4, 206, 208
Lichfield xxv, xxxiii, 310, 350–8, 375, 380
Liddel Moat 66
Liddel Water 66
Lide's I, St 43
Lidiate Moss 203
Lilburn Tower 273
Lilford 256
Lilleshall Abbey 309, 317
Limebrook 164, 172, 177
Limen, R 197
Limington 332–4
Lincoln 3, 105, 116, 183, 221, 224–9, 234, 237–8, 251, 290, 295
Lincoln (diocese) 180
Lincolnshire xii, xxiii, xxx, xl, xlv, 6, 219, **221–38**, 251, 270, 426, 433
Lincot Wood 169
Lindis, R 226, 235–6, 273
Lindisfarne, I 114, 271, 465
Lindridge 377
Lindsey 131, 235–6
Lindsey, High 236
Lindsey, Low 235
Lingfield 362
Lingoed 169
Linne Briggs 272
Linshull 169
Linstock 271
Lire (Normandy) 177
Liskeard 55
Lisle 67
Litcham 251
Little Bedwyn 400
Little Bytham 221
Little Eye 303
Little Haseley 288, 301
Little Malvern 416
Little Marlow 11
Little Milton 290
Little Missenden 22
Little Sodbury 137–8, 141–2, 144, 146
Little Stretton 308
Little Thetford (Cambs) 251
Little Torrington 76
Little Totnes 81
Littleborough 194, 229
Littlecote 399
Littlehampton xlix, 364
Littleton 357
Liverpool 29, 31, 201, 206–7
Lizard Point 60
Llanameueri 472
Llanandras 469
Llanandrew 171
Llandaff 244, 247
Llanddew 472
Llandewi Brefi 476
Llandinam 478
Llandovery 472–4
Llanfarda Hill 315
Llangibby 244
Llangurig 473, 478
Llanidloes 415, 478
Llanllieni 469
Llanllieny 172
Llantarnam 24
Llanthony Priory (Glos) 128, 131
Llanthony Priory (Mon) xliv, 131, 249
Llanuihengle 246
Llanvaes 471
Llanvair Castle 244
Lledan 478
Llinpeder 476
Llinridde Lake 476
Llwyn hen dinas 315
Llyn Gogurne 476
Llyn Pencarreg 476
Llyn Teifi 477
Llyn, Craig Naw 477
Lockington 438
Lodden, R 9
Loden, stream 138
Lodenek 39
Loe, The 45, 60, 139, 345
Logaresburch 334
London ix, x, xiii, xv, xvi, xviii, xxi–xxiii, xxv, xxxiv, xl, xliii–xlv, xlvii, xlviii, 1–2, 5, 12, 16, 19, 21–2, 40, 52, 65, 74, 89, 124, 127, 145, 153–4, 168, 170, 177, 180, 184, 186, 194–5, 210–12, 230, **239–41**, 243, 248, 271, 286, 289–90, 300–1, 310, 315–17, 319, 345, 347, 356–7, 361–2, 371, 374, 379–81, 392, 409, 416
Long Ashton 400
Long Compton 294
Long Forest 308
Longdon 357
Longford 239–40
Longnor 313–14
Longton Castle 174
Lonsdale 208
Looe, East 55, 62–3
Looe, West 55, 62–3
Looe Creek 54–5, 62
Looe Water 41, 55
Loose 189
Loose, R 189

INDEX OF PLACES

Lostephan 63
Lostwithiel 52–5, 62
Loughborough 211, 213, 216–17, 220
Loughborough Park 216
Loughes Forest 274
Louth 231, 235–6
Louvain xvi
Lovett, Hampton 416
Low, South, R 273
Low Holland 233, 235
Low Lindsey 235
Low Studley 465
Lowde Water 181
Lowe Hill 426
Lowestoft 360
Lowther, R 385–6
Luckington 388
Lud, R 236
Ludborough 236
Ludbrook 236
Lude 236
Ludford 307
Ludgershall 387, 404
Ludgvan 42
Ludlow xxiv, xxvii, 130, 165, 169, 171, 173–4, 178, 304–8, 313–14, 316–19, 411
Luele 67
Luen, Castel 69
Lug Harneis 469
Lugg, R 164–5, 170–2, 174–5, 177, 469–70
Lugg Bridge 170
Luggan brook 472
Lugubalia 67
Lugwardine 170
Lulworth 268
Lulworth, East 102–4
Lulworth, West 102–4
Lumley Castle 114, 118
Lundy I 92, 475
Lune, R 205–6, 208–9
Lunecaster 208
Lunesandes 206
Lunesdale 208
Luton 1–2, 6
Lutterworth 211, 216–17, 220

Lydd 191, 198
Lydden, R 106
Lyddington 302
Lydford 35, 63, 92, 331
Lyme Regis 94, 97, 109, 196
Lymehille 189
Lyminge 191, 195
Lymme Hill 196
Lympne 189, 191, 195–7
Lynher, R 56–7
Lynhil 189
Lynn, King's xiii, 233, 252
Lyonshall 169, 174
Lyrpole 206
Lytchett Minster 103–4
Lythe 440, 443–4
Lyveden 266

Mablethorpe 233, 237
Macclesfield 30, 32
Macclesfield 28, 30–2
Machen 246–7
Machynlleth 415
Mackney 12
Maelienydd 469
Maer 318
Maes Glâs 247
Magnusfelde 145
Mahenclift 415
Maiden Bradley 344, 407, 416
Maiden Castle (Westmor) 386, 460
Maidenhead 8–9, 11
Maidstone 185–6, 189–90, 194
Maildulphsbury 388
Mainorpirrhe 475
Mairin 247
Makerfield, Newton in 204
Malkins Shelf 181
Malleting 461
Malmesbury xiii, xxvii, 74, 108, 124, 138, 387–91, 393
Malpas 28, 30–1, 33, 48
Malpas Roads 48
Malton xiii, 225, 417, 428, 437–9, 443–4

Malton, Old 438
Malvern 147, 177
Malvern, Great 411
Malvern, Little 416
Malvern Chase 177, 416
Malvern Hills 411, 416
Malzeard, Kirkby 449, 465
Man, I 207
Manchester xxi, xxxii, 26, 28, 30, 201–2, 206–7
Mandite, St 49
Manditus, St 49
Mangotsfield 137, 145
Manifold 70
Manningford 401
Manorbier 475
Mansfield 70, 278–9, 282
Mapheralt Castle 174, 176
Marazion 42, 59–60
Marbury 26, 169
Marches 131, 168, 172, 306, 313, 408
Mardale 385
Marden 164, 166
Margate 193
Markby Priory 237
Market Deeping 231, 233–4, 303
Market Drayton 310, 313, 316
Market Harborough 211
Market Rasen 235, 237
Market Weighton 428
Markingfield 466
Markyate 5, 179
Marlais brook 473–4
Marlais Park 473
Marlais, Aber– 473
Marlborough xlvii, 387, 400–1, 404
Marlow, Great 11
Marlow, Little 11
Marlwood 141
Marnhull 106, 108
Marrick 458
Marsh Chapel 233
Marshfield 139, 149, 247, 402
Marshland 455–6
Marshwood 97

Marshwood Park 340
Marske 458–9
Marteres Abbey (France) 223
Martin Mere 207
Marton 228–9, 381–2, 468
Marwood Park 117
Marylebone Brook 240
Marylebone Park 240
Masham 448, 463, 465–6
Massingham 251
Mathern 244
Matlock 70
Mattersey 280–1
Maun, R 282
Mavis Enderby 237
Mawes, St xxiv, 34, 49–50, 61, 65
Mawgan Bridge 45–6
Mawgan Creek 45–6
Mawnan 46–7
Maxey Castle 233–4
Maxstoke 382
Maxwel 28
Maytham 195
Meare 328–30, 348
Meaux Abbey xiii, 430
Medbourne 212, 253
Medlock, R 201
Medmenham Abbey 11
Medway, R 185, 189–90
Medwegetoun 190
Melbourne Castle 218
Melbury Park 109
Melbury Sampford 99, 108
Melchbourne 1–2, 182
Melcombe Regis 100
Melenithland 165
Melennith 165
Mells 320, 346–7
Melton Mowbray xiii, 211–12
Melwood Park 229–30
Mendip Forest 343
Mendip Hills 320, 322, 326, 329, 342–3, 346–7, 349
Mendip, Chewton 326
Meneage 41, 60
Menheniot 54–6

Menthorpe 435
Meole Bridge 308
Meon, East 158
Meon, R 158, 160
Mercia 125, 129, 148, 310, 325, 351–2, 354, 380, 406
Merdon Castle 154
Mere, The 422–3
Mere (Chesh) 31
Mere (Lincs) 229
Mere (Wilts) 108, 331, 404
Meredith lordship 245
Meriden 379
Merionethshire 314–15
Mersey Bar 29
Mersey, R 28–31, 201, 206–7
Merthen 46–7
Merton Priory xiii, 109, 362
Meteham 195
Metford 438
Metham 434
Michaelstow-y-Fedw 246
Michaelwood Chase 141
Michelboro 333
Michelborow 336
Middle Studley 465
Middleham 448–9, 456–9, 461, 463–5
Middlesex xli, **239–41**, 361
Middlesmoor 465
Middleton (Yorks) 455
Middleton in Teesdale 116
Middleton Park 378
Middleton Stoney 294
Middlewich 28, 32–3
Midford Brook 322
Midleton 200
Midsomer Norton 346
Milborne Port 107, 348
Milburne 419
Milcote 375
⊠Milford, South 419, 474
Mill Bay 77
Mill Brook 319
Millaton 42
Millbrook 56–7, 62
Millbrook Lake 56

Millbrook Water 107
Millom Castle 69
Milton (Som) 330
Milton, Great 289–90
Milton, Little 290
Milton Abbas 99
Milton Bridge
Milton Creek 188
Milton Regis 188, 192, 200
Milwyn, R 477
Minchin Buckland 337–8
Minchinhampton 146
Minehead 341
Minshull 33
Minster in Thanet 193
Minster Lovell 298
Mirrow Pill 54
Misbourne, R 181
Misperton, Kirby 438
Missenden, Great 22–3
Missenden, Little 22
Missenden Priory 22
Mitchell 39–40, 65, 248
Mitford 272, 397
Mitton 408, 416
Mochnant, brook 477
Modbury 41, 80–1
Moel y Golfa 479
Mohun's Ottery 72, 89–90
Molescroft Cross 462
Molton, South 92
Mongewell 12
Monkbridge 318
Monks Kirby 381
Monkton (Pembs) xliii, 475
Monkton, Nun 454, 459
Monkton Farleigh 390–1
Monkwearmouth 114, 118
Monmouth 132, 163–4, 169–70, 176, 242, 244, 247–9
Monmouthshire **242–9**, 467
Monnow, R 170, 176, 247–9
Montacute xiii, 23, 54, 62, 103, 320, 334–5, 339, 454
Monteburgh Abbey (Normandy) 91

INDEX OF PLACES 517

Montford Bridge 310
Montgomery xx, 310, 316, 415, 467–9, 478
Moor (Sussex) 364
Moor (Worcs) 416
Moor Chapel (Northumb) 67
Moor Hall (Warwicks) 313
Moor Head (Yorks) 465
Moor Park (Herts) 180–1
Moore Water
Moran, St 49
Morda, R 315
Mordiford 165, 170, 174, 177
Moreby 419
Morecambe Bay 206
Morelande 106
Moreton Corbet 304–5, 313, 317
Morgannock 370
Morlais (Brittany) 97
Morleys Hall ix, 201–4, 207
Morpeth 271–2, 274–5, 454
Mortham 458–9
Morthe Forest 311–12
Mortlake 362
Morton Bridge 464
Morval 41, 55
Morville 311
Morwell 56
Morwellham 56–7
Mossdale Moor 459
Mottisfont Priory 161, 338
Moulton (Lincs) 231
Moulton (Northants) 260
Moulton Park 260
Mount Ferrant Castle 438–9, 461
Mount's Bay 59–60
Mountsorrel Castle 215
Mousehole 42, 44, 59
Mouthey 313
Mowbray, Melton xiii, 211–12
Mowthwy 313
Moythik 309
Much Wenlock 172, 177, 304, 310–11, 317–19

Muchelney 348
Mulgrave 438–9, 461
Mullion I 60
Munden 180
Murton 275
Mychelborow 348
Myddle Castle 316
Myerscough Park 204
Myllam 461
Mylor Creek 48
Mynachoy 165
Mynydd Du 472, 477
Mynyddislwyn 246
Mynys, brook 473
Myte 284
Myton 445, 464

Nadder, R 395–6
Nant Bawddwr 473
Nant Caiach 246
Nant-Llys 477
Nantwich 28, 30, 32–3
Nappa 458, 461
Nar, R 251
Nare Head 50
Naunton 142
Naworth Castle 69
Nazarre, battle 335
Neasham 111
Neath xlviii
Needwood Forest 357
Negem College 237
Nene, R 2, 183, 254–9, 266
Neots, St xiii, 2, 4–5, 24–5, 182–3
Ness (Devon) 85
Nesswick 438
Neston 29
Neston Roads 29
Nether Bridge 384
Nether Stowey 338–9
Netherbury 98–9
Netherby 67
Netley xiii, 157
Nettlecombe 339
Netton 395
New Bridge (Corn x 2) 35, 56
New Bridge (Devon) 63

New Bridge (Westmor) 384
New Forest 151, 162
New Park (Glos)
New Park (Leics) 217
New Park (Notts) 280
New Park (Staffs) 357
New Port 141
New Radnor 165, 469–70
New Salisbury 394, 399
New Southampton 155
New Thame 300
New Winchelsea 365
New Windsor 18
Newark (Glos) 131
Newark (Notts) 213–14, 219, 223, 278, 280, 284, 356
Newbo Abbey 219
Newbridge (Corn) 53
Newbridge (Oxon) 298
Newbridge (Yorks) 465
Newburgh Lancs) 203
Newburgh (Yorks) xiii, 418
Newbury 8–9, 16
Newcastle-under-Lyme 355–6
Newcastle upon Tyne xiii, 114, 267–72, 274–6
Newchurch 470
Newenden 195
Newenham Abbey xiii, 92, 259
Newent 132, 177, 256
Newhagg Park 279
Newhall Tower 30
Newham 50
Newham Wood 48
Newland (Yorks) 430
Newlyn 42, 44, 59–60
Newminster Abbey 273, 454
Newnham Mills 318
Newnham on Severn 127, 132
Newnham Priory xiii, 1–4, 6
Newnton, North xvi, xlii, 401
Newnton, Water 387–8
Newpool 32

Newport, estuary 158
Newport (Mon) xlviii, 242, 244–7
Newport (Salop) 316–17
Newport Pagnell 21, 23, 223, 233
Newstead Bridge 303
Newstead Priory (Lincs) 232
Newstead Priory (Notts) xiii, 282, 420
Newton (Northants) 266
Newton (Yorks) 442
Newton Bushel 85–6
Newton Castle (Dorset) 348
Newton in Makerfield 204
Newton-le-Willows 207–8
Newton Poppleford 90
Newton St Cyres 88–9
Newton St Loe 345
Newton Tracy 75
Newton, Sturminster 94, 104, 348
Newtown 415, 478
Nibley 145–6
Nichol Forest 67
Nidd, R 428, 453–4, 459, 465
Nocton Park Priory 237
Norfolk 4, 120, 224, 230, **250-2**, 317, 339, 360, 366, 423, 444
Norham 118, 269, 273–4
Norman Cross hundred 183
Normanby Bridge 443
Normandy 40, 51, 65, 91, 129, 133, 149, 177, 259, 270, 370
Normanton 461
North Bradley 342
North Burton 462
North Cadbury 331
North Cave 433
North Curry 336
North Newnton xvi, xlii, 401
North Petherton 337
North Tamerton 35, 63

North Tyne, R 271–2, 274
Northallerton 113, 417, 446–7, 451, 459
Northallertonshire 446
Northampton xlv, 5, 140, 219, 253, 255–60, 264–6, 295, 300
Northamptonshire xxiii, 1, 49, 145, 212, **253-66**, 269, 295, 302, 343, 382
Northbourne 190
Northleach 121, 142, 145
Northmouth 193
Northton 84
Northumberland xii, xxi, 66, 68, 153, **267-76**, 363, 428–9, 435, 438, 445, 454–5
Northumbria 129, 131, 352
Northwich 26–8, 30–3
Northwick 416
Norton Conyers 465
Norton Disney 224
Norton-on-Tees 119
Norton Priory 30–1
Norton St Philip 322, 344
Norton, Chipping 142, 265, 294, 299, 382
Norton, Green's 257
Norton, King's 376, 414
Norton, Midsomer 346
Norwich xiii, 252
Norwood Park (Notts) 280
Norwood Park (Som) 348
Noseley 213, 218
Noss Creek 84
Nostell Priory 68, 417, 419, 424
Notley 23
Notter Bridge 56
Nottingham 277–8, 280, 282–5, 379, 417
Nottinghamshire xliv, 70, 219, 223, 228, 270, **277-85**, 417, 420
Nun Appleton 427
Nun Monkton Nuneaton 216, 353, 355, 367, 381
Nunne-Eiton 123

Nunney Brook 344
Nunney Delamare 137, 320, 344, 347

Oakham 303
Oakleaze Park 141
Oakley 293
Ock, R 13, 15–18
Odell 7
Offa's Dyke 316, 469
Offchurch 382
Offenham 372, 406
Old Malton 438
Old Radnor 165, 470
Old Sarum 393–5
Old Sodbury 138–9, 142
Oldbek 233
Oldford 33
Olney (Bucks) 6–7
Olney (Glos) 142
Olney Water 7
Ombersley 406, 409, 416
Oncaster 225
Onkaster 225
Onny, R 165, 307–8, 318
Onslow 314
Orchard Wyndham 339
Ore Stone 85
Oresworth 70
Oringgam 280
Ormskirk 207
Orwell 24
Osgodby 224
Osney Priory 292–3, 297
Ospringe 188, 198
Ostinghanger 189
Ostrepole Lake 159
Oswald's Ash, St 271
Oswald's Priory, St (Nostell) 68, 419, 424
Oswestry 304, 310, 314–17, 469
Osyth, St 21, 23
Otley 314, 427
Otmoor 294, 296
Otter, Brook 154
Otter, Burn 272
Otter, R 89–90
Otterbourne 154
Otterburn Castle 272

INDEX OF PLACES

Otterden 188
Otterford 89
Ottermouth 90
Otterton 90–1
Ottery Brook 36, 63
Ottery St Mary 88–90
Ottery, Mohun's 41, 72, 89–90
Oulton 31
Oundle 253–7, 262, 265–6
Ouse, R (Beds) 1–4, 6–7
Ouse (Ise), R 263–4
Ouse (Yorks), R 419, 428, 435–7, 454–5
Ouzel Water 7
Over Court 146
Overton 147
Ovingham 271
Owse 385
Owseburne 143
Owston (Lincs) 230
Owston Abbey (Leics) 212
Oxford ix, x, xii, xiii, xvi, xix, xxv, xxxi–xxxiv, xl, xlii, 14–17, 29, 120, 137, 156, 175, 220, 231, 266, 286, 291–301, 304, 307, 353, 360, 398
Oxfordshire xvi, xxiii, xlv, 12, 14, 23, 142, 145, 265, **286–301**, 382
Oxney, I 195, 198

Packington 382
Padstow 35, 38–41, 57–8, 64
Padstow Bay 58
Paignton 84
Painscastle 470
Panton 236
Panton Brook 236
Papplewick 282
Papworth St Agnes 183
Paris x, xi, xiv, 146
Park (Corn) 37
Parke Bahan 245
Parkwalls 64
Parnham 41
Partney, Ashby by 237
Pateley Bridge 450, 465

Patrington 433, 441
Paulton 326
Peak, The 70, 317
Pecforton 27
Peckleton 218
Peder, brook 337
Peebles 274
Pelene Point 54
Pembridge 171, 174
Pembroke xliii, 130, 168, 474–5
Pembrokeshire xx, xxxviii, xlviii, 467, 474–5
Penarth Point 51
Penbro 41, 44
Pencaire 41–2
Pencarreg, Llyn 476
Pencombe 43
Pencragan 476
Pencraig 470
Pendennis 47, 50
Pendinas 45, 49
Pendley 180
Pendragon Castle 385
Penfilly brook 171
Penfusis 47
Pengersick 41–2
Penguern 309
Penhill (Yorks) 456, 463
Penk, R 356
Penknek 52–3
Penkridge 356–7
Penlee Point 57
Penleighs Mere 304
Penllyn Mountain 314
Penpoll Creek 54
Penreth, Poole 47
Penrith 47, 68–9, 384–6
Penryn 41, 47–8, 61
Penryn Creek 47
Pensford 345
Pentewan 50
Pentire 58
Penwith 43
Penwith, hundred 63
Penwolase 57
Penwortham 203–4
Penzance 42, 59–60
Peover, R 28
Pepperhill 319

Perranzabuloe 45
Pershore xiii, 127, 146, 373, 405–6, 415
Peterborough Abbey xiii, 232, 255
Petersham 362
Peterstone 247
Petherton, North 337
Petherton, South 337
Petherton Park 336–7
Petteril 68
Petty Pool 27
Petworth xxiii, xlix, 268, 363–4, 366
Peveril Castle 70
Pewsey 401
Philaw Brigg 440
Phillack 43
Pickenham 251
Pickering 417, 438, 440, 442–4, 460
Pickering, Vale of xxiii, 417
Pickering Lythe, wapentake 440, 443–4
Piddle (Trent), R 103
Piddle Brook 372–3
Piercebridge 117, 447, 457
Pilkington Park 202, 207
Pillaton Hall 357
Pillenhaul 357
Pilleth 165
Pilton 74
Pilton Park 348
Pinnock Well 142
Pinsley, R 165, 171, 174
Pipe 352
Pipewell Abbey xliv, 212, 253–4, 261
Piran, St 46, 48, 60
Pitchford 314
Plaish 314
Plaister, Chapel 390
Pleshey 120, 199
Plompton 454, 465
Plym, R 77–80
Plym Bridge 78
Plymouth 55, 57, 62, 72, 77–9, 81, 83–4
Plympton Priory xiii, 36, 50, 61, 77–9

Plympton St Mary 78
Plympton St Thomas 79–80
Plynlimmon 477
Plynlimon 415
Pocklington 428–9
Poitiers 146, 219, 335
Pokeshaulle 200
Poles 85
Polesworth 355
Polperro 54, 62
Polruan 54, 62
Polson Bridge 35–6, 63
Polt Rosse, stream 68, 271
Polwheveral 46
Polwheveral Creek 47
Pomparles Bridge 330–1
Ponslithe 312
Pont Bassaleg 246
Pont, R 273
Pontefract xiii, xlv, 68, 256, 270, 417, 419, 423–4, 426, 455–6
Pontesbury 304, 312, 415
Pontesford Hill 312
Pontperlus 330
Pontrilas 169
Pontus Cross 54
Poole 94, 103–4
Poole Harbour 103–4
Poole Penreth 47
Poole, Porte 29
Porlock Bay 341
Port Isaac 38, 64
Portchester (Bristol) 135
Portchester Castle (Hants) 159
Porte Poole 29
Portenis 42
Port-Hoyger 243
Portington 434
Portland 94, 98, 101
Portquin 38, 64
Portsbridge 160
Portsdown 160
Portsea I 160
Portskewett 243
Portsmouth xxiv, 151, 158–60, 363
Postland, Great 231

Potton 6
Poul–Morlande 54
Poulpere Creek 46
Poulton 123
Powder, hundred 63
Powderham 83, 86, 89
Powick 313, 410
Powick Mill 318, 411
Powis Castle 478
Powys 315, 317, 319
Powysland 342, 473, 479
Poynton 30
Prees 304–5, 318
Prescot (Lancs) 207
Prescott (Glos) 148
Prestbury (Chesh) 30–1
Prestbury (Glos) 121, 147, 177
Presteigne 165, 171–2, 307, 469
Preston (Devon) 41
Preston (Lancs) 66, 203–6, 208–9
Prinknash 130
Pronte, R 384
Provence 297
Prudhoe 118, 268, 271
Pryven 41
Pucklechurch 142, 345
Puckleshall 200
Puddington 33
Pudsey 118–19, 458
Pumlumon 478
Purbeck Forest 102–3
Purse Caundle 97
Purse, Small, brook 169
Putford Bridge 76
Pydar, hundred 63
Pyddildour 103
Pylale 165

Quantock Hills 320, 339
Quantoxhead 339
Quappelode 235
Quarrendon 20–3
Quatford 312
Quedgeley 131
Queen Camel 332
Queenborough 192

Raby 110, 113, 115–16, 444
Radcot 297
Radegund's, St 184, 189, 192
Radford 277–8
Radley 16
Radnor 173
Radnor, New 165, 469–70
Radnor, Old 165, 470
Radnorshire 173
Raglan 249
Raglan Castle 245
Ragley 369
Rainworth Water 279
Rame Head 55, 57, 78
Rammey Mead 181
Rampton 228
Ramsbury 399–400
Ramsey xiii, 182–3, 254
Ramsgate 193
Rasen, Market 235, 237
Rat I 43, 59
Ratesborough 191
Ratesburgh 194
Rauceby 224–5
Ravensburgh 433, 441
Ravensworth, R 447, 457
Ravensworth (Yorks) 447–8, 457
Ravensworth-on-Tyne 118, 269
Rawcliffe 204
Rayle Pits 464
Rea Brook 308, 319, 416
Rea, R 318, 416
Reading (Berks) xiii, 8–10, 161, 164, 172, 174, 292, 334
Reading (Kent) 195
Reculver 188–9, 192–4
Red Bank 29
Red Castle 316
Redbourn 180
Redbridge 157
Redcliffe (Bristol) 134–6
Redden Burn 274–5
Reddon 56
Rede, R 272
Redesdale 272–3, 275

INDEX OF PLACES

Redford 278
Redruth 43, 57
Redstone Rock 407–8
Reigate 366
Rendcomb Park 124
Renhold Castle 5, 7
Repton 354
Resprin Bridge 53
Restormel 53, 62
Restronguet 48, 50
Retford, East 278–9
Retford, West 278
Revesby Abbey xiii, 236
Rewley Abbey 292
Rey Bridge 392
Rhae, Castle of the 16
Rhe, R 236
Rhe Brook 311
Rhymney 246
Rhymney, R 245–8
Rhymney Bridge 242, 245–7
Ribbesford 408
Ribble Bridge 204
Ribble, R 203–4, 206, 208–9
Ribblesdale 208
Ribchester 209
Riccal, R 438
Richards Castle 173–4
Richborough 191, 194, 199
Richmond (Yorks) xxvii, 385, 417, 447–8, 456–61, 464–5
Richmond upon Thames 362
Richmondshire 113, 208, 385, 417, 438, 446–7, 451, 456–61, 463–4
Richmont Castle 342–3, 346
Rickmansworth 20, 180–1
Ridley Park 32
Ridley 27
Rievaulx Abbey xiii, 438
Ringwood 395
Ripley 408
Ripon xliv, 417, 446, 449–51, 459–60, 463–5
Risca 246

Rising, Castle 252
Risinghoe Castle 3, 5, 7
Riven 203
Rivenpike 203
River (Kent) 192
Riverhill 364
Riverhill Park 366
Rivers (Sussex) 364, 366
Riviere Castle 41, 43
Rivington 203
Rivington Pike 203
Robertsbridge 195
Rocester Priory 314
Roche 49
Roche Hill 49
Rochester 186–7, 189–90, 192, 198, 200
Rochford, Stoke 6
Rockcliffe 67
Rockingham 212–13, 253–4, 261–2, 302–3
Rockstone 407–8
Rodden, R 314
Rodeby 191
Roden, R 305, 314, 318–19
Roden Mere 314
Rokecester 415
Rollesley 442
Rollright 142
Rollright 300, 382
Rolster Bridge 81
Romney 191, 197–8
Romney Marsh 197–8
Romsey 151, 399, 402, 404
Rooksbridge 330
Roomwood 282
Ross on Wye 132, 164, 170, 174, 177
Rossington 281, 421–2, 455
Rostherne 28
Rostherne Mere 28
Rothbury 268
Rother, R 195, 366
Rotherbridge 363–4
Rotherfield 366
Rotherfield Greys 297
Rotherham 183, 278, 417, 419–20
Rotherland 303

Rouen xvii
Round Table, Arthur's 385, 471
Rousdon 92
Routon 382
Row Brook 311
Rowden 390
Rowington 382
Rowton Bridge 310
Royal, Vale 27, 31
Royston xlix, 24, 179–80
Rufford xliii, 279, 282, 420
Rugby 367, 381–2
Ruislip Priory 241
Rume Water 279
Rumford 279
Runcorn 30, 206–7
Rushall 33
Rushton 254, 266
Rutherland 303
Ruthin 5, 266, 297, 314
Rutland 212, 219, 221, 232, 254, **302–3**
Rutupi 191
Rutupinum 191, 194
Rycote 288–9, 292, 300
Rye 52, 191, 195
Rye, R 438, 444
Ryedale 225, 443
Ryther 427
Ryton 281
Ryton, R 270, 420

Saffron Walden xiii
St Albans xiii, xliii, xlv, 2, 11, 180, 185, 303
St Allen 40, 65
St Asaph 168, 175
St Andrews Auckland 111, 115
St Audrie's 339
St Austell 50, 61
St Banka 41
St Blazey 51
St Margaret's at Cliffe 190–1, 262, 367, 371
St Cybi 244
St David's 172, 474
St Decumans 339
St Decun 339

St Denys 157
St Erth 44
St Germans 41, 55-7, 62
St Germoe 42
St Gluvias 48
St Guntle 247
St Gwynlliw 247
St Ives 44-5, 58, 182
St Justinian 57-8
St Keverne 46, 60
St Lide's I 43
St Mandite 49
St Mandits 49
St Mawes xxiv, 34, 49-50, 61, 65
St Moran 49
St Neots xiii, 2, 4-5, 24-5, 182-3
St Oswald's Ash 271
St Oswald's Priory (Nostell) 68, 419, 424
St Osyth 21, 23
St Piran 46, 48, 60
St Radegund's 184, 189, 192
St Scaf 48
St Sitha 312, 462
St Sythe 312
St Teath 38-9, 64
St Tereudacus's Chapel 242
St Twrog's Chapel 242, 248
Salcombe 83, 85
Salford (Lancs) 202
Salford (Warwicks) 372, 376
Salford Bridge 377
Salfordshire 202, 206-7
Salisbury xiii, xxiv, 12, 14, 86, 94, 96, 98, 107, 148, 151, 185, 321-2, 348, 387, 393-9, 401, 403-4
Salisbury Park 185
Saltash 41, 56-7, 62-3, 77
Salter's Bridge 354
Salterton 90
Saltfleet 233
Saltfleet Creek 236
Salthouse Roads 29
Saltmarsh 434
Saltwood 196

Salwarpe 409
Salwarpe Brook 409, 411
Sancton 428
Sandal 424-5
Sandbeck 439
Sanded Bay 190
Sandford 318
Sandhill 12
Sandiford Brook 27
Sandwich 184-5, 189-91, 193-4, 199
Sandwiche 104
Sarre 193
SarsdenSarum, Old 393-5
Saughall 29
Saveock 48
Savernake Forest 399, 401
Savick, brook 204
Sawley Abbey 206, 208-9
Sawley Ferry 70, 284
Sawtry Abbey xiii, 183
Saxton 427, 461
Scaf, St 48
Scarborough xxiii, 417, 428, 433, 440-3
Scardale 70
Scawsby Leazes 423
Schilleston Creek 78
Schrobbesbyri 309
Scilly Is 42-4, 59
Scluse, Le, battle 335
Scorborough 429, 462
Scorgate 142
Scotland 25, 66-8, 117, 147, 150, 232, 270, 272, 274, 284, 446
Scrooby 281, 420
Sculthorpe 423
Seamer 439, 455
Seaton (Devon) 91
Seaton (Yorks) 438
Seaton Bridge (Corn) 55
Seaton Delavel Castle 272
Seaton, R 55
Sedbergh Vale 208
Sedbury 458
Sedge Moor 329
Selaby 116
Selby xiii, 229, 466
Selling 188

Selwood Forest 320, 331, 343, 346-9
Selyf, Cantref 471
Sempringham xiii, 224, 232
Senghenydd 246
Seperwelle 187
Serpenhil 17
Settrington 439, 461
Seukesham 12-13
Seusham 14-15
Seven Hayes Chase 357
'Seven loos' 27
Seven Sisters 97
Seven, R 438
Severn, R xxv, 127-9, 131-3, 138-9, 142-3, 146-8, 304-5, 308-14, 316, 318, 407-11, 414-16, 478
Severn Sea xlviii, 37-8, 44, 58, 64-5, 75-6, 131-2, 138-9, 141, 143, 242-8, 320, 341, 475-6
Shabbington 293
Shaftesbury 94, 108-9, 149, 172, 344, 347-8, 391, 393, 404
Shalbourne 400
Shap 385
Sharford Bridge 377
Sharpham 348
Shawbury 318
Sheen 362
Sheffield 417, 420
Sheffield Park 420
Shefford 6
Sheinton 313
Shelve 307
Shenstone 350
Shenton 32
Shepeton 317
Sheppey 192, 198
Sheppey, R 326, 328
Shepton Mallet 320, 328
Shepway 191, 196
Sherborne xiii, xlv, 91, 94-8, 105-8, 332, 347-8, 388
Sherborne Water 107, 109,

INDEX OF PLACES

348
Sherburn 439, 443
Sherburn in Elmet 419, 461
Sheriff Hutton 437, 444
Sherwood Forest 277–8, 282
Shillingstone 106
Shipeye 191
Shiptonthorpe 428
Shipway 191
Shirburn 209, 288
Shire Lake 181
Shirhuten 444
Shonington 293
Short Ferry 226
Shotwick 29–30
Shoulby 218
Shrawardine Castle 310, 316
Shrewsbury xxv, 177–8, 248, 304–5, 307–14, 316–19, 415, 470, 478
Shrewsbury's 305, 420
Shropshire xx, xxxviii, xliii, 30, 32, 49, 163–4, 177–8, 253, **304–19**, 350, 367, 407, 415, 467–8, 479
Shugborough 356–7
Shustoke 382
Shute 90, 209
Shypwey 196
Sibdon 317
Sibdon Cawood Castle 317
Sibertswold 187
Sidingburne 198
Sidling, stream 99
Sidmouth 91
Sigglesthorne 462
Silbury Hill 400–1
Silchester xxviii, xlix, 151, 161–2
Silling 99
Simon's Well 315
Simonsbath 72, 341–2
Simonsbath Water 72
Simonsburn 272
Sinnington 438, 460
Sinodun 12

Sirhowey, Dyffryn 246
Siston 140
Sitha, St 312, 462
Sittingbourne 184, 188, 194, 198–200
Skeffington 213, 218
Skegness 233
Skell, R 450–1, 458–9, 464
Skelton 434
Skelton Castle 455
Skenfrith 248–9
Skerford 260
Skip Bridge 465
Skipsea 442
Skipton 441
Skipton Bridge 464
Slane (Ireland) 74
Slapton 83
Slaughter 142, 425
Slea, R 224
Sleaford 221, 224–5, 234
Sleap 318
Slimbridge 141
Slindon 364
Smalhed 195
Small Hythe 195
Small Lea Bridge 181
Smawley 181
Smeaton 446
Smeaton, Great 446–7
Smeaton Bridge 446–7
Smite, R 211, 280, 284
Snape 457
Snodhill 174, 176
Snorre Castle 424
Soar, R 214–17
Sockburn 110–11, 417, 438, 447
Sodbury 124, 137–42, 144–6
Sodbury, Chipping 124, 138–42, 145
Sodbury, Little 137–8, 141–2, 144, 146
Sodbury, Old 138–9, 142
Sodbury Hill 137–8, 145
Soham 360
Solway Firth 67
Somerby 223
Somerset xviii, xxiii, xxvi,

xlv, 34, 41, 74, 90, 92, 98, 105, 187, 231, **320–49**, 370, 374
Somerset Levels 320, 336
Sonning 9, 11
Sonskue Park 457
South Brent 81
South Burton 462
South Cadbury 320, 331–2
South Carlton 237
South Hams 85
South Milford 419, 474
South Molton 92
South Petherton 337
South Thoresby 237
South Wingfield (Derbs) 420
South Wraxall (Wilts) 391
Southall 240
Southam (Glos) 127, 147
Southam (Warwicks) xlvi, 295, 367, 380–2
Southampton x, xiii, xxiv, xlv, 76, 151–2, 154–9, 255, 366, 393, 399
Southampton Water 156–9
Southwell 280
Southwick xiii, 160
Southwold 360
Sow, R 356–7, 381
Sowe, R 382
Sowe Common 382
Sowey, R 329
Spain 77, 172, 256
Spalding xiii
Spaldwick 183
Spanne, The 342
Sparsholt 18
Speke 207
Spilsby 235, 237
Spitel 236
Spittle 126, 437
Spofforth 454
Spon 379
Spriddlestone 41
Springhill 142
Sprint, R 384
Spurn Head 417, 441–2
Spurstow 27, 32
Stafford 353, 355–7

Staffordshire xx, 31, 33, 314, 317–18, **350–8**, 377, 382, 416
Staindrop 113, 116
Staines 19–20, 239–40
Stainmore 385, 460
Stainsby 237
Stainton Beck 383
Stalbridge 94, 106–8
Stamford 221, 232, 234, 253, 262, 265, 302–3
Stamford Baron 265
Stamford Bridge 428, 443, 460
Standish 203
Stanford on the Hille 265
Stanhope 111–12, 117, 119
Stanway 125, 147–8, 406
Stanwick 460
Stapleford 106, 396
Starborough Castle 362
Start Point 83
Staughton, Great 2, 182
Staveley 294, 384
Staverton 392
Steane 264
Steart 341
Steeple Ashton 402
Steneford 301
Steple–Castelle 469
Stirling, battle 150
Stixwould Priory 237
Stockbridge 151, 157
Stockport 30–1
Stockton on Tees 117–19, 447
Stockton-on-the-Forest 437
Stodart 453
Stogursey 341
Stoke Albany 219
Stoke Bridge 310
Stoke Fleming 72, 82–3, 90, 93
Stoke Gifford 137
Stoke Gregory 336
Stoke-on-Trent 355
Stoke Poges 19
Stoke Rochford 6

Stoke sub Hamdon 334–5, 342
Stoke upon Tern 310
Stoke, Itchen 153
Stokeinteignhead 86
Stokesay Castle 306, 317
Stokke Hall 399
Stonar 190
Stone (Kent) 195
Stone (Staffs) 356–7
Stone Bridge (Bucks) 22
Stone Castle 185
Stone House Creek 77
Stone Street 192, 197
Stoneleigh 382
Stonor 297
Stonton Wyvill 212–13
Stony Stratford 21, 23, 303
Stoppord 30
Stour, R (Dorset) 104–9, 199, 331, 403, 405
Stour, R (Kent) 186, 190, 193–4
Stour, R (Worcs) 407–8, 415–16
Stourbridge 356, 416
Stourmouth 199, 416
Stourton (Wilts) 107, 347, 387, 403–4
Stourton Castle (Worcs) 356, 416
Stourton Caundle 107
Stow-on-the-Wold 121, 142, 298
Stowell 145
Stowey, Nether 338–9
Strad y Llan 315
Strata Florida xx, xxxiv, xxxviii, xliii, 467, 476–8
Stratford Langthorne xiii
Stratford on Avon 367, 372–6
Stratford sub Castle 395
Stratford, Stony 21, 23, 303
Stratton 37, 57, 64
Stratton, hundred 63
Streatlam 117
Strefford 308
Stretllan 315

Stretton Dale 308, 318
Stretton Sugwas 165, 176
Stretton, All 308
Stretton, Church 304, 308
Stretton, Little 308
Strigul 242
Strigulia 242–3
Strood, R 174
Stroud (Glos) 121
Stroud Place (London) 357, 416
Studforth Hill 453
Studley Priory 294
Studley, Low 465
Studley, Middle 465
Sturminster Marshall 104
Sturminster Newton 94, 104, 106–7, 348
Sturseley Castle 356
Sturton on the Street 229
Subbury 144
Sudeley Castle 125–7, 142, 146, 150, 371
Suffolk 25, 102, 120, 235, 251, 287, 299, 301, **359–60**, 431
Summergil, R 165
Sunderland Bridges 112, 115
Sunnebeck 446
Surrey 179, 241, 250, **361–2**
Sussex xxiii, xlix, 79, 194–5, 198, 211, 251, **363–6**
Sutton (Devon) 77–9
Sutton (Herefs) 164–6, 175
Sutton (Som) 345–6
Sutton (Staffs)
Sutton Chase 357, 377–8
Sutton Coldfield xxxiii, 350, 357–8, 367, 377–8
Sutton Courtenay 15
Sutton on Sea 237
Sutton on the Forest 418
Sutton upon Derwent 428
Sutton Valence 200
Sutton Walls 175
Sutton, Bishop 345
Sutton, King's 15, 265, 294
Swaffham 251

INDEX OF PLACES

Swale, R 208, 385, 445, 447–8, 456–60, 464, 466
Swaledale 438, 457–60, 464
Swan Pool (Corn) 47
Swan Pool (Lincs) 228
Swanage 104
Swell 142, 193
Swilgate, R 148
Swillington 426, 456
Swinburne 141, 273
Swine 119
Swineshead xiii
Swingfield 188
Sydenham 339
Symphorian 37–8
Symphorian's 38, 64
Syon Abbey 42, 91, 205
Sythe, St 312
Sywell 266

Tabley 28, 31
Tadcaster 427, 437, 461
Taff, R 474
Taidbrooke 468
Tale, R 89
Talley Abbey xliii, 473
Talmeneth 41
Tamar, R 35–6, 56–7, 62–3, 76–9, 393
Tame, R 350, 354–5, 357, 377–9, 382
Tame Bridge 357
Tamerton 63
Tamerton, North 35, 63
Tamworth 350, 353–7, 378–9, 381–2
Tanfield, East 451, 459
Tanfield, West 451, 457, 459
Taranell, brook 471
Tarporley 31
Tarraby 271
Tarrant Abbey 109, 396
Tarset Castle 269
Tateshaul 236
Tatham 209
Tattershall 226, 236, 252
Tatton 31
Taunton xiii, 320, 336, 339

Tavistock xiii, 35, 43, 56–7, 59, 63
Tavy, R 77
Taw, R 73, 75–6, 92
Tawstock 75
Tawton 74
Team, R 269, 273
Tean 357
Teath, St 38–9, 64
Teddesley Chase 357
Tees, R 110–11, 116–19, 417, 433, 441, 446–7, 457–60
Teesdale 110, 116–17
Teesmouth 117
Tehidy 43
Teifi, R 476–7
Teign, R 85–6
Teign Bridge 85
Teign Head 85
Teignmouth 85–6
Teme 165, 177–8, 305, 307–8, 313, 316, 318–19, 411, 415–16, 469
Teme Bridge 319
Temple Balsall 371, 382
Temple Bruer 226
Temple Ewell 192
Tenbury 307, 318, 405
Tenby 475
Tenterden 194, 198, 363
Tereudacus's Chapel, St 242
Tern 317
Tern, R 310, 316–19
Tern Bridge 318–19
Tern, Stoke upon 310
Ternhill 318
Terrington 444
Test, R 151, 157
Teston Bridge 189
Tetbury 124, 142, 146
Tetbyri 414
Tettenhall 356
Tew 299
Tewkesbury xiii, xxxv, 106, 121–2, 125, 127, 132, 134, 136–7, 142, 146–50, 406, 411, 414–15
Tewkesbury, battle 142
Tewkesbury Park 147

Thame xlii, 20–3, 286, 289–91, 293–4, 296, 300
Thame, R 20–3, 286, 289–91, 293–4, 296, 300
Thames, R xvi, xxxiv, xlix, 8–12, 18–20, 23, 142, 181, 185, 192, 239–40, 291, 296, 300, 361–2
Thanet 190, 193–4
Thaxted 185
Thelford 381
Thelsford 373
Thelwall 206
Thetford (Lincs) 231
Thetford (Norfolk) xiii, 359
Thetford, Little (Cambs) 251
Thirlwall 271
Thirsk 445
Thonock 229, 238
Thoresby, South 237
Thorn Bridge 226
Thornbury 129, 132, 140–1, 150
Thorne 198, 265, 422
Thorney xiii, 183
Thornham Castle 189
Thornhaugh 265
Thornhill 106–7
Thornhull 109
Thornton Bridge 444–5, 452, 460, 464
Thornton Curtis 224, 237
Thornton on Humber xiii
Thorp Perrow 465
Thorpe (prebend) 434
Thorpe (Yorks) 449
Thorpe le Street 428
Thorpe Waterville 256, 262
Thorsgill Beck 447
Thorverton Bridge 88
Thrapston 256–7
Throckmorton 414
Thrugh-bridge 392
Thurgarton xliv, 280
Thurland 209
Thurlaston 218
Thurstaston 29
Tickenhill 415
Tickenhill Park 408

Tickhill 22, 233, 278, 422
Tider uab Hohele 246
Till, R (Northumb) 268–9, 273–4
Till, R (Wilts) 396
Tilton 218
Tintagel 38, 58, 64
Tintern Abbey 243, 248
Tintinhull 334
Tipping Castle 67
Tirtre 249
Titchfield x, 158
Titterstone Clee 318–19
Tiverton 88, 92, 341
Toddington (Beds) 6
Toddington (Glos) 126, 148, 150
Toddington Water 125
Tofte Hall 31, 231
Tollerton 445–6
Tonbridge 189
Tone, R 336
Toneton 336
Tong (Salop) 313, 317–18
Tonge (Kent) 188, 198–9
Toomer Park 107
Toorne Wood 422
Topcliffe 445, 464
Topsham 86–7
Torbay 41, 84–5
Torey Brook 78–9
Torksey 221, 226, 228
Tormarton 139–40
Torre Abbey 83–5
Torre Mohun 84
Torridge, R 75–6
Torrington, Great xlv, 75–6, 92
Torrington, Little 76
Tortworth 139
Tortworth, R 141
Totnes xiii, 72–3, 79, 81–2, 88
Totnes, Little 81
Tourres, the 342
Tours (France) 325
Towbury Castle 414
Towcester 253, 260, 265, 303
Towkey 298

Towley Park 217
Townstal 83
Towton 427
Towton, battle 427, 461
Towy, R 472–3
Toxteth Park 207
Trallwng 314
TrecarTrecastle 472
Tredegar 245, 247
Tredelerch 246
Trefarrith 167
Trefusis Point 48
Tregaron xliii, 476
Tregelly 55–6
Tregny 49
Tregony 49, 61
Tregrug Castle 244
Treharrock 44
Trelawne 55
Trelill 38, 64
Trelowarren 41
Trematon 56, 63, 79
Tremayne 46–7
Trenewith 41
Trenewydd 342
Trent, R xxiii, 70, 103, 211–12, 223, 228–30, 270, 277–80, 282–4, 352–7, 434, 455
Trerice 37, 40, 44, 65
Treryn Castle 41, 43
Tresco 43
Tresilian 48
Trethevey 37
Treveglos 41
Trevena 38, 64
Trevethy 64
Trevethy Water 64
Trewennack 45
Trewinard 44
Trewyn 248
Trigg, hundred 63
Troggy Castle 243–4
Trothy Abbey 249
Trowbridge 320, 342, 391–3, 402–3
Trudoxhill 347
Truham 162
Truro 34, 48–9, 61
Truro Creek 48–9

Tubney 298
Tudlad, R 452
Tupholme Priory xiii, 236
Tutbury 355–7
Tutt, R 452
Tweed, R 232, 273–5
Tweeddale 274
Tweedmouth 274–5
Twineham 157
Twinehambourne 158
Twmbarlwm 246
Two Waters Mill 181
Twrog's Chapel, St 242, 248
Twyford (Berks) 9
Twyford (Hants) 154
Twyford Bridge (Kent) 189
Twyning 414
Twyneham 104, 395
Tyburn 270
Tyndale 274
Tyne, R 118, 269–75, 417
Tyne, North, R 271–2, 274
Tyne, South, R 271–4
Tynedale 271–2, 274–5
Tynemouth xiii, 114, 269, 271–5
Tyve, Diffrin 476
Tywardreath 34, 41, 46, 51, 61
Tywardreath Bay 50–1

Ubley 345–6
Uffington 232, 303
Ulcombe 188
Ulleskelf 427
Ulverscroft Priory 216, 220
Undal Water 7
Unk, R 469
Upavon 395, 401
Upholland Priory 206, 209
Upleadon 177
Upottery 89
Uppingham 302–3
Upton
Upton-on-Severn 131, 148, 405, 414–15
Upwey 100
Ure, R 208, 417, 448, 450–60, 463–6

INDEX OF PLACES

Ureby 225
Uredale 458–60
Urivallis 458
Use, R 23
Use, Lake 67
Usk 242, 244–6, 248–9, 471–2
Utkinton 31
Utrecht 465
Uttoxeter 355–7
Uxbridge 19, 181, 239–40, 416

Vale of Aylesbury 20–3
Vale of Belvoir 219, 232
Vale of Evesham 406, 415
Vale of Ewyas 249
Vale of Pickering xxiii, 417
Vale of Radnor 469
Vale White Horse 12–13, 17
Vale Royal 27, 31
Valley Burn 115
Vaudey Abbey 221–2, 232
Vennones 458
Vensela 457–8
Veor, Ardevora 49
Ver, R 180
Vineyard 130
Vousa, La 61
Vowtre 279
Vyes, The 401
Vyne, The 161

Wade 251
Wadebridge 35, 38–9, 64
Wade's Grave 439
Wadele 470
Wadley 298
Wainfleet 233–5, 237
Wakefield 417, 425–6, 461–2
Wakefield, battle 462
Wakefield Moor 426
Walcot 318
Wales viii, xvi, xvii, xx, xxxiii, xxxviii, xxxix, xli, xliii, xlvi, xlviii, liii, 26, 32, 132, 163, 168, 173–4, 201, 211, 242–4, 248, 266, 304, 308–9, 315–16, 341, 405, **467–79**
Walford Bridge 105
Walkington 433, 462
Wallasey 29
Wallingford 8, 11–12, 16–18, 122, 291
Wallington Castle 273
Walmer 191
Walretensis 465
Walsall 358
Walshford Bridge 465
Walsingham xiii, 423
Waltham xiii, 157, 160, 181
Walton (Liverpool) 206
Walton on Darwen 204
Wangford Hill 360
Wansbeck, R 268, 272–3
Wantage 8, 17–18, 404
Warden Abbey xiii, 4, 6–7
Wardle 32
Warebridge 158
Wareham xxiii, xxxii, xlix, 94, 100, 103
Waring, R 236
Wark Castle 273–4
Warkworth 268, 271, 273
Warley 77
Warminster 347, 392, 396, 402
Warrington 204, 206–9
Warsop 278, 282
Warter Priory 430
Warton 206, 280
Warwick xiii, xxiv, xxx, xxxiv, 295, 353, 367–73, 375, 380–2
Warwickshire xxx, xxxii, 216–17, 300, 313, 354, 356–7, **367–82**, 405
Wash, The 231, 233
Water Eaton 123
Water Head 84
Waterbeck, Hawes 385
Waterdown Forest 366
Watford 180
Watling Street 179, 225, 228, 259, 270, 302–3, 382, 385–6, 423, 426–7, 447, 452, 455
Watlington 288
Wattlesborough 314
Watton xiii, 438–9
Waverley xiii
Weald, Kentish 194, 198, 363
Wear, R 111–15, 117–19, 273
Weardale 110–12, 119
Weaver, R 28, 30, 32, 202
Wedgnock Park 372
Wednesbury 358
Weedon 253, 258–60
Weedon, stream 258–9
Weedon-in-the-Street 303
Weeford 353
Weighton, Market 428
Welbeck Abbey xiii, 282
Welbeck, stream 282
Weldon 260
Welland, R 212–13, 231–2, 253–4, 261, 302–3
Wellesbourne 373
Wellhope Burn 112
Wellingborough 2, 257
Wellington (Herefs) 170
Wellington (Salop) 314, 316–17, 319
Wellington Brook 170
Wellow 321
Wells xiii, xlv, 142, 320, 326–8, 330, 336, 342, 346, 349
Wells Water 328
Welshpool xliii, 310, 314, 415, 468–9, 478
Welstreme 293
Wem 305
Wendover 22
Wenfeld 420
Wenhaston 359
Wenlock, Much 172, 177, 304, 310–11, 317–19
Wenlock Edge 311
Wenning, R 209
Wensley (Derbs) 70
Wensley (Yorks) 448, 457–8, 463
Wensleydale 417, 451,

457–9, 464
Wensum, R 252
Went, R 423, 426
Wentbridge 423, 455
Wentland 242
Wentllooge 245
Wentllug 245
Wentlooge 242, 244
Wentlugh 244
Weobley 169, 174
Wereford 84
West Auckland 111
West Butterwick 230
West Coker, stream 97
West Deeping 303
West Derby 202–3, 206
West Derbyshire 201, 206–7
West Gilling 385
West Harptree Gurney 343
West Hythe 189, 196
West Ilsley 404
West Kirby 29
West Knoyle, xvi, xxvi, xlii
West Looe 55, 62–3
West Lulworth 102–4
West Retford 278
West Tanfield 451, 457, 459
West Wivelshire, hundred 63
West Wycombe 23
Westbury (Wilts) 342, 387, 402
Westbury on Severn 132
Westenhanger 189
Westminster xiii, 11, 120, 146, 161, 261, 296, 425
Westmorland xxxvi, 68, 112, 208, **383–6**, 452, 460, 464
Weston (Oxon) 288–9
Weston (Salop) 318
Weston (Som) 348
Westpark 457
Westwood Park 462
Wetheral Priory 68
Wetherby 417, 427, 454
Wetley Moor 357
Wey, R 100
Weymouth 100–2, 104, 109

Whalley 208–9, 282
Whaplode 231, 235
Wharfe, R 427–8, 437, 454, 461
Wharfedale 458
Wharton 174
Whatcroft 32
Whatstandwell Bridge 70
Wheatley 293
Whelford 123
Whelmstone 41
Wherwell Abbey xlix
Wherwell Stream 151
Whichford 294
Whickham 117
Whinfell Park 385
Whistones 410
Whitbourne 177
Whitby xiii, 433, 438, 441, 443, 461
Whitchurch 26, 304–5, 310, 313–14, 316, 318, 478
Whitcliff Park 141
White Abbey (Salop) 304, 317
White Castle 248–9
White Cliff 91–2
White Horse, Vale of 12–13, 17
White Ladies (Brewood) Priory 317
Whitechapel 272
Whitelackington 333, 336
Whitelake R 329
Whitesheet Hill 403
Whitington xxxvi
Whitland xliii, xlviii, 474–5
Whitley 382
Whitstable 189, 199
Whittington (Glos) 416
Whittington (Salop) 315–16
Whittington Moor 315
Whittington Park 315
Whittlesey 187
Whitton 268
Whitwell on the Hill 437
Whitwick 216
Whitwood 426
Whorlton 455

Whorwellsdown, hundred 402
Wibbemere 319
Wick (Glos) 146
Wick (Som) 343, 346
Wickham (Hants) 158, 160
Wickham (Surrey) 250
Wickwar 139
Widcombe 342
Widdrington 272–3
Wigan 203, 206–7, 209
Wigford (Lincoln) 227–8
Wight, I 102, 151, 158
Wigland 28
Wigmore 164, 169, 177, 316–17
Wikerford 227
Wilberfoss 428
Wile, R 100
Wilegripe 233
Wilksby 237
Willenhall Bridge 381
Willey 314
Willington (Beds) 1, 4
Willington (Northumb) 272
Williton 339
Willow Beck 445
Willowgtowne 379
Wilsford 225
Wilsford brook 225
Wilton (Wilts) xlii, 149, 394, 396, 403
Wilton (Yorks) 442
Wilton Castle (Herefs) 174
Wiltshire xi, xvi, xxvi, xlii, 8, 44, 123, 322, 342, 348, **387–404**, 407, 416
Wimborne, R 105
Wimborne Minster 94, 104–5
Wimborne St Giles 105
Wincanton 106, 320
Winchcombe xiii, xliii, 121, 125–7, 142, 150, 209, 406, 411, 414
Winchelsea xxiii, 52, 363–5
Winchester xiii, xxiv, xlv, 151–4, 156–7, 160–1, 363
Windermere 385

INDEX OF PLACES

Windrush, R 142, 298
Windsor 18, 20, 56, 163, 260, 268, 287–8, 356
Windsor Forest 8
Winfeld 420
Winforton 174
Wingfield (Derbs) 70
Wingfield (Suffolk) 360
Wingfield, South (Derbs) 420
Wingham College 185
Winmarleigh 204
Winnington 33
Winnow, St 53–4
Winterbourne, R 396
Winwick 207
Wirksworth 70–1
Wirral 26, 29–31, 33, 351
Wirrall Park 348
Wiscombe 91
Wiske Bridge 446, 459–60
Wiske, Kirby 446
Wiske, R 445–7, 459–60
Wistanstow 307
Wisteston 170
Witham Charterhouse 347
Witham, R 226, 228, 235–6
Withcote 217, 302
Witney 298
Witton Castle 438
Wivelshire, East, hundred 63
Wivelshire, West, hundred 63
Wiverton Hall 280
Woburn xiii, 6, 11, 23
Wold Grift 233
Wold, Stow on the 298
Wolfhall 395
Wollaton 379
Wolsingham 111–12, 117, 119
Wolverhampton 317, 319, 355–8
Wolvesey Castle (Winchester) 151–2, 154
Woman's Bridge 21
Wombridge 314, 317, 319
Wood Mill 154, 157
Woodford (Chesh) 31

Woodford (Wilts) 395
Woodford Bridge (Devon) 76
Woodsford Castle 100, 108
Wool Bridge 100
Woolwich 181, 190
Worcester xiii, xxv, xlvi, lii, 124, 127–9, 131–2, 169, 172, 177, 307, 313, 318, 376, **405–16**, 434
Worcestershire 300, 307, 318–19, 356, 375–7, 405–7, 410, 412, 415–16
Workington 66, 68
Worksop xiii, xxi, 277–9, 281–2, 420
Worm, R 164, 175–7
Wormbridge 169
Wormley 181
Wormsley 164, 170, 177
Worngy 41
Worthy 153–4
Wotton under Edge 138, 145–6, 438
Wragby 236
Wrangton 229, 423
Wraxall (Som) 346
Wraxall, South (Wilts) 391
Wreake, R 211
Wreigh, R 273
Wrek, R 303
Wrekin Hill 310, 319
Wrenbury 32
Wressle 417, 428–9, 434–5, 461
Wrete, R 303
Wrexham 314
Wroot 229
Wroot Cote 423
Wroxall Priory 372
Wroxeter 310, 415
Wroxton Priory 296
Wulvedon 49
Wych, Higher 28
Wychnor 352, 357
Wychough 28
Wychwood Forest 298–9
Wycliffe 458
Wycombe, High 23
Wycombe, West 23

Wye (Kent) 186, 189, 199,
Wye, R (Chilterns) 23
Wye, R (Derbs) 71
Wye, R (Herefs, Mon) 163–70, 174, 176, 242–3, 247–9, 470, 477–8
Wyke 107
Wykeham 444
Wylye, R 331, 395–6
Wymestun 41
Wymondham xiii, 251
Wynermerewath 385
Wynnell Bridge 381
Wynyates, Compton 373
Wyralshire 273
Wyre, R 204
Wyre Forest 318, 408, 415–16
Wyredale Forest 204

Yade Moor 117
Yalding 189
Yardley Wood 382
Yarkhill 174
Yarm 117, 119, 447, 455
Yarmouth 252
Yarrow 203
Yarty, R 92
Yealm, R 80, 84
Yealmbridge 35, 63, 80
Yedingham 428, 444
Yelling 25
Yeo, R 347
Yeovil 109, 320, 332, 347
Yeovilton 332
Yetminster 107
Ynysddu 246
York xiii, xxiii, xliv, xlv, 68–9, 92, 113, 117, 119, 129, 131, 186, 227–8, 384, 417–20, 425, 428, 434–7, 443–5, 449, 453–4, 458–9, 461–2, 465
York (Diocese) 204
Yorkshire xxi, xxiii, xxvii, xl, xli, xliv, xlv, 66, 185, 203, 209, 223, 267, 270, 274, 278, 383, **417–66**
Ystwyth, R 477

 **HOBNOB PRESS** has been publishing books since 1983, with an emphasis on West Country history, literature and biography. For a complete list of publications visit www.hobnobpress.co.uk. Two other titles relating to the history of travel may be of particular interest:

John Taylor, Travels and Travelling, 1616-1653, edited by John Chandler, 2nd enlarged edition, 2020, xviii, 493 pp, paperback, £18.95, ISBN 978-1-906978-91-4.

John Taylor (1578-1653), known in his lifetime and ever since as the 'Water-Poet', wrote some two hundred pamphlets on every conceivable subject of interest to his contemporaries. A native of Gloucester who became a London waterman, he employed his ebullient wit and facility with words to make a reputation, if not a fortune, from his writing in prose and verse. His descriptions of the fourteen journeys he made between 1616 and 1653 around Britain (and twice to the continent), are not only entertaining to read, but an important source for anyone interested in travel, places and society before, during and just after the Civil Wars. This expanded edition of a work first published in 1999 includes the two foreign adventures and a group of pamphlets describing carriers, coaches, inns and taverns, with brief introductions to each work, annotations and an index of places and people.

Dorian Gerhold, Stage Coaches Explained: the Bristol Example, 2012, iv, 326 pp, paperback, £17.95, ISBN 978-1-906978-15-0

This is the first book to tell in detail the story of a stage coach route and network, from the pioneering services of the 1650s to the fast coaches of the 1830s. It explains what changed and when, identifying the impact of better roads, horses and vehicles, including the work of turnpike trusts. The experiences of coachmasters and passengers are described. Some surprising conclusions are drawn, and the development of Bristol's coaches provides the key to understanding the stage coach system as a whole. It is a groundbreaking study by the acknowledged authority on pre-railway road transport.

John Chandler BA PhD FSA edits the Victoria County History in Gloucestershire and Wiltshire. He has written extensively about Wiltshire and is the proprietor of Hobnob Press. He lives in Gloucester.

www.ingramcontent.com/pod-product-compliance
Lightning Source LLC
Chambersburg PA
CBHW051531230426
43669CB00015B/2568